SCOTL...
WHERE TO GO,...

Editor: Barry Francis
Designer: John Hawkins
Advertising: Peter Whitworth
tel Basingstoke 20123
Maps: AA Cartographic Department

Produced and distributed by the Publications Division of The Automobile Association
Scottish Office: Fanum House, Erskine Harbour, Erskine, Renfrewshire PA8 6AT
Distributed overseas by The British Tourist Authority, 64 St James's Street, London SW1A 1NF

Phototypeset by Vantage Photosetting Co Ltd, Southampton, Hampshire
Printed and bound by William Clowes (Beccles) Ltd

Photographs are by courtesy of J Allen Cash; The British Tourist Authority; The Scottish Tourist Board; Spectrum Colour Library; Tom Weir and George Young

Published by The Automobile Association, Fanum House, Basingstoke, Hampshire RG21 2EA

The contents of this publication are believed correct at the time of printing, but the current position may be checked through the AA. While every effort is made to ensure that information appearing in advertisements is correct, no responsibility can be accepted by the AA for inaccuracies.

All rights reserved. No part of this publication may be reproduced, stored in a retrieval system or transmitted in any form or by any means – electronic, mechanical, photocopying, recording or otherwise, unless the permission of the AA has been granted beforehand.

© The Automobile Association 1982
ISBN 0 86145 104X   56313

CONTENTS

5 **Out and About in Scotland**
Tom Weir and Barry Francis go golfing, motoring, walking, fishing, skiing and pony-trekking

IN COLOUR

17 **Whisky Galore**
Derek Cooper raises his glass to Scotland's liquid gold

23 **The Highland Games**
Jenny Carter puts into words that colourful spectacle of sight and sound

28 **Atlas**
Twenty pages of detailed motoring maps

49 **The Inner Hebrides**
A romantic island journey described by Roger Prebble

59 **Royal Houses**
John Hutchinson tours some of Scotland's famous historic palaces

65 **Edinburgh**
Donald MacCormick enthuses over one of the world's great cities

GAZETTEER

76 Abbreviations and symbols
79 Explanation of entries
80 Hotels, guesthouses, farmhouses and inns
150 Picnic sites
152 Country parks
153 Forest parks
153 Long-distance footpaths
154 Hire firms
154 Camping and caravanning sites: by town
180   by region
181 Scotland by the Sea
182 Places of Interest
210 Edinburgh town plan
212 Glasgow town plan
214 **Day Drives**
Fourteen one-day tours of Scotland's most scenic routes

INTRODUCTION

Many people planning to visit Scotland for the first time – whether they are from south of the Border or from overseas – usually have a mental picture of a romantic country of wild highlands, mysterious cloud-wreathed islands, tall-turretted castles facing cold grey seas, and a hardy race of men and women who speak a muscial (if sometimes unintelligible) form of the English language.

Romantic it is, in legend and history; and the landscape, except for the industrial belt which stretches from the Clyde to the Firth of Forth, is beautiful and unspoilt. From the rolling hills of the Border country beyond Carter Bar to the rugged Grampians, from the picturesque lochs and glens of the Highlands and the hundreds of islands which surround the mainland like jewels in a crown, to the wide beaches on the dry, and often sunny, east coast, there is much for the tourist to see and enjoy.

Accommodation in Scotland is plentiful and varied in style and price. This book gives full details of hotels, ranging from the 5-Star Gleneagles to modest 1-Star establishments, and lists guesthouses, inns and farmhouses – sometimes remote but always offering a hospitable welcome – together with AA-inspected restaurants where you can be sure of getting a value-for-money meal. A separate list gives information on camp sites with facilities and standards which meet the AA's stringent requirements.

In addition there is a selection of places to visit where you can enjoy an hour or two under cover or spend a whole fascinating day – places such as castles, zoos, museums, gardens, woollen mills – even whisky distilleries.

And for those keen to get out-and-about by car, there are 14 day drives, hand-picked by the AA's route-planning experts for go-as-you-please motoring, covering the finest touring country in Scotland.

All the information you need to make your holiday trouble-free and enjoyable can be found here, together with articles of interest on various aspects of Scottish life, plus a full colour 20-page atlas section to help you locate the places which you will want to explore.

The perfect Highland holiday where you can see the trees from the wood.

From a fully inclusive price of just £98* per lodge, per week, or £40* per weekend, you and up to five friends can enjoy the relaxing beauty of the magnificent Scottish countryside from your very own timber lodge at Lochanhully.

Lochanhully, located near Carrbridge, faces South to the Cairngorm mountains with a complex of lodges set in the scenic splendour of the Spey Valley.

*Prices correct at time of going to press.

LOCHANHULLY LODGES

Send to: Lochanhully Lodges, Dept. 4, Carrbridge, Inverness-shire, Scotland, PH23 3NA. Please send me a brochure with details.

Mr./Mrs. _____

Address _____

_____

_____

Scotland's for me!   AA

© A joint Lochanhully Lodges and Scottish Tourist Board advertisement.

A Lochanhully Lodge holiday offers the widest possible range of relaxing holiday activities.

The site has its own lake, licensed bar and heated covered swimming pool and is ideally positioned for touring, walking, climbing, pony treking, skiing and fishing. You can even visit nearby whisky distilleries.

Each lodge is modern and functional in design and gives a degree of comfort that you and your family and friends will enjoy.

All the lodges are equipped with electricity, hot and cold water, a cooker, TV, fridge, linen and furnishings, all of a high standard and all included in the price together with electricity and V.A.T.

Two of the fifty units have been specially designed to accommodate accompanied wheelchair or physically handicapped visitors, at no extra charge.

Make your next holiday just that little bit different in the natural setting of a Lochanhully Lodge.

For a brochure complete the coupon or phone Carrbridge (047 984) 234.

OUT AND ABOUT IN SCOTLAND

Scotland offers a wide variety of pursuits to visitors keen to add a little spice to their touring through the country's spectacular scenery . . . there is angling in superb fishing rivers, golfing at some of the world's best golf courses, walking and pony-trekking on moors and hills, and skiing at well equipped centres

Golfing

Some say it was providence that endowed Scotland with so many areas obviously intended for golf. True or not, there is no doubt that whatever your starting point or whichever way you head your car you will never be far from a course. Indeed, it is so much a national game that it seems logical to put it first when talking about sport. Scotland, where the royal and ancient game began in the 15th century, offers golfers some of the most historic and challenging courses in the world. Not that the game found favour with all monarchs. King James II, in fact, was so concerned that archery was being neglected that in 1457 he banned golf. James III and James IV did likewise because they needed men to take up the bow not the club, but after a treaty with England in 1502 James IV relented and even took up the game himself. A bow-maker in Perth furnished him with balls and clubs and an item in the royal accounts reveals that the princely sum of two guineas was paid for the king's game of golf with the Earl of Bothwell. Royal women also took up the game enthusiastically. Mary Queen of Scots braved wagging tongues when she strode out on to the golf course just after her husband, Lord Darnley, had been assassinated.

St Andrews opened its course in 1552, Leith near Edinburgh in 1593 and links were set up 200 miles north at Dornoch in 1616. It was James I and VI who took the game to England. Today there are some 350 courses in Scotland. Most are seaside links with sandy soil and springy turf, but there are also many fine courses inland among magnificent scenery. Visitors can play in the northern isolation of Sutherland's Brora, or after a round at glorious Machrihanish in Argyllshire, be lulled to sleep by the Atlantic.

Golf is less of a class-conscious sport in Scotland than it can be south of the border, it plays an important part in social life at all levels. It is also still comparatively cheap and Sunday play is now the rule rather than the exception.

St Andrews, on the Fife coast, is a town dedicated to golf. The Old Course there is said to be the best loved in the world; certainly most of the top names in the golfing world have played there. Another world famous venue, Gleneagles, 37 miles from Edinburgh, has probably two of the finest inland courses anywhere. The great Henry Cotton called it 'a golfer's paradise' – and he should know.

Carnoustie, north from Fife across the Tay estuary, is a seaside town which has staged several British Open Championships. Its mighty course, swept almost constantly by an east wind, sorts out the men from the boys. Over the sea, in the Isle of Skye, good golfing is to be found at Portree and Sconser, but few courses can match Machrie on the island of Islay if you want to play golf in

A scenic course at Rothesay on Bute

Motoring

an away-from-it-all atmosphere. It is just one of the many golfing jewels which is likely to charm the visitor.

Gullane (pronounced Gullan) in Lothian has four courses, the best known of which is Muirfield – home of the Honourable Company of Edinburgh Golfers. On the Firth of Clyde the names of Gailes, Barassie, Troon (a tough course even for leading professionals) and Prestwick are other familiar golfing centres.

Today, an increasing number of travel firms organise special golf tours, and there are several hotels which own courses – Gleneagles and Turnberry being among the best known. Both are owned by British Transport. Even if they do not actually own a course, many hotels close to courses run golf weeks or give special terms to players.

Scotland is a marvellous country for touring by car. There are excellent roads and motorways linking the main towns and it is easy to get off the beaten track to take in the scenery and perhaps enjoy a quiet picnic. It is a country with a two-fold appeal because it is possible to enjoy not only the wild mountain and loch scenery of the Highlands, but also the less spectacular but, nevertheless, beautiful Lowland country with its strong literary and romantic undertones. Except for the mainly industrial area, concentrated in the narrow waist between the Forth and the Clyde, the land is sparsely populated and nowhere else in Britain can you find such peace and tranquility as away up in the remote Highlands.

Anyone visiting Scotland in the crisp, fresh spring has the advantage of long hours of daylight, but the grandeur of the Highlands is probably best seen in September when the hillsides are ablaze with purple heather and rusty bracken. Warm July and pine-scented August are the best months for seeing traditional events such as Highland Gatherings, colourful festivals and other summer events. It is worth noting that access to some hills is restricted during the August shooting season.

The Day Drives which begin on page 210 have been specially selected to cover some of the most picturesque and interesting areas that Scotland has to offer. If you have time to spare you may also find it convenient to choose suitable centres from which to explore the surrounding countryside and, with a road atlas, tours covering most of the less frequented districts can be planned. These should appeal particularly to anyone already familiar with the better known touring areas. You can work out dozens of permutations.

Any comprehensive tour of Scotland ought to include a visit to at least one of the many islands off the west coast, although you do not necessarily have to take your car.

The coastal road to Drumbuie village with Skye in the distance

The only ferries still in operation on the mainland are at Kylesku in the far north west and at Ardgour south of Fort William, plus those to the islands. Tidal and weather conditions can sometimes cause delays, but increased traffic in the holiday season also causes holdups. Certain ferries do not operate on Sunday either, so check in advance – this can be done through AA offices. Ferry crossings can often be avoided, but the detours necessary can add considerably to your mileage and costs.

Although there is superb scenery to be enjoyed beside main roads, take lesser-used roads wherever possible to see more unspoilt areas of the beautiful countryside. Some minor roads may still not be well maintained, but road surfaces in recent years have been substantially improved and there are only a few steep gradients. North west of a line from Fort William to Inverness there are still some single-track roads, but with care these need not be a problem as passing bays are provided. The fact that roads are designated A or B does not necessarily mean that their width and condition match those of roads farther south. This is also true of many roads in other mountainous parts of the country. Estimated journey times, should allow for lower average speeds.

In the Highlands, many garages and filling stations are closed on Sunday and there are often long distances between them; it is therefore important to keep your tank topped up.

Fishing

It goes almost without saying that the scope for salmon and trout fishing in Scotland's hundreds of rivers and lochs is unrivalled. What is not, perhaps, so well known is how cheap it can be – trout fishing permits in particular are never expensive. It is true to say that Scotland offers a larger variety of angling for game fish suited to all types of pocket than anywhere else in Britain. Salmon can be a different matter. Some beats on exclusive waters are admittedly pricey but there are opportunities elsewhere which do not cost a lot. Salmon fishing is available to the residents of many hotels, who can arrange permits. There are also a number of fishing 'schools', many of which are attached to hotels and where equipment can be hired.

The best times to fish are spring, early summer and in autumn – in fact, it is in these off-peak periods that Scotland can be at its most enjoyable. There are national and international competitions for sea angling presided over by a governing body, the Scottish Federation of Sea Anglers. This body sponsors open-boat and shore championships and publishes a special brochure listing the main festivals and competitions. The Federation is affiliated to the European Federation of Sea Anglers and runs European championships in Scotland every year. The main season is from May to October.

British records are broken regularly in Scottish waters; head of the list is a skate weighing 226lb and the record halibut (caught from a boat) weighed in at 234lb. Both these were taken in northern waters around the Orkney and Shetland Isles. Tope and shark can be found in Luce Bay and the British cod and haddock records are being hard pressed in the Firth of Clyde.

It may surprise trout anglers used to the waters of Southern England to learn that the humble worm is not despised by everyone in Scotland. There are days, in fact, when the worm is almost the only lure for trout. Nevertheless, wet-fly fishing is most extensively used on the

Trailer caravanners will find it more convenient to choose a centre and tour the surrounding area by car only.

The AA produces a special leaflet about roads in Scotland which tourists will find helpful and informative.

Hotel accommodation in the north west is limited. If you have not booked in advance when touring, it is as well to telephone ahead as early as possible. In the height of the holiday season always arrange hotel or guesthouse accommodation before setting out. Inclusive go-as-you-please holidays are sensible alternatives because they take care of hotel bookings, or you can use the local Bed-Booking services which are operated by certain Tourist Information Centres.

lochs, though it also has its uses in fast-flowing rivers and streams. On the whole, however, dry-fly fishing is used a lot on rivers and there are some days on lochs when only the dry fly will do. Visiting anglers in doubt should seek the advice of local tackle dealers.

The extensive opportunities for coarse fishing that exist in Scotland for grayling, perch, pike and roach have only been realised in the last few years. The right to fish for coarse fish and brown trout belongs to owners of land that adjoins the water, so they may fish for those species in that part of the river opposite their land. Someone having land adjoining a loch, however, may pursue coarse fish and brown trout anywhere in that loch.

Visitors may find that their interest in coarse fish is regarded with some amusement but permission to fish is generally readily forthcoming and in some cases payment is not requested. Any charge made is usually to cover any game fish which may be in that particular water. River-board licences can cause some confusion, particularly among visiting anglers from England. Scotland does not have a direct equivalent to the English River Board and direct fisheries boards are concerned only with the preservation of salmon fisheries; there are no powers that apply to coarse fisheries. So, there is no such thing as a Scottish River-board licence for coarse fish, and there is no close season for coarse fish, either.

If you intend to go fishing in Scotland it is best to plan your route and book your rooms at angling hotels in advance. Go protected against wet weather and do not be put off by it because trout can quite often be caught in all weathers. A useful publication, *Scotland for Fishing* is issued by the Scottish Tourist Board, 23 Ravelston Terrace, Edinburgh EH4 3EU. It gives comprehensive information on all aspects of fishing in Scotland, including maps, lists of angling clubs from which permits can be obtained, fishing hotels and summaries of the various rivers and lochs in which it is possible to fish.

Boat fishing near the eastern shore of Loch Lomond

Walking Into Adventure *by Tom Weir*

There is no doubt about it, most of us like a bit of adventure in our walking – the marked forestry path, the nature trail and the ascent to a viewpoint indicator, they all make a pleasant stretch for the legs. But how much more satisfying to have the Ordnance Survey map in your hand and the compass in your pocket for a hill-walk or the circuit of a difficult shore – like the stretch from Elgol in Skye to Loch Coruisk via the Bad Step.

First of all, however, you have to be certain that you have the ability to cope with what you have in mind. Walk in easy places before you choose difficult ones. The main problem is in recognising the difference between danger and difficulty and the first thing you have to recognise about Scotland is that its hills must be taken more seriously than anywhere else in Britain.

Let me quote you a few Scottish mountain accident figures for 1981 covering the past year. It records 21 dead out of 109 accidents, a figure that is close to the average for the preceding three years. Mostly they were slips or stumbles but not a few accidents were of a non-climbing nature.

Accidents were almost unheard of in the first 40 years in the life of the Scottish Mountaineering Club, when the first generation of urban outdoor men was opening up to the world the great classic routes on the Scottish hills and climbing the sharp rock peaks of the Cuillins for the first time. In that period, from 1890 onward, as the mountains taught the climbers the elements of their craft they became ever more ambitious, but without losing respect for the hills. It was the early climbers who pointed out that it could be winter on any day of the year on the high tops, and to survive you had to be able to cope with being caught in the chilling combination of wind, wet and cold.

But in the big outdoor boom of the mid-fifties, this fact was often ignored and too many people died of exposure on the Scottish hills due to lack of warm

The crystal-clear Pools of Dee

clothing. Wool next to the skin was the old defence, a good vest and pants, long shirt and two woollen pullovers. Today we cover these with a windproof anorak and trousers. They are not hard to carry – unwanted clothing on the climb weighs little in the rucksack, and with some spare food like chocolate bars in addition to the day's rations you are prepared for most things, though not the worst weather that Scotland can throw at you when it is folly to go out. So consider the weather. Satellite photographs have dramatically increased the accuracy of forecasting and should be taken as a good guide to the weather you might expect, although the actual timing of it is less predictable. Even without a television picture or radio broadcast you can always phone the nearest Met office for an up-to-date report. Then you can watch out for any changes and pull back to base if it looks as though you are going to be caught out.

It is as well to remember, too, that if you persist in the face of heavy rain, streams and rivers will be rising, perhaps dangerously, and you may find yourself cut off in certain wet glens. This happened in Knoydart last January when a climber of Himalayan experience was drowned at sea-level trying to cross the normally small stream of the Allt Coire na Ciche. Even on the popular West Highland Way long-distance path, the two streams near the top of Loch

Lomond can be the most difficult problem on the 95-mile route from the outskirts of Glasgow to Milngavie.

Some people say that these streams should be bridged, but others disagree. It is an emotive subject which many outdoor folk get het up about. Many regard such a thing as a bridge as taking the wild out of wilderness. Challenging walks, they say, should remain challenging and be tackled only by those who can meet the challenge. It is a die-hard point of view, perhaps more important in the big, empty country of Knoydart than on the eastern shore of Loch Lomond.

This brings me to the question of National Parks, which was a lively issue in Scotland in the late 1940s when land was cheap and five locations were suggested for purchase. These outstanding areas were:

> Loch Lomond/Trossachs; Glen Affric/Glen Cannich/Glen Strathfarrar; Ben Nevis/Glencoe/Blackmount; The Cairngorms; Loch Torridon/Loch Maree

Although given National Park Direction Orders, and landscape protection (which helped to protect them against developments), these areas were not designated as parks when England and Wales received theirs by special legislation. What Scotland got by way of compensation were Forest Parks, the first of which had been set up in 1935 around the fjord lochs of Argyll, integrating forestry and tourism into a network of access paths for walkers.

These timber-planted parks cover 300,000 acres of wonderfully diverse country for walking. The Queen Elizabeth Park stretches from the oakwoods fringing the eastern shore of Loch Lomond over the top of Ben Lomond to the Trossachs. Glenmore has Loch Morlich and a network of paths leading through ancient Caledonian pines rich in wildlife. Glen Trool in the Solway region – stretching north of Newton Stewart and east to Loch Ken – has gentle, low-ground riches as well as a

Ramblers on An Teallach above Dundonnel

high granite heart akin to the Cairngorms. At the time of writing, an ambitious cross-country route is in the making, stretching 204 miles from Port Patrick near the Mull of Galloway to Glen Trool and the Nith to Wanlockhead (the highest village in Scotland), thence to Beattock for Moffat and across the Border Hills to Galashiels and on to Cockburnspath and the North Sea. This will give a new opportunity for walkers, with accessible and, indeed, inaccessible stretches which should please all comers.

Scotland, of course, has a wealth of rights of way, thousands upon thousands of them, which have never been registered so none are marked on the current series of Ordnance Survey maps. But many of the important ones are signposted by the privately subscribed Scottish Rights of Way Society Ltd. On any of these paths no person has a right to challenge you to state your destination or give an account of your movements. It is the duty of local councils to register all rights of way in their district, but lack of staff is too often their excuse for not discharging it.

For walkers, deer stalking can be a

problem, especially in a great wilderness area like that between Loch Maree and Little Loch Broom where public paths lead through, and there is a great temptation to take to the hill. But remember that the owner maintains this wild land and pays a staff in order to shoot, so in August, September and October you should respect his right.

Better at this time of year to visit the ever-open properties of the National Trust for Scotland in Kintail, Glencoe, Ben Lawers or the wonderful country of Glen Torridon. Remember for your own good that wherever you are on private property you can be asked to turn back by a route which the owner can decide you shall take. Moreover he can claim damages, but he will have to prove it, so you are in a better position than in England where damage is inherent in the mere act of trespass. It is certainly not correct to say that there is no law of trespass in Scotland, as many people believe.

Generally speaking I think the best walking in Scotland can be found within those areas which the pioneers selected as the most suitable for National Parks. Of these Glen Cannich and Glen Strathfarrar have been reduced in value by hydro-electricity reservoirs inundating the cross-country paths between the North Sea and Atlantic, but Glen Affric is still a gem. The Caledonian pines are being conserved, fine walks have been laid out, and the path by Loch Affric to Kintail is one of the best long cross-country walks in Britain.

There is much to be said in favour of the Cairngorms, too, which is now the second biggest nature reserve in Europe. It comprises glens with remnants of ancient Caledonian pines, superb rock corries leading up to the most considerable extent of plateau above 4,000ft in Britain, and paths on the lower ground which lead gently into remote recesses or through the deep trench of the Lairig Ghru Pass between the Spey and the Dee.

The National Trust for Scotland looks after Glencoe, while Blackmount, stretching from Loch Tulla, is both a deer forest and a winter skiing venture. Perhaps one day we will have Special Parks rather than the old concept of National Parks. The Countryside Commission for Scotland has published a list of 40 areas of outstanding merit, stretching from the Solway to Shetland. These amount to 3,868 square miles and combine coastline, sea and freshwater lochs, rivers and woodlands and moorlands, together with some admixture of cultivated lands.

The end result, should it ever come to pass, aims at developing and improving facilities 'for the enjoyment of the Scottish countryside and for the conservation and enhancement of the natural beauty and amenity of that countryside'.

It is a noble aim, and one we should press for. There is still plenty of lonely wilderness – but it is too inaccessible to all except true believers who don't like any watering of the wilds. TOM WEIR.

TOM WEIR is vice president of The Scottish Rights of Way Society.

Skiing

Scotland cannot claim to have the sort of snow conditions to be found at the high-altitude continental resorts (the climate is arctic rather than alpine) but skiing is usually possible for about four months, from December.

It had a slow start when it was first introduced into Scotland over 70 years ago. Even 20 years ago there was only a small hut on Cairngorm. It was 'Jean's Hut', built by the father of a girl who died on an early skiing holiday. Since then the sport has grown to become immensely popular and today the mountain boasts the highest restaurant in Britain – the Ptarmigan, at 3,600ft.

It is possible to ski in many more Scottish mountains than will ever be developed for the sport, several in areas not regarded as suitable for holidays by those living south of the border. Cairngorm and Glenshee, in the Perthshire highlands, provide excellent accommodation, ski school facilities, and a range of equipment hire, and aprés-ski activities. The official season at Cairngorm is from mid-December until March, and at Glenshee it extends to April; between March and late April is the best time. But the weather is unpredictable in the Scottish mountains: quickly-descending chill mists, causing poor visibility, and damp, bitter cold frequently close in on the slopes. On the other hand, when conditions are at their best they are excellent. Although the mountains are not high (Cairngorm is 4,084ft) it is possible in spring, to ski in warm sunshine over a still perfect surface when snow in the Alps is rapidly deteriorating.

Aviemore village near the foot of the Cairngorms has been transformed into an international-style resort, with a multi-million-pound leisure centre with first-class accommodation for skiers. Facilities there include hotels and chalets, restaurants, swimming pool, skating rink, cinema, ten-pin bowling – and an artificial ski slope! Reaching the real slopes is easy, thanks to a fast access road which ends at a car park 2,000ft up,

The slopes of Happy Valley near the head of Glen Coe

just below the chairlift station. Near the car park is a beginners' tow, but the main tows are reached from the mid station of the two-stage double chairlift. Nearby, easy but varied skiing can be enjoyed in the wide bowl of Coire Cas. (A coire is a mountain recess – in Gaelic it means cauldron.) Advanced skiers will find good sport on the steeper, faster pistes of the White Lady which are reached from the chairlift top station or by tow from the middle station. A third coire, Coire na Ciste, is a steep, narrow run and is also reached from the top. There are eating places and toilets at all these stations.

Hotels throughout the Spey Valley cater for winter-sporters and many of them arrange evening entertainment. Some also have their own ski school and a resident instructor, equipment-hire service, and may provide transport to the slopes. Otherwise there are many ski schools in the area offering excellent tuition – particularly if they belong to the British Association of Ski Instructors. One well known school is at Carrbridge, half a mile from Lochanhully, where the AA runs a 'village' of Finnish-style, pine-built lodges, ideal for skiers' accommodation, or a self-catering Highland holiday. Details and a brochure are available from AA offices.

At Glenshee, which was one of the first centres to be developed for skiing, the snow does not stay as long as it does at Cairngorm, but extensive facilities for skiers are provided. There are now two chairlifts and twelve tows. The aprés-ski programmes are wide-ranging and scattered among hotels as far afield as Blairgowrie, about 20 miles away.

From the Glenshee hotels it takes only 15 minutes or so to drive to the nearest slopes. You can chairlift to the top of the 3,059ft Cairnwell, and when the shadows lengthen, chase the sun to the facing slopes by way of the Sunny Slope tow. If you are not intrepid enough to tackle the Tiger Run down this steep, and often icy, face of the mountain, it can be avoided by traversing screes to Buchart's Corrie – a wide, pleasant bowl with tows and ideal runs for novice and intermediate skiers. This also applies to one of the most recent developments for downhill only, at Lecht on the Cockbridge to Tomintoul road 20 miles south east of Grantown-on-Spey – an area of short runs but with several tows to make life easier.

If you are planning a family skiing holiday, the Snow Fun Week at Glenshee from 17 to 23 March is aimed equally at experienced skiers and beginners. There are races, cross-country skiing, tobogganing and even snowman building competitions, while in the evening, aprés-ski activities include barbecues, discos and folk nights.

For non-skiers, Scotland offers a range of other winter sports. The best known are curling (the country's ancient winter sport) and shinty, which is similar to hockey.

Aviemore Leisure Centre

Pony Trekking

You do not have to be an expert to enjoy a Scottish holiday on horseback. A lot of day trips and holidays cater especially for those of little or no experience in the saddle, under the guidance of an expert.

Pony trekking began at Newtownmore on Speyside. In its simplest form it offers a means of exploring rough, open country in the company of adventure-loving people. The pace is steady and the ponies are surefooted and sturdy. They know their job and many of them carry riders of any age, size and weight for long distances over moorland and mountain, along forest paths, through burns and rivers and up and down steep glens. Experienced riders are offered more ambitious trail riding on full-sized horses at two centres in the Borders, at Lauder and near Jedburgh, where the pace is faster and includes spells of trotting and cantering.

Riding can include anything from lessons in an equestrian centre or country estate to rough riding over open country. Whether the mount is a highland pony (or one of the other ponies native to Britain), a hunter or a hack, the rider will be asked to care for it by grooming and feeding, irrespective of where the riding is based – hotel, guesthouse or youth hostel.

Many trekking centres are recognised by one of the national associations sponsoring the sport, such as the Scottish Council of Physical Recreation or the Ponies of Britain Club, and it is advisable to choose one of these centres so you can be sure that the ponies are healthy and well trained, and that the tack is in good condition.

At all sponsored centres, trekkers are given a test on the first morning. If they are complete novices they are told exactly what they should do – most people find that it is easier than riding a bicycle. So well trained and docile are the mounts that it is hardly necessary to tell them to stop and turn; they know the treks like the back of their, well . . . hooves! You may find that your instructor asks you to walk the last half mile or so home and lead the pony. This allows it to cool down before its saddle is removed; a sweating horse can catch cold, and the rider benefits, too, because walking helps to loosen muscles which are quite likely to have become stiff on the ride.

Dress simply. A pair of old slacks (cords, if possible) will do if you do not own jodhpurs or riding breeches – jeans are not really suitable. There are times when you may have to lead your pony over rough ground, so strong, flat-heeled shoes or boots should be worn. A hooded anorak or windcheater will keep out the worst of the wet, and take sweaters, gloves and warm underwear for when it is cold. Also, it is a good idea to have boots with you because the stable work can be messy.

It is possible to hire ponies by the hour or the day from centres all over Scotland, particularly in the Borders, the south west, Spey Valley and Angus. But a word of warning: you are quite likely to grow so fond of your pony after 'living' together for days that your parting will be painful.

Homeward bound after a day's trekking

WHISKY GALORE

TV personality DEREK COOPER, who has written three books about whisky and has twice been awarded the Glenfiddich Gold Medal as Wine and Food Writer of the Year, sings the praises of Scotland's glorious liquid gold

Whisky Galore

by Derek Cooper

Nobody really knows. Is it the quality of the pure, soft water filtered through moss off some of the oldest granite rocks on earth? Is it the excellence of the barley and the skill with which it's malted? Is it the fragrance of the peat smoke that lingers in the bouquet? Is it a couple of centuries of experience handed down, often from father to son?

As I say, nobody really knows the secrets of the art of making the finest malt whiskies in the world. However assiduously they try in Finland or Japan they can't make whisky like this. No-one outside Scotland has ever succeeded in re-creating the subtlety and mellowness of what in Gaelic they call *uisge beatha* and which comes bearing internationally recognised names like *Laphroaig, Glenmorangie, Bowmore, The Glenlivet, Macallan* and *Glenfiddich*.

There are only two other drinks in the world which can compare with it – Cognac and Armagnac. Malt whisky has a history equally as old and equally as distinguished. Two hundred years ago whisky making in Scotland was a cottage industry that flourished in every island and almost every glen. That it was illegal made the operation infinitely more attractive. The remote possibility that a government officer might come riding over the hill and confiscate your still lent an element of sport to the proceedings. For decades proud Scots manifested their contempt for the punitive duties imposed on distillation by the English and went their own individual way – as Robert Burns proclaimed: 'whisky and freedom gang thegither'.

Famous names like *Balmenach, Cardow, Lochnagar, Highland Park, Ardbeg* and *Lagavulin* all sprang from the old days of smuggling. A change in legislation in the 1820s made it less hazardous and more lucrative for the smugglers to abandon their clandestine activities, and many an old 'bothy', that formerly worked only in the dead of night, grew into a legitimate distillery.

When you follow the so called 'Whisky Trail' round Scotland you will often be literally treading in the footsteps of smugglers who made their whisky secretly in the hills and then took it by pony train to the nearest town. Sometimes they went in the guise of a funeral party; at other times, if the revenue officers had been handsomely bribed, they rode into town openly.

The heartland of these operations was in the Spey Valley but the 117 present-day distilleries are scattered far and wide. You'll find malt whisky being made in Orkney, Skye and Jura and in remote glens throughout the Lowlands and Highlands. If you want to find a real whisky island you might take the car ferry to Islay. If the Spey Valley is the Bordeaux of whisky, Islay is its Burgundy, and its most renowned malts – *Bowmore, Bruichladdich, Lagavulin* and *Laphroaig* are prized by those who like their whisky to possess a strong, distinctive character.

All over Scotland millions of gallons of whisky lie gently maturing (and evaporating), ageing in oak until they are considered old and smooth enough to be sold either as single malts under their own names or married with grain whisky to make one of the hundreds of internationally famous blends.

Well over 98% of all the Scotch whisky drunk today comes in a blend of malt and grain whisky. Up to 20 or more malt whiskies contribute their own particular aroma and flavour. Some give body, some give weight and some lend delicacy, but each blend has its own character whether it leans towards the heaviness of the Islay malts or the lightness of the Lowland malts. Whiskies are much lighter today than they were 50 years ago, but the skill in blending remains unchanged.

The process of distillation uses a great quantity of water, which is why traditionally distilleries have always suspended their operations in the summer when rainfall is at its lowest.

Whisky by the tun – but the eagle-eyed exciseman is never far away

This 'silent season', as its known, is a time for the staff to take their holidays and for the annual ritual of repair and maintenance. You may well find that if you go visiting in July and August many distilleries are either closed or not fully operational.

In the 19th century most distilleries were built alongside the banks of a river or a burn so that there was a generous supply of cold water to cool the copper worm through which the whisky vapours rose, and plenty of hydraulic power to work the crushing plant and the pulleys and winches. Many a distillery was using water-power until well into this century.

The most prominent feature of an old distillery is the distinctive pagoda-shaped kiln where the green malt was dried and peated. A few 20th-century distilleries have kept the pagoda shape in their architecture, but nowadays only a handful of distilleries malt their own barley and the old malting floors and kilns have probably been converted into storage space.

A dozen quick facts about whisky

● *Malt whisky* is made solely from water, malted barley and yeast. It is twice distilled in onion-shaped copper stills.

● *Grain whisky* is made from maize and barley in a continuous still.

● No whisky may be legally sold until it has aged for at least three years in oak casks.

● As a rule, the less subtle grain whiskies do not noticeably improve much after three years in wood; most malt whiskies take much longer to reach the peak of perfection. Some are at their best at 8 years, others are best at 10 or 12 or 15 years. Older malts – 21 and 25 years – can also be bought.

● *Single malt* is a whisky produced exclusively in one distillery. It has become increasingly fashionable to drink single malts either as an aperitif or as a digestif.

● *Vatted malt* is a blend of several malts chosen to achieve the desired quality and harmony.

● *Blended whisky,* commonly referred to as 'Scotch', was developed in the mid-19th century as a blend of malt and grain whisky. The high-priced luxury blends tend to contain the finest old malt whiskies. The less you pay when it comes to a blend the less you get in both quality and style.

● Malt whiskies are usually divided into four categories: **Lowland Malts, Highland Malts, Campbeltown Malts** and **Island Malts.**

● Whisky is improved by the judicious admixture of water; not too much, not too little.

● *Liqueur whiskies* like Drambuie and Glayva are whisky-based drinks fortified with honey and herbs.

● If an age is specified on a whisky then none of the whiskies in the blend may be younger than the specified age.

● In England and Wales whisky is usually sold in measures of $\frac{1}{6}$ gill ($\frac{2}{3}$ fl oz). In Scotland the measure is habitually $\frac{1}{5}$ gill (1 fl oz). Ask for a *glass* of whisky and you will be deemed to be discreetly asking for a double.

fermented 'wort' is then given its first distillation in the wash still to produce what are known as 'low wines'. The low wines are redistilled in the spirit still until the time comes to start collecting the whisky itself which comes off the still as a clear, colourless liquid – one of the most heavily taxed liquids in the world.

You will notice that the stillman is not allowed to touch or taste the result of his labours. The whisky pours into a glass-sided brass case which has a large and shining lock on it. From there the spirit is filled into casks and removed to a bonded warehouse – with another large lock on it! It's a tantalising industry, discreetly patrolled at every stage by the eagle-eyed exciseman.

Distilleries like the one at Bladnoch (above left) can be seen on the Whisky Trail (above)

A great deal of heat is given off in the distilling process so if you come round a bend in the Highlands and see a chimney belching steam, more often than not you'll be approaching a distillery.

Not all distilleries are able to welcome visitors; they are either too small or lack the staff necessary to make the operation possible. If in doubt contact the nearest tourist office. Some distilleries, notable amongst them *Glenfiddich, The Glenlivet* (in Glenlivet), *Glenfarclas, Glengoyne* and *Bowmore,* have purpose-built reception centres and skilled guides who will explain all the mysteries of this peculiarly Scottish industry.

Although most distilleries now receive their malted barley from a central maltings, the process of making whisky remains remarkably similar to the way it was 100 years ago.

The malt first has to be dressed and ground before it is mashed with hot water and fermented with yeast. The

Every distillery has its own ideas on how the finest whisky should be made. Some favour small stills, some large. Some heat their stills with steam coils, others continue to fire them with coal. Some use heavily-peated malt to make their mash; others use a malt in which you can hardly detect the reek of peat.

Great care is taken when a still has to be replaced – they seldom last longer than 25 years – to ensure that its successor has an identical shape, down to the last curve. There is a strong inherited feeling that the character of a malt whisky is deeply influenced by the still in which it is born, and there is much truth in this.

Today many distilleries have electronic consoles and the stillman looks more like a captain on the bridge of a tanker than the traditional kettle minder. Chromatography and mass spectrometry, sensory evaluation techniques and combined resources of PhDs and chemical engineers have certainly quantified the art of distilling in recent years, but I like to think that the basic alchemy remains firmly unchanged – barley and water . . . and then *uisge beatha*!

The Whisky Trail Grampian Region has organised a 62-mile Whisky Trail which takes in *Glenfiddich, Tamdhu, Glenfarclas* and *Strathisla*. The tour can last from four to six hours depending on how many distilleries you visit and how long you linger. The road is signposted and takes in the village of Tomintoul (the highest in the Highlands) and the towns of Keith and Dufftown.
Of course if you are motoring, don't be tempted to sample the goods. Every distillery almost certainly will want to offer you a dram, but remember – drinking and driving just don't mix!

Derek Cooper is author of
A Guide to the Whiskies of Scotland
Enjoying Scotch (with Diane Pattullo)
The Whisky Roads of Scotland (with Fay Godwin)

The principal towns and villages which have a distillery either in their midst or nearby:

ABERFELDY	Aberfeldy	INVERNESS	Glen Albyn, Glen Mhor, Millburn
ABERLOUR	Glenallachie, Benrinnes	KEITH	Aultmore, Glen Keith, Strathisla, Strathmill
ALNESS	Teaninich, Dalmore		
BALLINDALLOCH	Glenfarclas, Cragganmore	KILLEARN	Glengoyne
		KIRKWALL (Orkney)	Scapa, Highland Park
BALMORAL	Lochnagar		
BANFF	Macduff, Banff	MONTROSE	Hillside, Lochside
BLACKFORD	Tullibardine	MUIR OF ORD	Ord
BRORA	Clynelish, Brora	MULBEN	Auchroisk
BUCKIE	Inchgower	NAIRN	Royal Brackla
CAMPBELTOWN	Springbank, Glen Scotia	OBAN	Oban
		PENCATTLAND	Glenkinchie
CARBOST (Skye)	Talisker	PETERHEAD	Glenugie
CRIEFF	Glenturret	PITLOCHRY	Blair Athol, Edradour
CROMDALE	Balmenach		
DALWHINNIE	Dalwhinnie	PORTSOY	Glenglassaugh
DOUNE	Deanston	ROTHES	Caperdonich, Glen Grant, Glenrothes, Glen Spey, Glenburn
DUFFTOWN	Balvenie, Glenfiddich, Convalmore, Glendullan, Mortlach, Dufftown, Pittyvaich		
		STONEHAVEN	Glenury Royal
		TAIN	Glenmorangie
		TOBERMORY (Mull)	Ledaig
ELGIN	Glenmoray, Linkwood	TOMATIN	Tomatin
		WICK	Pulteney
FALKIRK	Rosebank		
FETTERCAIRN	Fettercairn		
FORRES	Benromach		
FORT WILLIAM	Ben Nevis, Glenlochy		

The following distilleries are on Islay: Ardbeg, Bowmore, Bruichladdich, Bunnahabhain, Caol Ila, Lagavulin, Laphroaig, Port Ellen

THE HIGHLAND GAMES

The first Highland Games, in Falkirk 200 years ago, were principally a piping competition. Today, as writer and editor JENNY CARTER reports, they are a spectacle of sight and sound, the colourful programme including athletic and dancing events

The Highland Games

Hammer thrower at Dunkeld

No visitor to Scotland should miss the colourful spectacle of a Scottish Highland Games. From spring to late autumn, from the Borders to the outposts of the Highlands, these gatherings attract the cream of competitors, and spectators in their thousands. On all sides the swirl of the kilt and the colour of tartan assail the eye; pipe bands play their pieces in cheerful oblivion of the rival bands fifty yards away; dancers warm up for the competition, kilts swinging, feet flashing – and even the 'heavy' athletes don the kilt for the tossing of the caber and the throwing of the hammer.

The origins of these games are undoubtedly ancient – Queen Victoria, although she did much to revive interest in these gatherings, was by no means their instigator. In the 11th century King Malcolm Canmore, in need of a fast and fit messenger, held auditions by means of a race to the top of Craig Coinnich above Braemar – the very first, perhaps, of the famous Braemar Highland Gatherings still patronised by the Royal Family today. Many clan chiefs, indeed, held competitions among their followers or clansmen, to pick out the ablest for bodyguards and to keep them fighting fit between active service.

The medieval 'wappenschaws' or weapon-showings – used both as a competitive tournament and for the training of men – lent something to the structure of latter-day Games. So, too, did Lowland 'Beltane' celebrations of the coming of spring, and the Gaelic 'Lunasdal' or 'Lammas' celebration of autumn. In many parts of the country, gatherings had their beginnings in purely social events such as weddings, where the celebrations would include impromptu challenges of skill in one field or another, and where the whole population would become involved.

Many events still featured in today's gatherings grew out of the amusements of local workers. Blacksmiths, tired of the forge, would see how far they could throw their hammers, or iron weights. River beds were searched for suitably-sized, well-rounded stones to 'put'. And foresters, not to be outdone, invented their own trial of skill and strength using a tree-trunk (*cabar* in Gaelic). Running and jumping could be carried out anywhere with the minimum of equipment; and hill-racing, with such a creditable pedigree, was in some places retained as an event – the most notable survivor being the annual race from the Post Office in Fort William to the top of Britain's highest mountain, Ben Nevis, and back again – an incredible and highly demanding exercise.

Pipe bands at Braemar

by Jenny Carter

But these gatherings were always more than merely a chance to show off physical fitness; piping and dancing – important aspects of the martial tradition – were always popular. So much so, indeed, that at various times statutes were laid down prohibiting them. It would not have been wise to encourage these arts when more practical skills such as archery and swordplay were required in the interests of national defence. In the 1780s, however, following the lifting of the ban on the wearing of tartan imposed after the defeat of the Jacobite cause, many people felt it important to encourage these aspects of Scottish culture, and they once again became a prominent feature of the Games.

The structure of today's Highland Games, rooted so firmly in history, offers a unique test of skills. On the field, it is the 'heavy' events that are most popularly associated with Scottish athletics – the hammer, the stone, the caber, traditional tests of strength and manhood. 'Ye casting of ye bar' as tossing the caber was once known, is perhaps the most remarkable of all these tests; the trunk of a pine tree, sometimes as long as 25 feet, or weighing as much as 154 pounds, is grasped by the competitor at its thinner end. The object is to 'turn' the log on to its thicker end, so that it describes a semi-circle, and lands as nearly in a straight line away from the thrower as possible. It is an art that calls not merely for strength but also balance and timing; and there is no substitute for experience, for ground conditions can be as variable and difficult to read as the cabers themselves. At some gatherings the log may be sawn shorter if the competitors are unable to turn it. Other Games, such as those at Braemar and Crieff, use the same caber year after year so that it becomes a standing challenge to the athlete.

Many athletes who enter the Games are professionals, and the performances they achieve go largely unnoticed in the

Dunoon sword-dance competitors

record books. This is particularly true of the track events, and times set by competitors in the sprint events have often approached Olympic standards. An Edinburgh sprinter, Ricky Dunbar, ran 100 yards in 9.6 seconds, and in 1970 George McNeill ran 110 metres in 11 seconds flat. Today competitors in the light events wear running kit, but this was not always so, and one Peter Cameron achieved a high jump of 5 feet 7 inches wearing the kilt!

Highland dancing, delicate and graceful, might be thought to bear little relation to the field events. But do not be deceived by the spectacular lightness and fine footwork of these dancers – it is an art that demands both athleticism and fitness. Many dances have their roots in warlike traditions; the famous 'sword dance' – there are, in fact, several variations – is said to have been first performed in 1054 by King Malcolm Canmore after his defeat of one of Macbeth's chiefs. Seizing his fallen foe's sword, he crossed it with his own weapon, and jubilantly danced a jig over the two swords. Dancing over crossed swords was thereafter supposed to bring luck in battle – unless the swords were touched by the dancer's feet, when action was to be avoided at all cost. The Highland Fling, danced on one spot, is reputed to have been danced originally on the *targe*, or shield, thus circumscribing movement. The arms, lifted above the head, are said to represent the antlers of a stag.

While many traditional dances have their roots in war, others have been developed for women, with more intricate footwork and demanding more elegant body movements. Originally ladies wore the same garb as male competitors – that is, full kilt regalia. But a movement initiated by the Aboyne Highland Games Committee in 1952 reintroduced a traditional style of dress popular in the 17th century – a gathered or slightly pleated lightweight tartan skirt with a low-cut velvet bodice worn over a loose white blouse with elbow-length sleeves, and an *arisaid* or plaid flowing from the right shoulder. Many competitors in the dancing events are children, and their skill at the intricate steps can be quite remarkable. Standards of judging are high, and many of the great dancers have themselves become teachers and carried the skills of their art to all parts of the globe.

There are few sounds more evocative than the sound of the pipes caught on the breeze and blown up to the heather-clad hills. Even more strongly than Highland Dancing is the bagpipe rooted in martial history; for centuries the pipes were carried to the very forefront in battle, to incite the clansmen to bravery and to affright the enemy. But the piper played an important role in Highland pageantry, too, and it was his duty to compose music for the celebration of every important event.

There are written records of bagpipes all over the world, dating as far back as 4,000BC, so Scotland certainly cannot claim this instrument as her own invention. But the Scottish pipes are recognised as amongst the finest of such instruments; and certainly the tradition of piping in Scotland is one that has endured over the centuries. Although the pipes are no longer carried into war, most Scottish regiments have their own pipe bands; and anyone who has visited the Edinburgh Military Tattoo will know just how stirring is the

SCOTTISH CLANS

performance of the Lone Piper at the close of the ceremony, a dim figure high up on the Castle ramparts. And for the purposes of communication in the open, the pipes can have few peers, for their haunting sounds have been known to travel as far as ten miles in favourable conditions.

The classic music of the pipes is the *piobaireachd* – pronounced pibroch – and it is prizes in this class that are the most highly coveted. But reels, strathspeys, jigs and marches are also represented in piping competitions, for it should be remembered that this is the instrument of war as well as the instrument of leisure.

Some Games, notably Aboyne, are renowned for their dancing events, others such as Braemar or Ballater for their heavy events, and the Border Games for the light events. The Northern Meeting at Inverness and the Argyllshire Gathering at Oban, however, award the most coveted prizes for piping. If a piper wins the Gold Medal at the Northern Meeting, he will die happy.

When Bonnie Prince Charlie gathered his troops for battle, when Jacobite hearts were still happy and full of hope, he also started a new tradition. Instead of the lone piper, he massed together all the pipes under his command, as many as a hundred – the first pipe band.

Today at every Highland Games, pipe bands tumble out of their coaches into the grounds by the hundreds. No Highland Games would be complete without the highly popular Pipe Band Championships. The spectacle of these proudly kilted pipers marching in stately procession under the shadows of Scotland's mountains is a never-to-be-forgotten experience of spectacular sight and thrilling sound, which provides a fitting end to the day's varied and unusual entertainment.

THE TARTAN

The colourful, enigmatic tartan was banned by the English after they had smashed the Highland clan system beyond repair at the Battle of Culloden in April 1746 – not because it served any military purpose, but because it had associations with the Jacobite cause. The penalty for contravening the Act proscribing the wearing of tartan was six months for the first offence and transportation for the second. The Act was not repealed until 1782. It has been suggested that the different tartans acted as 'badges' of clan loyalty in battle, but this seems unlikely because the clansmen used to take off their brightly coloured plaids before a conflict and fight half naked.

Sir Walter Scott's romantic, if rather dubious, versions of Scottish history – which 19th-century England accepted as fact – are largely responsible for the modern tartan myth. Thanks to Scott, England at that time was inflamed with a love for all things north of the border and a need to identify with the poet's Highland heroes; indeed, the Waverley novels did wonders for the kilt. George IV visited Scotland in 1882, the first reigning monarch to do so for two centuries, and showed himself at Holyroodhouse in a kilt of Royal Stewart tartan. Scott took charge of the ceremonial, clad in Campbell trews, and Scotland entered a tartan age which continues to this day.

Haberdashers, well used to following the dicates of fickle fashion, were only too happy to cater for the fast-growing number of folk keen to wear the tartan. Anyone who had a claim, however tenuous, to Scottish ancestry could have his own tartan designed and made up to order.

Today, there is a bewildering array of tartans, some are genuinely old, others are the result of wishful thinking on the part of some of the estimated fifty million people of Scottish descent throughout the world. Still more are town or area tartans which are not connected with any clan or family. But no matter where they come from the designs are colourful and ingenious, as the accompanying small selection illustrates. The map of Scotland indicates the location of the clans associated with the tartans that are shown.

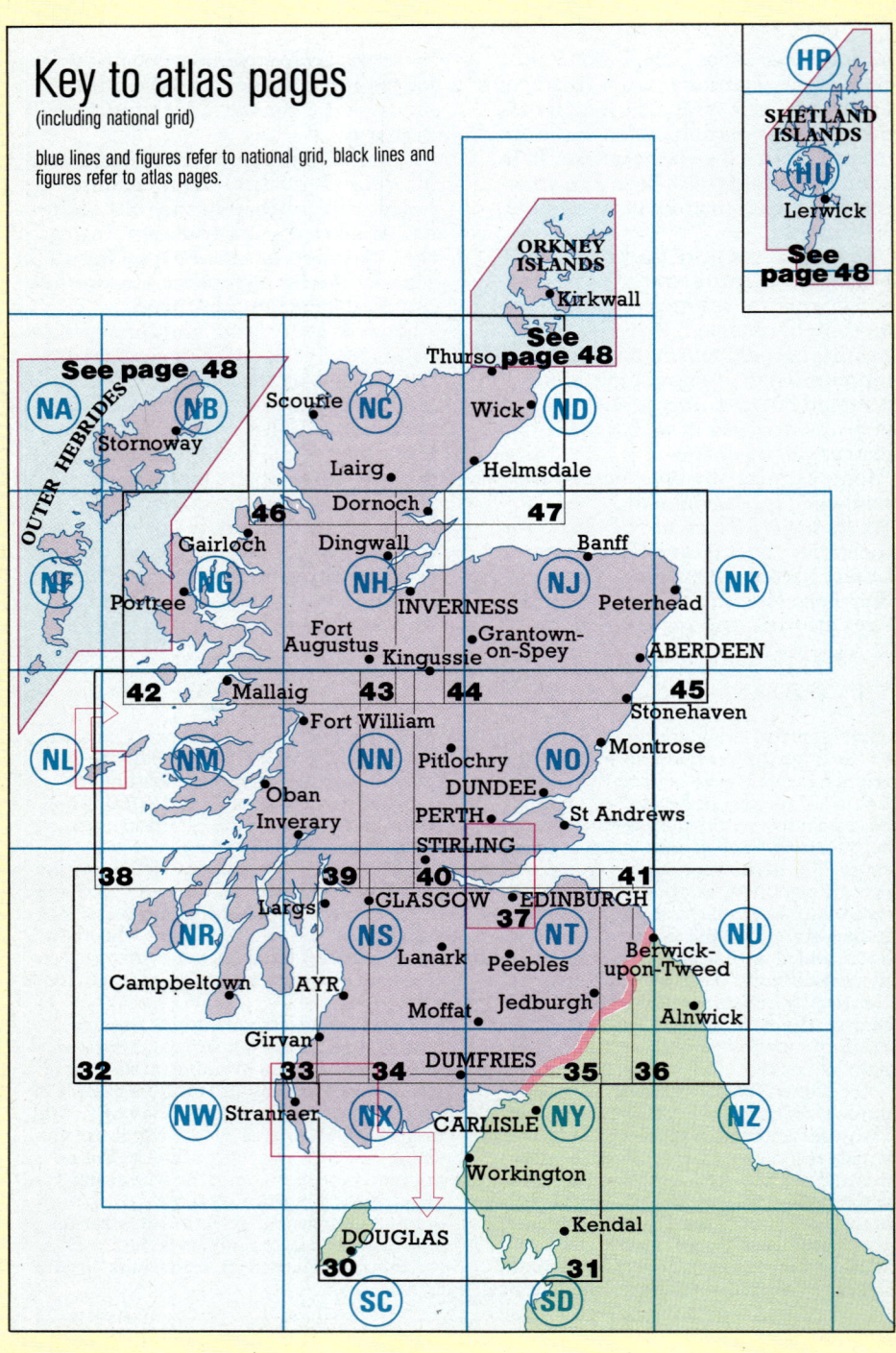

Atlas Legend

Motorways, junction numbers & service areas
Restricted motorway junction
Motorway under construction
Primary routes
Other A roads
B roads
Unclassified roads
Toll roads
Narrow roads with passing places
Rivers, lakes & lochs
AA service centres. 24 hr breakdown information service
AA service centres. Breakdown/information service normal hours
AA motorway information service centres. Normally 0900-1700 hrs. Callers only
AA road service centres. Breakdown & road service information. Normally 0900-1700 hrs
AA port service centres
AA & RAC telephones
PO telephone boxes in isolated areas of Northern Scotland
Places with AA hotels
Places with AA garages
Places with AA hotels & garages
Vehicle ferries between places in Great Britain
Continental vehicle ferries
Airports
Distance in miles between motorway junctions
Distance in miles between places and road junctions
AA viewpoints – leaflet available from Regional Headquarters
Tidal constant
Spot heights
Regional boundaries
Page overlaps and numbers of continuing pages

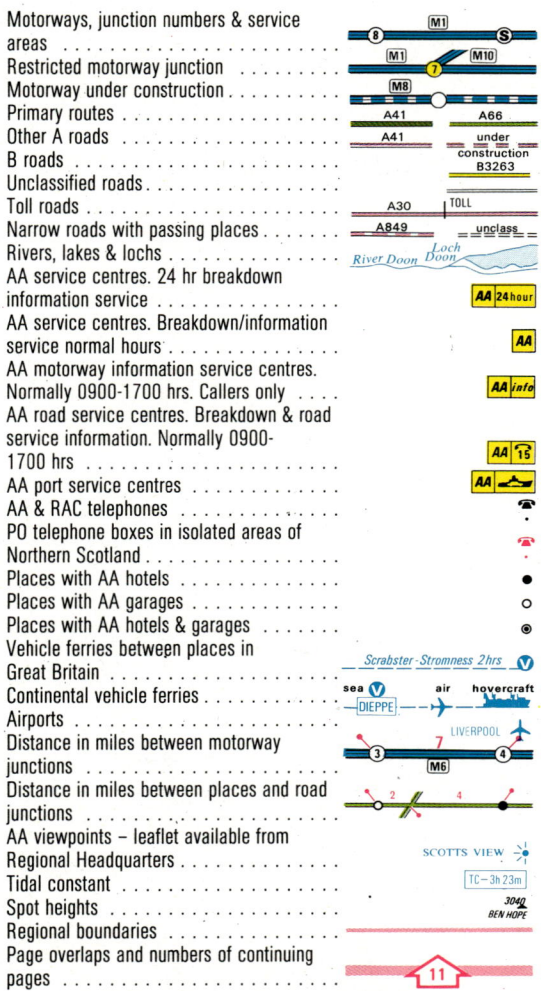

The National Grid Referencing system

The Ordnance Survey National Grid provides one system of reference common to maps of all scales. The country is first divided into major grid squares (100 kilometres) each square being designated by two letters (diag left). These major squares are then sub-divided into one hundred (10km) squares the graticules of which are numbered west to east and south to north from 1 to 9 (diag right). In the atlas the major squares appear in heavy blue lines and the sub-divisions are lighter.

2. figure referencing: A place listed in the gazetteer is referenced to the 10km square of the major square into which it falls and a two figure reference is sufficient to find that square. First the major square is located by its designating letters and then the 10km square by the intersection of the numbered graticules. (A gazetteer reference is prefixed by the appropriate atlas page number).

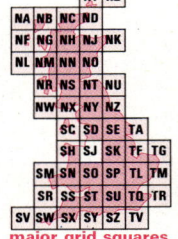
major grid squares

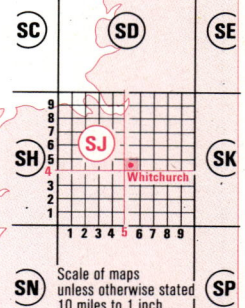

Example: The reference given for Whitchurch (Salop) is **Map23SJ54**. The first two figures **23** is the atlas page number. This is followed by the major square designation letters **SJ**. The next figure **5** is the numbered graticule of the major square sub-divisions when reading west to east (left to right) the last figure **4** the numbered graticule when reading south to north (bottom to top). The point of intersection of graticules **5** and **4** is the south-west (bottom left) corner of the 10km square containing Whitchurch (shaded in diag).

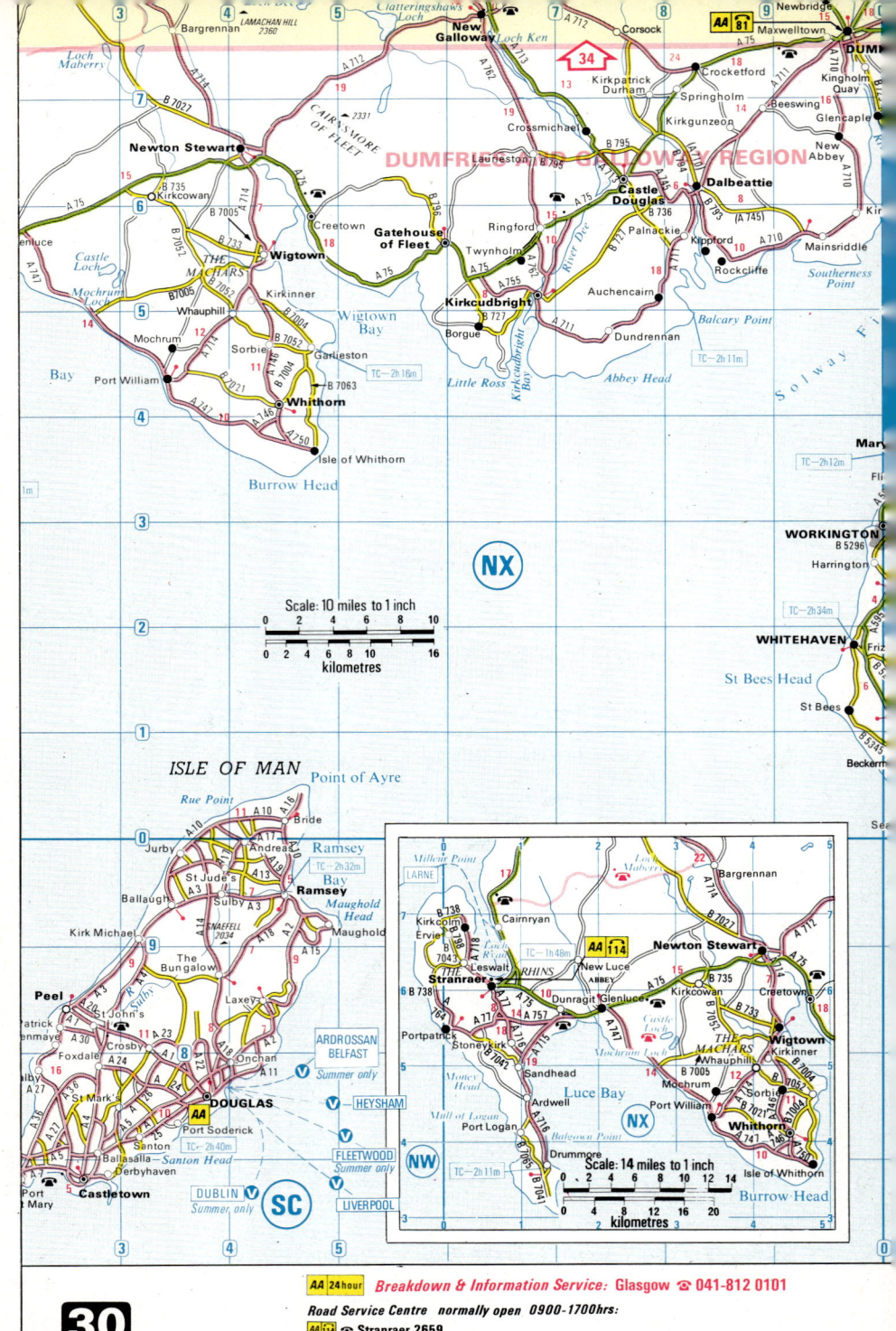

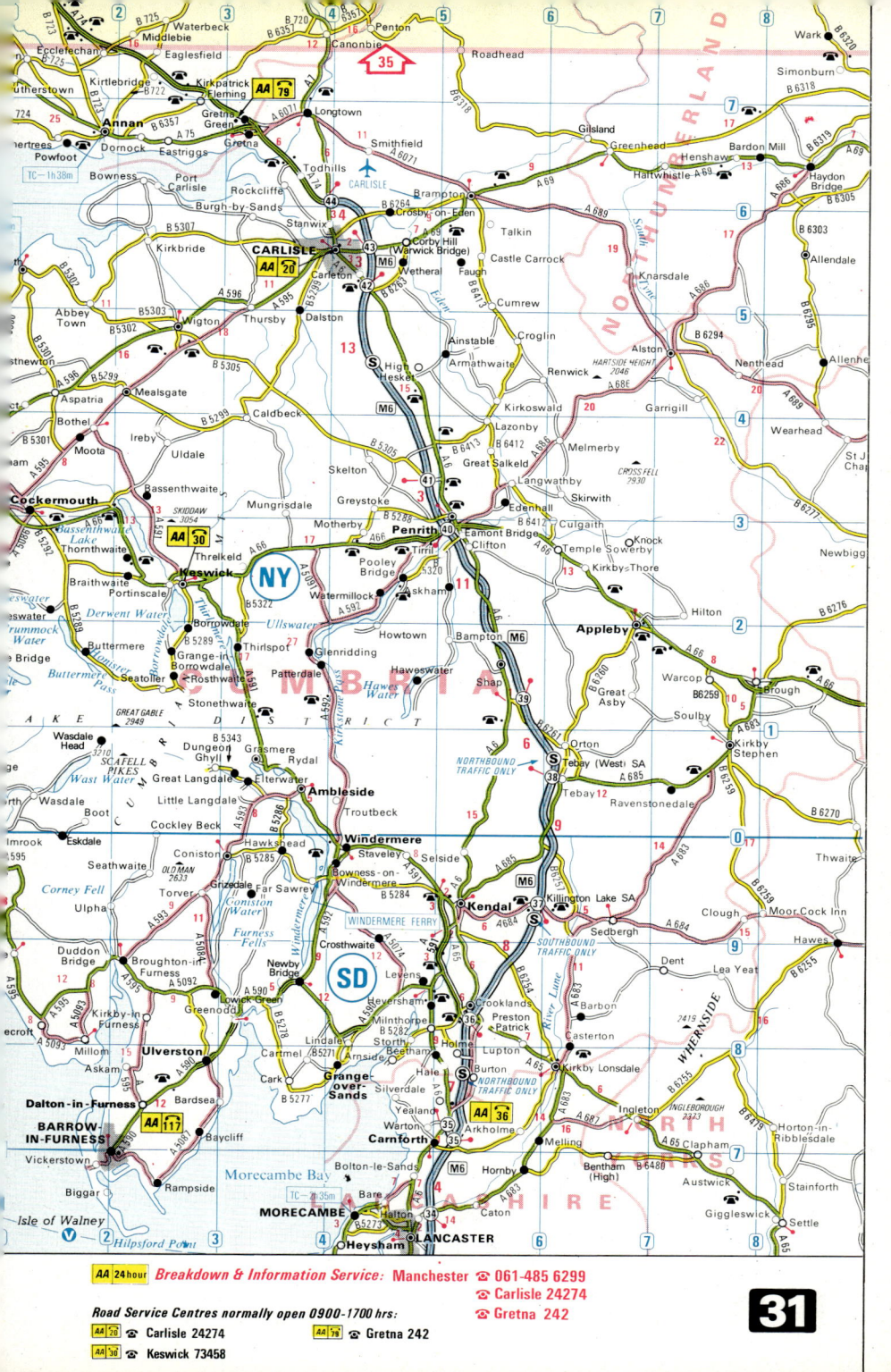

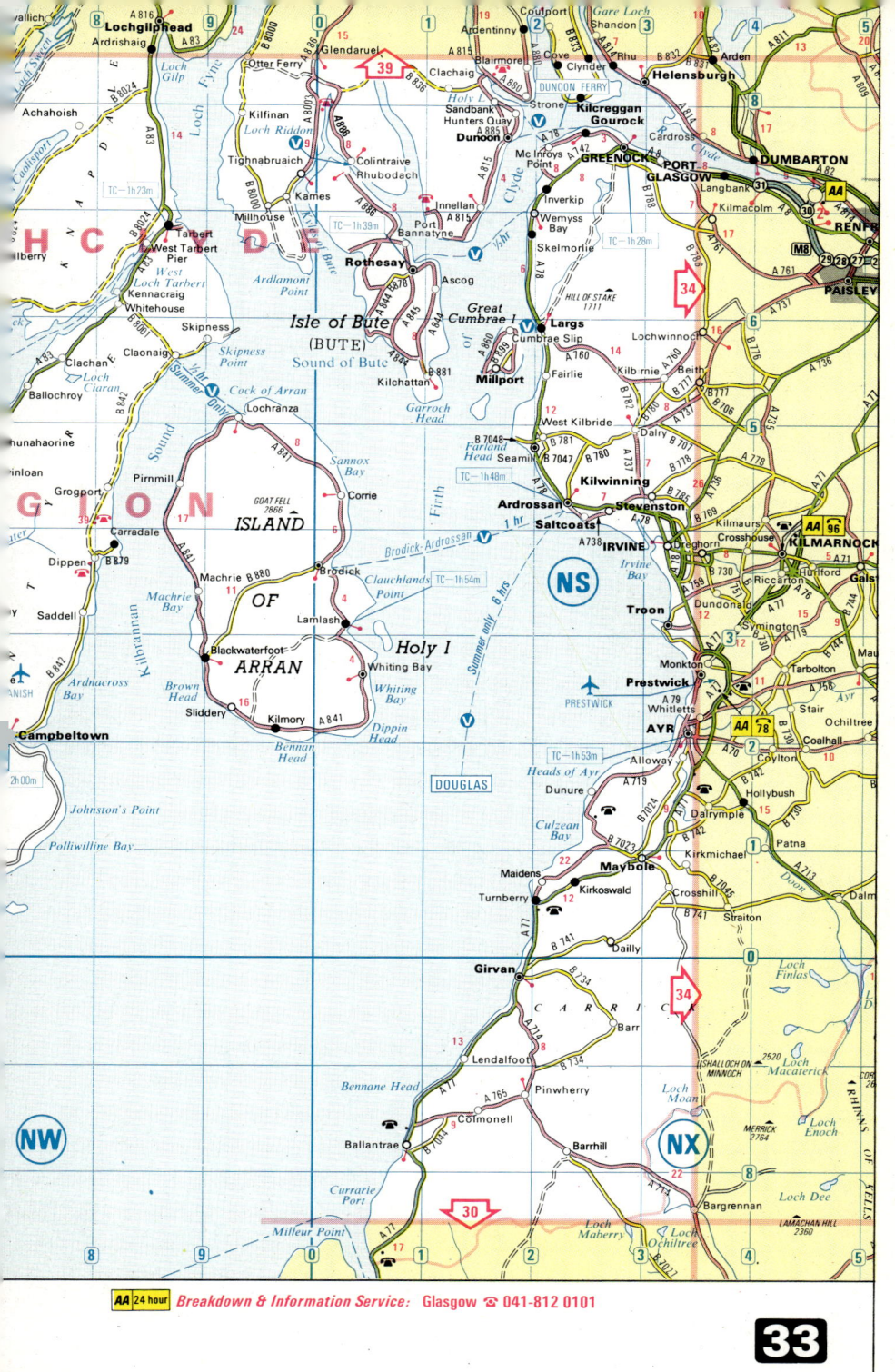

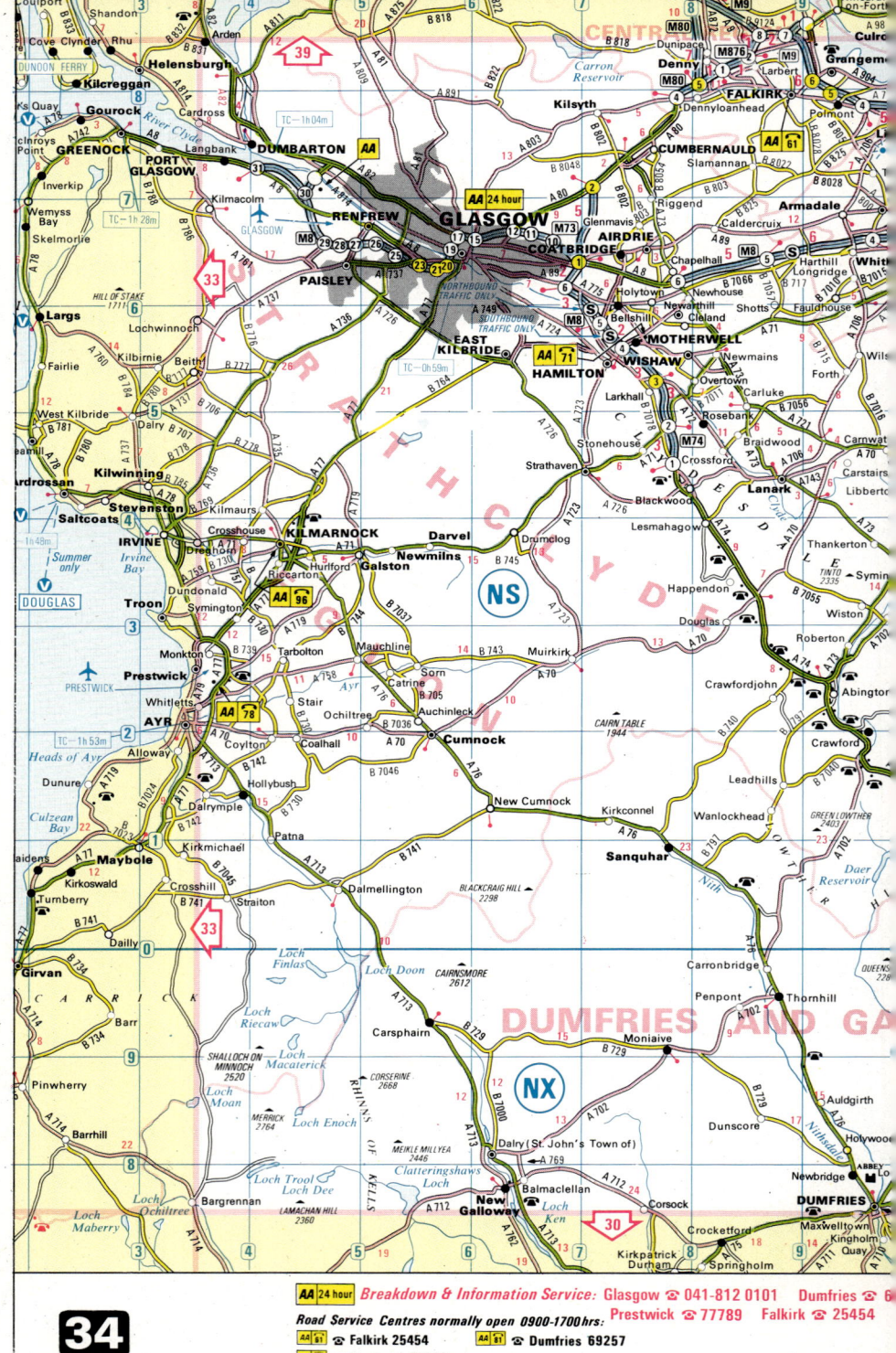

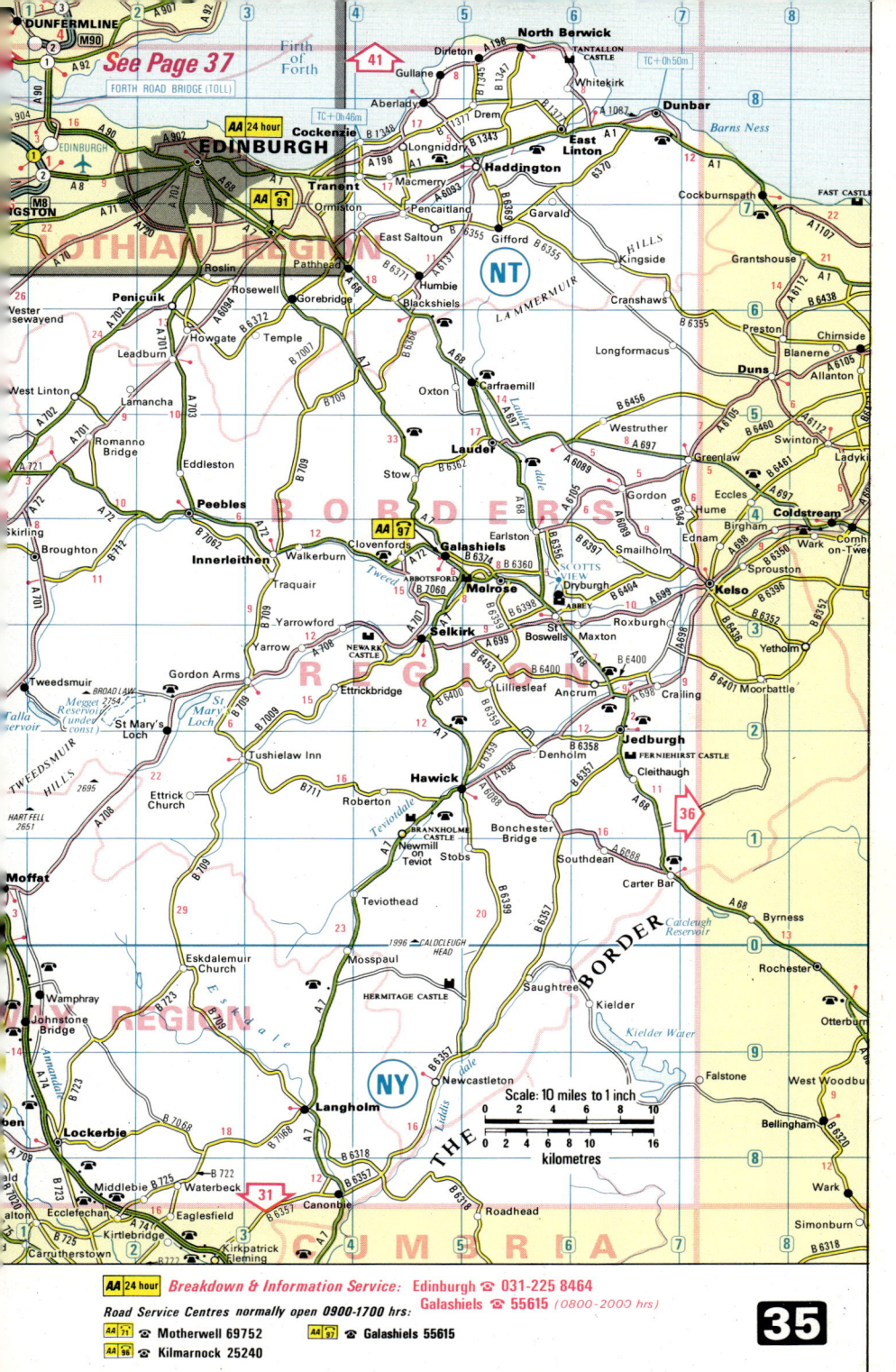

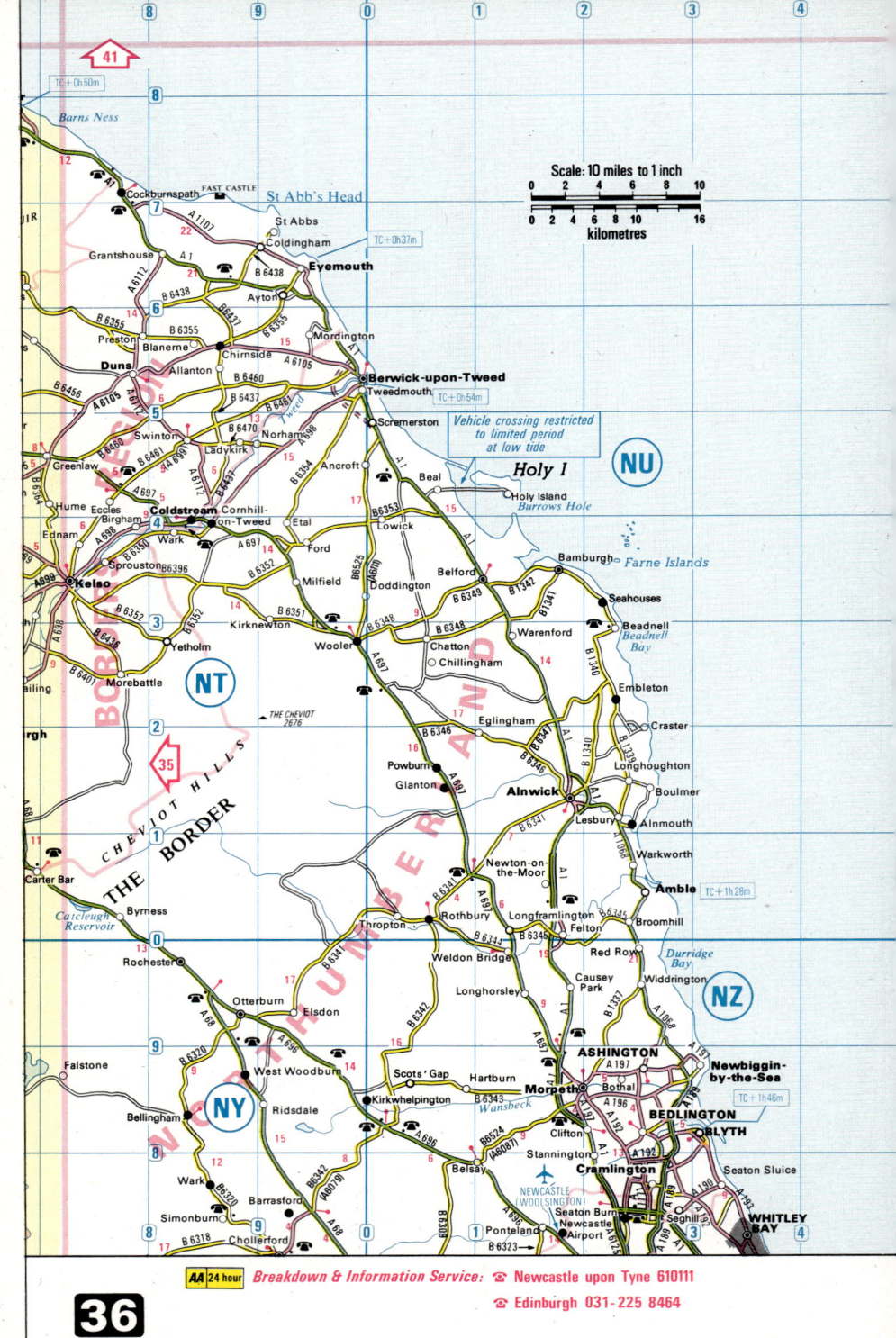

Edinburgh
at approx 5 miles to 1 inch

37

Rhum
Eigg
Muck
Sound of Rhum
Sound of Eigg
Eilean Shona
Loch Moidart
Sanna Point
HIGHLA
ARDNAMURCHAN
Kilchoan
Kentra
Acharacle
Salen
Glenborrodale
Point of Ardnamurchan
Ardmore Point
Auliston Point
Tobermory
TC + 4h 34m
Drimnin
Bonnavoulin
MORVERN
Loch Arienas
Claggan
Lochaline
Sound of Mull
Caliach Point
Calgary
Calgary Bay
Dervaig
Loch Frisa
Kilninian
Loch Tuath
ISLAND OF MULL
Salen
Fishnish
Craignure
Lochdonhead
Ulva
Loch Na Keal
Loch Ba
BEN MORE 3169
Staffa
Treshnish Isles
Iona
Fionnphort
Bunessan
Loch Scridain
Lochbuie
Loch Buie
Loch Spelve
Malcolm's Point
Mallaig
Morar
NORTH M
SOUTH MO
Arisaig
Sound of Arisaig
Loch Ailort
Lochailo
MOIDA
Kinloch
Sunart
Coll
Sorisdale
Clabhach
Arinagour
Coll-Oban 3¼ hrs
Crossapol Bay
Tiree
Caoles
Gott Bay
Scarinish
Hynish Bay
Tiree-Coll 1¼ hrs
Tiree-Oban 4½ hrs
TIREE
Middleton
Hynish
Balephuil Bay
Lochboisdale-Oban 5½ / 6 hrs
Castlebay-Oban 5½ / 6 hrs
STRATHCLYDE
Firth of Lorn
Easdale
Luing
Scarba
Gulf of Corryvreckan
Colonsay
Kiloran Bay
Kilchattan
Scalasaig
Colonsay-Oban
2½ hrs
Oronsay
JURA
Glendebadel Bay
Corpach Bay
Shian Bay
Ardlussa
Loch Righ Mór
Loch Tarbert
Sound of Jura
Tayvallich
Loch Sween
NL
NM
NR
NQ
42
32
Scale: 10 miles to 1 inch
0 2 4 6 8 10
0 2 4 6 8 10 16
kilometres

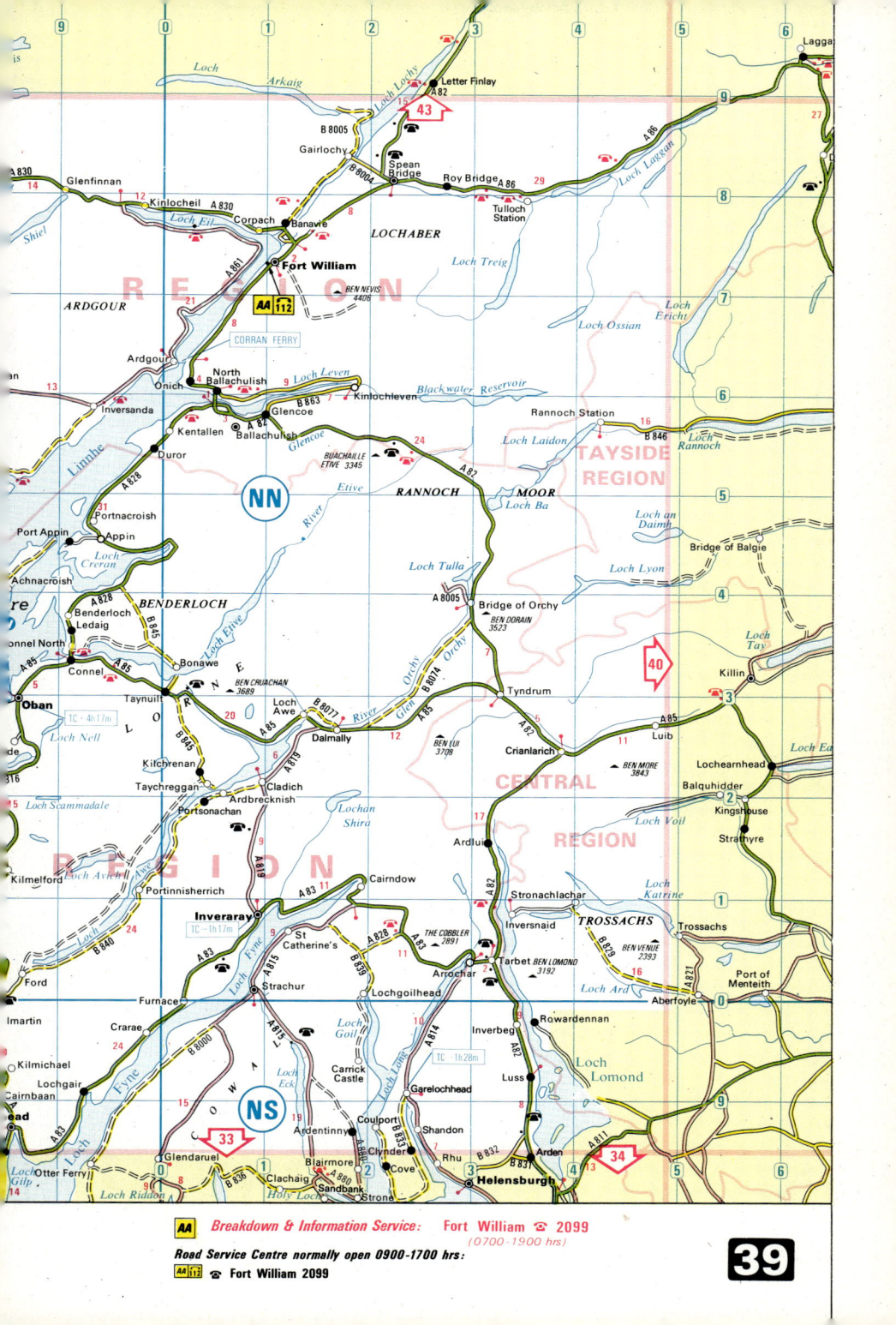

Breakdown & Information Service: Fort William ☎ 2099
(0700-1900 hrs)
Road Service Centre normally open 0900-1700 hrs:
AA ☎ Fort William 2099

39

40

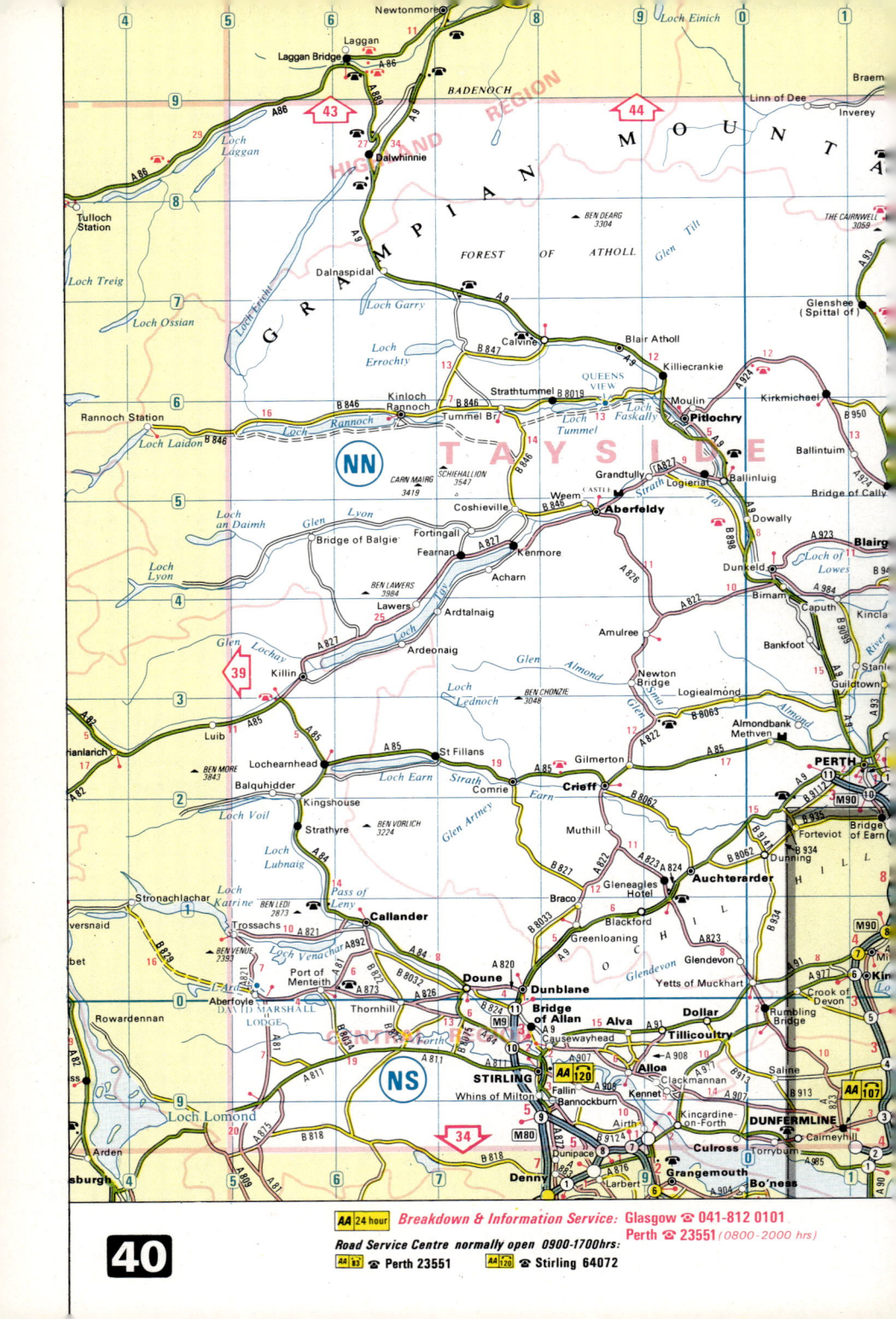

41

Grampian Region (north):
- Bridge of Cairn, Cambus o' May, Dinnet, Kincardine O'Neil, Marywell, Potarch, Banchory, Maryculter, Netherley, Newtonhill, Muchalls
- Ballater, B976, A93, B9017, B919
- Strachan, Cairn O' Mount 1488, Auchinblae, Drumlithie, Stonehaven (TC-0h11m), Stonehaven Bay
- Lochlee, Loch Muick, Glen Muick, Loch Lee, Glen Esk
- Howe of the Mearns, Fettercairn, Fordoun, Roadside, Laurencekirk, Inverbervie
- Clova, Glen Clova, Glen Prosen, Edzell, North Esk, Marykirk, Johnshaven, St Cyrus, Milton Ness
- Brechin, Memus, Tannadice, Farnell, Montrose (TC+0h39m)
- Cortachy, Kirriemuir, Southmuir, Forfar, Guthrie, Friockheim, Lunan, Lunan Bay, Inverkeilor
- Loch of Lintrathen, Dean Water, Glamis, Letham
- Meigle, Newtyle, Coupar Angus, Auchterhouse, Todhills, Newbigging, Woodhill, Muirdrum, Arbroath (TC+0h25m)
- Muirhead, Invergowrie, **DUNDEE** (AA 24 hour), Broughty Ferry, Monifieth, Carnoustie, Barry, Buddon Ness
- Wormit, Tayport, Newport-on-Tay, Tay Road Bridge (Toll) (TC+1h09m)
- Errol, Kilmany, Leuchars, St Andrews Bay

Fife Region:
- Dairsie, Guard Bridge, St Andrews (AA 113)
- Cupar, Ceres, Craigrothie, Kingsbarns
- Auchtermuchty, Ladybank, Kingskettle, Lathones, Largo Ward, Crail, Fife Ness
- Glenrothes, Upper Largo, Lundin Links, Kilrenny, Anstruther, Pittenweem, St Monans
- Leven, Earlsferry, Elie
- **KIRKCALDY** (AA 104) (TC+0h57m), Firth of Forth
- Dirleton, North Berwick, Gullane, Tantallon Castle, Whitekirk

Scale: 10 miles to 1 inch
0 2 4 6 8 10 miles
0 2 4 6 8 10 12 14 16 kilometres

Grid references: NO, NT

AA 24 hour Breakdown & Information Service:
Dundee ☎ 25585 Edinburgh ☎ 031-225 8464
St Andrews ☎ 76407 (0800-2000 hrs)

Road Service Centres normally open 0900-1700 hrs:
AA 113 ☎ St Andrews 76407

42

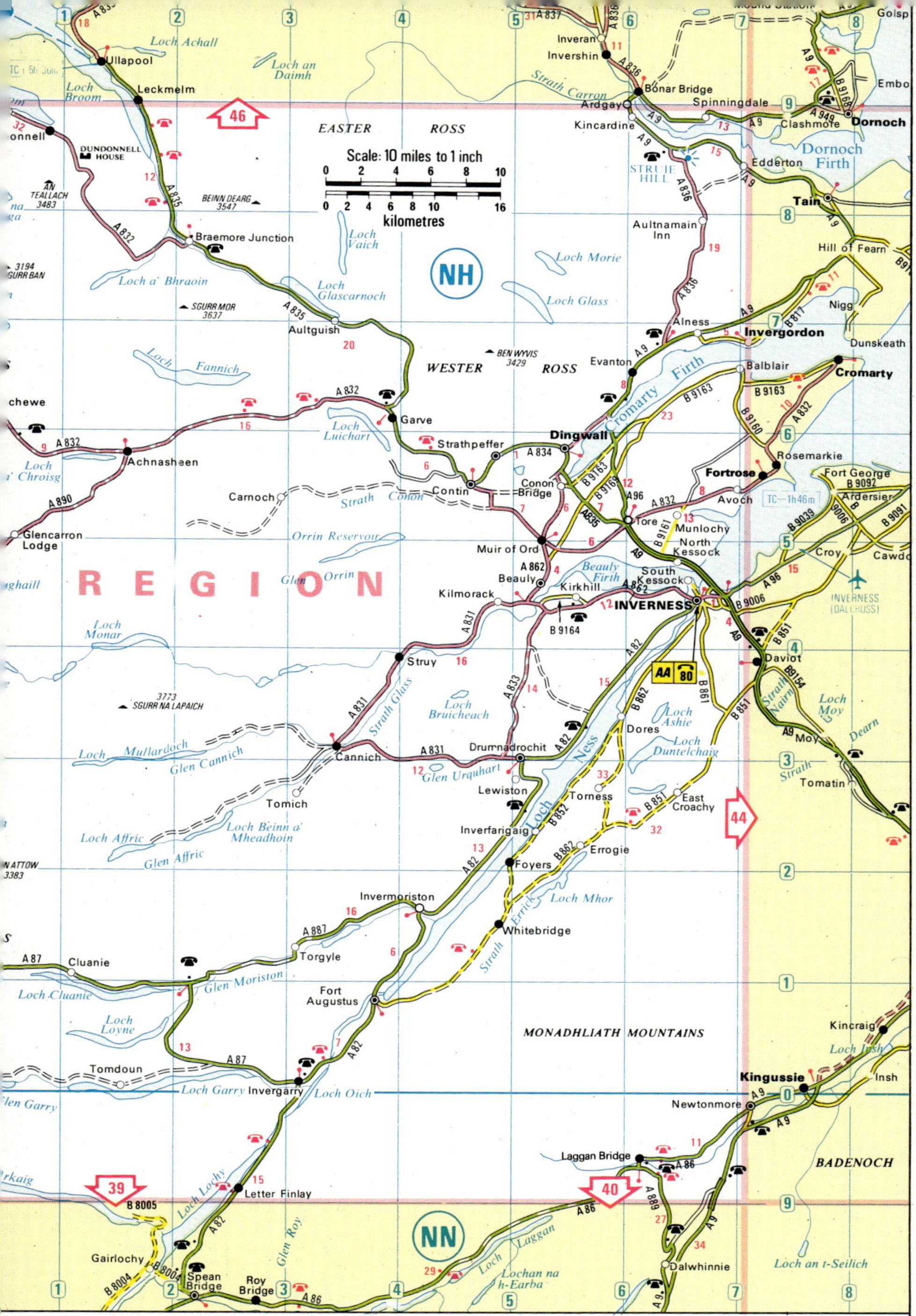

Scale: 10 miles to 1 inch
0 2 4 6 8 10
0 2 4 6 8 10 16
kilometres
NH
NN
46
39
40
44
EASTER ROSS
WESTER ROSS
REGION
MONADHLIATH MOUNTAINS
BADENOCH
Ullapool
Leckmelm
Loch Achall
Loch an Daimh
Loch Broom
DUNDONNELL HOUSE
AN TEALLACH 3483
BEINN DEARG 3547
Braemore Junction
Loch a' Bhraoin
SGURR MOR 3637
Loch Vaich
Loch Glascarnoch
Aultguish
Loch Fannich
Loch Morie
Loch Glass
BEN WYVIS 3429
Inveran
Invershin
Strath Carron
Bonar Bridge
Ardgay
Kincardine
Spinningdale
Clashmore
Dornoch
Golspie
Embo
Dornoch Firth
Edderton
STRUIE HILL
Tain
Aultnamain Inn
Hill of Fearn
Nigg
Alness
Invergordon
Dunskeath
Evanton
Cromarty Firth
Balblair
Cromarty
Garve
Loch Luichart
Strathpeffer
Dingwall
Achnasheen
Loch a' Chroisg
Kinlochewe
Carnoch
Strath Conon
Contin
Conon Bridge
Glencarron Lodge
Orrin Reservoir
Glen Orrin
Muir of Ord
Tore
Munlochy
North Kessock
Avoch
Fortrose
Rosemarkie
Fort George
Ardersier
Beauly Firth
South Kessock
Beauly
Kirkhill
Kilmorack
INVERNESS
INVERNESS (DALCROSS)
Croy
Cawdor
Daviot
Loch Monar
Struy
SGURR NA LAPAICH 3773
Strath Glass
Loch Bruicheach
Loch Mullardoch
Glen Cannich
Cannich
Drumnadrochit
Glen Urquhart
Lewiston
Loch Ness
Loch Ashie
Dores
Loch Duntelchaig
Strath Nairn
Loch Moy
Moy
Strath Dearn
Tomatin
Tomich
Loch Affric
Glen Affric
Loch Beinn a' Mheadhoin
Inverfarigaig
Torness
East Croachy
Errogie
Foyers
Loch Mhor
Whitebridge
Strath Errick
Invermoriston
Torgyle
Cluanie
Loch Cluanie
Glen Moriston
Fort Augustus
Loch Loyne
Tomdoun
Loch Garry
Glen Garry
Invergarry
Loch Oich
Kincraig
Loch Insh
Insh
Kingussie
Newtonmore
Laggan Bridge
Letter Finlay
Loch Lochy
Glen Roy
Loch Laggan
Lochan na h-Earba
Gairlochy
Spean Bridge
Roy Bridge
Dalwhinnie
Loch an t-Seilich
TC - 1h46m
A 835
A 832
A 890
A 831
A 833
A 82
A 87
A 887
A 86
A 889
A 9
A 96
A 834
A 862
A 836
A 949
A 837
B 9163
B 9169
B 9160
B 9161
B 9164
B 862
B 852
B 851
B 861
B 9006
B 9154
B 9092
B 9039
B 9091
B 817
B 8005
B 8004
AA 80

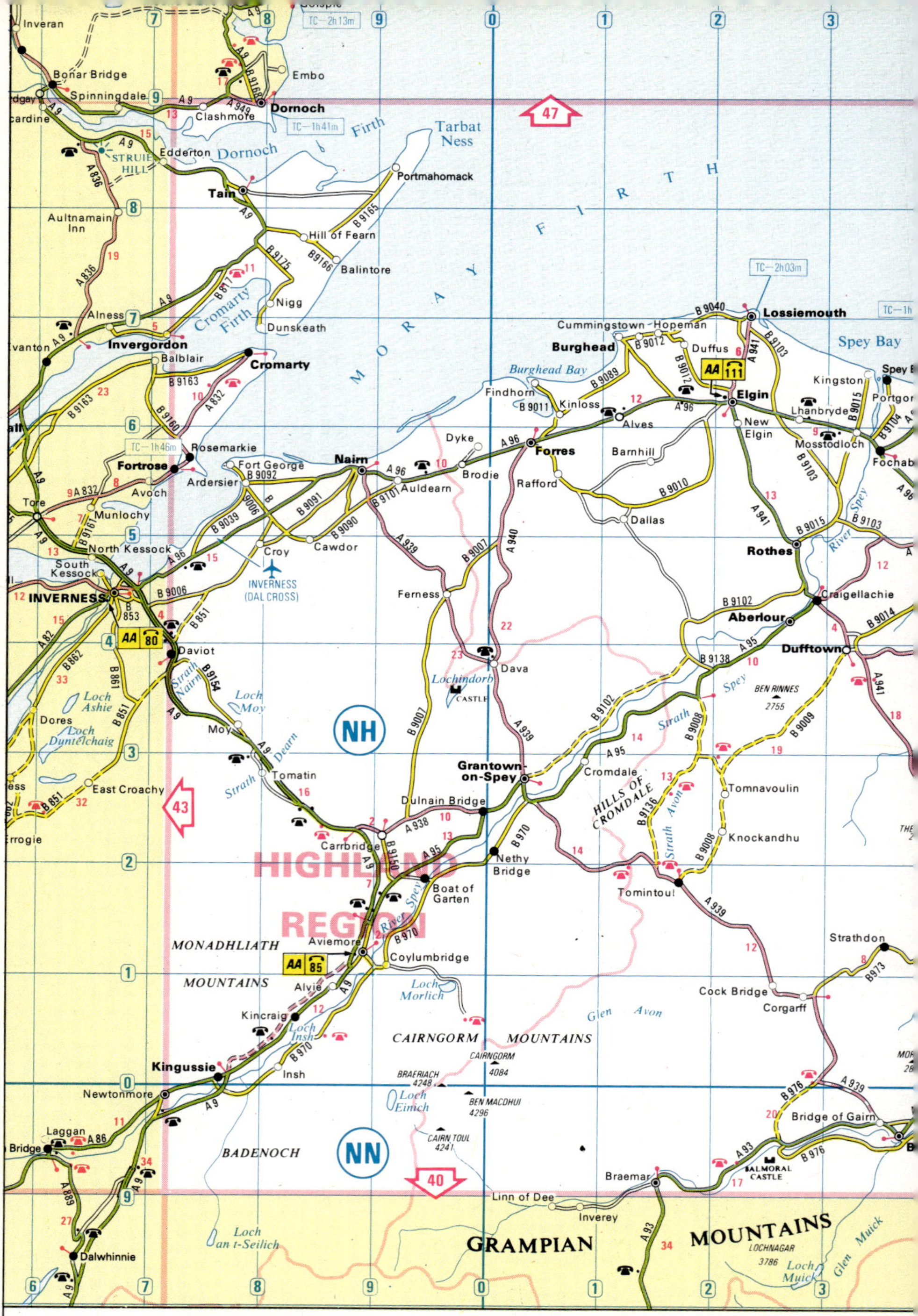

AA 24 hour **Breakdown & Information Service:** Edinburgh ☎ 031-225 8464 Glasgow ☎ 041-812 0101 Aviemore ☎ 810300 (0700-1900 hrs)

Road Service Centre normally open 0900-1700 hrs:

AA 80 ☎ Inverness 33213

Breakdown & Information Service: Edinburgh ☎ 031-225 8464   Glasgow ☎ 041-812 0101
Aberdeen 51231

45

Cape Wrath
Kyle of Durness
Faraid Head
Durness
SMOO CAVE
Whiten Head
Keoldale
Sandwood Loch
Talmine
Kyle of Tongue
Loch Eriboll
Sheigra
B 801
A 838
Kinlochbervie
Badcall
Tongue
Eriboll
Loch Inchard
Loch Hope
Rhiconich
FOINAVEN 2980
Loch Laxford
BEN HOPE 3040
Loch an Dherue
2504
BEN LOYAL
A 836
Handa I
Laxford Bridge
NC
BEN ARKLE
2582
Scourie
BEN STACK 2364
Loch Stack
Loch Meadie
Badcall
TC - 5h 41m
Loch More
REAY FOREST
Eddrachillis Bay
A 894
Loch an Leathaid Bhuain
Point of Stoer
Clashnessie Bay
BEN HEE 2864
Kylestrome
Altnaharra
Drumbeg
Loch Glendhu
Unapool
Loch Merkland
BEN KLIBRECK 3154
Nedd
B 869
Loch Glencoul
Clashnessie
KYLESKU FERRY
QUINAG 2653
Loch Fiag
Stoer
GLASVEN 2541
B 869
Loch Assynt
Crask
Overscaig
A 837
Lochinver
Inchnadamph
Loch Inver
BEN MORE ASSYNT 3273
Rubha Coigeach
Inverkirkaig
SUILVEN 2399
CANISP 2779
Loch Shin
Enard Bay
Loch Veyatie
Cam Loch
Reiff
Ledmore Junction
Glen Oykell
Loch Sionascaig
Knockan
Loch Ailsh
Polbain
HIGHLAND
Achiltibuie
Loch Urigill
Loch Lurgain
KNOCKAN CLIFF
A 835
Lairg
Summer Isles
COIGACH
Stornoway-Ullapool 3¼ / 3¾ hrs
A 837
Rosehall
A 839
B 864
Oykell Bridge
Strath Kinnaird
Strath Oykell
TC - 5h 36m
Inveran
Loch Achall
Loch an Daimh
Little Loch Broom
Ullapool
Invershin
Strath Carron
Laide
A 832
43
Bonar Bridge
Ardgay
Ardessie
Loch Broom
Leckmelm
EASTER ROSS
Kincardine
Dundonnell
DUNDONNELL HOUSE
NH
A 835
AN TEALLACH 3483
Loch na Sealga
BEINN DEARG 3547
A 9

47

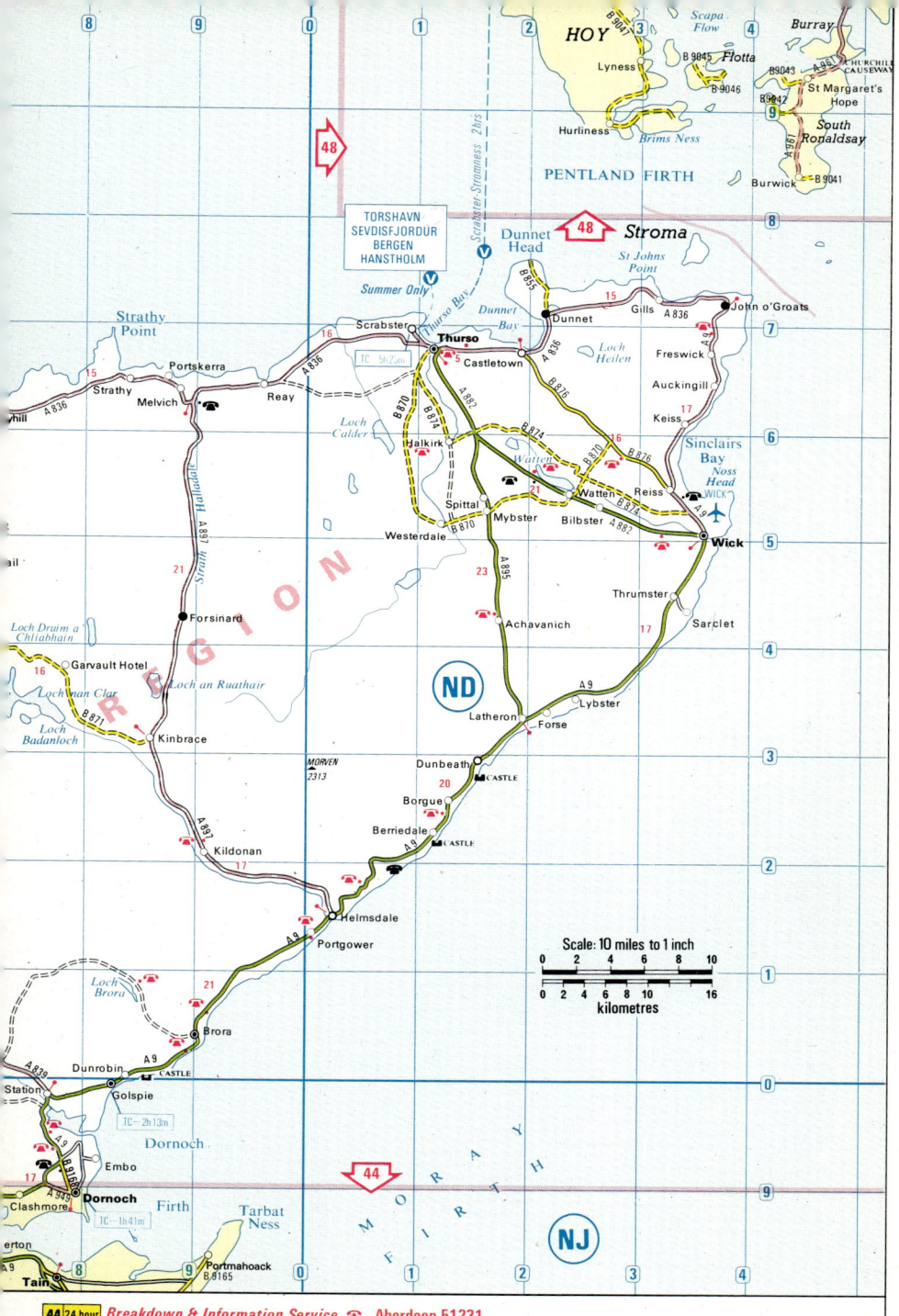

Outer Hebrides
Scale: 22·5 miles to 1 inch

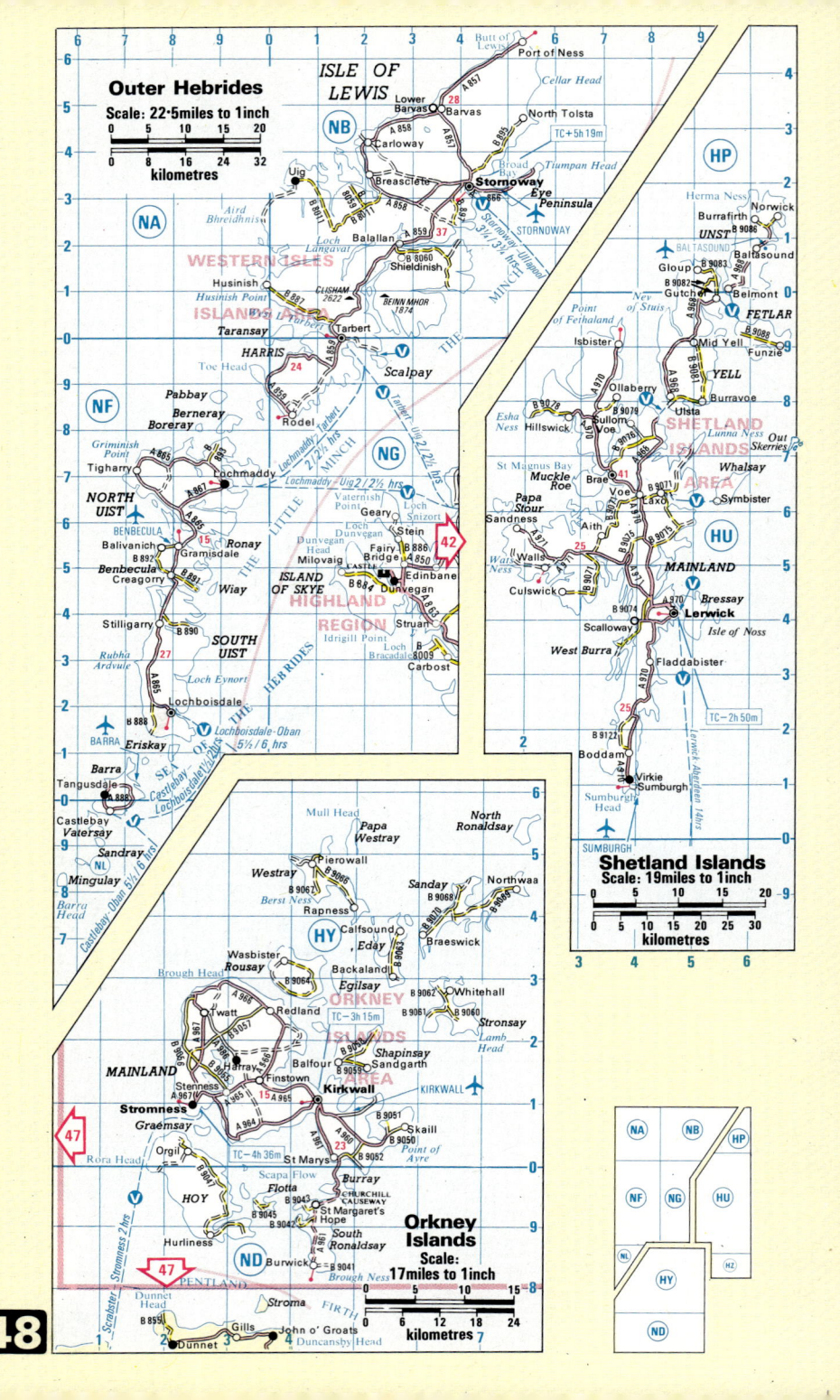

Shetland Islands
Scale: 19 miles to 1 inch

Orkney Islands
Scale: 17 miles to 1 inch

48

THE INNER HEBRIDES

Roads fan out to the wild Atlantic coastline and the romantic Sound of Mull, which curves north to the enchanting and romantic Inner Hebrides. ROGER PREBBLE discovers the charms that the islands hold

The Inner Hebrides by Roger Prebble

Beyond the lonely lighthouse on Ardnamurchan Point, the most westerly tip of the British mainland, lie the many enchanting isles of the Inner Hebrides, with strange sounding names such as: Muck, Eigg, Canna, Soay and Eagamol. Over the centuries these remote Scottish outposts have had their share of drama and hardship, but thanks to the islands' stark beauty it is a romantic impression that is always left in the minds of visitors. Indeed, many poets have extolled the region, and Robert Louis Stevenson's lines from the *Skye Boat Song* are ever-emotive of the lovely boat journeys in and around the isles –

'Mull was astern
Rhum on the port
Eigg on the starboard bow . . .'

A nautical position that could mean only one thing – you are heading for **Skye**. It would be difficult to dream up a more oddly shaped piece of land. Although only fifty miles long and little more than fifteen miles across at the widest point, the Isle of Skye has over 1,000 miles of craggy coastline. The waters around Skye have always been a formidable challenge to mariners, mainly because of the suddenly-changing currents and tides. Until the advent of steamboats, crossing from the mainland was a hazardous business. To and fro travel is a good deal safer these days and the three main access routes are Mallaig to Ardvasar across the Sound of Sleat, Glenelg to Kylerhea, and Kyle of Lochalsh to Kyleakin. The last of these passages is the most popular, since not only is it the shortest – about ten minutes on the car-ferry – but also the mainland departure point is the British Rail terminus of the scenic Inverness to Kyle of Lochalsh line. Once on the island, motorists will find that virtually all roads follow the coast, as the steep hills and ridges make inland travel very difficult. A notable exception is the A856 north of Portree, a road riddled with hairpin bends and narrow cliffside ledges high among the ridges of Trotternish.

Kyleakin is likely to be your first port of call. It was here that the King of Norway stopped off in 1263 on his way to Largs. The monarch's ill-fated journey ended on the coast of the Firth of Clyde where he was defeated by Alexander III – a battle resulting in the end of Norse power in the Western Isles. Looking out to the pier are the ruins of Castle Moil which, reputedly, also has Norwegian connections. This 14th-century stronghold is strategically placed on a small island, making it accessible only at low tide. Traditionally it was here that a Norwegian princess

A remote croft on the Isle of Skye

Weekaway Motoring Holidays
Why settle for anything less?

Why indeed, when Weekaway Motoring Holidays offer you the freedom of Scotland at your own pace staying at superb Ladbroke Hotels in some of Scotland's finest touring centres.

What can be more relaxing than to spend seven nights or longer, at your choice of comfortable Ladbroke Hotels — booked in advance by us to your exact instructions and requirements.

Your Weekaway includes so much. You can look forward to luxury bedrooms with a private bathroom, colour TV, radio and welcoming tea and coffee tray. Dinner and full Scottish breakfast set you up well for the next day.

And if all that isn't enough we even give you a suggested route itinerary should you need a little help on the way.

Weekaway is not the only tune to our bagpipes. You can be our guest for two days or longer at a hotel of your choice — we're in all the best places. Prices for two nights room and breakfast start at £25.00 per person.

And don't worry too much about the rest of the family. On all our holidays children under 14 enjoy free accommodation.

Ladbroke Hotels

With our choice, our welcome and our value for money why settle for anything less.

Phone 01-734 6000, or fill out the coupon for your copy of our full-colour Lazydays in Scotland brochure with details of these and other exciting holiday ideas.

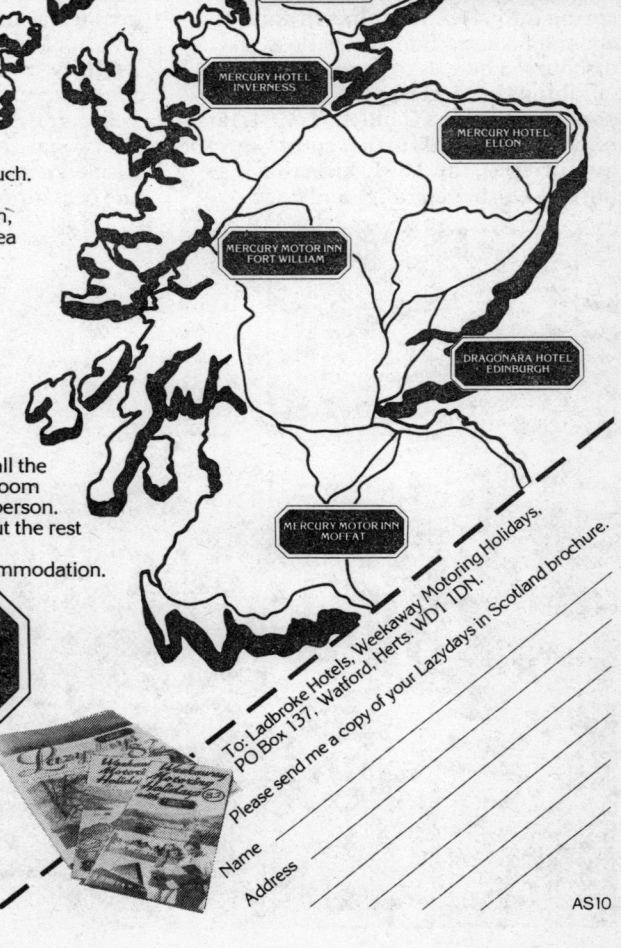

- MERCURY MOTOR INN ULLAPOOL
- MERCURY MOTOR INN WICK
- MERCURY HOTEL INVERNESS
- MERCURY HOTEL ELLON
- MERCURY MOTOR INN FORT WILLIAM
- DRAGONARA HOTEL EDINBURGH
- MERCURY MOTOR INN MOFFAT

To: Ladbroke Hotels, Weekaway Motoring Holidays, PO Box 137, Watford, Herts, WD1 1DN.
Please send me a copy of your Lazydays in Scotland brochure.

Name _____
Address _____

AS10

('Saucy Mary') guarded the strait.

The coastal route from Kyleakin to Broadford commands wonderful views, especially of the incomparable Cuillin Hills. Broadford is set in a pretty bay and ranks as the island's second-largest community. Its houses and hotels, as elsewhere on the island, tend to sprawl over a large area. There is also a small hospital here. Boating and fishing are both popular in the bay and hiking enthusiasts will find the village a handy base from which to explore the southern arm of the island.

On heading south-west from Broadford, the Red Hills immediately spring into view. Dr Johnson and his constant companion James Boswell discoursed here as to the merits of climbing Beinn Dearg (2,323ft), crossing Beinn na Caillich (2,403ft) and rejoining the road further south. For the less intrepid, the A881 skirts this horseshoe-shaped range and once beyond the hamlet of Torrin, provides drivers with lovely views of Loch Slapin.

The road comes to an end at Elgol, a small crofting community with boarding-house and cottage accommodation. Less than a mile south of here is Prince Charles's Cave, where the then fugitive Pretender, Charles Stuart, was once harboured and fed.

Trips by boat and coach excursion both take visitors from Elgol to the spectacular Loch Coruisk. As with many sights on Skye, the Loch's real splendour is nature's own. Glaciers have etched their icy fingers deep into the surrounding hills to form a giant geological amphitheatre.

West of Loch Coruisk are the Cuillins, a tightly-bunched range of hills with a highest point of 3,251ft (Sgurr Alasdair). Although covering only some fifty square miles, the hills, composed of black igneous rock, are rated as some of the best for rock-climbing in the whole of Europe. Inexperienced climbers should only attempt the lower slopes as mist and rain, coupled with unreliable compass-readings due to the magnetic nature of the rock, can make climbing unexpectedly dangerous.

Some six miles north of these hills the A850 splits at Sligachan Hotel. The A863 meanders north-westward from the fork via Glen Drynoch, affording fine views of Lochs Harport and Bracadale. Those who have read Gavin Maxwell's *Harpoon at a Venture* will know that large schools of shark occasionally put in an appearance off Bracadale, looking like a fleet of submarines.

Dunvegan is the terminus of the A863 and has facilities for fishing, boating and golf. But Dunvegan's main tourist draw is its castle. It is a daunting fortress, for over seven centuries the ancestral home of the MacLeod chiefs. At one time the castle was only accessible by sea, but now there is access via a bridge. James V, Dr Johnson, Sir Walter Scott and Queen Elizabeth II (1956) have all been entertained within Dunvegan Castle's walls. Today visitors can browse among Prince Charles Stuart memorabilia and see the letters of Samuel Johnson. Afterwards they can take a short boat trip from the castle jetty to see the resident baby seals.

Look out, too, for nesting herons high up in the lochside trees. A short trip north-westward along the bank of Loch Dunvegan, will reach the Skye Water Mill, and the Black House – a crofter's cottage with contents including a replica of the earliest type of whisky still.

The A850 heads north from here to Fairy Bridge, and then east through the sleepy hamlets of Edinbain and Bernisdale. After crossing River Snizort (Skye's longest river) the road turns south into Portree.

As there are fewer than 8,000 residents on the isle – one person for every 58 acres – it is not surprising that nowhere is very crowded. With 1,500 people, Portree, the island's capital, has by far the largest community. The village's Royal Hotel occupies the site of a thatched inn where Prince Charles bade his last farewell to Flora Macdonald. St Columba's episcopal church also has connections with Scotland's best-loved heroine. It has a special Flora Macdonald memorial window.

A combined tweed and wool mill provides work for many of the villagers. Surprisingly, Portree is surrounded by thickish woodland which recedes to heather-covered hills in the distance. The area's potential as a tourist centre has been developed since the war with golf, tennis, fishing, boating and coach excursions among the many attractions now on offer. If you plan visiting Portree in July there is an agricultural show as a bonus, or in August they have their very own Highland Games. Unfortunately, in common with the rest of Skye, Portree averages only sixty rain-free days a year.

For the first few miles north of Portree

New-born Atlantic seal pup

Left: loom-work at a Harris Tweed mill

on the A855 the view is dominated by The Storr, a 2,350ft peak. To the right, and below the mountain itself, is the Old Man of Storr, a 160ft rock pinnacle. As with other rock-faces in this Trotternish area, the Old Man has a slippery basalt surface and is consequently treacherous to climb. It was, however, successfully scaled in 1955. A few miles beyond Storr the road passes Lealt Falls. Although merely a small stream dropping into a chasm, the Falls have a certain primitive beauty. On and to the right of the A855 is Kilt Rock – a mainly basalt crag split in such a way as to resemble kilt pleats. Because of the danger of falling débris and landslips, the rock should be viewed from a safe distance. Further north still is the tiny parish of Staffin. The weird peak of Quiraing overshadows the whole of this crofting community. Although, in fact, a single mountain, Quiraing is so broken into pillars and jagged ridges that at first glance it appears as a miniature mountain group. Just beyond this is the Table, a huge grass-clad rock plateau that makes an ideal picnic site. Two

The stark Old Man of Storr

miles on from Quiraing is the village of Floddigarry, where Flora Macdonald lived for twenty years with her husband Allan Macdonald of Kingsburgh.

Once past the Aird, Skye's most northerly mainland region, the coast road passes the ruins of Duntulm Castle. Fladda Chuain lies some five miles offshore from Duntulm and was surely one of the most remote sites that followers of St Columba, the 6th-

The Uig-Tarbert car-ferry on Harris

century abbot and missionary, chose on which to build a chapel. Nowadays the puffins have the island all to themselves.

From Duntulm, and further south, the coastal route commands fine views across Little Minch, the strait separating Skye from the Outer Hebrides. The Kilmuir Croft Museum is along this stretch of road and, mornings only, local farming and domestic implements are on display, allowing visitors to glimpse the crofting life of northern Skye.

The oddly named Uig (Norse for 'bay') is a car-ferry terminal. From here passengers can cross to Tarbert on **Harris**, and Lochmaddy on **North Uist**. Uig makes a good base for those who enjoy a quiet fishing and boating holiday (the pier here is the longest in Scotland). South of Uig Bay and the fjord-like inlets of Loch Snizort is Kingsburgh, where Flora Macdonald died in 1790. Back south of Portree the A850 passes through Glen Varragill to rejoin the Broadford road at Sligachan Hotel.

Skye's southern region is Sleat (pronounced *Slate*). From Broadford the A851 passes the lonely peak of Cnoc Glac na Luachrach, enters Sleat and meets the coast at Isleornsay which is a village named after the neighbouring island (which is an island only when the tide is in). To the left of the main road heading south, the ruins of Knock Castle come into view. The remains were a one-time Macdonald stronghold and further south is the ancestral seat of Lord Macdonald himself, Armadale Castle. This vast Gothic fortress was designed by Gillespie Graham in the early 19th century. The southernmost tip of the Isle of Skye is the Point of Sleat – the only part of the island where you will find any sand.

Crofting is still an important way of life on Skye. A little over half the island is given over to rough grazing, but the main source of agricultural wealth is animal farming, notably beef cattle and sheep. As with other Highland islands, few vegetables can be successfully grown. Only potatoes and turnips (as fodder) are worth growing.

At Carbost is the Talisker Distillery, a mainstay in another important island industry. The building is over 150 years old and is one of the few remaining distilleries with a manually-operated malting process. Most of the distillery's half-million-gallon annual output is blended, but a small amount is bottled as pure Highland Malt Whisky.

Surprisingly, fishing is not as big an industry as you would normally expect on an island. The distance required to reach good fishing grounds acts as a deterrent to the many small-boat owners. Uig, however, is a fairly busy herring port, and at the south of the island both shellfish and lobster-catching are quite profitable ventures.

Easily the largest satellite island off Skye is **Raasay**. It is some thirteen miles long and three miles across at the broadest part. To the north are the ruins of Brochel Castle and, beyond, the isle of **Rona** where an isolated lighthouse gives warning of the treacherous inner sound. Access is via a private ferry from Sconser on the mainland at Loch Sligachan.

Dr Johnson spoke of it as an isle of gaiety in the 1770s, but these days, since the MacLeods have been forced to desert it, Raasay is better described as an isle of sadness. Only about 150 residents are on the island now.

Below Raasay is the now-deserted isle of **Scalpay**, where a ruined chapel bears testimony to the days of a previous community. Across the other side of Skye is **Soay**, an island overlooked by the Cuillin Hills. It was here that the author and naturalist Gavin Maxwell once set up a shark-fishing station. In the mid-fifties almost all Soay's inhabitants left to settle on **Mull**, and today it is occupied only by artists and bird-watchers.

Approximately 15 miles south of Soay lies the kidney-shaped isle of **Eigg**. It is only about five miles long and is dominated by An Sgurr, a 1,289ft peak. The only break in Eigg's hostile coastline is at the Bay of Laig where a sandy beach is lapped by the harbour waters. The Camas Sgiotaig Sands, to the north of the bay, make a sound uncannily like singing when they are walked across. The phenomenon is due to the underlying friction between the ground grains of quartz.

At the southernmost tip of the isle there is a shell-cum-sand beach at Galmisdale Harbour, but the mailboat only ventures to neighbouring **Castle Island**. The ferry meets her here and brings back the post through the rock-strewn haven.

Eigg is remarkable for its many weirdly formed caverns. One such is the Cave of St Francis where a vengeful MacLeod clan from Skye are said to have massacred over two hundred hapless inhabitants by starting a fire and blocking the only entrance. That was in the 16th century and the many human remains since found in the cave tend to bear out the macabre tale. Fewer than seventy people live on Eigg today and, predictably, crofting and fishing are the only occupations. The isle is walkable, but for the less energetic, a mini-bus runs in and around the tiny communities. There are no hotels as such, but it can sometimes be arranged for visitors to stay at crofters' homes.

Muck lies south-west of Eigg and probably derives its amusing name from *Muc*, the Gaelic for pig. It is possible that the isle was once noted for its pigs, but a more plausible reason is that Muck is shaped roughly like a pig. Certainly, James Boswell chronicled that it was as well that the owner of Muck was known as a laird (not Lord Muck!). The isle is a relatively low-lying dot in the sea and consequently very exposed. The usual point of access is Port Mor. The half a dozen hardy families here are again crofters and fishermen. A dyke system connects the isle with outlying **Eagamol** and **Horse Islands** to the north west. There is no accommodation or transport on Muck, which is perhaps why visitors like to return to 'get away from it all'.

Rhum is not unlike a miniature Isle of Wight in shape, being about eight miles long and nine miles wide. Here, though, the comparison ends. It is unenviably the wettest and most barren isle of the Inner Hebrides. It is also very mountainous. The lovely brittle peaks and rounded domes of the mountains are

56

All around Scotland Trusthouse Forte Value.

When you're choosing a hotel for your holiday it makes sense to choose from the best selection around – and you'll find that in the THF leisure brochures.

Because whatever it is you like about Scotland, you can enjoy it from the comfort of a THF Hotel.

THF have the largest number of hotels in Britain and offer you the widest choice: historic coaching inns, modern hotels, seaside hideaways, or the famous Post House Hotels. Each has its own distinctive character, comfort and cuisine, and friendly welcoming service.

Aviemore Post House Hotel. (0479) 810771.
Dundee Queen's Hotel. (0382) 22515.
Edinburgh Post House Hotel. 031-334 8221.
Glasgow Albany Hotel. 041-248 2656.
Glasgow Airport Excelsior Hotel. 041-887 1212.
Glenborrodale Glenborrodale Castle Hotel. (09724) 266.
Inverness Royal Hotel. (0463) 30665.
North Berwick Marine Hotel. (0620) 2406.
Peebles Tontine Hotel. (0721) 20892.
Perth Royal George Hotel. (0738) 24355.
Pitlochry Atholl Palace Hotel. (0796) 2400.

For details, contact your travel agent, write to us or phone for our Hightime Holidays and Weekend Bargain Breaks brochures, or contact the hotel direct.

Have a good holiday!

Yours faithfully
Trusthouse Forte Hotels

Send to THF PO Box 1, Altrincham, Cheshire WA14 5AB.
Please send me: ☐ Weekend Bargain Breaks ☐ Hightime Holiday ☐ Map/Price Guide to THF
Name
Address

AAS82

Or phone:
London 01-567 3444 · Manchester 061-969 6111
Belfast (Belfast) 46711 · Dublin (Dublin) 764401
Birmingham 021-236 3951 · Glasgow 041-221 6164
Leeds (0532) 431261 · Liverpool 051-236 0841
Edinburgh 031-226 4346 · Durham (0385) 62761
Cardiff (0222) 371589

Red deer with its fawn

like those drawn by a child. They rest on the surface of a seven-mile-deep volcanic root and their highest peak is Askival at 2,659ft. The whole of Rhum's population of about 40 lives at Kinloch, where the crofters' simple dwellings are overshadowed by Kinloch Castle. The building, made from Arran sandstone, was the whim of an English textiles magnate at the height of Edwardian extravagance. For long known as the 'Forbidden Island', Rhum was acquired by the Nature Conservancy Council in 1957. The society's motive was to study the resident deer (Rhum is now *the* spot in Britain for red deer), but it has also resulted in visitors now having access to the few fertile acres around Kinloch and Loch Scresort. There is no actual accommodation on the isle, but camping is permitted with prior permission. Boats leave Mallaig on the mainland for Rhum about four times a week.

Further towards the open Atlantic Ocean is **Canna** and, although this five-square-mile outpost is only four miles north-west of Rhum, its climate is strikingly different. The nearby islet of **Sanday**, together with Compass Hill and Carn a Ghaill ensure that there is shelter for Canna from all directions except east. This results in very good growing conditions, not only for flowers but for vegetables, too. Fuchsias, especially, do very well, as do globe artichokes – which many a gardener would envy. Several varieties of fruit all thrive around the tranquil Canna harbour area, and the brilliant yellow of the daffodils which bloom here in mid January are an early herald of spring.

Seven miles south-west of Canna, past Umaolo (a 24ft basalt rock looming out of the sea) is **Heiskeir**. In days gone by weatherbeaten crofters tended the isle's ten rough acres, but nowadays only the lighthouse-keepers brave the elements to share Heiskeir with the innumerable kittiwakes, eider ducks and migratory arctic terns.

ROYAL HOUSES

Scotland has many reminders of the country's kings and queens, their palaces and houses. JOHN HUTCHINSON, publicity editor for the Scottish Tourist Board, describes some of the more famous historic buildings which can be enjoyed by millions of visitors

The Royal Houses of Scotland

For over a thousand years Scotland had its own kings and queens, fiercely independent of their counterparts and rivals in England. They ruled, too, with a different kind of authority as King or Queen of Scots, the people not the land. This was an idea which traced its ancient origins to the Celtic nation of the *Ard Righ* the High King, Chief of Chiefs.

They fought long and hard for centuries against the English from the south and the Vikings from the north. They built castles to defend their country, grim reminders of their war-like inheritance; and, as times grew more peaceful, they built palaces and halls to reflect the new ideas of taste and style and to display their country's growing prosperity. They travelled about their sparsely populated country at the head of an army or on royal progress, and moved their capital on several occasions; and so throughout Scotland, there are reminders of her kings and queens, their palaces, castles and houses, still to be enjoyed today.

One of the oldest buildings in Scotland with royal connections is the tiny chapel of St Margaret, high on the volcanic castle rock of Edinburgh. It was built in Romanesque style about 1076 by Margaret, King Malcolm Canmore's saintly Queen, a lady of Saxon origin who married the Celtic king and began the slow introduction of feudal ideas to Scotland. The ferry she established between North and South Queensferry was named after her.

Edinburgh Castle was used as a royal residence from time to time throughout the Middle Ages and its defences were greatly strengthened by David II. The great keep where he died in 1371 can still be seen today. Mary Queen of Scots gave birth to James VI, the future James I of England, in a tiny panelled room close to that which today holds the Regalia, the Crown, Sceptre and sword, known as the Honours of Scotland.

But the castle was an uncomfortable and draughty place to live and so the court moved down the medieval backbone of the city of Edinburgh, the Royal Mile, to the Palace of *Holyroodhouse*, still the official residence of the Queen in Scotland.

The palace was originally the guesthouse of the abbeys from which it takes its name: Holy Rood means Holy Cross. Legend has it that King David I founded the abbey in gratitude for having been saved from being gored to death by a stag through the miraculous appearance of a cross. The abbey was severely damaged during the Reformation, but the palace, considerably rebuilt by James V, continued to be one of the main seats of the Scottish Crown despite damage and fire.

Here Mary Queen of Scots spent six

The esplanade of Edinburgh Castle

by John Hutchinson

years from 1561; here she had her dialogues with John Knox and married Darnley and Bothwell; and here she watched the murder of her secretary David Rizzio. The rooms today are largely as they were in her day.

In 1603, James VI of Scotland succeeded to the English throne. The Crown moved to London and regular Court life left Holyrood. The Palace was much enlarged, however, by Charles II, to the designs of Sir William Bruce. A wing was added to match that of Mary's days, and spacious apartments were created; but Holyrood had to wait until 1745 to see regular Court life again, and that for only one month under Prince Charles Edward Stuart.

Today the Palace is again the scene of Court functions, if only for a short time each summer, but in that time the elegant rooms resound once more with music and people, and glitter with jewels and resplendent gowns, just as they did in centuries gone by.

But the capital city has by no means a monopoly of royal houses in Scotland.

On the rocky West Highland coast, three miles north of Oban, stands *Dunstaffnage*, a fine and well-preserved 13th-century castle with a long and colourful connection with Scottish kings and a Hereditary Royal Captain. Here the early kings of Dalriada had a stronghold, and here, it is said, the Stone of Destiny was kept before its removal to Scone and then to the Coronation Chair in Westminster Abbey.

Hillside approach to imposing Stirling Castle

To the south, on the Isle of Bute in the Firth of Clyde, is the mighty circular castle of *Rothesay*, one of the few in Scotland still with its water-filled moat. The castle under its Hereditary Keeper, Lord Bute, has had a stormy history, suffering damage under Cromwell, and partial destruction at the hands of Argyll. The Dukedom of Rothesay is traditionally the premier Scottish title of the eldest son of the reigning monarch. Prince Charles, the Prince of Wales, is also Duke of Rothesay, Earl of Carrick, Baron Renfrew, Great Steward of Scotland and Lord of the Isles.

Royal castles with their Hereditary Royal Captains date from an age when the Crown was trying hard to assert its influence in the north against rival clan factions, and in the south both against the English and against the great Border lords and their bands of reivers. These castles were, above all, military strongholds, and usually uncomfortable places to live in.

But as medieval Scotland evolved, partly at least, into Renaissance Scotland, a very new style of royal building was developed. In much of this change in royal life style, King James IV (1488 to 1513) in particular led the way. He was himself the ideal of a Renaissance Prince. He was good looking, strong and chivalrous. His Court was the centre of a growing intellectual life in Scotland and under his patronage Scottish poetry, writing and architecture flourished as never before. Under his influence, and that of his music-loving father James III and his son, James V, the Scottish Royal palaces were transformed.

Stirling Castle was extensively remodelled with the Great Hall of James III, the Palace of James V, and the Chapel Royal of James VI as its chief attractions. Built in secular Gothic style, the Great Hall was used as a parliament house, and for state occasions, then languished for centuries as a military barracks. Today, careful restoration is now returning James III's magnificent hall to its medieval splendour. The Palace is best known for the remarkable ceiling of the King's presence chamber, decorated with the 'Stirling Heads', carved wooden roundels of which 28 have been preserved; while the Chapel Royal, built in 1594 in classical Renaissance style, has remained largely unaltered to this day.

Those same talented Stuart Kings enlarged the tiny Palace of *Falkland* to create the Renaissance gem to be seen today, set at the foot of the Lomond Hills of Fife. It has a magnificent south range in French style, and a Royal tennis court, added in 1539, which is still played on.

Falkland was really built as a hunting lodge and a pleasant country retreat away from the cares and intrigues of Edinburgh, and was greatly used and appreciated by James III, James V, and his daughter, Mary Queen of Scots.

Linlithgow, on the contrary, was built almost from the beginning as a royal palace, and built particularly by James IV and James V in a mixture of Gothic and Renaissance styles, with magnificent proportions. Set high above the loch which was stocked with eel and fish, the palace windows still have a glorious view over the Lothian countryside. Here James IV's wife, Margaret Tudor, sister of Henry VIII of England, waited in vain for her husband's return from Flodden in 1513. Here in 1542 the future Mary Queen of Scots was born, as her father James V lay dying at Falkland.

Linlithgow, too, was occupied by Prince Charles Edward Stuart in 1745, and had a brief return to glory before its disastrous destruction by fire the following year.

Both the Royal palaces of Holyroodhouse and Linlithgow were extensively remodelled in the 1600s when the Crown was no longer permanently resident in Scotland. The other (and often forgotten) Scottish Royal palace, at *Dunfermline*, also began its final days of glory at that time. Originally the Abbey guesthouse, the building was partially rebuilt by Anne of Denmark, James VI's wife, and here her son, the future Charles I of both Scotland and England was born in 1600. Fifty years later, his son, later to be Charles II, maintained a Court in the palace during the Commonwealth of Cromwell.

Dunfermline Palace was in ruins by 1700; Linlithgow was destroyed in 1746; and Falkland and Stirling ceased to be used as Royal residences; so all the emphasis was concentrated on the Palace of Holyroodhouse and on the new Royal residence developed on Deeside at Balmoral.

Balmoral Castle, a favourite retreat of our royal family

Balmoral will for ever be linked with Queen Victoria and her consort, Prince Albert. Together they bought the estate in 1852 and, along the lines he suggested, built the present castle. Around it they laid out gardens, planted trees and made long excursions over the hills to the south towards Lochnagar and Glen Muick, and further west, to the Queen's View on Loch Tummel and Blair Castle at Blair Atholl. Close associations and traditions were formed then which survive to this day; associations with Crathie Church where stands a monument to John Brown, Victoria's faithful servant; and with Braemar and the Royal Highland Gathering. The Royal Family today still attends church at Crathie and enjoys the fresh air on those same lands south of the castle. Each year they attend the brilliant spectacle of the Royal Braemar Gathering. This is always held on the first Saturday in September, and is one of the most popular attractions in the Scottish calendar.

These royal houses hold their special place because they were all built for the sovereign. Other places throughout the country deserve attention because of their association with a particular king or queen.

In the north-east of Scotland, north of Royal Deeside, the Peel Ring of *Lumphanan* is a large medieval earthwork where, it is said, Malcolm Canmore slew King Macbeth in 1057 to take over his throne. Nearby is *Kildrummy*, one of the most impressive medieval castles in the country. It was besieged in 1306 during the Wars of Independence when Robert the Bruce's wife and family had taken refuge there. They escaped, but his brother, Nigel, was betrayed and hanged by the English.

Robert the Bruce, Scotland's great warrior King, finally triumphed over his ancient enemy at *Bannockburn* near Stirling, where today his equestrian statue dominates the battlefield. He had been crowned, as had his predecessors for centuries, on the Stone of Scone on the Mote Hill at *Scone*, north of Perth. Today the Stone is in Westminster Abbey in London, but the Mote Hill is still to be seen in the grounds of the magnificent Scone Palace.

The ancient abbey of *Arbroath*, on the coast, founded in 1178 by King William the Lion, will forever be linked with the noble Declaration of 6 April 1320, which acknowledged Bruce as King and asserted the independence of Scotland. The beautiful red sandstone ruin is now the focal point of the Arbroath Abbey Pageant which recreates the atmosphere and events of the time. Bruce is associated also with the Isle of Arran, where there is a room dedicated to him in the castle at *Brodick* and a cave at

Blackwaterfoot bears his name. He attended the consecration of the largest cathedral in Scotland, *St Andrews* in 1318 and was finally buried, along with a number of other kings and queens, in the abbey at *Dunfermline*.

Mary Queen of Scots was born in the palace of *Linlithgow* and all around the eastern lowlands of Scotland there are reminders of her tragic life. In 1547, aged only four, she sought refuge in the priory of *Inchmahome*, now ruined, but beautifully situated on an island in the Lake of Menteith. She lived on the island for several weeks and a little garden that was once part of the priory is named after her. Twenty years later she lived on another island, in the middle of *Loch Leven* near Kinross, imprisoned in the castle there until a young admirer helped her to escape.

Happier days of her reign are recalled at *Crichton* (where she attended a close family wedding in 1562), *Craigmillar*, where the castle was a favourite refuge from the intrigues of Court life at Holyrood, and *Borthwick*, where in 1567 she spent her honeymoon with Bothwell in his castle. Fascinating relics of her life are to be found in Queen Mary's House, an attractive building in *Jedburgh*.

In more recent years, the number of Royal Houses of Scotland has been extended to include *Glamis*, the romantic castle north of Dundee where the Queen Mother grew up and where Princess Margaret was born.

So the royal tradition of building and rebuilding goes on, continuing the pattern which has left a legacy of palaces, houses and castles throughout Scotland to be enjoyed today.

The Old Bridge of Dee at the edge of the Balmoral estate

MULL

A Holiday Across the Water?

One of our attractive self-catering chalets on the beautiful island of Mull could be the answer –

Our chalets are easy to run, sleep 4/5 people and are fully equipped; all linen is provided. Ideal for families with young children.

From £35 for a three night stay and from £65 for a full week.

For details ring John King at 06884 270 (24 hour service).
Glen Houses, Dervaig,
Isle of Mull

Everything's big about our atlas, except the price.

Big Road Atlas of Britain.
Only £2.95.
Available from the AA, all good bookshops and newsagents.

AA Publications

Clan HIGHLAND HOLIDAYS

Clan Hotels offer 3 excellent centres and 4 delightful hotels for that short refreshing break or extended stay. The locations of each hotel offer first class bases to tour the splendid Highlands whether by car, foot, or public transport.

The Park Hotel in Oban is just a short way from the ferry to the captivating islands of Mull, Iona and Staffa. Glencoe and Inveraray are only a short drive away.

The Drumossie in Inverness is an ideal centre for touring this historical region. Loch Ness (and all her attractions), Glen Affric and Aviemore are within easy reach.

In Nairn, famous for its beaches and golf courses, you have a choice of 2 four star hotels — the Golf View and the Newton. Both have excellent sporting facilities including tennis, golf, swimming pool, sauna and games room.

Main Summer Holidays ● Spring and Autumn Breaks ● Inclusive Golfing Holidays ● Fishing and Shooting ● Motoring Holidays ● Private Parties.

Midweek and weekend bargain breaks are available with special rates for 2, 3 and 4 day stays. Prices per person, per night, dinner, bed and breakfast depends on Hotel chosen — From £14.50 including V.A.T. to £20.00.

For colour brochures and full details on any of the above holidays plus our special off season and group rates contact

CLAN HOTELS.
DEPT AA.
25 WELLINGTON STREET.
GLASGOW G2 6JJ.
TELEPHONE: 041-221 2891

Scotland's for me!

EDINBURGH

Despite admitting to being a Glaswegian, DONALD MacCORMICK, from television's Newsnight, writes with affection about the fascination and grandeur of one of the world's great cities

Edinburgh

Any one of the five million visitors who come to Edinburgh each year is bound to be exhilarated by the sheer physical grandeur of the place. No matter how widely travelled the visitor may be, he or she will surely find Edinburgh one of the most visually striking of all the world's great cities. Fortunately, it is also one of the easiest to explore on foot. In one day's determined expenditure of energy and shoe-leather, it would be possible to take in at least half of all the principal sights.

The central and most scenic part of Edinburgh is dominated by three rugged hills and adorned by the numerous imposing buildings. The spreading ramparts of Edinburgh Castle tower some 300 feet over the celebrated Princes Street – the most beautiful and elegant of shopping streets in Scotland, if not in Britain. It's a splendid sight to walk down this long, straight thoroughfare from the east end just before dusk and see the Castle and the tall, terraced houses of the Royal Mile silhouetted against the sky. About a mile distant to the east, and twice as lofty, the peak and crags of Arthur's Seat can be seen in all their natural splendour. They in turn look directly northwards across to the Calton Hill. This is another jagged heap of rock rising out of city streets and rather quaintly surmounted by Edinburgh's famous uncompleted model of the Parthenon in Athens.

by Donald MacCormick

From the easily-reached vantage point of that architectural folly, it's appropriate that the visitor should be able to look down and around at an almost bewildering variety of handsome buildings – each one well worth a visit. In a verdant park at the foot of Arthur's Seat is the elegant Royal Palace of Holyroodhouse. It was lived in for six years by Mary Queen of Scots, was enlarged in the 17th century, and is now the official residence in Edinburgh of the Queen. In appearance the Palace carries echoes of the French chateaux of the Loire, which is fitting enough remembering the political links between Scotland and France in the 17th and 18th centuries. In the middle of Princes Street stands the Gothic spire of the Scott Monument, commemorating the novelist Sir Walter Scott. (It's possible, if you're feeling fit, to climb up the 287 steps inside.) And nearby there are also the pleasing neo-classical buildings housing the city's two main art galleries, the Royal Scottish Academy and the National Gallery of Scotland.

Up the hill from there, on the ridge running along from the Castle, are the elaborate, Norman-style arches of St Giles's Cathedral, the High Kirk of Edinburgh; and the spacious 17th-century building of Parliament House, which was the Scottish seat of government until the Act of Union with England in 1707, and which now houses

St Giles's Cathedral

Left: Edinburgh Castle and Princes Street

Scotland's supreme courts. The Castle itself, a short walk away, is, of course, primarily a massive military fortification – first recorded as a tribal stronghold in 600AD and still the headquarters of the army in Scotland. But it is also a rich storehouse of Scottish history, containing among other treasures the ancient Crown, Sceptre and Sword of State of Scotland.

Also worth visiting, as one of Edinburgh's more modern historic buildings, is the Old Royal High School, another neo-classical structure sitting on Calton Hill at the east end of the central area. This was once intended to house the new Scottish Assembly, or sub-parliament, proposed by the Devolution legislation of the late 1970s. But the scheme was abandoned after the insufficiently conclusive Scottish Referendum of 1979, and since then the building, though fully renovated and prepared as the home for a modern legislative assembly, has remained empty and largely unused. It is, too, still the subject of strong political controversy in Scotland and as such, at the time of writing, is closed to the public and kept under strict security. Any visitor interested in constitutional matters, however, will no doubt want to have a look at the parliament building where nobody parleys.

It would be a pity, while discussing the physical character of Edinburgh, not to add some mention of the Old and New Towns – the Old being that labyrinthine quarter huddling on the southern side of the ridge running down from the Castle to Holyroodhouse, and the New (in fact it dates from 1767) being the spacious, and gracious, Georgian area lying just to the north of Princes Street. Each of these parts has, of course, its own outstanding individual buildings, some of them described already; but it's their quite distinctive overall atmospheres that make both Old and New such rewarding territory to stroll through.

The Old Town, with its main thoroughfare, the Royal Mile, is the medieval part of the city, in which hundreds of tall and ancient tenements cluster together round narrow wynds and alleyways, cheek by jowl with landmarks like St Giles's, and the house where the religious leader John Knox once lived. Many of the tenements have been converted into modern flats, but the old access passages, or 'closes', remain – some of them bearing descriptive plaques at the entrances.

By contrast with the higgledy-piggledy structure of the Old Town, the New Town over on the far side of Princes Street is a measured and symmetrical example of 18th-century town planning, and is probably the finest (and certainly the largest) area of Georgian architecture in Europe. Although the spacious squares and crescents, built of golden sandstone, are now studded with legal and commercial offices, the New Town is still seventy-five per cent residential.

So far as Edinburgh events are concerned, obviously the most famous, and the one that most reflects the grand, prestigious and historic aspects of the city, is the Edinburgh International Festival, held every year during the last fortnight of August and the first week of September. This is one of the most important cultural events in the international calendar, and each Festival attracts well over 90,000 visitors from all over the world. Music, drama and art are all represented at international level, not to mention the separate but concurrent

A bird's eye view of Edinburgh

John Knox's house in the Old Town

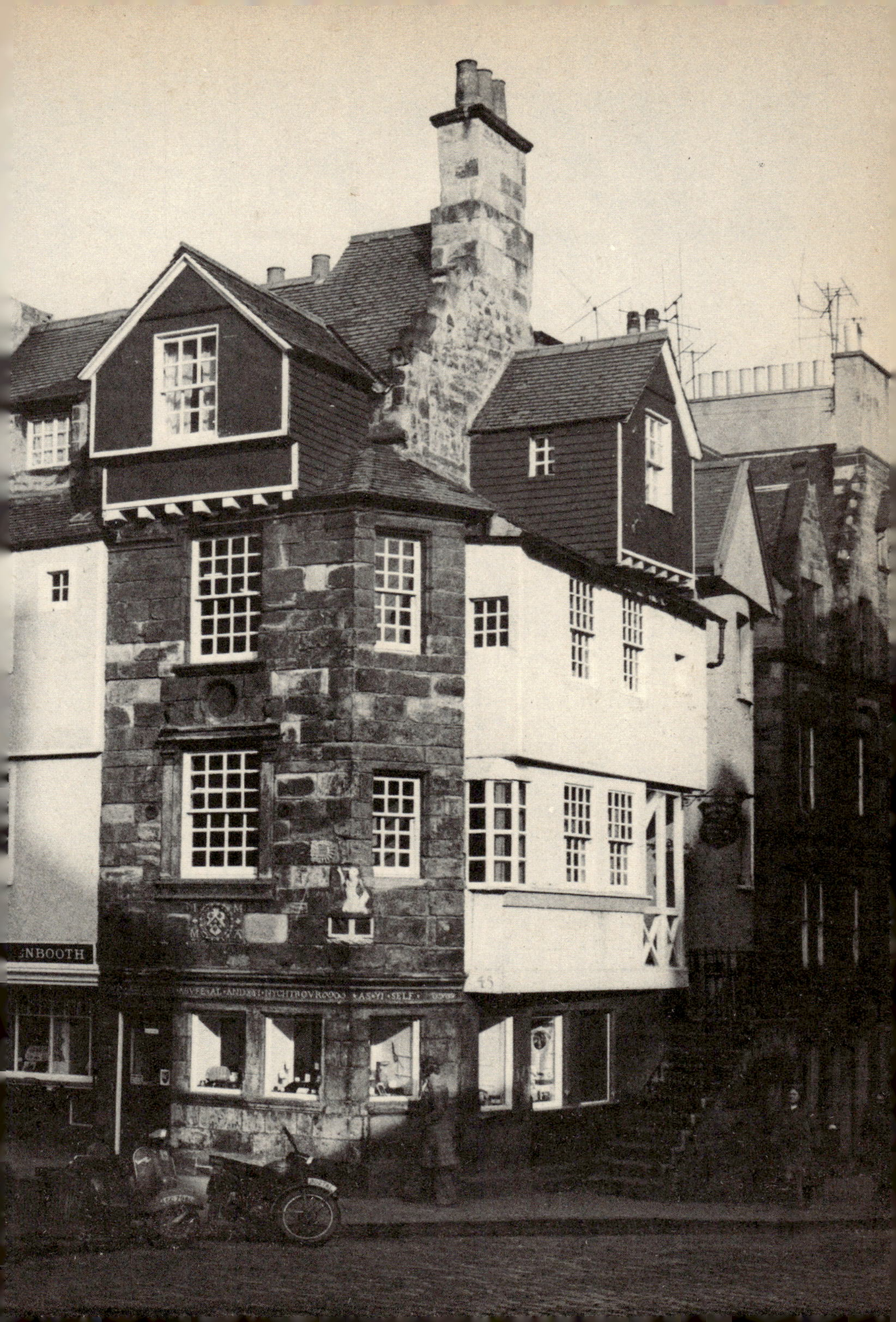

NBOOTH

The Georgian architecture of Charlotte Square

Film Festival, all helping to turn the city during these three weeks into a kind of living 'Who's Who' of all the arts. Naturally, much of the Festival is a serious, though not solemn, affair, with the concert hall audiences in particular often donning the civilised glamour of formal evening clothes. But there's a more relaxed and spontaneous side as well, which has been greatly encouraged over the years by the mushroom growth of the Edinburgh Festival Fringe. In 1981, nearly a thousand different shows of every conceivable kind were on offer on the Fringe, performed by professional, amateur and student groups in any and every school, church hall or old garage that could somehow be pressed into service as an auditorium. There was even one theatrical group who would come along and enact a play for you in your own hotel bedroom – and informality can't go much farther than that!

Another famous feature of Festival time in Edinburgh is the military tattoo, performed under floodlights every evening on the Castle Esplanade. Invariably, parades of Scottish pipers and drummers form part of this spectacular event, but each year there is also at least one presentation by soldiers or sailors from abroad. Obviously, military precision and dramatic effects of sound and lighting are the key elements in the tattoo; but here, too, there is often a mood of relaxed enjoyment, the atmosphere of a big night out, among the spectators piled up on the tiered seating overlooking the spectacle. The evening always ends with a haunting bagpipe tune played by a solitary, spotlit piper.

During the Festival, and indeed throughout the year, Edinburgh is extremely well provided with places to eat and drink, in terms of variety as well as of quantity. As you might expect, however, Sundays tend to be a bit more difficult. The central area around

Princes Street boasts a whole clutch of high-class restaurants, and there are more, too, scattered round the halls and theatres behind the Castle. There is also a handful of very good, country house-style eating places on the periphery of the city or just outside it. For 'fast food' there are the usual hamburger and baked potato places, but special mention must be made of the excellent collection of self-service restaurants in and around Hanover Street, just inside the New Town, which serve mostly delicious vegetarian dishes and good drinkable wine at extremely keen prices.

Then, of course, there are the Edinburgh pubs – many of which, by the way, also do good plain bar meals. The main, and best-known, concentration of pubs is in Rose Street, which runs parallel to Princes Street, and which is the favourite celebratory pub-crawl for revellers after rugby internationals at Murrayfield. For anyone in need of more modest refreshment, and who likes old, unspoiled pub interiors with gleaming dark wood, generous mirrors and lots of well-polished glasses hanging up, Rose Street is well worth a visit. Visitors from south of the border should note, too, that Scottish licensing laws allow some pubs to serve drinks right through the day.

A couple of other places of interest not covered so far, and perhaps of particular interest to children (of all ages) are the fascinating Museum of Childhood, in the High Street opposite John Knox's house, which has a splendid collection of old clothes, toys and games; and the 'Camera Obscura' up on Castlehill, which is sited on top of a look-out tower and affords a kind of distorting-mirror tour of the city's rooftops and spires.

Nor should it be forgotten that Edinburgh has several large and pleasant public parks, my own favourite being the Royal Botanic Gardens at Stockbridge on the northern fringe of the New Town. This has some splendidly exotic glasshouses, and also provides a superb setting for the ravishing Scottish National Gallery of Modern Art.

In addition to the parks, there are many other places for outdoor or athletic activity. There's an attractive zoo out to the west, on the way to Edinburgh Airport, and an Olympic-size Royal Commonwealth swimming pool lies on the south side. Beyond that, on the Pentland Hills at the southern edge of the city, there's the largest artificial ski-slope in Britain.

Finally, in some of these places and in others, a whole range of bracing walks are to be enjoyed – perhaps the best of all being the scramble to the summit of Arthur's Seat. For further information about these, consult the Tourist Information Centre at 5 Waverley Bridge, right in the city centre by the railway station.

Alternatively, write to:
The Scottish Tourist Board
23 Ravelston Terrace
Edinburgh EH4 3EU

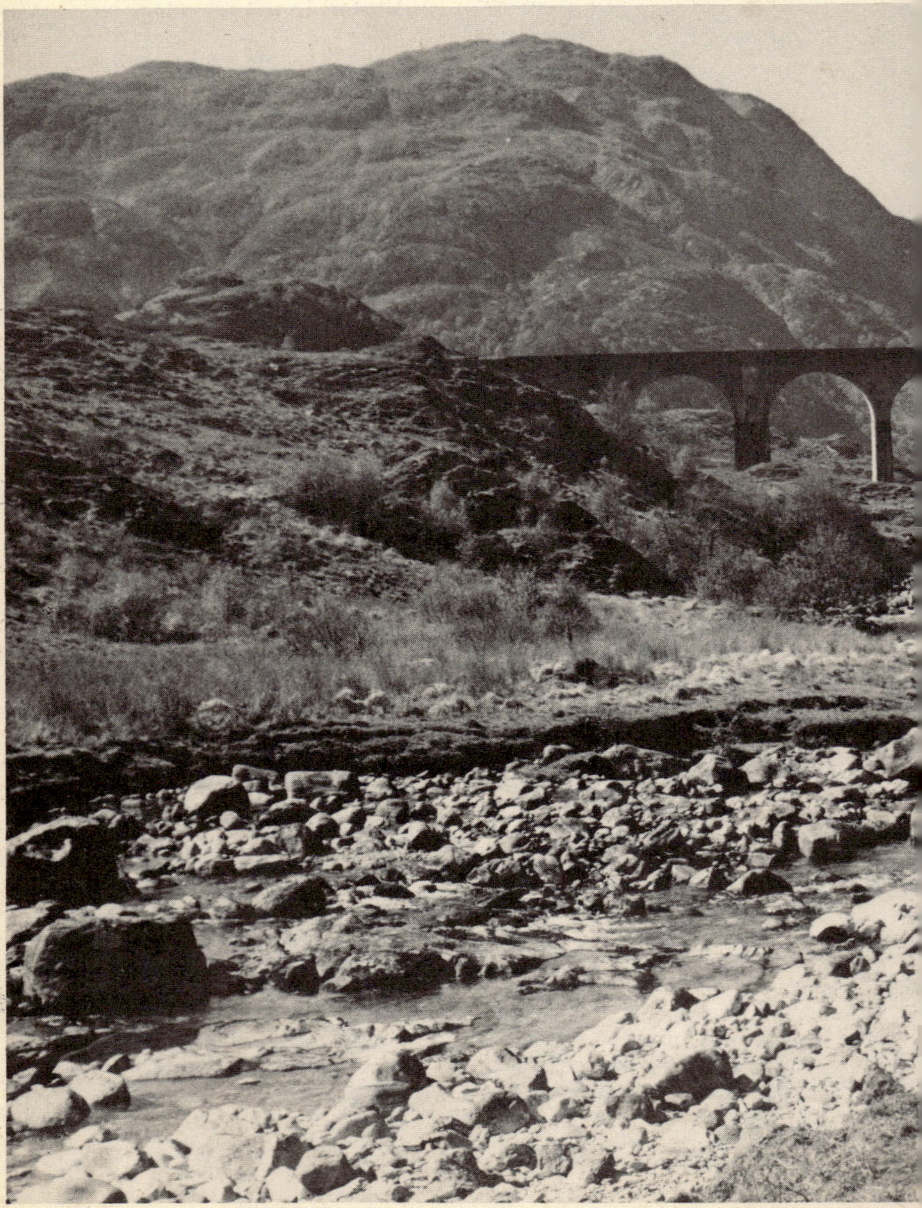

GAZETTEER

ABBREVIATIONS AND SYMBOLS

For how to read a gazetteer entry see page 79.

Town headings

AA	AA office
☎	telephone — unless stated, the name of the exchange is the same as the placename; at hotels the number is usually for reception
D	district (see 'Population', page 79)
Ec	early closing
ex	except
fy	ferry
Map	figures and letters which follow give the service atlas page number and the national grid reference (see atlas page 28)
Md	market day

Hotels, Restaurants, Guesthouses, Farmhouses & Inns

Explanations of criteria used in classification and of various symbols may be found at the foot of the next column and on page 77.

✻	1981 prices
☎	Telephone
	Private bathroom with own toilet
	Private shower with own toilet
	Four-poster beds
☽	Night porter
	Air conditioning throughout
	Room(s) set aside for non-smokers
	Central heating throughout
	No dogs allowed overnight in hotel bedrooms
P	Open parking for cars
	Garage or covered space
	No parking on premises
	No coach parties accepted
	Garden over ½ acre
	Indoor swimming pool
	Outdoor swimming pool
♦9	9-hole golf course
♦18	18-hole golf course
	Tennis court(s)
	Fishing
∩	Riding stables on premises
	Special facilities for children
	Type of cooking
	Afternoon tea
	Morning coffee
&	The hotel can accommodate disabled persons
S%	Service charge levied and included in prices

Hotels only

ꞯ	This symbol shows that the hotel offers cheaper off-season weekends
®	Tea/coffee-making facilities in bedrooms
alc	á la carte
sB&B	Single room including breakfast per person per night
sB&B⇌	Single room with private bath and toilet and breakfast per person per night
sB&B	Single room with private shower and toilet and breakfast per person per night
dB&B	Double room (2 persons) including breakfast
dB&B⇌	Double room (2 persons) with private bath and toilet and breakfast
dB&B	Double room (2 persons) with private shower and toilet and breakfast
CTV	Colour television
Etr	Easter
fr	from
mdnt	midnight
RS	Restricted service
TV	Black and white television
Wine	Minimum price of full bottle of wine (eg 70cl)
xmas	Special Christmas programme for residents

Credit cards

The numbered boxes below indicate the credit cards which hotels and restaurants accept

1	Access	4	Carte Blanche
2	American Express	5	Diners
3	Barclays Visa	6	Euro

Abbreviations & symbols applicable to GH, FH & Inns only

(A..)	Annexe. The number following the letter A indicates the number of rooms
B&b	Bed and breakfast per person per night
Bdi	Inclusive dinner bed and breakfast. When B&b prices not shown, rate always charged whether dinner taken or not
D	Dinner/evening meal
fb	Family bedroom
FH	Farmhouse
GH	Guesthouse
hc	Number of bedrooms with hot and cold water
lake/sea/river	Some bedrooms overlooking lake/sea/river
L	Lunch price (only inns show prices)
Lic	Licensed
Ł	No lunches included in weekly price
M	No main meals included in weekly price
nc	No children eg nc . . . no children under . . . years of age
rm	Total rooms in main building where 100% hot and cold water not provided
rs	Restricted service or accommodation
sn	Snacks available
Tem	Temperance
W	Weekly terms

For Camping & Caravanning see page 154

Where to stay, where to eat

The AA's full time and highly qualified team of inspectors regularly inspects all AA-recommended tourist accommodation in Britain and Ireland. Establishments are required to meet and constantly maintain minimum standards, details of which, together with the criteria for classification by the AA, are set out in the following booklets obtainable from AA Regional Headquarters.

HH5	Hotels and The Automobile Association
HH12	Notes on the listing of guesthouses, private hotels, farmhouses and inns.
HH62	Notes on caravan and camp site classification.

Hotels

Hotels are classified by stars; each classification reflects the provision of facilities and services rather than comparative merit. The range of menus, service and hours of service are appropriate to the classification, although hotels often satisfy several of the requirements of a classification higher than that awarded.

★ Good hotels and inns, generally of small scale and with modest facilities and furnishings, frequently run by the proprietor himself. All bedrooms with hot and cold water; adequate bath and lavatory arrangements; main meals with a choice of dishes served to residents; menus for residents and meal facilities for non-residents may be limited, especially at weekends.

★★ Hotels offering a higher standard of accommodation, more baths and perhaps a few private bathrooms/showers; lavatories on all floors; wider choice of meals (but these may be restricted, especially to non-residents).

★★★ Well-appointed hotels with more spacious accommodation and at least 40% of the bedrooms with private bathrooms/showers; full meal facilities for residents every day of the week but at weekends service to non-residents may be restricted.

★★★★ Exceptionally well-appointed hotels offering a high standard of comfort and cooking with 80% of the bedrooms providing private bathrooms/showers. At weekends meal service to non-residents may be restricted.

★★★★★ Luxury hotels, offering a very high standard of accommodation, service and comfort. All bedrooms have private bathrooms/showers.

⊕ Approved hotels which do not conform to the minimum classification requirements in respect of porterage, reception facilities, and choice of dishes; facilities for non-residents are often limited.

Red stars
★ (red) The award of red stars is based on a subjective assessment to highlight hotels considered to be of outstanding merit within their normal star ratings, offering something special in the way of welcome and hospitality. The award is normally withdrawn when the hotel undergoes a change of ownership.

White stars
☆ The method used to indicate establishments high in amenities but with deliberately limited personalised services, designed and operated to cater predominantly for the short-stay guest. Under this heading will be found some motels and motor hotels with bedroom facilities mainly on a self-service basis. It is emphasised that white stars are an indication of a type of hotel.

Country house
♨ Hotels which display many of the characteristics of a traditional country house, set in secluded rural surroundings. Reception and service facilities may be of a more informal nature than in conventional hotels of similar classification.

Restaurants
✗ Restaurants are inspected by the AA who classify them by knife-and-fork symbols ranging in number from one to five, reflecting comfort, service and cooking. The basic requirements for a recommendation are a high standard of cooking, prompt and courteous service, a pleasant atmosphere and value for money.

A high standard of cooking and service is expected from restaurants throughout the British Isles, but differing national or regional tastes and styles are taken into account.

Rosette awards
❀ Each year the AA presents rosette awards to hotels and restaurants where the cooking, wine and service can be particularly recommended. The award can be of one, two or, exceptionally, three rosettes, and full details of such establishments can be found in the annual publication *Hotels and Restaurants in Britain* available from AA offices.

Merit symbols
H Denotes hospitality, friendliness and service well above the average for hotels similarly classified.
B Denotes bedrooms significantly better than those to be expected within the star classification.
L Denotes lounges, bars and public areas significantly above the standard implied by the star classification.

Note: Only three-, four- and five-star hotels have so far been considered for merit awards.

Guesthouses, farmhouses and inns
These establishments are not graded by the AA, but they are regularly inspected and have to maintain minimum standards and meet stipulated criteria.

Camping and caravanning sites
▶ The AA inspects camping and caravanning sites throughout the British Isles and classifies them with between one and five pennant symbols. Each classification indicates the type of site and its range of facilities. To provide a qualitative comparison between sites, the AA has introduced an assessment, taking account of three major aspects of a site: environment, sanitary installations and other equipment.

By combining both the pennant and qualitative schemes, members are now better able to choose a site best suited to their needs.

Picnic sites/transit picnic sites
The AA inspects and lists two distinct types of picnic sites. A picnic site is one considered worthy of a visit and must be equipped with litter bins. Listed transit picnic sites are conveniently situated for breaking a journey and are equipped with litter bins, toilets, drinking water and furniture; they are not necessarily of scenic interest.

General information
Annexes
Annexes may lack some of the amenities available in the main hotel building; the exact nature of the accommodation should be checked at the time of reservation. Note that the gazetteer only gives information on recommended annexes.

Children
Not all establishments accept children of all ages, and those that do vary in the special facilities provided for them. Readers are advised to check with the establishment before booking. When reserving cots, readers should ensure that the highest safety requirements are met.

Disabled persons
Anyone with any form of disability should notify proprietors so that appropriate arrangements can be made to minimise difficulties, particularly in the event of an emergency.

Fire precautions
When the programme of registration and inspection

has been completed by the authorities responsible no premises, as encompassed by the Fire Precautions Act, 1971 will be allowed by the Home Office to operate without a certificate. Our inspectors, while checking whether the necessary steps are being taken to obtain a certificate, will continue to inspect emergency notices, fire-fighting machinery and fire exits. You are strongly urged to read and understand emergency notices for your own and other people's safety.

To the best of the AA's knowledge at the time of going to press, every establishment listed in this publication has applied for, and has not been refused, a fire certificate.

Gazetteer entry
When establishments names are shown in *italics* the particulars have not been confirmed by the management.

Hygiene
The local authority is responsible for conditions of hygiene in hotels but our inspectors, during regular classification visits, also inspect kitchens, storerooms etc to assure themselves that satisfactory standards of cleanliness and hygiene are being maintained.

Licensing regulations
All hotels are licenced unless otherwise stated. Licensing hours within Scotland are set out under the Licensing (Scotland) Act 1976. Various restrictions in licensed premises are placed on minors depending on whether they are aged under 18, over 16 or under 14. Details are available in a leaflet from AA Regional Headquarters.

Meals
Residents may obtain breakfast, lunch and dinner at all AA-appointed hotels but service to non-residents at weekends, and to a lesser extent at lunch, may be restricted in all but five-star establishments.

Seeking to maintain a balance between the high cost of staff and an acceptable price to consumers, some hotels have introduced an element of self-service at some meals, particularly for breakfast and at weekends. Times shown are for latest time evening meal can be ordered **not** necessarily when meal is served.

Opening dates
Hotels and restaurants show inclusive dates when **closed**. GH, FH & Inns show inclusive opening dates.

Prices
Prices should be checked before booking as they are likely to fluctuate significantly during the currency of this book. The effects of inflation, possible variations in the rate of VAT and other factors may influence prices. The prices are approximate and are intended as a comparative guide only. Readers are advised always to obtain quotations when making enquiries or reservations. Remember, there is invariably a higher charge for a private bathroom, and the application of VAT and service charges varies from hotel to hotel.

Reports
Readers' comments on establishments are welcome, and report forms can be obtained from AA offices. Any criticism should be brought to the hotel management's notice immediately so that the problem can be dealt with promptly. If a personal approach fails, members should inform the AA within a week stating whether or not their name can be disclosed to the hotel, so that an investigation can be made.

Reservations
It is advisable to book early, especially during the holiday season. You should inform the hotel staff at once of any delay or change of plan, since you may be held legally responsible for part of the charge if the room booked cannot be relet.

Some hotels, especially those in short-season holiday centres, do not accept advance bookings for bed and breakfast only; others, particularly in the larger towns, find it necessary to ask for a deposit from chance visitors who are staying for one night only; others charge for dinner, bed and breakfast, whether or not dinner is taken. *En pension* terms are normally offered for periods of three days or more. Many hotels, particularly at seaside resorts, do not take bookings from midweek to midweek and will only accept period bookings at a full-board rate. The hotel industry's Voluntary Code of Booking Practice was introduced in June 1977. Its prime object is to ensure that the customer is clear about the precise services and facilities he is buying, and what price he will have to pay, before he commits himself to a contractually binding agreement. The guest should be handed a card at the time of registration, with a full tariff including the total obligatory charge, and details may also be displayed prominently at the reception office. The Tourism (Sleeping Accommodation Price Display) Order 1977 was introduced in February 1978. It compels hotels, motels, guesthouses, inns and self-catering accommodation with four or more letting bedrooms to display in entrance halls the maximum and minimum prices charged for each category of room. This order complements the Voluntary Code of Booking Practice.

Every effort is being made by the AA to encourage the use of the Voluntary Code in appropriate establishments.

Reservation services
AA Travel Agencies can reserve accommodation at company and consortia hotels throughout Great Britain and Ireland. A list of companies is available on request.

Telephone surcharge
To cover high equipment installation and rental costs a surcharge is sometimes imposed on telephone calls made through the hotel switchboard. Members are advised to ascertain the rate of surcharge prior to placing a call.

Gazetteer

Explanation of entries

Arrangement of gazetteer
Within each section of the gazetteer, place names are arranged alphabetically including individual place names on off-shore Islands.

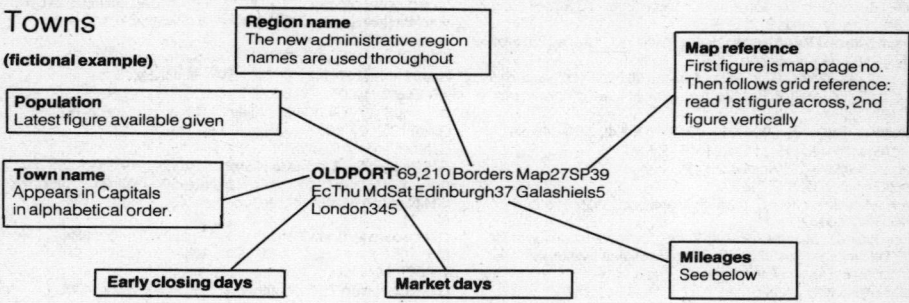

Towns
(fictional example)

Population — Latest figure available given

Town name — Appears in Capitals in alphabetical order.

Region name — The new administrative region names are used throughout

Map reference — First figure is map page no. Then follows grid reference: read 1st figure across, 2nd figure vertically

OLDPORT 69,210 Borders Map27SP39
EcThu MdSat Edinburgh37 Galashiels5
London345

Early closing days

Market days

Mileages — See below

Population
Population figures are given after the names of many towns and villages. These are from the 1971 census. In few cities, where the name of the District is the same as the principal town, the population of the township is given, followed by the population of the post 1975 District Council area in brackets ie (D210,000).

Postal addresses
The name shown after each placename is the administrative region in which the place is situated; it is not the correct postal address.

Map references
The map reference for each place consists of the page number of the atlas at the beginning of the book and the national grid reference; the national grid is explained on atlas page 28 and the second page of the service atlas has a list of the symbols and other markings used throughout.

Early closing days
The information can only be a general guide. Some shops may operate a six-day week or some other variation.

Mileages
After each entry a selection of mileages is given to other towns. These are calculated to the nearest mile, using the AA recommended route between town centres; the abbreviation *(fy)* indicates that a ferry crossing is included. Supplementary mileage information which is described in the legend may be obtained from the atlas, pages 28 to 48.

Gazetteer location policy
The AA applies the following principles in deciding under which towns establishments will be listed.
1. All establishments within three miles of a larger town, in particular when part of a continuous urban belt, may be consolidated under that town unless a county change is involved.
2. White star hotels, which cater for the motorist in particular, are given dual listing, firstly under their actual location and secondly under a larger town if it is within six miles.
3. Most major airports have an individual gazetteer heading.

There may be a few map entries unsupported by text. This is because the maps have to be completed before final amendments are made to gazetteer copy.

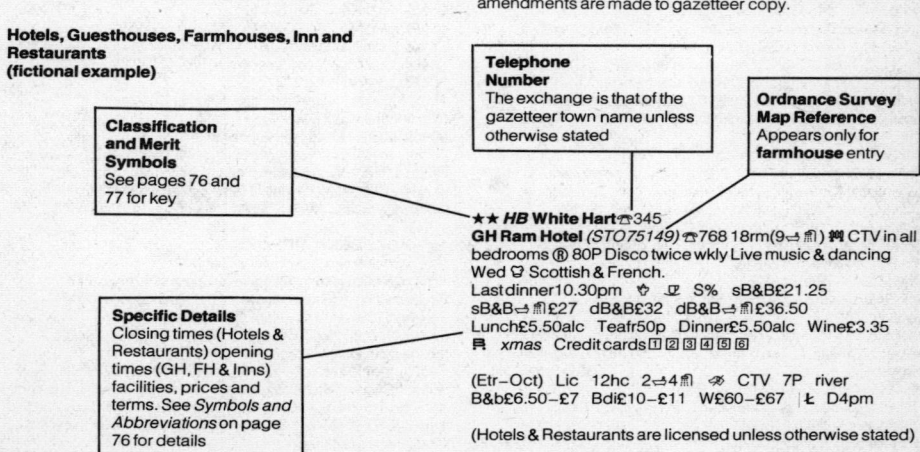

Hotels, Guesthouses, Farmhouses, Inn and Restaurants
(fictional example)

Classification and Merit Symbols — See pages 76 and 77 for key

Telephone Number — The exchange is that of the gazetteer town name unless otherwise stated

Ordnance Survey Map Reference — Appears only for **farmhouse** entry

★★ *HB* White Hart ☎345
GH Ram Hotel *(STO75149)* ☎768 18rm(9⇌🛏) 🛏 CTV in all bedrooms ® 80P Disco twice wkly Live music & dancing Wed ♀ Scottish & French.
Last dinner 10.30pm ♀ 🖳 S% sB&B£21.25
sB&B⇌🛏£27 dB&B£32 dB&B⇌🛏£36.50
Lunch£5.50alc Teafr50p Dinner£5.50alc Wine£3.35
🍴 xmas Credit cards ① ② ③ ④ ⑤ ⑥

(Etr-Oct) Lic 12hc 2⇌4🛏 🚿 CTV 7P river
B&b£6.50-£7 Bdi£10-£11 W£60-£67 | ₤ D4pm

(Hotels & Restaurants are licensed unless otherwise stated)

Specific Details — Closing times (Hotels & Restaurants) opening times (GH, FH & Inns) facilities, prices and terms. See *Symbols and Abbreviations* on page 76 for details

79

Aberdeen – Aberdeen Airport

AA ABERDEEN 208,569 Grampian Map45NJ90 EcWed/Sat MdFri Banff47 Braemar62 Fraserburgh43 Huntly39 London538 Stonehaven15 **See also Aberdeen Airport**

☆☆☆***Holiday Inn Bucksburn*** Old Meldrum Rd, Bucksburn (3m N A947) (Holiday Inn) ☎713911 Telex no71308
99⇌🛏 Lift ♪ 🎨 📺 CTV in bedrooms 180P ⌂(heated) Disco Sun Cabaret Sun ♀ International. Last dinner 10.30pm ✧ 🍷 🍴 Credit cards ①②③④⑤⑥

☆☆☆***Skean Dhu Altens*** Souter Head Rd, Altens (3m S off A956) ☎877000 Telex no739631
221⇌🛏 Lift ♪ 📺 CTV in all bedrooms ⓡ 500P ⊅(heated) squash Cabaret Fri & Sat ♀ International. Last dinner11pm ✧ 🍷 S%
✽sB&B⇌🛏£35.25–£36.90 dB&B⇌🛏£42.55–£45.85 Lunch£4.95&alc High Tea£1.45–£7.80 Dinner£5.95&alc Wine£4.20 🍺 xmas
Credit cards ①②③④⑤⑥

★★★★***Station*** Guild St (British Transport) ☎27214 Telex no73161
Closed Xmas; 60rm(42⇌) Lift ♪ 📺 CTV in 42 bedrooms TV in 18 bedrooms ⓡ 45P Conference facilities available ♀ English & French. Last dinner 9.30pm S%
✽sB&Bfr£23.75 sB&B⇌fr£35.75 dB&Bfr£35.70 dB&B⇌fr£49.50 Lunch fr£1.95 Tea fr£2.15 Wine£4.75 🍺 Credit cards ①②③④⑤

★★★***Caledonian*** 10 Union Ter (Thist'e) ☎29233 Telex no73758
80rm(50⇌30🛏) 1🛏 Lift ♪ ✈ 📺 CTV in all bedrooms ⓡ 17P ♿ International. Last dinner11.30pm ✧ 🍷 S%
✽sB&B⇌🛏fr£38.75 dB&B⇌fr£45.50
Lunch£3.20–£3.35&alc Dinner£6.95–£7.95&alc Wine£3.37 🍺 Credit cards ①②③④⑤⑥

★★★***Imperial*** Stirling St (Swallow) ☎29101 Telex no73365 RS Xmas & New Year; 109rm(10⇌90🛏) Lift ♪ 📺 CTV in all bedrooms ⓡ ⪢ ♫ Disco wkly Live music & dancing 6nights wkly ♀ English & French. Last dinner10pm ✧ 🍷 S% ✽sB&B⇌🛏£23.25–£29.35
dB&B⇌🛏£27.35–£37.55 Lunch fr£3.25&alc High Tea fr£2.50 Dinner fr£5&alc Wine£3.55 🍺 Credit cards ①②③④⑤⑥

★★★***Marcliffe*** Queens Ter ☎51281 Telex no73225
A granite faced, terraced building situated on the western approach road to Aberdeen, with modern furnishings and décor.
40rm(15⇌25🛏) Lift ♪ 📺 CTV in all bedrooms ⓡ 30P ♨ sauna bath ♀ English & French. Last dinner 9.45pm ✧ 🍷 S% ✽sB&B⇌🛏£26 dB&B⇌🛏£32
Wine£4.80 🍺 Credit cards ①②③④⑤⑥

☆☆☆***Royal Darroch*** Cults (3m SW A93) (Reo Stakis) ☎868811 Telex no739138
67⇌🛏 Lift ♪ 📺 CTV in all bedrooms ⓡ 200P Live music & dancing Sat ♀ English & French. Last dinner10pm ✧ 🍷 ✽sB&B⇌fr£30 dB&B⇌fr£38 Lunch fr£2.95&alc Tea fr45p Dinner fr£7.50&alc Wine£3.75 🍺
Credit cards ①②③④⑤⑥

☆☆***Dee Motel*** Garth Dee Rd ☎321474 Telex no73212 Annexe: 75rm(31⇌44🛏) ♪ 📺 CTV in all bedrooms ⓡ 150P Live music & dancing Tue–Thu, Sat & Sun Conference facilities available Last dinner 9.45pm ✧ 🍷 S%
sB&B⇌🛏fr£18.50 dB&B⇌🛏fr£23.50
Continental breakfast Lunch fr£3.75 Tea fr65p
Dinner fr£4.20&alc Wine£3 🍺 xmas
Credit cards ①②③④⑤⑥

★★***Gloucester*** 102 Union St (Allied) ☎29095 Telex no76357
71rm(30⇌41🛏) Lift ♪ 📺 CTV in 23 bedrooms TV in 48 bedrooms ⓡ Disco 6 nights wkly Live music & dancing 3 nights wkly ♀ Last dinner 8.30pm ✧ 🍷 sB&B⇌🛏 fr£24 dB&B⇌🛏 fr£33 Lunch fr£6 Tea fr£1.75
Dinner fr£7.50&alc Wine£2.20 🍺 xmas
Credit cards ①②③④⑤⑥

★★***Gordon*** Wellington Rd (Ind Coope (Alloa)) ☎873012

21rm(12⇌) ♪ 📺 CTV in all bedrooms ⓡ 100P
Last dinner 9.30pm ✧ S% sB&Bfr£14 sB&B⇌fr£17
dB&Bfr£22.50 dB&B⇌fr£28 Lunch fr£4 Dinner fr£4
Wine£2.30 🍺 Credit cards ①②③④⑤⑥

★★***Lang Stracht*** Lang Stracht (Scottish & Newcastle) ☎38712
Modern concrete structure, just off ring road.
40rm(2⇌🛏) Lift ♪ CTV 30P Disco wkly ♀ Mainly grills.
Last dinner 8.45pm ✧ 🍷 🍴 Credit cards ①②③④⑤⑥

★★***Northern*** 1 Great Northern Rd (Swallow) ☎43342 Telex no53168
57rm(27⇌) Lift ♪ 🎨 📺 CTV in all bedrooms ⓡ 10P
Last dinner 9.30pm ✧ 🍷 S% ✽sB&B£15.55
sB&B⇌£21.60 dB&B£28.75 dB&B⇌£33.30
Lunch£3.20–£4.60&alc Tea£1.40 High Tea£3–£4.50
Dinner£5–£7.75&alc Wine£3.40 🍺
Credit cards ①②③④⑤⑥

GH *Broomfield Private Hotel* 15 Balmoral Pl ☎28758 8hc (1fb) CTV 16P 🎨 S% B&bfr£8.50 Bdifr£12 D6pm

GH *Carden Hotel* 44 Carden Pl ☎26813 7hc nc5 CTV 6P 🎨

GH *Crown Private Hotel* 10 Springbank Ter ☎26842
8hc (2fb) ⫸ nc4 CTV S% B&b£8 Bdi£11.50
W£50 M D5pm

GH *Dunromin* 75 Constitution St ☎56995 5hc (1fb) CTV 🎨 S% B&b£6–£7

GH *Klibreck* 410 Great Western Rd ☎36115 Closed Xmas & New Year 7hc (2fb) ⫸ CTV 3P 🎨 S%
✽B&bfr£7 Bdifr£10.50 Wfr£45.50 M D3pm

GH *Mannofield Hotel* 447 Great Western Rd ☎35888 Lic 10rm 7hc (2fb) nc5 CTV 14P 🎨 ✽B&bfr£13.80
Bdifr£19.55 Wfr£136.85 Ł D6pm

GH *Tower Hotel* 36 Fonthill Rd ☎24050 Lic 7hc (3fb)
CTV 8P 🎨 S% ✽B&b£9 Bdi£13.25 W£83.50 Ł D6.45pm

GH *Urray House* 429 Great Western Rd ☎35204 6hc (3fb) nc5 CTV 8P 🎨 S% D3pm

GH *Western* 193 Great Western Rd ☎56919 6hc (2fb) ⫸ CTV 8P 🎨 S% B&bfr£7

×××***Fiddlers*** 1 Portland St ☎52050
Closed Sun; Lunch not served Sat; 45seats 15P
♀ International. Last dinner 10.30pm
Credit cards ②③④⑤

×××***Dickens*** 347 Union St ☎20318
75seats 🍴 ♀ International. Last dinner 11pm
Lunch£3.15 Dinner£7.50–£10&alc
Credit cards ①②③④⑤⑥

××***Gerard's*** 50 Chapel St ☎571782
Closed Sun; 80seats 🍴 ♀ French. Last dinner 11pm
✽Lunch£2.60–£2.95&alc Dinner£12alc
Credit cards ①②③④⑤⑥

××***Pinocchio*** 58–60 Justice Mill Ln ☎24599
Closed Sun, 60seats 🍴 ♀ International.
Last dinner 10.30pm Credit cards ①②③⑤

××***Shapla*** 13 King St ☎55999
100seats 🍴 ♀ Indian. Last dinner 11.30pm
Credit cards ②③⑥

×***Poldino's*** 7 Little Belmont St ☎27777
A modern Italian restaurant in quiet street near city centre.
Closed Sun, Xmas & New Year's Day; 75seats 🍴
♀ Italian. Last dinner 10.45pm Lunch£3.50&alc
Dinner£7.50alc Wine£4.50 Credit cards ①②③⑤

✈ **ABERDEEN AIRPORT** Grampian Map45NJ81
London544 Aberdeen6 Banff41

☆☆☆***Holiday Inn Aberdeen Airport*** Riverview Dr, Farburn, Dyce (Commonwealth) ☎Aberdeen770011 Telex no739651
154⇌🛏 ♪ 🎨 📺 CTV in all bedrooms 200P ⌂(heated) sauna bath Disco 6 nights wkly ♀ International.
Last dinner 11pm ✧ 🍷 🍴 Credit cards ①②③⑤

☆☆☆***Skean Dhu Aberdeen Airport*** Argyll Rd (adj to main entrance 1m N of A96) ☎Aberdeen725252 Telex no739239
148⇌🛏 ⓡ 📺 CTV in all bedrooms ⓡ 300P ♨ ⊅(heated) Conference facilities available ♀ International.

Last dinner 11pm ⚭ ⏸ S% sB&B⇨🛁£41.25–£49.90
sB&B⇨🛁£43.55–£52.85 Lunch£1.20–£1.80&alc
Tea£1.75alc HighTea£2.50alc Dinner£5.95&alc
Wine£4.80 🍷 Credit cards ①②③④⑤

☆☆**B Skean Dhu Dyce** Farburn Ter, Dyce (off A947)
☎Aberdeen723101 Telexno73473
222⇨🛁 ♪ CTV in all bedrooms ® 300P squash Live music Sun Conference facilities available ♿ English & French. Last dinner 11pm ⚭ S%
✻sB&B⇨🛁£33.15–£34.25 dB&B⇨🛁£36.55
Lunch fr£3.95&alc Dinnerfr£5.90&alc Wine£4.20 🍷 xmas Credit cards ①②③④⑤

ABERDOUR 1,576 Fife Map 40 NT18 EcWed Dunfermline 8 Edinburgh 18 Kirkcaldy 9 London 435
★★**Woodside** High St ☎860328
Attractive palm tree fronted hotel. Interesting cocktail bar was once a lounge in the Orient Line vessel Orontes.
12rm(2⇨4🛁) CTV in 10 bedrooms 35P 🛥 ⚭
Last dinner 8.45pm ⚭ sB&Bfr£15.50
sB&B⇨🛁fr£18.50 dB&Bfr£27 dB&B⇨🛁fr£31
Lunch£8alc Dinner£8alc Wine£5.30 Credit cards ①②③
✕✕**Sir Patrick Spens** ☎860414
19seats P Lunch£2.30alc Dinnerfr£5 Wine£4

ABERFELDY 1,589 Tayside Map 40 NN84 EcWed
Md alt Thu Crianlarich 37 Crieff 24 Dunkeld 18 London 464 Perth 32 Pitlochry 15
★★**Palace** ☎20359
Four storey grey and red stone Victorian building just outside town centre in market town by River Tay.
Closed Nov–8 Apr; 18rm(1⇨2🛁) Annexe: 7rm ✕ ♪ CTV 30P 🛥 Live music & dancing 3 nights wkly
Last dinner 8.30pm ⚭ sB&B£10–£12
sB&B⇨🛁£11–£13 dB&B£20–£24 dB&B⇨🛁£22–£26
Lunch£3–£3.50&alc Tea£1.20 HighTea£3
Dinner£5.50–£6.20&alc Wine£3.50 🍷
★★**Weem** Weem (1m NW on B846) (Inter-Hotels) ☎20381

12rm(3⇨) CTV ® 16P 🛥 ⚭ Last dinner 8.30pm ⚭ ⏸
✻sB&B£8.50 sB&B⇨🛁£9.50 dB&B£17 dB&B⇨🛁£19
Bar lunch£1.90–£3.30 Teafr35p Dinner£5 Wine£3.10
🍷 Credit card ②
⊛**Station** Dunkeld St ☎20372
7rm CTV ® 24P Live music & dancing nightly during season
Last dinner 7.30pm ⚭ ⏸ S% sB&B£7–£7.50
dB&B£13–£14 Lunch£2–£3 Tea£2–£2.25
Dinner£4.50–£5 Wine£2 🍷 S%
GH Balnearn Private Hotel Crieff Rd ☎20431 13hc
(2fb) CTV 13P 2🛥 ⚭ B&b£10.35 Bdi£14.55
W£80.50 ⚔ D7pm
GH Guinach House Urlar Rd ☎20251 Mar–Oct Lic
8hc (2fb) CTV 8P S% B&b£8.50–£10
Bdi£12.50–£15 W£80–£95 D7pm
GH Nessbank Private Hotel Crieff Rd ☎20214 Mar–Oct rsNov–Feb Lic 7hc CTV 7P B&bfr£10.50
Bdifr£15.50 Wtrf£95 ⚔ D6pm
FH Mr A. Kennedy **Tom of Cluny** (NN875515) ☎20477
Small hillside farmhouse reached by long steep tarmac/rough drive. Magnificent views southward across the River Tay and Aberfeldy.
3rm (1fb) CTV 2P river 136acres mixed S%
B&b£5–£6 Bdi£7.50–£8.50 D8pm
✕**Ailean Chraggan** Weem (1m N B846) ☎20346
Closed Nov–Mar; 45seats 40P bedrooms available
♿ Scottish, English & French. Last dinner 8.30pm

ABERLADY 737 Lothian Map 35 NT47 EcWed Edinburgh 17 Haddington 5 London 422 North Berwick 8
★★**Kilspindie House** Main St ☎319
White painted stone building (dating from 1638) with crow stepped gables and recent extension to side.
13rm(5⇨) ♪ CTV TV available in bedrooms ® 40P 3🛥 Live music & dancing Sat 🎵 Last dinner 9pm ⚭ S%
sB&B£10–£11 sB&B⇨🛁£11–£13.50 dB&B£20
dB&B⇨🛁£24 Lunchfr£1.60 HighTea£3.05–£4.50
Dinnerfr£5.80&alc Wine£3.10 🍷 Credit cards ①③

Marcliffe Hotel

1-5 Queen's Terrace, Aberdeen.
Tel: 51281
Telex: 73225

The Marcliffe Hotel is privately owned, situated overlooking one of Aberdeens many beautiful parks, yet is only half a mile from the City Centre. Approximately half an hours drive from the airport and ten minutes away from the rail station.

All our 40 bedrooms have private bathroom and colour television, with several luxury rooms also available.

There are three function suites available for all types of functions, *ie* conferences, dinners, weddings, exhibitions and stockrooms, catering for numbers of up to 150 persons.

The Hotel is one of the most popular West End meeting places, at lunchtime and from early evening onwards.

Under the same ownership as the Atholl Hotel.
Mr. – Mrs. J. Stewart Spence, Proprietors.

ABERLOUR 837 Grampian Map44NJ24 EcWed
Craigellachie2 Grantown22 Inverness54 London568
★★*Aberlour* High St ☎287
Centrally situated three storey hotel.
18rm(10⇌🛁) 🍴 CTV 15P 6🅿 Last dinner 8.30pm ✢ ⚲ 🐕
★★*Dowans* ☎488
16rm(12⇌🛁) ✕ 🍴 CTV ® 30P 3🅿 ⚲ 🐕
Last dinner8.15pm ⚲ 🐕 *Lunch£3.75–£5.25
Tea65p–£1.10 High Tea£3.50–£5 Dinner£5.50–£6.90
Wine£2.75
★*Lour* The Square ☎224
Popular for fishing and surrounded by distilleries.
9rm 🍴 CTV 7P ♨ Mainly grills. Last dinner8.30pm
✳sB&Bfr£10.65 dB&Bfr£21.30 Lunchfr£3.50
High Tea£2.50–£4.30 Dinner£5.60–£7.50&alc
Wine£1.95

ABINGTON 184 Strathclyde Map34NS92 EcWed
Carlisle59 Glasgow37 Lanark17 London366 Moffat18
FH Mr G. Hodge **Craighead** (NS914236) ☎Crawford356
Large farm building in courtyard design. Set amid rolling
hills on the banks of the river Duneaton. Main building dates
from 1780. Off unclassified Crawfordjohn road. 1m N of
A74/A73 junc.
May–Oct 3rm (1fb) ⚲ CTV 8P 4🅿 river
800acres mixed S% B&bfr£5.50 Bdifr£8.50 D6pm
FH Mr D. Wilson **Crawfordjohn Mill** (NS897242)
Crawfordjohn ☎Crawfordjohn248
Two-storey, brown-brick farmhouse. Set in its own land. Off
A74 1m SE of Crawfordjohn on unclassified rd.
May–15 Oct 3rm (1fb) TV 4P 🍴 180acres arable
dairy S% B&bfr£6 Bdifr£8 Wfr£52 Ł D6.30pm
FH Mrs M.E. Hamilton **Kirkton** (NS933210) (1m S A74)
☎Crawford376
May–Sep 3rm ⚲ nc7 CTV 3P river 750acres beef
sheep S% B&b£5–£5.50
FH Mrs J. Hyslop **Netherton** (NS908254) (on unclass road
joining A74 & A73) ☎Crawford321
3hc (1fb) ⚲ CTV 4P 🍴 3000acres sheep S%
13rm(4⇌1🛁) 🍴 CTV 60P ⚲ ⚲ Last dinner8.45pm

ABOYNE 1,040 Grampian Map45NO59 EcThu
Aberdeen31 Banchory13 Braemar28 London549
★★*Balnacoil House* ☎2252
Country house type hotel standing in own grounds on the
banks of the River Dee.
13rm(4⇌1🛁) 🍴 CTV 60P ⚲ ⚲ Last dinner8.45pm
✢ ⚲ S% sB&B£15 sB&B⇌🛁£17 dB&B£24
dB&B⇌🛁£26 Lunch£4 Dinner£7.50 Wine£4 🐕
Credit cards ③⑤
★★*Birse Lodge* ☎2253
Victorian granite Dower House of Huntley estate. Standing
in 5¼ acres of private grounds near village green and River
Dee.
Closed mid Oct–mid Mar; 17rm(7⇌1🛁) Annexe: 4⇌ 🍴
CTV 30P ⚬ ⚲ Last dinner8pm ✢ ⚲ sB&B£13–£15

sB&B⇌🛁£14–£15 dB&B£26–£28 dB&B⇌🛁£28–£30
Bar lunchfr£1.50 Tea£1 Dinner£8–£9 Wine£4.20
Credit card ②
★★*Huntley Arms* (Inter-Hotel) ☎2101
Hotel stands beside field in which the Aboyne Games are
played.
55rm(16⇌🛁) ♪ 🍴 CTV ® 100P 4🅿 ⚲ billards sauna bath
Disco 3nights weekly Live music & dancing twice wkly ⚬
Last dinner9pm ✢ ⚲ 🐕 Credit cards ①②③⑤
★*Charleston* ☎2475
Small converted private house, just off the main road,
overlooking field where the Aboyne Games are played.
7rm TV 30P ⇌ Music Sat Music & dancing Sun
Last dinner7pm ✢ ⚲ Credit cards ②③

ACHARACLE Highland Map38NM66 Fort William47
Mallaig29 Salen2 London563
FH Mrs M. Macaulay **Dalilea House** (NM735693)
☎Salen253
A splendid turreted house with surrounding grounds giving
excellent views over farmland, hills and Loch Shiel. A blend
of the ancient and modern.
Mar–mid Oct 6hc (1fb) 8P 14,000acres beef sheep
S% B&bfr£7.50 Bdifr£12.10 Wfr£80.50 Ł D7pm

ACHNASHEEN Highland Map43NH15 EcWed Dingwall30
Gairloch29 Inverness45 London610
★★*Achnasheen* ☎243
Original building (1870) has close associations with
Inverness to Kyle of Lochalsh railway line. Of special
interest to railway enthusiasts, as it is part of the station.
14rm(7⇌1🛁) CTV 30P Last dinner8.15pm ✢ ⚲ 🐕
Credit cards ①②③④⑤
★★⚲ *H Ledgowan Lodge* (Best Western) ☎252
Telex no75605
Fine solidly built red sandstone building, formerly a
shooting lodge, set amid tall pines overlooking Strath Bran.
Closed Dec–Feb; 17rm(9⇌🛁) 🍴 TV ® 30P 2🅿 ⚲
Last dinner8.30pm ✢ ⚲ S% sB&B£14–£15
sB&B⇌🛁£16–£17 dB&B£23–£26 dB&B⇌🛁£27–£31
Lunch£4–£5 Tea75p–£1.50 Dinner£6.75–£8.50
Wine£3.50 🐕 Credit cards ①②③④⑤⑥

AIRDRIE 38,833 Strathclyde Map34NS76 EcWed
Carlisle92 Glasgow11 Lanark17 London399
★★*Tudor* Alexander St (Ind Coope (Alloa)) ☎64144
21rm(7⇌🛁) ♪ CTV in all bedrooms ® 150P ♨ European.
Last dinner9.30pm ✢ ✳sB&B£15.50
sB&B⇌🛁£19.50 dB&B£22.50 dB&B⇌🛁£29.50
Lunch£7alc Dinner£8.50alc Wine£3.40 🐕
Credit cards ①③⑤
✕✕*Postillion* 8–10 Anderson St ☎67525
Attractive restaurant housed in Staging Post hotel, which is
located on town centre one way street.
Lunch not served Sat & Sun; 50seats P bedrooms
available Last dinner9.30pm Lunch£3.90&alc
Dinner£11alc Credit cards ①③⑤

The Huntingtower Country Restaurant

Open for Lunch — Mon-Sun 12.30-2.00pm
Dinner Mon-Sat 7.15-9.30pm
Closed Sunday Nights
Bar Lunches also Served

**Huntingtower Country Restaurant
Telephone Almondbank 241**

HighTea£2.95   Dinner£8.50alc   Wine£4.20

ALMONDBANK 158 Tayside Map40NO02 Crieff15 London456 Perth4
××**Huntingtower Country** Crieff Rd (off A85) ☎241
Dinner not served Sun; 50seats 40P bedrooms available ♀French.   Last dinner 9.30pm
Lunch£5.50 – £6.50&alc   Dinner£8.50 – £10.50&alc   Wine£4.35   Credit cards ①②③④⑤

ANNAN 6,291 Dumfries & Galloway Map31NY16 EcWed MdThu/Fri alt Tue Carlisle19 Dumfries16 London326 Moffat28
★★**Queensberry Arms** (Osprey) ☎2024
A whitewashed two-storey building in the centre of Annan which is 10 miles from the English border.
27rm(5⇌) ⋈ CTV CTV in all bedrooms ® 40P 12🏠 ⚓ Live music & dancing Fri & Sat ♀Scottish & French.
Last dinner 9.30pm   ⋇   ♫   S%   Wine £14.05
sB&B♫17.50 dB&B♫23 dB&B⇌♫27.50
Lunch£3.50&alc Tea£1 HighTea£2.50 Dinner£5&alc   Wine£3.50   ♬   xmas Credit cards ①②③④⑤
★**Corner House** High St (Mount Charlotte) ☎2754
30rm(1♫) ⋈ CTV 50P Disco 3 nights wkly Live music & dancing wkly Last dinner8pm ⋇ ♫ S% sB&B£8 – £9 sB&B♫£9.80 – £11   dB&B£13.80 – £14.50
dB&B♫£16.10 – £18.50 Lunch£2.50 – £3 Tea£1 – £1.25
HighTea£2.50 – £3   Dinner£3 – £4&alc Wine£4.90 ♬
Credit cards ①②③⑤
GH Ravenswood St Johns Rd ☎2158 Mar – Jan Lic
9hc (2fb) ⋇ CTV S% B&b£7.50 – £8
Bdi£11 – £11.60 W£77 – £80.50 Ł D5pm
FH K.E. Yates **Beechgrove** (NY213652) ☎2220
Attractive redstone house with pleasant garden, surrounded by pastureland. Views of Solway Firth.
5hc (4fb) CTV 10P ⋈ sea non-working S%
✻B&b£7.60 – £9.60   Bdi£12.60 – £14.60 D7.30pm

ANSTRUTHER 2,962 (with Kilrenny) Fife Map41NO50 EcWed Elie6 Edinburgh50 London467 St Andrews14
★★★**Craws Nest** Bankwell Rd ☎310691 Telexno727396
A resort hotel in small East Fife fishing village.
31rm(1) ⋈ CTV CTV in all bedrooms ® ⋇ 200P 3🏠 ⚓ sauna bath Disco Fri/Sun Live music & dancing Sat Cabaret alternate Sun ⋇ Last dinner9pm ⋇ ♫ S%
sB&B⇌♫£15 – £19 dB&B⇌♫£30 – £36 Lunchfr£4
Dinnerfr£6.50 Wine£3.55 ♬ xmas
Credit cards ①②③④⑤⑥
★★**Smugglers Inn** High St ☎310506
Original inn dates back to 1300 and in the days of Queen Anne it was a noted tavern.
9rm(6⇌♫) ⋈ CTV 16P ⇔ ♀English & French.
Last dinner 9.30pm ⋇ Credit cards ①②③⑤⑥
★**Royal** Rodger St ☎310581
9rm(1⇌1♫) ⋈ CTV ® ⇔ Last dinner6.30pm ⋇ S%
sB&B£9.50 sB&B⇌♫£10.50 dB&B£19 dB&B⇌♫£21
Lunch£1.75 HighTea£3 Wine£2.40 ♬

ARBROATH 23,207 Tayside NO64 EcWed Dundee18 London490 Montrose13 Perth38
★★**Seaforth** Dundee Rd ☎72282
19rm(4⇌) ⋈ CTV 150P ⚓ Live music & dancing Sat Last dinner9pm ⋇ ♫ S% sB&Bfr£13.20 sB&B⇌fr£15.40 dB&Bfr£25.30 dB&B⇌fr£30.80 Lunchfr£4&alc
Teafr£1 Dinnerfr£6&alc Wine£5.50
Credit cards ①②③⑤
★**Towerbank** James St ☎75987
7rm ⋈ CTV ® 12P ⇔ ♀English & French.
Last dinner 10.30pm ⋇ S% sB&B£12 dB&B£18
Lunch£1.50 – £3.60   Dinner£6.50&alc   Wine£4.35
Credit cards ①⑤
××**Carriage Room** Meadowbank Inn, Montrose Rd ☎75844
Closed Mon, Lunch not served Sat, Dinner not served Sun; 54seats 120P Live music & dancing Thu & Sat ♀French. Last dinner 10pm ✻Lunch£3.65

ARDBRECKNISH Strathclyde Map39NN02 Crianlarich26 Lochgilphead31 Inveraray12 London469
FH Mrs H. F. Hodge **Rockhill** (NN072219) ☎Kilchrenan218
Loch-shore farm. Trout and perch fishing (free), and on the farm's private loch, by arrangement.
Apr – Sep 6hc (4fb) nc5 CTV 8P ⋈ lake 200acres sheep S% B&bfr£7 Bdifr£11 Wfr£66 Ł
(W only mid Jul – Aug)   D7pm

ARDEN Strathclyde 34MapNS38 Glasgow21 Dumbarton8 Helensburgh5 Tarbet14 London435
★★★**B Lomond Castle** ☎681
Converted private house overlooking Loch Lomond towards Ben Lomond. Set in large grounds with its own jetty at lochside.
21⇌ Ɗ ⋈ CTV in all bedrooms ⋇ 120P ⇔ ⚓ (heated) ⋐(hard) sauna bath ♀Continental. Last dinner 10.30pm
⋇ ⋇sB&B⇌fr£30 dB&B⇌£50 – £56 Lunchfr£7&alc
Tea£2.75   Dinner£10.25&alc   Wine£5.50 ♬   xmas
Credit cards ①②③⑤⑥
FH Mrs R. Keith **Mid Ross** (NS359859) ☎655
Farmhouse pleasantly located close to Loch Lomond 3m N of Balloch off A82.
May – Oct 3hc (2fb) CTV P ⋈ lake 32acres mixed S% B&b£5.50

ARDENTINNY Strathclyde Map39NS18 EcWed Dunoon14 Glasgow68 London471 Tarbet33
★★**Ardentinny** (Inter Hotel) ☎209
RS Nov – Mar; 10rm(4⇌3♫) ⋈ CTV ® 20P ⚓ ♀Scottish & Continental. Last dinner9.45pm ⋇ ♫ S%
sB&B⇌♫£14.50 – £15.50 dB&B⇌£24 – £27
dB&B⇌♫£27 – £30 Barlunch£2 – £4&alc
Dinner£6.50 – £9&alc   Wine£3.50 ♬

ARDERSIER Highland Map44NH75 Nairn7 Inverness11 London569
FH Mrs L. E. MacBean **Milton-of-Gollanfield** (NH809534) ☎2207
Stone farmhouse set on north side of A96 5m W of Nairn.
Apr – Oct 3rm 2hc (1fb) ⋇ ⋈ CTV P 365acres mixed S% B&b£5 – £6

ARDFERN Strathclyde Map39NM80 Lochgilphead16 Oban24 Dalmally34 London498
★**Galley of Lorne** ☎Barbreck284
10rm(2⇌) ⋈ CTV 25P ⇔ ⚓ & Last dinner 9.30pm ⋇ ⋇
sB&Bfr£9.78 sB&B⇌fr£11.50 dB&Bfr£19.56
dB&B⇌fr£23 Lunchfr£2.50 Dinnerfr£6.75 xmas
Credit cards ①⑤
FH Mrs G. McKinlay **Corranbeg** (NM801045) ☎Barbreck207
Large rambling farmhouse in quiet spot. Surrounded by beautiful scenery.
Whit – Sep 3rm (1fb) ⋇ P lake 208acres mixed S% B&b£5 Bdi£9 W£63 D5pm
FH Mrs M. C. Peterson **Traighmhor** (NM800039) ☎Barbreck228
Farmhouse offering magnificent views towards Loch Craignish.
Apr – Oct 3rm (1fb) ⋇ ⋈ CTV 8P lake 75acres mixed S% B&b£6 Bdi£10 Wfr£70 Ł D5pm

ALYTH 1,757 Tayside Map41NO24 EcWed MdSat Blairgowrie5 Dundee17 London473 Perth21
★★★⚐ **Lands of Loyal** Loyal Rd ☎2481
Originally built by William Deilvy in 1850, this three storey building stands on elevated ground above the town of Alyth, with fine views over Strathmore towards the picturesque Sidlaw Hills.
Closed Xmas & New Year; 14rm(7⇌♫) 1🖂 TV 15P 4🏠 ⇔
⚓ ⋐ ♀English & French. Last dinner 8.30pm ⋇ ⋇ ♬
Credit cards ②⑤

ARDLUI Strathclyde Map39NN31 Crianlarich9 Glasgow44 London446 Tarbet8
★★**Ardlui** ☎Inveruglas243
Three storey white-painted house with gardens running down to shores of Loch Lomond.
11rrm(1⇌) CTV 50P ⇌ ⌿ Live music 5 nights wkly Last dinner8.30pm ⋄ ⌐ S% sB&B£12.40–£13.65 dB&B£22.53–£24.78 dB&B⇌£24.78–£27.12 Barlunch£2alc Tea60palc Dinner£6alc Wine£3.31

ARDRISHAIG 946 Strathclyde Map33NR88 EcWed Glasgow85 Lochgilphead2 London488 Tarbet50
★★**Royal** ☎Lochgilphead3239
On northern edge of town, looking out across Loch Fyne.
20rm(4⇌) CTV ® 50P 3⌂ ⇌ ⌿ Live music & dancing Sat Last dinner9pm ⋄ ⌐ S% ✱sB&B£10.50–£12 sB&B⇌£12–£13.50 dB&B£21–£24 dB&B⇌£24–£27 Barlunch£2.15alc Teafr45p Dinner£6.50–£7.50 Wine£3.80 ⏚ xmas Credit cards ② ③ ⑥

ARDROSSAN 11,166 Strathclyde Map33NS24 EcWed Ayr21 Glasgow30 Irvine8 London424
GH Ellwood House 6 Arran Pl ☎61130 7hc (1fb) CTV sea S% B&b£6

ARDUAINE Strathclyde Map39NM80 EcWed Glasgow102 Lochgilphead18 London504 Oban19
★★★**HL Loch Melfort** ☎Kilmelford233
Closed mid Oct–8Apr; 8rm(2⇌) Annexe: 20⇌ ⏧ CTV 50P ⇌ ⌿ ♀English & French. Last dinner8.30pm ⋄ ⌐ sB&B£15–£20 sB&B⇌£15–£20 dB&B£30–£40 dB&B⇌£30–£40 Continental breakfast Barlunch£2–£4 Tea80p–£1.50 HighTea£2.50–£4 Dinner£9–£10.50 Wine£3.50 Credit cards ① ③

ARINAGOUR Isle of Coll, Strathclyde Map38NM25 EcThu
Car carrying service from Oban
★**Isle of Coll** ☎Coll334
9rm CTV CTV available in bedrooms ® 30P ⌿ sauna bath Live music nightly (summer only) Last dinner8pm ⋄ ⌐ sB&B£12 dB&B£23 Lunch£6 Tea£1 Dinner£7.50&alc Wine£2.10 ⏚ xmas Credit cards ① ⑤ ⑥

ARRAN, ISLE OF Strathclyde Map43 **See Blackwaterfoot, Brodick, Corrie, Lamlash, Lochranza, Sannox, Sliddery and Whiting Bay.** Car carrying services operate between Ardrossan and Brodick

AUCHENCAIRN 215 Dumfries & Galloway Map30NX75 Dalbeattie8 Dumfries21 Kirkcudbright11 London362
★★★**H Balcary Bay** ☎217
Closed Nov; 10rm(4⇌1⏧) 2☐ ⏧ CTV 80P ⇌ ⌿ billiards ♀Scottish, French & Italian. Last dinner9.30pm ⋄ ⌐ S% sB&B£15–£22 sB&B⇌⏧£17–£23 dB&B£30–£44 dB&B⇌⏧£34–£46 Lunch£4.50alc Tea£1alc Dinner£8.50&alc Wine£2.45 ⏚ xmas Credit cards ① ② ③ ④ ⑤ ⑥

FH Mrs D. Cannon **Bluehill** ☎228
Farm offers panoramic views overlooking the Solway Firth and the English lakeland hills.
May–Sep 4hc (1fb) ⏃ nc12 CTV P ⏧ 120acres dairy B&b£6–£6.50 Bdi£9.50 D6pm

AUCHTERARDER 2,845 Tayside Map40NN91 EcWed Crieff11 London438 Perth14 Stirling9
★★★★★**L Gleneagles** ☎2231 Telex no76105
Closed end Oct–mid Apr; 206⇌ Lift ⏈ ⏧ CTV in all bedrooms ® P ⌿ ▣(heated) ⏃⏃ squash sauna bath Live music & dancing nightly Conference facilities available ♀English & French. Last dinner9.15pm ⋄ ⌐ S% ✱sB&B⇌£39.50–£46.50 dB&B⇌£74.50–£102.25 Lunchfr£11 Teafr£3.25 Dinnerfr£14 Wine£5.70 Credit cards ① ② ③ ④ ⑤ ⑥

★★**Ruthven Tower** Abbey Rd ☎2578
Converted private house in quieter part of town, within own grounds.
Closed New Year's Day; 10rm(2⇌1⏧) Annexe: 8⇌⏧ ⏧ CTV TV available in bedrooms 40P ⇌ ⌿ & ♀English. Last dinner9pm ⋄ ⏚

★**Crown** 112–114 High St ☎2375
Victorian building situated on corner, in small town on A9.
13rm CTV ® 6P Disco twice wkly Last dinner9pm ⋄ ⌐ ⏚

AUCHTERHOUSE Tayside Map41NO33 Dundee8 Coupar Angus11 Perth23 Forfar18 Arbroath24 London475
⊛★★★⏚**HB Old Mansion House** ☎366
Closed 1&2 Jan; 6rm(5⇌1⏧) 1☐ ⏧ CTV in all bedrooms ® 50P ⇌ ⌿ ⏢(grass) squash sauna bath ♀Scottish & French. Last dinner9.30pm ⋄ ⌐ sB&B⇌⏧£27.50–£30 dB&B⇌⏧£35–£37.50 Lunch£5.50–£5.95&alc Dinner£12alc Wine£4.65 ⏚ Credit cards ① ② ⑤

AULTBEA 146 Highland Map42NG88 EcWed Gairloch13 Inverness80 London645 Ullapool45
★★**Drumchork Lodge** (Inter-Hotels) ☎242
18rm(3⇌) Annexe: 4⇌ CTV ® 50P ♀English & Continental. Last dinner8.30pm ⋄ ⌐ S% sB&B£13.75–£15.95 sB&B⇌£15.95–£18.15 dB&B£26.40–£30.80 dB&B⇌£28.60–£33 Barlunchfr£1.95 Tea£1–£1.50 Dinner£6.60–£7.15 ⏚ Credit cards ① ② ③ ⑤ ⑥

★**Aultbea** ☎201
Closed Nov–9Apr; 9rm(1⇌) TV ® 30P ⌿
Last dinner8.30pm ⋄ ⌐ sB&Bfr£11 sB&B⇌fr£13.50 dB&Bfr£22 dB&B⇌fr£24.50 Lunch£3alc Tea£1.50 HighTea£3alc Dinner£6 Wine£2.30 Credit cards ① ③

AVIEMORE 1,224 Highland Map44NH81 EcWed Grantown-on-Spey15 Inverness33 Kingussie12
☆☆☆☆**Coylumbridge** (Reo Stakis) ☎810661 Telex no75272
133⇌ ⏈ ⏧ CTV in all bedrooms ® 80P ⌿ ▣(heated) ⌕

Balcary Bay Hotel

Tel: Auchencairn 217 & 311   **BTA Commendation**

The hotel is located in one of the most secluded and enchanting situations on the edge of Balcary Bay, in 4 acres of parkland. Although the hotel has been modernised and tastefully decorated, it retains most of its old character and atmosphere. Visit our Raiders Cave for snacks and refreshments in the original 17th Century smugglers cellars. There are 2 lounges, one with colour TV, a cocktail bar and a restaurant offering such imaginative delicacies as Galloway Beef, Heston Isle Lobsters, Prawn and Sole and, of course, Balcary Bay Salmon. A wide choice of Italian food is also offered. Fresh vegetables, fruit and salads are utilised to the full. There is an extensive wine list.
The Hotel is under the personal supervision of
Franco & Lynne Galgani.
AUCHENCAIRN, by CASTLE DOUGLAS

Aviemore contd – Ayr

The Ladbroke Freedom Inn, Aviemore, is the Centre of Attractions

Fishing, sailing, climbing, hill walking, skiing, pony trekking, cycling, swimming, ice skating — Aviemore offers all these and more!

Amidst the magnificent Cairngorms the Freedom Inn is ideal for self catering family holidays and has a restaurant and two fine bars. You'll find plenty of exciting holiday ideas in our Lazydays brochure — try a Scottish Weekaway — tailor made for touring in your own car, or take a Welcome Break from as little as £30.00 per person bed & breakfast.

For your Lazydays brochure, 'phone 01-734 6000 or write to PO Box 137, Watford, Herts. WD1 1DN.

Ladbroke Freedom Inn,
Aviemore Centre,
Aviemore,
Inverness-shire. PH22 1PE.
Tel: (0479) 810781

Ladbroke Hotels

sauna bath Disco Thurs & Fri Live music & dancing Thurs, Sat & Sun Conference facilities available ♀ English & French. Last dinner 10.30pm ✩ ⚜ *sB&B⇌fr£26 dB&B⇌fr£36 Lunchfr£2.95&alc Tea fr50p Dinner fr£7&alc Wine£3 🍴 xmas
Credit cards ① ② ③ ④ ⑤

☆☆☆**Strathspey** (Thistle) ☎810681 Telex no 75213
Six storey ultra-modern building of spacious design standing within Aviemore Sports Centre.
90rm(89⇌1 ⋒) Lift ♪ ⚜ ⋒ CTV in all bedrooms ®
150P ⚓ sauna bath Disco Mon–Fri Live music & dancing 6 nights wkly ♪ Conference facilities available ♀ Scottish & French. Last dinner 11pm ✩ ⚜ S% *sB&B⇌⋒£38 Lunch£5alc Tea£1 Dinner£7.40&alc Wine£4.40 🍴 xmas Credit cards ① ② ③ ④ ⑤

☆☆☆**Badenoch** (Osprey) ☎810261
New building of ultra-modern design, situated within Aviemore Sports Centre.
77rm(61⇌) Lift ♪ ⚜ CTV CTV in 61 bedrooms ® 20P ⇌ Disco Thur Conference facilities available ♀ Scottish & French. Last dinner 9.30pm ✩ ⚜ S% dB&B£12.80 sB&B⇌£22.40 dB&B£22.40 dB&B⇌£30.80 Lunch£3.50&alc Tea£1 High Tea£2.50 Dinner£5&alc Wine£3.50 🍴 xmas Credit cards ① ② ③ ④ ⑤

☆☆☆**Ladbroke Freedom Inn** Aviemore Centre (Ladbroke) ☎810781
93⇌ ⋒ Lift ♪ ⚜ TV in bedrooms ⇌ 100P Conference facilities available ♀ International. Credit cards ① ② ③ ⑤

☆☆☆**Post House** Aviemore Centre (Trusthouse Forte) ☎810771
103⇌ Lift ♪ ⚜ CTV in all bedrooms ® 140P ♪ Conference facilities available Last dinner 9.30pm ✩ ⚜ S% sB&B⇌£27.80–£30.30 dB&B⇌£40.60–£44.10 ® 🍴 xmas Credit cards ① ② ③ ④ ⑤

★★**Alt-Na-Craig** ☎810217
A red sandstone Victorian villa with modern extension standing in own grounds on main road in centre of Highland village.
Closed Nov; 10rm(1⇌) CTV ® 20P 2⌂ ⚓ Last dinner 8pm ✩ ⚜ S% sB&B£9.90–£11 sB&B⇌£11.70–£12.80 dB&B£19.80–£22 dB&B⇌£21.60–£23.80 Lunch fr£3.20 Tea fr30p Dinner fr£5 Credit card ③

★★**Cairngorm** (Best Western) ☎810233 Telex no 75261
Victorian stone house with modern extension, situated on main road, and adjacent to Aviemore Centre.
24rm(10⇌ ⋒) CTV 30P 4⌂ ⚓ Last dinner 8.30pm ✩ ⚜ Credit cards ① ② ③ ④ ⑤

★★**Lynwilg** ☎810207
18th-C coaching inn with small modern extension. Beside the main road approximately 2 miles south of Aviemore village and overlooking Loch Alvie.
Closed Nov–Jan; RS Xmas & New Year; 13rm(3⇌ ⋒) CTV 40P 5⌂ ⚓ ⚓ Last dinner 8.30pm ✩ ⚜ Credit cards ② ⑤ ⑥

GH Aviemore Chalets Motel Aviemore Centre ☎810618

Lic 76 ⋒ (72fb) CTV 300P ⚜ S% B&B£8.40–£9.50 Bdi£12.65–£14 W£109–£120 D10pm

GH Corrour House Inverdruie ☎810220 Dec–Oct Lic 10rm 9hc (5fb) CTV 12P ⚜ S% B&B£11.50 Bdi£18.40 W£128.80 L D6.30pm

GH Craiglea Grampian Rd ☎810210 11hc 1 ⋒ (4fb) ♪ CTV 10P S% B&B£7–£8 W£45.50–£52.50 M

GH Ravenscraig ☎810278 5rm 4hc (2fb) CTV 10P ⚜ S% B&B£7.50–£8.50 Bdi£11–£12.50 W£72–£80 L

✕✕**Winking Owl Roadhouse** ☎810646
Converted cottage in own grounds, situated in Aviemore village.
Closed Sun & Nov–mid Dec; Lunch not served; 65 seats 50P Last dinner 9.15pm Credit cards ① ② ③ ⑤

AYR 47,991 Strathclyde Map 33 NS 32 Ec Wed Md Tue/Thu Carlisle 105 Girvan 23 Glasgow 34 Kilmarnock 13 London 411

★★★**Belleisle** Belleisle Park ☎42331
17rm(9⇌5 ⋒) 1 ⋒ ♪ ⚜ CTV in all bedrooms ® 200P ⚓ ⌂18 Live music & dancing Sat ♀ English & French. Last dinner 9pm ✩ ⚜ S% sB&B£14–£19.50 sB&B⇌ ⋒£16–£21.50 dB&B£17–£28.50 dB&B⇌ ⋒£21.50–£32.50 Lunch£3–£3.50&alc Tea£1.50–£1.25 High Tea£2.30–£2.50 Dinner£4.50–£5&alc Wine£3 🍴 xmas
Credit cards ① ② ③ ④ ⑤

☆☆☆**Caledonian** Dalblair Rd (Allied) ☎69321 Telex no 76357
118rm⇌ Lift ♪ ⊞ ⚜ CTV in 59 bedrooms, TV in 59 bedrooms ® ⇌ 70P sauna bath Disco 5 nights wkly Live music & dancing 3 nights wkly ♪ Conference facilities available ♀ English & French. Last dinner 10.30pm ✩ ⚜ sB&B⇌fr£20 dB&B⇌fr£32 Lunch fr£6 Tea fr£2 Dinner fr£4.50 Wine£2.10 🍴 xmas
Credit cards ① ② ③ ④ ⑤ ⑥

★★★**HB Pickwick** 19 Racecourse Rd ☎60111
15rm(10⇌5 ⋒) ♪ ⚜ CTV TV in all bedrooms ® ⇌ 100P ⇌ ⚓ ♀ French. Last dinner 9.15pm ✩ ⚜ sB&B⇌ ⋒£18 dB&B⇌ ⋒£32 Lunch£4.50alc Tea£2&alc High Tea£3.50&alc Dinner£7&alc Credit cards ③ ⑤

★★★**Savoy Park** Racecourse Rd ☎266112
Red sandstone building standing in 3 acres of gardens.
20rm(13⇌ ⋒) ♪ ⚜ TV available in bedrooms 100P ⚓ ♪ ♀ French. Last dinner 8.30pm 🍴 Credit card ①

★★★**Station** Burns Statue Sq (Reo Stakis) ☎263268 Telex no 778704
74rm⇌ Lift ♪ ⚜ CTV in all bedrooms ® 50P ♀ English & French. Last dinner 10pm ✩ ⚜ *sB&B⇌£23 dB&B⇌fr£32 Lunch£5alc Tea fr40p Dinner£7alc Wine£3 🍴 xmas Credit cards ① ② ③ ⑤ ⑥

★★**Ayrshire & Galloway** 1 Killoch Pl (Scottish & Newcastle) ☎262626
24rm(8⇌) ♪ CTV TV in 8 bedrooms 15P Last dinner 8.15pm ✩ ⚜ S% sB&B£11.50–£14 sB&B⇌£11.50–£16 dB&B£22 dB&B⇌£22–£26 Lunch£3 High Tea£1.60–£4 Dinner fr£4.50 Wine£3.65 🍴 Credit cards ① ② ③ ④ ⑤

★★**Balgarth** Dunure Rd, Alloway (2m S A719) ☎42603
15rm(3⇌4 ⋒) ⚜ CTV 80P ⚓ ♀ French. Last dinner 9.30pm ✩ ⚜ *sB&B£11 sB&B⇌ ⋒£13 dB&B£22 dB&B⇌ ⋒£24 Bar lunch£2.25–£5.15 Tea50p–£1.50 High Tea£2.10–£4 Dinner£4.95–£7 🍴 xmas
Credit cards ① ⑤

★★**Berkeley** Barns St ☎263658
10rm(3⇌2 ⋒) 1 ⊞ CTV TV available in bedrooms ⇌ 18P ⚓ ♀ French. Last dinner 8.45pm ✩ ⚜ S% sB&B fr£13.50 sB&B⇌ ⋒ fr£15.50 dB&B fr£28 dB&B⇌ ⋒ fr£30 Lunch fr£3.90 Tea fr85p High Tea fr£3.20 Dinner fr£5.95 Wine£3.25 🍴 xmas Credit cards ① ⑤

Ayr contd – Ballater

★★**Burns Monument** Alloway (2m S on B7024) ☎42466
9rm(6⇄1fl) ⁴⁴ CTV ® ⌀ 12P ⏚ Last dinner 8.30pm ✧
⏛ ✻sB&B£16 dB&B⇄fl£20 Bar lunch fr£1.75
Dinner£8alc Wine£3.80

★★**Elms Court** 21 Miller Rd ☎264191
19rm(9⇄1fl) ♪ ⁴⁴ TV in all bedrooms ® 50P ⊕
♀ Scottish, English & French. Last dinner 9.30pm ✧ ⏛
✻sB&B£10.50 sB&B⇄fl£11.50 dB&B£21
dB&B⇄fl£23 Bar lunch£1–£3 Tea 50p–£1.50
High Tea£1.95–£3.75 Dinner£5 Wine£3.75 *xmas*

★★**Gartferry** Racecourse Rd ☎262768
Built in late 18th-C using stone from original Ayr Prison. Hotel is situated on south side of the town.
13rm(2⇄5fl) ⁴⁴ CTV ® 150P Live music & dancing wkly Cabaret wkly ♀ International. Last dinner 9.30pm ✧ ⏛
S% sB&B£10–£10.50 sB&B⇄fl£12.30–£13.60
dB&B£19–£21 dB&B⇄fl£22.50–£24.75
Lunch£3.50–£5 Tea£1.75–£2.25 High Tea£3–£4.25
Dinner£5.50–£8.50alc Wine£3.95 🅿 *xmas*

★★**Marine Court** Fairfield Rd ☎267461
15rm(10⇄2fl) Annexe:9rm(5⇄4fl) 1🛏 ♪ ⁴⁴ CTV CTV in all bedrooms ® 80P ⏚ Live music & dancing wkly
♀ French. Last dinner 11pm ✧ ⏛ S%
sB&B£12.50–£14 sB&B⇄fl£12.50–£15
dB&B⇄fl£25–£30 Lunch fr£2.95 Tea fr£1
High Tea fr£2 Dinner fr£6.90 Wine£3.75 🅿 *xmas*
Credit cards ① ② ③ ⑤ ⑥

★**Fort Lodge** 2 Citadel Pl ☎65232
6rm ⁴⁴ CTV ⌀ 7P ⊕ Last dinner 7pm ✧
Credit cards ① ② ③ ⑤ ⑥

★**Monkwood** Carrick Rd ☎60952
11rm(2⇄2fl) ⁴⁴ CTV P Last dinner 9pm ✧ ⏛
✻sB&B£9 sB&B⇄fl£12 dB&B£15 dB&B⇄fl£18
Lunch 60p–£4 Dinner£8.80alc Wine£3.65

GH Clifton Hotel 19 Miller Rd ☎264521 Lic 11hc 4fl (1fb) ⌀ nc5 CTV 16P B&B£6.50–£7
Bdi£10.50–£12 W£70–£75 D5.30pm

GH Inverlea 42 Carrick Rd ☎266756 7hc (1fb) CTV 4P S% B&B£5–£7 Bdi£7–£9 (W only Oct–Apr) D5pm

GH Kingsley Hotel 10 Alloway Pl ☎262853 6hc (4fb) ⌀ CTV P ⁴⁴ S% B&B£8 Bdi£12 W£54–£77.05 ⏚ D8pm

GH Lochinver Hotel 32 Park Circus ☎265086 Closed Xmas & New Year Lic 8hc (1fb) ⌀ CTV 3P ⁴⁴ S%
✻B&B£5.75 Bdi£9.20 W£64.40 ⏚ Dam (W only Jul & Aug)

GH Windsor Hotel 6 Alloway Pl ☎264689 10hc (5fb)
CTV ⁴⁴ B&B£9.50–£10.50 Bdi£13–£14 W£85–£90
⏚ D4.30pm

FH Mr & Mrs A. Stevenson **Trees** (NS386186) ☎Joppa 270
Comfortable accommodation in a quiet location. 4m E on unclassified road, between A70 and A713.
Etr–Sep 3rm (1fb) ⌀ CTV P ⁴⁴ 125acres beef
S% B&B£5.10–£6 Bdi£9–£9.50

✕✕**Kylestrome** Miller Rd ☎26247
100seats 30P bedrooms available. Last dinner 10pm
✻Lunch£4.50alc Dinner£8alc Wine£3.70
Credit cards ① ② ③

✕**Carle's** 27 Burns Statue Sq ☎262740
Closed Sun; 70seats ♀ International. Last dinner 10.30pm

✕**Fouter's Bistro** 2A Academy St ☎61391
Situated in narrow cobbled street; stone floor with authentic 'Bistro' atmosphere.
Closed Mon, Xmas, New Year, last wk Sep & 1st wk Oct;
Lunch not served Sun; 42seats 🅿 ♀ French & Italian.
Last dinner 10.30pm Lunch£3.50alc Dinner£9.50alc
Credit cards ① ② ③ ④ ⑤

AYTON 410 Borders Map 36 NT96 EcThu
Berwick-upon-Tweed 8 Duns 12 Edinburgh 49 London 356
INN Royal Oak Hotel High Gr ☎722361 Lic 5hc
(1⇄fl) CTV D9.15pm

BALFRON STATION Central Map 37 NS58 Glasgow 20
Callander 17 Stirling 19 London 422
FH *Clachanry* (NS512888) ☎Balfron 335
Pleasant little hillside farmhouse with reasonable access from the main road.
Apr–Sep 3rm ⌀ TV 3P ⁴⁴ 135acres mixed

BALLACHULISH Highland Map 39 NN05 EcWed
Crianlarich 39 Fort William 13 London 504 Oban 36
See also North Ballachulish
★★★ *L* **Ballachulish** ☎239
Large, Victorian building on roadside; gardens overlook Loch Linnhe and Ardgour Mountains.
Closed 5 Oct–Apr; 34rm(16⇄) ♪ CTV P
Last dinner 8.30pm ✧ ⏛ sB&B⇄fr£18.30
sB&B⇄fr£21.30 dB&B fr£30.60 dB&B⇄fr£36.60
Tea fr£0.90 Dinner fr£6.90 Wine£4.20 🅿
Credit cards ① ② ③ ④ ⑤ ⑥

GH Lyn-Leven White St ☎392 8hc ⌀ CTV 9P ⁴⁴
lake S% B&B£4.50–£5.90 Bdi£8–£9.40 D8pm

BALLANTRAE 262 Strathclyde Map 33 NX08 Girvan 13
London 424 Newton Stewart 31 Stranraer 18
INN Ardstinchar Main St ☎383 4fl 6P ⁴⁴ river S%
B&b£7 Bdi£10 Bar lunch£1.50–£2.50 D9.30pm

BALLATER 992 Grampian Map 44 NO39 EcThu winter
Aberdeen 42 Braemar 17 London 519 Perth 68
★★ *Craigard* 3 Abergeldie Rd ☎55445
Closed Nov–Mar; 15rm(8⇄fl) ✈ CTV ® 20P ⊕ ⏚ ⌀
Last dinner 8pm ✧ ⏛ Credit cards ② ③ ⑤
★★ **Darroch Learg** ☎55443
Attractive red stone house standing on hillside in 4 acres of garden and woodland overlooking golf course and River Dee.
Closed Nov–Jan; 16rm(11⇄fl) Annexe: 9rm 1🛏 ⁴⁴ CTV
CTV in 2 bedrooms ® 25P ⏚ Last dinner 8.30pm ✧
⏛ S% sB&B fr£8.80 sB&B⇄fl£11.20–£14

GARTFERRY HOTEL ★★
44 Racecourse Road, Ayr
Telephone (0292) 262768 or 81472

Bedrooms tastefully furnished, with free tea and coffee making facilities.
The Captain's Table: Local and International cuisine at its best. Open from 5.15 till 9.30 pm, 7 days a week.
Victoria Lounge Bar: Ayr's finest carvery lunches served seven days a week, from 12 midday to 2pm.
Commodore Suite able to cater for functions of all descriptions, for 10 to 300 people. Special Weekend Rates.

Balmacara Hotel ★★
by Kyle of Lochalsh
on The Wester Ross Coastal Route   Tel Balmacara (059986) 283

Our hotel is privately owned, caters for a maximum of 50 guests, is warm, clean and comfortable and overlooks the waters of Lochalsh and the mountains of Skye. Most rooms with private bath.
It is an ideal centre from which to enjoy our magnificent countryside. Coloured Brochure and Tariff on application.

---

dB&Bfr£17.60 dB&B⇨♨£22.40–£28
Lunch£2.50–£3.50 Tea£1.25 HighTea£3 Dinner£6.50
Wine£3 ℝ
GH Moorside Braemar Rd ☎55492 Apr–Oct Lic 8hc
1⇨3♨ (2fb) nc5 CTV 10P ♨ S% B&bfr£8
Bdifr£12 Wfr£78 ⌧ D7pm
GH Morvada ☎501 Apr–Oct Lic 7rm 6hc 2♨ (2fb)
CTV 6P ♨ S% ✻B&bfr£6.50 Bdifr£10 D6.30pm
GH Netherley 2 Netherley Pl ☎792 Feb–Oct 10rm
9hc (1fb) nc2 CTV S% ✻B&B£6 Bdi£10 W£60 ⌧ D7pm

BALLOCH 1,484 Strathclyde Map37NS38 EcWed
Dumbarton5 Glasgow19 London425 Tarbet16
★★**Balloch** (Ind Coope (Alloa)) ☎Alexandria52579
Attractive small hotel in town centre on the bank of the River Leven.
13rm(6⇨) CTV ® 30P Disco twice wkly ♀ European.
Last dinner9pm ⌧ ✻sB&B£11.50 sB&B£15
dB&B£18.50 dB&B⇨£24 Lunch£5.50alc
Dinner£6.50alc Wine£3.40 ℝ Credit cards 1 2 3
INN Lomond Park Hotel Balloch Rd ☎Alexandria52494
7hc 1⇨2♨ ⇌ CTV 50P ♨ S%
✻B&b£10–£14 W£70–£98 M

BALMACARA 107 Highland Map42NG82 EcWed
Fort William71 Kyle of Lochalsh4 London595 Shiel Bridge12
★★**HL Balmacara** ☎283
Roadside hotel with fine views across Loch Alsh towards Skye.
23rm(18⇨2♨) CTV 35P Last dinner8.30pm ⌧
sB&B£15 sB&B⇨♨£15.50 dB&B£30 dB&B⇨♨£31
Lunch£3.75 Tea50p Dinner£6.50 Wine£3.50
Credit card 3

BALMAHA Central Map37NS49 Glasgow22 Stirling26 London423
GH Arrochoile ☎231 Apr–Oct 6hc (2fb) ✿ CTV 12P ♨ S% B&b£5 W£35 M

BALQUHIDDER Central Map39NN52 Callander13 Crianlarich22 Crieff25 London443
✕✕**Ledcreich Hotel** ☎Strathyre230
Classification awarded for dinner only.
Closed Tue; 40seats 30P bedrooms available
♀ International. Last dinner9pm Dinnerfr£11.25
Wine£4 Credit cards 1 2 3 5

BANAVIE 137 Highland Map39NN17 London516
Fort William3 Inverness65 Mallaig44
★★**Moorings** ☎Corpach550
RS Oct–May; 14rm(4⇨1♨) ♨ CTV ® 25P ⇌ Children
under 10yrs not accommodated Last dinner8pm ⌧
sB&B£8–£10 dB&B£16–£24 dB&B⇨♨£20–£30
Barlunch£1.50–£5 Tea£1.75 Dinner£8–£11
Wine£3.80 ℝ

FH Mrs A.C. MacDonald **Burnside** (NN138805)
Muirshearlich ☎Corpach275
Small, stone-built farmhouse with open views over Caledonian Canal, Loch and north face of Ben Nevis. 3m NE off B8004.
Apr–mid Oct 3hc CTV 3P 75acres mixed S%
B&b£5 Bdi£7.50 W£50 ⌧ D7pm

BANCHORY 2,555 Grampian Map45NO69 EcThu
Aberdeen18 Braemar40 London539 Stonehaven16
★★★(red)♨**Banchory Lodge** ☎2625
This Red Star hotel, a Georgian building by the Water of Feugh, is beautifully decorated and furnished. Very well cooked food meals appreciated by the predominantly sporting clientele.
Closed 15Dec–28Jan; 27rm(21⇨1♨) 2⇌ CTV CTV in 8bedrooms TV in 4bedrooms ® 50P 3♨ ⇌ ⌧ sauna bath
⇌ ♀ English & French. Last dinner9.30pm ⌧ ⌧ S%
✻sB&B£17.25–£18.40 sB&B⇨♨£19.40–£19.55
dB&B£34.50–£40.25 dB&B⇨♨£34.50–£40.25
Lunch£4.50–£6 Teafr£2 Dinnerfr£10.50 Wine£3.80
Credit cards 2 3 4
★★★♨**H Raemoir** ☎2622
18th-C mansion set in own grounds in elevated position 3 miles north of town.
18rm(14⇨) Annexe: 5rm(4⇨1♨) ⌧ CTV CTV available in bedrooms ® 200P 10♨ ⇌ ♨ ⌧ International.
Last dinner9.30pm ⌧ ⌧ ✻sB&Bfr£17
sB&B⇨♨fr£18 dB&Bfr£34 dB&B⇨♨fr£36
Lunchfr£3.50 Teafr60p HighTeafr£3.50 Dinnerfr£9
Wine£4.05 ℝ xmas Credit cards 1 2 5
★★★**Tor-na-Collie** ☎2242
25rm(15⇨10♨) Lift CTV CTV in all bedrooms ® 60P ⇌ ⌧
⌕ squash billiards Last dinner9.30pm ⌧ ⌧ S%
sB&B⇨♨fr£16.50 dB&B⇨♨fr£33 Lunch£3.50 Tea£1
Dinner£7&alc Wine£4 ℝ xmas
Credit cards 1 2 3 4 5 6
★★**Burnett Arms** ☎2545
Rough cast and granite fronted building in main street of pleasant Deeside town.
17rm(6⇨5♨) ♨ CTV CTV available in bedrooms 40P 4♨
⇌ ♀ Scottish & European. Last dinner8pm ⌧ ⌧ S%
✻sB&B£14 sB&B⇨♨£15 dB&B£23 dB&B⇨♨£25
Lunch£4.25 Tea£1.20 HighTeafr£3.50 Dinner£6.50
Wine£3.80 ℝ xmas Credit cards 3 5

BANFF 3,847 Grampian Map45NJ66 EcWed Aberdeen47
Cullen14 Huntly21 London585
☆☆☆**Banff Springs** Golden Knowes Rd ☎2881
Well-appointed modern hotel, standing to the west of the town, on hillside with splendid views over Moray Firth.
Closed 1–3Jan; 30rm(25⇨5♨) ♨ CTV in all bedrooms ® 150P ♀ French. Last dinner9pm ⌧ ⌧
S% dB&B⇨♨£17 dB&B⇨♨£34 Lunch£3.25
Tea£1.75 HighTea£2.50 Dinnerfr£5.10&alc
Wine£3.80 ℝ Credit cards 1 2 3 5 6

87

★★ **HL County** 32 High St ☎5353
A Georgian town house fronted by willow trees set right in the centre of town, but with the ambience of a small country house hotel.
8rm(4⇌1⋔) Annexe: 4rm 2☐ ᛗ TV in all bedrooms ® ⌾ 15P 1🐾 ⇌ ⌇ Children under 13yrs not accommodated ♀International ⇘ ⌇ sB&B£15−£19 sB&B⇌⋔£16−£20 dB&B£30−£38 dB&B⇌⋔£32−£40 Lunch£2.80−£6.40&alc Tea50p−£1 Dinner£6.25−£9.75&alc Wine£4.25 🍺 xmas Credit cards ① ② ③ ④ ⑤ ⑥
★ **Fife Lodge** Sandyhill Rd ☎2436
6rm CTV TV available in bedrooms 100P ⌇ Live music & dancing wkly Last dinner8.15pm
GH Carmelite House Private Hotel Low St ☎2152 Closed Xmas & New Year Lic 8hc (3fb) ⌾ CTV 6P S% B&b£6.50−£7.50 Bdi£9−£10.50 W£60−£65 ⱡ D5pm
GH Ellerslie 45 Low St ☎5888 6hc (1fb) ⌾ CTV S% B&b£5.50 Bdi£7.75 W£50 ⱡ D3pm

BANKFOOT 868 Tayside Map40 NO03 Dunkeld6 London461 Perth9 Stirling42
××**Hunters Lodge** ☎325
60 seats 50P bedrooms available Last dinner9pm S% ✻Lunch£5.50alc HighTea£3.50 Dinner£5.50alc Credit cards ① ② ③ ⑤ ⑥

BARBRECK Strathclyde Map39 NM80 Lochgilphead15 Oban23 London497
FH Glenview (NM841079) Turnalt Farm ☎277
Apr−Oct 4rm ⌾ CTV 4P 3,500acres sheep D6pm

BARRA, ISLE OF Western Isles Map48 **See Borve and Tangusdale**

BARRHEAD 18,843 Strathclyde Map37 NS45 EcTue Glasgow8 Kilmarnock18 London413 Paisley4
★★ **Dalmeny Park** Lochlibo Rd ☎041-881 9211
18rm(10⋔) ⊞ ᛗ CTV CTV in all bedrooms ® 120P ⌇ Live music & dancing Sat ⌾ ♀English & Continental. Last dinner9.30pm ⇘ ⌇ S% ✻sB&B£19 sB&B⋔£23 dB&B£23.50 dB&B£26.50 Lunch£4.50&alc Tea£1&alc Dinner£6&alc Wine£4.75 🍺 Credit cards ① ② ③ ⑤ ⑥

BATHGATE 14,232 Lothian Map34 NS96 EcWed MdFri Edinburgh23 Glasgow27 Lanark19 London414
☆☆☆**Golden Circle** Blackburn Rd (Swallow) ☎53771 Telex72606
75rm(55⇌20⋔) Lift ♪ ᛗ CTV in all bedrooms ® 150P Last dinner9.30pm ⌾ ⌇ S% sB&B⇌£27 dB&B⇌⋔£36 Lunch£3.50&alc Dinner£6.30&alc 🍺 Credit cards ① ② ③ ④ ⑤ ⑥
★★ **Dreadnought** Whitburn Rd (Scottish & Newcastle) ☎630791
Closed New Years Day; 18rm(11⇌⋔) ᛗ CTV 30P ☐ Disco 3nights wkly Last dinner9pm ⌇ ♪ Credit cards ① ② ③ ④ ⑤ ⑥
×××**Balbairdie** Bloomfield Pl ☎55448
Closed Sun; 40seats ♀Scottish & French. Last dinner10pm Credit cards ① ② ③ ⑤
××**Bridge Castle Hotel Restaurant** ☎Armadale30228
A fine castle, dating from 12th-C, which has been converted into an hotel. There are bars in the outhouses.
Closed 1Jan; 44seats 150P bedrooms available ♀Scottish & French. Last dinner10pm ✻Lunch£2.50−£5.50&alc Dinner£6.50&alc Wine£4.45 Credit cards ① ② ③ ⑤

BEARSDEN 25,437 Strathclyde Map37 NS57 EcTue/Sat Dumbarton11 Glasgow6 London408 Stirling27
☆☆**Burnbrae** Milngavie Rd (Reo Stakis) ☎041-942 5951 Telex no778704
Custom-built modern hotel set back from A81 on outskirts of town.
15rm(13⇌) ♪ ᛗ CTV in all bedrooms ® 100P ♀English &

French. Last dinner10.30pm ⇘ ⌇ ✻sB&Bfr£18.50 sB&B⇌fr£24.75 dB&B⇌fr£34 Lunch£5alc Dinner£7alc Wine£4.20 🍺 Credit cards ① ② ③ ⑤ ⑥
××**La Bavarde** 9 New Kirk Rd ☎041-942 2202
Closed Sun, Mon, 3 last wks Jul, last wk Dec & 1st wk Jan; 50seats 🍺 Last dinner9.30pm ✻Lunch£2.50−£2.75 Dinner£7alc Wine£3.90 Credit cards ① ② ④ ⑤ ⑥
×**Ristorante da Riccardo** 130 Drymen Rd ☎041-943 0960
Attractive little restaurant and delicatessen, with modern shop frontage in town centre.
Closed Sun, Mon, 1st wk Feb & 1st 3 wks Aug;
Unlicensed; No corkage charge; 40seats ♀Italian. Last dinner10.15pm Lunchfr£2.30&alc Dinner£3−£9&alc Credit card ①

BEATTOCK 309 Dumfries & Galloway Map35 NT00 Carlisle40 Edinburgh53 London247 Moffat2
★★**Auchen Castle** (Inter-Hotels) ☎407 Telex no77205
Closed mid Dec−mid Feb; 20rm(16⇌⋔) Annexe: 10⇌⋔ ᛗ CTV CTV in all bedrooms P 3🐾 ⌇ ⌾ ♀English & French. Last dinner9pm ⇘ ⌇ 🍺 Credit cards ① ② ③ ④ ⑤ ⑥
★★**Beattock House** ☎403
Converted mansion dating from 1812 and standing in 6½ acres of ground.
7rm(2⋔) ᛗ CTV ® 25P ⌇ ⇘ Last dinner9.30pm ⇘ ⌇ S% sB&B£12.50−£13.75 sB&B⋔£12.50−£13.50 dB&B£25−£27 dB&B£25−£27 Lunchfr£4.25 Teafr£1.95 HighTeafr£3.50 Dinnerfr£6.85 Wine£4.45 🍺
★★**Old Brig Inn** ☎401
Situated in the Moffat turn off on the A75, the Old Brig Inn is a comfortable stone built country hotel.
8rm(1⋔) ᛗ CTV ® 10P 4🐾 Last dinner8.30pm ⇘ S% sB&B£12.50 dB&B£21.50 dB&B⋔£24 Lunch£4 Dinner£6.50alc Wine£4.40 Credit cards ② ⑤

BEAULY 1,141 Highland Map43 NH54 EcThu Dingwall9 Invermoriston27 Inverness13 London578
★★ **Lovat Arms** ☎2313
An impressive red sandstone building with ornate stonework, standing on main road in the centre of town.
17rm(4⇌⋔) ① ᛗ TV in all bedrooms P ⇘ Disco wkly Live music & dancing wkly Last dinner8.45pm ⇘ ⌇ 🍺 Credit card ②
★★**Priory** The Square ☎2309
12rm(6⇌) ᛗ CTV ₧ Disco Fri Live music & dancing Fri Cabaret twice wkly Last dinner9pm ⇘ ⌇ S% sB&B£9.50−£12.50 sB&B⋔£10.50−£13.50 dB&B£17−£21 dB&B⇌£19−£23 Lunch£3.50 Tea80p−£1.30 HighTea£2.40−£5 Dinner£6.50−£8 Wine£3.10 🍺 Credit cards ① ② ③ ⑤ ⑥
GH Chrialdon Station Rd ☎2336 Jun−Oct rsApr & May Lic 11hc (4fb) CTV 14P S% B&B£6−£6.50 Bdi£9.75−£10.25 D7.45pm
GH Gruinard ☎2417 Apr−Oct 6hc (2fb) TV 6P

BEESWING Dumfries & Galloway Map30 NX86 Dumfries7 Dalbeattie7 London344
FH R.H. Littlewood **Garloff** ☎Lochfoot225
Pleasant farmhouse set at end of farm road on south-east side of A711 6m west of Dumfries.
6hc (2fb) ⌾ CTV 6P ⇘ 220acres dairy S% B&B£6.32−£6.90 Bdifr£11.73 Wfr£76.95 D5pm

BELLSHILL 18,166 Strathclyde Map34 NS76 EcWed Glasgow10 Lanark16 London395 Motherwell2
★**Hattonrigg** Hattonrigg Rd (Scottish & Newcastle) ☎748488
8rm(4⇌⋔) ♪ ⋇ CTV ⌾ 100P Disco wkly Live music & dancing twice wkly Cabaret wkly Last dinner10pm ⇘ Credit cards ① ② ③ ⑤

BIGGAR 1,737 Strathclyde Map35 NT03 EcWed Md livestock Thu Carlisle70 Edinburgh29 Lanark13 London376 Moffat30

Close enough for comfort

Only 45 minutes from Aberdeen, the Banff Springs Hotel is situated above Boyndie Bay, overlooking a glorious beach.

Guests can fish on the Deveron, try sailing or sea angling or put in a round of golf at one of 4 nearby courses.

The magnificent view from the dining room is matched by the excellence of the cuisine. We pride ourselves on the range and standard of dishes we serve.

Above all we try to give you service second to none, so Banff Springs to mind for your next holiday. Whether for a weekend or weeks... Banff Springs to mind.

BANFF SPRINGS HOTEL

Scotland
Golden Knowes Road, Banff AB4 2JE
Telephone 02612-2881

Biggar contd – Boghead

★★**Toftcombs** ☎20142
Red sandstone building standing in its own grounds ½m NE of Biggar on A702.
Closed 1Jan; 8rm ⌘ CTV P ♨ Live music & dancing Sat Lastdinner8.30pm ✿ ⌛ S% ✻sB&Bfr£10
dB&Bfr£20 Lunchfr£3.80 Teafr£1.10
HighTea£3.10–£5 Dinner£5.80–£6.25&alc Wine£3.03
Credit cards ① ③

BIRNAM Tayside Map40NO04 Perth14 Dunkeld1 Pitlochry13 London462
GH Waterbury House Murthly Ter ☎Dunkeld324 6hc (1fb) CTV P ⌘ S% B&B£5.50–£6 Bdi£9.50–£1
W£39–£66 ⌛ D6pm

BLACKWATERFOOT Isle of Arran, Strathclyde Map33NR92 Brodick11 Lochranza18 WhitingBay16 London432
★★**Kinloch** (Inter-Hotels) ☎Shiskine286
55rm(25⇌) ⌘ CTV CTV available in bedrooms ® 50P ♨ ▨(heated) sauna bath Conference facilities available Lastdinner10pm ✿ ⌛ S% sB&B£11.15–£12
sB&B⇌£12.95–£14 dB&B£22.30–£24
dB&B⇌£25.90–£28 Lunch£3 Tea30–40p
Dinner£5.25–£6&alc Wine£2.50 ⊟ Credit cards ② ④
INN Greannan Hotel ☎Shiskine200 Apr–Oct 12hc
CTV 40P ⌘ S% B&b£7.30–£7.50 Bdi£11–£11.30
W£77–£79.10 ⌛ Barlunch£1–£2 D£5.50

BLAIR ATHOLL 437 Tayside Map40NN86 EcWed London82 Perth35 Pitlochry7 Stirling64
★★**Atholl Arms** ☎205
Large greystone roadside hotel, built and furnished in traditional Scottish style.
28rm(4⇌)1 ⌘ CTV 24P 3⌂ Lastdinner8.30pm ✿ ⌛ S% sB&B£9.75–£12 dB&B£19.50–£24
dB&B⇌£21.50–£26 Lunchfr£3 Teafr£1
HighTea£2.50–£3.50 Dinner£6–£7.50 Wine£3 ⊟
xmas   Credit cards ① ③
★★**Tilt** Bridge of Tilt ☎253
Two-storey stone building with attractive modern extension, good views of surrounding countryside.
21rm(7⇌⌘) Annexe: 6⇌⌘ ⌘ CTV 6⌂ ♬ Music & dancing wkly Lastdinner8.30pm ✿ ⌛ ⊟
Credit cards ② ④ ⑤

BLAIRGOWRIE 5,760 (with Rattray) Tayside Map40NO14 EcThu MdTue Dundee19 Dunkeld12 London468 Perth16
★★**B Angus** ☎2838 Telexno76526
70rm(62⇌⌘) Lift ⌘ CTV in bedrooms 30P ▨(heated) ♨ squash sauna bath Cabaretwkly ⚃ Conference facilities available Lastdinner8.30pm ✿ ⌛ ⊟
Credit cards ① ② ③
★★**Stormont Lodge** Upper Allan St ☎2853
8rm(3⌘) ⌘ CTV TV in 3bedrooms ® 40P ♨ Children

under 6yrs not accommodated ⌘ Scottish, English & French. Lastdinner8.30pm ✿ sB&Bfr£13.30
sB&B⌘fr£15.30 dB&Bfr£25 dB&B⌘fr£29
Lunchfr£5.50 Dinnerfr£7.50 Wine£5 ⊟ *xmas* Credit cards ① ③
★**Golf View** Rosemount ☎2895
7rm(3⇌⌘) ⌘ CTV CTV in 3bedrooms TV in 4bedrooms ®
✿ 70P ♨ Lastdinner9.30pm ✿ ⌛ S%
sB&B£11.50–£13 sB&B⇌⌘£14.50 dB&B£22–£25
dB&B⇌⌘£26–£28 Lunch£3–£3.75 Tea£1–£1.50
HighTea£2.50–£3.50 Dinner£4–£7.50&alc Wine£2.50
⊟ *xmas* Credit cards ② ③ ④ ⑤
★**Rosemount Golf** Golf Course Rd, Rosemount ☎2604
9rm(2⇌2⌘) ⌘ TV in all bedrooms ® ✿ 50P ♨
Lastdinner10pm ✿ ⌛ sB&Bfr£8.50
sB&B⇌⌘fr£9.50 Lunch£3alc Tea75palc
HighTea£4alc Dinner£5alc Wine£3
GH Kintrae House Hotel Balmoral Rd ☎2106
Lic 9hc (3fb) CTV 16P ⌘ S% B&b£8.50 Bdi£13
Wfr£91 ⌛ D9pm

BLAIRLOGIE Central Map40NS89 Stirling4, Alva4, Alloa5, London419
✕✕ **Blairlogie House Hotel** ☎Alva61441
Closed 1–30Jan; 40seats 30P bedrooms available Lastdinner9pm Credit cards ① ③ ⑤

BOAT OF GARTEN 406 Highland Map44NH91 EcThu Aviemore6 Inverness30 London542 Perth91 Tomintoul18
★★★**Boat** ☎258
Grey stone building dating from 1898 and offering good scenic views, situated adjacent to railway station.
36rm(31⇌⌘) ✈ ⌘ CTV CTV in all bedrooms 40P 6⌂ ♨ Conference facilities available Lastdinner9pm ✿ ⌛ ⊟
Credit cards ① ② ③ ⑤
★★**Craigard** Kinchurdy Rd ☎206
Late Victorian shooting lodge converted to hotel in 1931. Situated in 2¼ acres of grounds with direct access to golf course.
22rm(7⇌1⌘) CTV 30P 4⌂ ➳ ♨ Lastdinner8pm ✿
⌛ sB&B£12–£13 dB&B£24–£26 dB&B⇌⌘£26–£28
Lunch£3.75 Dinner£6.50 Wine£3.95 ⊟
Credit cards ① ② ③ ⑤ ⑥
GH Moorfield House Hotel Deshar Rd ☎646
Jan–Oct Lic 5hc (2fb) ⊘ nc5 TV 12P ⌘
✻ B&b£7.50–£8 Bdi£10.50–£12 W£70–£80 ⌛ D5.30pm

BOGHEAD Strathclyde Map34NS74 Strathaven6, Glasgow26, London370
FH I. McInally **Dykehead** *(NS772417)*
☎Lesmahagow892226
Rough cast, two-storey farmhouse just fifty yards from Strathaven/Lesmahagow road.
Mar–Oct 2rm (1fb) CTV 3P 1⌂ ⌘ 200acres dairy sheep S% B&b£5 W£35 M

KINLOCH HOTEL
Blackwaterfoot Isle of Arran
Telephone Shiskine
STD (0770-86) 286

AA ★★

Situated in its own grounds which run down to the sea shore, and overlooking the Kilbrennan Sound to the hills of Kintyre. This thoroughly up-to-date and pleasant hotel is 2 minutes from the Blackwaterfoot golf and tennis courts, with two fine beaches and perfectly safe bathing.
56 bedrooms — 26 with private bathrooms. Heated indoor swimming pool and sauna.
Lawrence and Robin Crawford — Resident Proprietors.
Fully licensed. Write or phone for colour brochure and tariff and details of our inclusive ferry charge package deal.

Bridge of Cally Hotel
Perthshire PH10 7JJ
Tel. Bridge of Cally 231

Situated on the A93 Braemar Road overlooking the River Ardle surrounded by woodland and the Perthshire hills. Fishing, golf, pony trekking, skiing all available nearby. Open all year. Four bedrooms with private bath. Fully licensed. Restaurant. Residents' lounge with colour TV. Brochure and tariff on application.

BONAR BRIDGE 519 Highland Map46NH69 EcWed Dingwall27 Inverness49 Lairg11 London614
★★**Bridge** ☎Ardgay204
Two-storey stone house on main road with views of Kyle of Sutherland.
Closed 1Jan; 16rm(4⇌2♒) ♨ CTV ® 20P Last dinner8pm
❀ ⊒ *sB&B£11–£12.50 sB&B⇌♒£12.50–£14.50
dB&B£20–£23 dB&B⇌♒£23–£25.50
Barlunch£2.40alc Dinner£5alc Wine£2.70 ✱
Credit cards ① ② ③ ⑤ ⑥

★★**Caledonian** ☎Ardgay214
Two-storey, stone building standing on main road, overlooking Kyle of Sutherland.
8rm(3⇌3♒) Annexe: 16rm(1⇌3♒) ⊞ ♨ CTV ® 20P ⚓
Live music & dancing wkend Cabaret twice wkly (summer)
♨ Lastdinner8pm ❀ ⊒ S% sB&B£9–£10.50
sB&B⇌♒£10.50–£12.50 dB&B£18–£21
dB&B⇌♒£21–£25 Lunch£3–£3.50 Tea85p–£1.20
HighTea£2.60–£3.40 Dinner£6–£6.50 Wine£3.05
GH Glengate ☎Ardgay318
Mar–Oct 3hc CTV 4P sea S% B&b£6

BONNYRIGG 7,569 (with Lasswade) Lothian Map35NT36 EcWed Edinburgh8 Jedburgh43 London373
★★★★ ♨ ✿ **BL Dalhousie Castle** (Prestige)
☎Gorebridge20153 Telexno72380
Fine red stone castle dating back to the 12th C situated in open countryside nine miles south of Edinburgh city centre.
22⇌♒ 1☐ ♭ ♨ CTV in all bedrooms 50P ⇔ Conference facilities available S% sB&B⇌♒fr£42.32
dB&B⇌♒fr£52.90 Lunch£4.50–£5.50 Tea£1–£2
Dinner£7.50–£9.50&alc Wine£4.50 ⚓ xmas
Credit cards ① ② ③ ⑤

BORELAND Dumfries & Galloway Map35NY19 Lockerbie7 Langholm18 London340
FH Mrs I. Maxwell *Gall (NY172901)* ☎229
Situated on a hill looking towards the Moffat Hills.
Apr–Oct 2hc ❀ ✿ CTV 2P 1,066acres beef sheep
S% B&b£5.50–£6.50 Bdifr£9.50

BORGUE Dumfries & Galloway Map30NX64 London371 Dumfries33 Kirkcudbright6 NewtonStewart25
★★**Senwick House** Brighouse Bay ☎236
9rm(4⇌) ♨ CTV CTV in 3bedrooms ® ✿ 50P ⚓ ⚓ (hard)
Live music & dancing nightly in season Last dinner9.30pm
❀ ♨ dB&B£10.90–£13.20 sB&B⇌£12.60–£14.95
dB&B£21.80–£26.40 dB&B⇌£25.20–£29.90
Lunch£3.50–£4 Tea£1.50 HighTea£4–£6
Dinner£6.50–£7.50 Wine£2.50 ✱ xmas

BORVE Isle of Barra, Western Isles Map48NF60 Castlebay3 London504 (ferry via Oban)
FH Mrs M. MacNeil *Ocean View (NF655014)*
☎Castlebay397
Detached bungalow standing in natural farmland facing west over Atlantic Ocean.
3rm (3fb) ❀ TV P sea 3acres sheep
B&b£6–£6.50 Bdi£9.50–£10

BOTHWELL Strathclyde Map34NS75 Hamilton2 Glasgow13 Coatbridge6 London394
★★**Silvertrees** Silverwells Cres ☎852311
7⇌♒ Annexe: 17⇌♒ Lift ♭ ♨ CTV CTV in 19bedrooms ® P ⇔
100P 4♦ ⇔ ⚓ Last dinner9pm S%
*sB&B⇌♒fr£17.50 dB&B⇌♒fr£24 Lunch£4.50&alc
HighTea£2.40 Dinner£5&alc Wine£4.20 xmas
Credit cards ① ② ③ ⑤

×××**Da Luciano** 2 Silverwells Cres ☎852722
100seats 60P ⚓ English, French & Italian.
Lastdinner10.45pm S% Lunch£3.20&alc
Dinner£10alc Wine£5 Creditcards ① ② ③ ④ ⑤ ⑥

BOWMORE 947 Isle of Islay, Strathclyde Map32NR35 **Car carrying services operate from Kennacraig (mainland) to ports:** PortAskaig11 PortEllen11
★★**Lochside** Shore St ☎244
7rm(2⇌) ♨ CTV CTV available in bedrooms ® P ⇔
Last dinner9pm ❀ S% sB&Bfr£15 dB&Bfr£28
dB&B⇌fr£31 Barlunch£1alc Dinner£6.50alc
Wine£1.95 Credit cards ① ② ③

★**Bowmore** Jamieson St ☎327
8rm ♨ TV 10P ⚓ Last dinner8.30pm ❀ ⊒

BRAE 121 Shetland Map48HU36 Lerwick27
★★★**Brae** ☎456
29⇌ ♭ ♨ CTV in all bedrooms ® 80P Last dinner9.30pm
❀ S% sB&Bfr£29.25 sB&B⇌fr£44.25
dB&B⇌fr£53.50 Lunchfr£3.50 Dinnerfr£7&alc Wine£6
Credit cards ① ③ ⑤ ⑥

BRAEMAR 394 Grampian Map44NO19 EcThu (except Jun–Sep) Ballater17 London502 Perth51 Pitlochry41
★★★**Invercauld Arms** ☎605 Telex no739169
Large stone-built, early Victorian building on outskirts of village. Built on the site where the old Pretender's standard is said to have been raised.
57rm(40⇌♒) ♨ CTV ® 100P 2♦ ⚓ ⚓ ♥ Scottish & French. Lastdinner8.30pm ❀ ⊒ sB&B£10–£14.50
sB&B⇌£14.50–£18.50 dB&B£21–£29
dB&B⇌£25–£37 Lunchfr£2.95&alc Teafr90p
Dinnerfr£7.25&alc Wine£3.50 ✱ xmas
Credit cards ① ② ③ ⑤ ⑥
GH Braemar Lodge ☎617 June–Sep rsMay Lic
12hc (3fb) TV 12P ♨ S% B&b£7.50–£8.50
Bdi£13–£14.50 D6.30pm
GH Callater Lodge ☎275 26Dec–midOct Lic 9hc
(1fb) 42P ♨ S% B&b£9.54 Bdi£16 D8pm

BRECHIN 6,727 Tayside Map41NO56 EcWed Md cattle Tue Aberdeen40 Forfar13 London496 Perth43
★★**Northern** Clerk St ☎2156

91

Brechin contd – Cairnie

Closed Xmas & New Year's day; 24rm(4⇔12🚿) CTV 24P 3🦽 Last dinner 8.30pm ⌕ S% ✱sB&B£10 sB&B⇔🚿£12 dB&B£20 dB&B⇔£20 Lunch£3.50 High Tea£1.50–£4 Dinner£4–£6 Wine£2.50 Credit cards ②③

FH Mr J. Stewart **Wood Of Auldbar** (NO554556) Aberlemno ☎Aberlemno 218
Fairly large farmhouse well back from road amid farmland and woods 5m SW on unclassified road, between B9134 and A932.
3rm (1fb) ⚓ CTV 3P 🐎 187acres mixed S% B&b£4.50–£5 Bdi£7–£7.50 W£49

BRIDGE OF ALLAN 4,651 Central Map40 NS79 EcWed Callander 15 Glasgow 33 London 422 Perth 31 Stirling 4
★★**Royal** Henderson St (Best Western) ☎832284 Telex no 778982
Large building dating from 1836 standing on main road in centre of town.
34rm(13⇔1🚿) Lift ♪ 🍴 CTV CTV in 14bedrooms 50P Last dinner 8.45pm ⌕ ⚓ ✱sB&B£18 sB&B⇔🚿£20.25 dB&B£32 dB&B⇔🚿£35 Lunch£4.25&alc Tea50p High Tea£3.25 Dinner£7.50&alc Wine£3.45 🍺 xmas Credit cards ①②③④⑤

BRIDGE OF CALLY Tayside Map40 NO15 Blairgowrie 6 London 474 Perth 22 Pitlochry 20
★**HB Bridge of Cally** ☎231
10rm(3⇔1🚿) 🍴 CTV 40P 🚗 ⚓ Last dinner 8.30pm ⌕ 🍺 S% sB&B£10–£12 dB&B£18–£21 dB&B⇔🚿£21–£24 Lunch£2.80–£3.75 Tea70p–£1.20 Dinner£6.75 Wine£3.50 🍺 Credit cards ①③

BRIDGE OF EARN 348 Tayside Map40 NO11 EcThu MdFri Edinburgh 40 London 457 Perth 4 Stirling 32
★★**Moncrieffe Arms** ☎2931
13rm(4⇔1🚿) 🍴 CTV 80P 2🦽 ⚓ ♀ French. Last dinner 9pm ⌕ 🍺 sB&B£15 sB&B⇔🚿£17 dB&B£24.75 dB&B⇔🚿£26.75 Lunch£3.80&alc Dinner£5.80&alc Wine£3.65 🍺
Credit cards ①②③④⑤

BROADFORD 310 Isle of Skye, Highland Map42 NG62 EcWed Armadale 17 Kyleakin 8 Portree 36 Uig 43
★★**Broadford** (Best Western) ☎204
Original inn dating from 1611, considerably altered and extended.
Closed Nov–Mar; 19rm(3⇔11🚿) Annexe: 9rm(2⇔7🚿) CTV ® 50P ⚓ ♀ Scottish & French. Last dinner 9pm ⌕ S% ✱sB&B£12.88–£14.20 sB&B⇔🚿£15.35–£17.20 dB&B£25.30–£27.60 dB&B⇔🚿£29.90–£31.85 Bar lunch£1.80–£2.80 Dinner£6.32–£7.47 Wine£2.40 Credit cards ①③
GH Hilton ☎322 Apr–Oct 10rm ⚓ TV 10P 🍺

BRODICK 630 Isle of Arran, Strathclyde Map33 NS03 EcWed Corrie 6 Kilmory 18 Lochranza 14 **Car carrying service from Ardrossan**
☎**Glenartney** ☎2220
Two-storey rough-cast house on hill overlooking Brodick Bay.
Closed Oct–Feb; 19rm(2fb) 🍴 CTV TV in 3bedrooms ® 8P Last dinner 7.30pm ⌕ sB&B£7–£8 dB&B£14–£16 dB&B🚿£16.50–£18.50 Lunch£2.50 Dinnerfr£4.50 Wine£3.15 🍺

BRORA 1,436 Highland Map47 NC90 EcWed Dornoch 17 Helmsdale 12 Inverness 76 London 641
★★**Royal Marine** Golf Rd ☎252
11rm(4🚿) 🍴 CTV ® 30P 8🦽 ⚓ ♪ Live music & dancing wkly ⌕ Last dinner 8.30pm ⌕ ⚓ sB&B£10.35–£15.65 sB&B🚿fr£18.15 dB&Bfr£31.30 dB&B🚿fr£36.30 Lunchfr£4.50 Teafr£1.50 High Tea£3 Dinnerfr£6.60 Wine£2.85

BROUGHTON 975 Borders Map35 NT13 EcWed Edinburgh 29 Lanark 18 London 372 Peebles 13
★★**H Greenmantle** ☎301
Modern building with cottage-type exterior in centre of village. Set in two acres of grounds off the main road.
6rm(2⇔🚿) CTV 50P ⚓ ♀ Scottish & French. Last dinner 9pm ⌕ 🍺 Credit cards ③⑤

BUCHLYVIE Central Map37 NS59 Stirling 15 Glasgow 24 London 430
FH J. McArthur **Balwill** (NS548927) ☎239
White-painted farmhouse and buildings set off main road in the upper Forth Valley.
Etr–Sep 2rm 1hc (1fb) ⚓ CTV 3P 🍴 200acres beef S% B&b£6 Bdi£8

BUCKIE 8,188 Grampian Map45 NJ46 EcWed Aberdeen 68 Cullen 8 Elgin 17 Inverness 55 London 598
★★**Cluny** High St ☎32722
Victorian building on corner site in main square with views out to sea. Internally modernised to a high standard.
Closed 1st & 2nd Jan; 10rm(8⇔2🚿) Annexe: 6rm(3⇔1🚿) 🍴 CTV in 14bedrooms TV in 2bedrooms ® 20P Last dinner 9.30pm ⌕ S% ✱sB&B⇔🚿£12.50 dB&B⇔🚿£21.30 Lunch£2.50 Tea£1.25 High Tea£2–£4 Dinner£4.50&alc Wine£3.50 🍺
Credit cards ①②③⑤
★★**St Andrews** St Andrews Sq ☎31227
15rm(9⇔1🚿) 🍴 CTV CTV in 3bedrooms 10🦽 billiards Disco twice wkly Live music & dancing twice wkly Last dinner 7pm ⌕ S% sB&B£10 sB&B⇔£12 dB&B£18 dB&B⇔£23 Lunchfr£1.90 Teafr£1 High Teafr£2.50 Dinnerfr£5.50&alc Wine£2.75 🍺
FH M.E.B. McLean **Mill of Rathven** (NJ446657) ☎31132
Farmhouse with attractive garden. On edge of village of Rathven and surrounded by arable land and several outbuildings.
Closed Xmas 3rm CTV 3P S% B&b£6.50 Bdi£8–£10.50 D6pm

BURNHOUSE Strathclyde Map34 NS35 Glasgow 18 Irvine 8 Kilmarnock 10 London 496
FH Mr & Mrs Robertson **Burnhouse Manor** (NS383503) ☎Dunlop 406
Large farmhouse in own grounds. Visible and well signposted from main Paisley/Irvine road. Off B706.
Closed 2nd & 3rd wk Oct & New Year rsSun (Nov–Etr) & Mon (B&b only) 6hc (1fb) ⚓ CTV 40P 🍴 111acres arable beef S% B&B£6.50–£7.50 Bdi£11–£12 D8.30pm

BURNTISLAND 5,588 Fife Map41 NT28 London 435 Cowdenbeath 5 Dunfermline 11 Kirkcaldy 6
★**Leonard** 110–112 Aberdour Rd ☎872629
6rm 🍴 CTV P Live music & dancing Sun Last dinner 9pm ⌕ 🍺 Credit cards ①②③⑤
GH Forthaven 4 South View, Lammerlaws ☎872600 4hc (2fb) TV 4P river S% B&b£5 W£30 M

BUTE, ISLE OF Strathclyde Map43 **See Rothesay**

CAIRNBAAN 135 Strathclyde Map39 NR89 Glasgow 86 Lochgilphead 2 London 488 Oban 36
★★**Cairnbaan Motor Inn** ☎Lochgilphead 2488
Old inn with extensions, situated near Crinan Canal.
Annex: 16⇔🚿 ® 100P 4🦽 ⚓ Last dinner 10pm ⌕ 🍺
Credit cards ①②③④⑤

CAIRNIE Grampian Map45 NJ44 Huntly 5 Keith 6 Dufftown 13 London 581
FH Mrs P. M. F. Moir **Smallburn** (NJ469341) ☎Cairnie 219
(Approach road to farm is from southside of A96 mid way (approx 6m) between Huntly and Keith at signpost Wyndraw 1m of Cairnie.)
Apr–Oct 2rm (1fb) ⚓ CTV 6P 400acres mixed S% B&b£5.50–£6 Bdi£8–£8.50 W£50–£54 Ł D6pm

CALLANDER 1,826 Central Map40NN60 EcWed ex summer Edinburgh53 Glasgow37 London434 Perth40 Stirling16
★★★⚁L **Roman Camp** ☎30003
Closed mid Oct–8Apr; 10rm(6⇨) Annexe: 5rm(3⇨) 1🛏 🍴 CTV in all bedrooms ⓡ 30P 3🅿 ⚁ ↯ Last dinner9pm ☸ S% sB&B£20.50–£22.50 sB&B⇨£20.50–£23.50 dB&B£28 dB&B⇨£43.50 Lunch£7.25alc Dinner£10–£12alc Wine£5 Credit card②

★★**Ancaster Arms** Main St (Scottish & Newcastle) ☎30167
A red sandstone Victorian building with tower standing in main street of Scottish country town.
25rm CTV 150P Live music & dancing Sat ♀ English & French. Last dinner8.45pm ☸ S% ✱sB&B£14 dB&B£21 Lunch£2.75–£3.25 Tea£1.10 HighTea£3.35 Dinner£6.50alc 🍺 Credit cards ①②③④⑤⑥

★**Pinewood** Leny Rd, Strathyre ☎30111
Converted stone house, dating from 1900, with white painted wood extension, standing back from main road with mature trees and shrubs in grounds.
RS mid Oct–Mar; 16rm(2⇨) 🍴 CTV 30P ✿ ↯ ♀ Scottish, French & Italian. Last dinner8.15pm ☸ S% sB&B£6.86–£9.48 sB&B⇨£10.75–£11.39 dB&B£17.72–£18.96 dB&B⇨£21.50–£22.78 Lunch£3.79 Tea35–40p Dinner£5.06–£5.69 Wine£4.50 xmas Credit card ①

★**Waverley** Main St ☎30245
13rm CTV ⓡ ☔ Live music & dancing twice wkly Last dinner9pm ☸ S% sB&B£8 dB&B£16 Lunch£3.50 Tea£1.10 HighTea£3 Dinner£5.50&alc Wine£2.50 🍺 xmas Credit cards ①③

GH Abbotsford Lodge Stirling Rd ☎30066 Lic 19rm 18hc (7fb) CTV 20P 🍴 S% B&b£7.20 Bdi£12.40 W£79.90 ↯ D7pm

GH Annfield 18 North Church St ☎30204 Apr–Oct 8hc (1fb) CTV 9P 🍴 S% B&b£5.50–£6

GH Ashlea House Hotel Bracklinn Rd ☎30325 Mar–Nov 20hc 2⇨🍴 (3fb) ✿ CTV 17P 🍴 D7.15pm

GH Edina 111 Main St ☎30004 9hc (2fb) CTV 7P S% B&b£5.47–£6.21 Bdi£8.92–£10.17 Wfr£64.50 ↯ D7.30pm

GH Highland House Hotel South Church St ☎30269 Mar–Oct Lic 10hc 4🍴 (1fb) ✿ CTV 🍴 river B&b£7.50–£10 Bdi£14–£16.50 W£94–£110 ↯ D7.30pm

GH Kinnell 24 Main St ☎30181 Mar–Nov 9hc (2fb) CTV 8P river S% B&b£6.25–£7 Bdi£10.50–£11.50 W£80 ↯ D7.30pm

GH Lubnaig Leny Feus ☎30376 Mar–14Oct Lic 10hc 10⇨🍴 (A2🍴) ✿ nc7 CTV 14P 🍴 (W only mid May–mid Sep) D8pm

GH Rock Villa 1 Bracklinn Rd ☎30331 Etr–midOct 7hc (1fb) ✿ 7P 🍴 S% B&b£5.50–£6

GH Tighnaldon Private Hotel 156 Main St ☎30703 Etr–Oct, Xmas & New Year Lic 6hc (1fb) ↯ TV river ✱B&b£5–£5.50 Bdi£9–£10 W£60–£65 ↯ D6pm

CAMPBELTOWN 6,326 Strathclyde Map33NR72 EcWed MdMon Glasgow135 London538 Oban89 Tarbert38
★★**Ardshiel** Kilkerran Rd ☎2133
Three-storey Victorian house in quiet residential area not far from town centre and harbour.
Closed Oct to Mar; 12rm CTV 10P ↯ Last dinner8pm ☸ Credit cards ①③

GH Westbank Dell Rd ☎2452 Feb–Nov 7hc CTV

CAMPSIE GLEN Strathclyde Map37NS67 Glasgow12 Lennoxtown1 Kirkintilloch5 London413
✕✕✕**Campsie Glen** Lennoxtown310666
130seats 200P bedrooms available Live music & dancing Wed, Fri & Sat ♀ Scottish & French. Last dinner11pm Lunch£4–£6.50&alc Tea£1–£3 Dinner£7.50–£12.50&alc Wine£7.50 Credit cards ①②③④⑤⑥

CANNICH 203 Highland Map43NH33 EcThu/Sat Invermoriston25 Inverness28 London580
★★**Glen Affric** ☎214
Closed 20Oct–8Apr; 23rm(5⇨) CTV 30P ↯ Last dinner8pm ☸ ↯ S% sB&B£9.50 dB&B£19 dB&B⇨£21 Lunch£3.50 Tea85p HighTea£3 Dinner£6

CANONBIE 234 Dumfries & Galloway Map35NY37 Carlisle14 Dumfries31 Langholm6 London322
★★**Cross Keys** ☎205
9rm(4⇨) 🍴 CTV ⓡ 25P ✿ ↯ ♀ English & French. Last dinner9pm ☸ ↯ S% sB&B£8.50–£9.50 sB&B⇨£10–£12 dB&B£15–£17.50 dB&B⇨£22.50–£25 Lunch£4.25–£5.50 Teafr£1.50 Dinner£6.50–£10 Wine£3.60 🍺 Credit cards ①②③⑤⑥

INN Riverside ☎295 (Closed last 2wks Jan) Lic 7hc ✿ CTV 25P 🍴 D8.30pm

CAPUTH Tayside Map40NO03 Dunkeld5 Perth12 Blairgowrie8 London460
FH Mrs R. Smith **Stralochy** (NO086413) ☎250
Situated in lovely spot looking down a valley, trees merging in Sidlaw hills.
May–Oct 3rm (1fb) ↯ TV 3P 239acres arable S% Bdifr£7 Wfr£49 ↯ D4pm

CARFRAEMILL Borders Map35NT55 Lauder4 Edinburgh23 London357
★★**Carfraemill** (Osprey) ☎Oxton800
9rm(2⇨) 🍴 CTV CTV in 2bedrooms ⓡ 20P ✿ ♀ Scottish & French. Last dinner9.30pm ☸ ↯ S% sB&B£11.45 sB&B⇨£15.25 dB&B£20 dB&B⇨£25.50 Lunch£3.50&alc Tea£1 HighTea£2.50 Dinner£5&alc Wine£3.50 🍺 xmas Credit cards ①②③④⑤

CARNOUSTIE 7,389 Tayside Map41NO53 EcTue Dundee13 London485 Perth33
★★★**Bruce** Links Pde ☎52364
36rm(22⇨) 🍴 CTV CTV in 24 bedrooms TV in 12bedrooms 60P ↯ Conference facilities available ♀ Scottish & French. Last dinner8.45pm ☸ ↯ sB&B£15–£18 sB&B⇨£15–£18 dB&B£30–£44 dB&B⇨£30–£44 Lunch£3.90–£4.50&alc Dinner£5.50–£6.50&alc Wine£3.70 ↯ Credit cards ①②③⑤⑥

★★**Earlston** 24 Church St ☎52352
21rm(1⇨🍴) CTV 80P Last dinner9.30pm ☸ ↯ sB&B£10.35 sB&B⇨🍴£12.65 dB&B£20.70 dB&B⇨🍴£25.30 Lunch£4.02 Tea£1.38 Dinner£4.95&alc Wine£3.85 Credit cards ①③⑤

★★**Glencoe** Links Pde ☎53273
Three-storey stone house with modern extensions overlooking sea & golf course.
10rm(2⇨5🍴) 🍴 CTV CTV available in bedrooms 10P ✿ ♀ Scottish & French. Last dinner9pm ☸ ↯ S% sB&B£10 dB&B£22 dB&B⇨🍴£22 Lunch£3–£6&alc Tea£1–£1.50 HighTea£2.25–£4 Dinner£5.50–£8 Wine£4 Credit cards ①③⑤⑥

★**Station** ☎52447
12rm 🍴 CTV 20P 6✿ Live music & dancing Sat Cabaret Sat Last dinner9pm ☸ ↯ Credit cards ①⑤

🄶 **Carlogie House** ☎53185
Closed 1–3Jan; 11rm(2⇨9🍴) ⚁ 🍴 CTV in all bedrooms ⓡ ↯ 150P 2✿ ↯ ♀ Scottish & French. Last dinner9.30pm ☸ ↯ S% ✱sB&B⇨🍴£16.50 dB&B⇨🍴£33 Lunch£3.50&alc Tea£1 HighTea£2.50 Dinner£5.50 Wine£5 🍺 Credit cards ①②③⑤⑥

GH Dalhousie Hotel 47 High St ☎52907 Feb–Dec Lic 7rm 5hc (2fb) CTV 6P sea S% B&b£7 Bdi£11 W£77 ↯ D8.30pm

CARRADALE 262 Strathclyde Map33NR83 EcWed

Carradale contd – Clachan

Campbeltown15 London524 Tarbert24
★★**Carradale** ☎223
Closed Nov–Feb; 16rm(4🛁) Annexe: 6rm(3🛁) 🍴 CTV 20P 🚗 ⚲ squash sauna bath Last dinner8.30pm ✤ 🍷 🍺
S% ✽sB&B£10–£10.50 sB&B🛁£11.50–£12.10
dB&B£20–£21 dB&B🛁£23–£24.20 Lunch£4 Tea80p
High Tea£3.45 Dinner£6.50 Wine£2.66 🍺
GH Ashbank Hotel ☎650 Etr–Oct Lic 5hc (2fb) ⊘
CTV 7P sea ✤Bdi£12 Wfr£72 ⚲ D8.30pm
GH Drumfearne ☎232 Apr–Sep 6rm 5hc (3fb) ⊘
TV P D6pm
GH Duncrannag ☎224 Apr–Sep Tem 11hc 8P
GH Dunvalanree Portrigh ☎226 Etr–Sep 12hc (3fb)
⊘ nc2 TV 9P 🍴 sea S% ✽B&b£5–£6
Bdi£7–£7.50 W£49 ⚲ D3pm

CARRBRIDGE 416 Highland Map44 NH92 EcWed
Grantown-on-Spey10 Inverness26 London540
★**Rowan Lea** ☎212
7rm 🔔 CTV ⓇR 7P 🚗 Live music Fri & Sat
Last dinner8.30pm ✤ 🍷 S% sB&B£8.20–£9.20
dB&B£16.40–£18.40 Bar lunch£1.20–£2
Dinner£4.50–£5.50 Wine£3.27 🍺 Credit cards ① ③
GH Ard-na-Coille Station Rd ☎239 4hc (1fb) TV 7P
🍴 river S% ✽B&bfr£6 Bdifr£10.50 Wfr£70 ⚲
D2pm
GH Dalrachney Lodge Private Hotel ☎252 Closed Nov & Dec (except Xmas) 9hc (3fb) nc5 CTV 10P 🍴
river B&bfr£8 Bdifr£12 D7pm
GH Old Manse Private Hotel Duthil (2m E A938) ☎278
Closed Nov 9hc (2fb) CTV 9P 🍴 B&b£7.50
Bdi£11.50 W£70 ⚲ D1pm
✕**Landmark** ☎613
Closed Nov–Mar; 80seats 🍽 English & French.
Last dinner9pm S% ✽Lunch£2.50–£5&alc Tea55p
High Tea£1.95–£2.50 Dinner£4.95–£7
Credit cards ① ② ③

CARRONBRIDGE Central Map34 NS78 Stirling8, Denny9, Kilsyth4, London414
FH Mr A. Morton **Lochend** (NS759350) ☎Denny822778
Modernised, 18th-century hill farm. Pleasant farmyard with rose garden in centre. Set in quiet, isolated position. 1½m off unclass rd towards Bannockburn.
Jun–Sep 2rm 1hc ⊘ nc3 TV P 🏠 🍴 380acres
beef sheep S% B&b£5.50–£5.75 Bdi£6.50–£6.75

CARRUTHERSTOWN Dumfries & Galloway Map35 NY17 Dumfries20, Annan7, London333
FH Mrs J. Brown **Domaru** (NY093716) ☎260
Modern, detached, two-storey farmhouse built at side of farm road. About 300 yards from farm buildings.
Carrutherstown ½ mile.
Apr–Oct 3rm 2hc TV in all bedrooms 3P 🍴
140acres dairy S% B&bfr£5 Bdifr£8 Wfr£56 ⚲
D6.30pm

CARSPHAIRN Dumfries & Galloway Map34 NX59 Ayr25
Dumfries36 London387 New Galloway12
★★**Salutation** ☎250
RS Nov–Apr (accommodation limited); 16rm(2⇔🛁) 🍴 CTV ⓇR 12P Last dinner8pm ✤ 🍷 🍺

CASTLE DOUGLAS 3,385 Dumfries & Galloway
Map30 NX76 EcThu Carlisle53 Dumfries18 Kirkcudbright10 London359
★★★**Douglas Arms** King St ☎2231
White-painted former coaching inn standing in town centre.
27rm(11⇔) 🍴 CTV CTV in 4bedrooms 8P 10🏠
Last dinner9pm ✤ 🍷 S% sB&B£15–£17
sB&B⇔£17.50–£19.50 dB&B£27–£29
dB&B⇔£32–£34 Lunch£3.60–£4 Tea£1.25–£1.35
High Tea£3–£8 Dinner£6.70–£8.70 🍺
Credit cards ① ② ③ ④ ⑤

★★🍽**Ernespie House** ☎2188
Stone mansion dating from 1870 standing in own grounds of 17¼ acres on outskirts of town.
16rm(4⇔1🛁) 🍴 TV ⓇR 100P ⚲ Last dinner8pm ✤ 🍷
S% sB&B£10–£11.50 sB&B⇔🛁£11.50–£12.50
dB&B£20–£23 dB&B⇔🛁£23.50–£25
Lunch£2.50–£3.75&alc Tea£1–£1.50
High Tea£2.50–£3.75 Dinner£5.50–£6.50 Wine£2 🍺
xmas Credit card ②
★★**Imperial** King St ☎2086
14rm(3🛁) 🍴 CTV 25P 5🏠 Last High Tea7pm ✤ 🍷
sB&B£9 dB&B£18 Bar lunch£1–£2.50 Tea75p–£1
High Tea£1.80–£3.50 Wine£3.40 🍺 Credit cards ① ③
★★**King's Arms** St Andrew's St ☎2626
15rm(4⇔2🛁) 🍴 CTV 15P 🚗 🍽 French. Last dinner8pm
✤ S% sB&B£10.50–£13.50 sB&B⇔🛁£14–£17.50
dB&B£21–£27 dB&B⇔🛁£28–£35 Lunch£3.50
High Tea£5 Dinner£8 Wine£2.25 🍺
Credit cards ② ③ ⑤ ⑥
★**Merrick** 193 King St ☎2173
6rm CTV ⓇR ⊘ 9P 🚗 Last dinner8pm S% ✽sB&Bfr£7
dB&Bfr£14 Lunch fr£1.75&alc Dinner fr£2.50&alc
Wine£3
GH Rose Cottage Gelston ☎2513
5rm ⊘ nc3 CTV 14P 🍴 S% B&b£6.50–£7
Bdi£8.50–£9.50 W£45.50–£66.50 ⚲ D5pm

CAWDOR Highland Map44 NH85 Nairn6, Inverness14, London564
FH *Little Budgate* (NH834503) ☎267
Small, cottage-style farmhouse set amid fields.
Cawdor 1 mile.
May–Sep 2rm (A 2hc) ⊘ P 50acres arable

CHAPELHALL 3,928 Strathclyde Map34 NS76 EcWed
Airdrie2 Glasgow14 Edinburgh33 London400
GH Laurel House Hotel 101 Main St ☎Airdrie63230
Lic 6rm 5hc (1fb) ⊘ CTV 6P 🍴 ✽B&b£8.50
Bdi£11

CHAPELTON 499 Strathclyde Map37 NS64 EcWed (all day 1st Wed of month) East Kilbride5 Glasgow13 London393
FH Mr R. Hamilton **East Drumloch** (NS678521) ☎236
Large stone-built farmhouse with a modern, well-furnished interior.
4rm (2fb) CTV P 260acres beef S% B&b£5.50–£6
W£40–£47 **M**
FH Mrs E. Taylor **Millwell** (NS653496) ☎East Kilbride43248
Small, 18th-century farm set in tree-studded land.
3rm CTV 4P 94acres dairy S% B&b£5 Bdi£6.50

CHARLESTOWN 366 Fife Map40 NT08 Dunfermline4 Edinburgh8 London435
★*Elgin* (off A985) ☎Limekilns257
5rm Annexe: 2⇔🛁 🍴 TV 40P 2🏠 🚗 ⚲ 🍽 English & French.
Last dinner9.30pm Credit cards ① ⑥

CHIRNSIDE 888 Borders Map36 NT85 EcWed Berwick-upon-Tweed9 Edinburgh49 London357
★★🍽**Chirnside Country House** ☎219
Early Victorian country mansion set in 56 acres of tree-studded grounds.
Closed Xmas; 14rm Lift CTV 30P ⚲ 🍽 English, Scottish & Continental. Last dinner8.45pm ✤ 🍷 sB&Bfr£11
dB&Bfr£22 Lunch fr£5 Tea fr£1.50 High Tea fr£3.50
Dinner fr£7 Wine£4 🍺 Credit cards ① ② ③ ⑤

CLACHAN Isle of Skye, Highland Map48 NG40 Portree14, Kyleakin24 London612
FH Mr & Mrs C. MacDonald **Windyridge** (NG492666)
☎Staffin222
Small, white-painted croft with blue-tiled roof. At north end of Island in a very pleasant situation.
mid May–mid Oct 3rm (1fb) ⊘ nc5 CTV 6P
10acres sheep S% ✽B&b£5 Bdi£7.50 D7pm

Willowburn hotel

ISLE OF SEIL, BY OBAN ARGYLL
Telephone BALVICAR 276

MEMBER INTER-HOTEL (SCOTLAND)

Drive onto the Isle of Seil, over the only bridge to span the Atlantic, where we offer you a warm welcome, good food and a "get away from it all" holiday.
Willowburn lies in four acres of ground reaching down to the sea. This is the lovely island where 'Ring of Bright Water' and 'Kidnapped' were filmed. Centrally heated. Open all year, except November.

CLACHAN-SEIL Strathclyde Map38NM71 EcWed Lochgilphead12 London518 Oban13
❀★**Willowburn** (Inter-Hotel) ☎Balvicar276
(Rosette awarded for dinner only.)
RS Nov (no accommodation); 6rm(1⇌) ⌇ CTV ⓡ 25P ⇌ ⌇
♀English & French. Last dinner8.30pm
*sB&B£12–£15.40 dB&B£21–£27.50
dB&B⇌£26–£29.70 Lunch£3 Dinner£7alc Wine£2.60
🍷 Credit cards①②③⑤⑥

CLARENCEFIELD Dumfries & Galloway Map31NY06
Annan7 Dumfries10 London333
FH Mrs S. C. Hogg **Kirkbeck** (NY083705) ☎284
Attractive farmhouse with a high standard of décor. Near to Solway coast. Fishing and golf. N on A724.
Apr–Oct 3hc (1fb) ⌇ CTV 3P ⌇ 106acres arable pigs S% B&b£5 Bdi£7.50 W£50 Ł D8pm

CLEISH Tayside Map40NT09 Perth22 Dunfermline9 London438
❀★**Nivingston House** ☎Cleish Hills216
(Rosette awarded for dinner only.)
Closed Mon, mid Oct–mid Nov & 1st wk Jan; Dinner not served Sun; 76seats 40P bedrooms available ♀French.
Last dinner9pm S% ✱Lunchfr£6.75 Dinnerfr£12.75
Wine£4.20 Credit cards②③

CLOVA Tayside Map41NO37 Brechin31 Kirriemuir16 London499 Perth47
★★**Ogilvy Arms** Glen Clova (Clova village) ☎222
7rm(4⇌) CTV ⓡ 40P ⌇ ⌇ sB&B£11.50
sB&B⇌£12.50 dB&B£23 dB&B⇌£25
Barlunch40p–£3.75 Tea40p–£1 HighTea£2.50–£3.50
Dinner£5.25–£8 Wine£2.60
★★⛤B **Rottal Lodge** Glen Clova (3m SE on B955 on east bank of river) ☎224
Closed Dec–Mar 12rm(7⇌) ⌇ TV 12P ⇌ ⌇
¤International. Last dinner 8.15pm ⌇ S%
*sB&B£25.98 sB&B⇌⌇£25.98 dB&B£44.26
dB&B⇌⌇£44.26 Lunch£3.45–£5.75 Tea£1.38
Dinner£6.82 Wine£3.05 🍷

CLYDEBANK 46,915 Strathclyde Map37NS47 EcWed
Dumbarton8 Glasgow7 London409
★★**Radnor** Kilbowie Rd (Osprey) ☎041-9522875
Modern four-storey brick building occupying fine site overlooking Clydeside.
12⇌ Lift ⌇ CTV CTV in all bedrooms ⓡ 40P ⇌ ⌇Scottish & French. Last dinner9.30pm ⌇ S% sB&B⇌£15.25
dB&B⇌£25.50 Lunch£3.50&alc Tea£1 HighTea£2.50
Dinner£5&alc Wine£3.50 🍷 Credit cards①②③④⑤

CLYNDER 192 Strathclyde Map33NS28 EcWed Glasgow35 London437 Tarbet16
★★**Clynder** (Osprey) ☎248
11rm ⌇ CTV ⓡ 40P ⇌ ♀Scottish & French.
Last dinner9.30pm ⌇ ⌇ S% sB&B£11.75 dB&B£21
Lunch£3.50&alc Tea£1 HighTea£2.50 Dinner£5&alc
Wine£3.50 🍷 xmas Credit cards①②③④⑤

COATBRIDGE 50,945 Strathclyde Map34NS76 EcWed Airdrie2 Glasgow9 London397
✰✰✰**Coatbridge** Glasgow Rd (Scottish & Newcastle) ☎24392
Modern custom-built hotel set on west side of town overlooking Drumpelier golf course.
22⇌ ⌇ D ⌇ CTV CTV in all bedrooms ⓡ ⌇ 200P Disco Sun
Live music & dancing Thu–Sat Cabaret Sat ♀French.
Last dinner9.30pm ⌇ S% sB&B⇌⌇£23
dB&B⇌⌇£30 Lunch£5.75&alc Dinnerfr£5.75&alc
Wine£3.45 🍷 Credit cards①②③④⑤

COCKSBURNSPATH 233 Borders Map36NT77 EcThu Berwick-upon-Tweed21 Edinburgh36 London369
★**Cockburnspath** ☎217
Small, white-painted coaching inn (18th century) with attractive interior décor, situated on main road of village.
6rm ⌇ CTV ⌇ 12P Last dinner8.30pm ⌇ ⌇
sB&B£7.50 dB&B£15 Barlunch£1.35–£2.30 HighTea
£2–£4 Dinner£5.50alc Wine£2.75

COLBOST Isle of Skye, Highland Map48NG24 Dunvegan6 Kyleakin52 Portree24 London640
✗**Three Chimneys** ☎Glendale258 Closed Mon
& 19Oct–6Apr; 35seats 15P Last dinner8.30pm
Lunch£alc Dinner£8.50alc Wine£2.90

COLDINGHAM 423 Borders Map36NT96 EcThu Berwick-upon-Tweed12 Edinburgh46 London360
INN Anchor ☎338 Lic 4rm 3hc ⌇ CTV P ⌇ ⌇
D8pm £4

COLDSTREAM 1,429 Borders Map36NT83 EcThu London342 Berwick-upon-Tweed14 Edinburgh48 Kelso9 North Berwick47
★**Majicado** 71 High St ☎2112
Converted sandstone house dating from 1860, close to River Tweed.
7rm ⌇ CTV 🅿 Last dinner 8.30pm ⌇ sB&B£8
dB&B£18 Lunch£3.20alc Dinner£8.50alc Wine£3.50

COLL, ISLE OF Strathclyde Map50 See **Arinagour**

COLLIN Dumfries & Galloway Map34NY07 Dumfries4 Annan12 Lockerbie10 London338
★★★⛤**Rockhall** ☎427
9rm(4⇌1⌇) CTV CTV in 2bedrooms ⓡ 100P ⌇ Live music & dancing wkly ♀International. Last dinner9pm ⌇ ⌇
sB&B£18.50–£20 dB&B£30–£34 dB&B⇌⌇£33–£41
Lunch£5.50–£6.50&alc Tea£1.25alc
Dinner£5.50–£7.50&alc Wine£3.15 🍷
Credit cards①②③⑤⑥

FALLS OF LORA HOTEL
Connel, Argyll PA37 1PB
Tel: Connel 483

Overlooking Loch Etive, Oban 5 miles. An ideal centre for a touring, walking and sailing holiday or just relaxing in a friendly atmosphere. A fine Victorian Hotel beautifully appointed with a modern centrally heated extension. The accent being on personal attention by the resident owners, comfort, good food and traditional highland hospitality.
Open all year, out of season mini breaks, children sharing parent's room — free accommodation.
Fishing, water-skiing and pony trekking can be arranged.
Open to non-residents, bar snacks and À la Carte available till 9.30 pm.

COLONSAY, ISLE OF Strathclyde Map50 **See Scalasaig**

COMRIE Tayside Map40 NN72 EcWed Crieff7 London443 Perth24 Stirling23
★★**Comrie** Drummond St ☎239
Attractive ivy-clad roadside hotel in quiet central Highland village.
Closed Nov–mid Apr; 10rm(4⇨🛏) Annexe: 2⇨ 🛏 CTV 26P 🚗 Children under 5yrs not accommodated Last dinner 8.30pm ♥ ⌑
★★**Royal** ☎200
Built in 1765. Prints of photographs in cocktail bar recall visits by Queen Victoria and her much-loved servant John Brown, and Lloyd George.
11rm(6⇨) Annexe: 5rm(2⇨1🛏) 1⌑ CTV TV available in bedrooms ® 30P 3🚗 ♥ ♀Scottish & French.
Last dinner 9.30pm ♥ *sB&B⇨£8.50–£10.35 sB&B⇨🛏£9.50–£11.50 dB&B⇨£17–£20.70 dB&B⇨🛏£19–£23 Lunch£2.50alc Dinner£6.95 🍺 Credit cards ① ⑥
GH Mossgiel ☎567 Closed Nov, rsDec-Etr 6hc nc2 CTV 6P 🚗 ♥ S% B&b£5 Bdi£8.50 W£59.50 ⌑ D5pm
FH Mrs J. H. Rimmer **West Ballindalloch** (NN744262) ☎70282
Cosy, small farmhouse with neat garden set amid hills in secluded glen. Comrie 4 miles.
Apr–Sep 2rm (1fb) ⊛ CTV 3P 1,500acres sheep S% B&b£5–£5.50

CONNEL 300 Strathclyde Map39 NM93 EcWed FortWilliam43 London500 Oban5
★★**Falls of Lora** ☎483
30rm(12⇨1🛏) ♪ CTV CTV in 20bedrooms 40P 🚗 ⌑ 🍴 ♥ ♀Scottish & French. Last dinner 9.30pm ♥ ⌑ sB&B£8.50–£14 sB&B⇨🛏£17.50–£21.50 dB&B£13–£23 dB&B⇨🛏£23–£28 Lunch£2.50–£3.50 Tea£1–£2 HighTea£2.50–£3.50 Dinner£6.75&alc Wine£3.25 🍺 Credit cards ① ② ③ ⑤ ⑥
★★**Lochnell Arms** Connel North ☎408
9rm(4⇨) CTV 50P 🚗 ⌑ ♥ Last dinner 10pm ♥ ⌑ S% sB&B£7–£11 sB&B⇨£8–£12 dB&B£14–£22 dB&B⇨£16–£24 Lunch£3–£5 Teafr75p Dinner£5.50–£6.50 Wine£3.80 🍺 Credit card ①
★★**Ossians** Connel North ☎322
Modern architect designed hotel situated some 250yds from northern end of Connel Bridge and looking across Loch Etive.
Closed 10 Oct–9Apr; 14rm(4⇨) CTV 50P 🚗 ⌑ Last dinner 7.30pm ♥ ⌑ sB&B£10.99–£11.54 dB&B£21.98–£23.08 dB&B⇨£23.58–£25.38 Barlunchfr£1 Teafr80p Dinnerfr£6.30 Wine£4.50 🍺

CONTIN 244 Highland Map43 NH45 EcThu Dingwall17 Inverness22 London587
★★**Craigdarroch Lodge** Craigdarroch Dr ☎Strathpeffer265
19rm(8⇨3🛏) CTV ® 20P 🚗 ⌑ ⇝ billiards ♣ ♀English & Continental. Last dinner 8.30pm ♥ ⌑ *sB&B£7–£12.50 sB&B⇨🛏£25 Dinnerfr£7.95 Wine£3.45 xmas
★**Achilty** Strathpeffer355
Closed Oct–mid Apr; 12rm 🛏 TV ® 10P 2🚗 🚗 ⌑ Last dinner 8pm ♥

CORRIE 143 Isle of Arran, Strathclyde Map33 NS04 EcWed Brodick6 (ferry to Ardrossan) Lochranza8
GH Blackrock House ☎282 Mar–Oct 9hc (4fb) CTV 8P 🛏 sea S% B&b£6.50–£7.50 Bdi£9–£9.50 W£63–£66.50 ⌑ D6pm

CORTACHY Tayside Map41 NO35 Forfar11 London486 Perth34
★★**Royal Jubilee Arms** Dyke Head ☎225
12⇨ Annexe: 17🛏 🚗 CTV CTV available in bedrooms ®

Dykehead, Cortachy,
By Kirriemuir Angus, Scotland

Special "Value for Money" room rates all with private facilities plus suites. Reputation for High Quality food available all day at attractive prices. Special Wine selection and offers.
Close to many famous sights, historic buildings, golf courses, winter sports, hunting, fishing, walking and "The most beautiful view in the world."
For an hour, night, day, week or a month we doubt you will find its equal.
Tel. Cortachy (057 54) 225 or 213 for details

Royal Jubilee Arms Hotel

150P Live music & dancing Fri, Sat & Sun Cabaret Fri & Sat ♣ ♥ Scottish & French. Last dinner 11pm ✧ ⌂ S% sB&B⇌🕿£8.50–£11 dB&B⇌🕿£15–£20 Lunch£3alc Tea85p High Tea£3alc Dinner£5–£5.40 Wine£1.95 ☎ xmas Credit cards ①②③④⑤

COVE 1,412 (with Kilcreggan) Strathclyde Map33 NS28 Glasgow41 London443 Tarbet21
★★**Knockderry** 🕿 Kilcreggan 2283
13rm (5⇌🕿) CTV 50P ♣ ⌂ Live music Sat (Jun–Aug) Last dinner 8.30pm ✧ ⌂ ☎ Credit cards ①②③⑤

CRAIGELLACHIE 382 Grampian Map44 NJ24 EcThu Aberdeen58 Elgin14 Huntly19 Inverness52 London570
★★★**Craigellachie** 🕿204
Well-established fishing hotel in Highland distillery village. Fine views towards River Spey.
Closed Oct–Feb; 31rm (23⇌2🕿) CTV 40P ♣
Last dinner 8.20pm ✧ ⌂ S% sB&B£13–£15 sB&B⇌🕿£15 dB&B£26 dB&B⇌🕿£30 Lunchfr£3.50 Tea fr£1.50 Dinner£6.50–£7&alc Wine£3.30

CRAIGHOUSE 113 Isle of Jura, Strathclyde Map32 NR56 EcTue Feolin Ferry8 **Car carrying service to Port Askaig (Islay) thence for service to mainland**
★★**L Jura** 🕿 Jura 243
Overlooks sheltered bay.
20rm (4⇌) CTV ® 18P ♣ ⌂ ♥ Scottish & French.
Last dinner 9pm ✧ ✶sB&B£18.75 dB&B£37.50 dB&B⇌£41.26 Lunch£4.35 Dinner£8.75 Wine£2.65
☎ Credit cards ①②③⑤

CRAIGNURE Isle of Mull, Strathclyde Map38 NM73 EcThu Fishnish pier6 Tobermory22 **Car carrying services operate from Oban, also Lochaline to Fishnish**
★★★**Isle of Mull** (Scottish Highland) 🕿351 Telex no 778215
Modern hotel, ¼ mile from car ferry terminal, looking out across Craignure Bay to the distant mainland.
Closed Nov–Mar; 60rm ♪ CTV 80P ♣
Last dinner 8.15pm ✧ ⌂ S% sB&B⇌🕿£21.30 dB&B⇌£36.60 Bar lunch£2alc Dinner£7.50 Wine£3.95 Credit cards ①②③④⑤

CRAIL 1,029 Fife Map41 NO60 EcWed Edinburgh52 London464 Perth42 St Andrews10
★**Croma** Nethergate 🕿239
Conversion of two adjoining houses with white-painted stone exterior. Residential situation in quiet road in east coast fishing port.
10rm (2⇌) ⚡ CTV 10P ♣ ⌂ ♣ Last dinner 10pm ✧ S% sB&B£8–£9 sB&B⇌£8–£9 dB&B£16–£18 dB&B⇌£16–£18 Bar lunch£1.50–£1.75 Tea£1.25–£1.50 High Tea£2.50–£2.75 Dinner£5.50–£6 Wine£4
★**Marine** Nethergate 🕿207
12rm CTV ℙ ⌂ Children under 6yrs not accommodated Last dinner 8.30pm ✧ ⌂
GH Caiplie House 51–53 High St 🕿564
7hc (2fb) CTV 12P B&b£6.50–£7.50 Bdi£10–£11 W£63–£70 ⌂ D8.30pm

CREETOWN 769 Dumfries & Galloway Map30 NX45 EcThu Carlisle80 Glasgow93 London387 Newton Stewart7
★★**Ellangowan** 🕿201
9rm CTV ® 3P 6🕿 Live music & dancing twice mthly Last dinner 8pm ✧ ⌂ S% ✶sB&B£7.25–£7.50 dB&B£14.50–£15 Bar lunch£1–£3.50&alc Tea80p High Tea£2.20–£3.50&alc Dinner£4.50
GH Mayburn 🕿317
Etr–Sep 5hc (2fb) ⌂ TV 5P D7.30pm
INN Creetown Arms Hotel St Johns St 🕿282
6hc CTV 20P S% B&bfr£7.50 Bdifr£10.50 Wfr£75 ⌂ sn L£2–£5.50 D9pmfr£5.50&alc

CRIANLARICH 160 Central Map39 NN32 EcWed Callander30 Glasgow52 London465 Tarbet17
GH Glenardean 🕿236
Lic 6hc (3fb) CTV 5P ⚡ river S% B&b£5.50–£6 Bdi£8.25–£9 W£51–£54 ⌂ D7pm
GH Mountgreenan 🕿286
Closed Xmas Day 5hc (1fb) CTV P ⚡ S% ✶B&bfr£5 D6.30pm

CRIEFF 5,812 Tayside Map40 NN82 EcWed MdTue London440 Perth17 Stirling22
★★**Cultoquhey** 🕿3253
Closed Oct–Apr; 12rm CTV 50P 3🕿 ⌂ Last dinner 8pm ✧ ⌂
★★**Drummond Arms** James Sq 🕿2151
34rm (13⇌) Lift CTV 30P 2🕿 Live music & dancing Thu Cabaret Thu ♥ Scottish & French. Last dinner 9pm ✧ ⌂ sB&B£8.75–£9.75 sB&B⇌£10–£11 dB&B£17.50–£19.50 dB&B⇌£20–£24 Lunch£3–£4.50 Tea35p–£1.50 High Tea£2.50–£4.25 Dinner£4–£6.50 Wine£3.85 ☎ xmas
Credit cards ①②③
★★**George** King St 🕿2089
24rm (4⇌) ⚡ CTV 6P billiards Cabaret Tue ♥ French.
Last dinner 8.30pm ✧ ⌂ S% sB&B£8.50–£9.50 sB&B⇌£11.50–£13.50 dB&B£17–£18 dB&B⇌£20–£22 Lunch£2.50–£3.50&alc Tea£1.50–£2 High Tea£3–£3.50&alc Dinner£2–£6.50&alc Wine£2.50 ☎ Credit cards ③⑤
★★**B Murray Park** Connaught Ter 🕿3731
Situated in quiet residential area with fine views from upper floors across the Earn Valley to Ochil Hills.
15rm (10⇌) CTV TV in 2bedrooms CTV in 1bedroom 60P ♣ ⌂ ♣ Last dinner 9.15pm ✧ ⌂ sB&B£11.50 sB&B⇌£13.50–£18 dB&B£21 dB&B⇌£27 Lunch£4.85alc Dinner fr£7.85&alc Wine£4
Credit card ⑤
★**B Gwydyr** Comrie Rd 🕿3277
Former private mansion overlooking MacRosty Park on the west side of Crieff and commanding fine views of delightful Perthshire scenery.
Closed Xmas & New Year; RS Nov–20 Dec & 4 Jan–Etr; 10rm ⚡ CTV ® 18P 1🕿 ♣ ⌂ Last dinner 8.30pm ✧
Credit card
★**Star** East High St 🕿2632
10rm (1🕿) ⚡ CTV 20P sauna bath ♥ Scottish & French.
Last dinner 9pm ✧ ⌂ ✶sB&B£9 dB&B£16 dB&B🕿£17.50 Lunch£3.30&alc Tea£1.10 High Tea£2.30 Dinner£6&alc Wine£3.50 ☎
Credit cards ①②⑤⑤
GH Comely Bank 32 Burrell St 🕿3409
Feb–Nov 6hc (2fb) CTV S% B&b£6 Bdi£8.50 W£52 ⌂ D6pm
GH Heatherville 31 Burrell St 🕿2825
5hc (3fb) ⚡ CTV 5P S% ✶B&b£5.50–£6

Murraypark Hotel

**Connaught Terrace, Crieff, Tayside, Perthshire.
Telephone: Crieff (0764) 3731**

Year after year people return to the Murraypark Hotel, to enjoy once again its very special pleasures. A friendly welcome superb food and quiet comfort in the heart of beautiful Perthshire.
Murraypark is a medium size hotel with 15 bedrooms — 10 with private bathroom.
Under the personal management of the owners Ann and Noel Scott who, living on the premises, make it their sole aim to take excellent care of their guests and help to provide them with the type of holiday they wish.

Crieff contd–Daviot

Bdi£8.50–£9 D5pm
GH Lockes Acre Hotel Comrie Rd ☎2526
Apr–Oct Lic 6hc (2fb) CTV 5P ⊘ S% B&b£7 Bdi£12 D6.30pm

CRINAN Strathclyde Map38NR79 Glasgow90 Lochgilphead7 London493 Oban36
★★★ *L Crinan* ☎235 Telex no778817
Closed Nov–mid Apr; 22⇌🛏 Lift 🎵 CTV 35P ⬥
Last dinner 9pm 🚭 Credit cards ①②⑤

CROCKETFORD 102 Dumfries & Galloway Map30NX87 Carlisle44 Dumfries10 Glasgow85 London351
★★*Galloway Arms* Stranraer Rd ☎240
Closed Nov; 11rm(1⇌) Annexe: 2rm 🎵 CTV TV in 3 bedrooms ® 40P ⬥ ⚓ ♨ Scottish & French.
Last dinner 10pm 🚭 S% sB&B£10–£12 sB&B⇌£12–£14 dB&B£19–£23 dB&B⇌£23–£27 Lunch£4–£5 Tea£1.50–£1.80 HighTea£2–£5 Dinner£6–£10&alc Wine£3.50 ⊛
★*Lochview Motel* ☎281
Closed Xmas; 9rm(7🛏) 🎵 CTV ℗ ⊘ 60P ⬥ Live music & dancing Sat (winter only) Last dinner 10pm 🚭 🏐 S% sB&B£12 sB&B🛏£12 dB&B£18 dB&B🛏£18 Lunch£1.70–£3.50 Tea£1.25 HighTea£2.60–£3.50 Dinner£7alc Wine£3.10 Credit cards ①③

CROFTAMIE Strathclyde Map37NS48 Glasgow17 Stirling24 Drymen2 London430
✕*Red House Grill* ☎Drymen358
Closed Mon & Nov 48 seats 30P Last dinner 9.30pm

CROIK Highland Map46NH49 Bonar Bridge12 Dingwall38 London613
FH Mrs K. M. Moffat **Forest** *(NH454914)* ☎The Craigs322
1870 farmhouse in beautiful location but very isolated. 10 miles off single track road from Ardgay.
Apr–Sep 3rm ⊘ CTV 5P river 3,000 acres mixed S% B&bfr£4.50 Bdifr£8.50 D8pm

CROMARTY 503 Highland Map34NH76 Dingwall24 Inverness38 London603
★★ *Royal* Marine Ter ☎217
11rm CTV CTV in 2 bedrooms ® 12P 🚗 ⬥ Disco wkly Live music & dancing wkly ♨ Last dinner 8.30pm 🚭 🚗 ⊛

CROSSMICHAEL 317 Dumfries & Galloway Map30NX76 Castle Douglas4 Carlisle54 Dumfries20 Glasgow95 London361
★★🍴*Culgruff House* ☎230
Baronial mansion set in secluded, wooded grounds in the heart of farming land high above the village.
16rm(1⇌) 🎵 CTV 50P 8🏠 ⬥ ♨ Scottish, English & French.
Last dinner 8pm 🚭 sB&B£9.78 dB&B£18.40 dB&B⇌£23 Lunch£3.50–£4&alc Tea50p–£1.50 HighTea£3–£3.50 Dinner£6.50–£7.50&alc Wine£4 ⊛ Credit cards ①②③⑤

CULLEN 1,221 Grampian Map45NJ56 EcWed Aberdeen60 Banff14 Elgin22 London599
★★★ *L Seafield Arms* Seafield St ☎40791
25rm(17⇌) 🎵 CTV CTV in all bedrooms ® 30P
Last dinner 10pm 🚭 🚗 S% sB&B£17.95 sB&B⇌£20.70 dB&B£33.40 dB&B⇌£38.40 Lunch£3.85 Dinner£6.70–£7.15&alc Wine£3 ⊛ Credit cards ①②③④⑤⑥
★★*Cullen Bay* ☎40432
18rm(1⇌) 🎵 CTV ℗ ⊘ 150P 4🏠 ⬥ 🏊 billiards ♨ Last dinner 8.30pm sB&B£12–£12.80 sB&B⇌£14 dB&B£32 dB&B⇌fr£33.50 Lunch£4&alc Dinner£5.50&alc Wine£3.25 ⊛
Credit card ③
GH Wakes Seafield Pl ☎40251 Apr–Oct Lic 23rm 22hc (3fb) CTV 20P B&b£5.50–£6.50 Bdi£8–£9 W£45–£50 ⬥ D5pm

CULLODEN MOOR Highland Map44NH74 Inverness6 Nairn12 London557
FH Mrs E. M. C. Alexander **Culdoich** *(NH755435)* ☎268
18th-century, two-storey farmhouse in isolated position near Culloden battlefield and Clava standing stones.
Etr–Oct 2rm (1fb) ⊘ TV P 200 acres mixed S% B&B£5.50–£6 Bdi£8–£8.50 D6pm

CUMNOCK 6,348 (with Holmhead) Strathclyde Map34NS51 EcWed MdFri Ayr16 Glasgow36 London395
★★*Dumfries Arms* Glaisnock St ☎20282
7rm(2🛏) 🎵 CTV 50P Disco Fri Last dinner 8pm 🚭 🚗
✽sB&B£10.10 sB&B🛏£12.65 dB&B£17.70 dB&B🛏£20.24 Lunch£4&alc Dinner£4&alc Wine£2.60
★★*Royal* 1 Glaisnock St ☎20822
12rm 🎵 CTV CTV in 1 bedroom TV in 1 bedroom 8P 2🏠
Last dinner 9pm 🚭 🚗 sB&B£10 dB&B£20 Lunch£1–£1 Tea80p–£1 HighTea£3–£3.60 Dinner£5–£6.50 Wine£4 Credit card ①

CUSHNIE Grampian Map45NJ51 Ballater18 Alford8 Banchory19 London532
FH *Brae Smithy Croft* *(NJ520108)* ☎Muir of Fowlis215
Approach from A980 (3m) W or B9119 (3m) N.
Apr–Sep 3rm CTV P 🎵 20 acres arable

DALBEATTIE 3,649 Dumfries & Galloway Map30NX86 EcWed Castle Douglas7 Dumfries13 Kirkcudbright19 London354
★★*Pheasant* ☎610345
10rm(2⇌) 🎵 CTV CTV available in bedrooms ⚑
Last dinner 8.30pm 🚭 ✽sB&Bfr£11 sB&B⇌fr£14.95 dB&Bfr£22 dB&B⇌fr£26 Bar lunch fr£1.30 HighTea£3 Dinner£7alc Wine£3.50

DALMALLY 283 Strathclyde Map39NN12 EcWed Crianlarich17 Fort William50 Glasgow69 London482 Oban24
★★*Carraig Thura* Lochawe ☎210
16⇌🛏 🎵 CTV ℗ ⊘ 40P ⬥ ♨ Last dinner 8.30pm 🚭 🚗 sB&B£10–£14 sB&B⇌£14–£16 dB&B£18–£24 dB&B⇌🛏£22–£28 Lunch£3–£4 Tea£1–£2 HighTea£3–£4 Dinner£5–£8 Wine£3 ⊛

DALRY (ST JOHN'S TOWN OF) 432 Dumfries & Galloway Map34NX68 Ayr35 Dumfries27 London368 Newton Stewart22
★★*Lochinvar* ☎210
18rm(2⇌) ✕ CTV 40P 1🏠 ⬥ ♨ Children under 5yrs not accommodated Last dinner 7.30pm 🚭 S% sB&B£9.34 sB&B⇌£10.84 dB&B£18.74 dB&B⇌£21.74 Bar lunch fr£2 Dinner fr£5.50 Wine£2.50

DALWHINNIE Highland Map40NN68 Pitlochry31 Fort William46 Inverness57 London502
★★*Loch Ericht* ☎257
27rm(23⇌4🛏) 🏐 CTV ℗ 80P Last dinner 8.30pm 🚭 🚗 S% sB&B🛏fr£10.75 dB&B🛏fr£19 Lunch£2–£3 Tea25p–£1.80 HighTea£2.50–£4.50 Dinner£5.50 Wine£3.05 ⊛ Credit cards ③⑤

DAVIOT Highland Map44NH73 Inverness7 London559
★★*Meallmore Lodge* ☎206
Situated on the main north road, south of Daviot, this converted sandstone and granite shooting lodge was built in 1869 for the Mackintoshes of Moy
11rm(3⇌) 🎵 CTV 50P 4🏠 ⬥ ♨ Last dinner 9.30pm 🚭
🚗 sB&B£10.50–£14.50 sB&B⇌£12.50–£16.50 dB&B£21–£29 dB&B⇌£25–£33 Lunch£4.50&alc Tea75p–£1.50 HighTea£3–£3.50 Dinner£6.50–£7.50&alc Wine£3.80 ⊛ xmas Credit cards ① ⑤
FH Mrs E. MacPherson **Lairgandour** *(NH720376)* ☎207
In a quiet location, near to Culloden Moor, Loch Ness and the Cairngorms. Lies E of A9 at junction with B9154.
Apr–Sep 5rm 3hc (3fb) ⊘ CTV 5P 1,000 acres

mixed S% B&bf£5-£5.50 Bdifr£7.50 Wfr£48

DINGWALL 4,379 Highland Map43NH55 EcThu MdWed
Inverness21 London586
★★**National** High St ☎62166
A handsome red sandstone building dating from 1900 in main shopping street.
42rm(3⇌) CTV CTV in 3bedrooms 50P Last dinner8.45pm
♥ ♫ S% sB&Bfr£13.55 sB&B⇌fr£21.36
dB&Bfr£26.94 dB&B⇌fr£32.74 Lunch£3.45 Tea£1.50
Dinner£6.65 Credit cards ① ③
★**Royal** High St ☎62130
Three-storey stone building in main street.
19rm(6⇌2🛁) ♫ 💷 CTV CTV in all bedrooms ® 20P Disco 3nights wkly Live music & dancing wkly ♀ European.
Last dinner9pm ♥ ♫ sB&B£10-£12.90
sB&B⇌🛁£15.90 dB&B£20-£22.90
dB&B⇌🛁£25.90-£27.90 Lunch£2.50-£3.50
Tea£1.50 High Tea£2.50-£4.95 Dinner£3.25-£6.80
Wine£2.95 🍴 Credit cards ① ② ③ ⑤

DIRLETON 392 Lothian Map35NT58 Edinburgh22
London393 North Berwick3
★★★**HB Open Arms** ☎241 Telex no727887
Small select hotel in picturesque setting by village green, close to 13th-C castle ruin.
7rm(6⇌1🛁) 🎧 CTV CTV in all bedrooms 60P ♿ ♣ ♀Scottish & French. Last dinner10pm ♥ sB&B⇌🛁£29
dB&B⇌🛁£43 Lunch£5 Dinner£11 Wine£4.30 🍴
Credit cards ① ② ③ ④ ⑤
INN Castle ☎221 rsNov-Apr 5hc (A 4hc) CTV 12P
💷 B&b£10.50 Bdi£16 W£95 ♣ Bar lunchfr£1.50
D8.30pmfr£5.50

DORNIE Highland Map42NG82 Fort William67 Kyle of Lochalsh9 London583
FH Mrs M. Macrae Bungalow *(NG871272)* ☎231
Farmhouse situated on main A87.
rsEtr-Oct 3hc (1fb) ♿ nc5 4P mixed S% B&b£5.50-£6

DORNOCH 895 Highland Map44NH78 EcThu Dingwall41
Inverness62 Lairg22 London627
★★**Burghfield House** ☎212
Scottish baronial-style turreted mansion built for Lord Rothermere in 1910, standing in 5½ acres of tree studded grounds.
Closed 16Oct-Mar; 18rm(2⇌) Annexe: 39rm(2⇌) ♫ 💷
CTV 100P ♿ ♣ ♿ Disco twice wkly ♿ ♀ Scottish & French.
Last dinner8.30pm ♥ ♫ £14.50 sB&B⇌fr£17
dB&Bfr£29 dB&B⇌🛁fr£34 Lunchfr£5.20
Dinnerfr£8.60 Wine£3.14 🍴 Credit cards ② ③ ⑤
★★**Dornoch Castle** Castle St ☎216
450-year-old castle, former seat of Bishops of Caithness; standing in centre of town overlooking Dornoch Firth.
Closed 6Oct-8Apr; 10rm(1⇌) Annexe: 10⇌ Lift 💷 CTV ®
14P ♿ Last dinner9pm ♥ ♫ sB&B£11.50-£13.50
sB&B⇌£13.50-£15.50 dB&B£21-£25
dB&B⇌£23.50-£27.50 Bar lunchfr£5op Teafr£1.10
Dinnerfr£7 Wine£3.20 🍴 Credit card ⑤

DOUNBY Orkney Map48HY22 Kirkwall14 Stromness9
London704 (ferry Stromness-Scrabster)
FH Chinyan (HY307200) ☎Harray372
Small farm cottage overlooking Loch Harray. Free loch fishing.
2rm ♿ ♿ TV P lake 342acres arable beef D2pm

DRUMNADROCHIT 359 Highland Map43NH53
Invermoriston13 Inverness15 London568
★★**(red)**♣ **Polmaily House** ☎343
Run like a private house party, with excellent food and attentiveness to guests' comfort, this lovely Edwardian house in 20 acres of grounds is a Red Star hotel.
Closed Oct-8Apr; 9rm(5⇌) 1🛁 💷 25P ♿ ♣ ⇌ (Hard)

Children under 8yrs not accommodated ♀ International.
Last dinner9pm ♥ ♫ *sB&Bfr£10 dB&Bfr£18
dB&B⇌£20-£26 Bar lunchfr£1.50 Dinner£8.50
Wine£2.50 🍴 Credit cards ① ②
★★**Drumnadrochit** Loch Ness ☎218
26rm 💷 TV ♿ ♿(Hard) ♿ ∩ ♀French & Continental.
Last dinner8pm
★**Benleva** ☎288
RS Nov; 7rm(4🛁) CTV ® 30P ♿ ♣ Live music & dancing twice wkly ♀Scottish & French. Last dinner9pm ♥ ♫
sB&Bfr£11 sB&B⇌🛁fr£13.80 dB&Bfr£11.50
dB&B⇌🛁fr£13.80 Bar lunchfr£1.60-£4.20 Teafr60p
Dinner£4.25&alc Wine£3.20 🍴 Credit card ③
INN Lewiston Arms Hotel Lewiston ☎225
4hc (A 4hc) ♿ CTV 40P S% B&B£7.50
Bdi£12.50-£15 W£52 M Bar lunch£2alc
D8.30pmE5.50alc

DRYBRIDGE Grampian Map45NJ46 Buckie2 Elgin17
Cullen7 London599
××**Old Monastery** (1m E off Deskford Rd) ☎Buckie32660
Closed Sun, Mon, 3wks Oct & Feb; 32seats 15P
♀Scottish & French. Last dinner9.30pm Lunch£4alc
Dinner£7.50alc Wine£3.75

DRYBURGH Borders Map35NT53 Jedburgh13 Lauder13
London345 Melrose6
★★★♣**L Dryburgh Abbey** ☎St Boswells22261
Telex no727396(Dryburgh)
Turreted mansion dating from 1848 standing in 11 acres of parkland on the banks of the River Tweed.
29rm(10⇌2🛁) 3🛁 💷 CTV ® 100P 2♿ ♣ ♿
Last dinner8.30pm ♥ ♫ S% *sB&Bfr£19.80
dB&Bfr£39.20 dB&B⇌🛁fr£43.80 Lunchfr£5.95
Teafr£1.50 Dinnerfr£8.85 🍴 xmas Credit cards ① ② ③ ④ ⑤

DRYMEN 659 Central Map37NS48 EcWed Dumbarton12
Glasgow19 London432 Stirling22
★★★**H Buchanan Arms** (Scottish Highlands) ☎588
Telex no778215
Originally an 18th-C coaching inn, now modernised and extended, set by roadside in centre of small village.
23rm(21⇌) ♫ CTV in all bedrooms ® 50P ♿ ♣
Last dinner9.15pm ♥ ♫ ♫ sB&B⇌£19.25
sB&B⇌£22.25 dB&B£32.50 dB&B⇌£38.50
Lunchfr£5&alc Dinnerfr£8.50&alc Wine£3.95 🍴
xmas Credit cards ① ② ③ ④ ⑤

DULNAIN BRIDGE 119 Highland Map44NH92 EcWed
Grantown-on-Spey3 Inverness32 London543
❀★★★♣**H Muckrach Lodge** ☎257
(Rosette awarded for dinner only.)
9rm 💷 ® ♿ 50P 3♿ ♣ Last dinner8.15pm
★★**BL Skye of Curr** ☎345
8rm(1⇌) 💷 CTV ® 20P ♿ ♣ Last dinner8.30pm ♥ ♫
sB&B£10-£12 dB&B£20-£24 dB&B⇌£23-£27
Lunch£3-£3.50 Tea50p Dinner£7.50 Wine£3.25 🍴
Credit cards ① ② ③ ⑤

DUMBARTON 25,440 Strathclyde Map37NS37 EdWed
Glasgow15 London420 Stirling35 Tarbet21
★★**Dumbuck** Glasgow Rd (Scottish & Newcastle) ☎63818
RS Xmas & New Year; 25rm(10⇌🛁) ♫ 💷 CTV in all bedrooms 200P ♿ ♀ European. Last dinner9pm ♥ 🍴
Credit cards ① ② ③ ④ ⑤
×**Akram's** St Mary's Way, Church St ☎63121
80seats P Disco Fri & Sat ♀ Pakistani & Tandoori.
Last dinner11.30pm Credit cards ① ③ ⑤
×**Upstairs Downstairs** Riverside Ln ☎67828
Closed Sun & New Year's Day; 36seats ♀Mainly grills.
Last dinner9.30pm

DUMFRIES 29,431 Dumfries & Galloway Map34NX97
EcThu MdWed Carlisle35 Edinburgh79 Glasgow75
London341

The Station Hotel
★★★

Situated close to the town centre, the Station Hotel is an ideal base for visiting South West Scotland. Many rooms have private facilities, all have colour television, radio and tea/coffee making facilities.
The Hotel offers good food, 2 bars, a lift to all floors and a welcoming atmosphere.

★★★**Cairndale** English St ☎4111 Telexno777170
Closed New Years Day; 44rm(29⇌) Lift ♪ CTV CTV in all bedrooms 60P 1🐾 Last dinner 9pm ⋄ ⚯ S%
sB&B£20.50 sB&B⇌£22.50 dB&B£32 dB&B⇌£34
Lunch£5.50−£6.50&alc Tea£1.75 HighTea£2.50−£7
Dinner£7−£8&alc Wine£3.50 ♬
Credit cards ①②③④⑤⑥

★★★**Station** 49 Lovers Walk ☎4316
30rm(10⇌8⋔) Lift ♪ CTV CTV in all bedrooms ® 60P ♿
Last dinner 9pm ⋄ ⚯ ✻sB&B£16.50
sB&B⇌⋔£18.50 dB&B£22.50 dB&B⇌⋔£24.50
Lunch£3&alc HighTea£3.35 Dinner£6&alc Wine£3
♬ Credit cards ①②③⑤

★★**County** High St (Inter-Hotels) ☎5401 Telexno777205
The lounge was Bonnie Prince Charlie's headquarters in 1745.
50rm(10⇌6⋔) Lift ♪ CTV in all bedrooms ® 20P
Last dinner 10.30pm ⋄ SB&B£19.50 sB&B⇌⋔fr£19
dB&Bfr23 dB&B⇌⋔fr£27 Lunchfr£3.50
Dinnerfr£6.50 Wine£3.30 ♬
Credit cards ①②③⑤⑥

★**Embassy** Newbridge (2½ NW on A76) (Scottish & Newcastle) ☎Newbridge233
Small Regency country house standing in 16 acres of gardens with own trout stream.
6rm 🍴 CTV 100P ♨ 🎵 Disco fortnightly Last dinner 10pm ⋄ ⚯ S% ✻sB&B£9 dB&B£18 Lunch£1.75−£3
Tea60p−£1 HighTea£1.75−£3 Dinner£3−£5.50

★**Moreig** 67 Annan Rd ☎5524
10rm(1⇌) 🍴 CTV ® 40P ♿ Live music & dancing Sat Cabaret Sat ♥ Mainly grills. Last dinner 7pm ⋄
sB&B£8.50−£9.30 sB&B⇌⋔fr£8.50 dB&Bfr£17
dB&B⇌⋔£20 Lunch£2.50−£3.20
HighTea£4.50−£6.50 Dinner£6−£8 Wine£4.50 ♬

★**Skyline** 123 Irish St ☎62416
Closed New Years Day; 6rm(2⇌) 🍴 CTV CTV in bedrooms on request ⓓ 20P Last dinner 8.30pm ♬
Credit cards ②⑤

★**Swan at Kingholm** Kingholm Quay ☎3756
11rm CTV ® 50P ♿ Last dinner 8pm ⋄ ⚯ ♬
★**Winston** Rae St ☎4433
Closed Xmas & New Year; 14rm 🍴 CTV 6P
Last dinner 7.30pm ⋄ ⚯ ✻sB&B£8.05 dB&B£16.10
Lunch£2.50 Tea£1−£2 Dinner£3.50 Wine£3 ♬
GH Fullwood Private Hotel 30 Lovers Walk ☎2262
5hc (2fb) TV S% B&b£5.50 W£37.50 M
Bdi£10 W£65 Ł D5pm
GH Newhall House 22 Newall Ter ☎2676
Lic 7rm 6hc (3fb) CTV 7P 🍴 S% ✻B&b£7
Bdi£10 W£65 Ł D5pm
××**Bruno's** Balmoral Rd ☎5757
Closed Tue; Lunch not served; 70seats ⚯English, French & Italian. Last dinner 10pm Dinner£10alc
Wine£4.50

DUNBAR 4,627 Lothian Map35NT67 EcWed Berwick-upon-Tweed30 Edinburgh28 London378 North Berwick13

★★**H Bayswell** Bayswell Park ☎62225
RS Oct−Mar; 13rm(5⇌) CTV ® 16P ♿ Last dinner 7.30pm
⋄ ⚯ S% ✻sB&B£12−£14.40
sB&B⇌£16.80−£19.80 dB&B£20.40−£24
dB&B⇌£28−£33 Lunch£3−£8 Tea£1.25−£2
HighTea£3−£5 Dinner£5.50−£8&alc Wine£3.50 ♬
Credit cards ①③
GH Cruachan East Links Rd ☎63595 6hc (1fb) CTV
🍴 sea S% B&bfr£7 Bdifr£10 Wfr£67 Ł
GH Marine 7 Marine Rd ☎63315 11hc (3fb) ⓓ CTV
🍴 S% B&b£4.45−£6.50 Bdi£7−£8.50 W£44−£54
Ł D6pm
GH St Laurence North Rd ☎62527 Etr−Oct 6hc ⓓ
sea S% ✻B&bfr£6.50 Bdifr£10 Wfr£60 Ł D5pm
GH Springfield House Edinburgh Rd ☎62502
Apr−Oct 6hc (2fb) CTV 9P 🍴

DUNBLANE 5,409 Central Map40NN70 EcWed Glasgow32 London425 Perth28 Stirling6
★★★**Dunblane Hydro** (Reo Stakis) ☎822551
Telexno778704
Imposing late 19th century five-storey stone building, standing on elevated site in own spacious grounds on the northern outskirts of city.
126⇌ Lift ♪ 🍴 CTV in all bedrooms ® 1000P ♿ ▤(heated) ⚲(hard) sauna bath Disco Sat ♿ Conference facilities available ♥English & French. Last dinner 9.30pm ⋄ ⚯
✻sB&B⇌fr£24 dB&B⇌fr£36 Lunchfr£3.85&alc
Tea fr50p Dinnerfr£7.25&alc Wine£4.20 ♬ xmas
Credit cards ①②③⑤⑥
GH Altair Neuk Hotel Doune Rd ☎822562 Lic 8hc 2⋔ (2fb) CTV 10P 🍴 S% B&bfr£10 Bdifr£16 D8.45pm

DUNDEE 191,517 Tayside Map41NO33 EcWed MdTue Aberdeen68 Edinburgh57 Glasgow80
★★★**Angus** Marketgate (Thistle) ☎26874 Telexno76456
Modern hotel forming part of shopping centre.
58rm(43⇌⋔) Lift ♪ ✗ 🍴 CTV in all bedrooms ® 7P Live music & dancing nightly ♿ Conference facilities available ♥Scottish & French. Last dinner 10pm ⋄ ⚯ S%
sB&Bfr£28.90 sB&B⇌⋔fr£35.90 dB&Bfr£33.80
dB&B⇌⋔fr£45.80 Lunch£5−£6&alc Tea60p−£1
Dinner£7.60−£8.50&alc ♬ Credit cards ①②③④⑤⑥
☆☆☆**Invercarse** 371 Perth Rd, Ninewells (Thistle) ☎69231
Telexno76608
Extended private house, standing in own grounds.
27rm(5⇌22⋔) ♪ ▤ ✗ 🍴 CTV CTV in all bedrooms ® 250P
ⓓ ♿ Live music & dancing weekends ♥French.
Last dinner 9.45pm ⋄ ⚯ S% ✻sB&B⇌⋔£33.50
dB&B⇌⋔£45 Lunchfr£3.95&alc Dinnerfr£5.95&alc
Wine£3.85 ♬ Credit cards ①②③⑤
☆☆☆**Swallow** Kingsway West, Invergowrie (3½ W off A972 Dundee Ring Road) (Swallow) ☎641122 Telexno53168
Closed Xmas & New Year; 69⇌ 2☐ ♪ ▤ 🍴 CTV in all bedrooms ® 100P ♿ ⓓ ♥Scottish & French.
Last dinner 9.45pm ⋄ ⚯ S% ✻sB&B⇌£14−£26.85

dB&B⇨£28–£32 Lunch£3.25–£3.95&alc Tea30–45p Dinner£5.45–£6.75&alc Wine£3.32 ₽
Credit cards ① ② ③ ⑤ ⑥
★★**Cambustay** 8 Dalhousie Rd (Ind Coope (Alloa)) ☎79290
8rm CTV ® 100P ⚓ Last dinner 9.30pm ✧ S%
sB&B£12.50 dB&B£21 Lunch£4.50
Wine£2.30 ₽ Credit cards ① ② ③
★★**Kellyfield** Drumgeith Rd (Reo Stakis) ☎454522
A converted private house standing in own grounds on edge of housing estate.
8rm(1⇨🏠) 🎵 CTV in all bedrooms ® ⊘ 100P Live music & dancing Thu & Sun ♀ Mainly grills. Last dinner9pm ⚲
Credit cards ① ② ③
★★**Queens** 160 Nethergate (Trusthouse Forte) ☎22515
56rm(11⇨1🏠) Lift ♪ 🎵 CTV in all bedrooms ® 40P ⊚
Last dinner9.15pm ✧ ⚲ S% sB&B£19.60–£21.10
sB&B⇨🏠£22.10–£24.10 dB&B£28.20–£30.20
dB&B⇨🏠£33.20–£35.70 ₽ Credit cards ① ② ③ ④ ⑤ ⑥
★★**Tay** Whitehall Cres ☎21641 Telex no 76296
Five-storey city centre hotel on Tay Road Bridge approach road.
87rm(31⇨) Lift ♪ CTV in all bedrooms ® ♣ Disco 3 nights wkly Conference facilities available ♀ Italian.
Last dinner9pm ✧ ⚲ S% sB&Bfr£17
sB&B⇨🏠fr£22.25 dB&Bfr£19.50 dB&B⇨🏠fr£32.50
Lunch fr£4 High Tea fr£3 Dinner fr£5 Wine£4 ₽ *xmas*
Credit cards ① ② ③ ⑤ ⑥
★★**Tay Park** Broughty Ferry (3m E A930) ☎78924
Fine country mansion, situated in its own terraced grounds commanding magnificent views of the River Tay estuary and opposite Fife shore.
11rm(4⇨) ♪ 🎵 CTV in all bedrooms ® 100P ⚓ ⊚
✱International. Last dinner9.30pm ✧ ⚲ S%
✱sB&Bfr£13 sB&B⇨fr£18.30 dB&Bfr£23.60
dB&B⇨fr£32.60 Lunch£5.40&alc Tea£1.20–£1.90
High Tea£2.50–£5 Dinner fr£6.80 Wine£4 ₽
Credit cards ① ② ③ ⑤

DUNDONNELL Highland Map43 NH08 Gairloch30 Inverness62 London627 Ullapool26
★★**Dundonnell** ☎204
RS Nov–Feb; 26rm(20⇨🏠) 🎵 60P ⚓ Last dinner8.30pm
✧ ⚲ Credit cards ② ⑤

DUNFERMLINE 53,418 Fife Map35 NT08 EcWed **See also Kingseat** Crieff31 Edinburgh17 London435 Perth30 Stirling22
✩✩✩**King Malcolm** Queensferry Rd, Wester Pitcorthie (Thistle) ☎22611
Modern low-rise hotel in residential situation on the outskirts of town.
48⇨🏠 ♪ ✗ 🎵 CTV CTV in all bedrooms ® 60P ⚓
Disco Sun Cabaret Wed ♀ French. Last dinner9.30pm
⚲ S% ✱sB&B⇨🏠£34.20 dB&B⇨🏠£31.80–£47.60
Lunch£4.75&alc Tea£1.25 Dinner£7.50&alc
Wine£3.50 ₽ Credit cards ① ② ③ ④ ⑤ ⑥
★★**Brucefield** Woodmill Rd ☎22199
Converted Victorian mansion dating from 1845 and standing in own grounds.
9rm(6⇨) 🎵 CTV TV in 3 bedrooms 70P Last dinner8pm ✧
⚲ S% ✱sB&B⇨🏠fr£9 sB&Bfr£12 dB&Bfr£17
dB&Bfr£25 Lunchfr£3 Tea£1.50 High Tea fr£3
Dinner fr£6.10 Wine£3.75 Credit card ①
★★**City** 18 Bridge St ☎22538
City centre hotel of considerable age standing on main road in shopping centre.
17rm(3⇨🏠) 🎵 CTV ® ⊘ 20P Last dinner8.45pm ✧
sB&B£13.22 sB&B⇨£17.25 dB&B£22.42
dB&B⇨£25.87 Lunch£3.93alc Tea£1.50alc
HighTea£4.31alc Dinner£7.76alc Wine£3.50

DUNKELD 273 Tayside Map40 NO04 EcThu Aberfeldy18 London463 Perth15 Pitlochry15
★★★👑L **Dunkeld House** ☎243

Closed Nov–13Jan; 28rm(23⇨🏠) 🎵 CTV in all bedrooms 50P 5⊚ ⚓ ✗ ⚲(hard) ♾ Live music & dancing Sat
♀ English & French. Last dinner9pm ✧ ⚲ ₽
Credit card ⑥
★★**Atholl Arms** Bridgehead ☎219
24rm CTV 20P ⚓ Last dinner8.15pm ⚲ S%
sB&B£11 dB&B£22 Bar lunch£1–£2.50
Tea£1.25–£1.50 Dinner£6–£7 Wine£3.90 ₽
Credit cards ① ② ③ ⑤ ⑥
★**Taybank** Tay Ter ☎340
RS Nov–Feb; 7rm CTV 30P ⇔ ⚓ Last dinner8pm

DUNLOP Strathclyde Map34 NS44 Glasgow17 Kilmarnock9 Paisley13 London415
FH Mr & Mrs R. B. Wilson **Struther** (*NS412496*) ☎346
Larger farmhouse in its own gardens. On edge of Dunlop village.
6hc (2fb) CTV 10P 50acres non-working
B&B£6.50–£7.50 Bdi£13.50–£14.50 W£90 ₺
D8.30pm

DUNNET 681 Highland Map47 ND27 Inverness140 John O'Groats12 London705 Thurso9
★★**Northern Sands** ☎Barrock270
13rm(1⇨) 🎵 CTV 100P ⇔ ♾ Live music & dancing Sat ⊚
♀ Italian. Last dinner8.45pm ✧ ⚲ sB&B£10
sB&B⇨£11 dB&B£20 dB&B⇨£22 Bar lunch£2alc
Tea£1.50alc HighTea£2.50alc Dinner£5alc
Wine£4.37 Credit card ③

DUNOON 8,899 Strathclyde Map33 NS17 EcWed
Glasgow76(fy26) Inveraray39 London479 Tarbet41
★★**Abbeyhill** Dhailling Rd ☎2204
11rm(8⇨3🏠) 🎵 CTV CTV in all bedrooms ® 40P ⚓
Last dinner8.30pm ✧ ⚲ sB&B£12 sB&B⇨🏠£15
dB&B£20 dB&B⇨🏠£25 Lunch£3 Teafr50p
High Tea£2 Dinner£7 Wine£3.60
★★**Ardfillayne** West Bay ☎2267
12rm(2⇨🏠) 🎵 CTV TV available in bedrooms 20P 1⊚ ⇔ ⚓
Last dinner11pm ✧ ⚲
★★**Ardnadam House** Ardnadam (3m N A815)
☎Sandbank210
6rm(2⇨🏠) 🎵 CTV CTV in 4bedrooms ® 20P ⇔ ⚓ Children under 5yrs not accommodated. ♀ English & French.
Last dinner9pm sB&B£15–£17.50 dB&B£25–£30
dB&B⇨🏠£30–£35 Dinner£8.50alc Wine£3.95
★★**Argyll** ☎2059
In central situation close to pier.
23rm(6⇨) CTV ® ⚓ Last dinner8pm ♣ ⚲
✱sB&B£7.50–£11.04 sB&B⇨£8.50–£13.34
dB&B£15–£22.08 dB&B⇨£14.24.38 Lunch£3.05
Tea fr40p High Tea£2.82 Dinner£4.20 Wine£2.95 ₽
Credit cards ① ⑥
★★**McColl's** West Bay (Osprey) ☎2764
58rm(12⇨) Lift ♪ 🎵 CTV CTV in 11 bedrooms ® 10P Live music & dancing 4nights ♀ Scottish & French.
Last dinner9.30pm ⚲ S% sB&B£13.05
sB&B⇨£16 dB&B£23 dB&B⇨£25.50
Lunch£3.50&alc Tea£1 High Tea£2.50 Dinner£5&alc
Wine£3.50 ₽ *xmas* Credit cards ① ② ③ ④ ⑤
★★**Queens** Marine Pde, Kirn ☎4224
Substantial stone building overlooking Firth of Clyde.
20rm 🎵 CTV 20P ⚓ Last dinner8.15pm
sB&B£10–£10.55 dB&B£20 Bar lunch£1.50–£2.50
Dinner£4.75–£6.50 Wine£2.96
★★**Royal Marine** Sea Front, Hunters Quay (2m N A815)
☎3001
34rm(1⇨) Annexe: 10rm(8🏠) ♪ 🎵 CTV CTV in 15bedrooms 24P ⚓ Disco Fri & Sat Live music & dancing wknds ⊚ Last dinner9pm ✧ ⚲ S% sB&B£15–£17
sB&B⇨🏠£17–£19 dB&B£28–£32
dB&B⇨🏠£32–£36 Lunch£1–£3.50 High Tea£1–£3
Dinner£3.50–£6.50&alc Wine£3.70 ₽ *xmas*
Credit cards ① ② ③ ⑥
GH Cedars Private Hotel Alexandra Pde ☎2425

Dunoon contd—**Eddleston**

Feb–Dec Lic 14hc 2⇌ (2fb) CTV ⋈ sea S%
*B&b£7.47–£8.91 Bdi£11.50–£12.93
W£72.45–£82.80 ᄂ D5.30pm

DUNSYRE Strathclyde Map35NT04 Lanark14 Peebles16 Edinburgh24 London388
FH Mr L. Armstrong **Dunsyre Mains** (NT074482) ☎251
A two-storey stone farmhouse dating from 1800 in courtyard style with splendid views and small garden.
Mar–Oct 3rm 2hc (1fb) ⊗ CTV P 400acres beef sheep S% B&bfr£5.50 Bdifr£9.50 Wfr£66 ᄂ D6pm

DUNTOCHER 3,532 Strathclyde Map37NS47 EcWed Dumbarton7 Glasgow9 London414
★★ **Maltings** Dumbarton Rd ☎75371
This timber built hotel lies just off the A82, about 1½m E of the Erskine Bridge.
29⇌⋒ D ⋈ CTV CTV in all bedrooms ® 150P Disco twice wkly Live music & dancing twice wkly Cabaret twice wkly ⊗ ♀ Scottish & French. Last dinner9pm ⋫ ♀ ⛿
Credit cards ② ③ ⑤ ⑥

DUNTULM Isle of Skye, Highland Map42NG47 Uig9 Portree25 Staffin9 Kyleakin59 Armadale67 London647
★ **Duntulm** ☎213
Closed Oct–9Apr; 15rm(3⇌3⋒) Annexe: 13rm TV 20P ᄂ ⋫ & Last dinner8.15pm ⋫ ♀ S% sB&B£8–£8.50 sB&B⇌⋒£9.50–£10.50 dB&B£17–£18 dB&B⇌⋒£21
Lunch£3.50alc Tea£1alc HighTea£2.50alc
Dinner£5.50alc Wine£3 ⛿

DUNVEGAN 301 Isle of Skye, Highland Map48NG24 Armadale57 Kyleakin49 Portree22 Uig28
★★ **Dunvegan** ☎202
6rm Annexe: 10rm(3⇌⋒) ⋈ 50P ⋒ ᄂ ⋫ Ω Live music 6nights wkly Live music & dancing 3nights wkly Cabaret 2nights wkly Children under 1yr not accommodated
Last dinner8pm ⋫ ♀ Credit cards ① ③
GH Argyll House Kensalroy, Roskhill (3m S A863) ☎230
Etr–Oct 6rm 5hc (1fb) TV 6P ⋈ lake S% B&b£5.25 Bdi£8 D7pm
GH Roskhill Roskhill (3m S A863) ☎317 Mar–Dec 5hc (2fb) TV 6P ⋈ S% B&b£6.50–£6.90
Bdi£10.25–£10.75 D6.15pm
FH Mr A. Munro **Feorlig House** (NG297422) ☎232
Two-storey, white-painted farmhouse dating from 1820. Situated off main road looking onto Loch Cavoy.
Apr–Sep 3rm TV 10P lake 1,112acres beef sheep S% B&b£5 Bdi£8.50–£10 W£59.50–£70 ᄂ D7pm

DUROR 102 Highland Map39NM95 Crianlarich45 Fort William19 London510 Oban31
★★ **L Stewart** (Inter-Hotel) ☎268 Telex no778866
Closed Nov–Jan; RS Feb & Mar; 29⇌⋒ ⋈ CTV TV available in bedrooms ® 50P ⋒ ᄂ ⋫ Music & dancing Sat ♀ Scottish, English & French. Last dinner8.30pm ⋫ ♀
sB&B⇌£15.50–£23.50 dB&B⇌£21–£37
Lunch£2.20alc Tea80p Dinner£8.50–£9.50
Wine£3.40 ⛿ Credit cards ① ② ③ ⑤ ⑥

EAGLESFIELD Dumfries & Galloway Map31NY27 Annan7 Dumfries20 Locherbie8 London326
FH Mrs S. Johnstone **Newlands** (NY240741)
☎Kirtlebridge269
Attractive white-faced farmhouse in secluded position at end of ½ mile drive.
May–Oct 2hc (1fb) ⊗ CTV 2P ⋈ 150acres mixed S% B&b£5 Bdi£7.50 W£52.50 ᄂ D6pm

EAGLESHAM 2,788 Strathclyde Map37NS55 EcTue London399 East Kilbride5 Glasgow10 Kilmarnock14
★★ **Eglinton Arms** Gilmour St (Scottish & Newcastle)
☎2631
12⇌⋒ D ⋈ CTV in all bedrooms ® 60P Disco Sun Live music & dancing Mon Last dinner9.30pm ⋫ ⛿

×× **Pepper Pot** Cross Keys Inn ☎2002
Closed Sun; 70seats 40P ♀ Scottish & French.
Last dinner9.30pm *Lunch fr£3.75&alc Dinner£10alc Wine£3.65 Credit cards ① ③ ⑥

EASDALE Strathclyde Map38NM71 EcWed Fort William65 Glasgow109 London521 Oban16
★★ ⚘ **Dunmor House** ☎Balvicar203
Delightful, white-painted house with views of the Atlantic and Isle of Scarba.
Closed 17Oct–Apr; 11rm(3⇌2⋒) TV ® 30P 6⛿ ⋒ ᄂ
Last dinner9pm ♀ sB&Bfr£15 dB&Bfr£23
dB&B⇌⋒fr£33 Lunch£3alc Tea£1.50alc
Dinner fr£7.50 Wine£4

EAST CALDER Lothian Map35NT06 Edinburgh12 Bathgate10 London403
FH Mr & Mrs D. R. Scott **Whitecroft** 7 Raw Holdings (NT095682) ☎Mid Calder881810
Surrounded by farmland and only ½ mile from Almondell Country Park. Good views of Pentlands to the south and Ochils and Forth road bridge to the north.
3rm (1fb) ⊗ CTV 3P ⋈ 5acres arable S% B&b£5.50 W£38.50 M

EAST KILBRIDE 76,000 Strathclyde Map37NS65 EcWed Glasgow9 Hamilton6 London399
☆☆☆ **Bruce** Cornwall St (Swallow) ☎29771 Telex no778428
Modern custom-built hotel forming part of New Town complex.
84⇌⋒ Lift D ⊞ ⋈ CTV in all bedrooms ® 32P 12⛿
Disco Sun Live music & dancing Thu Conference facilities available ♀ French. Last dinner10pm ⋫ ♀ S%
sB&B⇌⋒£26–£28.50 dB&B⇌⋒£36.50
Lunch£2.30–£2.90 Tea50–90p
Dinner£5.75–£6.50&alc Wine£3.95 ⛿
Credit cards ① ② ③ ④ ⑤ ⑥
☆☆ **Stuart** Cornwall Way (Thistle) ☎21161
29⇌⋒ Lift D ⋈ TV 200P Music & dancing Sat
Last dinner9.30pm ⋫ ♀ Credit cards ① ② ③ ④ ⑤ ⑥
★★ **Crutherland Country House** Stratheven Rd ☎37633
Closed 1&2Jan; RS Sun; 21rm(5⇌3⋒) D ⋈ CTV in all bedrooms ® 300P ⋒ ᄂ ⋫ Last dinner10pm S%
*sB&B⇌⋒£22 dB&B⇌⋒£30 Lunch£2.80&alc
Dinner£8&alc Wine£4.20 Credit cards ① ② ③
★★ **Torrance** Main St (Scottish & Newcastle) ☎25241
Large 200 year old former coaching inn, in centre of original village of East Kilbride.
26rm(7⇌⋒) D ⋈ CTV TV available in bedrooms 100P
Last dinner9pm ⛿ Credit cards ① ② ③ ⑤ ⑥

EAST LINTON 878 Lothian Map35NT57 EcWed Edinburgh23 London387 North Berwick9
★★★ **Harvesters** (Best Western) ☎395 Telex no8814912
An intimate Georgian house standing in 3½ acres of well-tended gardens beside the River Tyne. The interior is well decorated.
Closed 15Dec–19Jan; 6rm(4⇌⋒) Annexe: 7rm(4⇌⋒) ⋈ CTV ® 45P 1⛿ ⋒ ᄂ ⋫ Disco nightly ⋫ ♀ International.
Last dinner8.30pm ⋫ ⛿ Credit cards ① ② ③ ④ ⑤ ⑥

EAST MEY Highland Map47ND37 Thurso14 Wick20 London695
FH Mrs M. Morrison **Glenearn** (ND307739) ☎Barrock608
Small croft situated on the main coast road. Thurso 15 miles.
Etr–Oct 4rm (2hc) (2fb) CTV 5P sea 7½acres mixed
S% B&b£5–£5.30 Bdi£8–£8.50 D2pm

EDDLESTON Borders Map35NT24 Peebles5 Edinburgh19 Dalkeith16 London382
×× **Horse Shoe Inn** ☎225
Closed 25Dec & 1Jan; 60seats 30P Last dinner10pm

Edinburgh

*Lunch £3.95 – £9.95 &alc   Dinner £3.95 – £9.95 &alc
Wine £4.60   Credit cards ① ② ③ ⑤ ⑥

EDINBURGH plan – see page 210 456,512 Lothian Map 35 NT 27 MdTue cattle Wed Aberdeen 128 Ayr 73 Fort William 135 Glasgow 45 Inverness 161 London 405 Oban 124 Perth 44 Stirling 37

★★★★**Caledonian** Princes St ☎031-225 2433
Telex no 72179
213rm(205⇌) Lift ⊅ ﹫150P ♣ ♀English & French.
Last dinner 11pm   ⊅   S% *sB&B⇌﹫£31.40–£34
sB&B⇌£34.50–£36   dB&B⇌﹫£53.50–£67.50
Lunch £5–£6 Tea fr £1.45 Dinner fr £8 Wine £5.25 ♬
Credit cards ① ② ③ ④ ⑤ ⑥

★★★★**George** George St (Grand Met) ☎031-225 1251
200rm⇌﹫ Lift ⊅ 田 ﹫CTV CTV available in bedrooms
Conference facilities available ♀   S%
*sB&B⇌﹫£25–£32   dB&B⇌﹫£36–£44   Wine £4.75
♬   xmas   Credit cards ① ② ③ ④ ⑤ ⑥

★★★★**North British** Princes St ☎031-556 2412
Telex no 72332
A traditional style railway hotel, located in the city centre.
193rm(171⇌) Lift ⊅ ﹫16P Last dinner 10.30pm ♦
S%   *sB&B⇌£24.40   sB&B⇌£34.95   dB&B⇌£44.75
dB&B⇌£60.90   Lunch fr £4.50 &alc   Tea fr £1.75
Dinner £6 alc   Wine £5.50 ♬   Credit cards ① ② ③ ④ ⑤ ⑥

☆☆☆**Royal Scot** 111 Glasgow Rd (Swallow)
☎031-334 9191 Telex no 727197
258rm⇌﹫ Lift ⊅ ﹫CTV in all bedrooms ® 300P
sauna bath Conference facilities available ♀ International.
Last dinner 10.30pm   ⊅   S%   *sB&B⇌﹫£27
dB&B⇌﹫£37   Lunch £5.50 &alc   Tea £1.20
High Tea £3.75   Dinner £7.50 &alc   Wine £3.07 ♬   xmas
Credit cards ① ② ③ ④ ⑤ ⑥

★★★**Albany** 39–43 Albany St ☎031-556 0397
22rm⇌﹫ ⊅ ⊀ ﹫CTV in all bedrooms ® ♣ ♀ French, German, Italian & Swiss Last dinner 10.30pm ♦
sB&B⇌﹫£24–£34   dB&B⇌﹫£28–£44   Lunch £4.50 alc
Tea £1ea   Dinner £7.50 &alc   Wine £4.85 ♬   xmas
Credit cards ① ② ③ ⑤ ⑥

★★★**Barnton** Queensferry Rd, Barnton (Thistle)
☎031-339 1144 Telex no 727928
51rm(29⇌22﹫) Lift ⊅ ⊀ ﹫CTV in all bedrooms ® 100P
Live music & dancing Sat Conference facilities available
♀ Scottish & French. Last dinner 10pm   ⊅   S%
*sB&B⇌﹫£33.93   dB&B⇌﹫£40.25
Lunch £4.50–£4.90 &alc   Tea 50p–£1.95   High Tea £3.50
Dinner £6.50–£7.75 &alc ♬   xmas
Credit cards ① ② ③ ④ ⑤ ⑥

★★★**Braid Hills** Braid Rd, Braid Hills (2½m SA702)
☎031-447 8888
Built in 1886 and standing in own grounds, off A702, hotel offers wide panorama of Edinburgh and Pentland Hills.
50rm(23⇌1﹫) ⊅ ﹫CTV TV in 4 bedrooms CTV in 10 bedrooms 35P ♣ ♀ Scottish, English & French.
Last dinner 8.45pm   ⊅   sB&B £15–£18
sB&B⇌﹫£18.50–£20   dB&B⇌£27–£30
dB&B⇌﹫£32–£39   Lunch £4.80–£5.50 &alc
Tea £2–£2.75   Dinner £6–£8 &alc   Wine £3.50 ♬
Credit cards ① ② ③ ⑤ ⑥

★★★**Bruntsfield** 69–74 Bruntsfield Pl (Best Western)
☎031-229 1393
Conversion of six adjoining houses dating from 1862, overlooking Bruntsfield Links.
53rm(26⇌1﹫) Lift ⊅ ﹫CTV CTV in 31 bedrooms 20P ⇌
Conference facilities available ♀ Mainly grills.
Last dinner 9.45pm   ⊅   S%   sB&B⇌﹫£16.10–£20.30
sB&B⇌﹫£20.70–£25.30   dB&B £26.45–£31.05
dB&B⇌﹫£33.35–£40.25   Bar lunch £1–£3.50
Tea 50p–£1   Dinner £7 &alc   Wine £4 ♬   xmas
Credit cards ① ② ③ ⑤ ⑥

★★★**Carlton** North Bridge (Scottish Highland)
☎031-556 7277 Telex no 778215
97⇌ Lift ⊅ ﹫CTV in 92 bedrooms ® ♣ Conference facilities available Last dinner 9pm   ⊅   S%

sB&B⇌£24.20   dB&B⇌£42.40   Lunch fr £5 &alc
Dinner fr £7.50 &alc   Wine £3.95 ♬   xmas
Credit cards ① ② ③ ④ ⑤ ⑥

☆☆☆**Crest** Queensferry Rd (Crest) ☎031-332 2442
Telex no 72541
Modern hotel situated 1m from city centre on main road from Edinburgh to Forth Road Bridge.
120rm(60⇌60﹫) Lift ⊅ ﹫CTV CTV in all bedrooms ®
120P ♣ Last dinner 9.45pm   ⊅   S%
*sB&B⇌﹫fr £28.10   dB&B⇌﹫£38.20   Lunch fr £6
Tea 45p   Dinner fr £5.80 ♬   Credit cards ① ② ③ ④ ⑤ ⑥

★★★**Ellersly House** Ellersly Rd (Allied (Scotland))
☎031-337 6888 Telex no 76357
Former private mansion, now extended, west of city centre close to A8.
54rm⇌ Lift ⊅ ® 70P ♣ Live music & dancing 3 nights wkly
♦ ♀ English & French. Last dinner 9pm   ⊅
sB&B⇌﹫fr £21   dB&B⇌﹫fr £35   Lunch fr £6   Tea fr £1.50
Dinner fr £7.50   Wine £2.10 ♬   xmas
Credit cards ① ② ③ ④ ⑤ ⑥

★★★ **L Howard** Great King St ☎031-556 1393
Telex no 727887
26rm(18⇌0﹫) Lift ⊅ TV in 5 bedrooms CTV in 21 bedrooms ® 13P ♣ Conference facilities available Last dinner 9.45pm   ⊅   *sB&B⇌﹫£23–£24
dB&B⇌﹫£35–£39.50   Lunch £5.40 alc   Tea 60p alc
Dinner £9.50 alc   Wine £5.10 ♬
Credit cards ① ② ③ ④ ⑤ ⑥

☆☆☆**King James** 107 St James Centre (Thistle)
☎031-556 0111
160rm(116⇌44﹫) Lift ⊅ ⊀ ﹫CTV in all bedrooms ® 12P
Disco nightly Cabaret Mon–Sat (May–10 Oct) Conference facilities available ♀ Scottish & French. Last dinner 9.45pm
⊅   S%   sB&B⇌﹫£36.45   dB&B⇌﹫£47.40
Lunch £4.75 &alc   Dinner £6.50 &alc   Wine £3.37 ♬
Credit cards ① ② ③ ④ ⑤ ⑥

★★★**Oratava** 41–43 Craigmillar Pk ☎031-667 9484
Telex no 727401
54rm(45⇌9﹫) Lift ⊅ ﹫CTV in all bedrooms 80P Live music & dancing Fri/Sat (Oct–Apr) Cabaret Mon–Sat (May–Oct) ♀ International. Last dinner 9.45pm   ⊅
sB&B⇌﹫£19.75–£21   dB&B⇌﹫£27.50–£31
Lunch £2.30–£4 &alc   Dinner £7–£10 &alc ♬   xmas
Credit cards ① ② ③ ④ ⑤ ⑥

☆☆☆**Post House** Corstorphine Rd (Trusthouse Forte)
☎031-334 8221 Telex no 727103
208rm⇌ Lift ⊅ ﹫CTV in all bedrooms ® 158P ♣
Conference facilities available Last dinner 10.15pm   ⊅
⊅   S%   sB&B⇌﹫£30.30–£32.80
dB&B⇌﹫£42.20–£45.70 ♬   xmas
Credit cards ① ② ③ ④ ⑤ ⑥

★★★ **BL Roxburghe** Charlotte Sq (Prestige)
☎031-225 3921 Telex no 727054
78rm(49⇌14﹫) Lift ⊅ ﹫CTV in all bedrooms ® ♣
Conference facilities available ♀ International.
Last dinner 10pm   ⊅   S%   sB&B⇌﹫£20–£25
sB&B⇌﹫£25–£35   dB&B⇌£35–£48
dB&B⇌﹫£40–£60   Lunch £6 &alc   Tea £1.25
High Tea £3 &alc   Dinner £8 &alc   Wine £4.25 ♬
Credit cards ① ② ③ ⑤ ⑥

★★**Clarendon** Grosvenor St (Scottish Highland)
☎031-337 7033 Telex no 7788215
Closed Oct–Mar; 46rm(30⇌10﹫) Lift ⊅ CTV ® ♣
Last dinner 8.30pm   ⊅   S%   sB&B⇌﹫£19.35
sB&B⇌﹫£22.25   dB&B⇌£32.50   dB&B⇌﹫£38.50
Bar lunch £2 alc   Dinner £7.50   Wine £3.95
Credit cards ① ② ③ ④ ⑤ ⑥

☆☆**Commodore** West Marine Dr, Cramond Foreshore (Reo Stakis) ☎031-336 1700 Telex no 778704
Set in parkland on the Cramond foreshore, the hotel overlooks Firth of Forth.
49rm⇌ Lift ⊅ ﹫CTV in all bedrooms ® 150P ♀ English & French. Last dinner 9.45pm   ⊅   *sB&B⇌﹫fr £24
dB&B⇌﹫fr £34   Lunch fr £2.25 &alc   Tea fr 40p
Dinner fr £7.50 &alc   Wine £3 ♬   xmas

Edinburgh contd

Credit cards ① ② ③ ⑤ ⑥
★★**Grosvenor Centre** Grosvenor St (Crest)
☎031-226 6001 Telex no 72445
160rm(37⇨) Lift ⅅ ✠ CTV TV in all bedrooms ® Live music & dancing wkly Conference facilities available ♀ Scottish & French. Last dinner 9.30pm ⇕ ⅃ S% ✱sB&B£20.45 sB&B⇨£30.70 dB&B£30.05 dB&B⇨£39.05
Lunch£5.25&alc High Tea£1.75&alc Dinner£5.25
Wine£3.95 ℝ xmas Credit cards ① ② ③ ⑤ ⑥
★★**Hailes** 2 Wester Hailes Centre (Scottish & Newcastle)
☎031-442 3382
RS Sat & Sun; 17⇨ ⅃ ⅅ ✠ CTV ® ✻ 750P ➞ Disco Sat
Live music & dancing Fri ♀ French. Last dinner 9.30pm ⇕ ⅃ S% sB&B⇨ⅿ£22.50 dB&B⇨ⅿ£25 Lunch£5alc Tea40-65p Dinner£5alc Wine£3.50
Credit cards ① ③ ⑤ ⑥
★★**Harp** St John's Rd, Corstorphine (3½m W on A8) (Osprey) ☎031-334 4750
20rm(8⇨) ⅅ ✠ CTV CTV in 8 bedrooms ® 60P ♀ Scottish & French. Last dinner 9.30pm ⇕ ⅃ S% sB&B£14.50 sB&B⇨£18 dB&B£25 dB&B⇨£29.50
Lunch£3.50&alc Tea£1 High Tea£2.50 Dinner£5&alc
Wine£3.50 ℝ xmas Credit cards ① ② ③ ④ ⑤
★★**Iona** Strathearn Pl ☎031-447 6264
Situated in quiet district on south side of Edinburgh.
17rm ✠ CTV ® 20P ➞ ⅃ Last dinner 8.30pm sB&B£13 dB&B£25 Lunch£3.50 High Tea£2.50 Dinner£5.50alc Wine£3.25
★★**Mount Royal** 53 Princes St (Allied (Scotland))
☎031-225 7161 Telex no 76357
156rm(156⇨50ⅿ) Lift ⅅ ✠ TV in all bedrooms ®
Last dinner 8.30pm ⇕ ⅃ S% sB&B⇨ⅿ fr£22
dB&B⇨ⅿ fr£33 Bar lunch fr£2 Dinner fr£7.50
Wine£2.10 ℝ Credit cards ① ② ③ ④ ⑤
★★**Murrayfield** 18 Corstorphine Rd (Ind Coope (Alloa))
☎031-337 1844
22rm(7⇨) Annexe 14rm ⅅ CTV CTV in all bedrooms ® 40P
Last dinner 9.30pm ⇕ ⅃ S% ✱sB&Bfr£17
sB&B⇨ fr£19.50 dB&Bfr£27 dB&B⇨ fr£29.50
Lunch fr£3 Tea fr40p Dinner fr£5.95 Wine£2.30 ℝ
Credit cards ① ② ③ ⑤ ⑥
★★**Old Waverley** Princes St (Scottish Highland)
☎031-556 4648 Telex no 778215
72rm(46⇨) Lift ⅅ CTV CTV in all bedrooms ® ℙ
Conference facilities available Last dinner 8.45pm ⇕ ⅃ S% sB&B£19.95 sB&B⇨£22.95 dB&B£33.90
dB&B⇨£39.90 Lunch£2alc Dinner fr£7.50 Wine£3.95
ℝ xmas Credit cards ① ② ③ ⑤ ⑥
★★**St Andrew** 8-10 South St Andrew St ☎031-556 8774
A traditional hotel, set in the city centre, just off Princes Street.
42rm(9⇨ⅿ) Lift ⅅ ✠ CTV CTV in 9 bedrooms ® ℙ
♀ Scottish & French. Last dinner 9pm ⇕ S%
✱sB&B£17-£19 sB&B⇨ⅿ£19-£21 dB&B£28-£32
dB&B⇨ⅿ£32-£36 Lunch£3.50-£4 Dinner£4.50-£5
Wine£1.50 ℝ Credit cards ① ② ③ ④ ⑤

The Ladbroke Dragonara Hotel, Edinburgh, is the Centre of Attractions

This recently built hotel is only a few minutes away from Princes Street, Edinburgh Castle and the Royal Mile. It's superb restaurant overlooks the Water of Leith and the Granary Bar is tastefully renovated from an original 19th century mill.

You'll find plenty of exciting holiday ideas in our Lazydays brochure — try a Scottish Weekaway — tailor made for touring in your own car, take a Welcome Break from as little as £30.00 per person bed & breakfast.

For your Lazydays brochure, 'phone 01-734 6000 or write to PO Box 137, Watford, Herts. WD1 1DN.

Ladbroke Dragonara Hotel,
Belford Road,
Edinburgh EH4 3DG
Tel: 031-332 2545

★**Georgian** 5-6 Dean Ter ☎031-332 4520
12rm(6⇨6ⅿ) ✠ CTV TV in all bedrooms ® ℙ
Last dinner 10pm ⇕ ⅃ S%
✱sB&B⇨ⅿ£11.13-£15.06 dB&B⇨ⅿ£19.48-£24.60
Bar lunch fr£1.20&alc Tea fr50p High Tea fr£1.50
Dinner fr£4.50&alc Wine£3.25 xmas Credit card ②
○ **Ladbroke Dragonara** Bells Mills Belford Rd (Ladbroke)
☎031-332 2545 146⇨ 88P
GH Adam Hotel 19 Lansdowne Cres ☎031-337 1148 Lic
9hc (1fb) CTV ⅃ D6pm
GH Ben Doran Hotel 11 Mayfield Gdns ☎031-667 8488
Closed 23-30 Dec 9hc (5fb) CTV 7P S%
B&b£6-£7.50 W£35-£48 M (W only Nov-Jun)
GH Boisdale Hotel 9 Coates Gdns ☎031-337 4392 11hc
3⇨ (4fb) CTV ✠ S% B&b£5.50-£10
Bdi£8-£12.50 D7.30pm
GH Clans Hotel 4 Magdala Cres ☎031-337 6301 8hc
(3fb) ✠ CTV ✠ S% B&b£7-£9.50
GH Cumberland Hotel 1 West Coates ☎031-337 1198
8hc (4fb) ✾ CTV 9P ✠ S% B&b£9-£11
W£56-£70 M
GH Dorstan Private Hotel 7 Priestfield Rd
☎031-667 6721 Closed Xmas & New Year 14hc 3⇨
1ⅿ CTV 10P ✠ S% B&b£8.22-£9
Bdi£14.54-£15.32 W£100 ⅃ Dam
GH Eden 12 Osbourne Ter ☎031-337 4185 6hc (2fb)
✾ 8P ✠ S% B&b£8-£9
GH Elmington House Private Hotel 45 Leamington Ter
☎031-229 1164 Lic 7hc 3ⅿ (2fb) CTV TV available
in some bedrooms ✠ S% B&b£6.50 Bdi£9 D6pm
GH Galloway 22 Dean Park Cres ☎031-332 3672 8hc
1⇨ⅿ (2fb) CTV ✠ D5pm
GH Glendale 5 Lady Rd ☎031-667 6588 7hc (2fb) ✾
nc3 CTV 8P ✠ S% B&b£7.50-£9
GH Glenisla Hotel 12 Lygon Rd ☎031-667 4098 9hc
(1fb) CTV 5P ✠ S% B&b fr£8.50 Bdi fr£12 D2.30pm
GH Golf View Hotel 2 Marchall Rd (off Dalkeith Rd)
☎031-667 4812 Apr-Oct Lic 11hc 4⇨ 2ⅿ (3fb)
CTV 12P ✠ S% B&b£8.05-£11.50
GH Greenside Hotel 9 Royal Ter ☎031-557 0022
Feb-Nov 12hc 1⇨ 1ⅿ (3fb) CTV ✠ river
B&b£10.35-£12.65
GH Grosvenor 1 Grosvenor Gdns, Haymarket
☎031-337 4143 7hc 2⇨ⅿ (3fb) TV ✠
GH Halcyon Hotel 8 Royal Ter ☎031-556 1033 *Where meal terms are included in the prices, these meals are taken at Peppermills Restaurant, 4A Royal Terrace.* Feb-Nov
16hc (6fb) ✾ CTV river S% B&b£6.90-£9.20
Bdi£10.90-£13.70 W£71.47-£89.46 ⅃
D7.30pm
GH Hillview 92 Dalkeith Rd ☎031-667 1523 8hc 1⇨
nc3 CTV 4P ✠ S% B&b£6.50-£7.25
Bdi£10.45-£11.50 W£72.50-£79 ⅃
D4.30pm
GH Kildonan Lodge Hotel 27 Craigmillar Pk
☎031-667 2793 Lic 8hc (5fb) nc5 CTV 15P ✠
B&b£9.20 D9.30pm
GH Kirkridge 8 Kilmaurs Ter ☎031-667 6704 *Students taken during university terms* 7hc (1fb) TV in all
bedrooms ✠ S% B&b£6-£7.50 W£36-£45 M
GH Park Lodge 13-15 Abercorn Ter, Portobello
☎031-669 9325 14rm 1hc 6⇨ (4fb) ✾ CTV
8P ✠ sea S% B&b£7.50-£9 Bdi£10.50-£12
W£70-£80 ⅃ D10am
GH Quinton Lodge 24 Polwarth Ter ☎031-229 4100
Closed Xmas & New Year 6hc (2fb) ✾ CTV 8P ✠
D6.30pm
GH Salisbury Hotel 45 Salisbury Rd ☎031-667 1264
15hc 2ⅿ (4fb) CTV 12P ✠ S% B&b£6.50-£10
Wfr£40 M
GH Sharon 1 Kilmaurs Ter ☎031-667 2002 9hc (3fb)
✾ CTV 5P ✠ S% B&b£6.50-£9.50
GH Southdown 20 Craigmillar Pk ☎031-667 2410 8hc
(4fb) ✾ CTV 8P ✠ B&b£5-£6.50 Bdi£8.50-£9.50
D6pm

GH Thrums Private Hotel 14 Minto St, Newington
☎031-667 5545 Lic 6hc 1🛏 (2fb) CTV S%
B&b£7–£8
FH Mrs Jack **Tower Mains** (NT267693) Liberton Brae
☎031-664 1765
Farmhouse in its own grounds within residential area, but backed by farmland. Overlooks golf course, city centre at Arthur's Seat.
Apr–Oct 5hc (2fb) CTV P ⚔ 200acres arable S%
B&b£5.30–£6
×××× **Prestonfield House** Priestfield Rd ☎031-667 8000
120seats 200P bedrooms available ♀ Scottish & French. Last dinner 9pm ✻Lunch£12alc Dinner£16alc
Credit cards ① ② ③ ④ ⑤ ⑥
××× **Café Royal** West Register St ☎031-556 1884
Classification refers to first floor main restaurant.
150seats 𝐏 ♀ French. Last dinner 10.30pm
Credit cards ① ② ③ ④ ⑤
××× **Oscars** Drumbrae Road South ☎031-339 8262
Closed Sun; 80seats P ♀ Continental.
Last dinner 10pm ✻Lunch fr £3.95 Dinner£10alc
Wine£4.90 Credit cards ① ② ③ ⑤
××× **Ristorante Cosmo** 58A North Castle St
☎031-226 6743
Italian restaurant situated in New Town of Edinburgh, five minutes' walk from Princes St.
Closed Sun & Mon; Lunch not served Sat; 62seats 𝐏
♀ Italian. Last dinner 10.15pm ✻Lunch£10alc
Dinner£11.50alc Wine£4.30 Credit cards ① ③ ④ ⑤
×× **Al Amin** 17–19 Forrest Rd ☎031-225 7396
♀ Asian
×× **Alp-Horn** 167 Rose St ☎031-225 4787
Closed Sun, Mon, 2wks Xmas & last 3wks Sep; 46seats
𝐏 ♀ French & Swiss. Last dinner 10pm ✻Lunch £5
Dinner£12alc Credit card ①
×× **Beehive** Grassmarket ☎031-225 7171
1st floor restaurant in old stone building, situated in the older part of the city in front of Edinburgh Castle.
Closed Sun; 60seats Disco Fri & Sat ⚔ Mainly grills.
Last dinner 10.30pm Credit cards ① ② ③ ⑤ ⑥
×× **Cousteau's Sea Food** 109 Hanover St ☎031-226 3355
Closed Sun; 50seats 𝐏 Last dinner 10.30pm
✻Lunch£5&alc Dinner£15alc Wine£4.25
Credit cards ① ② ③ ⑤
×× **Denzlers** 80 Queen St ☎031-226 5467
Closed Sun & local hols; 130seats 𝐏 ♀ Swiss.
Last dinner 9.45pm ✻Lunch£8.25alc Dinner£11alc
Wine£4.12
×× **Handsel** 22 Stafford St ☎031-225 5521
Closed Sun; Lunch not served Sat; 58seats 𝐏
♀ Scottish & French. Last dinner 10.30pm
Lunch£4.95&alc Dinner£8.25&alc Wine£5
Credit cards ① ② ③ ④ ⑤
⊛×× **Howtowdie** 27a Stafford St ☎031-225 6291
Closed Sun; 45seats 𝐏 ♀ Scottish & French.
Last dinner 10.30pm ✻Lunch£8.75–£12.75&alc
Dinner£8.75–£12.75&alc Credit cards ① ② ③ ④ ⑤
×× **Hunters Tryst** Oxgangs Rd ☎031-445 3132
Modernised former coaching inn.
80seats 40P ♀ International. Last dinner 10pm
✻Lunch£3.50&alc Dinner£6&alc
Credit cards ① ② ③ ④ ⑤
×× **Old Bell Inn** 233 Causewayside ☎031-668 1573
Closed Sun; 40seats 𝐏 ♀ British & French.
Last dinner 10pm
×× **Ristorante Milano** 7 Victoria St ☎031-226 5260
Closed Sun; 65seats ☎ ♀ Italian. Last dinner 11pm
Lunch£8alc Dinner£12alc Wine£4.50
Credit cards ② ③ ④ ⑤
×× **Shamiana** 14 Brougham St ☎031-229 5578
Lunch not served; 50seats 𝐏 ♀ Indian.
Last dinner 11.30pm S% ✻Dinner£6–£10 Wine£3.45
Credit cards ① ② ③ ④ ⑤
×× **Town & Country** 72 Rose St, North Ln ☎031-225 3106
Closed Sun; 32seats 𝐏 ♀ International.
Last dinner 10.30pm ✻Lunch£3.40–£4.40&alc

Edinburgh contd– Elgin

Dinner£7.50alc Wine£3.50 Credit cards ① ② ③ ⑤ ⑥
× **Anatolian** 13 Dalry Rd ☎031-346 0204
Closed Sun; Lunch not served; 32seats ♀ Turkish.
Last dinner 11.30pm Credit cards ② ③ ⑤
× **Casa Española** 61–65 Rose St ☎031-225 5979
80seats 40P bedrooms available ♀ Continental.
Last dinner 10.30pm Credit cards ① ③
× **Casa Siciliana** 11 Lochrin Ter ☎031-229 1605
Closed Sun; 70seats 𝐏 ♀ International.
Last dinner 11pm ✻Lunch fr £3&alc Dinner£10alc
Wine£4.20 Credit cards ① ② ③ ⑤ ⑥
× **Le Caveau** 13B Dundas St ☎031-556 5707
Closed Sun, 1st 2wks Jul & Public Hols; 50seats 𝐏
♀ French. Last dinner 10pm Lunch£5alc Dinner£7alc
Wine£3.70
× **Chez Julie** 110 Raeburn Pl ☎031-332 2827
Closed Sun, Xmas, 1 & 2Jan; Dinner not served Mon;
38seats 𝐏 ♀ British & French. Last dinner 10pm
× **Creperie Restaurant Française** 8A Grindley St
☎031-229 5405
Closed Sun; 60seats 𝐏 ♀ French.
Last dinner 10.15pm ✻Lunch£3.50&alc Dinner£8alc
Credit cards ① ⑥
× **Doric Tavern** 15–16 Market St ☎031-225 1084
Closed Sun; 44seats 𝐏 ♀ Scottish & French.
Last dinner 9.30pm Lunch fr £1.80&alc Dinner fr £3&alc
Wine£3.40
× **Duncan's Land** Gloucester St ☎031-225 1037
Dinner not served Mon; 35seats 𝐏 Last dinner 10pm
✻Lunch£3alc Dinner£10alc Wine£3.70
⊛× **Flappers** 8 West Maitland St ☎031-228 1001
Closed Sun; Lunch not served Sat; 32seats 𝐏
♀ French & Italian. Last dinner 10.45pm Credit card ②
× **Lafayette** 22 Brougham Pl ☎031-229 0869
Closed Sun; 28seats 𝐏 ♀ French.
Last dinner 10.30pm ✻Lunch£2.65–£3&alc
Dinner£10alc Wine£4.50
× **Snobs** 1 Dean Bank Ln ☎031-332 0003
Closed Sun; 25seats 𝐏 ♀ Italian.
Last dinner 11.30pm ✻Lunch£3–£5&alc Dinner£8alc
Wine£4.10 Credit cards ① ②
At **Musselburgh** (6m E A198)
☆☆ **Drummore** North Berwick Rd ☎031-665 2302
37⇌🛏 P

EDZELL 658 Tayside Map41 NO56 Ec Thu Aberdeen36
London510 Montrose12 Perth49
★★★ **Glen Esk** High St ☎319
Closed 1Jan; 24rm (10⇌4🛏) 🍴 ℬ 108P ⚓ ♫ billiards
Last dinner 8.45pm ✵ ⚒ ✻sB&B£14.37
sB&B⇌🛏£16.67 dB&B£28.74 dB&B⇌🛏£33.34
Lunch£3.50&alc Dinner£6&alc Credit cards ② ⑤
★★ **Central** ☎218
A small three-storey hotel, standing in quiet street in this village which lies to the south of the Grampian mountains.
20rm (1⇌5🛏) 🍴 CTV TV in 1bedroom CTV in 6bedrooms
80P 2⚓ billiards Last dinner 8.30pm ✵ ⚒ S%
sB&B£8.85–£9.50 sB&B⇌🛏£12–£13
dB&B£17.70–£18.50 dB&B⇌🛏£24–£26
Lunch£2.50–£3 Tea£1–£1.20 High Tea£2.50–£3.40
Dinner£4.50–£5.50&alc Wine£2.20 🍴
★★B **Panmure Arms** High St (Inter-Hotel) ☎420
Telex no 76534
Attractive mock-Tudor hotel situated in quiet village on edge of the Highlands.
17rm (3⇌1🛏) 🍴 CTV CTV in 17bedrooms 30P
🚿(heated) ⚓ squash sauna bath Live music & dancing Sat
Last dinner 9pm ✵ S% ✻sB&B£15

ELGIN 17,589 Grampian Map44 NJ26 Ec Wed Md cattle Fri
Aberdeen67 Cullen22 Inverness39 London581 Perth134
☆☆☆ **Eight Acres** Sheriffmill ☎3077
Modern hotel on A96 on western outskirts of town.
40rm (21⇌19🛏) 🍴 CTV TV in 39bedrooms CTV in
1bedroom 60P ⚓ squash Disco Sat Conference facilities

105

Elgin contd–Falkland

available ♥ French & Italian. Last dinner 8.45pm ✻ S%
sB&B⇌🛏£26 dB&B⇌🛏£44 Lunch£5.50&alc
Dinner£8.25&alc Wine£3.55 ₽ xmas
Credit cards ① ② ③ ⑤ ⑥

★★**Laichmoray** Station Rd ☎2558
Greystone hotel standing opposite goods station in south end of town.
Closed New Year's Day; 26rm 🍴 CTV 60P ⚓ ♋
Last dinner 8.30pm ✻ ♫ Credit cards ① ③ ⑤

★**Grove** Pluscarden Rd ☎2958
6rm 🍴 CTV TV in 1 bedroom ⓡ ⊛ 50P ⚓ ↳
Last dinner 8.30pm ✻ ♫ S% ✻sB&B£8.50
dB&B£15 Lunch£1.60alc Tea£1alc High Tea£2.75alc
Dinner£4alc Wine£4.50 xmas

★**St Leonards** Duff Av ☎7350
Converted private house standing in own grounds in residential area of town.
17rm(6⇌2🛏)🍴 CTV ⓡ 60P ⚓ ♋ ♥ Scottish, English & Continental. Last dinner 8.30pm ✻ ♫ S% sB&B£12
sB&B⇌🛏£14 dB&B£21 dB&B⇌🛏£25 Lunch£3
Tea£1 HighTea£2.50–£4.50 Dinner£6.50–£7.50
Wine£3.50 ₽

✕✕**Enrico's** 15 Grey Friars St ☎2849
Closed Sun, Xmas & 1–3 Jan; 58 seats ₽ ♥ English & Italian. Last dinner 9.30pm ✻Lunch£2&alc
Credit cards ② ③ ⑤

ELIE 830 (with Earlsferry) Fife Map41 NO40 EcWed
Edinburgh44 Kirkcaldy18 London461 Perth37
St Andrews13

★★**Golf** Bank St ☎330259
Mansion in the Scottish Baroque style with outlook over the Firth of Forth and golf course at the back door.
21rm(6⇌1🛏) 🍴 CTV CTV in 1 bedroom 50P ⚓ ♋ Live music & dancing wkly ♋ Last dinner 9pm ✻ ♫ ₽
sB&B£12.08–£13.50 dB&B£24.16–£27
dB&B⇌🛏£26.46–£29.30 Bar lunch£1.75–£3.25
Tea£1.75–£2.25 High Tea£3–£3.50
Dinner£6.33–£7&alc Wine£4.25 ₽ xmas
Credit cards ① ③ ⑥

GH Elms Park Pl ☎330404 Lic 6rm (2fb) ⊛ CTV 8P
🍴 B&B£7 Bdi£11 W£73 ₤ D6pm

✕**Upstairs, Downstairs** 51 High St ☎330374
Closed Tue & Nov–Feb; 24 seats Last High Tea 6.30pm
Lunch£1.50–£2.50&alc Tea fr£1.50 High Tea£3–£4.50
Dinner£5–£8.50 Wine£3

ELLON 2,898 Grampian Map45 NJ93 EcWed MdMon
Aberdeen16 London555 Peterhead18
☆☆☆**Ladbroke Mercury Motor Inn** (Ladbroke) ☎20666
Telex no 739200
40⇌🛏 ♫ 🍴 CTV available in bedrooms 100P ⚓
Last dinner 10pm ✻ ♫ ₽ Credit cards ① ② ③ ④ ⑤ ⑥

★**Buchan** ☎20208
17rm(1⇌🛏) CTV TV available in bedrooms 60P ↳
Last dinner 6.30pm ✻ ♫

★**New Inn** Market St ☎20425
12rm(2⇌4🛏) 🍴 CTV 68P Last High Tea 7pm ✻ ♫ S%
sB&B£11 sB&B⇌🛏£12 dB&B£22 dB&B⇌🛏£24
Lunch£3 Tea 75p High Tea£3 Dinner£5
Credit cards ① ② ③ ⑤ ⑥

ERSKINE 10,700 Strathclyde Map37 NS47 Dumbarton7
Glasgow12 London420 Renfrew6
☆☆☆**Crest** North Barr, Inchinnan (Crest) ☎041-812 0123
Telex no 777713
185⇌🛏 Lift ♫ ⓡ CTV CTV in all bedrooms ⓡ 350P ⚓ Live music & dancing Sat Conference facilities available
♥ International. Last dinner 10pm ✻ ♫ sB&B⇌🛏£36.40
dB&B⇌🛏£51.80 Lunch£6.30 Dinner£6.90&alc
Wine£5.55 ₽ Credit cards ① ② ③ ⑤

ETTRICK Borders Map35 NT21 Hawick19 Langholm26
Innerleithen18 London355
FH J. R. Hall **Thirlestane Hope** (NT285167)
☎Ettrick Valley229
Quaint, white-painted farm in border hill country. Small burn flows through farmland. Good access by ⅟₂ mile track.
Mar–Oct 2⇌ (1fb) CTV P 900 acres non-working
S% B&B£5.50–£6 Bbi£9–£10 D4pm

EVANTON 562 Highland Map43 NH66 EcThu Dingwall6
Inverness28 London592
★★**Novar Arms** ☎830210
Two-storey building alongside main road in centre of village.
13rm CTV 60P 2🅟 ♥ International. Last dinner 10pm ✻
♫ S% sB&B£9 dB&B fr£9 dB&Bfr£18 Lunch£4.50
Tea£1.50&alc High Tea£2.50–£7&alc Dinner£7&alc
Wine£3.50 ₽ Credit card ③

FALKIRK 36,589 Central Map34 NS87 EcWed MdSat
Edinburgh25 Glasgow23 London417 Stirling10
☆☆☆**Park** Arnot Hill, Camelon Rd (Reo Stakis) ☎28331
Telex no 778704
55⇌🛏 Lift ♫ ⓡ CTV CTV in all bedrooms ⓡ 100P Conference facilities available ♥ Scottish & French. Last dinner 9.30pm
✻ ✻sB&B⇌fr£23.75 dB&B⇌fr£34 Lunchfr£2.50&alc
Teafr50p Dinnerfr£7&alc Wine£3.90 ₽
Credit cards ① ② ③ ⑤ ⑥

✕✕**Hatherley** Arnot Hill Ln ☎25328
Closed Sun; Lunch not served Wed; 32 seats 25P
♥ Danish. Last dinner 9.30pm

✕**Pierre's** 140 Graham's Rd ☎35843
Closed Sun, Mon & 29 Jun–17 Jul; Lunch not served Sat;
40 seats ₽ ♥ French. Last dinner 9.30pm
✻Lunchfr£3.50&alc Dinnerfr£6.95&alc Wine£3.85
Credit cards ① ② ③

FALKLAND Fife Map41 NO20 Glenthrothes6 Kirkcaldy12
Auchtermuchty3 London452
✕✕**Covenanter** ☎224

Eight Acres Hotel *(ELGIN)*

45 BEDROOMS WITH BATH/SHOWER TV RADIO ETC IN ALL ROOMS SPACIOUS PUBLIC ROOMS/GROUNDS. EXCITING WEEKEND ENTERTAINMENT

Situated against beautiful back-drop of oak woods outskirts of town, on main Elgin, Inverness Road

ELGIN
TEL. 3077

The Ladbroke Mercury Hotel, Ellon, is the Centre of Attractions

This small modern hotel set in the heart of Aberdeenshire is the ideal base for visiting the nearby Whisky distilleries of Glenfiddich and Glenfarclas and the granite city of Aberdeen The Rowan Tree restaurant prides itself on its Scottish specialities and there's also a friendly bar where you can enjoy a quiet drink.

You'll find plenty of exciting holiday ideas in our Lazydays brochure — try a Scottish Weekaway — tailor made for touring in your own car, or take a Welcome Break from as little as £25.00 per person bed & breakfast.

For your Lazydays brochure, 'phone 01-734 6000 or write to PO Box 137, Watford, Herts. WD1 1DN.

Ladbroke Mercury Hotel,
Ellon,
Aberdeenshire. AB4 9NP
Tel: (0358) 20666

Ladbroke Hotels

Closed Mon; 36seats 12P bedrooms available
Last dinner 9pm ✽ Lunch£4&alc Dinner fr£6.50&alc Wine£4 Credit cards ② ③ ⑤

FEARNAN Tayside Map40NN74 EcSat Aberfeldy10 Crianlarich27 London474 Perth42
★**Tigh-an-Loan** ☎Kenmore249
Closed Oct–8Apr; 10rm CTV 20P ⇌ ♨
Last dinner7.30pm ❦ ☐ sB&B£10.50 dB&B£21
Bar lunch£2 Dinner£6 Wine£3.20

FENWICK Strathclyde NG ref NS44
★★**Fenwick** ☎478
12rm CTV CTV in all bedrooms ⓡ 120P ♀ French.
Last dinner 9.30pm ❦ ☐ ✽sB&Bfr£12.50
dB&B fr£19.50 Bar lunch fr£2.50 Lunch fr£3.75&alc
Tea fr£1.25 Dinner£7.50alc ♪ Credit cards ① ② ④ ⑤ ⑥

FINTRY Central Map37NS68 Stirling16 Glasgow19 London422
FH Mrs M. Mitchell **Nether Glinns** (NS606883) ☎207
Well-maintained farmhouse situated among rolling hills. Access via signposted ¼ mile gravel drive.
15Apr–Sep 3rm (1fb) CTV 6P river 150acres arable dairy S% B&B fr£5.50

FOCHABERS 1,238 Grampian Map44NJ35 EcWed Aberdeen58 Elgin9 Huntly19 Inverness48 London594
★★**Gordon Arms** ☎820508
15rm(6⇌) Annexe: 2rm(1⇌1♨) ⇭ CTV CTV in 15bedrooms ⓡ 50P ⇌ Last dinner9.15pm ❦ ☐ S%
sB&B£18 sB&B⇌♨£20 dB&B£28 dB&B⇌♨£30
Lunch£3–£3.50&alc Tea£1.50–£2 High Tea£2.50–£5
Dinners£5–£8&alc Wine£4.80 ♪

FORDOUN Grampian Map41NO77 Laurencekirk4 Stonehaven11 Aberdeen25 London319
FH Mrs M. Anderson **Ringwood** (NO743774) (2m N on A966) ☎Auchenblae313
Small modernised villa in open setting amidst farmland and with its own neat garden and outhouse. Very high standard of décor and furnishings. 1m north-west of village on B966.
Feb–Nov 4hc (1fb) ⇌ CTV 6P ⇭ 17acres arable S% B&B£6–£7 Bdi£9–£10.50 W£60–£70 ⚥ (Wonly Oct–Nov & Feb–May) D6pm

FORFAR 11,395 Tayside Map41NO45 EcThu MdMon/Fri Aberdeen54 London483 Montrose18 Perth37
★★**County** Castle St ☎62878
12rm ⇭ CTV ♪ Last dinner9pm ❦ S% sB&B£9.50
dB&B£16.50 Lunch£2.90 High Tea£2.90 Dinner£4.40
Wine£3.35
★★**Royal** Castle St ☎62691

Closed 1–4Jan; 17rm(8⇌) ⚥ ⇭ CTV TV in 8bedrooms ⓡ ⇌
10P 10⇭ ♪ Live music & dancing twice wkly Cabaret twice wkly ♀ French. Last dinner9pm ❦ ☐ sB&B£14.50
sB&B⇌♨£17 dB&B£24 dB&B⇌♨£28
Lunch fr£3.50&alc Tea fr£1&alc High Tea fr£2&alc
Dinner fr£5.95&alc Wine£3.50 Credit cards ② ⑤

FORRES 5,620 Grampian Map44NJ05 EcWed Elgin12 Grantown-on-Spey23 Inverness27 London569
★★**Ramnee** ☎72410
Fine, two-storey stone villa standing back from main road in well-kept grounds
Closed Jan; 20rm(10⇌♨) Annexe: 2⇌♨ ⇭ CTV TV in all bedrooms ⇌ 50P 1⇭ ⇌ ♀ English, French & Italian.
Last dinner9pm ❦ Credit card ②
★★**B Royal** ☎72617
Three-storey stone building with wrought iron entrance porch and balcony, standing in quiet area of the town opposite market and adjacent to station.
20rm(12⇌1♨) ⇭ CTV CTV in all bedrooms ⓡ ⇌ 40P ⚥
Live music & dancing Fri–Sun Last dinner8.30pm ❦ S%
sB&B£11.50 dB&B£20.70 dB&B⇌♨£23 Lunch£2.80
High Tea£2.10–£4.90 Dinner£5.75 Wine£2.99
Credit cards ① ⑥
★**Heather** Lyler St ☎72377
6rm(1⇌2♨) ⇭ CTV ⓡ P ♪ Last dinner6.30pm S%
sB&B£10 dB&B£18.40 dB&B⇌♨£24 ⚥ S%
Bar lunch£1.20–£3 High Tea£2.50–£3.50 Dinner£6.50
Wine£3.40 ♪
GH Regency 66 High St ☎72558 Lic 7hc CTV S%
B&b£5–£6 D6pm
×× **Elizabethan Inn** Mundole ☎72526
Located west of Forres, this converted and extended cottage stands on the banks of the River Findhorn.
Closed last wk May, last wk Sep, 1st wk Oct, 1st wk Jan & 2days Xmas; Dinner not served Wed; 45seats P
Last dinner8.30pm

FORSINARD Highland Map47NC84 Helmsdale25 Inverness112 London677 Thurso30
★★**Forsinard** ☎Halladale221
13rm(9⇌2♨) ⚥ ⇭ CTV ⓡ 30P ⚥ ⇌ ₺ Last dinner8pm
❦ ☐ ✽sB&B£13.25 dB&B£26.50 dB&B⇌♨£26.50
Lunch fr£4.20 Tea fr£1.50 High Tea fr£2.15
Dinner fr£5.75 Wine£4

FORT AUGUSTUS 670 Highland EcWed Map43NH30
Fort William32 Invermoriston6 Inverness34 London548
★★**Inchnacardoch Lodge** Loch Ness (Inter-Hotels)
☎6258
17rm(6⇌♨) 1⇌ ⇭ CTV 50P 2⇭ ⇌ ♨ ☊ Live music & dancing Fri & Sat ⇌ Last dinner10pm ❦ ☐
Credit cards ① ② ③ ④ ⑤
★★**Lovat Arms** ☎6206
Neat stone-built house with extensive views of Loch Ness and surrounding mountains.
Closed Nov; 26rm(2⇌) Annexe: 6rm ⇭ CTV ⓡ 50P ⚥
Last dinner8pm ❦ ☐ S% ✽sB&B£12.10–£13.50
dB&B£24.20–£27 dB&B⇌£27.20–£30 Lunch£4.25
Tea£1 Dinner£7 Wine£2.20 ♪
★**Caledonian** ☎6256
Closed Oct–8Apr; 13rm(1♨) CTV ⓡ 20P ⚥
Last dinner10pm ❦ ☐ S% sB&B£8.50–£9.50
dB&B£17–£19 Lunch£3–£3.50 Tea35–75p
High Tea£2–£2.50 Dinner£4.50–£5 Wine£2.50 ♪

FORTROSE Highland Map44NH76 Inverness13 Dingwall16 London507
★★**Royal** Union St ☎20236
11rm CTV ⇌ 12P ♪ Last dinner9pm ❦ ☐ S%
sB&B£6.50–£7.50 dB&B£13–£14
Continental breakfast Lunch£3.50 Tea£1.25
High Tea£3–£3.50&alc Dinner£5.50–£6.50&alc
Wine£2 ♪ xmas

107

Fort William – Gairloch

FORT WILLIAM 4,352 Highland Map39NN17 EcWed (not summer) Edinburgh135 Glasgow104 Inverness66 London516 Oban49 Perth105

❋❋❋★★★★(red) ♨**Inverlochy Castle** (3m NE A82) ☎2177
Beautifully situated between loch and mountain, this Red Star hotel is thought by many to be among the best in the world. Queen Victoria stayed here when it was privately owned, and ambience, food and service are still fit for a queen.
Closed 5Nov–4Apr; 14⇌ ♪ CTV in all bedrooms ⊛ P ⇌ ♨ ♨(hard) ↳ billiards ♀ International. Last dinner9pm S% sB&B⇌£65 dB&B⇌£90 Dinner£21&alc Wine£6 Credit cards ①②③⑤

★★★**Alexandra** ☎2241 Telexno777310
Conversion and extension of purpose-built Victorian stone hotel standing on corner site. Situated just outside main shopping centre of town and adjacent to Railway Station.
93rm(68⇌) Lift ♪ ♨ CTV 40P Last dinner9pm ♥ S% sB&B£10.50–£18.50 sB&B⇌£12.50–£22 dB&B£16.50–£31.20 dB&B⇌£21–£37.60 Barlunch£1.50 Tea£1 Dinner£7.50 Wine£3.25 ⌻ Credit cards ①②③⑤⑥

☆☆**Ladbroke Mercury** (on A82) (Ladbroke) ☎3117
Modern low rise standing by main road on southern outskirts of town, with splendid hill views over Loch Linnhe.
61⇌ ♨ ♨ TV available in bedrooms 60P sauna bath Conference facilities available Last dinner10pm ♥ ⌻ ⌻ Credit cards ①②③④⑤⑥

★★**Grand** Gordon Sq ☎2928
This pre-war, three-storey hotel stands on a corner site in the shopping centre.
33rm(19⇌) ♪ CTV CTV in 12bedrooms ⓡ 25P Last dinner8.30pm ♥ ⌻ sB&B£9.50–£13.50 sB&B⇌£9.50–£16 dB&B£18–£19–£28 Lunch fr£3.25 Tea fr£1.50 Dinner fr£6.25 Wine£3.25 ⌻ Credit cards ①②③⑤⑥

★★**Highland** Union Rd (Galleon) ☎2291
An imposing Victorian building with ornate panelled main hall and stairway. Hillside situation with panoramic views of town, Loch Linnhe and Ardgow hills.
52rm(12⇌♨) Annexe: 8⇌ ♪ ♨ CTV P ♨ Last dinner8.30pm ♥ ⌻ sB&B fr£13.50 dB&B fr£22 dB&B♨fr£25 Lunch fr£5.50 Dinner fr£5.50 ⌻ xmas Credit cards ①③

★★**Imperial** Fraser's Sq ☎2040
An extended three-storey Victorian building standing in a side street off the main shopping area, with views over Loch Linnhe.
43rm(3♨) ♨ CTV CTV in 2bedrooms ⓡ 30P Live music & dancing Tue & Thu Cabaret Fri Last dinner8.30pm ♥ S% sB&B♨£9.80–£10.80 dB&B£18–£20.70 dB&B♨£21.90–£25.20 Lunch£3.60–£4.20 Dinner£4.60–£5.50 Wine£3.40 ⌻

★★**Milton** ☎2331 Telexno777210
A modern purpose-built tourist hotel standing at northern outskirts of town.
Closed Oct–Apr; 62rm(10⇌) ♪ ♨ CTV 100P ♨ Disco Fri&Sat Live music & dancing Mon–Thu Last dinner9pm ♥ ⌻ S% sB&B⇌£16.50 sB&B⇌£20 dB&B£27.20 dB&B⇌£33.60 Tea£1 Dinner£6.50 Wine£3.25 ⌻ Credit cards ①②③⑤⑥

★★**Nevis Bank** Belford Rd ☎2595
23rm(6⇌♨) ♨ CTV 20P Last dinner8pm ♥

★★**Stag's Head** High St ☎4144
Closed late Sep–late Apr; 46rm(7⇌♨) Lift ♪ ♨ CTV Last dinner8.30pm ⌻ Credit cards ①②③④⑤⑥

GH Benview Beford Rd ☎2966 Mar–Nov 15hc (2fb) CTV 20P B&b£6.90–£9.20 Bdi£11.50–£13.80 D7pm

GH Guisachan Alma Rd ☎3797 15hc (4fb) CTV 14P ♨ lake S% B&b£6–£7.50 Bdi£9–£11.50 W£63–£80.50 ⌻ D5.30pm

GH Hillview Achintore Rd ☎4349 Apr–Sep 9hc (2fb) CTV 9P ♨ lake S% ✻B&b£5.50 Bdi£9.50

GH Innseagan Achintore Rd ☎2452 Apr–Oct Lic

The Ladbroke Mercury Motor Inn, Fort William is the Centre of Attractions

Set amid breathtaking Highland scenery overlooking Loch Linnhe, this modern hotel is the ideal base for exploring Glencoe and Ben Nevis. Enjoy a round of golf at the Spean Bridge Golf Club, then relax in the cocktail bar and an excellent meal in the Lochside restaurant with a splendid panoramic view.
You'll find plenty of exciting holiday ideas in our Lazydays brochure — try a Scottish Weekaway — tailor made for touring in your own car, or take a Welcome Break from as little as £25.00 per person bed & breakfast.

For your Lazydays brochure, 'phone 01-734 6000 or write to PO Box 137, Watford, Herts. WD1 1DN.

Ladbroke Mercury Motor Inn,
Achintore Road,
Fort William
Inverness-shire. PH33 6RW
Tel: (0397) 3117

Ladbroke Hotels

26hc 12⇌ (2fb) CTV 30P ♨ lake S% B&b£6–£8.50 Bdi£10.50–£13 D7pm

GH Loch View Heathercroft, off Argyll Ter ☎3149 Etr–Oct 7hc 1⇌ (3fb) CTV 8P ♨ lake S% B&b£5.50–£6

GH Rhu Mhor Alma Rd ☎2213 Mar–Oct 7hc (2fb) ⊛ CTV 7P lake S% B&b£6–£6.50 Bdi£9–£9.50 D5pm

GH Stronchreggan View Achintore Rd ☎4644 Apr–Oct 7hc (5fb) ⊛ CTV 7P ♨ lake S% Bdi fr£10 Wfr£70 ⌻ D6.30pm

FOYERS 276 Highland Map43NH42 Fort Augustus14 Fort William46 Inverness19 London562

★**Foyers** ☎Gorthleck216
Attractive roadside inn set on hillside above Loch Ness, 19 miles west of Inverness on B852.
10rm ♨ CTV ⓡ 25P ⇌ ♨ Last dinner7.30pm ♥ ⌻ S% sB&B£8 sB&B£16 Lunch£1.50alc Tea50p&alc Dinner£3.90&alc

GH Foyers Bay House Lower Foyers ☎Gorthleck631 6hc (2fb) CTV P 4⇌ ♨ lake S% ✻B&b£6.25 Bdi£11.25 W£70 ⌻ D8.30pm

FREUCHIE 869 Fife Map41NO20 EcThu London450 Dundee20 Kirkcaldy10 StAndrews18

★★**Lomond** Parliament Sq ☎Falkland329
9rm(1⇌) ♨ CTV TV in 9bedrooms ⓡ 60P ⇌ sauna bath ♀ Scottish & French. Last dinner9pm ♥ S% sB&B£12–£13 sB&B⇌♨£14–£15 dB&B£23–£25 dB&B⇌♨£26–£27 Lunch£5–£5.50&alc High Tea£3.30–£4.50&alc Dinner£6.25–£6.75&alc Wine£4 ⌻ Credit cards ①③

FYVIE Grampian Map45NJ73 Aberdeen27 Turriff9 Ellon16 London564

FH Mrs A. Runcie **Macterry** *(NJ786424)* ☎555
Two-storey farmhouse with adjoining farm buildings in rural setting.
May–Sep 3rm 1hc ⊛ nc3 CTV 3P 105acres arable S% B&b£6–£7 Bdi£10.50–£12 Dnoon

GAIRLOCH 125 Highland Map42NG87 EcWed (not summer) Fort William127 Inverness74 London635 Ullapool56

★★**Gairloch** (Scottish Highland) ☎2001 Telexno778215
Three-storey sandstone Victorian building standing on the edge of Loch Gairloch in West Highland village.
50rm(42⇌) Lift ♪ CTV ⓡ 50P ♨ ↳ Last dinner9pm ⌻ S% sB&B£18.30 sB&B⇌£21.30 dB&B£30.60 dB&B⇌£36.60 Bar lunch£2alc Dinner£7.50 Wine£3.95 Credit cards ①②③⑤⑥

★**Creag Mhor** Charlestown ☎2068 Telexno75605
Closed Nov; 9rm(2⇌) CTV ⓡ 15P ⇌ ↳ Last dinner8pm ♥ ⌻ S% ✻sB&B fr£10.78 dB&B fr£17.96 dB&B⇌fr£20.86 Bar lunch fr80p Tea fr60p Dinner£5.75–£6.25 Wine£2.90 xmas

> **Always try to book your accommodation well in advance**

GH Horisdale House Strathgairloch ☎2151 Apr–Sep rsMar & Oct 9hc (3fb) ≉ nc7 CTV 20P ⚓ lake S% B&b£7–£8 Bdi£11–£12 W£73–£80 ⅃ D5pm

GALASHIELS 12,788 Borders Map35NT43 EcWed MdFri Edinburgh33 Jedburgh16 London350 Peebles19
★★**King's Knowes** Selkirk Rd ☎3478
Red sandstone mansion dating from 1869 in nine acres of grounds overlooking River Tweed. Interior reflects Italian influence.
10rm(7⇨) ᵐ CTV CTV in all bedrooms ® 50P ⚓ ≉(hard) Last dinner9pm ◊ S% sB&B£21 sB&B⇨£24 dB&B£32 dB&B⇨£36 Lunch£6.50alc Dinner£6.50alc Wine£3.15 Credit cards ① ② ⑤ ⑥
★**Royal** Channel St (Scottish & Newcastle) ☎2918
Three-storey stone building with decorative wrought iron work balcony to second floor, situated in main shopping thoroughfare.
22rm(1⇨) CTV ® ₱ Last dinner8.45pm ◊ S% sB&B£16.50 dB&B£20 dB&B⇨£26 Bar lunch£1.20alc Dinner£3.75alc Wine£4 ₱ xmas Credit cards ① ③ ⑥
✕**Redgauntlet** 36 Market St ☎2098
Closed Tue; Lunch not served; 40seats ₱ ♀Scottish, French & Italian. Last dinner10pm ✱Dinner£8alc Wine£3 Credit card ①

GARTMORE Central Map37NS59 Aberfoyle3 Callander11 Glasgow25 London439
GH Baad Springs Farm ☎Aberfoyle207 Apr–Oct Lic 3rm 1⇨2 ᵐ (1fb) CTV 6P S% ✱B&b£8 Bdi£13 W£50 D5pm

GARVE Highland Map43NH26 EcThu Dingwall14 Inverness28 London593
★★**Garve** ☎205
Large, three-storey white-painted building standing on main road in shadow of Ben Wyvis.
Closed Oct–Mar; 32rm(16⇨) ᵐ CTV 60P 6⚑ ⚓ ♀English & French. Last dinner9pm ◊ ⚏ S% ✱sB&B£11–£12.50 sB&B⇨£12.50–£14.50 dB&B£22–£25 dB&B⇨£25–£29 Lunch£4–£6 Tea50p–£1.50 Dinner£7.50 Wine£2.70 ₱ Credit cards ① ③ ⑤

GATEHEAD Strathclyde Map34NS33 Kilmarnock3 Troon7 Ayr12 London409
FH Mrs R. Elliot **Old Rome** *(NS393310)* ☎Drybridge850265
Situated in a completely rural setting 300 yards off the A759 to Troon (5 miles). Farmhouse has charm and character and dates from 17th century.
3hc CTV 20P 6⚑ ᵐ 10acres non-working S% B&b£5–£6.50 Bdi£8–£10.50 D9pm

GATEHOUSE OF FLEET 837 Dumfries & Galloway Map30NX55 EcThu Ayr55 Carlisle68 Kirkcudbright9 London375
★★★**Cally** (Trusthouse Forte) ☎341
Closed Jan; 88⇨ Lift ⅅ CTV CTV in all bedrooms ® 25P ⚓ ⇨(heated) ✎(hard) ⚓ sauna bath ♨ Last dinner9.30pm ◊ ⚏ S% sB&B⇨£23.10–£25.10 dB&B⇨£38.20–£41.20 ₱ xmas Credit cards ① ② ③ ④ ⑤ ⑥
★★★**L Murray Arms** (Best Western) ☎207 Telex no8814912
A modernised and extended 17th-C posting house. Burns wrote 'Scots wha Hae' whilst staying here.
12rm(9⇨1 ᵐ) Annexe: 10rm(7⇨) ⅅ ᵐ CTV CTV in 6bedrooms ® 20P ⚓ ✎(hard) ⚓ Last dinner9pm ◊ ⚏ S% sB&Bfr£19.50 sB&B⇨ ᵐ fr£21 dB&Bfr£39 dB&B⇨ ᵐ fr£42 Lunchfr£3.75 Teafr£1.20 HighTeafr£3 Dinnerfr£7.50&alc Wine£3.50 ₱ xmas Credit cards ① ② ③ ⑤ ⑥

GATTONSIDE Borders Map35NT53 Galashiels3 Selkirk8 Jedburgh15 London345
✕✕**Hoebridge Inn** ☎Melrose3082
Closed Mon (Oct–Apr); Lunch not served; 46seats 30P ♀English & Continental. Last dinner10pm ✱Tea£1alc Dinner£6.50alc Wine£4.90 Credit card ①

GIFFNOCK 10,987 Strathclyde Map37NS55 EcTue/Wed Glasgow5 London408 Paisley7
★★★**MacDonald** Eastwood Toll (Thistle) ☎041-638 2225 Telex no779138
Modern sandstone building at Eastwood Toll roundabout (A77), on southern outskirts of Glasgow.
58⇨ ᵐ ⅅ ᵐ CTV CTV in all bedrooms ® 200P 6⚑ ⚓ billiards Live music & dancing Fri–Sun Conference facilities available ♀French. Last dinner10pm ◊ ⚏ Credit cards ① ② ③ ⑤ ⑥
★★**Redhurst** Eastwood Mains Rd (Reo Stakis) ☎041-638 6465 Telex no778704
Modern custom built L-shaped building in residential suburb about 5 miles from Glasgow city centre.
16rm(12⇨) ⅅ ᵐ CTV CTV in all bedrooms ® 50P ♀English & French. Last dinner9.55pm ◊ ✱sB&B⇨fr£18.50 sB&B⇨fr£24.75 dB&B⇨fr£34 Lunch£3.25&alc Dinner£7alc Wine£3 ₱ Credit cards ① ② ③ ⑤ ⑥

GIFFORD 575 Lothian Map35NT56 EcMon/Wed Edinburgh20 Haddington5 Jedburgh41 London373
★★**Tweeddale Arms** ☎240
8rm(1⇨2 ᵐ) ᵐ CTV 14P Last dinner8.30pm ◊ ⚏ ✱sB&B£10–£12.50 sB&B⇨ ᵐ £11–£14 dB&B£20–£25 dB&B⇨ ᵐ £22–£28 Lunch£3.75–£4.25 Tea£1.20 HighTea£3 Dinner£6.95 Wine£3.55 ₱ Credit cards ② ③ ④
★**Goblin Ha'** ☎244
Early Victorian painted stone inn, standing in centre of attractive village.
7rm ᵐ TV ⚓ ⚓ Last dinner9pm ◊ ⚏

GIRVAN 7,660 Strathclyde Map33NX19 EcWed Ayr23 Carlisle116 Glasgow57 London423 Stranraer30
★**Carrick Arms** Dalrymple St ☎2261
7rm(1⇨) CTV 25P ⚓ ♨ Last dinner9pm ◊ S% ✱sB&B£7.50–£9 dB&B£14–£17 dB&B⇨£18–£19 Lunch£2.75alc Dinner£5alc Wine£3.45
★**Hamilton Arms** (Osprey) ☎2182
11rm ᵐ CTV CTV in 1bedroom TV in 1bedroom 6⚑ Disco Thu Last dinner7pm ◊ ⚏ S% sB&B£8–£10 dB&B£14–£18 Lunch£2–£3 Tea50p HighTea£2–£4 Dinner£5–£7 Wine£4.80
★**Westcliffe** Louisa Dr ☎2128
RS Oct–Mar (no lunch); 21rm(7⇨) ᵐ CTV ® ✎ ₱ Last dinner6.30pm sB&Bfr£8 dB&Bfr£15 dB&B⇨ ᵐ fr£18 Lunchfr£2.50&alc HighTeafr£2.50&alc Dinnerfr£3.50&alc Wine£3.90 Credit cards ① ③

GLAMIS Tayside Map41NO34 Forfar5 Perth25 Kirriemuir5 Dundee12 London480
✕✕**Strathmore Arms** ☎248
Nicely-appointed country restaurant and bar, in historic village with famous Glamis Castle nearby.
Closed Sun & Mon, (Oct–Apr) 60seats ♀Scottish, English & French. Last dinner9pm ✱Lunch£4.40 Dinner£8alc Wine£3.50 Credit cards ② ⑤

GLASGOW plan – see page 212 809,679 Strathclyde Map37NS56 Ayr34 Edinburgh45 Fort William104

Glasgow contd

Inverness 172 London 402 Oban 93 Perth 60 Stirling 26

★★★★**Albany** Bothwell St (Trusthouse Forte)
☎041-248 2656 Telex no 77440
251⇌ Lift ♪ ⁂ CTV in all bedrooms ® 25P Conference facilities available Last dinner 10.45pm ♥ ♫ S%
sB&B⇌£39.10–£42.60 dB&B⇌£51.20–£55.70 ₱
Credit cards ①②③④⑤

★★★★**Central** Gordon St (British Transport)
☎041-221 9680 Telex no 777771
211rm(150⇌20⁂) Lift ♪ ⁂ CTV in all bedrooms ₱ ♿
Conference facilities available ♀ English & French.
Last dinner 10.30pm ♥ S% *sB&B£25 sB&B⇌⁂£34
dB&B£30 dB&B⇌⁂£40 Lunch£3.25&alc
Dinner£17.50alc Wine£4.75 ₱ Credit cards ①②③④⑤

★★★**Bellahouston** 517 Paisley Rd West (Swallow)
☎041-427 3146 Telex no 778795
71⇌ Lift ♪ ⁂ CTV in all bedrooms ® 150P ♀ English & French. Last dinner 9.30pm ♥ ♫ S%
*sB&B⇌⁂£19.80–£25 dB&B⇌⁂£25–£35
Lunchfr£3.40 High Tea fr£2.50 Dinnerfr£5 Wine£3.40
₱ xmas Credit cards ①②③④⑤

☆☆☆**Glasgow Crest** Argyle St, Anderston (Crest)
☎041-248 2355 Telex no 779652
Closed Xmas; 117⇌⁂ Lift ♪ ⁂ CTV in all bedrooms ®
Conference facilities available ♀ European.
Last dinner 9.30pm ♥ S% *sB&B⇌⁂£26.60
dB&B⇌⁂£36.70 Lunch£3.25–£4.20&alc
Dinner£3.75–£5&alc Wine£3.25 ₱
Credit cards ①②③④⑤

☆☆☆**Ingram** Ingram St (Reo Stakis) ☎041-248 4401
Telex no 778704
90⇌ Lift ♪ ⁂ CTV in all bedrooms ® 30P Conference facilities available ♀ English & French. Last dinner 9.45pm
♥ ♫ *sB&B⇌fr£28 dB&B⇌fr£37 Lunchfr£2.25&alc
Tea fr50p Dinnerfr£7&alc Wine£3 ₱
Credit cards ①②③⑤⑥

★★★**North British** 50–51 George Sq (British Transport)
☎041-332 6711
Large four-storeyed building with a modern extension forming part of the north side of Glasgow's famous George Square.
130rm(91⇌⁂) Lift ♪ ⁂ CTV in all bedrooms ® 150P ♿
Conference facilities available Last dinner 10.30pm ♥
♫ ♥ *sB&B⇌⁂£16–£18.50 sB&B⇌⁂£20–£27
dB&B£29.50–£35 dB&B⇌⁂£33–£39.50
Lunchfr£5.50&alc Tea fr£3.50&alc High Tea fr£3.50
Dinnerfr£6.50&alc Wine£4.80 ₱ xmas
Credit cards ①②③④⑤⑥

☆☆☆**Pond** Great Western Rd (Reo Stakis) ☎041-334 8161
Telex no 778704
Modern hotel on north-west suburbs of city.
137⇌ Lift ♪ ⁂ CTV in all bedrooms ® 200P Live music & dancing Tue ♀ English & French. Last dinner 10pm ♥ ♫
*sB&B⇌fr£28 dB&B⇌fr£36 Lunchfr£2.95&alc
Tea fr45p Dinnerfr£7&alc Wine£3 ₱
Credit cards ①②③⑤⑥

★★★**Tinto Firs** 470 Kilmarnock Rd (Thistle)
☎041-637 2353 Telex no 778329
This modern hotel is situated on the A77, in a residential area south of the city.
30rm(24⇌⁂) Lift ♪ ⁂ CTV in all bedrooms ® 46P Live music & dancing Fri ♀ Scottish & Continental.
Last dinner 9.30pm ♥ sB&B⇌£27–£28
sB&B⇌⁂£33–£34 dB&B⇌⁂£41–£42
Lunchfr£4.90&alc Dinnerfr£6.50&alc Wine£3.70 ₱
Credit cards ①②③④⑤⑥ NB

★★**Buckingham** 31 Buckingham Ter (Inter-Hotels)
☎041-334 4847 Telex no 777205
31rm(13⇌⁂) Lift ♪ ⁂ CTV CTV in all bedrooms ® 6P
Last dinner 8pm ♥ ♫ Credit cards ①②③⑤⑥

★★**Ewington** Queens Dr, Queens Park ☎041-423 1152
48rm(4⇌⁂£33–£34 dB&B⁂£41–£42 Lift ♪ ♿ CTV 12P ⁂ billiards
*sB&B⇌⁂£11.78–£12.65 sB&B⇌⁂£14.95–£15.53
dB&B£23–£24.75 dB&B⇌⁂£25.88–£27.60
Lunch£2.50–£3.50 Tea fr£1.50 High Tea fr£3
Dinnerfr£5.90

★★**Lorne** 923 Sauchiehall St (Thistle) ☎041-334 4891
86rm(48⇌⁂) Lift ♪ ⁂ CTV in bedrooms ∅ 8P 22♿
♀ Mainly grills. Last dinner 9.30pm ♥ ♫ ₱
Credit cards ①②③④⑤

★★**Newlands** 260 Kilmarnock Rd (Scottish & Newcastle)
☎041-632 9171
Set in the southern suburbs of the city, this small hotel is conveniently situated on the A77 road and adjacent to a commuter station.
17rm(15⇌⁂) ♪ ⁂ CTV CTV in all bedrooms ® ♀ Scottish & French. Last dinner 9.30pm ♥ ♫ sB&B⇌fr£15.50
dB&B⇌fr£29 Bar lunch fr£1 Dinnerfr£4 Wine£3.30 ₱
Credit cards ①②③④⑤

☆☆**Shawlands** 30 Shawlands Sq, Shawlands Shopping Centre (Scottish & Newcastle) ☎041-632 9226
Modern hotel forming part of a modern shopping precinct on the south side of the city.
20⇌⁂ Lift ♪ ⁂ TV in all bedrooms ® 100P ♀ Scottish & French. Last dinner 8.30pm ♥ ♫ S% sB&B⇌⁂£25
dB&B⇌⁂£32 Bar lunch £1.50alc Tea 75p alc
Dinner£6.50alc Wine£3.30 ₱
Credit cards ①②③④⑤

★★**Sherbrooke** 11 Sherbrooke Av, Pollokshields
☎041-427 4227
7rm(5⇌⁂) ⁂ CTV CTV in bedrooms ∅ 50P ♿ ♱
♀ Mainly grills. Last dinner 10.30pm ♥

O Grosvenor Great Western Rd (Reo Stakis) ☎041-339 8811
96⇌

O Holiday Inn Glasgow Argyle St, Anderston (Holiday Inns) ☎041-226 5577 300⇌

GH Burnbank Hotel 67–85 West Prince's St
☎041-332 4400 36hc 5⇌⁂ (4fb) CTV ⁂ D7pm

GH Chez Nous 33 Hillhead St, Hillhead ☎041-334 2977
Lic 14hc (2fb) CTV 9P ⁂ S%
B&b£6.90–£7.50 Bdi£11.65–£12.25 D4.30pm

GH Dalmeny Hotel 62 St Andrews Dr, Nithsdale Cross
☎041-427 1106 Lic 10hc 2⇌ 2⁂ (1fb) ∅ CTV
20P ⁂ S% B&b£12.42–£20.13

GH Devonshire Hotel 5 Devonshire Gdns, Gt Western Rd, Kelvinside ☎041-334 1308 Tem 22hc 2⇌ 2⁂ (5fb)
CTV 8P ❄ *B&b fr£8.05 Bdi fr£12 D8pm

GH Kelvin Private Hotel 15 Buckingham Ter, Hillhead
☎041-339 7143 14hc (2fb) ∅ CTV 5P ⁂ S%
B&b£10–£12.50 W£65–£82.50 M

GH Linwood House 356 Albert Dr, Pollokshields
☎041-427 1642 16hc (2fb) ∅ CTV 7P ⁂ S%
B&b£7.50–£8.50

GH Marie Stuart Hotel 46–48 Queen Mary Av, Cathcart
☎041-423 6363 Closed 1 Jan Lic 34hc 8⇌ 1⁂
(4fb) CTV 20P ⁂ S% *B&b£12.50 Bdi£16.50
D7.30pm

GH Smith's Hotel 963 Sauchiehall St ☎041-339 7674
26hc (7fb) ∅ CTV ⁂ S% B&b£8.05–£10.35

GH Wilkie's 14–16 Hillhead St, Hillhead ☎041-339 6898
Closed Xmas & New Year 13hc (12fb) CTV 5P
B&b£6.50–£7.50

×××**Ambassador** 19–20 Blythswood Sq ☎041-221 2034
Closed Sun & Public Hols; Lunch not served Sat (bar only); 100 seats ₱ Live music & dancing Tue–Sat
♀ International. Last dinner 11pm ♥ Lunch£4.80&alc
Dinner£12alc Wine£5 Credit cards ①②③⑤

××**L'Ariosto** 92–94 Mitchell St ☎041-221 0971
144 seats ₱ Live music Mon ♀ French & Italian.
Last dinner 11pm S% *Lunch£3.30–£4.80&alc
Dinner£10alc Wine£4.80 Credit cards ①②③⑤

××**Basement at Archie's** 27 Waterloo St ☎041-221 3210
Closed Sun; Lunch not served Sat; 48 seats ₱
♀ International. Last dinner 11pm Lunch£5–£5.50alc
Dinner£5–£5.50alc Wine£3.50 Credit cards ①②③⑤⑥

✹××**Colonial** 25 High St ☎041-552 1923
Closed Public Hols, Xmas, New Year & Etr; 60 seats ₱
♀ French. Last dinner 11pm Lunch£2.50–£4.50&alc
Dinnerfr£6&alc Credit cards ①②③⑤⑥

Glasgow Airport–Glenborrowdale

××Kensingtons 164 Darnley St, Pollockshields ☎041-424 3662
Closed Sun & Mon; Lunch not served Sat; 30 seats ♬
♀International. Last dinner 10.30pm S%
✻Lunch£5.23–£6.88 Dinner£12alc Wine£4.35
Credit cards ①②③⑤

××Pendulum 17 West Princes St ☎041-332 1709
Closed Sun, 1wk New Year & 3–18 Aug; Lunch not served Sat; Dinner not served Mon; 50 seats ♀Continental.
Last dinner 10pm ✻Lunch fr£2.50&alc Wine£4.70
Credit cards ①②

××Poachers Ruthven Ln ☎041-339 0932
Closed Sun; 55 seats 8P Last dinner 11pm
✻Lunch£8alc Dinner£10alc Wine£4.15
Credit cards ①②③⑤

××Le Provençal 21 Royal Exchange Sq ☎041-221 0798
Closed Sun; 48 seats ♬ ♀French. Last dinner 11pm
Credit cards ①②③④⑤

××Shish Mahal 45 Gibson St ☎041-339 8256
Unlicensed; No corkage charge; 110 seats ♬
♀Indonesian & Pakistani. Last dinner 11.30pm
Credit cards ①②③⑤

×Buttery 654 Argyll St ☎041-221 8188
45 seats 100P ♀Scottish & Continental.
Last dinner 9.30pm ✻Lunch fr£3.15&alc Dinner£8.50alc
Credit cards ①②③⑤

×Danish Food Centre 56–60 St Vincent St ☎041-221 0518
Closed Sun & Public Hols; 86 seats ♀Danish.
Last dinner 10.30pm S% ✻Lunch fr£3.50 Wine£3.50
Credit cards ①②③⑤

×Koh-I-Noor 4 Gibson St ☎041-339 4257
Closed Xmas day; Unlicensed; 104 seats ♬ ♀Indian.
Last dinner 11.30pm Credit cards ①②③⑤

×Loon Fung 417 Sauchiehall St ☎041-332 1240
90 seats ♀Cantonese. Last dinner 11.45pm
Lunch£1.65 Dinner£3alc Credit cards ②③⑤

×New Oriental 41 Hope St ☎041-221 1950
Closed 1–2 Jan; 60 seats ♬ ♀Cantonese.
Last dinner 11.30pm Lunch£2–£2.50
Dinner£5.50–£7&alc Wine£5.50 Credit cards ①②③⑤

×Trattoria Lanterna 35 Hope St ☎041-221 9160
Closed Sun; 52 seats ♬ ♀Italian.
Last dinner 10.15pm ✻Lunch£3.80&alc Wine£3.70
Credit card ②

×Ubiquitous Chip Ashton Ln, off Byres Rd ☎041-334 5007
Closed Sun; 120 seats ♬ ✼ ♀International.
Last dinner 10.45pm ✻Lunch£5alc Dinner£9alc
Wine£3 Credit card ②

At **Bearsden** (6m NW A81)
✰✰**Burnbrae** Milngavie Rd (Reo Stakis) ☎041-942 5951
15rm(13⇨) 100P

At **Stepps** (5m E A80)
✰✰✰**Garfield** (Scottish & Newcastle) ☎041-779 2111
21⇨🚿 120P

GLASGOW AIRPORT Strathclyde Map 37 NS46
Glasgow 8 London 413 Paisley 2 Renfrew 3
★★★★**Excelsior** Abbotsinch (Trusthouse Forte)
☎041-887 1212 Telex no 777733
305⇨ Lift ♪ ⊞ ♨ CTV in all bedrooms ® 35P Conference facilities available Last dinner 10pm ✿ ♫
SB&B⇨£35.60–£38.60 dB&B⇨£47.20–£51.20 ♬
Credit cards ①②③④⑤

✰✰✰**Normandy** Inchinan Rd, Renfrew (2m NE A8)
(Reo Stakis) ☎041-886 4100 Telex no 778897
142⇨ Lift ♪ ♨ CTV in all bedrooms ® 150P Disco Fri, Sat & Sun Conference facilities available ♀English & French.
Last dinner 10.45pm ✿ ♫ ✻sB&B⇨fr£30
dB&B⇨fr£38 Lunch fr£3.75&alc Dinner fr£7&alc
Wine£3 ♬ Credit cards ①②③⑤⑥

★★★**Dean Park** 91 Glasgow Rd, Renfrew (3m NE A8)
☎041-886 3771 Telex no 779032
120⇨ ♪ ♨ CTV CTV in all bedrooms ® 250P ♣ Children under 15yrs not accommodated Conference facilities

available ♀English & French. Last dinner 9.30pm ✿ ♫
sB&B⇨£21.50–£23 dB&B⇨£31–£33
Lunch£3.75–£4.25&alc Tea 60p–90p
High Tea£2.50–£3.50 Dinner£6.25–£6.75&alc Wine£4
♬ xmas Credit cards ①②③⑤⑥

★★★**Glynhill** Paisley Rd, Renfrew (2m E A741)
☎041-886 5555 Telex no 779536
Modern low rise hotel situated on outskirts of town.
80rm(78⇨🚿) 2⃣ ♪ ♨ CTV CTV in all bedrooms ® 200P
Live music & dancing 4 nights wkly Conference facilities available ♀International. Last dinner 10.15pm ✿ ♫
sB&B⇨£25.50 sB&B⇨🚿£27.50 dB&B⇨🚿£34
Lunch£4.50&alc Tea 50p High Tea£3.75 Dinner£7&alc
Wine£3.95 ♬ xmas Credit cards ①②③

★★**Ardgowan** Paisley (3m S) ☎041-887 2196
A modern brick and concrete built hotel, situated about five minutes' walk from the town centre.
18rm(6⇨12🚿) 1⃣ Lift ♪ ♨ CTV CTV in all bedrooms ®
50P Live music & dancing Sat ♀English & Continental.
Last dinner 9.30pm ✿ ✻sB&B⇨fr£19
dB&B⇨🚿fr£29 Lunch£2.30–£4 Tea fr75p
Dinner£4.95&alc Wine£3.40

★★**Rockfield** 125 Renfrew Rd, Paisley (2m SE A741)
(Ind Coope (Alloa)) ☎041-889 6182
20⇨ CTV in all bedrooms ® 75P ♀European.
Last dinner 8.30pm ✿ ♫ ✻sB&B⇨£19.50
dB&B⇨£29.50 Lunch£5.50alc Dinner£6.50alc
Wine£3.25 ♬ Credit cards ①②③

✰☆**Watermill** Lonend, Paisley (3m S) (Reo Stakis)
☎041-889 3201 Telex no 778704
Pleasantly located in the centre of Paisley, this four-storey hotel is a conversion from the original mill and stable buildings. A waterfall at the rear adds to its character.
51⇨ Lift ♪ ♨ CTV in all bedrooms ® 50P ♫ Mainly grills.
Last dinner 10pm ✿ ♫ ✻sB&B⇨fr£25.50
dB&B⇨fr£34 Lunch£3.50–£6&alc Tea fr40p
Dinner£3.50–£6&alc Wine£4.05 ♬
Credit cards ①②③⑤

GH Ardgowan 92 Renfrew Rd, Paisley ☎041-889 4763
11 Jan–19 Dec 6hc (3fb) TV available in some bedrooms 6P ♨ S% B&b£8.50–£10.50

GH Broadstones Private Hotel 17 High Calside, Paisley
☎041-889 4055 8hc (2fb) CTV 12P ♨ S%
B&b£9–£10

×××**Ristorante Piccolo Mondo** 63 Hairst St, Renfrew
(3m NE) ☎041-886 3055
Italian restaurant and function suite with modern red-brick façade; set on corner site in town centre.
Closed Sun; 270 seats 52P Live music & dancing nightly Cabaret Wed, Fri & Sat ♀English, French & Italian. Last dinner 10pm Lunch£3.02–£4.95&alc
Dinner£5.32–£8.25&alc Wine£3.20
Credit cards ①②③④⑤⑥

×**Junction Diner** 2 New St, Paisley (3m S) ☎041-889 4104
Closed Sun; 42 seats 12P Disco Mon, Wed, Fri & Sat
♀European. Last dinner 11pm S%
✻Lunch£1.70–£2.60&alc Dinner£7alc Wine£4.10
Credit cards ②③

×**Shezan Tandoori** 82 Glasgow Rd, Paisley
☎041-889 6485
58 seats ♬ ♀Indian. Last dinner mdnt

At **Erskine** (4m NW A8)
✰✰✰**Crest** North Bar, Inchinnan (Crest) ☎041-812 0123
185⇨ 350P

GLENBORROWDALE Highland Map 38 NM66
Fort William 56(fy40) Lochaline Pier 38 London 572(fy556)
★★**Clan Morrison** ☎232
Closed end Oct–mid Mar; 6⇨🚿 ♨ 60P ♣ ♪ ♣ ♿
Last dinner 8.30pm ✿ ♫

★★🍴**BL Glenborrowdale Castle** (Trusthouse Forte)
☎266
Closed Nov–Feb; 23rm(2⇨) ♪ CTV in all bedrooms ® 40P
♣ ♣ Last dinner 9.30pm ✿ ♫ S%
sB&B£22.10–£24.10 dB&B£34.20–£37.20

111

Glenborrowdale contd–Glenrothes

dB&B⇌£42.20–£46.70 Credit cards ① ② ③ ④ ⑤

GLENCAPLE 275 Dumfries & Galloway Map30NX96
Carlisle32 Dumfries5 London339
★★**Nith** ☎213
10rm(1⇌2⇌) ⊕ TV in all bedrooms ® 60P billiards sauna bath Disco Sat Live music & dancing Sat
Last dinner 8.30pm ✧ ⌀ ✻sB&B£10 sB&B⇌⌀£10
dB&B£18 dB&B⇌⌀£20 Lunch£2.40alc
Tea80p–£1.20 High Tea fr£2.90 Dinner£6alc
Wine£3.50 Credit card ①

GLENCARSE Tayside Map41NO12 Dundee16 London458 Perth6
★★L **Newton House** ☎250
Former dower house situated on the edge of the village, bordering the main Perth to Dundee road.
7rm ⊕ CTV ⇌ 50P ⬚ ♡ Scottish & French. Last dinner 9pm
✧ sB&B£14–£16 dB&B⇌£21–£23 Lunch£5
Dinner fr£8.50&alc Credit cards ① ③

GLENCOE 195 Highland Map39NN15 Crianlarich36 Fort William16 Glasgow88 London501
★★**Glencoe** ☎Ballachulish245
A roadside, painted stone building, which has been modernised and extended. It stands at the head of Glencoe overlooking Loch Leven and the mountains.
15rm(2⇌) ⊕ CTV 40P Last dinner 8pm ✧ ⌀
✻sB&B£6.50–£8.50 sB&B⇌£9.50–£10.50
dB&B£13–£17 dB&B⇌£17–£21 Bar lunch£3.50
Tea45p Dinner fr£3 Wine£3.60
★★**Kings House** (12m SE A82) ☎Kingshouse259
Stone inn dating from early 1700s; used as a barracks for George III after the Battle of Culloden (1746).
Closed Nov–Feb; 22rm(10⇌) 60P ⬚ International.
Last dinner 8.15pm ✧ ⌀ sB&B£13 sB&B⇌£15
dB&B£24 dB&B⇌£28 Bar lunch fr£1.50 Teafr45p
High Tea fr£1.50 Dinner fr£6 Credit cards ① ② ⑥
★**Clachaig Inn** ☎Ballachulish252
10rm(4⇌) ⊕ 30P ⇌ Last dinner 7.45pm ✧ S%
sB&B£8–£10 dB&B£16–£18 dB&B⇌£18–£20
Bar lunch 30p–£2.50 Dinner£4–£8 Wine£3.80
GH Dunire ☎Ballachulish318 6hc (4fb) TV 10P ⊕
S% ✻B&B£5.50–£6 Bdi f£8–£8.50 D6.30pm
GH Scorrybreac ☎Ballachulish354 Jan–Oct 5hc
(2fb) ⊕ nc5 CTV 8P ⊕ lake S% B&b fr£5.50
Bdi fr£8.50 D6.30pm

GLENDEVON Tayside Map40NN90 Edinburgh32 London443 Perth23 Stirling20
××**Tormaukin Hotel** ☎252
Closed Jan & Feb; 74seats 100P bedrooms available
♡ International. Last dinner 9.30pm
✻Bar lunch£3.50&alc Dinner£8.50alc Wine£4.30

GLENEAGLES Tayside Map40NN91 **See Auchterarder**

GLENFARG 319 Tayside Map40NO11 EcThu Kinross7 Kirkcaldy18 London451 Perth11
★★**Bein Inn** ☎216
10rm(7⇌) ⊕ CTV TV in 7bedrooms ® 100P 12⬚ ⬚
Last dinner 9.30pm ✧ ⌀ ✻sB&B£11.75 sB&B⇌£16
dB&B£17 dB&B⇌£21.50 Lunch£3–£6 Tea60p–£1
High Tea£3 Dinner£5–£11&alc Wine£3.90   xmas
Credit cards ① ③ ⑥

GLENLUCE 725 Dumfries & Galloway Map30NX25 EcWed
Girvan37 London408 Newton Stewart15 Stranraer10
★**King's Arms** Main St ☎219
Small hotel set in centre of village on main road between Newton Stewart and Stranraer.
RS Nov–Mar; 8rm(2⇌) CTV 16P ⊕ Last dinner 8pm ✧
⌀ ✻sB&B£8.05 dB&B£16.10 dB&B⇌£18.40
Lunch£2–£2.50&alc Tea50p&alc Dinner£4–£6&alc
Wine£3

GLENMAVIS Strathclyde Map34NS76 Airdrie1 Coatbridge2 Glasgow14 London400
FH Mrs P. Dunbar **Braidenhill** (NS742637)
☎Glenboig872319
300-year-old farmhouse on the outskirts of Coatbridge. About ½ mile from town boundary N off B803.
3hc (1fb) CTV 4P ⊕ 50acres arable S% B&b£7

GLENROTHES 37,500 Fife Map41NO20 EcTue Kirkcaldy7 Kinross12 London451 Perth22
★★★**⚑ Balgeddie House** Leslie Rd ☎742511
Large mansion dating from 1936 standing in six acres of gardens and tree covered land on hillside.
Closed 1 & 2 Jan; 19rm(13⇌) ⊕ CTV in all bedrooms ⇌ 50P
⬚ ⬚ ♡ English & French. Last dinner 9pm ✧ ⌀
sB&B£17.85–£25.20 sB&B⇌£26.70–£29.20
dB&B£35.70–£38.10 dB&B⇌£40.76–£45.90
Lunch£7.50alc Tea fr60p Dinner£6.50&alc Wine£4.95
  Credit cards ① ② ③
★★**Golden Acorn** Central Av (Osprey) ☎752292
Modern hotel beside new town shopping centre.
24rm(20⇌) Lift ⌀ CTV CTV in all bedrooms ® 300P Live music & dancing Sat ♡ Scottish & French.
Last dinner 9.30pm ✧ ⌀ S% sB&B£13.05
sB&B⇌£16 dB&B£21 dB&B⇌£25.50
Lunch£3.50&alc Teafr£1 High Tea fr£2.50
Dinner fr£5&alc Wine£3.50   xmas
Credit cards ① ② ③ ④ ⑤
★★**Greenside** High St, Leslie (2m W A911) ☎743453
Three storey Victorian stone house with modern extensions standing in main road at eastern approach of village on outskirts of industrial Glenrothes.
16rm(9⇌) ⌀ CTV CTV in 9bedrooms ® 50P 4⬚
♡ English & French. Last dinner 8.45pm ✧ S%
✻sB&B£15.80 sB&B⇌£19.60 dB&B£24.65
dB&B⇌£28.75 Lunch£2.95&alc Dinner fr£3&alc
★★**Rothes Arms** South Park Rd (Scottish & Newcastle)

The Bein Inn
Glenfarg ★★

Perthshire PH2 9PY
Telephone (05773) 216

Nestling in beautiful Glenfarg, eight miles south of Perth, just off the M90, is where you will find the Bein Inn. The public rooms are in the traditional style, comfortable and full of atmosphere. The bedrooms, most with private bath and TV, are spacious, bright and modern. Edinburgh, Perth, Dundee and St. Andrews, are all within easy motoring distance.
A golfers paradise with St. Andrews, Gleneagles, Carnoustie and many more within easy reach.
Special Bargain-Break prices available for Spring/Autumn.
Send for brochure and terms.
Personally supervised by Mike and Elsa Thompson

Dalmunzie House, The Hotel in the Hills, Glenshee, Perthshire PH10 7QG

Dalmunzie Hotel; Scotland's highest, is set in 6000 acres of Perthshire Highlands and therefore provides the peace and beauty for which so many desire.

The hotel is of a very high standard, having 22 bedrooms, many of which have private bathrooms. The lounges and cocktail bar are comfortable and spacious. The hotel has its own golf course, tennis court; fishing and there is a games room for the younger set. Apply to T. Campbell for further information.

Telephone Glenshee (025 085) 224/5

☎753701
15rm(7⇌) ♪ 卌 CTV in all bedrooms ® ⊘ 100P Disco 5nights wkly Live music & dancing 5nights wkly Lastdinner9pm ♡ S% *sB&B£14.50 sB&B⇌£18.50 dB&B£23.50 dB&B⇌£28 Lunchfr£3.50&alc Dinnerfr£3.50&alc Wine£3.45 🅿
Creditcards 1 2 3 4 5

GLENSHEE (Spittal of) Tayside Map40 NO16 Braemar16 Perth35 Pitlochry25 London487
★★ ⚑ **Dalmunzie** ☎224
Closed 25Oct–18Jan; 19rm(10⇌) Lift 30P 2🏰 ⇌ ⚓ ❀(hard) ⋓ Lastdinner8pm ♡ ⚷ S%
*sB&B£14–£16 dB&B£26–£34 dB&B⇌£32–£40 Barlunch75p Tea£1–£1.45 Dinnerfr£7.50 Wine£4.15
🅿 Creditcards 1 4

GOLSPIE 1,374 Highland Map47 NH89 EcWed Dornoch11 Helmsdale17 Inverness70 London638
★★ **Golf Links** ☎3408
A converted red stone manse dating from 1870. Sea front location, near to harbour and golf course.
10rm(5⇌) 卌 CTV 16P 🎾 ⚓ Lastdinner8pm ♡ ⚷
sB&B£13.50–£15 sB&B⇌£15.50–£17 dB&B£25–£28 dB&B⇌£29–£32 Barlunch£1.75alc Dinnerfr£8 Wine£3.60 🅿
★★ **Sutherland Arms** Old Bank Rd ☎3216
17rm(1⇌1🛁) 1🍽 🎾 卌 CTV 20P 2🏰 ⚓ ⋓ ♀English & French. Lastdinner8pm ♡ ⚷
GH Glenshee Station Rd ☎3254 6hc (2fb) ⊘ CTV 12P 卌 S% B&b£5–£5.50

GOREBRIDGE Lothian Map35 NT36 Edinburgh11 Galashiels22 Haddington14 Dalkeith5 Peebles18 London370
★★ **HL Auld Toll** Newtonloan Toll ☎21253
10rm(2⇌1🛁) 卌 CTV ® ⊘ 50P Live music & dancing wkly

♫ ♿ Lastdinner9.30pm ♡ *sB&B£8.50
sB&B⇌🛁£10 dB&B£17 dB&B⇌🛁£20
Lunch£3.25&alc Dinner£2.95–£4.50 Wine£3.70

GOUROCK 11,152 Strathclyde Map33 NS27 EcWed Glasgow27 Greenock4 Largs15 London432
☆☆☆ **Gantock** Cloch Rd (Reo Stakis) ☎34671
Telexno778704
Modern building situated one mile southwest of town, with views out across the Clyde.
63⇌ ♪ 卌 CTV in all bedrooms ® 80P Conference facilities available ♀English & French. Lastdinner10pm ♡ ⚷
*sB&B⇌fr£24.75 dB&B⇌fr£34 Lunchfr£2.90&alc Teafr25p Dinner£8.50alc Wine£4.70 🅿 xmas
Creditcards 1 2 3 5 6
GH Claremont 34 Victoria Rd ☎31687 6hc (2fb) CTV 卌 river S% B&b£7 W£49 M

GRANGEMOUTH 24,347 Central Map34 NS98 EcWed Edinburgh24 Glasgow28 London421 Stirling15
★★ **Leapark** 130 Bo'ness Rd ☎486733
Detached stone mansion, standing in own grounds, close to town centre.
35rm(5⇌) ♪ 卌 CTV in 14bedrooms TV in 21bedrooms 150P ⚓ Disco Sun Live music & dancing Tue ♀International. Lastdinner9.30pm ♡ ⚷ S%
*sB&Bfr£18.50 sB&B⇌fr£20.50 dB&Bfr£26 dB&B⇌fr£28 Barlunch£1–£2 Tea60p–£1.50 Dinner£3.50–£10&alc Wine£3.20 xmas
Creditcards 1 2 3 5 6

GRANTOWN-ON-SPEY 1,591 Highland Map44 NJ02 EcThu Kingussie27 Inverness35 London546
★★ **Ben Mhor** High St ☎2056
24rm(20⇌4🛁) 卌 CTV TV in all bedrooms 20P
Lastdinner8.30pm ♡ ⚷ sB&B⇌🛁£10–£12.50 dB&B⇌🛁£20–£22 Lunch£3.50–£4 Tea50p–75p

---

GOLF LINKS HOTEL

Golspie (Tel 3408) Sutherland
AA ★ ★

Magnificently Situated Beside Beach and Golf Course. The Third Tee is 100 yards from the Hotel.
Excellent Licensed Hotel Overlooking the Dornoch Firth.

10 Bedrooms, 5 with private bathroom, Central Heating throughout, TV Lounge, 3 self-catering units, Hairdressing Salon.

Ideal Centre for Touring & Bird Watching. Fishing in Angling Association Lochs.

Grantown-on-Spey contd – Hamilton

High Tea £3 – £4.50 Dinner £6.50 – £7.50 &alc Wine £4.50
Credit cards ① ⑤ ⑥

★★**Coppice** Grant Rd ☎2688
Detached two-storey stone building dating from 1890, standing in two acres of grounds.
24rm CTV 40P ♨ Last dinner 8pm ⚑ ⚑ S%
✱sB&B £8 – £12 dB&B £12 – £18 Bar lunch £1 – £2.50
Tea £1 High Tea £2.50 – £4 Dinner £4 – £5 Wine £2.90

★★**Garth** Castle Rd ☎2836
Charming conversion of 18th-C house.
14rm Annexe: 3⇨ ♨ ⚑ CTV 8P 2♨ ⚑ ♨ ♨ (grass)
♨ International. Last dinner 9.30pm ♨ ⚑ S%
sB&B £9 – £10 sB&B ⇨ ♨ £10 – £11 dB&B £18 – £20
dB&B ⇨ ♨ £21.80 – £23 Lunch £2.75 – £3.80
Tea 40 – 60p High Tea £2 – £3.50 Dinner fr £5.95 &alc
Wine £3.10 ⚑ xmas Credit cards ③ ⑤ ⑥

★★**Rosehall** The Square ☎2721
14rm(4⇨2♨) ⚑ CTV TV available in bedrooms ⓑ 20P ⚑
Last dinner 8pm ♨ S% sB&B ♨ £11 – £12
sB&B ⇨ ♨ £16.65 – £18.50 dB&B £22 – £24
dB&B ⇨ ♨ £23.50 – £26 Lunch £3 – £4.50
High Tea £3.50 – £4.50 Dinner £6.50 Wine £3.20 xmas

★★**Seafield Lodge** Woodside Av ☎2152
Converted detached house dating from 1910 standing in quiet residential street.
RS Nov – Mar; 14rm(3⇨6♨) ⚑ CTV 50P ♨ ⚑
Last dinner 8.15pm ♨ sB&B ♨ £11.50 – £12.50
sB&B ⇨ ♨ £13.22 – £14.67 dB&B £23 – £25
dB&B ⇨ ♨ £26.45 – £28.75 Bar lunch £2 – £3.50
Dinner fr £7 Wine £4.10 ⚑ Credit card ②

◉ **Dunvegan** Heathfield Rd ☎2301
Closed 19 – 29 Dec; 9rm ⚑ CTV 9P 1♨ ⚑
Last dinner 7.30pm ♨ sB&B £8.25 – £9.25
dB&B £16.50 – £18.50 Bar lunch £50p Tea 50 – 90p
Dinner £5 Wine £3.50 ⚑

◉ **Holmhill** Woodside Av ☎2645
10rm ⚑ CTV 12P 2♨ ⚑ ♨ Last dinner 7.45pm S%
sB&B £7.95 – £8.95 dB&B £15.90 – £17.90 Dinner £4 – £5
Wine £3.20

◉ **Ravenscourt** Seafield Av ☎2286
Closed Nov – 27 Dec; Unlicensed; 9rm ⚑ CTV 10P ⚑ ⚑
Last dinner 7.30pm ♨ ♨ S% sB&B £7 – £8
dB&B £14 – £16 Dinner £4 – £5

GH Braemoray Private Hotel Main St ☎2303 Feb – Nov
Lic 7hc 3⇨ ♨ (1fb) CTV 6P ⚑ D7.30pm

GH Dar-il-Hena ☎2929 Etr – Oct 7hc (3fb) CTV 10P
⚑ S% B&B fr £7.75 Bdi fr £12 Wfr £80 Ł D7pm

GH Dunachton off Grant Rd ☎2098 Jan – Oct 7hc (2fb) ⚑ CTV 8P ⚑ B&B £6.90 – £7.40
Bdi £10.25 – £10.90 W £65 – £72 Ł D7pm

GH Kinross House Woodside Av ☎2042 Closed Xmas
6hc (2fb) ⚑ S% ✱B&B fr £8.50 Bdi fr £12.90
Wfr £87 Ł D4.30pm

GH Pines Hotel Woodside Av ☎2092 Etr – Sep 10hc (2fb) ⚑ CTV 4P S% B&B fr £7 Bdi fr £11 D7pm

GH Riversdale Grant Rd ☎2648 7hc (3fb) ⚑ CTV 8P ⚑ S% B&B £6.50 – £7 Bdi £9.50 – £10
W£63 – £66.50 D6pm

GH Umaria Woodlands Ter ☎2104 7hc (4fb) TV 10P
S% ✱B&B £6.50 – £7 Bdi £10.50 – £11 Wfr £70 Ł D5pm
✕**Craggan Mill** ☎2288
Closed Nov; Lunch not served winter months; 45 seats
25P Live music Sat ⚑ British & Italian. Last dinner 10pm
✱Lunch £5 alc Dinner £6.50 alc Wine £3.40

GREENOCK 66,456 Strathclyde Map33 NS27 EcWed
Glasgow23 Gourock2 London429 Wemyss Bay8
★★★**Tontine** 6 Ardgowan Sq (Best Western) ☎23316
Telex no 779801
19th-C building, with extension wing, situated on square in west end of town.
32rm(23⇨21♨) ♨ ⚑ CTV in all bedrooms ⓑ 20⚑
Last dinner 9pm ♨ S% sB&B £21 sB&B ⇨ ♨ £23
dB&B £33 dB&B ⇨ ♨ £37 Lunch fr £4.75
High Tea fr £3.75 Dinner fr £6.75 &alc Wine £4.75 ⚑

Credit cards ① ② ③ ⑤ ⑥
✕**La Taverna** 6 West Blackhall St ☎25391
Closed Sun; 48 seats Last dinner 9.45pm
Credit cards ① ⑤

GRETNA 1,907 Dumfries & Galloway Map31 NY36 EcWed
Annan8 Carlisle10 Dumfries24 London317
★★**Gretna Chase** (¼m S on B721 in England) ☎517
10rm(1⇨2♨) ⚑ CTV ♨ 40P ⚑ ♀ English & French.
Last dinner 9.30pm ♨ sB&B £14 sB&B ⇨ ♨ £16 – £26
dB&B £24 dB&B ⇨ ♨ £28 Lunch £4.50 &alc
Dinner £6 alc Wine £3.40 ⚑

★★**Royal Stewart Motel** ☎210
Bungalow-style motel on the outskirts of the town which is now bypassed.
Closed Sep; RS Oct, Feb & Mar; 13rm(8⇨ ♨) ⚑ CTV CTV
available in all bedrooms 17P Last dinner 9pm ⚑

★★**Solway Lodge** Annan Rd ☎266
3rm Annexe: 10rm(7⇨) ⚑ CTV ⓑ 40P Last dinner 9pm ♨
⚑ ✱sB&B £11.50 sB&B ⇨ £14 dB&B £20.70
dB&B ⇨ £20.70 Lunch £3.25 Tea fr 50p
Dinner £4.85 – £7.20 &alc Wine £3.20

GH Surrone House Annan Rd ☎341 Lic 6⇨ ♨ (5fb)
⚑ CTV 20P ⚑ ✱B&B £10.35 Bdi £15.35

GRETNA GREEN 130 Dumfries & Galloway Map31 NY36
Carlisle10 Dumfries25 Lockerbie15 London317
★★**Gretna Hall** ☎257
The original marriage house of Gretna Green; catering mainly for tourists.
Closed Jan; 51rm(6⇨) Annexe: 28♨ 1⚑ ♯ CTV ⓑ P ⚑
Live music & dancing twice wkly (summer only)
Last dinner 9.30pm ♨ sB&B £11 – £12.50
sB&B ⇨ ♨ £13 – £14.50 dB&B £22 – £25
dB&B ⇨ ♨ £26 – £29 Lunch £5 Dinner £6 alc
Wine £3.10 ⚑ xmas Credit cards ① ② ⑤ ⑥

GH Greenlaw ☎361 Etr – Oct 8hc (1fb) CTV 8P sea
S% B&B £5.50 – £6

GUILDTOWN Tayside Map40 NO13 Perth6 Blairgowrie10
London458
INN Angler's Rest Main Rd ☎Balbeggie329 Lic 5hc ⚑ nc3 CTV 40P ⚑ D9.30pm

GULLANE 1,701 Lothian Map35 NT48 EcWed Dalkeith16
Edinburgh19 London395 North Berwick5
★★★(red)⚑ **BL Greywalls** Duncar Rd ☎842144
Telex no 727796
This country house, designed by Lutyens, has a homelike atmosphere. Its comfort and good food have been acknowledged by the award of Red Stars.
Closed mid Oct – mid Apr; 26rm(23⇨) ♯ ⚑ CTV 50P ⚑ ⚑(hard) ♨ Last dinner 9pm ♨ ⚑ sB&B £28
sB&B ⇨ £32 dB&B £56 dB&B ⇨ £64 Lunch £4 alc
Tea £1.50 alc Dinner £10 Wine £5
Credit cards ① ② ③ ⑤ ⑥

★★**Bissets** ☎842230
Victorian building in two acres of grounds situated in the centre of small village.
RS Xmas; 26rm Annexe: 8rm CTV ⓑ 25P 3⚑ ⚑
Last dinner 9pm ♨ ⚑ ✱sB&B £10 – £12
dB&B £18 – £22.40 Lunch fr £3.95 Tea fr £1.20
High Tea fr £2.50 Dinner fr £6.50 Wine £3.80 ⚑ xmas
Credit card ③

◉✕**La Pontinière** Main St ☎843214
Closed Wed & Oct; Lunch not served Sat; Dinner not served Mon, Tue, Thu, Fri & Sun; 34 seats 10P ⚑
♀ French. Lunch £6.50 – £7.50 Dinner £9.50 Wine £4
✕**Tartufo** Main St ☎842233
Closed Mon; Lunch not served Tue – Sat; 35 seats ⚑
♀ Italian. Last dinner 10.30pm Dinner £7 – £10
Wine £4.50 Credit cards ② ③ ⑤

HAMILTON 45,176 Strathclyde Map37 NS75 MdTue cattle
Glasgow10 Lanark15 London393 Motherwell3

★★**Commercial** 29 Townhead St (Osprey) ☎282757 Telex no778278
White-fronted hotel with modern extension to rear, located on busy one-way street in the town centre.
20rm(10⇌) ♪ ♨ CTV CTV in 9bedrooms ® 30P ⚓
♀ Scottish & French. Last dinner 9.30pm ⚙ ♫ S%
sB&B£12.45 sB&B⇌£16.25 dB&B£20 dB&B⇌£25.50 Lunch£3.50&alc Tea£1 High Tea£2.50 Dinner£5&alc Wine£3.50 ☒ xmas Credit card ⑤
★**Royal** New Cross (Ind Coope (Alloa)) ☎285926
Small hotel on corner site above shops in centre of town.
6rm(1⇌) ♨ CTV ® ♬ European. Last dinner 8.45pm ⚙ ♫ *sB&Bfr£11.50 dB&Bfr£18.50 Lunch£5.50alc Dinner£6.50alc Wine£3.40 ☒ Credit cards ① ③ ⑤
×× **Costa's** 17–21 Campbell St ☎283552
Closed Sun & 1Jan; 52seats ♬ ♀ International. Last dinner 10.30pm Lunch£2.60&alc Dinner£8alc Wine£4.50 Credit cards ① ② ③ ⑤ ⑥
×**Il Frate** (Friar Tuck) 4 Barrack St ☎284319
Closed Sun; 52seats ♀ Italian. Last dinner 11pm

HARDGATE 3,729 Strathclyde Map37NS47 EcWed Clydebank2 Dumbarton8 Glasgow8 London413
★★**Cameron House** Main St ☎Duntocher73535
17rm(4⇌13♨) Lift ♪ ♨ CTV in all bedrooms ⚓ 50P ⚓ Live music & dancing Sat Last dinner 9.15pm ⚙ ♫ S%
sB&B⇌♨£16 dB&B⇌♨£22 Lunch£1.30–£1.80 Dinner£5.75–£7&alc Wine£3

HARRAY Orkney Map48HY31 EcFri Kirkwall11 Stromness10 **(car ferry to Scrabster)**
★★**Merkister** ☎366
RS Oct–Mar; 19rm(2⇌♨) CTV 30P ⚓ Last dinner 9pm ⚙ ♫

HARRIS, ISLE OF Western Isles Map48 **See Scarista and Tarbert**

HAUGH OF URR Dumfries & Galloway Map30NX86 Dumfries15 Castle Douglas5 Dalbeattie4 London352
FH Mrs G. J. MacFarlane **Markfast** *(NX817682)* ☎220
Typical modernised farmhouse. Situated at the gateway to Galloway's historic and picturesque scenery with wide choice of beaches, fishing, etc.
3rm (3fb) ⚓ TV 3P 140acres beef S% B&b£5 Bdi£7 W£49 ⚓ D3pm

HAWICK 16,378 Borders Map35NT51 EcTue Carlisle44 Jedburgh14 London352 Selkirk12
★★**Crown** High St (Osprey) ☎3344 Telex no778278
Centrally-situated in main shopping street adjoining 19th-C stone buildings.
32rm(6⇌) ♨ CTV CTV in 6bedrooms ® 12P ♀ Scottish & French. Last dinner 9.30pm ⚙ ♫ S% sB&B£12.45 sB&B⇌♨£16.29 dB&B£22 dB&B⇌£27.50 Lunch£3.50&alc Tea£1 High Tea£2.50 Dinner£5&alc Wine£3.50 ☒ xmas Credit cards ① ② ③ ④ ⑤
★★**Kirklands** West Stewart Pl ☎2263
Late Victorian sandstone house standing in quiet residential area of town.
Closed Xmas; 6rm(2⇌1♨) Lift ♨ CTV in all bedrooms ® 20P ⚓ ♀ English & French. Last dinner 8.30pm ⚙ sB&B£14 sB&B⇌♨£15.50 dB&B£25 dB&B⇌♨£27 Lunch£2.60–£3&alc Dinner£7.50–£8&alc Wine£3.20 ☒
★★**Teviotdale Lodge Country** (7m S off A7) ☎Teviotdale232
RS Oct–Mar; 8rm(2⇌) 1☐ ♨ CTV in all bedrooms ® ⚓ 30P ⚓ ⚓ Last dinner 8pm S% sB&B£11 dB&B£22 dB&B⇌£24 Lunch£2–£4 Dinner£6–£9 Wine£4 ☒ Credit cards ① ③

HELENSBURGH 13,956 Strathclyde Map33NS28 EcWed Dumbarton8 Glasgow23 London428
★★★**Queen's** East Clyde St ☎3404

Originally established by Henry Bell, the pioneer of steam navigation.
21rm(10⇌♨) ♪ ♨ CTV CTV in 1bedroom 60P ⚓ ⚓
♀ French. Last dinner 9pm ⚙ Credit cards ① ② ③
★★**Cairndhu** Rhu Road Lower ☎3388
13rm(5⇌♨) ♪ CTV ⚓ 60P ⚓ Last dinner 9pm ⚙
Credit cards ② ③ ⑤
GH Aveland 91 East Princes St ☎3040 6hc (2fb) nc5 CTV 6P river S% B&b£6–£6.50 Bdi£9–£9.50 W£57–£67 ⚓ D6pm
FH Duirland *(NS299872)* Glen Fruin ☎3370
A comfortably-sized farmhouse situated away from main road.
Jun15–Sep 3hc ⚓ nc5 CTV 5P 2⚓ 775acres mixed
×**Ruby Chinese** West Clyde ☎4080
First-floor restaurant overlooking Firth of Clyde in town's main street.
88seats ♬ ♀ English & Chinese. Last dinner 11.30pm

HOLLYBUSH 101 Strathclyde Map34NS31 London392 Ayr6 Dumfries55 Girvan19
★★★⚓ **Hollybush House** ☎Dalrymple214
Closed 25–27 Dec; 12rm(7⇌♨) ♨ CTV 40P 6⚓ ⚓ ⚓
♀ French. Last dinner 9.30pm ⚙ ♫
Credit cards ① ② ③ ⑥
FH A. Woodburn **Boreland** *(NS400139)* ☎Patna228
Two-storey farmhouse with rough cast exterior, situated on the banks of the River Doon. West off A713 south of village.
Jun–Sep 3rm (2fb) ⚓ TV 10P ♨ 105acres dairy S% B&bfr£5.50

HOWGATE Lothian Map35NT25 Edinburgh11 Penicuik2 Peebles12 London397
×× **Old Howgate Inn** Wester Howgate ☎Penicuik74244
Old coaching house reputed to have been used by pilgrims on their way south from Edinburgh.
Closed Xmas Day & 1–2Jan; 50seats 50P ♀ Danish. Last dinner 10pm ✱ Lunch£10alc Dinner£10alc

HUMBIE Lothian Map35NT46 Haddington9 Lauder12 Edinburgh18 Dalkeith11 London376
★★★⚓ **HBL Johnstounburn House** (1m S A6137) ☎696 Telex no727897 (DOOCOT)
Originating in 1625, this fine country house hotel stands in sheltered walled gardens amongst mature trees and yew hedges. It was extended in the 18th & 19th C eventually being converted into a hotel in 1980. A particular feature is the 18th-C dovecote.
11rm(9⇌2♨) ♨ CTV in all bedrooms ® 100P 1⚓ ⚓ ⚓
♀ French. Last dinner 9pm ⚙ ♫ sB&B⇌♨£15–£28 dB&B⇌£30–£40 Bar lunch£1.50–£5 Tea£1–£3 Dinner£10.50–£11.50&alc Wine£4.80 ☒ xmas Credit cards ① ② ③ ⑤

HUNA Highland Map47ND37 Wick18 Thurso18 London693
GH Haven Gore ☎John O'Groats314 5hc (3fb) CTV 8P ♨ sea S% B&b£5–£6 Bdi£8–£9

HUNTLY 4,124 Grampian Map45NJ53 EcThu MdWed Aberdeen39 Banff21 Keith11 London575
★★★⚓ **Castle** ☎2696
Closed Jan & Feb; 24rm(6⇌3♨) 1☐ ♨ CTV 20P 3⚓ ⚓ ⚓ Last dinner 9.45pm ⚙ sB&B£14.50 sB&B⇌♨£16.50 dB&B£27 dB&B⇌♨£29 Lunch fr£3 Tea fr£1 High Tea fr£4 Dinner fr£6.50 Wine£3.89 ☒ Credit cards ③ ⑤
★★**Gordon Arms** The Square (Scottish & Newcastle) ☎2536
14rm CTV ® 6P Last dinner 8pm ⚙ ♫ sB&Bfr£11.50 dB&Bfr£19.50 Lunch£2.25–£3 Tea£1.05 High Tea£1.70–£3.66 Dinner£4alc
Wine£3.45 ☒ Credit cards ① ② ③ ④ ⑤ ⑥

Come for a meal · for a weekend · for a week or more

Standing in its own grounds on the outskirts of Huntly, the Castle Hotel, hospitable as befits its heritage . . . for this was formerly the ancient home of the Gordons . . . offers every comfort, spacious lounges, varied menus and a well-stocked cellar. Fully licensed. Write for illustrated brochure.
THE RIVER DEVERON PROVIDES EXCELLENT FISHING BOTH ON HOTEL WATER, AND ON OTHER BEATS AVAILABLE TO GUESTS.

CASTLE HOTEL huntly
ABERDEENSHIRE
Tel: Huntly 2696

INCHNADAMPH Highland Map46NC22 Dornoch50 Inverness85 Lairg33 London650
★★*Inchnadamph* ☎Assynt202
Closed Nov–Feb; 30rm(7⇌🛁) TV 30P 4🐕 ⇌ ♋
Last dinner8pm ♢ ♋

INVERARAY 468 Strathclyde Map39NN00 EcWed (not summer) Glasgow59 Lochgilphead25 London462 Oban38
★**Fernpoint** Ferryland ☎2170
Closed Nov–Feb; 6rm(5🛁) 🎗 🍴 CTV CTV in 5bedrooms ®
12P ⛳ 🛥 Last dinner10pm ♢ ♋ S%
sB&B£9.75–£11.75 sB&B⇌£11.75–£14.75
dB&B£19.50–£23.50 dB&B⇌£23.50–£29.50
Bar lunch£2.35–£4.85&alc Tea£1–£1.85
High Tea£2.95–£4.95 Dinner£6&alc Wine£4.35 🍷
Credit cards ① ② ③ ⑤

INVERGARRY 178 Highland Map43NY30 Fort William25 Invermoriston14 Inverness41 London541
★★♿**Glengarry Castle** ☎254
A Victorian mansion with ruins of Invergarry Castle in the grounds.
Closed 15Oct–7Apr; 30rm(9⇌) 🍴 CTV 45P ⛳ 🛥(hard)
Last dinner8.15pm ♢ ♋ S% sB&B£11–£12.25
dB&B£22–£24.50 dB&B⇌£26.50–£29
Lunch£3.75–£4 Tea£1.15–£1.35 Dinner£6–£6.75
Wine£3
GH *Graigard* ☎258 Apr–Oct Lic 7hc (2fb) ⌀ nc5 6P D6.30pm
GH *Lundie View* Aberchalder (3m NE A82) ☎291 Lic 6hc (3fb) CTV 8P 🍴 S% ✻B&bfr£5.50 Bdifr£9 Wfr£61 ⛳ D7.30pm
FH Mrs G. Swann *Ardgarry* (NH286091) ☎226
Warm and comfortable traditional Scottish farmhouse and lodge dated 1868 in a quiet position off A87.
Mar–Oct 1hc (A3hc) (1fb) CTV 6P 10acres mixed
S% B&b£6–£6.50 Bdi£9–£9.50 W£63–£66.50 ⛳

D4pm
FH Mrs L. Brown **Faichem Lodge** (NH286014) ☎314
Modernised old stone house.
3hc (1fb) CTV 4P 🍴 7½acres mixed S%
B&b£5–£6 Bdi£9–£10 D7pm

INVERKEITHING 6,139 Fife Map35NT18 EcWed Dunfermline4 Edinburgh13 Kirkcaldy13 London431
★**Queens** Church St ☎413075
13rm 🍴 CTV ⇌40P Last dinner9pm ♢ ♋ S%
✻sB&Bfr£10.50 dB&Bfr£18 Bar lunch85p–£1.75
Tea50p High Tea£2–£3 Dinner£5.50–£5.85&alc
Wine£3.21

INVERKIP 751 Strathclyde Map34NS27 EcWed London429 Glasgow30 Greenock6 Largs8
★★**Langhouse** Langhouse Rd ☎Wemyss Bay521211
8rm(3⇌) 🎗 CTV ® 30P ⛳ ♋ Last dinner8.45pm
♋ sB&B£13.75 sB&B⇌£15.90 dB&B£24.75
dB&B⇌£28.75 Lunch£4.25 Tea£1.50 High Tea£4.50
Dinner£6.75 Wine£3.25 *xmas*

INVERMORISTON 114 Highland Map43NH41
Fort William29 Invergarry14 Inverness28 London555
GH *Tigh Na Bruach* ☎Glenmoriston51208 Etr–mid Oct
7rm 5hc (2fb) nc5 12P lake B&bfr£8.05
Bdifr£12.65 Wfr£72.45 ⛳ D7.30pm

INVERNESS 36,595 Highland Map43NH64 EcWed MdSat
Dingwall21 Fort William66 London565 Nairn16
★★★★♿**HL Culloden House** Culloden Moor (2m E off A96) ☎Culloden Moor461 *(due to change to Inverness 790461 during the currency of this guide)* Telex no75402
21⇌ 3🛁 ♪ 🍴 CTV in all bedrooms 50P 🐕 🛥 sauna bath
Last dinner10pm ♢ ♋ sB&B⇌£36.80–£39.68
dB&B⇌£51.75–£57.50 Lunch fr£7.50&alc Tea fr£2.50
Dinner fr£9.60 Wine£4 Credit cards ① ② ③ ⑤

FERNPOINT HOTEL — Inveraray

Inveraray's most historic building (built 1751)
Located by pier on lochside.

**Come and visit our
JACOBEAN RESTAURANT & BAR**
Bar lunches: 12-6.00pm.
Evening restaurant: 6.30-10pm.
Bar hours: 11am-11pm Mon to Sat.
12-11pm Sunday.

Accommodation available in rooms with en suite facilities.

Tel: Inveraray 2170

Children welcome in our restaurant and garden.

Inverness contd

☆☆**Caledonian** Church St (Allied (Scotland)) ☎35181
Telex no76357
120⇌ Lift ♪ ⌸ ⓡ 70P Disco 3nights wkly Live music & dancing 6nights wkly & Conference facilities available
♡English & French. Last dinner 10pm ✣ ⌓
sB&B⇌fr£22 dB&B⇌fr£38 Lunch fr£6 Tea fr£2
Dinner fr£8 Wine£2.50 ℞ *xmas*
Credit cards ① ② ③ ④ ⑤

★★★**HBL Kingsmills** Damfield Rd (Best Western)
☎37166 Telex no75566
Conversion of 18th-century Provost's House, standing in three acres of gardens.
54⇌ 㡀 ♪ CTV CTV in all bedrooms ⓡ 100P ♨ squash
Conference facilities available Last dinner 9.45pm ✣ ⌓
sB&B£12.50 – £18.50 sB&B⇌㡀£18.30 – £35
dB&B£20 – £28 dB&B⇌㡀£28 – £48 Lunch£3alc
High Tea£2.50alc Dinner£6.50 – £8.75&alc Wine£4.95
℞ Credit cards ① ② ③ ④ ⑤ ⑥

☆☆**Ladbroke Mercury Hotel** (& Conferencentre) Nairn Rd (junction A9/A96) (Ladbroke) ☎39666 Telex no75377
84⇌ 㡀 Lift ♪ CTV in bedrooms 150P Conference facilities available Last dinner 10.30pm ✣ ℞
Credit cards ① ② ③ ④ ⑤

⊛★★★**Station** Academy St (British Transport) ☎31926
Telex no75275
Attractive large building forming part of the city's railway station.
65rm(52⇌) Lift ♪ TV in 13bedrooms CTV in 52bedrooms
5P ✱Scottish, English & French. Last dinner 9pm ✣ ⌓
S% ✱sB&B£15 sB&B⇌£28.35 dB&B£23
dB&B⇌㡀£44 Lunch fr£5 Tea fr£1.95 Dinner fr£8&alc
Wine£4.75 ℞ Credit cards ① ② ③ ④ ⑤

⊛★★(red) ♨**Dunain Park** ☎30512
(Rosette awarded for dinner only)
A very personal hotel with individuality and character which has earned a Red Star award. Much of the food is home-grown as well as home-cooked.

The Ladbroke Mercury Hotel, Inverness, is the Centre of Attractions

Inverness — the capital of the Highlands — a city full of interest. From here you can visit the beautiful and mysterious Loch Ness and the historic battle field of Culloden. The hotel has a choice of two bars and an impressive restaurant — the Eight Pointer.

You'll find plenty of exciting holiday ideas in our Lazydays brochure — try a Scottish Weekaway — tailor made for touring in your own car, or take a Welcome Break from as little as £25.00 per person bed & breakfast.

For your Lazydays brochure, 'phone 01-734 6000 or write to PO Box 137, Watford, Herts. WD1 1DN.

Ladbroke Mercury Hotel,
Nairn Road,
Inverness, IV2 3TR.
Tel: (0463) 39666

⌾ Ladbroke Hotels

Closed mid Nov – mid Mar; 6rm(4⇌) 1🚻 ♪ CTV 30P 1🅿 🚗
♨ ♡International. Last dinner 9pm ✣ ⌓
dB&B£30 – £42 dB&B⇌£35 – £48 Bar lunch£5alc
Tea£4alc Dinner fr£13

★★**Beaufort** 11 Culduthel Rd ☎222897
21rm(19㡀) ♪ CTV in all bedrooms 53P 🚗
Last dinner 10pm ✣ ⌓ sB&B㡀£16.50 – £18.50
dB&B㡀£31 – £33 Lunch£4 – £6 Tea£1 – £1.50
Dinner£7 – £9 Wine£6 ℞ *xmas* Credit cards ① ③

★★**Craigmonie** Annfield Rd (Scottish & Newcastle)
☎31649
Gabled and turretted red sandstone mansion dating from 1832 with modern extension.
10rm ♪ CTV 30P Live music & dancing Sun
Last dinner 8.30pm ✣ ⌓ Credit cards ① ② ③ ④ ⑤

★★**Cummings** Church St ☎32731
38rm(4⇌1㡀) Lift ♪ CTV TV available in bedrooms 25P
Cabaret nightly in season Last dinner 8pm ✣ S%

Kingsmills Hotel Inverness ★★★
the hotel you always look for, but seldom find —
— a first class country hotel in town!

Set in three acres of woodland and gardens, only one mile south of the centre of town, this lovely converted 18th-century mansion reflects the unhurried atmosphere of days gone by, yet combines truly high standards of cuisine and modern comforts with friendly, personal service. Our 54 bedrooms have private bathrooms, colour television, telephones and radio, and offer the choice of luxury bed sitting-rooms, family rooms, really superb 'doubles' and very well appointed twin and single bedded rooms. Private Squash Courts and adjacent to the fine 18 hole Inverness Golf Course. Parking for 100 Cars.

Kingsmills Hotel is personally supervised by the Proprietors, Angus and Lilian Macleod, who look forward with their staff to the pleasure of welcoming you.

Please write for our brochure and tariff, Kingsmill Hotel, Culcabock Road, Inverness.
Telephone: 0463 37166
Telex: 75566

Inverness contd – **Isle Ornsay**

sB&B£13–£15 dB&B£25–£29 dB&B⇌⇧£29–£33
Lunch£3.50–£4.50 Tea85p HighTea£3.50–£5.50&alc
Dinner£5.50–£7 Wine£3 🅿

★★**Drumossie** Perth Rd ☎36451 Telexno777967
81rm(42⇌9⇧) Annexe: 20⇌1☒ ♪ CTV CTV in
40bedrooms ® 80P 🎵 Live music & dancing 3nights wkly in
summer ⛱ ♚ European. Last dinner 8.30pm ⚲
sB&B£14–£17.50 sB&B⇌⇧£16–£19 dB&B£24–£32
dB&B⇌⇧£28–£36 Lunchfr£3.75 Dinnerfr£7 Wine£4
🅿 *xmas* Creditcards ① ② ③ ⑤ ⑥

★★**Glen Mhor** 10 Ness Bank (Inter-Hotels) ☎34308
*Conversion of Tarradale stone mansion dating from 1870.
Set in quiet residential area of town.*
Closed 31Dec–4Jan; 21rm(5⇌8⇧) ⇧ CTV in all bedrooms
® 16P ⚑ ♚ International. Last dinner 9pm ⚲ ⚵ S%
*sB&B£8.50–£13.50 sB&B⇌⇧£12–£19.50
dB&B£17–£27 dB&B⇌⇧£24–£50 Lunchfr£1.65&alc
HighTeafr£2.80&alc Dinnerfr£6.50&alc Wine£4 🅿
Creditcards ① ② ③ ⑤

★★**Glenmoriston** 20 Ness Bank ☎223377
Telexno778215
21rm(10⇌⇧) ® 🎵 Last dinner 10.30pm ⚲ ⚵ 🅿
Creditcards ① ② ③ ④ ⑤ ⑥

★★**Muirtown** 11 Clachnaharry Rd (Scottish & Newcastle)
☎34860
*Low-rise complex with the accommodation in modern
timber-clad chalets. On main road to north of town
overlooking river.*
Annexe: 36rm(20⇌16⇧) Lift ⇎ ⇧ CTV in all bedrooms
® 60P 🎵 Last dinner 9pm ⚲ S% 🅿
Creditcards ① ② ③ ⑤ ⑥

★★**Palace** Ness Walk ☎223243 Telexno777210
38rm(7⇌) Annexe: 41⇌ Lift ♪ CTV® 30P
Last dinner 9pm ⚲ ⚵ S% 🅿 European. Last dinner 9pm
sB&B£12.50–£22 dB&B£16.60–£31.20
dB&B⇌£21–£37.60 Barlunchfr£1.50 Tea£1
Dinner£7.50 Wine£3.25 🅿 Creditcards ① ② ③ ⑤ ⑥

★★**Queensgate** Queensgate ☎37211 Telexno75235
Closed Xmas & New Year; 60⇌ Lift ♪ CTV CTV in
32bedrooms ⇎ ⚑ sauna bath ♨ Conference facilities
available Last dinner 9pm ⚲ ⚵ S%
sB&B⇌£13.50–£20 dB&B⇌£20–£35 Lunchfr£3.50
Teafr£1.50 Dinnerfr£6&alc Wine£3.50 🅿
Creditcards ① ② ③ ⑤ ⑥

★★**Royal** Academy St (Trusthouse Forte) ☎30665
48rm(19⇌) Lift ♪ ⇧ CTV in all bedrooms ® ⚑
Last dinner 9.15pm ⚲ ⚵ S% sB&B£18.60–£20.10
sB&B⇌£21.60–£23.60 dB&B£30.20–£32.70
dB&B⇌£33.20–£35.70 🅿 Creditcards ① ② ③ ④ ⑤ ⑥

★**Redcliffe** 1 Gordon Ter ☎32767
Closed Nov–8Apr; 7rm(2⇌) ⇧ CTV ® ⚑ ⇎ ⚵ English &
French. Last dinner 8.30pm ⚲ S% sB&B£12
dB&B⇌£27 dB&B⇌⇧£24 Barlunch£1.50–£2.50
Dinner£7.50&alc Wine£3.50 🅿

⊕ **Tower** Ardross Ter ☎32765
*On a corner site at the end of a terraced row, dated 1875,
and near the town centre, overlooking the River Ness and
the Castle.*
Closed Sun (Nov–8Apr); 9rm ⇧ ⇧ CTV 4P ⇎
Last HighTea 7.30pm ⚲ S% sB&B£8.05 dB&B£16.10
Lunch£3 HighTea£3 Tea£1 Creditcard ③

GH Abermar 25 Fairfield Rd ☎39019 11hc 3⇌⇧ (3fb)
CTV 9P ⇧ S% B&b£5.50–£6.50 W£38.50–£45.50
M

GH Ardnacoille House 1A Annfield Rd ☎33451
Apr–27Nov Tem 6hc (2fb) ⇎ nc10 CTV 6P ⇧
S% B&b£5.50–£6.50 Bdi£9.50–£10.50 W£63–£70
L D2pm

GH Arran 42 Union St ☎32115 7hc (2fb) TV S%
B&b£5.50–£6

GH Craigside House 4 Gordon Ter ☎31576 Mar–Oct rs
Nov & Feb (dinner only if ordered) 6hc 2⇧ (1fb) ⇎
nc13 4P ⇧ S% B&b£7.50–£8.50 Bdi£13–£15
W£88–£92 L D6pm

GH Four Winds 42 Old Edinburgh Rd ☎30397 25Dec &
1Jan 6hc (2fb) CTV 15P ⇧ S% B&b£6–£6.50
W£40 M

GH Leinster Lodge 27 Southside Rd ☎33311 6hc (2fb)
CTV 8P ⇧ S% B&b£6

GH Lyndale 2 Ballifeary Rd ☎31529 Closed Xmas & New
Year 6hc (1fb) CTV 6P B&b£5–£6

GH Moray Park Hotel Island Bank Rd ☎33528 7hc
(4fb) ⇎ CTV 10P ⇧ S% B&b£7.70 Bdi£13.60
W£89.50 L D5pm

GH Riverside Hotel 8 Ness Bank ☎31052 9hc (3fb) ⇎
CTV river S% B&b£7–£8.50 Bdi£12–£13.50
W£82–£92 L D7pm

GH *Tigh a' Mhuillinn* 2 Kingsmill Gdns ☎38257 6hc
CTV 8P D2pm

×× **Dickens** 77–79 Church St ☎224450
60seats ♚ International. Last dinner 11pm
*Lunchfr£2&alc Dinner£10alc Wine£5

× **Bishop's Table** Eden Court Theatre, Ness Walk ☎39841
Closed Sun; 134seats 200P Live music & dancing Sat
Last dinner 9pm *Lunch£2.35–£4.65
HighTea£3.10–£5.10 Dinner£6.90&alc Wine£3.50
Creditcard ③

INVERSHIN Highland Map46NH59 Dornoch17
Inverness52 London617 Tain19

★★⊕ **Aultnagar Lodge** (2½m N A836) ☎245
RS Dec–Mar; 27rm(2⇧) 10☒ Lift CTV ® 50P 4⇎ 🎵
Cabaret Wed ♪ Last dinner 9pm ⚲ ⚵ S% sB&B£8
sB&B⇌⇧£9 dB&B£18 dB&B⇌⇧£20
Lunch£3–£3.50 Tea£1.50 HighTea£4.50
Dinner£5.50–£6 Wine£2 🅿 *xmas*

★★**Invershin** ☎202
Closed 1st wk Jan; 12rm(4⇌1⇧) Annexe: 12rm(6⇌3⇧) ⇧
CTV in 20bedrooms TV in 4bedrooms ® 50P 🎵 ⇎ ♨
Last dinner 9.30pm ⚲ ⚵ S% sB&B£8.50–£9.50
sB&B⇌⇧£9.50–£10 dB&B£19–£20
dB&B⇌£20–£22 Lunchfr£3 Teafr£1 HighTeafr£3
Dinner£5–£6.50 Wine£2 🅿 Creditcards ① ③ ⑤

INVERURIE 5,617 Grampian Map45NJ72 EcWed
Aberdeen17 Huntly23 London555 Old Meldrum5

★**Gordon Arms** The Square ☎20314
11rm CTV ® ⚑ ⇎ Last dinner 8pm ⚲ ⚵ S% *sB&B£9.75
dB&B£17.50 Lunch£2.50 HighTea£1.50–£3.50
Dinner£4.25 Wine£3.20

× **J.G.'s** Market Pl ☎21378
Closed Sun; Dinner not served Mon; 50seats 25P
Last dinner 9.30pm

ISLAY, ISLE OF Strathclyde Map42
See Bowmore, Port Askaig & Port Ellen

ISLE OF SKYE Highland Map13NG
See Broadford, Clachan, Dunvegan, Isle Ornsay,
Portree, Uig and Waterloo

ISLE OF WHITHORN 222 Dumfries & Galloway
Map30NX43 EcWed Dumfries72 London414 Newton
Stewart21 Stranraer35

⊕★**Queens Arms** ☎369
(Rosette awarded for dinner only.)
10rm(4⇌) CTV ® ⇎ 10P ⇎ Last dinner 9.45pm ⚲
sB&B£9.50 dB&B£19 dB&B⇌£21 Barlunch£3alc
Dinner£5.75–£6.50&alc Wine£3.20

ISLE ORNSAY Isle of Skye, Highland Map42NG61
Armadale Pier8 Broadford10 Kyleakin15

★★**Duisdale** ☎202
Closed Nov–Mar; 23rm(2⇌) CTV ® 25P 🎵
Last dinner 8.30pm ⚲ ⚵ S% *sB&B£10.50–£11.50
dB&B£21–£23 dB&B⇌£25–£27 Barlunch£3.50alc
Teafr£1.25 HighTeafr£3.75 Dinnerfr£7.85 Wine£3.65
🅿

★★ Kinloch Lodge ☎214 Telex no 75442 (Donald G)
12rm(6⇌) TV ⓑ 30P 🐕 ♨ & Last dinner 8pm
S% sB&B£14.50–£16.50 sB&B⇌£17.80–£19.80
dB&B£29–£33 dB&B⇌£35.60–£39.60 Bar lunch £2.50
Tea 90p High Tea £2 Dinners £9.40–£10.40 Wine £4

★ Hotel Eilean Iarmain Camus Croise, Sleat ☎266
Telex no 75252
8rm Annexe: 5rm 2🛏 15P 🐕 Last dinner 8.30pm 🇻 🍺
S% ❋sB&B£10–£16.50 dB&B£20–£33
Lunch £3.25–£5.50 Tea 60p–£1.55 High Tea £2.50–£5
Dinner £6.50–£9.50 Wine £3.80 xmas

GH Post Office House ☎201 Feb–Oct 4rm 3hc TV
10P S% B&b£5–£6

JEDBURGH 3,917 Borders Map 35 NT62 EcThu
Edinburgh 48 Hawick 14 Kelso 11 London 332

★★ Jedforest Country House ☎Camptown 274
Mansion dating from 1870, standing in 50 acres of tree-studded parkland bordering the River Jed.
RS Nov; 7rm Annexe: 4🛏 CTV TV in 4 bedrooms ⓑ 40P ♨
🎵 Last dinner 8.30pm 🇻 S% sB&Bfr£11.40
sB&B🛁 fr£16.45 dB&Bfr£18.98 dB&B🛁 fr£22.75
Lunch fr£4.50 Dinner £5–£7 Wine £3.20

GH Ferniehirst Mill Lodge ☎3279 Closed Nov Lic
11hc 6⇌ 3🛁 🐕 nc12 16P 🍽 river
B&b£9.77–£11.50 Bdi£17.25–£18.97 W£125.92 ♨
D8.30pm

GH Kenmore Bank Oxnam Rd ☎2369 6hc (2fb) 🛇
CTV 5P 1🏛 🍽 river S% ❋B&B£6 Bdi£12.50
W£80 ♨ D8.30pm

✕Carters Rest ☎2414
Closed Sun (Nov–Etr); 80 seats P 🍺 Mainly grills.
Last dinner 9pm ❋Lunch fr£3.50&alc Wine £3.50
Credit cards ②

JOHN O'GROATS 195 Highland Map 47 ND37
Inverness 142 London 705 Thurso 20 Wick 17

★★ John O'Groats House ☎203
Said to be the most northerly house on the British mainland, it overlooks the harbour with views across Stroma to the Orkneys.
Closed Nov–Mar; 18rm 🍽 CTV 50P 5🏛 ♨ 🎵 🍺 Scottish & French. Last dinner 9pm 🇻 🍺 sB&B£9–£12
dB&B£20–£24 Lunch £2.50–£3&alc Tea£1.50&alc
High Tea£3.50–£4.75 Dinner £6.50alc Wine £3 🍺
Credit cards ① ③

★ Sea View ☎220
This stone building stands on the roadside overlooking Pentland Firth and Isles of Stroma and Orkney.
9rm 🍽 CTV 20P 2🏛 ♨ Last dinner 8pm 🇻 🍺

JOHNSTONE BRIDGE Dumfries & Galloway Map 35 NY19
Carlisle 32 Dumfries 17 London 340 Moffat 9

★★ Dinwoodie Lodge Main Rd ☎289
A lodge house on the A74 positioned at the turn off for Newton Wamphray.
8rm 🍽 TV in all bedrooms ⓑ 100P 4🏛 ♨ &
Last dinner 9.30pm 🇻 ❋sB&B£10.50 dB&B£18
Lunch £4–£4.60 Tea £1.50 High Tea £3.45–£5.50
Dinner £6alc Wine £3.90 Credit cards ① ② ③ ⑤ ⑥

JURA, ISLE OF Strathclyde Map 42
See Craighouse

KEITH 4,208 Grampian Map 45 NJ45 EcWed Aberdeen 50
Elgin 17 Huntly 11 London 586

★★ Royal Church Rd ☎2528
14rm(3⇌) 🍽 CTV 20P 4🏛 Last dinner 9pm 🇻 🍺
sB&B£11.50–£12.65 sB&B⇌£13.80–£14.95
dB&B£20.70–£23 dB&B⇌£25.30–£28.90
Lunch£3.45–£4.45 Tea 60p–£1.50 High Tea£3–£4.45
Dinner £6.50–£8 Wine £2.80 🍺 xmas
Credit cards ① ③ ④ ⑤ ⑥

GH Aultgowrie 124 Moss St ☎2052 5hc (1fb) 🛇 CTV
4P 2🏛 🍽 S% B&b£6 Bdi fr£9 W£58.80 ♨ D5pm

FH Mrs J. Jackson **Haughs** (NJ416515) ☎2238
Attractively decorated farmhouse. 1 mile from Keith off A96.
May–15 Oct 4hc (1fb) 🛇 CTV 8P 2🏛
220 acres mixed S% B&b£5–£5.50 Bdi£7.50–£8
W£50–£54 ♨ D9pm

FH Mr & Mrs J. H. Farquhar **Mains of Tarrycroys** (NJ404537) Aultmore ☎2586
Attractive stone farmhouse with large farmyard and several outbuildings surrounded by arable land.
4rm 2hc (1fb) 🛇 nc5 TV 6P 43 acres arable S%
B&b£5.50 Bdi£8.50 Wfr£56 ♨ D7pm

FH Mrs E. C. Leith **Montgrew** (NJ453517) ☎2852
Farmhouse with several outbuildings and pleasant views. 2m E off A95.
May–Sep 4rm 1hc (1fb) 🛇 CTV 4P 211 acres arable
beef S% B&bfr£4.25 Bdifr£6 Wfr£42 ♨ D7pm

FH Mrs G. Murphy **Tarnash House** (NJ442490) ☎2728
Two-storey, stone farmhouse with well-maintained garden to the front. Surrounded by farmland 1m S off A96.
May–Oct 4hc (1fb) 🛇 CTV 10P 1🏛 🍽
100 acres arable S% B&b£5.50

KELSO 4,957 Borders Map 36 NT73 EcWed Berwick-upon-Tweed 24 Edinburgh 43 Jedburgh 11 London 343

★★★ Cross Keys The Square (Inter-Hotels) ☎3303
Modernised coaching inn standing in cobbled square in town centre.
26rm(9⇌4🛁) Lift 🎵 🍽 CTV in all bedrooms ⓑ 12P
Last dinner 9pm 🇻 ❋sB&B£13.45–£14.45
sB&B⇌🛁 fr£14.45–£15.45 dB&B£24.90–£26.90
dB&B⇌🛁 £26.90–£28.90 Lunch £3.75 Tea£1.25
High Tea £3.75 Dinner £6.50&alc Wine £4.60 🍺
Credit cards ① ② ③ ⑤ ⑥

★★★ Ednam House Bridge St ☎2168
Large Georgian house built in 1761, set in 3 acres of grounds, on the banks of the River Tweed.
Closed Xmas & New Year; 32rm(18⇌2🛁) 🍽 CTV 100P 2🏛
🐕 ♨ Last dinner 9pm 🇻 sB&Bfr£15.87
sB&B⇌🛁 fr£18.51 dB&Bfr£31.74 dB&B⇌🛁 fr£37
Lunch fr£4.20 Tea fr£1.50 Dinner fr£7.60&alc

★★ House o'Hill ☎2594
Two-storey house in elevated position with superb views over town and River Tweed.
Closed 2wks Jan; 7rm(1⇌) 🍽 CTV CTV in 5 bedrooms 100P
♨ 🐾 (hard) Children under 3yrs not accommodated
Last dinner 8.30pm 🇻 sB&Bfr£12.65
dB&B£22–£26.40 dB&B⇌£29.70 Lunch fr£2.75
Tea fr£1.50 High Tea fr£4 Dinner fr£6.50 🍺

★ Queens Head Bridge St ☎2636
Coaching inn dating from 1780, standing in centre of border town.
9rm(1⇌) 🍽 CTV 🍺 🍴 French. Last dinner 9pm S%
sB&B£8.90–£12.80 sB&B⇌£10.20–£15
dB&B£16.40–£20.60 dB&B⇌£19–£23.45
Bar lunch £1.45–£2.50 High Tea £2.95–£3.15
Dinner £6.40–£6.80 Wine £3.25 🍺 Credit card ①

GH Bellevue Bowmont St ☎2588 8hc (2fb) 🛇 CTV
8P S% B&b£5.50 Bdi£9 D5pm

KENMORE 211 Tayside Map 40 NN74 EcThu (not summer)
Aberfeldy 6 London 470 Perth 38 Pitlochry 21

★★★ Kenmore Village Sq ☎205
Reputed to be Scotland's oldest inn. Robert Burns is said to have stayed here.
30rm(19⇌) Annexe: 18rm(18⇌2🛁) Lift CTV 75P 🐕 ♨
Last dinner 9pm 🇻 ❋sB&Bfr£10 sB&B⇌🛁 fr£15
dB&Bfr£20 dB&B⇌🛁 fr£31 Lunch fr£4.50 Tea fr£1
Dinner fr£7.50 Wine £3.75 Credit cards ① ③

KILCHOAN Highland Map 38 NM46 Fort William 68(fy53)
Lochaline Pier 51 London 584(fy569) Mallaig 30

★★ Kilchoan ☎200
Closed Nov–Mar; 7rm(5⇌🛁) TV in all bedrooms ⓑ
🛇 24P 🐕 ♨ 🍺 Scottish & French.
Last dinner 8pm

KILCHRENAN Strathclyde Map51NN02 Crianlarich35 Inveraray31 London500 Oban19
❀★★★(red) ⚜ **Ardanaiseig** ☎333
Dramatically situated in beautiful gardens beside Loch Awe, this hotel offers the joys of a Highland holiday within its own grounds. British country house cooking at its best and comfortable appointments have helped to earn it three Red Stars.
Closed Nov–8Apr; 16rm(14⇌) 🍴 30P 🚗 ⚓ (hard) ↺ billiards ♀ Scottish & French. Last dinner 10pm ◊ ⚓
S% sB&B£33.50–£38.50 dB&B£67
Lunch£1.20–£7.50 Tea85p–£1.65 Dinner£14&alc
Wine£3.85 Credit cards ① ② ③
★★⚜ **Taychreggan** Lochaweside ☎211
Closed mid Oct–mid Apr; 22rm(11⇌🍴) TV 35P 🚗 ⚓
♀ International. Last dinner 9pm ◊ ⚓
Credit cards ① ② ③ ⑤ ⑥

KILCREGGAN 1,412 (with Cove) Strathclyde Map33NS28
EcWed Glasgow39 Invereray44 London444
★★**Kilcreggan** ☎2243
Closed New Years Day; 10rm(3⇌4🍴) 🍴 CTV CTV available in bedrooms 40P ⚓ ♀ Scottish & French. Last dinner 8pm
◊ S% sB&B£12.50–£14.50 sB&B⇌🍴£14.50–£16.50
dB&B£23–£27 dB&B⇌£27–£31 Bar lunch£1–£2.50
Dinner£6.50–£7 Wine£2.80 Credit cards ① ③ ⑤

KILDRUMMY 206 Grampian Map45NJ41 London541
Aberdeen34 Braemar43 Huntly16
★★★⚜ HL **Kildrummy Castle** (Best Western) ☎288
Closed 6Jan–4Mar; 13rm(9⇌1🍴) 3🍴 🍴 CTV CTV in all bedrooms ⓡ 30P ⚓ ↺ billiards ♀ Last dinner 9.30pm ◊
⚓ sB&B£12.50–£15.50 sB&B⇌🍴£14.50–£17.50
dB&B£25–£31 dB&B⇌🍴£29–£35 Lunchfr£6&alc
Tea fr£1.75 Dinner fr£9.50&alc Wine£4 🍺 xmas
Credit cards ① ② ③ ④ ⑥

KILLEARN 1,086 Central Map37NS58 EcWed
Dumbarton15 Glasgow18 London427 Stirling21
★★**Black Bull** (Ind Coope (Alloa)) ☎50215
Inn dating from 1880 in small country town. Garden at rear.
12rm(5⇌) 🍴 CTV ⓡ 40P ⚓ ♀ European.
Last dinner 8.30pm ◊ ⚓ ✱sB&B£11.50 sB&B⇌£15
dB&B£18.50 dB&B⇌£24 Lunch£7alc Dinner£8.50alc
Wine£3.40 🍺 Credit cards ① ② ③ ⑤

KILLIECRANKIE Tayside Map40NN96 EcThu (not summer) Braemar44 London479 Perth31 Pitlochry4
★★H **Killiecrankie** ☎Pitlochry 3220
Set amidst woodland and well-tended gardens, this attractive white-painted house is located near to National Trust beauty spot.
Closed mid Oct–mid Apr; 12rm(10⇌🍴) 🍴 CTV 30P 🚗 ⚓
⚓ Last dinner 8.30pm ◊
GH Dalnasgadh House ☎237 Etr–Oct 6hc (2fb) ⚓
CTV 10P 🍴 S% B&b£6.50–£7.50

KILLIN 600 Central Map40NN53 EcWed Aberfeldy23
Callander22 London456 Perth44
★★**Bridge of Lochay** ☎272
18th-C drover's inn on outskirts of town close to River Lochay.
Closed Oct–8Apr; 18rm(4⇌1🍴) CTV ⓡ 40P 4🛏 🚗 ⚓
Last dinner 8.45pm ◊ ⚓ S% sB&B£10.50 dB&B£21
dB&B⇌🍴£25 Lunchfr£3.60 Dinnerfr£6.50 🍺
★★**Killin** (Best Western) ☎296
Three-storey hotel dating from 1946 replacing original courthouse and standing on banks of River Lochay in 6 acres of grounds.
Closed Nov–Mar; 30rm(6⇌6🍴) Lift 🍴 CTV CTV available in 3 bedrooms 50P 2🛏 ↺ Last dinner 8.30pm ◊ ⚓
sB&B£12.50 sB&B⇌🍴£16.50 dB&B£22.55
dB&B⇌🍴£28 Lunch£4.25 Tea30p Dinner£7.15
Wine£2.75 🍺 Credit cards ① ② ③ ⑤ ⑥
★★**Morenish Lodge** ☎258
Originally a shooting lodge, built in 1820 for the Earl of Breadalbane, set in 10 acres of grounds.
Closed Oct–Apr; 12rm(3⇌) ⚓ CTV ⚓ 30P 5🛏 🚗 ⚓ ↺
Children under 5yrs not accommodated Last dinner 8pm
◊ ⚓ sB&B£10 dB&B£20 dB&B⇌£23 Bar lunch£2
Tea£1.50 Dinner£7 Wine£2.20
★**Craigard** ☎285
Converted stone town house dating from 1867, standing on main road in town centre.
10rm CTV 10P Live music & dancing mthly Last dinner 8pm
◊ ✱sB&B£6.50–£9.50 dB&B£13–£17
Bar lunch50p–£2.50 Dinner£4.60–£6.40 Wine£3.25
★**Falls of Dochart** Main St ☎237
Closed Nov–8Apr; 8rm(4⇌🍴) CTV 50P 2🛏 ♀ Scottish & Continental. Last dinner 8.30pm

KILMACOLM 3,348 Strathclyde Map34NS36 EcWed (3rd Wed each month all day closing) Dumbarton18 Glasgow17 London424 Paisley10
FH J. A. Blair **Pennytersal** (NS338714) ☎2349
Well-maintained building and courtyard set in rolling farmland. Kilmacolm 2 miles.
Jun–Sep 3rm 2hc (1fb) ⚓ TV P 125acres mixed
S% ✱B&B£5

KILMARNOCK 50,318 Strathclyde Map34NS43 EcWed
MdMon/Fri Ayr13 Glasgow21 Hamilton28 London410
☆☆☆**Howard Park** Glasgow Rd (Swallow) ☎31211
Telex no53168
Closed Xmas & New Year; 46rm⇌🍴 Lift 🌙 🍴 CTV in all bedrooms ⓡ 200P ♀ English & French.
Last dinner 9.30pm ◊ S% ✱sB&B⇌🍴£22.30
dB&B⇌🍴£29.70 Lunch£3.50&alc Dinner£5.60&alc
Wine£2.90 🍺 Credit cards ① ② ③ ④ ⑤ ⑥
✗**Coffee Club** 30 Bank St ☎22048
Unlicensed; 100seats 🅿 Last dinner 10pm
✱Lunchfr£1.75&alc Tea fr£1.75&alc
High Tea fr£1.75&alc Dinner fr£7alc

Kildrummy Castle Gardens Trust

Situated on the Alford-Strathdon road, A97, off the A944, Aberdeenshire. Alpine, shrub and water gardens. Collection of stones and bygones. Open daily 9-5pm. April-October. Car Park 10p (inside hotel entrance), admission 30p each. Coach parties by appointment.

Tel: Kildrummy (STD 03365) 264 & 277
Kildrummy Castle Hotel 288
Kildrummy Inn 277   *Plants for sale*

Killiecrankie Hotel
By Pitlochry, Perthshire ★★
Tel: Pitlochry 3220

Fully licensed country Hotel in 6 acres overlooking Pass of Killiecrankie, 4 miles north of Pitlochry on A9. Twelve bedrooms, 10 bathrooms, excellent restaurant, good wine, bar meals to 10.00 pm. Golf, fishing, shooting, sailing, trekking, hill walking, bird watching in vicinity. *Non-residents, children & dogs very welcome.*

Resident Proprietors: Duncan & Jennifer Hattersley Smith, & Emma.

KILMARTIN Strathclyde Map39NR89 Oban30 Glasgow92 Lochgilphead9 London494
INN Kilmartin Hotel ☎250 5hc CTV 13P sea S% B&B£8.25–£8.80 Bdi£11.75–£12.92 Bar lunch£2alc D8.30pm £6alc
✕ *Cairn* ☎254
Closed 24 & 25Dec, 1Jan, Feb & 1st 2wks Nov; Dinner not served Sun; 60seats 20P International. Last dinner 9.30pm Credit cards ② ③ ⑤

KILMORY Isle of Arran, Strathclyde Bute Map33NR92 EcWed Brodick17 Lochranza25
★★**Lagg** Sliddery255
Closed Nov–Feb 16rm(7⇨㊅) CTV 40P Last dinner 9pm ✶sB&B£11 sB&B⇨㊅£12 dB&B£22 dB&B⇨㊅£24 Lunchfr£1 Teafr60p HighTeafr£1.80 Dinnerfr£6.50 Wine£2.80

KILWINNING Strathclyde Map33NS34
⊛✕✕**High Smithstown** (off A737 1m N of Kilwinning Station) ☎53689
Closed Sun, Mon & 12–27Oct; Lunch not served; 32seats 16P French. Last dinner 9pm Dinner£8.75–£11.25 Wine£4.25 Credit card ②

KINCLAVEN Tayside Map40NO13 Blairgowrie6 Dundee19 London464 Perth12
★★★♨*BL* **Ballathie House** ☎Meikleour268 Telex no 727396 (Ballathie)
Victorian mansion on the banks of the River Tay. Just north of Stanley on an unclassified road.
Closed Dec–14Jan; 22rm(22⇨2㊅) Annexe: 16⇨ CTV in 22bedrooms TV in 16bedrooms ® 50P Last dinner 9.45pm sB&B⇨㊅£18–£25 dB&B⇨㊅£38–£48 Lunch£3–£5 Dinner£9–£12 🍺
Credit cards ① ② ④ ⑤ ⑥

KINCRAIG 106 Highland Map44NH80 EcWed Inverness39 Kingussie6 London528
★★**Ossian** ☎242
Closed 6Jan–15Feb; 9rm TV 20P Last dinner 9pm S% ✶sB&B£12 dB&B£24 Dinner£5.50alc Wine£3.75
⊛ *Suie* ☎344
Converted stone house built in 1910 standing in own grounds by main road through small village.
9rm 30P (grass) Children under 6yrs not accommodated Last dinner 7pm Credit cards ② ③

KING EDWARD Grampian Map45NJ75 Banff6 Turriff6 Aberdeen41 London578
FH *Blackton* (NJ726583) ☎205
A well-run working farm catering for family holidays. Banff 6 miles.
May–Oct 5hc CTV 6P 113acres arable beef D6pm

KINGHORN Fife Map35NT28 Kirkcaldy3 Burntisland2 London456
GH *Odin Villa* 107 Pettycur Rd ☎890625 Lic 7㊅ (1fb) CTV 14P sea S% B&b£9.50–£11.50 Bdi£13–£16 W£85–£100 D9pm

KINGSWELLS 228 Grampian Map45NJ80 Aberdeen6 Banchory15 London541 Stonehaven21
FH Mrs M. Mann *Bellfield* (NJ868055) ☎Aberdeen740239
Modernised and extended farm cottage on quiet road and set amid farmlands. 4m W of Aberdeen city centre off A944.
3hc (2fb) CTV 6P 200acres arable dairy S% B&b£5 Bdi£8 D5pm

KINGUSSIE 1,040 Highland Map44NH70 EcWed Grantown-on-Spey27 Inverness45 London522 Pitlochry45
★★**Duke of Gordon** Newtomore Rd ☎302

Killin Hotel
KILLIN, PERTHSHIRE
Tel: Killin 296 and 573

30 bedrooms, all with hot and cold water, Private suites if desired. 8 miles salmon fishing on Loch Tay (boats with out-board motors), golf, boating. Fully licensed, cocktail bar, etc. Central heating. Lift. Extensive parking space. A heart-warming combination of fine food, solid comfort and individual service. Excellent cellar, 3 well-stocked bars.
Open 1st April to 31st October.
Proprietors: Mr & Mrs D Proctor.

Kingussie contd – Kirkcudbright

An Edwardian building with a tower, topped by wrought iron and a pair of stone lions at entrance.
47rm(8⇨) Lift CTV 50P ⚓ billiards Disco Fri
Last dinner 8.45pm ✢ ⚲ sB&B£13 sB&B⇨£15 dB&B£24 dB&B⇨£27 Lunch£3 – £3.50
Tea30p – £1.50 HighTeafr£2.75 Dinnerfr£6 Wine£3.40
🍴 Credit cards ① ② ③ ⑤

★**Silverfjord** Ruthven Rd ☎292
Situated close to station in Spey Valley town with outlook towards Cairngorm mountains.
8rm(2⇨) CTV ® 5P ⚓ ♀ European. Last dinner 8pm ✢ ⚲ S% sB&B£9 – £12 dB&B£18 – £24 dB&B⇨㎡£24 – £28 Bar lunch£3 Tea90p
Dinner£6 – £7&alc Wine£5 🍴 Credit cards ① ② ③

GH Sonnhalde East Ter ☎266 Jan – Nov 6hc (2fb) TV 8P ⚓ S% ✳B&B£7 – £7.50 Bdi£12 – £12.50 Wfr£84 ⚓ D8pm

KINLOCHBERVIE 143 Highland Map46NC25 EcWed
Dornoch69 Inverness107 London672 Thurso91
★★★**Kinlochbervie** ☎275
Modern, two-storey white painted building on hillside overlooking sea.
Closed 20Dec – 4Jan; 10⇨ 🍴 CTV CTV in all bedrooms ® 40P ⚓ Last dinner 8.30pm ✢ ⚲ S% ✳sB&B⇨£17.25 dB&B⇨£34.50 Bar lunch£2.50alc Tea80p alc
Dinner£8alc Wine£3.50 🍴

KINLOCH RANNOCH 241 Tayside Map40NN65 EcWed (not summer) Aberfeldy18 London495 Pitlochry20
★★**Dunalastair** ☎323
RS Nov – Apr; 23rm(10⇨) ♪ 🍴 CTV ® 30P 6🅿 ⚓ ⚓ Last dinner 8.30pm ⚲ sB&B£10.95 sB&B⇨£13.95 dB&B£21.90 dB&B⇨£27.90 Lunch£4.95 Tea35p – £2 HighTea35p – £2 Dinner£6.95 Wine£2.95 🍴
Credit cards ① ② ③ ⑤ ⑥
★★**Loch Rannoch** ☎201
Impressive late 19th-C hillside hotel with views of Loch Rannoch.
17⇨ ♪ ⚲ 🍴 CTV in all bedrooms ® 40P ⚓ ⛅(heated) sauna bath Live music & dancing Wed & Sun ⚓ ♀ European. Last dinner 9.30pm ✢ ⚲ S% sB&B⇨£21 dB&B⇨£32 Bar lunch£1 – £1.80 Teafr£1.50 HighTeafr£1.60 Dinner£6.25 – £8.25&alc Wine£3.95 xmas Credit cards ① ② ③ ⑤

KINROSS 3,082 Tayside Map40NO10 EcThu MdMon
Dunfermline13 Kirkcaldy16 London445 Perth18
★★★**Green** 2 The Muirs (Best Western) ☎63467
Telex no 76684
Fully modernised former coaching inn standing in 6 acres of gardens.
48rm(41⇨7㎡) ♪ CTV available in bedrooms 60P ⚓ ⛅(heated) ⚓ ⚓ squash sauna bath Live music & dancing Fri & Sat ⚓ Conference facilities available ♀ International. Last dinner 9pm ✢ ⚲ S% ✳sB&B⇨㎡£19.50 dB&B⇨㎡£38 Lunch£5.50&alc Tea£2.50alc
HighTea£4.50 Dinner£7 – £8&alc Wine£4.05 🍴
Credit cards ① ② ③ ⑤ ⑥
★★**Bridgend** ☎63413
10rm(3⇨㎡) 🍴 CTV 50P ⚓ Music & dancing 3nights wkly Last dinner 8pm ⚲
★**Kirklands** High St ☎63313
9rm CTV 30P ⚓ ⚓ Last dinner 8pm ✢ S% sB&B£10 dB&B£20 Lunch£2.50 HighTea£2.10 – £3.75 Wine£3.75 🍴
✕✕**Windlestrae** ☎63217
Closed Tue, Jan & 1st wk Oct; 50seats 50P bedrooms available ♀ French. Last dinner 8.55pm S% Lunchfr£6 Dinner£16alc Wine£4.50
Credit cards ① ② ③

KIPPEN 529 Central Map37NS69 EcWed Dumbarton24 Glasgow28 London428 Stirling10
FH Mrs J. Paterson **Powblack** (NS670970) ☎260

Pleasant farmhouse near the River Forth on the Kippen to Doune road.
May – Sep 2hc (1fb) CTV 4P 🍴 300acres mixed
✕**Vinery** (Crosskeys Hotel) Main St ☎293
20seats 8P bedrooms available Last dinner 9.15pm

KIPPFORD 168 Dumfries & Galloway Map30NX85 London354 Dumfries17 Kirkcudbright24
★**Anchor** ☎205
RS Oct – 9Apr; 9rm 🍴 CTV 10P Last dinner 8.30pm ✢ S% sB&B£9 dB&B£18 Bar lunch25p – £3 HighTeafr£3 Dinnerfr£5 – £6.50alc Wine£3

KIRKBEAN Dumfries & Galloway Map30NX95 Dumfries12 Dalbeattie14 London349
GH Cavens House ☎234 Closed 15Dec – 15Jan Lic
6rm 3⇨ 2㎡ (1fb) ⚓ CTV P ⚓ S% B&B£9 – £9.50 Bdi£15.50 – £16

KIRKCALDY 50,063 Fife Map41NT29 EcWed Dundee30
Dunfermline14 Edinburgh26 London444
★★★**Dean Park** Chapel Level ☎61835
19⇨㎡ ♪ 🍴 CTV in all bedrooms ® 200P ⚓ ⚲ ♀ Live music & dancing twice wkly Cabaret twice wkly
Last dinner 10pm ✢ ⚲ Credit cards ① ② ③ ⑤
★★**Station** 4 Bennochy Rd (Osprey) ☎62861
34rm(9⇨) ♪ 🍴 CTV CTV in 6 bedrooms ® 20P ♀ Scottish & French. Last dinner 9.30pm ✢ ⚲ S% sB&B£11.45 sB&B⇨£16.25 dB&B£20 dB&B⇨£25.50 Lunch£3.50&alc Tea£1 HighTea£2.50 Dinner£5&alc Wine£3.50 🍴 xmas Credit cards ① ② ③ ④ ⑤
✕✕✕**Oswald Room** Dunnikier House Hotel, Dunnikier Park ☎68393
Closed Sun; 50seats 100P bedrooms available ♀ French. Last dinner 10pm ✳Lunchfr£5&alc Dinnerfr£5&alc Credit cards ① ② ③

KIRKCOLM 346 Dumfries & Galloway Map30NX06 EcWed Girvan37 London424 Newton Stewart32 Stranraer6
★★⚓**Knocknassie House** Ervie (3½m W off B738) ☎Ervie217
6rm(1⇨1㎡) 🍴 CTV TV in 1bedroom CTV in 1bedroom ® 20P ⚓ ⚲ Last dinner 9pm ✢ ⚲ S% sB&B£11 sB&B⇨㎡£13.50 dB&B£22 dB&B⇨㎡£27
Lunch£2 – £5.50 Dinner£5.50alc Wine£2.80
★**Corsewall Arms** Main St ☎228
13rm(1⇨) 🍴 CTV 30P Last dinner 7pm ✢ S% sB&B£7.45 dB&B£14.90 dB&B⇨£15.90
Bar lunch65p – £1.75 Dinner£4 Wine£2.20

KIRKCONNEL Dumfries & Galloway Map34NS71 Ayr29 Glasgow58 Dumfries31 London372
FH Mrs E. A. McGarvie **Niviston** (NS691135) ☎346
Pleasant, well-maintained farm delightfully set in elevated position overlooking Nithsdale.
May – Oct 2rm (1fb) CTV P 1🅿 345acres beef sheep S% B&b£4.70 Bdi£7.50 W£52 ⚓ D previous night

KIRKCUDBRIGHT 2,680 Dumfries & Galloway
Map30NX65 EcThu Ayr56 Dumfries28 London369 Stranraer52
★★**Royal** St Cuthbert St ☎30551
20rm(7⇨㎡) 🍴 CTV 6P 5🅿 ⚓ Last dinner 9pm ✢ ⚲
★★**Selkirk Arms** High St ☎30402
Robert Burns wrote the 'Selkirk Grace' here.
Closed 31Dec, 1&2Jan; 17rm(2⇨) Annexe: 10rm(2⇨) CTV ® 18🅿 ⚓ ⚲ Live music Tue ⚓ Last dinner 7.30pm ✢ S% sB&B£11 – £12.40 dB&B£22 – £24.80 dB&B⇨£25.80 – £28.80 Bar lunch£1 – £3.50 Dinner£6.50 – £7.25 Wine£3 🍴 Credit cards ① ⑥
✕**Ingle** St Mary St ☎30606
Closed Mon & Feb; Lunch not served; 60seats ♀ Italian. Last dinner 9.30pm S% Dinner£6.50&alc Winr£4.45 Credit cards ① ② ③

KIRKHILL Highland Map43NH54 Inverness8 Dingwall12 Invermoriston27 London569
FH Mrs C. Munro **Wester Moniack** (NH551438) ☎Drumchardine237
Small, modern, two-storey house with a relaxing, tranquil atmosphere.
Apr–Oct 2hc (1fb) ⚜ CTV 3P ⌘ 600acres mixed S% B&b£4.50–£5 Bdi£7.50–£8 W£50–£54 ⌘ D5.30pm

KIRKMICHAEL Tayside Map40NO06 Dundee32 London480 Perth28 Pitlochry13
★★**H Log Cabin** ☎Strathardle288
13rm(8⇨) Lift ⌘ CTV CTV available in bedrooms ® 60P ⌘ ⚜ ⇨ ∩ Live music & dancing Wed & Fri (in season) ⚜ ♕ Scottish & Continental. Last dinner9pm ☼ ⌘
✻sB&B£12–£16 sB&B⇨£14–£18 dB&B£24–£32 dB&B⇨£28–£36 Bar lunch£2.50–£3.50 Tea fr50p High Tea fr£3 Dinner£8–£9 Wine£4 ⌘ xmas
Credit cards ① ② ③ ⑤

★ **Aldchlappie** ☎Strathardle224
RS Nov–Mar; 7rm CTV 25P 4⌘ ⌘ ⌘ ⌘ Last dinner9pm ⌘
❋★**Strathlene** ☎Strathardle347
8rm(1⇨) ⌘ CTV 4P ⌘ Last dinner8.30pm ☼ ⌘ sB&B£8–£9 sB&B⇨£9.50–£10.50 dB&B£16–£18 dB&B⇨£17.50–£19.50 Bar lunch£2.50alc Tea£1.25 Dinner£6.50 Wine£3.50

KIRKOSWALD Strathclyde Map33NS20 Maybole5 Girvan8 Ayr15 London422
★**Kirkton Jean's** 45 Main St ☎220
Annexe: 9⇨⌘ ⌘ TV available in 9bedrooms 60P ⌘ Last dinner9pm ☼ ⌘ ✻sB&B⇨⌘£9 dB&B⇨⌘£18 Lunchfr£3 Tea fr£1.50 High Tea fr£3 Dinner fr£4 Wine£3

KIRKTON OF DURRIS Grampian Map45NO79 Banchory5 Aberdeen14 Stonehaven14 London537
FH Mrs M. Leslie **Wester Durris Cottage** (NO769962) ☎Crathes638
Attractive roadside cottage with well-tended garden. Farm 200yds.
May–mid Oct 2rm (1fb) 4P 300acres arable S% B&bfr£4.15

KIRKWALL 4,814 Orkney Map48HY41 EcWed
Car carrying services from Stromness (16 miles) to Scrabster (Thurso)
★★**Ayre** Ayre Rd ☎2197
27rm(4⇨⌘) ⌘ CTV 24P ⌘ sauna bath Disco wkly Live music & dancing wkly Last dinner8.30pm ☼ ⌘ Credit cards ① ② ③

★★**Kirkwall** Harbour St (Allied (Scotland)) ☎2232 Telex no76357
Stone building near pier head with views over bay.
38rm(11⇨) Lift ♫ ⌘ CTV Disco 3nights wkly ⚜ Last dinner8pm ☼ ⌘ sB&Bfr£13 sB&B⇨fr£16 dB&Bfr£25 dB&B⇨fr£30 Lunchfr£5 Tea fr£2 Dinnerfr£7 ⌘ Credit cards ① ② ③ ④ ⑤

GH Foveran (½m SW A964) ☎2389 Closed Oct Lic 10hc CTV 12P ⌘ D9pm
FH Mrs M. Hourie **Heathfield** (HY413108) St Ola ☎2378
Two-storey, stone farmhouse on a gently sloping hill. There are distant views over Scapa Flow.
3hc (2fb) ⚜ 4P ⌘ 500acres mixed S% ✻B&bfr£5 Bdifr£8.50 D5.30pm

✕✕**Foveran** St Ola ☎2389
Classification awarded for dinner only.
Closed mid Oct–mid Nov; Dinner not served Sun & Mon, mid Nov–Apr; 45seats 20P bedrooms available Last dinner9.30pm Lunch£4.50alc Dinner£8.50alc Wine£4.75 Credit cards ① ② ③

KIRRIEMUIR 4,328 Tayside Map41NO35 EcThu Dundee17 Forfar6 London486 Perth29

★**Airlie Arms** St Malcolm's Wynd ☎2847
Homely hotel in town centre.
7rm ⌘ CTV 6P Last dinner8pm ☼ ⌘ S% ✻sB&B£6.50–£7 dB&B£13–£14 Bar lunchfr£1 Tea fr75p High Tea fr£2.30 Dinner fr£4 Wine£3.80

KNOCK Isle of Skye, Highland Map42NG60 Armadale Pier5 Broadford13 Kyleakin *(fy to Kyle of Lochalsh)* 17
★★**Toravaig House** Knock Bay (Inter-Hotels) ☎Isle Ornsay231
Large house dating from 1935 standing in 8 acres of grounds in a remote location at south of island.
Closed Nov–Feb; 10rm(4⇨) ⌘ CTV ® 20P 2⌘ ⌘ ⌘ ⌘ Last dinner8pm ☼ ⌘ sB&B£10.50–£12 dB&B£21–£24 dB&B⇨£24–£28 Lunch£4 Tea£2 Dinner£7–£8 Wine£3.80 ⌘ Credit cards ② ⑤

KYLE OF LOCHALSH 687 Highland Map42NG72 EcThu **car ferry to Kyleakin (Skye)** Dingwall69 Fort William75 Inverness80 London591
★★★**Lochalsh** (British Transport) ☎Kyle4202
Situated in prominent position, with fine views across Kyle of Lochalsh to Skye.
45rm(29⇨) Lift ♫ ⌘ CTV CTV available in bedrooms 4P 12⌘ ⚜ ♕ English & French. Last dinner9pm ☼ ⌘ S% ✻sB&Bfr£21.50 sB&B⇨£24.80–£27.10 dB&Bfr£40.65 dB&B⇨⌘fr£48.35 Bar lunchfr£2 Tea£2.50alc Dinnerfr£7&alc Wine£4.75 ⌘
Credit cards ① ② ③ ④ ⑤

GH Retreat ☎Kyle4308 Etr–Oct 14hc (2fb) nc3 TV 14P 2⌘ S% B&b£6.95–£7.50

KYLEAKIN 268 Isle of Skye, Highland Map42NG72 EcWed Broadford8
★★**Marine** ☎Kyle4585
RS 23Oct–14Apr; 23rm Annexe: 28rm CTV 12P Last dinner8.15pm ☼ ⌘ sB&B£10.50–£11.50 dB&B£21–£23 Lunch£3–£4.50 Tea65p–75p Dinner£5.50–£6.50

LAGGAN BRIDGE Highland Map43NN69 Fort William39 Kingussie11 London513 Pitlochry38
★**Monadhliath** ☎276
8rm ⌘ TV 60P 1⌘ ⌘ ⚜ ♕ Scottish & French. Last dinner6pm ☼ ⌘

LAIRG 572 Highland Map46NC50 EcWed Dornoch22 Inverness59 London624 Tain26
★★★**Sutherland Arms** (Scottish Highland) ☎2291 Telexno778215
Stone hotel with views over River Shin and dam.
Closed Oct–Apr; 29rm(19⇨1⌘) CTV ® 30P ⌘ ⚜ ⌘ Last dinner8.30pm ☼ ⌘ S% sB&B£18.30 sB&B⇨⌘£21.30 dB&B£30.60 dB&B⇨⌘£36.60 Bar lunch£2alc Dinner£7.50 Wine£3.95
Credit cards ① ② ③ ④ ⑤

GH Carnbren ☎2259 Apr–Sep 3hc CTV 4P ⌘ lake S% B&bfr£5.50

FH Mr A. Mackay **Alt-Na-Sorag** (NC547123) 14 Achnairn ☎2058
Attractive farmhouse with good views of Loch Shin. Lairg 5m.
May–Sep 3rm (1fb) CTV 4P 1⌘ lake 125acres mixed S% ✻B&Bfr£5

FH Mrs V. Mackenzie **5 Tirryside** (NC570110) (3½m N off A838) ☎2332
Two-storey stone farm building situated in rolling farmland with distant views of Loch Shin. Roadside location.
May–Sep 3rm CTV P lake 50acres mixed S% B&bfr£5

FH Mrs M. Sinclair **Woodside** (NC533147) West Shinness ☎2072
Homely house surrounded by fields and overlooking Loch Shin. Lairg about 7 miles.
May–Sep 3rm ⚜ CTV 4P lake 360acres mixed S% B&b£5

Lamlash–Lawers

LAMLASH 613 Isle of Arran, Strathclyde
Map33NS03 EcWed (not summer) Brodick4 **(car to ferry to Ardrossan)**
★ *Lamlash* (Ind Coope (Alloa) Ltd) ☎208
Live music & dancing twice wkly Cabaret twice wkly
Lastdinner10pm ✧ ⌸ Credit cards ①②③⑤
GH *Glenisle Hotel* ☎258 Mar–Oct 3⇨🅿 (A3rm)
(6fb) CTV 16P sea Dnoon
GH Marine House Hotel ☎298 Apr–Sep 19hc 6🅿
(6fb) CTV 16P 🕸 sea S% ✶B&bfr£6.90
Bdifr£8.63 Wtrf£64.40
✕ *Carraig Mhor* ☎453
Closed Sun, Mon, Feb & Nov; 26seats Lastdinner9pm
S% ✶Lunch£2.20alc Dinner£7.50alc
Wine£3.10

LANARK 8,843 Strathclyde Map34NS84 EcThu MdMon
Glasgow25 Hamilton14 London382 Peebles30
★★ **Cartland Bridge** ☎4226
Closed 1Jan; 15rm 🕸 CTV 🅿 300P 🚗 ⚓ ⏚ Live music &
dancing Sat ⌾ French. Last dinner 9.30pm ✧ S%
sB&Bfr£16 dB&Bfr£30 Lunchfr£6&alc
Dinnerfr£7.50&alc Wine£4.50 🍏 Credit cards ①②③⑤
★★ **Clydesdale** Bloomgate (Ind Coope (Alloa)) ☎3565
10rm(1⇨) 🕸 TV TV in all bedrooms ® 100P ⌾ European.
Lastdinner9pm ✧ ⌸ ✶sB&B£10 sB&B⇨🅿£14
dB&B£17.45 dB&B⇨🅿£23 Lunch£5alc
Dinner£6.50alc Wine£3.15 🍏 Credit cards ①②③⑤
✕ *San Remo* 75 High St ☎61062
Closed Sun; 70seats ⌾ Italian. Last dinner 11pm
Credit cards ①②③⑤

LANGBANK 375 Strathclyde Map34SN37 EcSat
Glasgow16 Greenock17 London422 Paisley10
★★★ ⚓**BL Gleddoch House** ☎711 Telexno779801
RS Sat; 18rm(16⇨2🅿) 1⌸ 🕸 CTV CTV in all bedrooms
® 150P 2🚗 ⚓ ⏚ (heated) ⌇⌇ squash 🅾 sauna bath ⛳
Lastdinner9.30pm S% ✶sB&B⇨🅿£35–£40
dB&B⇨🅿£45–£50 Lunch£4.95–£6.50&alc
Dinner£11–£11.50 Wine£5 🍏 *xmas*
Credit cards ①②③④⑤

LANGHOLM 2,522 Dumfries & Galloway Map35NY38
EcWed Carlisle21 Dumfries31 Hawick24 London328
★★ **Eskdale** Market Pl ☎80357
Hotel is built on the site of the former Kings Arms Inn, a famous coaching hostelry, in the Langholm market place.
14rm(3🅿) 🕸 CTV 12P Last dinner 8pm ✧
sB&B£9–£9.50 sB&B🅿£10.50–£11 dB&B£17–£18
dB&B🅿£20–£21 Lunchfr£1.85 Teafr£1
High Teafr£2.90 Dinnerfr£5.35 Wine£3.15 🍏
Credit cards ①③

LARGS 9,343 Strathclyde Map33NS25 EcWed
Ardrossan11 Glasgow32 Greenock14 London436
★★ **Marine & Curlinghall** Broomfields (Inter-Hotels) ☎674551
Originally two hotels, now linked to form one building. Situated in own grounds on sea front, with views of islands in Firth of Clyde.
50rm(36⇨) 1⌸ 🌙 🕸 CTV CTV in 36 bedrooms ® 150P ⏚
billiards Disco wkly Live music & dancing wkly
Lastdinner8.30pm ✧ S% ✶sB&B£20 sB&B⇨£23.50
dB&B£31 dB&B⇨£35 Lunch£4.40 Tea£1.40
Dinner£7 🍏 Credit cards ①②③⑤
★★ **Castle** Broomfields (Osprey) ☎673302
40rm(14⇨) 🕸 CTV ® 25P ⏚ ⌾ Scottish & French.
Lastdinner9.30pm ✧ S% sB&B£10.75
sB&B⇨£15.25 dB&B£19 dB&B⇨£25.50
Lunch£3.50&alc Tea£1 High Tea£2.50 Dinner£5&alc
Wine£3.50 🍏 *xmas* Credit cards ①②③④⑤
★★ **Elderslie** John St, Broomfields ☎686460
Stone-built 19th-century building commanding a magnificent view, on sea front at Largs.
RS Nov–9Apr; 25rm 🕸 CTV ® 40P ⏚ Last dinner 8.30pm

S% ✶sB&B£12 dB&B£24 Lunch£3.25
Dinner£5.50&alc Wine£2.75 🍏 *xmas* Credit cards ①③
★★ **Mackerston** ☎673264
Closed Nov–Mar; 56rm(3⇨) Lift 🕸 CTV 15P ⏚ ⛳
Lastdinner7.30pm ✧ ⌸ S% sB&B£10.50–£11.90
sB&B£12.50–£13.90 dB&B£21–£23.80
dB&B⇨£25–£27.80 Lunch£3.60 Tea40p Dinner£5.70
Wine£2.20 🍏 Credit cards ①②③
★★ **Queens** North Esp ☎673253
14rm ⌸ 🕸 CTV 🅿 ⏚ Disco Live music & dancing Cabaret ⛳
Last High Tea 9pm ✧
★★ **St Helens** Greenock Rd ☎672328
Detached stone building with gardens, set back off the main road and looking out across Firth of Clyde.
28rm(4⇨) ⏚ 🕸 CTV ⛳ 36P ⏚ Children under 4yrs not accommodated ⌾ Scottish & Italian. Lastdinner8pm ✧
⌸ sB&B£10–£12 sB&B⇨£13.22–£13.80
dB&B£21.85–£23 dB&B⇨£25.30–£26.45
Lunch£3.17–£4.32&alc Tea46p–69p&alc
Dinner£5.17–£6.32&alc 🍏 Credit cards ①②③
★★ **Springfield** Greenock Rd ☎673119
41rm(2⇨12🅿) Lift ⏚ 🕸 CTV 60P ⏚ Live music & dancing twice wkly Cabaret twice wkly Last dinner 8.30pm ✧ S%
sB&B£10.50–£12 sB&B⇨🅿£12–£13.70
dB&B£18–£20 dB&B⇨🅿£21–£24 Lunch£3.80–£5
Tea75p–£1.50 High Tea£2.50–£5 Dinner£5.80–£10
Wine£2.80 🍏 *xmas* Credit cards ①②③⑤⑥
GH Aubery 22 Aubery Cres ☎672330 Etr–Sep 6hc
(2fb) nc3 TV 6P S% ✶B&B£5.50 Bdi£7 W£49 ⏚
D5.30pm
GH Douglas House 42 Douglas St ☎672257 Jun–Sep
Lic 14hc (2fb) ⛳ CTV 12P 🕸 ✶B&bfr£6.90
Bdifr£8.62
GH Gleneldon Hotel 2 Barr Cres ☎673381 Mar–Dec
Lic 11hc (2fb) ⛳ CTV 12P 🕸 ✶B&b£8.50–£9.50
Bdi£12.50–£14 Wtrf£88 ⏚
GH Holmesdale 74 Moorburn Rd ☎674793 Closed Oct,
Xmas & New Year 8hc ⛳ CTV 4P 🕸 S% B&b£6
Bdi£9 W£63 ⏚ Dam
GH Sunbury 12 Aubery Cres ☎673086 Apr–mid Oct
5hc (3fb) CTV 6P sea S% B&b£6 Bdi£9.50 W£63
⏚ D4.30pm

LATHERON Highland Map47ND13 Helmsdale20 Wick17
Thurso24 London658
FH Mrs C. Sinclair **Upper Latheron** (ND195352) ☎224
Two-storey house in elevated position with fine views out across North Sea. Farm also incorporates a pony stud.
May–Sep 4rm (1fb) ⛳ CTV 6P sea
200acres mixed S% B&bfr£5

LATHONES Fife Map41NO40 London458 Dundee18 Elie8
Kirkcaldy18 St Andrews5
★ *Lathones* ☎Peat Inn 219
Annexe: 6rm(5⇨🅿) 🕸 TV 40P 🚗 Live music wkly
Lastdinner9.30pm ✧ ⌸ Credit cards ①②③④⑤⑥

LAUDER 637 Borders Map35NT54 EcThu Edinburgh26
Galashiels13 Kelso16 London355
★ **Loanside** 2 Edinburgh Rd ☎305
Two-storey Victorian stone house standing on main road at northern end of Border village.
12rm 🕸 CTV ⛳ 40P Live music & dancing Sat
⌾ International. Last dinner 11pm ✧ ⌸ S% sB&B£12
dB&B£24–£25 Lunch£2.90–£5.45 Tea£1.50
High Tea£2.50–£4.25 Dinner£14 Wine£2.95 🍏 *xmas*
Credit card ③

LAURENCEKIRK 1,417 Grampian Map41NO77 EcWed
MdMon/altSat Aberdeen30 Forfar25 London508
Montrose10
GH Eastview Private Hotel ☎468 8rm 6hc (2fb) CTV
8P D7.30pm

LAWERS Tayside Map40NN63 Aberfeldy14 Perth46

124

Callander30 London464
FH *Croftintygan* (NN676389) ☎Killin534
Secluded stone farmhouse standing on hillside with dramatic views over Loch Tay. Between A827 and lochside. May–Sep 6rm 4hc TV lake 3,000acres mixed

LECKMELM Highland Map43NH19 Dingwall42 Inverness57 London621 Ullapool3
★ ⚭ *Tir-Aluinn* ☎Ullapool2074
Closed Oct–19May; 15rm(3⇨🛁) CTV 20P 🚗 ⚓
Last dinner8pm ⚓

LEDAIG Strathclyde Map39NM93 Crianlarich38 Fort William42 London503 Oban8
★★★(red) ⚭**Isle of Eriska** ☎371
Hospitality is the quality that elevates this hotel on its island site – part farm, part garden – to Red Star standard. The early-Victorian mansion is comfortably furnished and food is excellent.
Closed Nov–Mar; 24⇨ 🛁 P 🚗 ⚓ (hard) ⚓ ⚓ ♿
Conference facilities available Last dinner8.30pm S%
sB&B⇨£37–£45(incl dinner)
dB&B⇨£74–£90(incl dinner) Lunchfr£6 High Teafr£6
Dinnerfr£13 Wine£3.75 Credit card②

LERWICK 6,307 Shetland Map48HU44 EcWed/all day
Car-carrying service from Aberdeen
★★★**Kveldsro House** ☎2195
Closed Xmas & New Year; 14rm(9⇨🛁) 🍴 CTV CTV in all bedrooms ℝ 🚗 28P ⚓ Children under 12yrs not accommodated Last dinner9pm ♡ ⚓ *sB&Bfr£19.50 sB&B⇨🛁fr£27.50 dB&B⇨🛁fr£38.50 Lunch£5
Tea50p Dinner£7–£8&alc Wine£3.50
★★**Lerwick** Scalloway Rd (Thistle) ☎2166
Telex no75128
60⇨ 🅳 🚗 🍴 CTV in all bedrooms ℝ 60P Live music & dancing Sat ♀French. Last dinner9.30pm ♡ S%
sB&B⇨£38 dB&B⇨£44 Lunch£4.40–£4.75
Dinner£5.75–£6.75&alc Wine£3.75 🍽
Credit cards①②③④⑤
★★**Queens** ☎2826
Conversion of several stone buildings dating from 1850 standing off main road, overlooking harbour.
24rm(8🛁) 🍴 CTV CTV in 8bedrooms ℝ ⚓
Last dinner8.30pm ♡ ⚓ S% sB&B£26–£28
sB&B🛁£32–£34 dB&B£32–£36 dB&B🛁£44–£46
Lunch£2.20–£2.50 Tea50p–£2 High Tea£1.75–£5
Dinner£7.50–£10 Wine£3.20 🍽
GH Glen Orchy Lee Knab Rd ☎2031 6hc (1fb) ⚓
CTV 🍴 sea *B&b£7–£9 W£49–£63 M

LESLIE Fife Map41NO20 Glenrothes2 Kirkcaldy10 Milnathort9 London445
GH Rescobie ☎Glenrothes742143 Lic 8hc 3🛁 CTV 14P 🍴 S% *B&b£10.50–£14.75 Bdi£15.75–£20 Dam

LETHAM 170 Fife Map41NO31 Cupar5 Dundee15 London461 Perth19
★★★⚭**BL Fernie Castle** ☎209 Telex no727369
14th-C fortified house standing in secluded grounds with a small lake.
11rm(6⇨5🛁) 1⎕ 🍴 CTV in all bedrooms ℝ 200P ⚓ Live music & dancing Sat ♀French. Last dinner9pm ♡
sB&B⇨🛁£19.50–£29.50 dB&B⇨🛁£40
Lunch£4.25&alc Dinner£6.75&alc Wine£4.10 🍽
xmas Credit cards①②

LETTERFINLAY Highland Map43NN29 Fort William17 Inverness49 London533
★★*L* **Letterfinlay Lodge** (off A82) ☎Invergloy222
Converted stone shooting lodge dating from 1870 standing in 12 acres on the banks of Loch Lochy.
RS Dec–Feb; 15rm(5⇨🛁) ⎕ 🍴 CTV 100P 🚗 ⚓ ⚓
Last dinner8.30pm ♡ ⚓ S% sB&B£10–£12

sB&B⇨🛁£13–£15 dB&B£24–£27 dB&B⇨🛁£26–£29
Lunch£1–£2.75 Tea£2 Dinnerfr£6.95 Wine£2 🍽

LEVEN 9,463 Fife Map41NO30 EcThu Kirkcaldy9 London453 Perth29 St Andrews14
★★**Caledonian** High St (Osprey) ☎24101
Three-storey modern stone hotel (earliest section dating from 1648), with modern extension to rear, standing in centre of town.
36rm(16⇨) 🅳 CTV CTV in 16bedrooms ℝ 38P ♀Scottish & French. Last dinner9.30pm ♡ ⚓ S% sB&B£11.45
sB&B⇨£15.25 dB&B£20 dB&B⇨£25
Lunch£3.50&alc Tea£1 High Tea£2.50 Dinner£5&alc
Wine£3.50 🍽 *xmas* Credit cards①②③④⑤

LEWIS, ISLE OF Western Isles Map20
See Shieldinish, Uig and Stornoway (ferry service to mainland)

LEYSMILL Tayside Map41NO64 Arbroath6 Brechin10 Dundee20 London499
GH Spynie ☎Friockheim328 Etr–Sep Lic 5hc (2fb)
TV 8P 🍴 S% *B&bfr£7 Bdifr£10 Wfr£65 ⚓ D8pm

LINLITHGOW 6,158 Lothian Map34NS97 EcWed Edinburgh18 Falkirk7 London421 Stirling20
FH W. Erskine **Woodcockdale** (NS973760) ☎2088
Modern two-storey house lying about 50 yards from farmyard and outbuildings.
4rm (2fb) ⚓ CTV 12P 🍴 300acres dairy S%
B&bfr£6 Bdifr£8 Wfr£50 ⚓ D4pm
⊕×××**Champany** (2m NE off A904) ☎Philipstoun532
Closed Sun; Lunch not served Sat; 70seats 🍴
♀International. Last dinner10pm Credit cards②⑤

LINWOOD 10,510 Strathclyde Map37NS46 EcTue Glasgow10 London416 Paisley3 Renfrew6
★★**Golden Pheasant** Moss Road (Ind Coope (Alloa)) ☎Johnstone21266
A purpose-built hotel standing at the edge of this small commercial and industrial town.
12⇨ 🍴 CTV CTV in all bedrooms ℝ 100P ♀European.
Last dinner8.15pm ♡ ⚓ *sB&B⇨£14 dB&B⇨£23
Lunch£5.50alc Dinner£6.50alc Wine£3.25 🍽
Credit cards①②③⑤

LOCHBOISDALE 382 Isle of South Uist, Western Isles Map48NF71 EcThu **Car-carrying service from Oban**
★★*Lochboisdale* ☎332
Two-storey building dating from approx 1850, standing close to rocky foreshore and harbour.
18rm(6⇨🛁) 🍴 TV 30P ⚓ ⚓ ♀International.
Last dinner8.30pm ♡ ⚓ Credit cards①②③

LOCHCARRON 1,160 Highland Map42NG93 EcThu Achnasheen22 Fort William87 Inverness66 London603
★**Lochcarron** ☎226
7rm(4⇨) Lift 🅳 🍴 ⚓ 🍴 CTV ℝ 20P ⚓ Last dinner8pm ♡
⚓ sB&B⇨£8–£10 sB&B⇨£10–£12 dB&B£16–£20
dB&B⇨£20–£24 Barlunch£1.50–£3 Tea£1–£1.20
Dinner£6–£7 Wine£2.50 Credit cards①③

LOCHEARNHEAD 175 Central Map40NN52 EcWed Callander14 Crieff20 London448 Perth37
★★★**Lochearnhead** ☎237
Three-storey building overlooking Loch Earn.
Closed Nov–mid Feb; 51rm(17⇨) Annexe: 8rm 🅳 ⎕ CTV 150P 10⚓ ⚓ ⚓ (grass) ⚓ squash ⚓ Conference facilities available ♀French. Last dinner9pm ♡ ⚓
sB&B£12:50–£16 sB&B⇨£16–£19 dB&B£25–£32
dB&B⇨£32–£38 Lunchfr£5.18 Teafr£1.38
High Teafr£5.18 Dinnerfr£8.62 Wine£3.20
Credit cards①②③⑤
★★**Clachan Cottage** Lochside ☎247
A modernised conversion and extension of two 250-year-old cottages, overlooking Loch Earn and surrounding

Lochearnhead contd – Macduff

Perthshire hills.
Closed Nov–Mar; 30rm(9⇌) ⋈ CTV ⓡ 70P ⋋ billiards
Disco wkly Live music & dancing 3 nights wkly
Last dinner 8.30pm ✧ ⌿ 🄿 Credit cards ① ② ③ ⑤

★**Mansewood Country House** ☎213
Closed Nov–Mar; 6rm(2⇌1⋒) ⋌ CTV ⓡ 10P ⋋
♀ International. Last dinner 8.30pm ✧ ⌿
sB&B£14.40–£16 sB&B⇌⋒£18–£20
dB&B£21.60–£24 dB&B⇌⋒£27–£30 Lunch£2–£2.50
Tea80–90p Dinner£6–£7 Wine£3.60 🄿

LOCHGAIR Strathclyde Map39 NR99 Glasgow76
Inveraray17 Lochgilphead8 London479
★★*Lochgair* ☎233
19rm(9⇌⋒) ⋌ ⋈ CTV ⓡ 60P ⋋ ⌣ Live music
& dancing Sat & Sun in winter Last dinner 8.30pm ✧ ⌿
🄿 Credit cards ② ③ ④ ⑤

LOCHGILPHEAD 1,200 Strathclyde Map39 NR88 EcTue
Glasgow83 Inveraray25 London486 Oban37
★★*Stag* Argyll St ☎2496
29rm CTV 20P ♀ Scottish & French. Last dinner 9pm ✧
⌿ sB&B£9.50 dB&B£19 Bar lunch fr£2 Tea85p
High Tea£3 Dinner£5.50–£6.50 p *xmas* Credit card ③

LOCHINVER 283 Highland Map46 NC02 EcTue Dornoch47
Inchnadamph14 Inverness99 London662
★★★*Culag* ☎209
Closed Oct–Apr; 47rm(19⇌) Lift ⅅ ⋈ ⋌ CTV ⓡ 50P ⇔ ⋋
⌣ ♿ ♀ Scottish & French. Last dinner 8.30pm ✧ ⌿ S%
sB&B£14.30 sB&B⇌£16.40 dB&B£28.80
dB&B⇌£32.80 Bar lunch£1–£2.50 Tea50p–£1.50
Dinner£4.50–£6.50&alc Wine£2.50 🄿
Credit cards ① ③
GH Ardglas ☎257 Mar–Oct 8hc (4fb) CTV 20P ⋈
sea S% ✳B&B£5.50–£6
GH Hillcrest Badnaban (2m S on unclass rd) ☎391 4hc
CTV 4P ⋈ sea S% ✳B&B£6–£7 Bdi£11.50–£12
D6.30pm (W only Oct–Apr)
GH Park House Hotel Main St ☎259 Lic 4hc CTV
20P ⋈ river S% B&Bfr£9.20 D9pm

LOCHMADDY 307 Isle of North Uist, Western Isles
Map48 NF96 EcThu **Car-carrying service from Uig (Skye).
Also linked with service to Tarbert (Lewis)**
★★*Lochmaddy* ☎331
20rm(1⇌⋒) ⋈ TV 50P ⌣ Live music twice wkly
Last dinner 9pm ✧ ⌿

LOCHRANZA Isle of Arran, Strathclyde Map33 NR95
Blackwaterfoot18 Brodick14 London438
GH Kincardine Lodge ☎267 Apr–Oct 8hc (4fb) 6P
sea D7pm

LOCHWINNOCH 2,064 Strathclyde Map34 NS35 EcWed
Glasgow17 Largs13 London425 Paisley10
✕**Gable End** 45 High St ☎842775
50seats 20P ♀ Scottish & French. Last dinner 9pm ✧
Credit cards ① ② ③ ⑤

LOCKERBIE 3,189 Dumfries & Galloway Map35 NY18
EcTue MdTue/Thu/Fri Carlisle25 Dumfries13 London332
Moffat15
★★*Dryfesdale* ☎2427
Closed Xmas–New Year; 11rm(4⇌1⋒) ⋈ CTV CTV in
2bedrooms TV in 10bedrooms 100P ⋋ O
Last dinner 9pm ✧ ⌿ S% ✳sB&B£15
sB&B⇌⋒£17.50 dB&B£20.50 dB&B⇌⋒£25
Lunch£3.80 Tea60p Dinner£6alc Wine£3.20 🄿
Credit cards ② ③ ⑤
★★**L Lockerbie House** ☎2610
30rm(16⇌⋒) ⋌ CTV CTV in 12bedrooms ⓡ 150P ⋋ ⌣
O sauna bath Live music & dancing wkly
Last dinner 8.30pm ✧ Credit cards ① ③ ⑤
★★**Queens** Annan Rd ☎2415

14rm(1⇌7⋒) ⋈ CTV ⓡ 200P ⋋ ⌣ O ♀ English &
French. Last dinner 9.30pm ✧ ⌿ ✳sB&B£10.50
sB&B⇌⋒£12 dB&B£18 dB&B⇌⋒£21
Lunch£3.75&alc Tea£1.25–£1.75 High Tea£2–£5
Dinner£5.95&alc Wine£3.30 *xmas* Credit cards ① ③
★★**Somerton House** Carlisle Rd ☎2583
RS 25Dec & 1Jan; 6rm(3⇌) ⋈ CTV ⓡ 90P 1🏠 ⇔ ⋋
♀ Mainly grills. Last dinner 8.00pm ✧ ⌿
✳sB&B£10–£10.50 sB&B⇌£10.50–£11
dB&B£19–£21 dB&B⇌£21–£23
Bar lunch£2.30–£4.50 Tea45–85p
High Tea£1.85–£2.50 Dinner£5–£5.60
★**Blue Bell** ☎2309
12rm ⋈ CTV 40P Last dinner 8pm ✧ S%
sB&B£9.20 dB&B£18.40 Lunch fr£2.90 Tea40p–£1
High Tea£1.50–£5.50 Dinner£1.50–£5.50 Wine£3
Credit cards ① ③ ⑤
★**Kings Arms** ☎2410
16rm CTV 12🏠 Last dinner 8pm ✧ ⌿ sB&Bfr£10
dB&Bfr£20 Lunch£2.40alc Tea40p alc Dinner£4alc
Credit cards ① ③
★**Townhead** Townhead St ☎2298
Closed Nov–Feb; 10rm ⋈ CTV 20P ⇔ Last dinner 7.30pm
✧ ⌿ S% sB&B£9 dB&B£15 Lunch£2–£2.50&alc
Tea£1&alc High Tea£2–£5&alc Dinner£2.50–£5&alc
Wine£2.50
GH Rosehill Carlisle Rd ☎2378 6hc (3fb) CTV 4P ⋈
S% B&b£6

LOGIERAIT Tayside Map40 NN95 Aberfeldy9 London469
Perth23 Pitlochry6
★**Logierait** ☎Ballinluig253
Small roadside hotel beside the Tay.
7rm ⋈ CTV 100P 3🏠 ⇔ ⋋ ⌣ Live music & dancing wkly
Last dinner 8pm ✧ S% sB&B£10 dB&B£20
Bar lunch70p–£4.50 Tea50p Dinner£6 Wine£3.10 🄿

LOSSIEMOUTH 5,903 (with Branderburgh) Grampian
Map44 NJ27 EcThu Elgin5 Inverness44 London586
★★**Stotfield** ☎2011
Closed 28Oct–8Apr; 50rm ⅅ ⋈ CTV billiards Live music &
dancing twice wkly Last dinner 7pm ✧ S%
sB&B£12–£15 dB&B£21–£26 Bar lunch fr90p
Wine£3.40 🄿

LUNAN BAY Tayside Map41 NO65 Arbroath9 London499
Montrose5 Perth47
★★*B* **Lunan Bay** ☎Inverkeilor265
9rm(8⇌1⋒) ⋈ CTV CTV in all bedrooms ⓡ ⌿ 100P ⋋ ⌣
Last dinner 8.45pm ✧ sB&B⇌⋒£22 dB&B⇌⋒£29
Lunch£12alc Dinner£12alc Wine£5
Credit cards ① ② ③ ⑤

LUSS 141 Strathclyde Map39 NS39 Glasgow27 London430
Stirling38 Tarbet9
★★**Colquhoun Arms** ☎225
23rm(1⇌⋒) ⋈ CTV ⌿ 50P Last dinner 9pm ✧ ⌿
Credit cards ② ⑤
★★**Inverbeg Inn** Inverbeg (3m N on A82) (Inter-Hotels)
☎678 Telex no 777205
Attractive roadside inn with wooden shutters.
14rm(7⇌) ⅅ ⋈ CTV CTV in 6 bedrooms 80P 2🏠 ⋋ ⌣ ♿
♀ Scottish & French. Last dinner 11pm ✧ ⌿ S%
sB&B£10.50–£14.50 sB&B⇌£12.50–£16.50
dB&B£17–£25 dB&B⇌£21–£31 Lunch£1–£8
Tea fr£1 High Tea£1–£8 Dinner£5.50–£15&alc
Wine£4.50 🄿 *xmas* Credit cards ② ③ ④ ⑤

MACDUFF 3,707 Grampian Map45 NJ76 EcWed
Aberdeen46 Banff2 Fraserburgh25 London582
★★**Deveron House** 27 Union Rd (Inter-Hotel) ☎32309
Closed 3–16Jan; 17rm(7⇌7⋒) ⋈ CTV CTV in all bedrooms
ⓡ 18P Disco wkly Live music & dancing twice wkly
Last dinner 9.30pm ✧ ⌿ sB&B£11.50–£13.50
sB&B⇌⋒£14.50–£16.50 dB&B£21–£25

dB&B⇨⋒£24–£30 Barlunch75p–£2.50 Tea75p–£1
HighTea£2.95–£3.95 Dinner£6.50–£7&alc Wine£3.75
🅿 xmas Credit cards ①②③⑤
★★**Fife Arms** Shore St ☎32408
Situated in town centre overlooking harbour.
13rm(3⇨3⋒) 🏨 🍴 CTV ® 24P Lastdinner8pm ⇨ 🚗
S% sB&B£10–£12 sB&B⇨⋒£12.50–£15
dB&B£13–£21 dB&B⇨⋒£18–£22 Lunchfr£3
Teafr50p HighTeafr£2 Dinnerfr£5 Wine£3.40 🅿
Credit cards ① ③ ⑤

MALLAIG 903 Highland Map42NM69 EcWed **Car-carrying service to Armadale (Skye): summer only, not Sun** Fort William47 London563
★★**Marine** ☎2217
Adjacent to harbour and railway station.
24rm(6⇨) 🏨 ♨ 🍴 CTV ® 10P ♿ Lastdinner8pm ⇨ 🚗
sB&B£7–£9.50 sB&B⇨⋒£12 dB&B£12–£19
dB&B⇨£23 Lunch£3–£3.50 Tea50p–£1 HighTea£3
Dinner£4.50–£5.50 Wine£3.50 🅿 Credit cards ②⑤
★★**West Highland** ☎2210
Large stone building dating from 1900, standing on raised site overlooking fishing port and islands of Rhum, Eigg and Skye.
Closed Nov–Mar; 26rm(7⇨) 🍴 CTV ® 30P 🚗
Lastdinner8.30pm ⇨ 🚗 sB&B£12.96–£16
dB&B£21.60–£27.50 dB&B⇨£23.75–£29.70
Lunch£3.40 Tea60p Dinnerfr£7 🅿
Credit cards ①②③④⑤⑥

MARYBANK Highland Map43NH45 Dingwall5 Inverness19 Ullapool41 London580
FH Mr R. MacLeod **Easter Balloon** (NH484535)
☎Urray211
Roadside farmhouse standing in its own garden on edge of village.
Etr–Sep 5rm (2fb) ♨ CTV 10P 230acres mixed
S% ✱B&B£5 Bdi£8 D8pm

MAUCHLINE Strathclyde Map34NS42 Ayr11 Cumnock8 Kilmarnock15 London400
✕**La Candela** 5 Kilmarnock Rd ☎51015
Lunch not served Sun; 40seats 15P 🍽European.
Lastdinner10pm ♨Lunch£2.10alc HighTea£2.50alc
Dinner£4.50alc Wine£3

MEIGLE 357 Tayside Map41NO24 Dundee13 Forfar13 London471 Perth18
★★🔥**Kings of Kinloch** ☎273
Imposing 18th-C mansion set in own grounds off A94 situated 1½m W of Meigle. Rear views across Strathclyde.
Closed Feb; 7rm(1⇨) 🍴 CTV in bedrooms on request TV in bedrooms on request 45P 2🚗 ♨ 🚗 🍽Cosmopolitan.
Lastdinner9pm ⇨ 🚗 sB&B£14.62–£16.87
sB&B⇨£16.87–£18.87 dB&B£27 dB&B⇨£28.12
Lunch£4.50–£7 Tea60p–£1.30

The Ladbroke Mercury Motor Inn, Moffat is the Centre of Attractions

Moffat is the perfect centre for exploring Burns and Border country. There's fishing in the River Annan and a spectacular local attraction, the Grey Mare's Tail — one of Scotland's highest waterfalls. The hotel has earned a reputation for warmth and friendliness and the staff will be happy to advise you on the best bargains in woollens for which Moffat and the Border Towns are famous.

You'll find plenty of exciting holiday ideas in our Lazydays brochure — try a Scottish Weekaway — tailor made for touring in your own car, or take a Welcome Break from as little as £25.00 per person bed & breakfast.

For your Lazydays brochure, 'phone 01-734 6000 or write to PO Box 137, Watford, Herts. WD1 1DN.

Ladbroke Mercury Motor Inn,
Moffat,
Dumfries-shire. DG10 9EL
Tel: (0683) 20464

Ladbroke Hotels

HighTea£3.20–£6&alc Dinner£8.50&alc Wine£4.50

MELROSE 2,181 Borders Map35NT53 EcThu Edinburgh37 Galashiels5 London345 Selkirk8
★★**L Burt's** The Square ☎2285
Dating from 1722, this converted town house is of architectural interest.
19rm(5⇨2⋒) 🍴 CTV ® 30P 🚗 🍽Continental.
Lastdinner8.30pm ⇨ 🚗 S% sB&B£10.50–£11
sB&B⇨⋒£12.50–£13 dB&B£21–£22
dB&B⇨⋒£25–£26 Lunch£4.50–£4.75 Tea50p–£1
HighTea£3.75 Dinner£7–£7.50 Wine£3.25
Credit cards ①②③④⑤⑥
★★**George & Abbotsford** ☎2308
Three-storey stone coaching inn standing on main road in centre of Border town.
21rm(12⇨1⋒) CTV ® 40P 6🚗 ♿ 🍽Scottish, French & Italian. Lastdinner8.30pm ⇨ sB&B⇨£10–£12
sB&B⇨⋒£12–£14 dB&B£18–£20
dB&B⇨⋒£22–£25 Lunch£3.50&alc HighTea£3.50
Dinner£6&alc Wine£4 Credit cards ①②③④⑤⑥
★ **Bon-Accord** The Square ☎2645
Conversion of two adjoining stone houses dating from 1805, with shuttered windows.
8rm 🍴 CTV Live music Sun Live music & dancing Sat
Lastdinner8pm ⇨

MILNATHORT 1,099 Tayside Map40NO10 EcThu MdMon Kinross2 London446 Perth16 StAndrews28
★**Thistle** New Rd ☎Kinross63222
6rm CTV 40P Disco Sun Live music & dancing Fri & Sat
🍽Mainly grills. Lastdinner8pm ⇨ S% sB&B£9
dB&B£18 Lunch£6alc HighTea£3.50 Dinner£6
Wine£3

MILNGAVIE 10,908 Strathclyde Map37NS57 EcTue/Sat Clydebank7 Glasgow8 Kirkintilloch8 London413

Beechwood Country House Hotel
Moffat, Dumfries-shire DG10 9RS.
Tel. Moffat 20210

Beechwood is a gracious country house where good food and comfort are of paramount importance. Emphasis is placed on the use of locally produced meat, game, vegetable and dairy produce. There is a carefully chosen wine list. Residents and Table license. Self-catering lodges in the grounds of the Hotel are available. Write or phone for details of these and the Hotel.

BEECHWOOD

Milngavie contd—**Moniaive**

The Ladbroke Mercury Motor Inn, Moffat is the Centre of Attractions

Moffat is the perfect centre for exploring Burns and Border country. There's fishing in the River Annan and a spectacular local attraction, the Grey Mare's Tail — one of Scotland's highest waterfalls. The hotel has earned a reputation for warmth and friendliness and the staff will be happy to advise you on the best bargains in woollens for which Moffat and the Border Towns are famous.

You'll find plenty of exciting holiday ideas in our Lazydays brochure — try a Scottish Weekaway — tailor made for touring in your own car, or take a Welcome Break from as little as £25.00 per person bed & breakfast.

For your Lazydays brochure, 'phone 01-734 6000 or write to PO Box 137, Watford, Herts. WD1 1DN.

Ladbroke Mercury Motor Inn,
Moffat,
Dumfries-shire. DG10 9EL
Tel: (0683) 20464

Ladbroke Hotels

★★★**Black Bull** Main St (Thistle) ☎041-956 2291
Telex no778323
27rm(23⇌3🛁) 🎵 🍴 CTV in all bedrooms ® ⚡ 65P Live music Sun ♥English & French. Last dinner 9.30pm ✳
S% sB&B⇌🛁£29.25 dB&B£27.50 dB&B⇌🛁£37.50 Lunch £3.25&alc Dinner £7alc Wine £3.25 ♉
Credit cards ① ② ③ ⑤ ⑥

FH Mrs L. Fisken **High Craigton** (NS525766) ☎041-956 1384
Two-storey, stone-built farmhouse with numerous outbuildings. Good access road.
2hc (2fb) CTV 10P 🍴 1,100acres sheep S% B&b£5 W£35 ⓜ

MOCHRUM Dumfries & Galloway Map30NX34 EcWed
London408 Newton Stewart15 Stranraer25
★ **Greenmantle** ☎Port William357
This 17th-C building was formerly a manse and was converted to an hotel some ten years ago. It stands in its own gardens in centre of small country village.
7rm(6⇌) 🍴 TV ⚡30P ⚡ Last dinner 8.30pm ✳
sB&B🛁£12 dB&B£24 Bar lunch40p-£2.15
Dinner £6-£6.50&alc

MOFFAT 2,042 Dumfries & Galloway Map35NT00 EcWed
Carlisle41 Lanark35 London349
☆☆☆ **Ladbroke Mercury Motor Inn** Ladyknowe (Ladbroke) ☎20464
A modern two storey building at the foot of the main square.
51⇌🛁 🎵 🍴 CTV CTV available in bedrooms 70P
Last dinner 10pm ✳ ⚡ ♉ Credit cards ① ② ③ ④ ⑤ ⑥
★★**Annandale** High St ☎20013
Closed Dec – mid Mar; 25rm Annexe: 5⇌ 🍴 CTV TV in 5 bedrooms ® 50P ♥English & German.
Last dinner 8.30pm ✳ sB&B£9-£11 sB&B⇌£13-£15
dB&B£18-£22 dB&B⇌£22-£26

Bar lunch£1.75-£3.80 Dinner fr£5.75&alc Wine£3.30
♉ Credit cards ① ② ③ ⑤ ⑥
★★**Balmoral** High St ☎20288
Two storey hotel with characteristic shutters.
Closed Nov–Feb; 20rm(2⇌) CTV 10P 2🛎 Last dinner 9pm
✳ ⚡ sB&B£12 sB&B⇌£13.50 dB&B£19
dB&B⇌£21 Lunch£3.25 Tea£1.50 High Tea£3.25
Dinner£5.25 Wine£3 Credit cards ① ② ③ ⑤
★★🛏 **HB Beechwood** ☎20210
A 19th-C country house standing in its own grounds in a secluded position on the outskirts of the town.
8rm(3⇌3🛁) 🍴 CTV ® ⚡ 20P ⚡ Last dinner 9pm ✳
⚡ sB&B⇌🛁£12.50-£14 dB&B£22-£26
dB&B⇌🛁£25-£28 Bar lunch£2-£4 Tea£1-£1.50
Dinner£6&alc Wine£3 ♉ Credit cards ① ② ③ ④ ⑤ ⑥
★★**Moffat House** High St ☎20039
14rm(5⇌3🛁) CTV ® 25P 6🛎 ♥Scottish & French.
Last dinner 9pm ✳ ⚡ S% sB&B£12.50-£13.50
sB&B⇌🛁£14.50-£15.50 dB&B£25-£27
dB&B⇌🛁£29-£31 Lunch£4.75&alc Tea£1.50
High Tea£3.50-£5.50 Dinner£7.50&alc Wine£4.75 ♉
Credit cards ② ③ ⑤
GH Arden House High St ☎20220 Jan–Oct 8hc 4🛁
(2fb) CTV 10P 🍴 S% ✱B&b£5.50-£7
Bdi£8.50-£9 W£59-£65 £ D6.45pm
GH Buchan 13 Beechgrove ☎20378 8hc (2fb) CTV
7P 🍴 S% B&b£4.50-£5 Bdi£7.50-£8 W£52-£56
£ D7pm
GH Hartfell House Hartfell Cres ☎20153 Mar–Dec 9hc
(3fb) TV 10P 🍴 B&b£6.90 Bdi£11.50 W£40 £
D7pm
GH Robin Hill Beechgrove ☎20050 Etr–Oct 6hc (2fb)
CTV 6P 🍴 S% ✱B&b£6-£7
GH Rockhill 14 Beechgrove ☎20283 Mar–Oct 10hc
(3fb) CTV D6.15pm
GH St Olaf Eastgate, off Dickson St ☎20001 Apr–early
Oct 7hc (3fb) 4🛎 ✱B&b£5 Bdi£8.50 D6.15pm

MONEYDIE Tayside Map40NO02 Perth6 Crieff15
Pitlochry25 London454
FH Mrs S. Walker **Moneydie Roger** (NO054290)
☎Almondbank239
A substantial, two-storey farmhouse standing amid good arable land. Perth 7 miles.
Apr–Sep ✳ 1P 143acres mixed S% B&b£5-£5.25

MONIAIVE 342 Dumfries & Galloway Map34NX79 EcThu
Dumfries16 Glasgow68 London357
★★**Woodlea** ☎209
Closed Xmas; 13rm(2⇌) CTV TV in 17 bedrooms ® 40P ⚡
⚡(heated) 🌿(grass) sauna bath ⚡ Last dinner 8.30pm
✳ ⚡ S% sB&B£9.70-£10.70 sB&B⇌£16.50-£18
dB&B£19.40-£21.40 dB&B⇌£27-£29.70
Lunch£3.70-£4 Tea£1.40-£1.55 High Tea£2.50-£3
Dinner£6.30-£7&alc Wine£3.65 ♉
★**Craigdarroch Arms** ☎205

Moffat House Hotel

High Street, Moffat

From the comfort and serenity of Moffat House you can set out to explore the romantic border country — visit stately homes, is one hour from Edinburgh, 2 hours from the Lake District. You can fish, shoot, go hill walking or pony trekking; golf, tennis and many other sports can be arranged at a moments notice. Your holiday can be as restful or as active as you want to make it. Ring us on Moffat 20039. (0683)

Montrose

8rm ⊞ CTV 8P 🅟 Last dinner 9pm ᛎ 🏧 sB&B£8–£10
dB&B£16–£20 Lunch£2.50–£4.50&alc
Tea75p–£1&alc High Tea£2.75–£4.50&alc
Dinner£5–£6&alc Wine£3

MONTROSE 10,112 Tayside Map41 NO75 EcWed Md
cattle Wed Aberdeen38 Brechin9 London499 Perth48
★★★**Links** Mid Links ☎2288
22rm(18⇨) ⅅ 🏧 CTV 🅟 50P ᛤ Last dinner 10.45pm ᛎ
ᛎ S% ✳sB&B£17.50 sB&B⇨£20 dB&B£25

dB&B⇨£28 Lunch£3.45–£5.50 Dinner£4.50–£7.50
Wine£3.95 🅿 Credit cards ① ③ ⑤
★★★**Park** John St ☎3415 Telex no76357
59rm(41⇨🛁) ⅅ 🏧 CTV CTV in all bedrooms ® 100P 4🏋 ⌁
🅟 Conference facilities available Last dinner 9.30pm ᛎ
ᛎ 🅿 Credit cards ① ② ③ ⑤ ⑥
★★**Corner House** 134 High St ☎3126
15rm(5⇨) 🏧 CTV ® 🅟 ♀ English & French.
Last dinner 9pm ᛎ ᛎ ✳sB&Bfr£15 sB&B⇨fr£19
dB&Bfr£24 dB&B⇨fr£28 Bar lunch£2 Tea£1

DRIVE ON!

The end o' the road

Don't stop! It's an American in disguise.

Don't be fooled by cheap or expensive imitations. If you want to see the *real* Scotland, the AA has several books on it. But if what you want is to get a lift out of your motoring, the AA has a magazine for it – DRIVE&TRAIL monthly. Twelve times a year, it brings you the very best in car tests, investigations, columnists, cartoons plus pages and pages on everything you need to enjoy the great outdoors – camping equipment tests, campsite reports, caravans, motorvans and helpful hints all backed by the authority and expertise of the AA. We don't stop at borders or even coastlines – Scottish, English, Irish or Welsh – if you speak English and run a car, DRIVE is for you.

We're on sale every month at your local newsagent or AA office, but you can also have every issue delivered to your doorstep by taking out an annual subscription. Drop a line to DRIVE&TRAIL subscriptions, FREEPOST, Basingstoke, Hants RG21 2EA and we'll send you full details of some extra-special offers that go with a year's DRIVE. You don't even need to stamp your envelope. Now there's a saving that even an Englishman couldn't refuse!

drive AND TRAIL

Join our clan

Montrose contd – **Nairn**

High Tea £3 Dinner £6alc Wine £4.60
GH Linksgate 11 Dorward Pl ☎2273 6hc (3fb) CTV 6P D9am
FH Mrs A. Ruxton **Muirside of Gallery** (NO671634) ☎Northwater Bridge 209
Situated in beautiful countryside facing the Grampian Mountain range, and only 5 miles from the seaside.
2rm 1hc (1fb) TV 3P 110acres arable S%
✱B&b £4.50–£5 Bdi £8–£8.50 W£56 ⚓ D7pm

MONYMUSK 167 Grampian Map45 NJ61 Aberdeen 19 Braemar 47 Inverurie 9 London 548
★★**Grant Arms** ☎226
10rm(1⇌) ♨ CTV ⓑ 5P ⚲ Last dinner 8.30pm ♥ ⚓
✱sB&B £11.70 sB&B⇌ £12–£13.20 dB&B £24 dB&B⇌ £26.40 Lunch £3.25 Tea 22p–£1 High Tea £2.50 Dinner £6 Wine £3.98 Credit card ⑤

MOODIESBURN Strathclyde Map37 NS67 Glasgow 8 Stirling 18 Kirkintilloch 6 London 405
GH El Ranchero Western 6 Cumbernauld Rd (On A80) ☎Glenboig 874769 rs 25Dec–1Jan (B&b only) 5hc (2fb) CTV 30P D6.45pm

MORAR 184 Highland Map42 NM69 EcWed London 558 Fort William 45 Mallaig 3
★★**Morar** ☎Mallaig 2346
Closed 20Oct–Mar; 28rm(8⇌) CTV ⓑ 50P ⚓ ♥ ♀French.
Last dinner 8.30pm ♥ sB&B £9–£15 sB&B⇌ £12–£18 dB&B £20–£24 dB&B⇌ £23–£27 Lunch £3–£4 Tea 50–70p High Tea £3.50–£4 Dinner £5–£7 Wine £3.50 ♬

MORNINGSIDE 164 Lothian Map35 NT27 **See Edinburgh**

MOTHERWELL 73,116 (with Wishaw) Strathclyde Map34 NS75 EcWed **See also Wishaw** Glasgow 13 Lanark 14 London 393 Stirling 30
★★★**Garrion** Merry St (Scottish & Newcastle) ☎64561 51rm(27⇌8♨) Lift ♪ ♨ CTV in all bedrooms ⓑ 100P Disco twice wkly Conference facilities available
Last dinner 9.30pm ♥ ⚲ S% ✱sB&B £16 sB&B⇌ £21 dB&B £23 dB&B⇌ ♨ £28 Lunch £2.75–£3.75&alc Tea 60p–£1 Dinner £5.25&alc Wine £3.45 ♬ Credit cards ①②③④⑤

MOY Highland Map44 NH73 Inverness 13 Kingussie 32 Grantown on Spey 23 London 548
GH Invermoy House Tomatin ☎271 Lic 7hc 1♨ ⚓ CTV 10P ♨ lake S% B&b £5.75–£6.33 Bdi £9.20–£9.78 W£59.80–£64.40 ⚓ D6pm

MUIRHEAD 8,322 (with Chryston) Strathclyde Map37 NS66 EcWed Glasgow 19 London 404 Stirling 29
★★**Crow Wood House** (Scottish & Newcastle) ☎041-779 3861
Closed 1 & 2Jan; 18⇌♨ ♪ ♨ CTV ⓑ 80P Last dinner 9pm

♥ sB&B⇌♨ £21 dB&B⇌♨ £32 Lunch £4.25–£5&alc High Tea £2.50–£3.50 Dinner £6–£7.50&alc Wine £3.50 ♬ Credit cards ①②③
××**La Campágnola** 112 Cumbernauld Rd ☎041-779 3405
Closed Sun; 60 seats 20P ♀International.
Last dinner 11pm Lunch £3.25&alc Dinner £16alc Wine £4.75 Credit cards ①②③⑤

MUIR OF ORD Highland Map43 NH55 EcThu Dingwall 7 Invermoriston 29 Inverness 15 London 580
★★**Ord Arms** ☎870286
Attractive sandstone building set back from A9 on the northern outskirts of the town.
12rm(⇌♨) ♨ CTV in all bedrooms ⓑ 200P 6♣ ⚓ ⚲ ♀Scottish & French. Last dinner 9pm ♥ Credit card ①
★★⚐ **Ord House** ☎870492
Closed 21Oct–Apr; 17rm(8⇌♨) CTV 25P ⚓ ♀English & French. Last dinner 9pm ♥ ⚲ Credit card ⑤

MULL, ISLE OF Strathclyde Map50 Car-carrying services operate between Lochaline–Fishnish and Oban–Craignure. See Craignure, Salen and Tobermory

MUSSELBURGH 17,067 Lothian Map35 NT37 EcThu Dalkeith 5 Edinburgh 6 London 409 North Berwick 18
☆☆**Drummore** North Berwick Rd ☎031-665 2302
Annexe: 37♨ ♪ CTV in all bedrooms ⓑ ♣ Live music & dancing Tue & Sat ⚲ Conference facilities available ♀European. ⚓ S% sB&B♨ £14 dB&B♨ £24 Lunch £6alc Tea £1–£1.50 High Tea £3–£4 Dinner £8alc Wine £3.25 ♬ xmas Credit cards ①②③④⑤⑥
GH Parsonage 15 High St ☎031-665 4289 Jan–Nov 7hc 2⇌ (2fb) CTV TV in 3 bedrooms 10P ♨ S% B&b £6.50–£8 W£40–£55 M

NAIRN 5,890 Highland Map44 NH85 EcWed Md Thu Aviemore 39 Forres 11 Inverness 16 London 570
★★★★**Golf View** Seabank Rd ☎52301 Telex no 777969
Large stone hotel dating from 1895, standing in own grounds with views over Moray Firth.
55rm(45⇌10♨) Lift ♪ CTV in all bedrooms 35P ♣ ⚲ ⚲(heated) ⚲(hard) sauna bath Live music & dancing twice wkly Cabaret wkly ♣ ♀International. Last dinner 9.30pm ♥ sB&B⇌♨ £23–£26 dB&B⇌♨ £36–£40 Lunch fr £4.50 Tea fr £1.50 Dinner fr £7.50&alc Wine £4.25 ♬ xmas Credit cards ①②③⑤
★★★★ L **Newton** ☎53144 Telex no 777967 (Att. Clan)
Closed Nov–Mar; 34⇌ Annexe: 14⇌ Lift ♪ ♨ CTV CTV in all bedrooms ⓑ 50P ⚓ ⚲ sauna bath ♀International.
Last dinner 9.30pm ♥ ⚲ sB&B⇌ £25 dB&B⇌ £40 Lunch fr £4.50 Tea fr £1.75 Dinner fr £8&alc Wine £4.25 ♬ Credit cards ①②③⑤
★★★**Royal Marine** (Scottish Highland) ☎53381 Telex no 778215

DRUMMORE MOTOR INN HOTEL

**North Berwick Road,
Musselburgh, Edinburgh
Telephone: 031-665 2302**

Edinburgh's top value Motor Hotel is superbly placed just six short miles from Edinburgh's centre. We have 47 rooms each with toilet, shower, radio, colour television, telephone, inter-com and Teasmade facilities. We have the intimate Tartan Byre Restaurant, Cocktail and Lounge Bars and the Drummore and Rose Suites are available for conferences and can accommodate 200 and 100 respectively. All major Credit Cards accepted.

Closed Nov–Mar; 43rm (29⇨5🛏) Lift ♪ 🍴 CTV ⓡ 20P ⚓
⇨ & Last dinner 8.30pm ♀ ♫ S% sB&B£18.40
sB&B⇨£21.30 dB&B£30.60 dB&B⇨🛏£36.60
Bar lunch £2 alc Dinner £7.50 Wine £3.95
Credit cards 1 2 3 4 5

★★**Alton Burn** Alton Burn Rd ☎52051
Closed Nov–Mar; 24rm (5⇨) Annexe: 10rm 🍴 CTV 60P ⚓
⇨ (heated) 🌊 (hard) ♣ Last dinner 8.30pm ♀ ♫
sB&B£10–£12 sB&B⇨£12–£14 dB&B£20–£24
dB&B⇨£24–£28 Lunch fr £3.85 Tea fr £1
High Tea fr £3.50 Dinner fr £5.85 & alc Wine £3.50 ℉

★★**Clifton** ☎53119
A conversion of two adjoining three-storey buildings on corner site near to sea front.
Closed Nov–Feb; 17rm (9⇨) 2🛁 CTV 20P ⚓ ⚓ ♀ French.
Last dinner 9.30pm ♀ ♫ sB&B£12.50–£15
dB&B⇨£21.30 Lunch £2.50 alc Tea £2 alc
Dinner £7.50 alc Wine £4.70 Credit card 2

★★**Windsor** Albert St ☎53108
60rm (40⇨) Lift ♪ 🍴 CTV in all bedrooms ⓑ 30P Live music & dancing twicewkly Cabaret 3 nights wkly ♀
♀ English & Continental. Last dinner 9.30pm ♀ S%
✱sB&B£12.65 sB&B⇨£14.95 dB&B£19.90
dB&B⇨£29.90 Lunch £4.03 & alc Tea £1.75
High Tea £3.50–£5 Dinner fr £6.95 & alc Wine £3.50 ℉
xmas Credit card 3

★**Washington** 8 Viewfield St ☎53351
19rm (6🛏) CTV ⚓ 26P ⚓ Live music & dancing wkly
Cabaret wkly ♣ Last dinner 8pm ♀ ♫ S%
sB&B£8–£10 sB&B🛏£8–£10 dB&B£16–£18
dB&B🛏£18–£20 Lunch £2.50–£3 Tea 75p–£1.20
High Tea £2–£2.50 Dinner £4.50–£6 Wine £3.45 ℉
xmas

⊕ **Ross House** Seabank Rd ☎53731
Closed end Oct–mid Apr; 17rm CTV 17P ⚓
Last dinner 8pm ♀

GH **Greenlawns** 13 Seafield St ☎52738 Apr–Oct 6hc 2⇨ (3fb) CTV 8P D5pm
GH **Lothian House Private Hotel**
10 Crescent Rd ☎53555 Lic 9hc CTV 10P sea D7pm
✕**Taste Bud** 44 Harbour St ☎52743
Closed Oct; Lunch served summer only; 48 seats ℉
♀ International. Last dinner 9.20pm ✱Lunch £2–£6 & alc
Dinner £5.15–£8 & alc

NETHY BRIDGE 431 Highland Map 44 NJ02 EcThu
Aviemore 10 Inverness 35 Loundon 546 Tomintoul 14
★★★**Nethy Bridge** (Best Western) ☎203 Telex no 75261
Closed Oct–Apr; 63rm (60⇨1🛏) Lift ♪ CTV TV available in bedrooms 50P 20⚓ ⚓ ⭕ billiards ♣ Last dinner 9pm ♀
♫ S% sB&B⇨🛏£17 dB&B£34 dB&B🛏£34
Bar lunch fr £3 Dinner £7–£8 Credit cards 1 2 3 5

★**Mount View** ☎324
Situated in three acres of secluded tree-studded grounds on outskirts of village.
Closed Nov–26Dec; 11rm 🍴 CTV 20P ⚓ Last dinner 8pm
⇨ sB&B£9.10 dB&B£18.20 Bar lunch £1.90–£2.20
Dinner £5.24 Wine £2.50 ℉

NEW ABBEY 339 Dumfries & Galloway Map 30 NX96
Carlisle 42 Dumfries 7 London 349
★**Abbey Arms** 1 The Square ☎215
6rm 🍴 CTV ⓡ 6P ⚓ Last dinner 7pm ♀ ♫
✱sB&B fr £9.25 dB&B fr £18.50 Tea fr £1.40
High Tea £2.75–£5 Dinner £7 Wine £3.35

NEWBRIDGE 397 Lothian Map 35 NT17 EcMon & Wed
Edinburgh 9 Linlithgow 10 London 423
FH Mr & Mrs W. Pollock **Easter Norton** (NT157721) ☎031-333 1279
Small attractive farmhouse. Excellent position for motorway and Edinburgh Airport.
Apr–Sep 3rm (2fb) CTV P ⚓ 7 acres poultry S%
B&B fr £5

NEWBURGH 2,170 Fife Map 41 NO21 EcWed Cupar 11 Dundee 19 London 461 Perth 12
★★**Udny Arms** Main St ☎444 Telex no 739187
16rm (6⇨10🛏) 🍴 CTV in all bedrooms 30P ⚓ ⚓
Last dinner 9.30pm ♀ ♫ sB&B⇨🛏£20–£23
dB&B⇨£33.50–£36 Bar lunch £4 Dinner £10–£11.50
Wine £3.75 ℉ Credit cards 1 2 3

FH **Glen Duckie** (NO283188) ☎352
A large farm set amid rolling hills with main farmhouse dating from 16th century.
May–Sep 2rm ⚓ TV 4P 358 acres mixed

NEW CUMNOCK 5,007 Strathclyde Map 34 NS61 EcWed
Ayr 22 Dumfries 38 Glasgow 42 London 379
FH Mr & Mrs A. Howat **Polshill** (NS652132) ☎301
Pleasant, well-kept old mill house, parts of which date back 300 years.
Jun–Sep 2rm (2fb) ⚓ nc5 CTV 4P 230 acres beef
S% B&b£4.50–£5

NEW GALLOWAY 338 Dumfries & Galloway Map 34 NX67
Ayr 38 Carlisle 60 Dumfries 25 Glasgow 72 London 366
Newton Stewart 19
★**Crosskeys** ☎218
RS 2wks Feb & 2wks Nov; 8rm CTV 8P 2⚓ ⚓
Last dinner 8pm ♀ ♫ sB&B£10.60–£12
dB&B£21.20–£24 Lunch £4–£4.50 & alc
Tea £1–£1.20 alc High Tea £1.70–£4 & alc
Dinner £5.30–£5.80 & alc Credit cards 1 3

NEWINGTON Lothian Map 35 NT27
See Edinburgh

NEW SCONE Tayside Map 40 NO12
See Scone, New

NEWTON MEARNS Strathclyde Map 37 NS55 Glasgow 7
Kilmarnock 21 Paisley 9 London 408
✕✕**Mearns House** Mearnskirk ☎041-639 7576
Lunch not served Mon–Thu; 36 seats 20P ♀ French.
Last dinner 10.45pm Credit cards 1 2 3

NEWTONMORE 894 Highland Map 43 NN79 EcWed
Fort William 46 Inverness 48 Kingussie 3 London 519
Pitlochry 42
★★**Glen** Main St ☎203
Converted small stone house with modern extension to side and front.
9rm (4⇨🛏) 🍴 CTV 30P ⚓ Last dinner 7.30pm ♀ ♫
★★**Highlander Motel** (Inter-Hotels) ☎341 Telex no 75577
33🛏 🍴 CTV TV available in bedrooms ⓑ 100P ⚓
Disco wkly Live music & dancing wkly Conference facilities available Last dinner 7.30pm (winter) 9pm (summer) ♀
♫ sB&B🛏£15.35 dB&B🛏£26.70 Lunch £2.50–£6
Tea 40p High Tea £1.85 Dinner £5.85 Wine £3.45 ℉
xmas Credit cards 1 2 3 4 5 6

★★**Mains** Main St ☎206
25rm (8⇨14🛏) 🍴 CTV ⓡ 50P Disco wkly Live music & dancing wkly Last dinner 8pm ♀ ♫ sB&B£10–£12
sB&B⇨🛏£10–£12 dB&B£19–£23
dB&B⇨£19–£23 Lunch £4 Tea 80p High Tea £3.50
Dinner £7.50 Wine £3.50 ℉ xmas
Credit cards 1 2 3 5 6

⊕ **Badenoch** Station Rd ☎246
Closed Oct–Mar; Unlicensed; 7rm ⓑ 10P ⚓ ⚓
GH **Alder Lodge** ☎376 Lic 7rm 6hc (3fb) CTV 10P
🍴 S% B&B£7 Bdi£11 W£70 £ D8.30pm
GH **Alvey House Hotel** Golf Course Rd ☎260
20Dec–Oct Lic 7hc (2fb) CTV 12P S%
B&b£7–£8 Bdi£10–£11 W£66–£74 £ D7pm
GH **Ard-na-Coille Hotel** ☎214 Jan–Oct Lic 12hc
1⇨4🛏 (3fb) CTV 20P 🍴 S% B&b£10.50–£11
Bdi£15.50–£16.50 D7.30pm
GH **Cairn Dearg** Station Rd ☎398 6hc (2fb) ♣ CTV

Newtonmore contd–Newton Stewart

BRUCE HOTEL
Newton Stewart

17 bedrooms, all with private bathroom. Single, twin and double. Central heating, radio, telephone and colour television in all rooms. Facilities for making coffee or tea are provided in all bedrooms.

WIGTOWNSHIRE.
Tel: (0671) 2294

A small privately owned hotel offering a high standard of comfort, service and food. Fire certificate granted.
★★★AA
British Tourist Authority Commendation Award.

8P S% B&b£6–£7 Bdi£10–£11.50 W£67–£77 ᒪ D5pm
GH Coig-na-Shee Fort William Rd ☎216 Apr–Oct rs Feb & Mar 6hc (1fb) CTV 8P ⚜ S% B&b£8.50–£9.50 Bdi£13.50–£15 W£85–£95 ᒪ D6.30pm
GH Glenquoich Glen Rd ☎461 Closed Xmas 6rm 5hc (3fb) ⚜ CTV 6P S% B&bfr£7.50 Bdifr£12.50 Wfr£50 M D7pm

NEWTON STEWART 1,983 Dumfries & Galloway Map30NX46 EcWed MdWed/Fri cattle Dumfries51 Girvan30 Kirkcudbright27 London393 Stranraer25
★★★**B Bruce** Queen St ☎2294
16⇌ ⚜ TV in 2 bedrooms CTV in 14 bedrooms ® 16P 3♨ ⚿ ♥ French. Last dinner/High Tea 8.30pm ♕ ⚲ S% sB&B£14–£16.50 sB&B⇌ 🛏£16–£18.50 dB&B£28–£33 dB&B⇌ 🛏£32–£37 Lunch£2.50–£8 Tea30–55p HighTea£2.50–£5 Dinner£7–£10.25 Wine£2.95 ᕈ xmas credit cards ① ② ③ ⑤

★★★⚜L **Kirroughtree** Minnigaff ☎2141
This 18th-C mansion is set in an elevated position in parkland, 2m outside town.
22rm(17⇌1🛏) Annexe: 2⇌ ♪ ⚜ CTV in all bedrooms ® 60P ⇌ ᒪ ♥ English & Continental. Last dinner 9.30pm S% sB&B£13–£16 sB&B⇌ 🛏£15–£18 dB&B£26–£32 dB&B⇌ 🛏£30–£36 Lunch£7.50alc Dinner£8&alc Wine£4.20 ᕈ xmas Credit card ⑤
★★**Creebridge House** ☎2121
26rm(4⇌) ♪ ⚜ CTV in 10 bedrooms ® 40P 1♨ ᒪ ⚿ ⚿ ♥ Scottish & French. Last dinner 9.30pm ♕ ⚲ S% sB&B£11.75–£12.50 sB&B⇌£13–£15 dB&B£23.50–£25 dB&B⇌£26–£30 Lunch£4–£5 Tea£fr1.45 Dinner£6.75–£8 Wine£3.80 ᕈ xmas Credit cards ① ② ③ ⑤
★★**Crown** 101 Queen St ☎2727
Closed Xmas; 9rm(4⇌1🛏) CTV TV & CTV available in bedrooms ® 20P ↩ Last dinner 8.30pm ♕ S% sB&B£11.50–£13.50 sB&B⇌ 🛏£15–£16.75

KIRROUGHTREE HOTEL
New Galloway Road, NEWTON STEWART, Galloway, SW Scotland. Telephone: (0671) 2141
AA ★★★

DO YOU ENJOY REALLY GOOD FOOD?
If so, you must try the cuisine prepared by our ambitious chefs, who have built up a reputation for producing the best food in the region.

Delightful Country House Hotel, built in 1719, full of traditional character, in 8 acres, with beautiful views.

- ★ Fully licensed, two cocktail bars, central heating.
- ★ All bedrooms, including 7 ground-floor bedrooms and family suites, have colour TV/Radio and private bathrooms.
- ★ Most bedrooms 5-star quality.
- ★ FREE GOLF for residents.
- ★ Permits for Salmon/Trout fishing from hotel, pony trekking nearby.
- ★ One of the mildest climates in Britain because of the Gulf-Stream.
- ★ HIGHLY RECOMMENDED FOR ITS PLEASANT ATMOSPHERE, COMFORT, TASTY FOOD AND WINES. Brochure on request.

North Ballachulish–Oban

dB&B£22.90–£26.35 dB&B⇨ ▥ £26.90–£30.25 Credit cards ① ② ③
★★**Galloway Arms** Victoria St ☎2282
Old building set between shops in centre of market town. 21rm(14⇨2▥) ₩ CTV 13P 12⚋ Last dinner9pm (winter) 11pm (summer) ♦ ♧ sB&B⇨ ▥ £12 dB&B£22 dB&B⇨ ▥ £24 Lunch£2.50–£7 Teafr£1.40 Dinner£6–£8 Wine£3.50 ♣ xmas Credit cards ① ② ③ ⑤ ⑥
★**Cairnsmore** Victoria St ☎2162
10rm CTV 20P 6⚋ ⚓ ♦ Mainly grills. Last dinner7pm ♦ sB&B£8 dB&B£16 Lunch£2.50alc High Tea£3alc Dinner£4alc Credit card ①
GH Duncree House Hotel Girvan Rd ☎2001 Lic 6hc (5fb) ♦ CTV 25P S% B&b£6 Bdi£9 Wfr£63 D5pm

NORTH BALLACHULISH 172 Highland Map39 NN06 EcWed Crianlarich40 FortWilliam12 London505 Oban37
★**Loch Leven** ☎Onich236
11rm CTV 50P 1⚋ ⚓ Live music & dancing alt Fri ♡ International. Last dinner9.30pm ♦ ♧
∗sB&B£8–£9 dB&B£16–£18 Lunch£4–£6 Teafr80p Dinner£10alc Wine£3.20 ♣ xmas

NORTH BERWICK 4,429 Lothian Map35 NT58 EcThu Berwick-upon-Tweed42 Dunbar13 Edinburgh24 London390
★★★L **Marine** Cromwell Rd (Trusthouse Forte) ☎2406 Telex no727363
Hotel in grand resort style, with excellent views across Firth of Forth.
85rm(75⇨10▥) Lift ♪ ₩ CTV CTV in all bedrooms ® 150P ⚋ ⇨ (heated) ⚭ (hard) squash sauna bath ♦ Last dinner9pm ♦ ♧ S% sB&B⇨ ▥ £23.10–£25.10 dB&B⇨ ▥ £41.20–£44.70 ♣ xmas Credit cards ① ② ③ ④ ⑤ ⑥
★★**Blenheim House** Westgate ☎2385
12rm(4⇨▥) CTV ⚓ 30P ⚓ ⚋ ⚓ Last dinner9pm ♦ ♣
★★**Nether Abbey** Dirleton Av ☎2802
RS Nov–Mar; 18rm(2▥) CTV 60P ⚓ ⚋ Last dinner8pm S% ∗sB&B£11.50 sB&B▥£11.50–£12.50 dB&B£23 dB&B▥£23–£25 Bar lunch£1.25–£1.50 Tea50p High Tea£2–£3 Dinner£5.50 Wine£3.80 ♣
★★**HPoint Garry** West Bay Rd ☎2380
Closed Nov–Feb; 15rm(2⇨6▥) ₩ CTV 12P ⚓ billiards Last dinner9pm ♦ ♧ S% sB&B£11.50 sB&B⇨ ▥ £13 dB&B£23 dB&B⇨ ▥ £26 Lunch£1.25–£4 Tea75p–£1.25 Dinner£5.25–£7.50&alc Wine£2.95
GH Belhaven Private Hotel Westgate ☎2573 mid Mar–Sep 6hc (2fb) sea
GH Cragside Private Hotel 16 Marine Pde ☎2879 Apr–Oct 6hc (1fb) CTV P ₩ sea S% ∗B&b£6 Bdi£10 W£65 ⚋ D7pm
✕Al **Vagabondo** 35 High St ☎3434
Closed Mon (Nov–Mar); Lunch not served Sun; 50seats

♡ Italian. Last dinner10.45pm Credit cards ① ③ ④ ⑤

NORTH UIST, ISLE OF Western Isles Map48 **See Lochmaddy**

OBAN 6,410 Strathclyde Map39 NM83 EcThu Crianlarich41 FortWilliam49 Glasgow93 Inverary38 London505
★★★L **Alexandra** Corran Esp (Scottish Highland) ☎62381 Telex no778215
Stone building with gables, tower and Regency-style porch leading to front. Views of Oban Bay.
Closed Nov–Mar; 56rm(38⇨2▥) Lift ♪ CTV ® 30P 20⚋ ⚓ Last dinner8.30pm ♦ ♧ S% sB&B£18.30 sB&B⇨ ▥ £21.30 dB&B£30.60 dB&B⇨ ▥ £36.60 Bar lunch£2alc Dinner£7.50 Wine£3.95 Credit cards ① ② ③ ④ ⑤ ⑥
★★★**Caledonian** Station Sq ☎63133 Telex no777210
Set in town centre close to railway and bus station, this five-storey Victorian building overlooks the bay and harbour.
Closed 16Oct–Apr; 72rm(34⇨) Lift ♪ ₩ CTV ⚑
Last dinner9pm ♦ ♧ S% sB&B£18.50 sB&B⇨ ▥ £22 dB&B£31.20 dB&B⇨ ▥ £37.60 Bar lunch£1.50 Tea£1 Dinner£7.50 Wine£3.25 ♣ Credit cards ① ② ③ ⑤ ⑥
★★★**Great Western** The Esplanade (Scottish Highland) ☎63101 Telex no778215
Large traditional hotel with imposing frontage, situated on Esplanade looking out across Oban Bay.
Closed Oct–Apr; 76rm(59⇨) Lift ♪ CTV ® 20P Disco 3nights wkly Last dinner8.30pm ♦ ♧ S% sB&B£18.30 sB&B⇨ ▥ £21.30 dB&B£30.60 dB&B⇨ ▥ £36.60 Bar lunch£2alc Dinner£7.50 Wine£3.95 Credit cards ① ② ③ ⑤ ⑥
★★★**Regent** The Esplanade ☎62341
Narrow sandstone building at end of Esplanade overlooking Oban Pier.
31rm(22⇨2▥) Lift ♪ CTV ® ⚑ ⚓ Last dinner8.30pm S% sB&B£11.88–£18.15 sB&B⇨ ▥ £14.19–£20.35 dB&B£23.76–£36.30 dB&B⇨ ▥ £28.38–£40.70 Lunch fr£5.35 Dinner fr£7.15 Wine£4.30 ♣ Credit cards ① ② ③ ④ ⑤
★★**Columba** North Pier ☎62183
Closed Nov–3Apr; 55rm(3⇨11▥) Lift ♪ CTV 9P Cabaret Tue, Fri, Sat & Sun Last dinner8pm ♦ ♧ S% ∗sB&B£10.35–£12.65 sB&B⇨ ▥ £12.45–£14.75 dB&B£20.70–£25.30 dB&B⇨ ▥ £24.90–£29.50 Lunch fr£3.50 Dinner fr£5.30 Wine£4.20
★★**Lancaster** Corran Esp ☎62587
Stone building with fine views of Oban Bay and Kerrara Island.
28rm(3⇨2▥) CTV ® 24P ⚓ ⚒ (heated) sauna bath Last dinner8pm ♦ ∗sB&B£11 dB&B£22 dB&B⇨ ▥ £24 Lunch£3 Dinner£5 Wine£3.25
★★**Marine** The Esplanade ☎62211
Building in the style of 1930's, situated on sea front overlooking bay and islands.

The Palace Hotel
OBAN
ARGYLL

Telephone 0631 62294

Situated on Oban's main street with panoramic view over Oban Bay, convenient for all bus and boat trips.

Good home cooking and personal supervision by the resident proprietors.

Several rooms with private bath. Reduced rates for children.

Small parties catered for in Licensed Restaurant.

Oban contd–Peebles

Closed Nov–Apr; 44rm(5⇌6♿) Lift ♪ CTV 10P
Last dinner 8.15pm ♥ ⚌ S% sB&B£10–£12.50
dB&B£20–£25 dB&B⇌♿£23–£27 Lunch£2.90
Tea fr 35p Dinner fr £6.55 Wine £3.60 Credit card [5]
★★**Park** The Esplanade ☎63621 Telex no 777967
81rm(22⇌17♿) Lift ♪ CTV ⓑ 16P Cabaret 3 nights wkly
(summer) ♀ European. Last dinner 8.30pm ♥
sB&B£14–£17.50 sB&B⇌♿£16–£19 dB&B£24–£32
dB&B⇌♿£28–£36 Lunch fr £3.75 Dinner fr £7 Wine £4
♬ xmas Credit cards [1][2][3][5][6]
★★**Rowan Tree** George St ☎62954
24rm(16⇌) ♪ ▦ ♿ CTV available in bedrooms 20P
♀ Scottish, English & French. Last dinner 9pm ♥ S%
sB&B£9.80–£16.15 sB&B⇌♿£11.30–£17.65
dB&B£19.60–£26.70 dB&B⇌♿£22.60–£29.70
Bar lunch£1.50–£3 Dinner£6.75–£7.50&alc
Wine£3.50 ♬ Credit cards [2][3]
★**King's Knoll** Dunollie Rd ☎62536
Converted stone manse, with well-maintained gardens, overlooking Oban Bay.
Closed Nov–Nar; 18rm ♿ CTV 12P ⚐ Last dinner 7.30pm
♥ ⚌ sB&B£7.50–£8.50 dB&B£15–£17
Lunch£3–£3.50 Tea£1 Dinner£4–£5 ♬
★**Palace** George St ☎62294
Closed 2wks Xmas–New Year; 16rm(6⇌1♿) CTV ♬
Last dinner 10.30pm ♥ ⚌ sB&B£7–£8
sB&B⇌♿£8.50–£9.75 dB&B£14–£16
dB&B⇌♿£17–£19.50 Lunch£2–£3.25 Tea 50p
Dinner£4–£5&alc Wine£3.20
GH Ardblair Dalriach Rd ☎62668 5May–27Sep 15hc
(A7hc) (4fb) ⚐ CTV 12P sea S%
B&b£5.50–£6.50 Bdi£9.50–£10.50 D6.30pm
GH Barriemore Private Hotel Esplanade ☎62197 wk
before Etr–mid Oct 14hc (4fb) nc6 CTV 17P sea
B&b£6.67–£8.75 Bdi£10.93–£12.08 D6.45pm
GH Crathie Duncraggen Rd ☎62619 May–Oct 9hc
nc3 CTV 12P sea
GH Glenburnie Private Hotel Esplanade ☎62089
May–Sep 13hc (3fb) ⚐ nc5 CTV 12P 1⚓ sea
✱B&B£6.95–£8.22
GH Heatherfield Private Hotel Albert Rd ☎62681
Apr–Oct 10hc (3fb) nc7 CTV 10P sea S%
B&b£6.33 Bdi£10.50 W£73 ★ D6pm
GH Kenmore Soraba Rd ☎63592 7hc (4fb) CTV 20P
♿ S% B&b£5.50–£6
GH Roseneath Dalriach Rd ☎64262 10hc (2fb) CTV
9P ♿ sea ✱B&b£5.75–£7.50 Bdi£8.50–£12 W£76
★ D6pm

OLD RAYNE 109 Grampian Map45 NJ62 London 564
Aberdeen 26 Huntly 13
★**Lodge** ☎205
2rm Annexe: 4⇌♿ ♿ CTV in 4 bedrooms ⓑ ⚐ 40P ⚐ ↔
billiards Last dinner 7pm ♥ S% sB&B£10.65
sB&B⇌♿£10.65 dB&B£17.04 dB&B⇌♿£17.04
Lunch£3.75 Tea 80p High Tea£3 Dinner£7 alc
Wine£3.50

ONICH Highland Map39 NN06 EcSat (ex summer)
Crianlarich 42 Fort William 10 London 507 Oban 39
★★**Allt-Nan-Ros** ☎210
In own grounds with splendid views over Loch Linnhe and surrounding hills.
Closed Nov–Mar; 20rm ♿ CTV 30P ♨ Last dinner 8.30pm
♥ ⚌ S% sB&B£8.63 dB&B⇌♿£17.26 Bar lunch fr £1.20
Tea fr 60p Dinner fr £5 ♬ Credit cards [1][2][3]
★★**L Creag Dhu** ☎238
Closed Nov–Mar; 20rm(5⇌3♿) ♿ CTV 25P ♨
Cabaret wkly Last dinner 8pm ♥ ⚌ S%
sB&B£11.50–£13.50 sB&B⇌♿£13.75–£16
dB&B£23–£27 dB&B⇌♿£27.50–£32
Bar lunch£2.50 alc Tea£1 alc Dinner£7–£9.50
Wine£3.65 ♬ Credit cards [1][2][3][5]
★★**Onich** ☎214
Conversion of two adjoining houses, dating from 1880, with modern extension, standing on lochside in own grounds. Views over Loch Linnhe and surrounding hills.
Closed 11 Oct–28 Apr; 25rm CTV 50P ♨ Cabaret Wed &
Sun Last dinner 8.30pm ♥ ⚌ S% sB&B fr £9.50
dB&B fr £19 Bar lunch fr £2.25 Tea fr £1.25 Dinner fr £7
Wine£3.75 Credit cards [1][2][3]
GH Glenmorven House ☎247 Etr–Oct 7rm 6hc
(2fb) 20P ♿ lake S% Bdi fr £12.25 W fr £85.75 ★
D8pm
GH Tigh-a-Righ ☎255 Closed 22Dec–7Jan Lic 5hc
(2fb) CTV 7P ♿ D8.30pm
FH Mr & Mrs A. Dewar **Cuilcheanna House** (NN019617)
☎226
Large Victorian house with gardens set in sloping fields leading to Loch Linnhe. Excellent views over lochs and mountains.
Etr–Sep 9rm 8hc (2fb) ⚐ 8P ♿ lake 120 acres
beef S% B&b£5.50–£6.50 Bdi£10.25–£11.25
W£69–£75 ★ D7pm

ORKNEY Map 48 **See Harray, Kirkwall, Rendall, St Margaret's Hope, and Stromness (for car-carrying service from Scrabster, Thurso)**

OVERSCAIG Highland Map 46 NC42 Durness 41
Inverness 76 Lairg 17 London 641
★**Overscaig** ☎Merkland 203
RS Oct–mid Apr; 10rm(4⇌♿) ♿ CTV ⓑ 20P ♨ ↔
Last dinner 8pm ♥ ⚌

PAISLEY 94,025 Strathclyde Map 37 NS46 EcTue MdMon
Dumbarton 13 Glasgow 7 Greenock 16 Kilmarnock 23
London 414
For accommodation and restaurant details see under Glasgow Airport

PATHHEAD 931 Lothian Map 35 NT36 EcWed Dalkeith 5
Edinburgh 12 Jedburgh 36 London 384
★★**Stair Arms** (Scottish & Newcastle) ☎Ford
(Midlothian) 320277
Old coaching inn with tastefully renovated interior retaining its old-world atmosphere. An old coach stands for the car park. Location is on the A68 to Edinburgh.
7rm ♿ CTV 100P 2⚓ ♨ Live music & dancing Sat
Last dinner 9.30pm ♥ Credit cards [1][2][3][4][5][6]

PEAT INN Fife Map 41 NO40 St Andrews 7 Elie 8 Cupar 7
London 462
✻××**Peat Inn** ☎206
Closed Sun, Mon, 1st 2wks Jan, 1wk May & 1wk Oct;
46 seats ♀ French. Last dinner 9.30pm S% Lunch£7
Dinner£10 alc Credit card [2]

PEEBLES 6,064 Borders Map 35 NT24 EcWed MdFri
Edinburgh 23 Galashiels 19 Glasgow 52 Hawick 33
London 382
★★★**Park** Innerleithen Rd (Swallow) ☎20451
Telex no 53168
Traditional Scottish building with modern extension, overlooking the River Tweed and Border hills.
24rm(17⇌2♿) 1⚏ ♪ ♿ CTV CTV in bedrooms ⓑ 60P ♨
Live music & dancing Sat (Nov–Mar) Last dinner 9pm ♥
⚌ S% Lunch£4.40 Tea£1.10 High Tea£4
Dinner£6.60&alc Wine£3.17 ♬ xmas
Credit cards [1][2][3][4][5][6]
★★★**Peebles Hydro** ☎20602 Telex no 72568
An impressive late Victorian building set in 30 acres of grounds with fine views over the River Tweed, surrounding hills and pine forests.
Closed 1–6Jan; 144rm(128⇌) Lift ♪ ♿ CTV in all
bedrooms ⓑ ⚐ 150P ♨ (heated) ⚐ (hard) squash Ω
billiards sauna bath Live music & dancing twice wkly ♫
Conference facilities available Last dinner 9pm ♥ ⚌
S% sB&B£18–£20 sB&B⇌♿£20–£24 dB&B£30–£34
dB&B⇌♿£37.50–£47.50 Lunch£4.50–£6.25 Tea 50p

Dinner£7–£9.50 Wine£4.75 ℞ xmas Credit cards ①③
★★★**Tontine** High St (Trusthouse Forte) ☎20892
Three storey hotel dating from 1808 with large modern extension to rear.
37rm(36⇌1🛁) 🌙 🍴 CTV CTV in all bedrooms ® 30P 4🛎
Last dinner9.30pm ✓ ♬ S%
sB&B⇌🛁£22.10–£24.10 dB&B⇌🛁£36.20–£39.20 ℞
xmas Credit cards ①②③④⑤⑥
★★ **HL Cringletie House** ⇌ Eddleston333
Closed Jan–mid Mar; 16rm(8⇌1🛁) Lift 🌙 CTV 40P 🏌
⛵(hard) 🗺 International. Last dinner8.30pm ✓ ♬
sB&B£16.50 dB&B⇌🛁£35 Lunch£6 Tea£1.75
Dinner£10 Wine£3.75
★★ **Kingsmuir** Springhill Rd ☎20151
10rm(7⇌) 🌙 🍴 CTV CTV in 7bedrooms ® 🚭 30P ✈ 🌙 ⛵
🎣 ↯ Last dinner8.30pm ✓ ♬ sB&B£19.50
dB&B£19.80 dB&B⇌🛁£23 Lunch£4 Tea£1.20
Dinner£5.50–£7.50&alc Wine£2.50 ℞
Credit cards ①③⑥
★★ **Venlaw Castle** Edinburgh Rd ☎20384
Built in 1872, this converted Baronial-style stone house stands in 6½ acres of wooded hill country on the site of the keep of the old Smithfield castle.
Closed 16Oct–14Mar; 12rm(1⇌4🛁) 🍴 CTV ® 20P 2🛎 ✈
🌙 Last dinner8.30pm ✓ S% sB&B£13–£15
sB&B⇌🛁£14–£16 dB&B£25–£28
dB&B⇌🛁£27–£29 Bar lunch£1.50–£4
Dinner£7–£8.50 Wine£3.40 ℞ Credit cards ①②④⑤⑥
★ **County** High St (Scottish & Newcastle) ☎20595
Centrally situated in Border town, stone-built inn dating from 14th-C, featuring vaulted 'Bastel House'.
6rm TV 3P Children under 4yrs not accommodated
Last dinner8.45pm ✳sB&B£7.50 dB&B£14.60
Lunch£2 High Teafr£2.80 Dinner£5 Wine£3.30
Credit card ①
★ **Riverside** Neidpath Rd ☎20776
Converted three-storey manse dating from 1865 with terraced gardens leading to banks of River Tweed.
8rm CTV 40P 1🛎 🌙 Last dinner8pm ✓
sB&B£8.50–£9.50 dB&B£17–£19 Lunch£2.80
High Tea£2.50 Dinner£4.50 Wine£3.20 ℞
GH 'Lindores' Old Town ☎20441 Closed Nov 5rac
(2fb) CTV 3P 🍴 S% B&b£6–£6.50 W£42–£45.50 Ⓜ

PENNAN Grampian Map45NJ86 Banff12 Fraserburgh12
Aberdeen43 London580
INN Pennan ☎New Aberdour201 8hc ✈ CTV 6P 🍴
S% ✳B&b£10.50 Bdi£17.50 Bar lunch90p–£2.75
D9.30pm£6.50&alc

PERTH 44,066 Tayside Map40NO12 EcWed MdFri
Braemar51 Dundee21 Edinburgh44 London452
Pitlochry27 Stirling33
☆☆☆**City Mills** West Mill St (Reo Stakis) ☎28281
Telex no778704

Built around an old mill. The mill stream passes under the hotel and can be seen in parts throughout glass floors.
78rm(76⇌) 🌙 🍴 CTV in all bedrooms ® 50P Live music & dancing Fri Conference facilities available 🗺 English & French. Last dinner10.30pm sB&B⇌fr£24
dB&B⇌fr£34 Lunchfr£5&alc Dinnerfr£5&alc
Wine£4.05 ℞ xmas Credit cards ①②③④⑤⑥
★★★**Isle of Skye** Queen's Bridge, Dundee Rd (Osprey)
☎24271
The hotel is on the north bank of river, opposite bridge.
33rm 🌙 🍴 CTV CTV in all bedrooms ® 70P Live music Tues, Fri & Sat Conference facilities available 🗺 Scottish & French. Last dinner9.30pm ✓ S% dB&B£12.05
dB&B£25 Lunch£3.50&alc Tea£1 High Tea£2.50
Dinner£5&alc Wine£3.50 ℞ xmas
Credit cards ①②③④⑤
★★★**Royal George** Tay St (Trusthouse Forte) ☎24455
Three-storey stone building overlooking River Tay.
43rm 🌙 🍴 CTV in all bedrooms ® 20P 12🛎
Last dinner9pm ✓ ♬ S% sB&B⇌£24.10–£27.10
dB&B⇌£35.20–£38.20 ℞ Credit cards ①②③④⑤⑥
★★★**Station** Leonard St (British Transport) ☎24141
Telex no76481
Traditional Victorian building adjacent to station.
54rm(41⇌) Lift 🌙 CTV CTV in all bedrooms 14P 🌙 ⛵
Conference facilities available ✓ ♬ S%
✳sB&B£15–£17.50 sB&B⇌£22–£25 dB&B£25–£32
dB&B⇌£30–£42 Lunchfr£3.50 Dinnerfr£7 Wine£4.85
℞ Credit cards ①②③④⑤⑥
★★ **Lovat** 90–92 Glasgow Rd ☎36555
Converted and extended private house on southern approach road (A9) to Perth.
24rm(12⇌1🛁) 🌙 🍴 CTV TV in 3bedrooms CTV in 21bedrooms 40P Live music & dancing wkly 🗺 French.
Last dinner10pm ✓ ♬ S% ✳sB&B£8–£11
sB&B⇌🛁£13.50–£19.50 dB&B£16–£22
dB&B⇌🛁£22–£27 Lunch£2.85–£3.50 Tea£1.50
High Tea£2.25–£4.75 Dinner£4.50–£5.75&alc
Wine£3.45 ℞ xmas Credit cards ①②③⑤
★★ **Queens** Leonard St (Travo) ☎25471
55rm(7⇌) Lift 🌙 🍴 CTV ® 20P Live music & dancing 3nights wkly 🗺 Scottish & English. Last dinner8.30pm ✓
♬ S% ✳sB&B£11.50 sB&B⇌£14.50 dB&B£20
dB&B⇌£23 Lunch£3.50 Teafr75p High Teafr£1.95
Dinner£4.95 Wine£3.25 ℞ Credit cards ①②③⑤⑥
★★ **Salutation** South St (Allied Scotland) ☎22166
Telex no76357
Established in 1699, this was the temporary HQ of Prince Charles Edward Stuart.
62rm(31⇌31🛁) 🌙 🍴 CTV CTV in all bedrooms ® ♪ Disco 3nights wkly Live music & dancing 3nights wkly Conference facilities available Last dinner9pm ✓
sB&B⇌🛁fr£16 dB&B⇌🛁fr£30 Lunchfr£6 Teafr£1.50
Dinnerfr£7.50 Wine£2.10 ℞ xmas
Credit cards ①②③④⑤⑥
★ **County** New Row (Scottish & Newcastle) ☎23618

Venlaw Castle Hotel

Peebles EH45 8QG
Tel: Peebles 20384 (STD 0721)

Venlaw Castle Hotel offers all the comforts of a modern hotel, with excellent cuisine, while retaining the atmosphere of gracious living of a bygone age.
The castle was built in 1782, in the Scottish Baronial style of architecture, on the site of the old Scottish keep of Smithfield Castle, and commands a magnificent view of the surrounding countryside.

LOVAT HOTEL
**90 Glasgow Road
Perth PH2 0LT
Tel (0738) 36555/6/7**

Our hotel is ideally situated for Touring, Golf, Fishing, etc. — it also offers an excellent cuisine and wines — very comfortable bedrooms with private bathrooms, colour TV's, etc., etc. — Conference facilities up to 200.

Two-storey building in town centre, near Motorail terminal.
9rm CTV 6P ♀ Mainly grills. Last dinner 8.45pm ⚬ ℞
Credit cards ① ② ③ ⑤ ⑥

GH Clunie 12 Pitcullen Cres ☎23625 7hc 1⇌ 1▥
(2fb) ⊘ CTV 7P ⋈ S% B&b£6.50 Bdi£10 W£70
£ D5pm

GH Darroch 9 Pitcullen Cres ☎36893 7hc (3fb) CTV
12P ⋈ S% B&b£6.50–£7.50 D9.15pm

GH Gables of Perth 24–26 Dunkeld Rd ☎24717 8hc
(4fb) CTV 6P ⋈ S% *B&b£6

GH Garth Dundee Rd ☎22368 6hc (3fb) CTV 3P
3▥ ⋈ river S% B&b£5.50–£6.50

GH Pitcullen 17 Pitcullen Cres ☎26506 10hc (2fb)
CTV 12P ⋈ S% B&bfr£6 Bdifr£9.50

××Timothy's 24 St John Street ☎26641
Closed Sun & Mon; 56seats ℙ ⌑Danish.
Last dinner 10pm

×Penny Post 80 George St ☎20867
So named as building housed one of Perth's first post offices in 1773.
Closed Sun; 64seats Last dinner 10pm Lunch£7alc Dinner£7alc Wine£3.80 Credit cards ② ⑤

PETERHEAD 14,994 Grampian Map45NK14 EcWed
Aberdeen34 Banff36 Fraserburgh18 London570
★★★**Palace** Prince St (Ind Coope (Alloa)) ☎4821
A city style hotel comprising original building extensions, internally modernised.
59rm(50⇌) Lift ⊅ ⊞ ⋈ CTV in all bedrooms ® 80P
Conference facilities available ♀Continental.
Last dinner 9.30pm ⚬ S% sB&B£13 sB&B⇌£18.50
dB&B£22 dB&B⇌£26.50 Lunch£3.85 Dinner£5.75
Wine£2.30 ℞ Credit cards ① ② ③ ⑤ ⑥

✩✩✩ **B Waterside Inn** Fraserburgh Rd ☎71121
Telex no739413
78⇌ Annexe: 40⇌ ⊅ ⋈ CTV in all bedrooms ® 250P ♨
Disco Fri & Sat Live music & dancing Sat Conference facilities available ♀English & French.
Last dinner 10.30pm ⚬ ⊥ S% sB&B⇌▥£16–£30
dB&B⇌£25–£40 Lunchfr£3.50&alc Tea75p–£1.75
High Tea£2.75–£4.50 Dinnerfr£7.50&alc Wine£3.95
℞ Credit cards ① ② ③ ⑤

PITCAPLE Grampian Map45NJ72 Inverurie5 Aberdeen21
Huntly18 London556
★★★**B Pittodrie House** ☎202
14rm(7⇌▥) 1⊞ ⋈ CTV in all bedrooms ® 30P ♨ ⊷(hard) squash billiards ♀French. Last dinner 9pm
Credit cards ① ② ③ ⑤

PITLOCHRY 2,473 Tayside Perths Map40NN95 EcThu
Aberfeldy15 Braemar41 London475 Newtonmore42 Perth27
★★★**Atholl Palace** (Trusthouse Forte) ☎2400
Telex no76406
92⇌ Lift ⊅ ⋈ CTV CTV in all bedrooms ® 180P ♨

⊡(heated) ⊷(hard) sauna bath ♨ Conference facilities available Last dinner 9.30pm ⚬ ⊥ S%
sB&B⇌£28.60–£31.10 dB&B⇌£41.70–£45.20 ℞
xmas Credit cards ① ② ③ ④ ⑤ ⑥

★★★**Fishers** Atholl Rd ☎2000
Well-established four storey hotel in town centre backed by fine gardens.
77rm(46⇌5▥) Lift ⊅ ⋈ CTV CTV available in bedrooms ⊘
55P 11⚘ ⊥ ⊷ Last dinner 8.30pm ⚬ ⊥ S%
sB&B£13.60–£18 sB&B⇌▥£16–£21
dB&B£25.60–£34 dB&B⇌▥£28.80–£38 Teafr80p
High Teafr£3 Dinnerfr£8 Wine£2.80 ℞
Credit cards ① ② ③ ⑤ ⑥

★★★**Green Park** ☎2537
An extended country house hotel standing on the banks of Loch Faskally and backed by woodland.
Closed Nov–Mar; 37rm(23⇌5▥) ⋈ CTV ® ⊘ 50P 4⚘ ⊘
⊥ ⊷ Conference facilities available ♀Scottish & French.
Last dinner 8pm ⚬ ⊥ S% sB&Bfr£14
sB&B⇌▥£16.50 dB&B£25.60–£34 dB&B⇌▥fr£33
Lunchfr£3.50 Dinnerfr£7 Wine£4 ℞

★★★**⚘ Pine Trees** Strathview Ter ☎2121
Closed Nov–Feb; 27rm(15⇌4▥) Annexe: 2⇌ ⋈ CTV CTV
available in bedrooms 60P 12⚘ ⊥ ⊷ ♀International.
Last dinner 9pm ⚬ ⊥ S% sB&B⇌▥£12–£15
sB&B⇌▥£14–£17 dB&B⇌£24–£30
dB&B⇌▥£25.50–£27.50 Lunch£5 Tea£1.50
Dinner£8&alc Wine£3 ℞ Credit cards ① ② ③ ④ ⑤ ⑥

★★★**Pitlochry Hydro** (Scottish Highland) ☎2666
Telex no778215
Set in own grounds, the hotel offers commanding views over the south west of town and valley.
Closed Oct–Apr; 62rm(58⇌) Lift CTV ® 60P 6⚘ ⊥ ⊷ ⊘
Last dinner 8.30pm ⚬ ⊥ S% sB&B£19.25
sB&B⇌£22.25 dB&B£32.50 dB&B⇌£38.50
Bar lunch£2alc Dinner£7.50 Wine£3.95
Credit cards ① ② ③ ④ ⑤ ⑥

★★★**Scotland's** 40 Bonnethill Rd (Best Western) ☎2292
50rm(21⇌25▥) Lift ⊅ ⋈ CTV CTV in 10 bedrooms ® 50P
Conference facilities available Last dinner 10.30pm ⚬
S% sB&B£17–£24.30 sB&B⇌▥£17–£24.30
dB&B£29–£42.60 dB&B⇌▥£29–£42.60
Lunch£5.40&alc Dinner£7.80&alc Wine£3.90 ℞
Credit cards ① ② ③ ⑤ ⑥

★★**Acarsaid** 8 Atholl Rd ☎2389
Closed 20Oct–6Apr; 20rm(14⇌4▥) CTV ® ⊘ 20P ⊥
Last dinner 7.30pm ⚬ ⊥ sB&B£9.50–£11
sB&B⇌▥£11–£12.60 dB&B£19–£22.50
dB&B⇌▥£22.50–£25.20 Lunch£3.50–£4.50
Tea50p–£1.25 Dinner£6 Wine£2.75

★★**Burnside** West Moulin Rd (Inter-Hotels) ☎2203
Centrally situated in a quiet residential part of the town with well-tended grounds and south-facing views.
Closed Nov–mid Mar; 16rm(11⇌5▥) Annexe:
6rm(1⇌1▥) ⋈ CTV ® 30P ⊥ ⊘ ♀Scottish & Continental.
Last dinner 8.30pm ⚬ ⊥ S% sB&Bfr£13.51

Pollokshields – Port of Menteith

sB&B⇌🛏£15.75 dB&Bfr£23.23 dB&B⇌🛏fr£27.71
Barlunchfr£3.25 Teafr95p Dinnerfr£6.50 Wine£3.40
🍴 Credit cards ② ③ ⑤ ⑥
★★**Claymore** 162 Atholl Rd ☎2888
Closed 24Oct–15Apr; 8rm(2⇌🛏) Annexe: 4rm(1⇌🛏) 🍴
CTV 30P 🐕 ♿ Children under 5yrs not accommodated
Last dinner 8.30pm 🍴
★★**Craigard** Strathview Ter ☎2592
Closed Nov–Etr 9rm(6⇌🛏) Annexe: 8rm(4⇌🛏) CTV ®
17P ♿ Last dinner 7.30pm ✲ ✲sB&Bfr£9.95
sB&B⇌🛏fr£11.55 dB&Bfr£17.50 dB&B⇌🛏fr£21
Lunchfr£2.40 Teafr75p Dinnerfr£6.50 Wine£3.35 🍴
★★**Craigvrack** West Moulin Rd ☎2399
19rm(9⇌🛏) 🍴 CTV ® 19P 2🅿️ 🐕 ♿ ♨ English & French.
Last dinner 8.30pm ✲ ♨ Credit card ①
★★**Dundarach** ☎2862
Formerly a private mansion house, set in ten acres of
wooded grounds, with views over river and surrounding
hills, yet within ¼ mile of town centre.
30rm(24⇌6🛏) 🍴 CTV 24P ♿ ♨ ♿ Last dinner 8pm ✲
♨ S% ✲sB&B⇌🛏£11–£12 dB&B⇌🛏£20–£22
Lunch£4–£5 Tea£1.20–£1.50 Dinner£7.50–£8
Wine£3.95 Credit card ⑥
★★**Wellwood** ☎2196
Charming little hotel on hillside above town. History dates
back to 1700.
RS Nov–9Apr; 18rm(9⇌🛏) Annexe: 5rm CTV 40P ⇌
♨ International. Last dinner 9pm ✲ ♨ S%
dB&B£26–£28.40 dB&B⇌🛏£30.60–£33 Lunch£5
Tea50p–£1 HighTea£3–£4.50 Dinner£7.50–£9&alc
Wine£3.30 🍴 Credit cards ① ② ⑤
★★**Wellwood** West Moulin Rd ☎2879
Closed Nov–Mar; 14rm(2⇌2🛏) CTV 20P 1🅿️ ♿ Children
under 8yrs not accommodated ♨ International.
Last dinner 7.45pm ✲ sB&B⇌🛏£9–£10.50
dB&B£18–£21 dB&B⇌🛏£22–£25 Barlunchfr£3.75
Dinnerfr£5.50 Wine£3.25 🍴
★**Airdaniar** 160 Atholl Rd ☎2266
Closed Nov–Etr; 10rm(1🛏) ♿ CTV ® 14P 🐕 ♿
Last dinner 7.30pm ✲ ♨ S% sB&B⇌🛏£11.80–£12.25
sB&B⇌🛏£12.80–£13.25 dB&B£19.60–£20.50
dB&B⇌🛏£21.60–£22.50 Barlunch£1–£2 Tea£1
Dinner£6 Wine£3.50 🍴
★**BL Birchwood** 2 East Moulin Rd ☎2477
11rm(6⇌2🛏) Annexe:4🛏 🍴 CTV TV available in
bedrooms ® 25P Last dinner 7.30pm ✲ ♨ S%
sB&B⇌🛏£8.50–£16 sB&B⇌🛏£9.75–£17.25
dB&B£17–£26.50 dB&B⇌🛏£19.50–£29.25
Lunch£3.75–£4.25 Tea£1.25–£1.50 Dinner£4.50–£5
Wine£3.25 🍴
★**Craig Urrard** 10 Atholl Rd ☎2346
Closed Dec–Feb; 10rm(2⇌🛏) Annexe: 2rm CTV 12P
♨ International. Last dinner 7.30pm ✲ 🍴
★**Dunfallandy House** Logierait Rd (2m S unclass road)
☎2648
8rm 🍴 CTV ® 20P 2🅿️ 🐕 ♿ Live music & dancing Wed, Fri
& Sat Cabaret Wed, Fri & Sat Last dinner 9.30pm ✲ S%
sB&B£8 dB&B£16 Barlunch£1.50alc Dinner£6.50alc
Wine£2.75 🍴 Credit cards ① ② ③
GH Adderley Private Hotel 23 Toberargan Rd ☎2433
14Apr–14Oct 10hc (1fb) ♿ nc10 CTV 9P S%
Bdi£11.50–£12.25 W£77.20–£80.50 ♿ D6.30pm
GH Balrobin Private Hotel Higher Oakfield ☎2901 late
May–late Sep 7hc 1⇌ 1🛏 (2fb) 10P S% B&b£10
Bdi£15 W£55 ♿ D7pm
GH Duntrune 22 East Moulin Rd ☎2172 mid Mar–mid
Oct 7hc (1fb) ♿ nc5 8P S% B&b£7–£7.50
Bdi£11–£11.50 W£71.50–£75.25 ♿ D6.30pm
GH Fasganeoin Hotel Perth Rd ☎2387 Apr–Sep Lic
9hc (4fb) ♿ TV 20P 🍴 river S%
B&b£9.50–£10.50 Bdi£14.50–£15.50 W£99–£106
♿ D7.30pm
GH Poplars Private Hotel Lower Oakfield ☎2129
Mar–Oct 9hc 7🛏 (2fb) CTV 14P 🍴 S%

B&b£6.50–£7.50 Bdi£11.50–£13 D6.30pm
GH Torrdarach Hotel Golf Course Rd ☎2136 7hc 1🛏
(1fb) CTV 9P 🍴 S% B&b£8.25–£8.75
Bdi£13.50–£14 W£89.50–£93 ♿ D6pm
FH Mrs M. M. Hay **Faskally Home** (NN918601) ☎2007
Pleasant 'U'-shaped farm with popular caravan site
attached. Set on west side of A9 on northern outskirts of
Pitlochry. Sheltered from Loch Faskally by trees.
Apr–mid Oct 8rm 6hc (2fb) P 100acres non-working
S% B&bfr£5.50

POLLOKSHIELDS Strathclyde Map37NS46
See Glasgow

POLMONT 2,153 Central Map34NS97 EcWed
Edinburgh22 Falkirk3 Glasgow31 London420
★★★**B Inchyra Grange** Grange Rd (Inter-Hotels)
☎711911 Telex no 777693
A converted mansion of considerable age and character
standing in nine acres of grounds with views over
Grangemouth and Firth of Forth.
30⇌🛏 D 🍴 CTV in all bedrooms ® 100P ♿ Live music &
dancing Sat & Sun Cabaret Sat Conference facilities
available Last dinner 9.30pm ✲
Credit cards ① ② ③ ⑤

POOLEWE Highland Map42NG88 EcThu Gairloch6
Inverness80 London641 Ullapool50
★★**Pool House** ☎272 Telex no 75605
Closed 15Oct–Mar; 14rm 🍴 CTV ® 24P
Last dinner 8.30pm ✲ ♨ S% sB&B£11.50–£14.50
dB&B£23–£29 Barlunchfr£2.75 Dinnerfr£6.75
Wine£3.30 Credit card ⑤

PORT APPIN Strathclyde Map39NM94 EcThu
Crianlarich55 Fort William29 London520 Oban26
✲★★(red) **Airds** ☎Appin236
(Rosette awarded for dinner only.)
This unassuming little Red Star hotel occupies the building
of an old ferry inn overlooking an island-studded loch. A
peaceful setting and good food make it ideal for a relaxing
holiday.
Closed Nov–Mar; 14rm(5⇌) 🍴 30P 🐕 Last dinner 8pm
✲ ♨ sB&B£13–£14.50 dB&B£26–£29
dB&B⇌£30–£33 Lunch£1.50–£3 Tea£1.50–£2.50
Dinner£10 Wine£3.20

PORT ASKAIG Isle of Islay, Strathclyde Map32NR46
EcTue **Car-carrying service from Kennacraig. Also
Feolin Ferry to Jura** Port Ellen19
★★**Port Askaig** ☎Kildalton245
Picturesque Highland inn.
10rm(4⇌🛏) 🍴 CTV 10P ♿ Children under 6yrs not
accommodated Last dinner 8.30pm ✲

PORT ELLEN 932 Isle of Islay, Strathclyde Map32NR34
EcTue **Car-carrying service from Kennacraig**
Port Askaig19
★★**Dower House** Kildalton (3m E A846) ☎225
5⇌🛏 CTV 12P 🐕 ♿ Last dinner 8.30pm ✲ ♨
GH Tighcargaman ☎2345 Lic 3hc 1⇌🛏
(A 6rm 4hc 1⇌🛏) (2fb) ♿ 9P 🍴 sea D8pm

PORTOBELLO Lothian Map35NT37
See Edinburgh

PORT OF MENTEITH Central Map40NN50 Callander7
Glasgow31 Stirling15 Aberfoyle4 London434
FH Mrs J. Fotheringham **Collymoon** (NN593966)
☎Buchlyvie268
Attractive white-painted farmhouse near lane. Situated just
off B8034.
Apr–Oct 3rm 1hc (3fb) ♿ CTV 3P 🍴 river
350acres mixed S% B&b£5.50 Bdi£8

137

PORTPATRICK 643 Dumfries & Galloway Map30NX05
EcThu Glenluce14 London423 Newton Stewart30
Stranraer8
★★★⚑ *HBL* **Knockinaam Lodge** (2m S on unclass rcad)
☎471
Closed 16Nov–Mar; 10rm(7⇨1🛁) 🍴CTV 45P 🚗 ⚓ ⟲
♀English & French. Last dinner8.45pm ✤ ⚷
sB&B⇨🛁£16–£19 dB&B£30–£32
dB&B⇨🛁£34–£42 Lunch fr£3.50&alc
Dinner£9.50&alc Wine£4.50 🅿 Credit card ②

★★**Fernhill** ☎220
Closed Nov–Feb; 11rm(8⇨) Annexe: 4rm(1⇨3🛁) 🍴CTV
® 40P ⚓ ⚭ Last dinner8.30pm ✤ S%
sB&B£12.50–£14.50 sB&B⇨🛁£15.50–£17.50
dB&B£23–£27 dB&B⇨🛁£27–£31
Bar lunch£1.20–£2.50 Tea fr50p Dinner fr£6.50
Wine£2.30 🅿 Credit cards ① ③

★★**Portpatrick** (Mount Charlotte) ☎333
Large building on cliffside with fine views down on to town and harbour.
Closed Nov–8Apr; 63rm(34⇨1🛁) Lift ♪ CTV CTV in
20bedrooms 60P ⚓ ⚭ (heated) ♣♠ ⚬♤(grass) billiards
Disco wkly Live music & dancing wkly ♀ Scottish, English
& French. Last dinner8.45pm ✤ ⚷ S%
sB&B⇨🛁£16–£19 sB&B⇨🛁£18–£23 dB&B£26–£36
dB&B⇨🛁£30–£40 Lunch£4.50–£5.50
High Tea£2.50–£3 Dinner£6.50–£7.50 Wine£4.90 🅿
Credit cards ① ② ③

★**Mount Stewart** South Cres ☎291
8rm(1⇨) 🍴CTV ® 20P ⚓ Last dinner9pm ✤ ⚷ S%
sB&B£10.50–£11 dB&B£21–£22 dB&B⇨🛁£24–£25
Bar lunch£1.50–£2 Tea£1.25–£1.50
Dinner£5.50–£6.50 Wine£3.54

GH Blinkbonnie School Brae ☎282 Apr–Sep 6hc
(1fb) CTV 8P 🍴 B&b£6.25 Bdi£10.50 W£73 ⚭
D5.30pm

GH Carlton 21 South Cres ☎253 Mar–Oct 8hc nc
CTV sea S% B&b£8 Bdi£12 D6pm

GH Melvin Lodge Dunskey St ☎238 Etr–Sep Tem
13hc (4fb) CTV 8P sea B&b£7.50 Bdi£9.50
D6.30pm

PORTREE 1,374 Isle of Skye, Highland Map42NG44
EcWed Broadford26 Dunvegan22 Uig17
★★★**Coolin Hills** ☎2003
Converted shooting lodge, with fine views over Portree Bay
19rm(8⇨) Annexe: 10rm(4⇨) 🍴CTV 100P ⚓ ⚭
Last dinner8pm ✤ S% ✽sB&B£10–£16
sB&B⇨🛁£12–£18 dB&B£20–£25 dB&B⇨🛁£22–£28
Lunch£3.50 Tea50p–£1.50 Dinner£5.50–£6.60
Wine£2.80 Credit card ⑥

★★**Rosedale** ☎2531
Closed Oct–Apr; 17rm(4⇨) 🍴CTV ® 20P ⚓
Last dinner8pm ✤ ⚷ ✽sB&B£11.25 dB&B£22.50
dB&B⇨🛁£27.50 Dinner£5.75 Wine£3.70

★★**Royal** ☎2525
25rm(17⇨) 🏛 🍴CTV 🅿 Last dinner8.30pm ✤ S%
✽sB&B£12–£14 dB&B£23–£26 dB&B⇨🛁£27–£30
Lunch£4 alc Tea£1.15 alc Dinner£5 alc Wine£4

★*B* **King's Haven** Bosville Ter ☎2290
Closed Nov–14Apr; 6rm(1⇨4🛁) ♪ CTV ® ⚓ ⚭
Last dinner10pm ✤ ⚷ S% sB&B£11
sB&B⇨🛁£13.30 dB&B£22 dB&B⇨🛁£24.30
Lunch fr£2 Tea fr£2 Dinner fr£8 Wine£3.70

GH Bosville Bosville Ter ☎2846 Apr–Oct 13hc 1⇨
1🛁 (3fb) CTV 8P sea S% ✽B&b£6.50–£7.50
Bdi£9.50–£11.50 W£52–£60 D7.45pm

GH Craiglockhart Beaumont Cres ☎2233 Closed Dec
rs Jan & Feb 4hc (A5hc) TV 4P 🍴 sea S%
B&b£6.90–£7.48 Bdi£10.35–£11.51 W£68–£75 ⚭
D7pm

FH Mrs M. Bruce **Cruachanlea** (NG513373) Braes
☎Sligachan233
Situated 6 miles SE of Portree on B883, overlooking sea to the Isle of Raasay. Hill views everywhere.

4hc (2fb) CTV 8P 🍴 sea 10acres arable sheep S%
B&b£5–£5.50 Bdi£8–£8.50 W£56–£59.50 ⚭ D7pm

FH No 1 Uigishadder (NG430463) ☎ Skeabost Bridge279
Small crofting farm situated high on moor in isolated position facing north-west. Portree about 4 miles.
Apr–Sep 3rm 6P 6acres arable

FH Mrs S. MacDonald **Upper Ollach** (NG518362) Braes
☎Sligachan225
Grey, stone crofting farm in 7 acres of hilly farmland with gardens and trees screening the house. Close to coastline 6½m SE of Portree on B883.
Mar–Oct 3rm (1fb) ⚓ TV 4P sea 7acres mixed
S% B&bfr£5.50 Bdi fr£8.75 D6pm

PORTSONACHAN Strathclyde Map39NN01 London470
Crianlarich27 Inverary13 Lochgilphead30
★★**Portsonachan** ☎Killchrenan224
20rm(3⇨1🛁) 🍴CTV ® 20P 3🏛 ⚓ ⚭ ⟲ ⚬
Last dinner9pm ✤ ⚷ 🅿

PORT WILLIAM 517 Dumfries & Galloway Map30NX34
EcThu London410 Newton Stewart17 Stranraer24
Whithorn9
★★★⚑**Corsemaizie House** ☎Mochrum254
Closed 15Jan–Feb; 15rm(13⇨🛁) 🍴CTV CTV in all
bedrooms ® ⚓ 35P ⚓ ⚭ ⟲ Scottish & French.
Last dinner9.15pm ✤ ⚷ Credit cards ① ③

★★**Monreith Arms** ☎232 13rm(1⇨) CTV 6P 3🏛
Last dinner8pm ✤ ⚷ S% sB&Bfr£9.25
sB&B⇨🛁fr£10.75 dB&Bfr£18.50 dB&B⇨🛁fr£20
Lunch fr£3 Tea fr£1 Dinner fr£5 Wine£3.95

POTARCH Grampian Map45NO69 Banchory6
Aberdeen24 Aboyne7 Alford19 London533
★**Potarch** ☎Kincardine O'Neil 339
Closed Jan; RS Nov & Dec; 6rm(2⇨) 🍴CTV ® 20P 2🏛 ⚓
⚭ Last dinner8.30pm ✤ ⚷ sB&B£9.50–£10.50
dB&B£17–£19 dB&B⇨🛁£19–£21
Bar lunch£2.30–£2.90 Dinner£5.80–£6.80&alc
Wine£3.95 🅿

POWFOOT 159 Dumfries & Galloway Map31NY16
Carlisle22 Dumfries15 Lockerbie16 London329
★★**Powfoot Golf** Links Av ☎Cummertrees254
A golfing hotel with views of the Solway.
20rm(7⇨) CTV ® 40P Last dinner8.15pm ✤ ⚷ S%
sB&B£9–£10 sB&B⇨🛁£12–£13 dB&B£17–£19
dB&B⇨🛁£22–£24 Lunch£3.50 alc Tea60p–£1.20
Dinner£6–£8 Wine£3.50 *xmas*

PRESTWICK 13,138 Strathclyde Map33NS32 EcWed Ayr3
Glasgow32 Irvine10 Kilmarnock11 London418
☆☆**Carlton Motor** (Osprey) ☎76811
37⇨ ♪ 🍴CTV CTV in all bedrooms ® 80P Live music &
dancing Fri & Sat ♀ Scottish & French. Last dinner9.30pm
✤ ⚷ S% sB&B⇨🛁£16.50 dB&B⇨🛁£27.50
Lunch£3.50&alc Tea£1 High Tea£2.50 Dinner£5&alc
Wine£3.50 🅿 *xmas* Credit cards ① ② ③ ④ ⑤

★★**Links** Links Rd ☎77792
Traditional seaside hotel overlooking Prestwick Championship Golf Course.
12rm(5⇨) 🍴CTV CTV in 5bedrooms 100P 2🏛 ⚓ ⚭
Last dinner8.30pm ✤ S%

★★**Parkstone** Esplanade ☎77286
Detached building situated on Esplanade looking out to Isle of Arran.
30rm(1⇨9🛁) 🍴CTV CTV in 10bedrooms ® ⚓ 60P
Last dinner8.30pm ✤ ⚷ S% sB&B£12.55–£14.25
sB&B⇨🛁£14.95–£16.95 dB&B£21.95–£24.85
dB&B⇨🛁£24.95–£27.95 Lunch£3.95–£4.45
Tea£1.40–£1.65 High Tea£2.85–£3.35
Dinner£6.15–£6.75 Wine£3.75 Credit card ②

★★**Queen's** Esplanade ☎70501
27rm(8⇨4🛁) ♪ 🍴CTV ⚓ 60P Disco Fri & Sun Live music &
dancing Thu ♀ French. Last dinner9.30pm ✤ ⚷ S%

*sB&B£11-£12 sB&B⇌ 🍴£12.50-£13.50
dB&B£22-£24 dB&B⇌ 🍴£25-£27 Bar lunch fr£1
Tea fr£1.50 High Tea fr£1.90 Dinner fr£5.50 ₧
Credit cards ① ② ③ ⑤ ⑥

★★**St Nicholas** 41 Ayr Rd ☎79568
13rm(4🍴) 🍴 CTV TV in 7 bedrooms ® ⇌ 50P
Last dinner 9pm ♥ S% *sB&B£9.32 sB&B🍴£10.32
dB&B£18 dB&B🍴£20 Lunch £2.50-£3
High Tea £2.20-£5.20 Dinner fr£4.25 &alc Wine £3.80

★**Auchencoyle** Links Rd ☎78316
6rm(3🍴) 🍴 CTV ® 20P ⇌ Last dinner 9pm ♥ S%
sB&B£7.25 dB&B£14.50 dB&B⇌£16.50
Bar lunch£1-£1.80 High Tea£1.80-£6
Dinner£5-£7 &alc Wine£2.95

★**Golden Eagle** 132 Main St ☎77546
6rm 🍴 CTV TV available in bedrooms 80P 4⚓ Live music &
dancing 5 nights wkly ♥ Mainly grills. Last dinner mdnt ♥
♫ S% sB&Bfr£8.25 dB&Bfr£14.50
Lunch£2.75-£3.75 Dinner£6.50-£17.25 &alc
Wine£4.50 Credit cards ① ② ③ ⑤ ⑥

★**North Beach** Links Rd ☎79069
Overlooks the golf links, near to the shore.
Closed New Years Day; 9rm 🍴 CTV ® 15P ⇌ Disco
3 nights wkly Cabaret wkly Last dinner 8pm ♥ ♫ S%
sB&B£9-£9.50 dB&B£17-£18 Bar lunch £1.50-£2
Tea 75p-£1.75 High Tea £2.50-£4.50 Dinner £4.50-£5
Wine £2.75

GH Kingcraig Private Hotel 39 Ayr Rd ☎79480 Lic 7hc
(1fb) 🍴 nc3 CTV 8P 🍴 S% B&b£6.25-£6.50
Bdi£10.25-£10.50 Wfr£65 £ D5.30pm

QUEENSFERRY (SOUTH) 5,372 Lothian Map35NT17
EcWed Dunfermline8 Edinburgh9 Linlithgow9 London428
☆☆☆**Forth Bridges Lodge** Forth Road Bridge (Grand Met)
☎031-331 1199
Situated close to southern approach to Forth Road Bridge,
affording splendid views over the Firth of Forth.
98⇌🍴 Lift ♪ 🍴 CTV CTV available in bedrooms P ♥
♫ S% *sB&B⇌🍴£20-£24
dB&B⇌🍴£28.50-£34.50 Wine£4.75 ₧ xmas
Credit cards ① ② ③ ④ ⑤ ⑥

RATHO Lothian Map35NT17 Edinburgh8 Linlithgow11
London426
✕**Bridge Inn** ☎031-333 1320
Closed Sun, Xmas Day & 1-2 Jan; 70 seats 50P
♥ English & French. Last dinner 10pm S%
*Lunch fr£2.05 &alc Dinner £6.50 &alc Wine £1.85
Credit cards ② ⑤

RENDALL Orkney Map48HY32 Kirkwall7 Stromness13
London708 (ferry Stromness-Scrabster)
FH Mrs H. R. Harcus **Lower Ellibister** (HY386213)
☎Evie224
Farmhouse set amid beautiful countryside with extensive
views across the bay to Kirkwall.

3rm (1fb) CTV 4P 344 acres mixed S% B&b fr£5
Bdi fr£8.50 Wfr£77 D6pm

RENFREW 19,075 Strathclyde Map48NS56 EcWed
Glasgow6 Greenock16 London412 Paisley3
For hotels and restaurants see Glasgow Airport.

RHU 1,540 Strathclyde Map33NS28 EcWed Dumbarton11
Glasgow25 London431 Tarbet17
★★★**Rosslea Hall** ☎820684
16rm(4🍴) 🍴 CTV in all bedrooms ® ⇌ 30P 1⚓ ⇌ ⚓ ⚓
Last dinner 9.30pm ♥ ♫ S% sB&B£12-£25
sB&B🍴£12-£25 dB&B£17-£36 dB&B🍴£17-£36
Lunch£1.75-£3.75 &alc Tea£1.50-£3
Dinner£6.50 &alc Wine£3.25 ₧ xmas
Credit cards ① ② ③ ⑤ ⑥

★**Ardencaple** (Ind Coope (Alloa)) ☎200
10rm(4⇌) CTV ® 40P Disco wkly ♥ European.
Last dinner 9pm ♥ ♫ *sB&B£11.50 sB&B⇌£15
dB&B£18.50 dB&B⇌£24 Lunch£7 alc Dinner£8.50 alc
Wine£3.40 ₧ Credit cards ① ② ③ ⑤

ROCKCLIFFE Dumfries & Galloway Map30NX85
Dalbeattie7 Dumfries20 London361
★★★⚓♿ **L Barons Craig** ☎225
Closed 11 Oct-Mar; 27rm(20⇌) CTV 50P 4⚓ ⇌ ⚓ ⚓
♥ International. Last dinner 9pm ♥ ♫ *sB&B£17-£19
sB&B⇌£24-£27 dB&B£32-£36 dB&B⇌£40-£48
Bar lunch£2 Tea£1.70 Dinner£8.90 Wine£4 ₧

ROGART Highland Map47NC70 Lairg11 Helmsdale25
Dornoch11 London621
FH Mrs C. F. Moodie **Rovie** (NC716023) ☎209
Farmhouse situated in the Strathfleet valley 4 miles from
sea. Rabbit shooting on farm and fishing locally in River
Fleet. S off A839.
Apr-Oct 7hc (1fb) CTV 6P 120 acres mixed S%
B&b£6-£6.50 Bdi£10-£10.50 W£70-£75 D6.30pm

ROSEBANK 101 Strathclyde Map34NS84 EcWed/all day
1st Wed of month Glasgow18 Hamilton8 Lanark7
London390
★★★**Popinjay** ☎Crossford441
Closed 1 & 2 Jan; 36rm(27⇌6🍴) 1⚑ ♪ 🍴 CTV in all
bedrooms ® 100P ⇌ ⚓ sauna bath ♫ Last dinner 9.30pm
♥ *sB&B£19 sB&B⇌🍴£21 dB&B⇌🍴£32
Lunch£4.50 &alc Dinner£6.50 &alc Wine£4 ₧
Credit cards ① ② ③ ⑤

ROSEHALL Highland Map46NC40 London623 Dingwall41
Lairg10 Lochinver37
★★**Achness** ☎239
Closed Oct-Feb; 5rm Annexe: 7⇌ CTV TV available in
bedrooms ® 22P ⇌ ♿ Last dinner 8pm ♥ ♫
sB&B£11.39 sB&B⇌£13.92 dB&B£22.78
dB&B⇌£26.56 Bar lunch£2.50 Tea 50p-80p

Rosslea Hall Hotel

Rhu Dunbartonshire
Telephone: 0436 820 684/5

Situated in attractive grounds, the Rosslea Hall has 17
comfortably furnished rooms with superb views of either the
loch or gardens. Each has its own private bathroom, with
telephone, radio, colour TV and tea and coffee making
facilities. A wide selection of excellent dishes and wines are
available for both lunch and dinner. Special weekend rates
available on request.
For further information phone 0436 820 684.

Rosehall contd – St Andrews

High Tea £3.50–£5 Dinner £6.50–£8 Wine £4.70

ROSEMARKIE Highland Map44NH75 EcThu Cromarty9 Fortrose1 Inverness29 (fy13) London594
★★**Marine** ☎Fortrose20253
Closed Oct–Mar; RS1–8Apr; 50rm(9⇨4🕮) CTV 50P 10🏛 ⇌ ⚓ & Last dinner 8.30pm ⚑ 🄼 sB&B£8–£10.50 sB&B⇨£9.50–£12 dB&B£16–£21 dB&B⇨🕮£19–£24 Lunch fr£4 Dinner fr£6 Wine £3 🄱

ROSLIN Lothian Map35NT26 Edinburgh8 Dalkeith6 Peebles17 London400
×**Ye Olde Original Rosslyne Inn** Main St ☎031-4402384 60seats 24P bedrooms available ♀Mainly grills. Last dinner 9pm

ROTHES 1,282 Grampian Map44NJ24 EcWed Elgin11 Inverness49 Keith12 London573
★★★🍴**L Rothes Glen** ☎254
Closed mid Nov–Feb; 19rm(8⇨) 1☐ CTV 40P ⇌ ⚓ ♀French. Last dinner 8.30pm ⚑ sB&B£21.60 sB&B⇨£23.25 dB&B£43.20 dB&B⇨£46.50 Lunch £5.50 Dinner £10 Wine £4
★**Station** 51 New St ☎240
10rm CTV 9P 2⇌ ⚓ Last dinner 9pm ⚑ S% sB&B£8 dB&B£16 Lunch £3.50–£3.75 High Tea £2.50–£7 Dinner £5–£5.50&alc Wine £3.90

ROTHESAY 6,286 Strathclyde Map33NS06 EcWed Colintraive (fy9) **Car-carrying services from Wemyss Bay**
★★★**Glenburn** Glenburn Rd ☎2500 Telex no778982 Imposing stone building with terraced lawns and fine view out across Rothesay Bay.
Closed Jan–mid Feb; 103rm(45⇨) Lift D ♫ CTV TV in 3bedrooms CTV in 4bedrooms ⇌ 60P ⚓ (hard) billiards Disco 3nights wkly Live music & dancing wkly Conference facilities available Last dinner 8.30pm ⚑ S% sB&B£15 sB&B⇨£16.50 dB&B£30 dB&B⇨£33 Lunch £3.50 Dinner £6.50 Wine £3.40 🄱 xmas Credit cards 1️⃣2️⃣3️⃣5️⃣
★★**Royal** Albert Pl (Osprey) ☎3044
20rm ♫ CTV ® 🅿 Disco wkly Live music nightly ♀Scottish & French. Last dinner 9.30pm ⚑ S% sB&B fr£11 dB&B fr£20 Lunch £3.50&alc Tea £1 High Tea £2.50 Dinner £5&alc Wine £3.50 🄱 xmas
Credit cards 1️⃣2️⃣3️⃣4️⃣5️⃣
★★**Victoria** Victoria St (Osprey) ☎3553
23rm(1⇨🕮) D CTV 🅿 Last dinner 9.30pm ⚑ 🄼 🄱
Credit cards 1️⃣2️⃣3️⃣5️⃣
★**Ardmory House** Ardmory Rd, Ardbeg ☎2346
10rm ♫ CTV TV in 6bedrooms ® 20P ⚓ ⇌ Last dinner 9.30pm ⚑ 🄼 🄱
GH Alva House Private Hotel 24 Mountstuart Rd ☎2328 May–Sep 6hc (1fb) ⇌ CTV sea S% B&b£7–£8 Bdi£8–£9 W£56–£63 D4pm
GH Morningside Mount Pleasant Rd ☎3526 Apr–mid Oct 6hc (A3hc) (2fb) CTV sea S% B&b£6.75 Bdi£9.25 W£54–£58 ₤ D6pm
GH St Fillans 36 Mountstuart Rd ☎2784 Apr–Sep 6hc (2fb) ⇌ CTV 6P ♫ sea S% B&b£6–£7 Bdi£7.50–£8.50
FH Birgidale Crieff (NS073591) ☎Kilchattan Bay236 Well cared for, attractively furnished farmhouse on south end of island. Well-maintained garden. 3m S off A845.
Apr–Oct 2rm nc4 TV 3P ♫ sea 300acres arable dairy

ROWARDENNAN Central Map39NS39 Dumbarton23 Glasgow27 London429 Stirling33
★★**Rowardennan** ☎Balmaha273
RS Nov–Feb; 9rm(1⇨🕮) ♫ CTV 50P ⇌ Last dinner 8.45pm ⚑ 🄼 🄱

ROY BRIDGE 202 Highland Map39NN28 Fort William12 London529 Newtonmore34 Spean Bridge3

★★**Glen Spean Lodge** ☎Spean Bridge224
15rm(1⇨🕮) ♫ TV 30P 3🏛 ⇌ Last dinner 8pm ⚑ 🄼

RUMBLING BRIDGE Tayside Map40NT09 EcWed Dollar5 Dunfermline11 Edinburgh28 London446
★★**Rumbling Bridge** ☎Fossoway325
A country hotel with a long established coaching inn history.
Closed Nov; 26rm CTV 100P ⚓ ⇌ ✱sB&B£9 dB&B£18 Last dinner 9.30pm
Lunch £3 Tea 25p–£1.20 High Tea £2.50–£4 Dinner £5.50–£6.25&alc Wine £3.80 🄱 xmas

RUSKIE Central Map40NN60 Callander7 Stirling13 London432
FH Mrs J. H. Bain **Lower Tarr** (NN624008) ☎Thornhill (Stirling)202
Large, well-maintained farm over 200 years old, with partly-modernised interior. Good views over rolling hill land.
Etr–Oct 2rm 1hc (1fb) ⇌ TV P 161acres mixed S% B&b£4.50–£5 Bdi£7.50 D4pm

RUTHERGLEN 23,956 Strathclyde Map37NS66 EcTue East Kilbride5 Glasgow3 Hamilton9 London399
★★**Burnside** East Kilbride Rd, Burnside, Cambuslang (Reo Stakis) ☎041-6341276 Telex no778704
16rm(13⇨) D ♫ CTV in 16bedrooms ® 100P ♀Scottish & French. Last dinner 9pm ⚑ 🄼 ✱sB&B fr£18.50 sB&B⇨fr£23 dB&B⇨fr£32 Lunch £5.50alc Tea fr70p Dinner £5.50alc Wine £4.20 🄱 Credit cards 1️⃣2️⃣3️⃣5️⃣
★★**Mill** Mill St (Scottish & Newcastle) ☎041-6475491
30rm(8⇨🕮) D ♫ CTV ® 300P ♀Scottish & French. Last dinner 9pm ⚑ 🄱 Credit cards 1️⃣2️⃣3️⃣4️⃣5️⃣

ST ANDREWS 13,137 Fife Map41NO51 EcThu Dundee13 Edinburgh56 Kirkcaldy27 London474 Perth32
★★★★**B Old Course** (British Transport) ☎74371 Telex no76280
Interesting modern building alongside 17th hole of Old Course. Fine views over golf course to St Andrews Bay.
72⇨ Lift D ♫ CTV CTV in all bedrooms 100P ⚓ Conference facilities available ⚑ 🄼 S% ✱sB&B⇨£29.75–£32.50 dB&B⇨£41–£55.75 Bar lunch fr75p alc Dinner £7.25&alc Wine £5.10 🄱
Credit cards 1️⃣2️⃣3️⃣4️⃣5️⃣
★★★★**Rusacks Marine** ☎74321
RS Jan–Mar; 50rm(49⇨1🕮) Lift D ♫ CTV in all bedrooms 25P ⇌ Live music & dancing Sat ⚓ ♀English & French. Last dinner 9.30pm ⚑ 🄼 S% ✱sB&B⇨🕮£19–£27 dB&B⇨🕮£38–£54 Lunch £3–£5&alc Tea £1.75 High Tea £3–£5&alc Dinner £7.95&alc Wine £4.95 🄱 xmas Credit cards 2️⃣3️⃣4️⃣5️⃣
★★★**HL Rufflets** ☎72594 Telex no76687
Charming country house dating from 1924 with modern extension standing in 10 acres with well maintained formal gardens to rear.
Closed mid Jan–mid Feb; 19rm(15⇨) Annexe: 3⇨ ♫ CTV ⇌ 100P 6🏛 ⚓ ♀Scottish & French. Last dinner 9pm ⚑ 🄼 sB&B⇨£18 sB&B⇨£21 dB&B£36 dB&B⇨£39 Lunch £3.75–£4&alc Tea £1.50 Dinner £7.25–£7.50&alc Wine £4.50 🄱 xmas Credit cards 2️⃣3️⃣5️⃣6️⃣
★★★**L St Andrews** 40 The Scores (Inter-Hotels) ☎72611 Telex no777205
Situated on the sea front with views over sandy beaches and rock pools.
RS Nov–Mar; 22rm(20⇨2🕮) Lift D ♫ CTV in all bedrooms ® 🅿 sauna bath Live music & dancing Sat Last dinner 9.30pm ⚑ 🄼 S% sB&B⇨🕮£12–£22.50 dB&B⇨🕮£24–£38 Lunch fr£4.50 Tea fr£1.75 High Tea fr£3.75 Dinner £8–£9 Wine £4.75 🄱
Credit cards 1️⃣2️⃣3️⃣5️⃣6️⃣
★★★**Scores** (Best Western) ☎72451
30⇨ Lift D ♫ ⚓ Last dinner 9pm ⚑ 🄼 sB&B⇨£17 dB&B⇨£34 Lunch £4.50 Dinner £8&alc Wine £4 🄱 Credit cards 1️⃣2️⃣3️⃣5️⃣6️⃣

★★**Star** ☎75701
Modernised coaching inn dating from early 1800s.
25rm(21⇨🛁) ♪ 🍴 CTV in all bedrooms ® 🐕
Last dinner9pm ✿ 🍺 Credit cards 1 2 5
★**Cross Keys** 85 Market St ☎72185
16rm(3⇨) 🍴 CTV 6P 1🛏 Last dinner8pm ✿ 🍺
sB&B£12 sB&B⇨£14 dB&B£20 dB&B⇨£22
Lunch£2.50 Tea50p HighTea£2.50 Dinner£6.50
Wine£2.30 Credit cards 2 3
★**Russell** 26 The Scores ☎73447
RS Nov-Mar (no accommodation 15Dec-15Jan); 8rm TV
TV in all bedrooms ® 🐕 🚸 Children under 3yrs not
accommodated Last dinner7pm ✿
sB&B£10.50-£11.50 dB&B£21-£23
Barlunch£2-£2.50 Dinner£5 Wine£3.75
GH Argyle Hotel 127 North St ☎733871 Apr-Oct Lic
18hc (4fb) nc2 CTV 🍴 S% B&b£6.50-£9.50
Bdi£11-£14 W£60-£90 ⚓ D4pm
GH Beachway House 4-6 Murray Pk ☎73319 Mar-Oct
rs Nov-Feb 11hc (4fb) CTV 🍴 *B&b£5.50-£7.95
Bdi£9.75-£12.20 W£65-£80 D2pm (W only Jul-early
Aug)
GH Cleveden House 3 Murray Pl ☎74212 6hc (1fb)
CTV 20P S% B&b£7-£7.50
GH Craigmore 3-5 Murray Pk ☎72142 Apr & Jun-Oct
rs Jan-Mar & May 12hc (5fb) CTV 🍴 B&b£6.95
Bdi£11.25 Wfr£75 ⚓ D6pm
GH Hazelbank Private Hotel The Scores ☎72466
Mar-Nov 10hc ✿ CTV 🍴 sea
GH Lorimer House 19 Murray Pk ☎76599 Apr-Oct
4hc (3fb) ✿ nc3 CTV 🍴 B&b£7-£8
GH Nithsdale Hotel The Scores ☎75977 Mar-Nov Lic
9hc CTV 🍴 sea
GH Number Ten 10 Hope St ☎74601 10hc (4fb) CTV
🍴 S% B&b£6-£7.50 Bdi£9.95-£11.45
W£65-£73.25 ⚓ D4.30pm
GH Yorkston Hotel 60-70 Argyle St ☎72019 Lic 12hc
(2fb) ✿ CTV 🍴 B&b£7.50-£9 Bdi£12.30-£13.40
W£86-£93 ⚓ D6.30pm
××**Grange Inn** Grange ☎72670
64seats 60P ♀Scottish & French. Lastdinner9.45pm
Credit cards 1 2 3 5 6
×**Pepita's** 11 Crails Ln ☎74084
Closed Sun & 24Dec-8Jan; Dinner not served Mon;
60seats 🐕 ♀French & Italian. Lastdinner9.30pm
Credit cards 1 2 3

ST CATHERINE'S Strathclyde Map39NN00 Strachur5
Inveraray16 Tarbet18 London452
GH Thistle House ☎209 6hc (1fb) 6P 🍴 sea
*B&bfr£8 Bdifr£13.90 Wfr£93.80 ⚓ D7pm

ST COMBS 738 Grampian Map45NK06 EcWed
Aberdeen44 Fraserburgh6 London579 Peterhead15
★★**Tufted Duck** ☎Inverallochy2481
18rm(11⇨7🛁) 🍴 CTV in all bedrooms ® 50P ✿ 🍺
♀French. Lastdinner9.30pm ✿ 🍺
sB&B⇨🛁£11-£16 dB&B⇨🛁£20-£32
Lunch£4.25&alc Tea£1 Dinner£5.95&alc Wine£4.50
🍺 Credit cards 2 3 5

ST FILLANS 160 Tayside Map40NN62 EcWed
Callander21 Crieff12 Glasgow58 London452
★★★**Four Seasons** ☎333
Closed Nov-Mar; 12rm(11⇨1🛁) Annexe: 6rm 🍴 TV in all
bedrooms ® 50P 🛏 🚸 ♀International.
Lastdinner9.45pm ✿ 🍺 S%
sB&B⇨🛁£20.50-£25.50 dB&B⇨🛁£41-£51
Lunch£6.30-£7&alc Dinner£8.90&alc Wine£4.80
🍺 Credit cards 1 2 3
★★**Drummond Arms** (Inter-Hotels) ☎212
Four storey turreted grey stone roadside hotel in attractive
position overlooking wooded shore of Loch Earn, with
steeply rising hills to rear.

Closed 17Oct-10May; 36rm(14⇨) CTV ✿ 50P ⚓ 🐕
♀English & French. Lastdinner8.15pm ✿ 🍺 S%
sB&B£10.95-£12.95 sB&B⇨£12.95-£14.95
dB&B£21.90-£25.90 dB&B⇨£25.90-£29.90
Lunch£3.50-£5.50 Tea75p-£1.75
HighTea£2.95-£4.50 Dinner£7-£9 Wine£3.75 🍺
Credit cards 1 2 3 4 5 6

ST MARGARET'S HOPE 210 South Ronaldsay, Orkney
Map48ND49 Kirkwall15
×**Creel** Front St ☎311
Closed Mon & Tue; Lunch not served; 45seats 🐕
♀British & French. Lastdinner10.30pm *Dinner£8alc
Wine£3.70

ST MARY'S LOCH Borders Map35NT22 Edinburgh45
London364 Moffat15 Selkirk19
★★**Rodono** ☎Cappercleuch232
Shooting lodge dating from 1866, standing on hillside
overlooking St Mary's Loch and Border hills.
Closed Nov-Feb; 11rm 🍴 CTV 30P 2🛏 ⚓ 🐕
♀International. Lastdinner9.30pm ✿ 🍺
*sB&B£9.20-£10 dB&B£18-£20 Lunch£3.20&alc
Dinner£6.15-£8.45&alc Wine£3.45 🍺

SALEN 181 Isle of Mull, Strathclyde Map38NM54 EcWed
Craignure11 **(car ferry to Oban)** Fishnish Pier8 **(car ferry to
Lochaline)** Tobermory10
GH Craig Hotel ☎Aros347 Closed Xmas & New Year
Lic 7hc ✿ 8P sea S% B&b£8.50-£11.50
Bdi£13-£14.50 W£90-£100 ⚓ D8pm
×**Puffer Aground** Main Rd ☎Aros389
Closed Sun, Mon (Apr-mid May) & Jan-Mar; RS Nov-Dec
(reservations only); 45seats 12P Lastdinner8pm
Lunch£4.20alc Teafr60p Dinnerfr£4.50&alc Wine£3.50

SANDYHILLS Dumfries & Galloway Map30NX85
Dumfries19 Dalbeattie7 London356
×**Granary** Barend (B794) ☎Southwick663
Closed Nov-1wk before Etr (ex Sat to Xmas & daily Xmas to
1Jan); 40seats bedrooms available ♀International.
Lastdinner9pm *Dinnerfr£7 Wine£3.90

SANNOX Isle of Arran, Strathclyde Map33NS04 Brodick8
Lochranza7 London432 (ferry)
GH Cliffdene ☎Corrie224 Dec-Sep 5hc (3fb) ✿
TV 6P river S% B&b£4.90 Bdi£7.20 W£50.40 ⚓
D4.30pm

SANQUHAR 2,073 Dumfries & Galloway Map34NS70
EcThu Cumnock17 Dumfries27 Glasgow54 London368
★**Nithsdale** High St ☎506
6rm 🍴 CTV 🐕 Live music & dancing wkly
Lastdinner8.30pm ✿ S% sB&B£8.75-£9.50
dB&B£17.50-£19 Lunchfr£3 Dinnerfr£5 Wine£3 🍺
Credit cards 1 2 3 6
GH Blackaddie House Hotel Blackaddie Rd ☎270 Lic
6rm 4hc 1⇨ (2fb) CTV 15P 🍴 river B&b£8
Bdi£12.50 W£48 🎵 D8.30pm

SCALASAIG Isle of Colonsay, Strathclyde Map38NR39
EcWed **Car-carrying service from Oban**
★**Colonsay** ☎316
10rm(1⇨) ⚓ 31P ✿ 🛏 🚸 ✿ ♀French. Lastdinner8pm
✿ 🍺 S% sB&B£13.50-£17 dB&B£13.50-£17
dB&B⇨£25-£27 Barlunch80p-£2 Tea80p-85p
HighTea£4.50-£4.90 Dinner£6.75-£7.95 Wine£3.10
🍺 xmas Credit cards 1 2 3 5 6

SCANIPORT Highland Map43NH63 Inverness4 Fort
Augustus30 London565
FH Mr D. A. Mackintosh **Antfield** (NH616371) ☎219
Large, two-storey building, ¼ mile off B852.

Scaniport contd – Spey Bay

May–Sep 2rm (2fb) ⊘ nc4 CTV 10P 354acres mixed

SCARISTA Isle of Harris, Western Isles Map48NG09 Tarbert14 Stornoway51 London652
FH Mrs M. Macdonald **Croft** (NG002926) 1 Scarista Vore ☎201
Small, well-maintained croft which doubles as local Post Office. Good position facing west overlooking golden sands and ocean.
Apr–Oct 2rm nc10 2P sea 19acres mixed S% B&b£6–£7 Bdi£10.50–£12

SCONE, NEW 3,830 Tayside Map40NO12 EcWed Edinburgh46 Forfar28 London454 Perth2
★★★⚐ **Murrayshall House** Montague ☎51171
7⇌🛏 🎗 CTV in bedrooms ⊘ 50P ⇌ ⚒
Last dinner10.30pm ♦ Credit cards ①③⑤

SCOURIE Highland Map46NC14 Durness26 Inverness104 Lochinver(fy)30 London669
★★**Eddrachilles** Badcall Bay ☎2080
14rm(4⇌10🛏) 🎗 TV in 8bedrooms CTV in 2bedrooms ®
35P ⇌ ⚒ ⇋ Last dinner8.30pm ♦ S%
sB&B⇌🛏£15.75–£17.80 dB&B⇌🛏£25.50–£28.80 Bar lunch£2–£3 Dinner£4.20–£4.75alc Wine£3.10 ₧
★★**Scourie** ☎2396
A shingle-clad building occupying the site and part of 17th-C Tower House, standing on rugged coast line overlooking Scourie Bay.
Closed 26Oct–14Mar; 22rm(10⇌3🛏) 30P ⇌ ⚒
Last dinner8.30pm ♦ ⇋ Credit card ③

SCRABSTER 273 Highland Map47ND06 EcThu Inverness133 London698 Thurso2 Tongue44
Car-carrying service to Stromness (Orkney)

SEAMILL Strathclyde Map33NS24 EcWed Ardrossan4 Glasgow33 Largs8 London428
★★**Inverclyde** 31 Ardrossan Rd ☎West Kilbride823124
Small detached building set close to roadside in Clyde coast village.
10rm 🎗 CTV CTV in 1bedroom TV in 1bedroom ® 25P ⚐ International. Last dinner9.15pm ♦ S%
✻sB&B£11 dB&B£22 Lunch£3.25alc Dinner£7.50alc Wine£3.70

SELKIRK 5,628 Borders Map35NT42 EcThu Edinburgh40 Galashiels6 Hawick12 London364 Peebles21
★**B Heatherlie Hill** Heatherlie Park ☎21200
Closed mid Oct – mid Nov; 6rm CTV TV in 1bedroom ⊘ 15P ⇌ ⚒ ⇋ Last dinner8pm ♦ ⇋ S% sB&B£10.50–£11 dB&B£21–£22 Bar lunch£1.50–£3 Tea£1.20 Dinner£7.50–£8 Wine£4.50 ₧

SHAWHEAD Dumfries & Galloway Map30NX87 Dumfries8 Castle Douglas12 New Galloway20 London345
FH Mrs M. D. Riddet **Henderland** (NX872746) ☎Lochfoot270
Small farmhouse about 5 miles from Dumfries. Golf, fishing and tennis are available.
May–Oct 3rm (2fb) CTV 3P 207acres dairy S% B&b£5–£6 W£35–£40 Ⓜ

SHAWLANDS Strathclyde Map37NS56 **See Glasgow**

SHETLAND Map48 **See Brae, Lerwick and Virkie. Car-carrying service operates between Aberdeen and Lerwick**

SHIELDAIG Highland Map42NG85 Lochcarron15 Achnasheen28 Gairloch37 Inverness72 London633
★**B Tigh an Eilean** ☎251
Closed Nov–Apr 14rm ⊘ 10P ⇌ ⚒ Children under 5yrs not accommodated Last dinner7.30pm ♦

SHIELDINISH Isle of Lewis, Western Isles Map48NB21 Stornoway18 Tarbert23

SKEABOST BRIDGE Isle of Skye, Highland Map42NG44 EcWed Kyle of Lochalsh(fy)40 Portree6 Uig12
★★★⚐L **Skeabost House** ☎202
Closed mid Oct–May; 21rm(10⇌) ♪ CTV ® 40P ⇌ ⇋ billiards Last dinner8pm ♦ ⚒ S% sB&B£13.20 sB&B⇌🛏£17.40 dB&B£26.40 dB&B⇌🛏£34.80 Buffet lunch£2.30 Tea£1.50 Dinner£7.50 Wine£3

SKELMORLIE 1,535 Strathclyde Map33NS16 EcWed Glasgow32 Greenock9 Largs6 London442
★★★⚐B **Manor Park** ☎Wemyss Bay520832
Imposing mansion set in its own grounds and formal gardens two miles south of Skelmorlie. The well and cupola above reception hall is a feature.
Closed 3Jan–mid Feb; 7rm(5⇌1🛏) 🎗 CTV available in bedrooms ® ⊘ 150P ⇌ ⚒ ⚐ Scottish & French.
Last dinner9.30pm ♦ ⚒ S%
dB&B⇌🛏£44–£60 Lunch£5.75 (Sunday only) &alc Tea£1.85 Dinner£8.50&alc ₧

SKINFLATS Central Map34NS98 Edinburgh25 Stirling12 Grangemouth3 London420
✕**Dutch Inn** Main Rd ☎Grangemouth3015
Closed Sun; 80seats 150P ⚐ Mainly grills.
Last dinner8pm

SKYE, ISLE OF Highland Map42
See Broadford, Carbost, Clachan, Duntulm, Dunvegan, Isle Ornsay, Knock, Kyleakin, Portree, Skeabost Bridge, Sligachan, Uig and Waterloo. From the mainland ferry services operate from Kyle of Lochalsh. Also from Mallaig and Glenelg; summer only, not Sun

SLIGACHAN Isle of Skye, Highland Map42NG42 Kyle of Lochalsh(fy)25 Portree10
★★★**Sligachan** ☎204
Two-storey stone building replacing original 18th-century coaching inn which stood nearby. Situated at head of Loch Sligachan.
Closed Oct–9May; 23rm(9⇌) 🎗 24P 6⇌ ⇌ ⇋ Children under 8yrs not accommodated Last dinner8.15pm ♦ ⚒ S% sB&B£18 sB&B⇌£19.50 dB&B£35 dB&B⇌£39.60 Lunch£4.50alc Tea£2 Dinner£8.50 Wine£3.50

SOUTH LAGGAN Highland Map43NN29 Fort William21 Fort Augustus11 London534
GH Forest Lodge ☎Invergarry219 Apr–Oct 6hc ⊘ nc3 CTV 8P 🎗 lake

SOUTH UIST, ISLE OF Western Isles Map48 **See Lochboisdale**

SPEAN BRIDGE Highland Map39NN28 EcThu **See also Letterfinlay and Roy Bridge** Fort Augustus23 Fort William10 London526 Newtonmore37
★★**Spean Bridge** ☎250
9rm(2⇌) Annexe: 16rm(14⇌) 🎗 CTV ® 50P 1⇌ ⇋ Live music & dancing monthly ♪ Last dinner10pm ♦ ⚒ ✻sB&B£9–£11 sB&B⇌£10–£12 dB&B£18–£22 dB&B⇌£20–£25 Bar lunch£2.15–£3 Tea35p–75p High Tea£2.50–£3.50 Dinner£6.50&alc Wine£4.50 ₧ Credit cards ①③⑤⑥
GH Coire Glas ☎272 Feb–Nov Lic 15hc 3🛏 (2fb) TV 15P 🎗 S% B&bfr£5.25 Bdifr£9.50 D7.30pm
GH Druimandarroch ☎335 Mar–Dec Lic 8hc (3fb) TV 9P 3⇌ river ✻B&b£6.50 Bdi£11.10 W£97.75 D7pm
GH Lesanne ☎231 5hc (1fb) ⊘ CTV 6P S% B&bfr£5.50 Bdifr£9.50 Wfr£65 Ŀ

SPEY BAY Grampian Map44NJ36 Aberdeen64 Huntly24

Elgin12 London598
★★**Spey Bay** ☎Fochabers820424
Closed New Years Day; 9rm(5⇨4🛏) 🍴CTV® 50P ⚲18
♨(hard) Live music & dancing Fri (in summer) Sat (in winter)
Last dinner7.30pm ♡ ⚥ *sB&B⇨🛏£12.58
dB&B⇨🛏£21.20 Lunch£2.60&alc Tea£1.15&alc
High Tea£1.50–£4&alc Dinner£5.28&alc Wine£2.84
🍴 Credit cards 5 6

STEPPS 2,916 Strathclyde Map37NS66 EcWed
Cumbernauld8 Falkirk19 Glasgow6 London402
☆☆**Garfield** Cumbernauld Rd (Scottish & Newcastle)
☎041-7792111
21⇨🛏 🍴 CTV in bedrooms 120P ⇔ Live music &
dancing Sat ♀French. Last dinner9pm ♡ ⚥ 🍴
Credit cards 1 2 3 4 5 6

STEWARTON 5,264 Strathclyde Map37NS44 EcWed/Sat
London417 Glasgow18 Kilmarnock7
❀★★(red)♨**Chapeltoun House** ☎82696
*Comfort is the keynote of this Red Star hotel. The rather
grand baronial-style house is set in 20 acres of informal
grounds, and both food and service are of a high standard.*
Closed Xmas, 1–7 Jan & 3wks Jul; 6rm(4⇨2🛏) 🍴CTV in all
bedrooms® ⇔ 50P ⇔ ⚲ Children under 12yrs not
accommodated ♀International. Last dinner9.30pm ♡
sB&B⇨🛏fr£25 dB&B⇨🛏fr£48 Lunchfr£6.50&alc
Dinner£12 Wine£4.70

STIRLING 29,818 Central Map40NS79 EcWed MdThu
Callander16 Dunfermline22 Edinburgh37 Glasgow26
London418 Perth33
★★★**Golden Lion** King St ☎5351 Telexno777546
75rm(30⇨7🛏) Lift ♪ 🍴CTV in all bedrooms ® 40P
Conference facilities available ♀English & French.
Last dinner9pm ♡ ⚥ S% sB&B£12.50–£15
sB&B⇨🛏£16.50–£21.50 dB&B£16.75–£26.50
dB&B⇨🛏£23.50–£35 Lunch£3–£3.50&alc
Tea90p–£1.15 High Tea£2.70–£3 Dinner£5–£6&alc
Wine£3 🍴 xmas Credit cards 1 2 3 5 6
☆☆**King Robert** Glasgow Rd (Scottish & Newcastle)
☎811666
*Modern low-rise building, lying on outskirts of town,
adjacent to Bannockburn Monument and battlefield.*
20⇨🛏 🍴CTV in all bedrooms 120P ⇔ Disco wkly
Last dinner9.15pm ♡ 🍴 Credit cards 1 2 3 4 5 6
★★**Station** 56 Murray Pl (Reo Stakis) ☎2017
Telexno778704
*Conversion of adjoining buildings, the earliest being a
former coaching inn. Standing on corner site in town centre
adjacent to railway station.*
25rm(10⇨15🛏) ♪ 🍴CTV in all bedrooms® ♀English &
French. Last dinner10.30pm ♡ ⚥
*sB&B⇨🛏fr£19.50 dB&B⇨🛏fr£30 Lunch£3&alc
Tea45p Dinner£5&alc Wine£4.05 🍴
Credit cards 1 2 3 5 6

★★**Terraces** 4 Melville Ter ☎2268
14rm(7⇨3🛏) ♪ 🍴CTV in all bedrooms ® 30P
♀International. Last dinner9pm ♡ ⚥ S%
*sB&Bfr£13 sB&B⇨🛏£15.50–£17.50 dB&Bfr£23
dB&B⇨🛏fr£27.50 Lunch£2.95–£5 Teafr£2.75
High Teafr£2.75 Dinnerfr£5.25&alc Wine£3.55 🍴
Credit cards 1 3 6
★**Kings Gate** 5 King St ☎3944
19th-C hotel standing in shopping area.
15rm(5⇨) 🍴CTV® 5P Last dinner8.30pm ♡ ⚥
*sB&B£10.35 sB&B⇨🛏£12.65 dB&B£16.10
dB&B⇨🛏£18.40 Lunch£3.20–£5&alc Teafr£1.20
High Tea£2.50–£4 Dinner£5.50–£6.50&alc Wine£4.80
★ **Royal** Queen St ☎5137
*Stone inn (listed building dating from 1780) standing on
corner site just outside main shopping centre.*
12rm(4⇨) 🍴CTV 🏫 ⇔ Mainly grills. Last dinner8.30pm
♡ ⚥ S% sB&B£10.50 sB&B⇨🛏£11.50 dB&B£17.50
dB&B⇨🛏£18.50 Barlunch£1.25alc Tea75palc
High Tea£1.90alc Dinner£6.50alc Wine£3.75
Credit cards 1 2 3
FH Mrs R. Johnston **Kings Park** (NS787936) ☎4142
*Large, modernised farmhouse situated on the outskirts of
the town and offering splendid views of Stirling Castle.*
Etr–Sep 3rm (2fb) ⇔ CTV 4P 🍴 230acres mixed
S% B&B£6
FH *Powis Mains* (NS819959) Causewayhead ☎3820
*Well-sited, stone farmhouse dating from 1840. Stands in
Forth Valley overlooked by Wallace Monument and Ochill
Hills. 3m NE A91.*
Jun–Sep 2rm ⇔ CTV 6P 250acres mixed
✕✕**Heritage** 16 Allan Park ☎3660
*An 18th-C painted stone building of architectural interest
situated in town at the foot of Castle Rock.*
Closed Xmas & 1 Jan; 75seats 15P bedrooms available
⚥ ♀French. Last dinner10pm Lunch£4–£7&alc
Dinner£4–£7&alc Credit card 2
✕✕**Hollybank** Glasgow Rd ☎812311
40seats 40P bedrooms available ♀International.
Last dinner10pm S% Lunch£5&alc
High Tea£3.50–£5.50 Dinner£10&alc Wine£3
Credit cards 1 2 3 5 6
✕**Riverway** Kildean Mkt ☎5734
400seats P ⚥ Live music & dancing Sat
Last dinner6.30pm Lunch£2.85–£4.50&alc Teafr£1.50
High Teafr£2.85 Dinnerfr£6.50 Wine£3.25 Credit card 5
✕**Trattoria La Romantica** 4 Viewfield Pl ☎64521
Closed Sun; 40seats 🏫 ♀European.
Last dinner10.45pm *Barlunch£1.50–£2.20&alc
Dinner£5&alc Wine£3.95 Credit cards 1 2 5

STONEHAVEN 4,866 Grampian Map41NO88 EcWed
Aberdeen15 Banchory16 Brechin25 London524
Montrose23
☆☆☆**Commodore** Cowie Park ☎62936 Telexno739111
40⇨🛏 ♪ 🍴CTV in all bedrooms® P ♀International.

HERITAGE HOTEL & RESTAURANT

16 Allan Park, Stirling
Tel: 3660

This elegant Georgian Town House (c 1820) combines good taste with good food. Leading guides recommend Georges Marquetty's fine French menu and wine cellar, complemented by the "gracious living" atmosphere of antiques and original paintings.

Chef/owner: Mr G Marquetty
Chevalier des Tastevin

Stonehaven contd–Strathmiglo

Last dinner 10pm ✦ ⌂ sB&B⇨ ㎜£22 dB&B⇨ ㎜£32
Lunch£2.95 Tea£1–£1.50 Dinner£5.95&alc
Wine£2.70 ₧ Credit cards ① ② ③ ⑤ ⑥
★★**County** Arduthie Rd ☏64386
14rm(8⇨) ⚐ CTV CTV in all bedrooms ® 80P ゚ squash sauna bath ♥ International. Last dinner 9.30pm ✦ ⌂
S% *sB&Bfr£10.50 sB&B⇨fr£12.50 dB&Bfr£19
dB&B⇨fr£20 Lunchfr£2.60 Teafr£1 Dinnerfr£6&alc
Wine£3.75
★★**St Leonard's** Bath St ☏62044
Closed 1 & 2 Jan; 14rm(3⇨㎜) ♪ ⚐ CTV TV in all bedrooms ® ゑ 40P ≋ ゚ ♀French. Last dinner 9pm ✦
Credit card ③
★**Crown** 26–30 Allardice St ☏62296
18rm ⚐ CTV CTV in all bedrooms ® 6P Last dinner 8.30pm ✦ S% sB&Bfr£14.95 dB&Bfr£20.70 Lunchfr£2
Teafr50p High Teafr£2.45 Dinner£5 Wine£4.65

STORNOWAY 5,418 Isle of Lewis, Western Isles
Map48 NB43 EcWed **Car carrying service to Ullapool**
Tarbert37
★★★**Caberfeidh** ☏2604
36⇨ Lift ⚐ CTV 100P ♨ ゚ ♀European.
Last dinner 9.30pm ✦ ⌂ S% sB&B⇨£14.75–£20.90
dB&B⇨£19.75–£29.90 Lunch£4&alc Dinner£8.75&alc
Wine£3.65 xmas Credit cards ① ② ③ ④ ⑤ ⑥
★★★**Seaforth** James St ☏2740
54rm(50⇨) Lift ♪ ⚐ CTV 25P Last dinner 9.45pm ✦ ⌂
*sB&B£15.50–£20.90 dB&B£19.75–£29.90
Lunch£2.25–£3.75 Tea50–60p
Dinner£6.50–£8.50&alc Wine£4.10 Credit cards ① ③
★★**Royal** Cromwell St (Scottish & Newcastle) ☏2109
A pleasant two-storey painted stone building overlooking inner harbour and Lewis Castle.
20rm ⚐ CTV ® ♟ Last dinner 9pm ✦ ⌂ S%
sB&B£12.75 dB&B£25.50 Lunch£3alc Tea£1alc
Dinner£5alc Wine£2.50 Credit cards ① ③
GH Ardlonan 29 Francis St ☏3482 Closed Xmas & New Year 5rm 3hc (1fb) ゑ CTV ⚐ S% *B&b£6
GH Park 30 James St ☏2485 7rm 6hc ⚐ CTV ⚐ S%
*B&b£7

STRACHUR Strathclyde Map39 NN00 EcWed Glasgow57 Inveraray21 London460 Tarbet22
★★★**Creggans Inn** ☏279 Telexno727396
A 15th-C inn offering views over Loch Fyne.
22rm(2㎜) ⚐ CTV TV in 20 bedrooms 70P ♨ ゑ ♀Scottish & French. Last dinner 8.45pm ✦ ⌂ *sB&B£19.80
sB&B㎜£22 dB&B£32.45 dB&B㎜£39.60 Lunchfr£5
Teafr£1.30 High Teafr£3.50 Dinner£8.50alc
Wine£4.90 ₧ xmas Credit cards ① ② ③
×× **Inver Cottage** Strathlachlan ☏396
A roadside cottage situated on Loch Fyne six miles SW of Strachur.
Closed Oct–Mar; 60seats ♀Scottish & French.
Last dinner 9.30pm

STRAITON Lothian Map35 NT26 Edinburgh5 Dalkeith4 Peebles18 London403
FH Mrs A. M. Milne **Straiton** (NJ273667) Straiton Rd
☏031-440 0298
Georgian farmhouse with garden, situated on southern outskirts of Edinburgh. Swing, climbing frame and lots of pets for the children.
Apr–Oct 4hc (3fb) ゑ CTV 10P 200acres mixed
S% B&b£6.50

STRANRAER 10,170 Dumfries & Galloway Map30 NX06
EcWed MdFri Ayr53 Carlisle111 Girvan30 Glasgow87
London418 Newton Stewart25
★★★**George** George St ☏2487
Former coaching inn showing fine examples of Victorian/Edwardian architecture.
28rm(12⇨) Lift ♪ ⚐ CTV 20P ♨ Last dinner 9pm ✦ ⌂
₧ Credit cards ① ② ③ ④ ⑤

★★★**North West Castle** ☏4413 Telexno777088
79⇨ Annexe: 4⇨ Lift ♪ ⚐ CTV in all bedrooms ® ゑ 100P
≋ ⚑(heated) billiards sauna bath Live music & dancing Sat ♨ Conference facilities available ♀International.
Last dinner 9.30pm ✦ ⌂ sB&B⇨£16
dB&B⇨£24–£30 (Continental breakfast) Lunchfr£5
Teafr£1.50 Dinnerfr£7.50 Wine£4.50 ₧ xmas
★**Bucks Head** 44 Hanover St ☏2064
13rm ⚐ CTV 16P 4♨ Disco wkly Live music & dancing wkly
Last High Tea7.30pm ✦ ⌂ sB&B£10 dB&B£19
Lunch£3.25–£5 Tea75p–£1 High Tea£2–£5 ₧
★**Enyhallow** Castle Kennedy (3½m E A75) ☏Dunragit256
7rm(5㎜) ⚐ CTV ® 30P ♨ Last dinner 9.30pm
*sB&B㎜£10.35 dB&B㎜£19.55 Bar lunch£1.80–£3
Dinner£5alc Wine£3
GH Lochview 52 Agnew Cres ☏3837 6hc (2fb) CTV
6P sea S% B&b£6 Bdi£9 W£60 ł Dnoon
×× **L'Aperitif** London Rd ☏2991
Closed Sun & 5wks Sep–Oct; 50seats 40P
♀International. Last dinner 9pm *Lunchfr£4
High Teafr£3.75 Dinnerfr£6.50
×× **Bay House** Cairnryan Rd ☏3786
55seats 24P Last dinner 9.30pm S% Lunch£2.10&alc
High Tea£3.50alc Dinner£6.50alc Wine£3.50
Credit cards ① ② ③

STRATHBLANE 755 Central Map37 NS57 EcWed
Glasgow12 Kilsyth11 London414 Stirling27
★★★**B Country Club** Milngavie Rd ☏Blanefield70491
Closed 1 Jan; 10rm(7⇨3㎜) ⚐ CTV in all bedrooms 120P
1♨ ≋ Live music & dancing Sun ♀Scottish, French & Italian. Last dinner 9.30pm ✦ ⌂ sB&B⇨㎜£23
dB&B⇨㎜£35 Lunch£6&alc Tea£1.25 Dinner£8&alc
Wine£4 ₧ Credit cards ① ② ③ ⑤ ⑥
★★**Kirkhouse Inn** ☏Blanefield70621
19rm(10⇨) ♪ ⚐ CTV CTV in all bedrooms 100P ♨
♀English & French. Last dinner 9.30pm ✦ ⌂ S%
*sB&B£17.50 sB&B⇨£20 dB&B£23.50
dB&B⇨£27.50 Lunch£4.50&alc Tea35–50p
Dinner£6.25&alc Wine£4.35 ₧ Credit cards ① ② ③ ⑤

STRATHAVEN 5,464 Strathclyde Map37 NS74 EcWed
Glasgow17 Kilmarnock20 Lanark14 London390
★★**Strathaven** Hamilton Rd ☏21778
7rm ⚐ CTV in all bedrooms ® 100P ♨ Disco wkly Live music & dancing wkly Cabaret wkly ♨ ♀English, French & Italian. Last dinner 9.30pm ✦ ⌂ sB&B£12 dB&B£24
Lunch£3.50&alc Tea£1&alc High Tea£2.50&alc
Dinner£5.50–£7.50&alc Wine£4.75 ₧ xmas
Credit cards ① ② ③ ④ ⑤ ⑥
GH Springvale Hotel 18 Letham Rd ☏21131 Lic 6hc
1㎜ (A8hc) (3fb) ⚐ CTV 8P ⚐ *B&b£7.50
Bdi£11 W£90 D7pm
FH Mrs E. Warnock **Laigh Bent** (NS701413) ☏20103
Attractive, stone-built farmhouse with outbuildings surrounding the courtyard. 1¾m SW of Strathaven on the A71.
Jun–Sep 2⇨ ゑ nc8 TV 4P 1♨ ⚐ 100acres beef
S% B&b£5 W£35 M
×× **Waterside** 31 Waterside St ☏22588
Dinner not served Mon Jan–Apr; 65seats 20P
♀French. Last dinner 10.15pm S% *Lunch£2–£10 ·
Dinner£9alc Wine£3.75 Credit cards ① ② ③ ⑤ ⑥

STRATHDON Grampian Map44 NJ31 Aberdeen46
Braemar26 Huntly27 London528
★**Colquhonnie** ☏210
10rm ⚐ CTV ® 20P 4♨ ゚ Last dinner 8pm ✦ ⌂
sB&B£7–£8 dB&B£14–£16 Lundh£3.50 Tea75p
High Tea£3 Dinner£7 xmas

STRATHMIGLO Fife Map41 NO21 Auchtermuchty2
St Andrews21 Perth14 London449
×× **Strathmiglo Inn** ☏252
Closed Thu; 28seats 6P Last dinner 9pm

Lunch £4.90 & alc   Dinner £10 alc   Wine £4.20
Credit cards 1 2

STRATHPEFFER 874 Highland Map43NH45 EcThu
Dingwall 5 Inverness 24 London 589 Ullapool 41
★★**Strathpeffer** ☎200
Closed mid Nov–Mar; 33rm(5⇌2🛁)CTV 30P sauna bath
Last dinner 8pm   S%   sB&B £8.75   sB&B⇌🛁£10
dB&B £17.50   dB&B⇌🛁£20   Lunch £3   Dinner £5.50
Wine £2.75
★**L Dunraven Lodge** Golf Course Rd ☎210
14rm 🍴 CTV ® 🎂 15P ⚓ Children under 12yrs not
accommodated   Last dinner 8pm   🍷   S%   ✻sB&B £8
dB&B £16   Dinner £6.50   Wine £3.75   🍺
★**Holly Lodge** ☎254
7rm(5⇌🛁)CTV ® 11P ⚓ ⚓ Last dinner 8.30pm   ⚓   🍷
GH Kilvannie Manor Fodderty ☎389 Lic 8hc (2fb) ⚓
CTV 15P D7pm
GH Rosslyn Lodge Private Hotel ☎281
Feb–Nov 15rm 14hc (5fb) ⚓ CTV 15P 🍴
D6.30pm

STRATHTUMMEL Tayside Map40NN86 Aberfeldy 17
London 484 Newtonmore 46 Pitlochry 9
★★⚓**Port-an-Eilean** ☎Tummelbridge 233
Closed mid Oct–Apr; 12rm(6⇌)🍴 20P 2🏠 ⚓ ⚓ ⚓
🍽 Scottish & French.   Last dinner 9pm   ⚓   🍷   sB&B £12
sB&B⇌£14   dB&B £24   dB&B⇌£27   Bar lunch £2alc
Tea 60p–£1.20   Dinner £6.50–£7.50   Wine £3.75

STRATHYRE 155 Central Map40NN51 EcWed Callander 8
Glasgow 45 Lochearnhead 5 London 442
★**Munro** ☎229
Closed Oct–Etr; 11rm ⚓ 20P 6🏠 ⚓ 🌐 International.
Last dinner 9pm   🍺
INN Strathyre ☎224   8⇌   ⚓ CTV 30P 🍴 S%
B&b £8.50–£11   Bdi £12.50–£17   W £100–£110   sn
L £5alc   D9pm £5alc

STRICHEN 962 Grampian Map45NJ95 EcWed
Aberdeen 37 Banff 21 Fraserburgh 9 London 572
⚓**Freemasons** High St ☎218
6rm CTV CTV in 1bedroom ® 20P ⚓ Last dinner 7pm   🍷
🍷   S%   sB&Bfr £8   dB&Bfr £14   Lunch fr £2   Tea fr 50p
High Tea fr £2   Dinner fr £3   Wine £2.75   Credit cards 1 2 3

STROMNESS 1,681 Orkney Map48HY20 EcThu
MdWed cattle Kirkwall 15 **Car ferry from Scrabster**
(Thurso)
★★**Stromness** ☎850298
Victorian four-storey sandstone building in narrow main
street, overlooking harbour.
Closed Jan–Mar; RS Nov & Dec; 40rm(35⇌🛁) Lift CTV 6P
⚓ ⚓ billiards   Last dinner 8pm   🍷   🍷
GH Oakleigh Private Hotel Victoria St ☎850447   Closed
New Year   Lic 7hc (A1hc)   (3fb)   ⚓   CTV 2P D5pm

STRONTIAN Highland Map39NM86 Ardgour 15 Fort
William 49 *(fy23)* London 565 Mallaig 50
★★⚓**Kilcamb Lodge** ☎2257
Situated on outskirts of village with grounds stretching down
to Loch Sunart.
11rm(3🛁) CTV ® 50P ⚓ ⚓ ⚓ Last dinner 8pm   🍷   🍷
S%   ✻sB&B £10–£12   dB&B £16–£20
dB&B⇌🛁£18–£22   Lunch £1.50–£3.80   Tea £1–£1.40
High Tea £1–£1.50   Dinner £6.50   Wine £3.50   🍺
★★**Loch Sunart** ☎2471
Situated in small Highland village on Loch Sunart, the hotel
looks out over the bay and down the loch.
Closed Nov–8Apr; 11rm(5⇌) 🍴 ® 25P ⚓ ⚓
Last dinner 7pm   🍷   🍷   S%   sB&B £12.50–£14
sB&B⇌£14–£15   dB&B £25–£27.50   dB&B⇌£28–£30
Bar lunch £1.50–£2.90   Tea 50p   Dinner £6.50–£7.50
Wine £2.95

STRUY Highland Map43NH43 EcFri/Sat Dingwall 19
Invermoriston 32 Inverness 21 London 586

STRATHPEFFER
Ross-shire

Strategically situated for exploring the scenic
grandeur of the North and West, offering unrivalled
facilities for a memorable holiday. 18-hole golf
course—full fishing facilities—rambling—climbing—pony-trekking
bowling—putting—or relaxing at nearby sandy beaches. Make Strathpeffer
your holiday centre and stay at the Strathpeffer Hotel, fully licensed,
h. & c. all rooms some with private facilities, colour T.V., public rooms
centrally heated, full fire certificate, large car park. Sauna.
Where comfort, personal attention and good food really matter.
Send for illustrated brochure.

THE STRATHPEFFER HOTEL
AA ★★
Resident Proprietors: Mr. and Mrs. T. Kennedy
Telephone: Strathpeffer (STD 09972) 200

Loch Sunart Hotel

Strontian, Argyll
Telephone Strontian 2471
WELL RECOMMENDED

19th-century Country House Hotel, overlooking one of Scotland's finest Lochs.
Smoking/Cocktail lounge, log fires, dinner by candlelight with excellent home cooking are some of the features of this family-run hotel. Hill-walking, climbing, sailing, sea or loch fishing (in private waters) in absolutely magnificent countryside. A very relaxing holiday.

★★**Cnoc** Erchless Castle Estate ☎264
Closed Dec–Mar; 10rm CTV ® 30P
Last dinner 8pm sB&B£10–£11 dB&B£18–£20
Lunch£3–£4&alc Tea£1.50–£2.50&alc
HighTea£2.50–£3.50&alc Dinner£6.50–£7.50&alc
Wine£3.50 Credit cards 3

SYMINGTON 433 Strathclyde Map34NS93 EcWed
Biggar13 Glasgow35 Lanark10 London373
★★**Tinto** (Scottish & Newcastle) ☎Tinto454
Closed 1Jan; 34rm(1⇨2) D CTV 100P 2 Live music & dancing Sat French. Last dinner 8.30pm
S% *sB&B£10.50–£15.50 sB&B£12.50–£20.50
dB&B£20.50–£24.50 dB&B£25–£29.50
Lunch£3–£3.50&alc Tea£1–£1.10 High Tea£2–£3.50
Dinner£4.50&alc Wine£2.45 xmas
Credit cards 1 2 3 4 5 6

★★**Wyndales House** (2m SW A73) ☎Tinto207
12rm 1 CTV CTV in 1bedroom ® 50P billiards sauna bath Mainly grills. Last dinner 9pm S%
sB&B£16.50 dB&B£20.90 Bar lunch 40p–£3.25
Teafr60p High Teafr£2.25 Dinner fr£5&alc Wine£3.90
xmas Credit cards 1 2 3 5

TAIN 2,151 Highland Map44NH78 EcThu Bonar Bridge15 Dingwall24 Inverness46 London609
★★★**Royal** High St ☎2013
25rm(22⇨) D CTV CTV in all bedrooms ® 8P
Last dinner 9.30pm *sB&B£11
sB&B£13.50 dB&B£27 Dinner£5.50&alc
Wine£4.60 Credit cards 1 2 3 5

TALLADALE Highland Map42NG97 Dingwall50 Gairloch10 Inverness64 London625
★★**Loch Maree** ☎Loch Maree200
Closed Dec–Mar; RS end Oct & Nov; 15rm
10P 4 sB&B£15–£17
dB&B£30–£34 Lunch£4–£4.50 Tea80–90p
Dinner£6.50–£7 Wine£3

TANGUSDALE Isle of Barra, Western Isles Map48NF60
Castlebay2 **Car-carrying service from Oban to Castlebay**
★★★**Isle of Barra** (Scottish Highland) ☎Castlebay383
Telex no778215
RS Oct–Apr; 41⇨ D CTV 30P
Last dinner 8.15pm S% sB&B£21.30
dB&B£36.60 Lunch£2alc Dinner£7.50 Wine£3.95
Credit cards 1 2 3 4 5 6

TARBERT 479 **Isle of Harris,** Map48NB10 EcThu
Stornoway37 **Car-carrying service from Uig (Skye) and via Lochmaddy (N Uist)**
★★**Harris** ☎Harris2154
24rm(11⇨1) CTV P Last dinner 8.30pm
sB&B£9 sB&B£12 dB&B£17 dB&B£22
Lunch fr£3.60 Teafr£1 Dinner£4.80–££5.50 Wine£2.50

TARBERT 1,391 Loch Fyne, **Strathclyde** Map33NR86
EcWed Md cattle Fri Campbeltown38 Glasgow97
Lochgilphead13 London500
★★★L **Stonefield Castle** ☎207
Stone castle in 100 acres of wooded grounds surrounded by hills, overlooking Loch Fyne.
Closed Jan–Mar; rs Oct–Dec; 34rm(28⇨4) Lift CTV ® 50P (heated) (hard) sauna bath Scottish, French & German. Last dinner 9pm *sB&Bfr£20
sB&B£fr£24 dB&B£fr£40 Bar lunch£3 Tea£1
High Tea£1.50 Dinner£10 Wine£3.95 xmas
Credit cards 1 2 3 4 5 6

★★**Bruce** Harbour St ☎577
11rm(2⇨9) CTV ® 5P Scottish, English & French.
Last dinner 9.30pm sB&B£fr£12
dB&B£fr£24 Lunch fr£4.50 Teafr£1 High Teafr£3.25
Dinner fr£7.95 Wine£3.50 xmas Credit cards 1 2 3

TAYNUILT 272 Strathclyde Map39NN03 EcWed
Crianlarich29 Fort William50 London493 Oban12
★**Polfearn** ☎251
14rm CTV ® 50P Children under 3yrs not accommodated Last dinner 8pm
sB&B£8.50–£10.50 dB&B£17–£21 Bar lunch£1–£3
Teafr£1 High Teafr£3 Dinner£7–£8 Wine£4

THORNHILL 1,510 Dumfries & Galloway Map34NX89
EcThu Cumnock29 Dumfries15 Glasgow62 London356
★★**Buccleuch & Queensberry** ☎30215
11rm(3⇨1) CTV ® 39P 4 Last dinner 8pm
S% sB&B£11.75–£12.75 sB&B£14–£15
sB&B£21.75–£23.75 dB&B£25–£27
Bar lunch£2.50alc Tea£1.25–£1.50 High Tea£3.50alc
Dinner£7.50alc Wine£3.50

★★L **Trigony House** Closeburn (2m S off A76)
☎Closeburn215
6rm(1⇨2) Annexe: 3rm CTV ® 30P
Last dinner 9.30pm sB&B£16 sB&B£19
dB&B£22 dB&B£30 Bar lunch80p–£3.50&alc
Tea50p–£1.50&alc Dinner£4.50–£5&alc Wine£3.05
FH Mr J. Mackie **Waterside Mains** (NS870971) ☎30405
Farmhouse set on banks of River Nith. Fishing parties catered for.
Etr–Ec 3hc (1fb) nc CTV 3P river
160acres arable dairy S% B&b£5–£5.50 Bdi£8–£8.50
D4pm

THURSO 9,107 Highland Map47ND16 EcThu MdTue
Helmsdale44 Inverness131 John O'Groats20 London696
Tongue44 Wick21
★★**Pentland** Princes St ☎3202
56rm(6⇨5) CTV CTV available in bedrooms
Last dinner 8.30pm sB&B£10.50 dB&B£21
dB&B£30 Lunch£2.50alc Tea75p High Tea£2.50
Dinner£4.50alc Wine£3.25
★ **St Clair** Sinclair St ☎3730

27rm(2⇌4🛁) D ⚔ CTV CTV available in bedrooms ⓡ 6🎛
Live music & dancing twice wkly Last dinner£3.50pm ✳
S% sB&B£10.92 sB&B⇌🍽£12.07 dB&B£21.84
dB&B⇌🍽£24.14 Lunch£2.90–£3.50 Tea60–80p
High Tea£2.90–£3.50 Dinner£5.20–£6 Wine£3.95

TOBERMORY 647 Isle of Mull, Strathclyde Map38NM55
EcWed Craignure21 **Car-carrying services operate between Lochaline–Fishnish and Oban–Craignure**
★★★**Western Isles** ☎2012
Closed Xmas; 29rm(13⇌) D ⚔ CTV 20P 6🎛 ⚓ ⌕ ⌠
Last dinner8.45pm ✳ ⌘ S% ✳sB&B£12.70–£18
dB&B£23–£32 dB&B⇌£25.40–£36 Bar lunch£3.50alc
Tea40–60p Dinner£6.95–£8.95 Wine£3.70 🍽
Credit cards ①②③④⑥

GH Suidhe Hotel 59 Main St ☎2209 Mar–Oct Lic 9hc
1⇌ (2fb) ⚔ CTV 5P ⌘ sea S% B&B£9–£10
Bdi£14–£15 W£90.65–£97.12 ⌕ D8.30pm

GH Tobermory 53 Main St ☎2091 Closed Xmas & New Year Lic 13hc (2fb) CTV 10P ⚔ sea S%
B&b£9.20–£10 Bdi£13.23–£14.50 W£86.25–£98 ⌕ D6.30pm

TOMDOUN Highland Map43NH10 Invergarry11
Invermoriston25 Fort William36 London552
FH Mrs H. Fraser **No 3 Greenfield** (NH201006) ☎221
Small modern bungalow set in isolated position in rugged, hilly countryside. 3m E, on S side of Loch Garry.
20May–Sep 3rm (1fb) TV 6P 172acres mixed S%
B&b£5–£5.50 Bdi£8.50 W£55 ⌕ D7pm

TOMINTOUL 306 Grampian Map44NJ11 Aberdeen64
Braemar33 Grantown-on-Spey14 London555
★★**Gordon Arms** The Square ☎206
Situated in village square with views of surrounding hills.
29rm(5⇌1🍽) CTV 20P ⌘ Last dinner8pm ✳
✳sB&B£8 sB&B£17 dB&B⇌🍽£19 Lunch£3 Tea50p
Dinner£5 Wine£3
★★**Richmond Arms** ☎209
27rm(8⇌) CTV ⓡ ⌕ ⌘ Ω Last dinner8.30pm ✳
✳sB&B£8.45 sB&B⇌£9.60 dB&B£16.90
dB&B⇌£19.20 Lunch£2.90 Tea5p High Tea£2.85
Dinner£4.95 Wine£3.12 🍽 Credit card③

TONGUE 129 Highland Map46NC55 EcSat Durness30
Inverness108 London661 Thurso24
★★**Ben Loyal** ☎216
13rm(2⇌) Annexe: 6rm ⚔ CTV 18P ⚓ Last dinner8pm ✳
⌘ sB&B£8–£11.50 dB&B£15.20–£23
dB&B⇌£21.50–£26.50 Bar lunch£1.75–£2.50
Tea£1.25 High Tea£2.50–£3 Dinner£6–£6.50 Wine£3
★★**Tongue** (Scottish Highland) ☎206 Telex no778215
Built in 1876 wity Victorian décor and furnishings.
Closed Oct–Apr; 21rm(10⇌) 3⌂ D CTV⊕ 30P ⌕ ⌘
Last dinner8.30pm ✳ ⌘ S% sB&B£18.30
sB&B⇌£21.30 dB&B£30.60 dB&B⇌£36.60
Bar lunch£2alc Dinner£7.50 Wine£3.95 🍽
Credit cards ①②③④⑤⑥

TORRIDON Highland Map42NG85 Lochcarron23
Achnasheen20 Gairloch30 Inverness64 London625
★★👑**Loch Torridon** ☎242
Closed Oct–Apr; 19rm(11⇌) CTV 30P ⚓ ⌕ ⌘
🍷Scottish & French. Last dinner9pm ✳ ⌘
sB&B£14.85 sB&B⇌£15.75 dB&B£23
dB&B⇌£27.50 Tea50p Dinner£7.30&alc Wine£3.75
Credit cards ①②③④⑤⑥

TROON 11,871 Strathclyde Map33NS33 EcWed Ayr8
Glasgow32 Irvine6 Kilmarnock10 London419
★★★★**Marine** (Scottish Highland) ☎314444
Telex no778215
In a fine position on the coast, overlooking golf course.
68⇌ Lift D ⚔ CTV in all bedrooms ⓡ 50P ⚓ ⌕ ⌠ ⌘
Live music & dancing wkly Conference facilities available

Tobermory–Tynet

🍷Scottish & French. Last dinner10.15pm ✳ ⌘ S%
sB&B⇌£26.20 dB&B⇌£46.70 Lunchfr£5&alc
Dinnerfr£8.50&alc Wine£3.95 🍽 xmas
Credit cards ①②③④⑤⑥

★★★**Sun Court** Crosbie Rd ☎312727
Spacious former home of wealthy industrialist, overlooking sea. Incorporates Real tennis court.
20rm(18⇌) ⚔ CTV in 20bedrooms 70P ⚓ ⌕ squash ⌘
🍷Scottish, French & Italian. Last dinner9.30pm ✳ S%
sB&B£19 sB&B⇌£22 dB&B£29 dB&B⇌£32
Lunch£6.50&alc Dinner£8.50&alc Wine£3.25 🍽
Credit cards ①②

★★**Ardnell** St Meddans St ☎311611
Large converted private house 100yds from railway station.
RS 1Jan; 9rm(3⇌) CTV CTV in 5bedrooms ⓡ 48P ⌕
Last dinner9pm ✳ ⌘ ✳sB&B£10.50 sB&B⇌£12.50
dB&B£21 dB&B⇌£25 Lunch£4.50 Tea£1.75
High Tea£3.25–£4.95 Dinnerfr£4&alc Wine£3

★★**Craiglea** South Beach ☎311366
22rm(12⇌) ⚔ CTV CTV in 12bedrooms ⓡ 14P 6🎛 ⚓ Live music & dancing Sat Last dinner8.45pm ✳ ⌘
sB&B£14.50–£16 sB&B⇌£15.50–£17 dB&B£23–£26
dB&B⇌£30 Lunch£5–£6&alc Tea50p
Dinner£6–£7.50&alc 🍽 xmas Credit cards ①②③

★★**South Beach** South Beach Rd ☎312033
24rm(6⇌) CTV CTV in 4bedrooms 40P ⌕
Last dinner8.30pm sB&B£14 sB&B⇌£15 dB&B£24
dB&B⇌£25 Lunch£3.75 High Tea£3.15–£4.95&alc
Dinner£6.45 Credit cards ①②③⑤⑥

××**L'Auberge de Provence** (Marine Hotel), Crosbie Rd ☎314444
Closed Sun; Lunch not served; 45seats 100P
🍷French. Last dinner10.15pm Dinner£13alc
Credit cards ①②③⑤⑥

TURNBERRY 164 Strathclyde Map33NS20 EcWed Ayr18
Girvan5 Glasgow52 London428 Stranraer35
★★★★**BL Turnberry** (British Transport) ☎202
Telex no777779
Gracious white building set in extensive grounds. Fine views over Firth of Clyde.
123⇌ Lift D ⚔ CTV CTV in all bedrooms 100P 4🎛 ⌕
⇌(heated) ⚓ ⌠ billiards sauna bath ⌕ Conference facilities available 🍷English & French. Last dinner9.30pm
✳ ⌘ S% ✳sB&B⇌£35–£42 dB&B⇌£58–£66
Lunchfr£7.50&alc Tea£2.25alc Dinnerfr£11&alc
Wine£5.50 🍽 xmas Credit cards ①②③④⑤⑥

TWEEDSMUIR Borders Map35NT12 EcSat Edinburgh37
London364 Moffat15 Peebles19
★★**Crook Inn** ☎272
Pre-war building in country setting occupying site of the old Crook Inn dating from 1604.
8rm(6⇌) ⚔ CTV⊕ 50P ⚓ ⌕ ⌘ 🍷Scottish & French.
Last dinner8.45pm ✳ ⌘ sB&B£14–£15
sB&B⇌£16–£17 dB&B£26–£28 dB&B⇌£28–£30
Bar lunch£3alc High Tea£3–£3.50 Dinner£7–£8&alc
Wine£3.95 🍽 xmas

TWYNHOLM 274 Dumfries & Galloway Map30NX65
Castle Douglas8 Kirkcudbright4 London368
★ **Burnbank** ☎244
Small village hotel situated in hollow beside the local burn.
6rm ⚔ CTV 10P ⚓ Last dinner9.45pm ✳ S%
✳sB&B£6.90–£8.05 dB&B£13.80–£16.10
Bar lunch£1–£3 Dinner£4–£7&alc Wine£2 🍽 xmas

TYNET Grampian Map44NJ36 London608 Banff22 Elgin12 Huntly21
★★**Mill Motel** ☎Clochan233
Converted mill on main road between Fochabers and the fishing town of Buckie.
Annexe: 15rm(12⇌3🛁) ⚔ CTV CTV in all bedrooms ⓡ 20P
Live music & dancing Wed & Sat Last dinner8.30pm
⌘ sB&B⇌🍽£14.65 dB&B⇌🍽£24 Lunch£2.50–£3

147

Tea £1-£1.50 High Tea £2-£3 Dinner £6-£8
Wine £2.25 Credit cards 1 2 3 5

UIG Isle of Lewis Western Isles Map 48 NB03 Stornoway 32 Tarbert 54 London 666 (ferry)
★★ ≝ *H* **Uig Lodge** ☎ Timsgarry 286
Built as a hunting and shooting lodge by Sir James Matheson over 100 years ago, this hotel stands in 200 acres of grounds on the western shores of the islands.
Closed 16 Oct–Mar; 11rm(4⇌) ⚲ ℝ 16P 🚭 ⚛ ✡
♥ International. Last dinner 9pm ♥ ♫ S%
sB&B £15.60 sB&B⇌£18.10 dB&B £27.50
dB&B⇌£32.50 Lunch £4-£6 Tea £1.50-£3.75
High Tea £3.50-£7 . Dinner £10 Wine £3 🍺
Credit cards 1 2 3 5 6

UIG Isle of Skye Highland Map 42 NG36 EcWed Kyle of Lochalsh(fy)51 **Car-carrying service to Lewis and North Uist**
★★**Uig** ☎205
Closed Oct–8 Apr; 12rm(7⇌5⌁) Annexe: 13rm(7⇌6⌁) ⚛
ℝ 20P ⚲ Children under 12yrs not accommodated ♿
Last dinner 8.15pm ♥ ♫ sB&B⇌⌁£14-£20
dB&B⇌⌁£28-£40 Bar lunch £2.50 Tea 80p
Dinner £7-£8.50 Wine £4 🍺 Credit cards 1 2 3 5
★ **Ferry Inn** ☎242
Painted stone house (formerly post office) set back from the road with splendid views over bay and harbour.
Closed New Year; 6rm(1⇌) ⚛ CTV ℝ 10P 🚭 Last High Tea 8.30pm ♥ ♫ S% sB&B £6-£8 sB&B⇌£7-£9
dB&B £12-£16 dB&B⇌£14-£18 Bar lunch 40p-£1.20
Tea 60p-£1 High Tea £1.75-£5&alc Wine £2.60 🍺
xmas Credit cards 1 3 6

FH Mrs J. Macleod **No 11 Earlish** (NG388614)(2m S of Uig off A856) ☎319
House and smallholding sheltered by conifers and lying approximately 300yds from main road.
early May–mid Oct; 3rm (1fb) TV 6P 36acres sheep
S% B&B £5-£5.50 W£33-£35

UIST (NORTH), ISLE OF Western Isles Map 48 **See Lochmaddy**

UIST (SOUTH), ISLE OF Western Isles Map 48 **See Howmore and Lochboisdale**

ULLAPOOL 807 Highland Map 46 NH19 EcTue (not summer) Gairloch 56 Inverness 60 Lairg 45 Lochinver 37 London 625
See also Leckmelm
☆☆**Ladbrooke Mercury Motor Inn** North Rd (on A835) (Ladbroke) ☎2314
Modern low rise complex standing on main north road on outskirts of fishing port.
Closed Nov–Mar; 60⇌ ⌁ TV in all bedrooms ℝ 80P ⚲ sauna bath Live music & dancing wkly Last dinner 10pm

The Ladbroke Mercury Motor Inn, Ullapool, is the Centre of Attractions

This comfortable modern hotel lies just north of the charming unspoilt fishing village of Ullapool. This part of the Western Highlands offers some truly magnificent scenery including the nearby 200' deep Corrieshalloch Gorge and Falls of Measach.
You'll find plenty of exciting holiday ideas in our Lazydays brochure — try a Scottish Weekaway — tailor made for touring in your own car, or take a Welcome Break from as little as £30.00 per person bed & breakfast.
For your Lazydays brochure, 'phone 01-734 6000 or write to PO Box 137, Watford, Herts. WD1 1DN.

Ladbroke Mercury Motor Inn,
Ullapool,
Ross and Cromarty,
IV26 2UD.
Tel: (0854) 2314

Ladbroke Hotels

♥ ♫ S% sB&B⇌£26.75-£27.75
dB&B⇌£41.50-£42.50 Lunch fr£5 Tea fr£2
High Tea fr£4 Dinner fr£7.50 Wine £5 🍺
Credit cards 1 2 3 5 6
★★★**Royal** (Best Western) ☎2181
RS Nov–Mar; 60rm(45⇌3⌁) ♪ ⚛ CTV ℝ 150P ⚲
Cabaret nightly ♿ ♥ British & French.
Last dinner 9.30pm ♥ ♫ sB&B⇌£13.50-£14.47
sB&B⇌⌁£16.75-£17.50 dB&B £25.80-£27.70
dB&B⇌⌁£31.30-£37.68 🍺 Credit cards 1 2 5
★★**Ceilidh Place** West Argyle St ☎2103
Closed Nov–Mar; 15rm(8⇌) 1⚛ ♪ ⚛ ♫ 30P
Last dinner 9.30pm ♥ ♫ S% ✱sB&B £13.50
sB&B⇌£16 dB&B £25 dB&B⇌£30 Lunch £2.50-£6
Tea £1-£2.50 High Tea £2.70 Dinner £3.60-£7.50&alc
Wine £4.50
★★**L Harbour Lights** Garve Rd ☎2222
Closed Dec & Jan; 22rm(13⇌6⌁) ⚛ CTV ℝ 40P ⚲ Live music 4 nights wkly ♥ Mainly grills. Last dinner 8.30pm
♫ sB&B £10.50-£13.50 sB&B⇌⌁£12-£15
dB&B £20.10-£22.10 dB&B⇌⌁£22.10-£25.10
Bar lunch £1.40 Dinner £6.50alc Wine £4.50
Credit cards 1 3 5
★**Ferry Boat Inn** Shore St ☎2366
Closed Dec–Feb; 12rm CTV 🏁 🚭 Last dinner 10pm
sB&B £8.50-£11.50 dB&B £15-£18.50
Bar lunch £1.40-£1.70 Dinner £5.50-£7.50 Wine £2.93
Credit cards 1 5 6

UPHALL 3,035 Lothian Map 35 NT07 EcWed Edinburgh 13 Linlithgow 7 Livingston 3 London 419
★★★≝*B* **Houstoun House** ☎Broxburn 853831
Telex no 727148
Closed 1 & 2 Jan; 27rm(24⇌3⌁) 11🛏 ♪ CTV in all bedrooms 100P 🚭 ⚲ ♥ International. Last dinner 9pm ♥
♫ S% ✱sB&B⇌⌁£24.50-£31 dB&B⇌⌁£38-£46

The Royal

In a superb situation on the shores of Loch Broom, the Royal has 61 bedrooms, 46 with private bath. Good food and a welcoming atmosphere, set in the grand Wester Ross scenery. For full details, telephone —
Ullapool 2181
A Best Western Hotel

Ullapool

The Ladbroke Mercury Motor Inn, Wick is the Centre of Attractions

Dating back to the 16th century, Wick is the perfect base to explore Northern Scotland. John O' Groats is a mere 17 miles away and also worth visiting is the Caithness glassworks. The hotel, in the centre of Wick, overlooks Riverside Park, and its Norseman Restaurant enjoys a popular local reputation.

You'll find plenty of exciting holiday ideas in our Lazydays brochure — try a Scottish Weekaway — tailor made for touring in your own car, or take a Welcome Break from as little as £25.00 per person bed & breakfast.

For your Lazydays brochure, 'phone 01-734 6000 or write to PO Box 137, Watford, Herts. WD1 1DN.

Ladbroke Mercury Motor Inn, Riverside, Wick, Caithness, KW1 4NL
Tel: (0955) 3344

Ladbroke Hotels

Continental breakfast Lunch£6.50 Tea45p Dinner£10.50 Wine£3 Credit cards②

VIRKIE Shetland Map48HU31 Lerwick24 **(car-carrying service to Aberdeen)**
★*Meadowvale* ☎Sumburgh60240
Modern timber clad two-storey building standing near to sea and overlooking Sumburgh Airport.
11rm(3⇨8⊓) CTV ⊘ 25P Lastdinner8pm ✻ ⚑

WAMPHRAY Dumfries & Galloway Map35NY19 EcWed Lockerbie10 London342 Moffat7
★*Red House* ☎Johnstone Bridge214
Closed Nov–8Apr; 6rm ⊪ CTV ® 20P ⇔
Lastdinner7.30pm ✻ sB&Bfr£11.50 dB&Bfr£23
Lunchfr£4 HighTeafr£4 Dinnerfr£6 Credit card⑤

WATERLOO Isle of Skye, Highland Map42NG62
Broadford1 Kyleakin7 Portree27 London595
GH *Ceol-na-Mara* ☎Kyle323 Etr–Sep 6hc (1fb) TV
6P sea S% ✻B&b£5.50 Bdi£10 W£70 ⊥ D9pm

WESTHILL 258 Grampian Map45NJ80 Aberdeen7
Alford19 London545 Stonehouse18
☆☆☆*Westhill Inn* ☎Aberdeen740388
Modern custom built hotel set just off A944 within developing area six miles west of Aberdeen.
39⇨ Annexe: 14rm(6⇨8⊓) Lift ⊅ CTV CTV in all bedrooms ® 220P sauna bath Conference facilities available ⚐ British & French. Lastdinner9.45pm ✻ S% sB&B⇨⊓£24 dB&B⇨⊓£30 Lunch£4 Dinner£6.25&alc Wine£3.60 ⚑ Credit cards①②③⑤

WEST LINTON 705 Borders Map35NT15 EcThu Biggar12
Edinburgh17 London388 Peebles14
GH *Rutherford Coaching House* ☎231 6hc (2fb)
CTV 12P 1⚋ ⊪ D9pm

WEST WEMYSS Fife Map41NT29 Kirkcaldy5 Leven6
Glenrothes8 London445
×××*Belvedere Hotel* Coxstalls ☎Kirkcaldy54167
Closed 26Dec & 1–2Jan; Dinner not served Sun;
60seats 30P bedrooms available ⚐ English & French.
Lastdinner9.30pm Lunch£5–£5.06&alc Dinner£10alc Wine£4.20 Credit cards①②

WHITEBRIDGE Highland Map43NH41 Fort Augustus10
Fort William42 Inverness25 London558
★★*Whitehouse* ☎Gorthleck226
Closed Jan; RSFeb, Mar, Nov & Dec; 12rm(2⇨3⊓) ⊪ CTV in all bedrooms ® 40P 3⚋ ⊘ ⊥ Lastdinner8pm ✻
⚑ sB&B£8.80 dB&B£17.50 dB&B⇨⊓£20
Lunchfr£4.50 Teafr80p Dinnerfr£6 Wine£3.10 ⚑
Credit cards①③⑤

Virkie – Wormit

WHITHORN 980 Dumfries & Galloway Map30NX44 EcWed
London411 Newton Stewart18 Stranraer33 Wigtown11
★*Castleriggh* ☎213
7rm ⊪ CTV ® 40P ⇔ ⊥ Disco Sat Lastdinner10pm ✻
⚑ ⚑ Credit cards①②③⑥

WHITING BAY 352 Isle of Arran, Strathclyde Map33NS02
EcWed (not summer) Brodick8 Lamlash4
★★*Whiting Bay* ☎247
A two storey building on sea front.
Closed Nov–Mar; 25rm(3⇨2⊓) CTV TV in all bedrooms ®
30P ⚋ ⊅ Disco 3nights wkly Live music & dancing wkly ⚗
Lastdinner9.30pm ✻ S% ✻sB&B£12.10
dB&B£23 dB&B⇨⊓£26.45 Lunch£2.50–£2.75
Tea50p–£1.20 HighTea£2.50–£3.50
Dinner£6.75–£8.75 Credit cards①②③⑤⑥
★*Cameronia* ☎254
RS Bookings only in winter for Grill room; 9rm ⊪ CTV TV on request in bedrooms ⊘ 13P ⇔ Lastdinner10pm ✻
Credit card①③
GH *Trareoch Hotel* Largie Beg ☎226 Apr–Sep Lic
8hc (2fb) ⊘ CTV 12P sea S% ✻B&b£9
Bdi£12.50 W£82.50 ⊥ D7pm

WICK 7,842 Highland Map47ND35 EcWed MdThu
Helmsdale37 Inverness125 John O'Groats17 London689 Thurso21
☆☆☆*Ladbroke Mercury Motor Inn* Riverside (Ladbroke) ☎3344
Closed Xmas; 48⇨ ⊅ ⊪ TV in 48bedrooms ® 30P
Conference facilities available Lastdinner9pm ✻ ⚑
sB&B⇨⊓£19.75–£21.75 dB&B⇨⊓£30.50–£32.50
Lunch£5.50–£6.50&alc Tea£2 HighTea£4
Dinner£7.50–£9.25&alc Wine£5 ⚑
Credit cards①②③⑤⑥
★★*Station* Bridge St ☎4545
Closed Xmas; 54rm(2⇨10⊓) Lift ⊅ ⊥ CTV CTV in 10bedrooms 40P Disco 5nights wkly Live music & dancing 3nights wkly Cabaret3nights wkly ⚗ Scottish & French.
Lastdinner8.30pm ✻ ⊘ ✻ sB&B£18.35
sB&B⇨⊓£20.25 dB&B£30 dB&B⇨⊓£32
Lunch£4.03 Tea95p HighTea£4 Dinner£6.90
Wine£3.50 ⚑ Credit cards①②③④⑤⑥
⊕ *Rosebank* Thurso St ☎3244
28rm(10⊓) CTV CTV in 10bedrooms 14P 2⚋ ⇔ Disco 3nights wkly Live music & dancing wkly Cabaret wkly
Lastdinner10pm ✻ S% sB&B£10–£14
sB&B⊓£14–£16 dB&B£20–£28 dB&B⊓£28–£32
Lunch£3.50 Dinner£6 Wine£3.50 ⚑

WISHAW 73,116 (with Motherwell) Strathclyde
Map34NS75 EcWed **See also Motherwell** Glasgow17
Lanark11 London392 Motherwell4
★★*Horse & Anchor* 206–212 Cambusnethan St ☎75603
8rm(7⇨⊓) ⊅ ⊪ CTV available in bedrooms ® 40P ⊥
⚗ Scottish & French. Lastdinner10.30pm ✻
Credit cards①②③⑥
★*Coltness* Coltness Rd (Ind Coope (Alloa)) ☎79491
11rm ⊪ CTV ® 100P Live music twice wkly ⚗ European.
Lastdinner8.30pm ✻ ✻sB&B£11.50 dB&B£18.50
Lunch£5.50alc Dinner£6.50alc Wine£3.25 ⚑
Credit cards①②③⑤

WORMIT Fife Map41NO32 EcWed Dundee5 London472
Perth26 St Andrews14
★★*Sandford Hill* ☎Newport-on-Tay541802
16rm(14⇨⊓) ⊪ CTV CTV in all bedrooms ® 50P ⊥
⇨ (hard) ⚗ Scottish & French. Lastdinner9pm ✻ ⚑
Credit cards①②③⑥

Always try to book your accommodation well in advance

Picnic Sites

All AA-listed Picnic Sites have been visited by an AA inspector and recommended as worthy of listing because they are sufficiently attractive and/or provide useful 'park and walk' access to the countryside. A transit Picnic Site may, though well equipped, be utilitarian in character but will be suitable for breaking long journeys for rest and refreshment.

BORDERS

Mayfield Riverside Walk Map 35 NT73 **(Kelso)**
Abbotsford Grove on river bank by Kelso Abbey (OS74 NT730337). Signposted in advance and at entrance, ¼m of grass and mature tree-studded land along the River Tweed. Fishing by permit. Bathing dangerous. Drinking water, furniture. Toilets. Parking 50.

Glentress Forest Map 35 NT23 **(A72)**
Off A72 2m E Peebles (OS74 NT284396). Signposted in advance and at entrance, area by small burn with access to forest trails. Information centre, furniture. Toilets. Parking 20.

Teviothead Map 35 NT40 **(A7)**
W side of A7 1m S of Teviothead Post Office (OS79 NT404038). Signposted in advance. Grassy riverside site with tarmac parking area. 10 acres. Drinking water, furniture. Toilets. Parking 12.

Cambridge Picnic Site Map 35 NT54 **(A697)**
A697 Lauder 3½m, at junction with unclassified road to Spottiswoode (OS74 NT585482). Signposted in advance and at entrance. Converted lay-by with grassed picnic areas. ½acre, furniture. Portaloo. Parking 20.

Meikle Harelaw Picnic Area Map 35 NT64 **(A697)**
Coldstream Carefraemill Road 3½m NW of Greenlaw. (OS74 NT657470). Signposted in advance and at entrance. Area cleared from section of old road. Grass with gorse and trees. Exceptional view. Furniture. Parking 30.

Rosetta Map 35 NT22 **(Off A703)**
On northern outskirts of Peebles ½m from town centre (0573 NT244415). Signposted in advance. Tree-studded grass slope in Rosetta Park. 2 acres. Park walks, walled gardens, licensed bar, furniture. Toilets.

St Mary's Loch Map 35 NT53 **(Off A6091)**
Mid-way between Selkirk and Moffat (OS73 NT238205). Grass on shingle between two lochs. 3 acres. Yacht club. Toilets. Parking 200.

Glenmayne Haugh Map 35 NT53 **(Off A6091)**
2m S of Galashiels on unclassified road between A6091 and A7 (OS73 NT504537). On south bank of River Tweed. 4 acres. Fishing, drinking water, furniture. Toilets. Parking 120.

Rankleburn Map 35 NT31 **(Off B709)**
¾m SE of Tushielaw on B711 off B709. (OS79 NT310169). Parking 100.

Cardona Forest Walks Map 35 NT23 **(B7062)**
3m E Peebles (OS73 NT295383). Signposted at entrance. 2 acres. Within Glentress Forest by small Burn. Access to various forest walks. Furniture. Parking 20.

Meldons Picnic Areas Map 35 NT24 **(Unclassified road)**
Three separate areas within ½m on unclassified road linking A72 and A703, through Meldon Hills (OS73 NT215435). Signposted in advance and at entrance. Close to Meldon Burn and many archaeological features. Cairn marker on each site with display of interesting items. Drinking water, furniture. Toilets. Parking 200.

CENTRAL

Strathyre Map 39 NN51 **(A84)**
Outside Strathyre village (OS57 NN562165). Signposted in advance and at entrance. Large grassy area beside river. 10 acres. Toilets. Parking 50.

Picnic Site Map 39 NN52 **(A85)**
Lochearnhead to Crianlarich road (OS51 NN559283). Signposted in advance and at entrance. rugged, elevated site. Parking 20.

Loch Lubhair Map 39 NN42 **(A85)**
3m from Crianlarich (OS51 NN426268). Wooded site in glen by Loch Lubhair. Access restricted to 6'6" high. Furniture. Parking 50.

Queens View Map 34 NS58 **(A809)**
4m S of Drymen (OS64 NS500830). Signposted at entrance. On the edge of moorland. 1 acre. AA Viewpoint. Access to hill walking. Parking 60.

David Marshall Lodge (Carnegie Building) Map 40 NN50 **(A821)**
¾m E of Aberfoyle (OS57 NN520014). Signposted in advance and at entrance. Extensive area of forestry land with parking and adjacent grassed picnic areas, grouped around central lake. Furniture, drinking water, restaurant, information centre, static displays and maps of local features. AA Viewpoint, disabled toilets. Parking 50.

Wilmirnog Map 40 NN60 **(A821)**
400 yds from junction with A84 (OS57 NN607082). Signposted at entrance. Landscaped site close to River Leny with access to the former Stirling-Oban railway now a footpath. Furniture. Parking 15.

Kincardine Bridge Map 34 NS98 **(A876)**
Near S access to bridge on A876. (OS65 NS912863). signposted at entrance. Toilets. Parking 50.

Galloch Map 39 NS39 **(Continuation of B837)**
On unclassified road approx 2½m S of Rowardennan (OS56 390950). Woodland site on shore of Loch Lomond.

Mealldhuinne Map 39 NS39 **(Continuation of B837)**
On unclassified road approx 1m S of Rowardennan on E side of loch (OS56 NS365974). Signposted in advance and at entrance. Natural woodland site with stream. 3 acres. Parking 70.

Milarrochy Map 34 NS49 **(B837)**
1m N of Balmaha (OS56 NS408928). Natural woodland on loch shore. 2 acres.

Rowardennan Map 39 NS39 **(Continuation of B837)**
On unclassified road adjacent to village (OS56 NS365985). On hillside adjacent to right of way to Ben Lomond. 3 acres. Access to hill walking. Parking 150.

DUMFRIES & GALLOWAY

Opposite Glenairlie Bridge Map 34 NS80 **(A76)**
On W side 4½m S of Sanquhar (OS71 NS835056). Signposted in advance and at entrance. Attractive riverside environment fenced from road. Furniture. Toilets. Parking 20.

Portpatrick Harbour Map 30 NW95 **(A77)**
A77, N side of harbour (OS82 NW999541). Safe bathing, drinking water. Toilets. Parking 100.

Grey Mare's Tail Map 35 NT11 **(A708)**
10m NE of Moffat (OS79 NT187147). Signposted at entrance. By large waterfall. Access to bridle path. Parking 30.

Sandhead Beach Map 30 NX15 **(A715/A716)**
Junction A715/A716 (OS82 NX100510).

Picnic sites

Overlooking Luce Bay. Safe bathing, drinking water.
Craignarget Shore Map 30 NX25 **(A747)**
Between Glenluce and Port William (OS82 NX255514). Overlooking Luce Bay, rocky coastline. Safe bathing. Parking 100.
St Medan, Monreith Map 30 NX34 **(A747)**
1m SE of Monreith village (OS83 NX380402). On shoreline. Rock fishing, safe bathing. Parking 100.
Port Logan Shore Map 30 NX14 **(B7065)**
At Port Logan (OS82 NX100410). Fishpond. Drinking water, furniture. Toilets.

FIFE
Craigmead, Lomond Hills Map 41 NO20
On unclassified road between Leslie and Falkland (OS56 NO227064). Signposted in advance at entrance. 2 acres in sheltered area with access to country walks. Furniture. Toilets with facilities for the disabled, open touring summer. Parking 30.

GRAMPIAN
Picnic Site Map 41 NO49 **(A93)**
2m W of Aboyne (OS44 NO495987) signposted in advance. Roadside site with outlook across Deeside. Airfield to South Deeside. Furniture. Parking 24.
Broddie Castle Map 44 NH95 **(A96)**
4.5m W Forres (OS27 NH979577). Signposted in advance and at entrance. 175 acres. Level grassy area set amidst mature woodland forming heart of castle ground. Woodland walks, pictish stone, adventure playground. Furniture. Toilets. Parking 150.
Picnic Site Map 45 NJ62 **(A96)**
E side A96 2m NW Pitcaple (OS38 NJ698251). Signposted in advance and at entrance. Grassed area screened from highway. Furniture and Portaloo Toilet. Parking 10.
Speymouth Map 44 NJ35 **(A98)**
½m E of Fochaber (OS28 SJ358587). Signposted in advance and at entrance. On forest road in woodland area. 5 acres. Forest walks, viewpoint, furniture. Toilets. Parking 30.
Potarch Green Map 45 NO69 **(B933)**
Off B933 near Potarch Bridge 4m W Banchory (OS37 607973). Signposted in advance at entrance. 5 acres. Flat grassy area surrounded by trees, close to River Dee and various forest walks. Furniture. Toilets. Parking 20.
Picnic Site Map 45 NJ41 **(A97)**
1m N Kildrummy Castle (OS37 NJ465175). Signposted at entrance. Simple grassed site planted with young trees. ½ acre. Furniture. Parking 10.
Un-named Transit Picnic Site Map 45 NJ53 **(A97)**
On outskirts of Huntly between town and by-pass roundabout. (OS29 NJ525395). Signposted in advance from by-pass. Pleasant enclosed grassed area. Drinking water. Toilets. Parking 50.
Well of Lecht Map 44 NJ21 **(A939)**
5m SE of Tomintoul (OS36 NJ235153). Signposted in advance and at entrance. Mountain streams, footpaths to old iron-stone mine. Drinking water. Parking 10.
Picnic Site Map 45 NK02 **(A975)**
2m N of Newburgh by Ythan Estuary (OS38 NK006284). Signposted at entrance. ½ acre. Outlook across estuary and bird sanctuary.

HIGHLAND
Landmark Visitors' Centre, Carrbridge Map 44 NH92 **(Off A9)**
Off A9 at Carrbridge (OS36 NH908224). Signposted in advance and at entrance. Tourist complex in heavily wooded area. Nature trail, sculptures, audio visual display. Drinking water, furniture. Toilets. Parking 200 (fee).
Foulis Ferry Map 43 NH56 **(A9)**
1m SW Evanton (OS21 NH599636). Signposted at entrance. Landscaped site on the Cromarty Firth. Restaurant, craft shop, furniture. Toilets. Parking 20.
Redburn Map 43 NH78 **(A9)**
2m SE Eddelton(OS21 NH735840). Signposted at entrance. Wooded roadside site with access to forest walks. Furniture. Parking 12.
Loch Linnhe Map 39 NN07 **(A82)**
3m S Fort William W side A82 (OS41 NN075705). Signposted in advance and at entrance. 1 acre. Small area utilising the natural rocky shore line of Loch Linnhe with fine views across the loch to the mountains of Morven. Furniture. Parking 10.
Loch Oich Map 46 NH39 **(A82)**
2m S Invergarry (OS34 NH302987). Signposted at entrance on Loch Oich. Drinking water, furniture. Toilets. Parking 20.
Glenn Finnan Transit Picnic Site Map 39 NM98 **(A830)**
At the head of Loch Shiel between Fort William and Mallaig (OS40 NM905808).
Loch Maree Map 43 NH06 **(A832)**
2½m NW of Kinlochewe (OS19 NH004647). Signposted in advance. Sheltered sites on loch shore. Nature reserve, walks, furniture.
Coldbackie Sands Map 46 NC66 **(A836)**
3m NE of Tongue (OS10 NC612600). 200yds from sheltered sandy bay with steep approach. Parking 8.
Sangomore Map 46 NC46 **(A838)**
At Durness (OS9 NC406675). Sandy bays. Near Smoo Cave. Parking 20.
Gludie Picnic Map 43 NH36 **(A832)**
At W end of Loch Luichart 5m W Garve (OS20 NH311625). Signposted at entrance. Riverside site close to loch, falls and hydro electric development. Furniture. Parking 7.
Dalcraig Map 43 NH41 **(B852)**
1m SW Foyers (OS34 NH493183). Signposted at entrance. 2 acres. Small level site set among bushes on S bank of River Foyers. Furniture. Parking 15.
Ralia Transit Picnic Site Map 43 NN79 **(B9150)**
At Junction with A9 sm S Newtonmore (OS35 NN703940). Signposted in advance and at entrance. Grassed undulating area with panoramic views. Viewpoint, drinking water, furniture. Toilets. Parking 50.

LOTHIAN
Bilsdean Transit Picnic Site Map 35 NT77 **(A1)**
N of Cockburnspath (OS67 NT766725). Signposted at entrance. Small roadside site with individual parking spaces by furniture and toilets. Parking 10.
Pencraig Picnic Place Map 35 NT57 **(A1)**
N side of A1 4m E Middleton 1m East Linton (OS67 NT573765). Signposted at entrance. On high ground within wooded area. 1 acre. Tourist Information Centre, drinking water, furniture. Toilets. Parking 20.

STRATHCLYDE
Cauldshore Map 33 NX19 **(A77)**
At Girvan (OS76 NX181980). Signposted in advance and at entrance. On sandy foreshore. 1½ acres, toilets, furniture.
Finnarts Bay Map 30 NX07 **(A77)**
3m N of Cairnryan (OS76 NX052757).

Picnic sites – Country parks

Signposted at entrance. Parking 100.
Duck Bay Map 39 NS38 **(A82)**
1m N of Balloch (OS56 NS380823). Signposted in advance and at entrance. Grassed area overlooking Loch Lomond. 1½ acres. Drinking water, furniture. Toilets.
Maidens Map 33 NS20 **(A719)**
In village of Maidens (OS76 NS213079). Signposted in advance and at entrance. Furniture. Toilets. Parking 100.
Garelochhead Map 39 NS29 **(A814)**
1m N of Garelochhead (OS56 NS236916). Signposted at entrance. Small trees on heather slopes. 10 acres. No overnight parking. Drinking water, furniture. Toilets. Parking 20.
St Columb's Bay Map 39 NM94 **(A828)**
10m NE of Oban (OS49 NM945413). Signposted at entrance. Cleared forest area. 10 acres. Furniture. Parking 100.
Jubilee Picnic Site Map 33 NS07 **(A8003)**
2m N of Tighnabruaich (OS63 NS000760). Signposted in advance and at entrance. Steep hillside with bays carved into thick undergrowth, cooking area in rocks. 2 acres. Pay telescope, drinking water, furniture. Parking 30.

TAYSIDE
Tummel Forest-Faskally Walk Map 40 NN95 **(A9)**
2m N Pitlochry (OS52 NN923592). Signposted in advance and at entrance. 10 acres. Forest walks, play area, wildlife hide, drinking water, furniture. Toilets. Ample parking (ticket machine).
Picnic Site, East Haven Beach Map 41 NO53 **(Off A92)**
1½m SE of Muirdrum 1½m NE of Carnoustie (OS54 NO591362). Access under low bridge and on single, unmetaled track to grass area giving access to sandy beach and coastal walks. Toilets. Parking 20.
Montrose Links Map 41 NO75 **(Off A92)**
1m off A92 E of Montrose (OS54 NO726582). Parking 200.
Victoria Park Map 41 NO64 **(Off A92)**
¾m E of Arbroath (OS54 NO653412). Public park bordering promenade. Drinking water, furniture. Toilets. Parking 200.
Birks O'Aberfeldy Map 40 NN85 *(A826)*
At Aberfeldy *(OS52 NN855485)*. Furniture.
Dalerb Map 40 NN74 **(A827)**
On N shore at east end of Loch Tay, ¾m from Kenmore (OS52 NN761452). Signposted at entrance. Landscaped field with access to rocky shore. Bathing dangerous. Furniture, drinking water, disabled toilets. Parking 50.
Allean-Tummel Forest Map 40 NN86 **(B8019)**
7m NW of Pitlochry ½m W Queens View (OS43 NN852602). Signposted in advance and at entrance. 2 acres. Hillside site with part excavated ring fort, forest walks. Drinking water, furniture. Disabled toilet. Parking 20.
Picnic Site Map 41 NO26 **(Off B951)**
Glen Isla (OS44 NO214604). Signposted at entrance. Grassy picnic site in attractive setting by the River Isla. 1½ acres. Furniture. Toilets. Parking 20.
Queens View Tourist Park Map 40 NN85 **(B8019)**
a. On B8019 (OS52 NN859600). Signposted in advance and at entrance. Forest walks, furniture. Parking 40.
b. 400yds W of above. Signposted in advance and at entrance. Extensive tree-studded area. AA Viewpoint Forestry Coimmission Tourist Information Centre. Parking 100.
Loch Leven Picnic Area Map 40 NT19 **(B9097)**
In National Nature Reserve 1½m NW of Ballingry and 3m SE Kinross S side of Loch Leven (OS58 NT160990). Signposted at entrance. Roadside car park giving access to Nature Reserve. Vane Farm Nature Centre ½m W. Extensive grass and gorse clad slopes bordering and overlooking loch. Drinking water. Toilets open during season and suitable for disabled. Parking 175.
Un-named Site Map 41 NO37 **(Off B955)**
At Oglilvy Arms Hotel, Clova Village (OS44 327731). Small site surrounded by trees close to a small burn at the head of Glen Clova. Hill walking, drinking water, furniture. Toilets. Parking 10.
Un-named Site Map 41 NO36 **(B955)**
8½m N River Esk (OS44 NO373653). Signposted at entrance. Two areas either side of road. Level grassy on river bank. Furniture. Parking 20.
Cullow Market, Glen Clova Map 41 NO36 *(B955)*
On E side of road, ¾m N of Dyke Head (OS44 386612). Signposted at entrance. Small wooded picnic site amidst hills, trees and farmland N of Dyke Head Village. Furniture. Parking 10.
Un-named Site at Glecca Bridge, Glen Clova Map 41 NO36 **(B955)**
(OS44 3746654). Where the road forks at Glecca Bridge 4m N Dyke Head. Attractive river bank picnic site on both banks of River South Esk by the old and new Glecca Bridge. Furniture. Parking 16.

Country Parks

Areas of land or land and water, normally not less than 25 acres in extent, designed to offer to the public, with or without charge, opportunity for recreational pursuits in the countryside.

FIFE
Craigtown Country Park Map 41 NO41 (OS59 NO477412) 2½m SW of St Andrews. Off unclassified road from B939 in St Andrews to Pitscottie. 50 acres.
Lochore Meadows Country Park
Map 40 NT19
(OS58 NT176950) At Crosshill on the B290 from Lochgelly to Ballingry centered in a district wasted by extensive coal mining and subjected to Britains largest land reclamation scheme. A loch surrounded by attractive countryside. Sailing, canoeing, boating, angling, ranger service, information centre.
Management: Fife Regional Council.

GRAMPIAN
Haddo Country Park Map 45 NJ83
(OS30 NJ867346) 20m N Aberdeen off B9005. 180 acres of mature parkland with lake and mixed woodland supporting a variety of wildlife. Picnic sites, footpaths, information centre, ranger service.
Management: Grampian Regional Council.

Haughton House Map 45 NJ51
(OS37 NJ583169). Wooded parkland within grounds of Houghton House. 50 acres. Nature trail, walks, narrow gauge railway, shop. Parking controlled by ticket machine.
Management: Grampian Regional Council.

LOTHIAN

Almondell and Calderwood Country Park Map 35 NT06
(OS65 NT076676 and NT092696) 10m W Edinburgh, 2m S Broxburn in Almond Valley, access from Mid and East Calder. Access signposted from A8 at Broxburn. Almondell between A98 and A71. Calderwood S of A71. Lies in a natural gorge featuring woodland and an artificial waterway. 240 acres. Nature trails, picnic areas, riverside and woodland walks, barbecue site. 90 acres. Calderwood has been left completely undeveloped, 130 acres, car parks, ranger service.
Management: Lothian County Council.

Beecraigs Country Park Map 34 NS97
(OS65 NS993742–NS998741) 2m S of Linlithgow. Mixed woodlands, grassland, loch and burns. 700 acres. Trout farm, deer farm, picnic and barbecue sites, orienteering course, daily permit fishing, ranger service. AA Viewpoint.
Management: Lothian County Council.

John Muir Country Park Map 35 NT67
(OS67 NT678792) W of Dunbar access from A1087 via three car parks, Linkfield, Shore Road, Belhaven and Castle Park, Dunbar. Coastal area of great natural beauty offering marked walks, cliff top walk, barbecue area, ranger service.
Management: East Lothian District Council.

STRATHCLYDE

Culzean Maybole Map 33 NS21
(OS70 NZ231102) Between Maidens and Dunure on A719. Castle and 531 acres estate with restored gardens, wooded walks, ponds, cliff walk, access to shore with dunes and rock pools, ranger naturalist service, park centre with exhibition and shop.
Management: National Trust for Scotland and Local Authorities.

Muirshiel Country Park Map 33 NS36
(OS63 NS318631) Signposted from Lochwinnoch access by road through Clader Glen. High valley admidst moorland, mixed habitat of moor, woodland and river. Picnic sites, nature trail, information centre, ranger service.
Management: Strathclyde Regional Council.

Castle Semple Water Park Map 33 NS35
(OS63 NS362596) Signposted from Lochwinnoch. Large loch launching facilities for sailing craft, rowing boats and canoes, hiring facilities for craft, angling facilities. Warden service.
Management: Strathclyde Regional Council.

Cornalees Bridge Centre Map 33 NS27
(OS63 NS249724) Beside moorland road from Greenock to Inverkip at the head of Shielhill Glen. Moorland and wooded glen. Walking trail, Information Centre, ranger service.
Management: Strathclyde Regional Council.

Palacerigg Map 34 NS77
(OS64 NS788738) 2m SE of Cumbernauld. 614 acres.

Strathclyde Regional Park Map 34 NS75
(OS64 NS715586) N and S of M74 between Hamilton and Motherwell. Access from A725 at M74 Junction 5. Constructed by clearance excavation of derelict land and diversion of the River Clyde. 2,000 acres including 200 acre artificial loch. Picnic areas, nature reserves, areas of scientific interest, scheduled areas of historical interest, sailing, canoeing, fishing, national rowing centre, ranger service.
Management: Strathclyde Park Joint Committee.

Forest Parks

Six figure map references have not been provided because of the large areas involved.

Border Forest Park Map 35 NY68/69
(OS79, 80 and 86) 145,000 acres of woodland hills and farms in Northumberland and Cumbria in England. Dumfries and Galloway and Borders in Scotland. The route of the Pennine Way long-distance walk crosses the park.

Argyll Forest Park Map 39 NS18/19
(OS56) Over 60,000 acres of rugged hills and lochs extending to Loch Goil and the Holy Loch near Dunoon.
Campsite: See Gazetteer under Ardgartan, Inverchapel, Inveruglas and Lochgoihead.

Galloway Forest Park Map 34 NX47
(OS76 and 77) 150,000 acres in the Galloway Highlands including Loch Trool and much of the Rhinns of Kells.
Campsite: See Gazetteer under Glen Trool and nearby Newton Stewart.

Glenmore Forest Park Map 44 NH90
(OS36) 12,500 acres in the Cairngorms, including some of Scotland's best ski-ing grounds, and Loch Morlich with its sandy shores and pine trees.
Campsite: For sites in vicinity see Gazetteer under Aviemore and Boat of Garten.

Queen Elizabeth Forest Park Map 39 NS49
(OS56) Over 40,000 acres of mountain, loch, moor and forest scenery. Over 60m of signposted walking routes.
Campsite: See Gazetteer under Gartmore and Balmaha.

Long-distance Footpaths

The following long distance paths have been approved, but except for the West Highland Way, it may be some years before they are fully implemented and established.

West Highland Way 98 miles (158 kilometres) Milngavie to Fort William. Officially opened October 1980.

Southern Upland Way 204 miles (328 kilometres)
Portpatrick to Cockburnspath.
Not open.

Speyside Way 609 miles (96 kilometres)
Glenmore (Cairngorms) to Spey Bay.
Not open.

Hire firm gazetteer

Listed below is a selection of firms hiring out camping and caravanning equipment. They are not necessarily recommended by the AA. The list is in alphabetical order under administrative regions, towns and the firms' names. Postal addresses may differ slightly as far as the regions are concerned.

KEY
- △ Tents/equipment
- ☎ Touring caravans
- 🚐 Motor caravans
- ── Luggage Trailers
- C Available for Continental use
- (NCC) National Caravan Council Member

CENTRAL
Stirling Borestone Caravans Ltd (NCC), 96 Glasgow Road, St Ninians. ☎Bannockburn 811787.

DUMFRIES & GALLOWAY
Dumfries Border Caravans, Annan Road. C ☎2917/3399.
Gretna The Braids Caravans, The Braids, Annan Road. ☎409 or Kirkpatrick Fleming 630.

STRATHCLYDE
Stoneyburn Knowepark Caravans (NCC), Main Street. ☎259.
Glasgow The Glen Caravan Co Glasgow Ltd (NCC), 1920 London Road, Shettlestow. ☎778 5212.
Greenock Black & Edgington Hire Ltd, Blacks Division, 70 East Hamilton Street. ☎41385.
Glasgow Halley Caravans Ltd (NCC), Glasgow Road, Milngavie. ☎956 1088.
Glasgow Millar, 11 Hayston Road, Kirkintilloch. ☎776 2807.
Rosneath UBC (Rosneath) Ltd, Nr Helensburgh, ☎Clynder 208 (Also collection depots in France).

TAYSIDE
Perth Gloagtrotter, Gartshore Buildings, Friarton Road. ☎33481.

Camping and Caravanning Sites

ABERCHIRDER Grampian Map 45 NJ65
▶**McRobert Park** *(NJ624527)* ☎Macduff 32861
[1] ❷ signposted
A small level grassy site, adjacent to playing fields just off the centre of this small town, 9 miles S of Banff on the A97. ½acre 15pitches May–Sep must book last arrival 21.00hrs last departure 09.00hrs 2🚐 3wc lit all night 4washbasins hc central hot water ⌐hc calor gas camping gaz paraffin ⛽ ⊖ ♪ pub 15△£2.10 or 15☎£1.80 or 15🚐£1 (awnings)

ABERDEEN Grampian Map 45 NJ90
▶▶**Hazelhead Caravan and Tent Site**
(NJ893057) Groats Rd, Apply to: Aberdeen City District Council, St Nicholas House, Aberdeen AB1 1XJ ☎23456 Ext 475 [2]❷△ signposted
A level grass site with mature trees, set in woodland countryside. 3m W of Aberdeen on A944. 6acres 165pitches 35static Apr–Sep must book Jun–Aug 5🚐 individual pitches 36wc lit all night 6cdp washbasins hc central hot water ⌐hc ⊙ (wash) (iron) calor gas ⊖ stables 🎬 cinema launderette 165☎£3.90 or 165🚐£3.90 or 165△£3.90 awnings

ABERFELDY Tayside Map 40 NN84
▶▶**Municipal Caravan Site** *(NN858495)*
Dunkeld Road, Apply to: Perth and Kinross District Council, Parks and Recreation Department, Area Office, Bank Street, Aberfeldy, Perthshire PH15 2AQ ☎20662
[1]❷△ signposted
A level grass site with a perimeter of mature trees, situated at the eastern end of the town and lying between main road and banks of the River Tay. Good views, from site, of surrounding tree-clad Perthshire hills. 3acres 110pitches 40static
Apr–Oct no bookings last departure 12.00hrs 4🚐 individual pitches △ 30wc lit all night 1cdp washbasins hc central hot water ⌐hc ⊙

children's playground ☎ ⊖ 🎬 cinema ♪ pub ⛽ 60☎£2.25 or 60🚐£2.25 50△£1–£1.50 (awnings)

ABERLOUR Grampian Map 44 NJ24
▶▶**Aberlour Gardens Caravan Park**
(NJ282432) ☎586 [2]❷△ signposted
Site within the beautiful setting of the Old Aberlour Estate with its walled gardens. 3acres 41pitches 17static
Apr–Oct last arrival 23.00hrs last departure 14.00hrs 4🚐 individual pitches ⓐ late arrivals enclosure 5wc lit all night 1cdp ⊙ 9washbasins hc 2central hot water ⌐hc ⊙ (wash, spin) dry iron cold storage children's playground calor gas camping gaz toilet fluid ☎ mobile⛽ ⊖ stables 🎬 ♪ launderette pub ⛽ 16☎£2.50 5🚐£2.50 20△£2.50 (awnings) ltr SA

ABOYNE Grampian Map 45 N059
▶▶▶**Aboyne Loch Caravan Park** *(NO538998)*
[3]❷△ signposted
Attractively sited caravan park set amidst woodland beside Aboyne Loch in scenic Deeside. no tents 8acres 65pitches 50static Apr–Sep no bookings late arrival 20.00hrs last departure 12.00hrs 10🚐 individual pitches 23wc lit all night 1cdp ⊙ 23washbasins hc 8⌐hc ⊙ supervised (wash, spin) (iron) children's playground calor gas ☎ ⊖ 🎬 ♪ 62☎£2.60–£3 3🚐£2.60–£3 (awnings)

ALFORD Grampian Map 45 NJ51
▶▶▶▶**Haughton House Caravan Site**
(NJ583169) ☎2107 [3]❷△ signposted
This impressive site with central mansion house dating back to 1800, is part of an estate set amongst woodland and beside the River Don. Approx ½m NW of Alford. Situated within country park. 10acres 70pitches 20static 26 Mar–4 Oct booking advisable July and Aug last arrival 18.00hrs last departure 10.00hrs 8🚐 individual pitches △ 15wc lit all night

154

1cdp ⌂ 20washbasin hc (10㋐hc) (5☉)
supervised (wash, spin, dry, iron) games room
TV children's playground calor gas camping
gaz toilet fluid ☎ ✉ putting green, bird aviary
and nature trails ⛐
➔ stables ⌨ launderette pub ⛐
40⛺£3.50 or 40🚐£3.50 30🚙£3.50 (awnings) ltr

ALVES Grampian Map 44 NJ16
▶▶▶▶**North Alves Caravan Park** (NJ122633)
c/o Moray Estates Development Co, Estates
Office, Forres, Morays IV36 OET ☎223
③⓿⚠ signposted
A pleasant, quiet, grassy site with views over
farmland. 7acres 45pitches 25static
Apr–Oct booking advisable Jul and Aug last
arrival 22.00hrs last departure 12.00hrs 6🚻
late arrivals enclosure 9wc lit all night 1cdp
18washbasins hc 6㋐hc 3☉ supervised (wash,
spin) iron games room CTV cold storage
children's playground calor gas toilet fluid ☎
off licence ⛐
45⛺£2.88–£3.45 or 45🚐£2.88–£3.45 or
45🚙£2.88–£3.45 awnings

AMISFIELD Dumfries & Galloway Map 35 NY08
▶▶**The Caravan Park** (NY002831) Glen Clova
☎710447
②⓿⚠ signposted
Adjacent to the busy A701, Moffat to Drumfries
road. A level grassy site bordered by trees and
on the edge of the village. 2acres 30pitches
Mar–Oct must book peak periods last arrival
22.00hrs 3🚻 8wc lit all night 1cdp ⌂
washbasins hc ㋐hc ☉ supervised ⊺ cold
storage calor gas
➔ stables ⌨ pub ⛐
30⛺£3.20 or 30🚐£3.20 or 30🚙£3.20 (awnings)
ltr

ANNAN Dumfries & Galloway Map 31 NY16
▶**Galabank** (NY193673) North St
①⓿⚠ signposted
Mainly level, grassy site situated on B722 off
A75 Dumfries–Carlisle road. 1acre 30pitches
Etr–Oct no bookings 1🚻 6wc lit all night
4washbasins hc (2㋐hc) 2☉
➔ stables ⌨ cinema ⌨ launderette ⛐
30⛺ or 30🚐 or 30🚙 (awnings) ltr

APPLECROSS Highland Map 42 NG74
▶**Applecross Campsite** (NG714443) ☎268
②⓿⚠
Level, grass site with trees and bushes, set
amidst mountains and moorlands, and adjacent
to sea and beach. Caravans should approach via
Shieldaig. Site is signposted from Applecross
village. 6acres 60pitches 6static
May–Sep rsApr & Oct no bookings 6🚻 12wc
16washbasins hc (8㋐hc) 2☉ (wash, dry) (cold
storage) children's playground calor gas
camping gaz ☎ ⛐
➔ launderette pub
60⛺ or 60🚐 or 60🚙 awnings ltr

ARDGARTAN Strathclyde Map 39 NN20

▶▶▶**Ardgartan Camp Site** (NN275030)
☎Arrochar 293
②⓿⚠ signposted
Level, grass and gravel site with trees, set in
hilly woodland country adjacent to sea, beach.
Loch Long and river. 3m SW of Arrochar on
A83. 10acres 200pitches
Apr–Sep Last arrival 20.00hrs 12🚻 individual
pitches ④ late arrivals enclosure 22wc lit all
night 2cdp washbasins hc central hot water
㋐hc ☉ supervised (dry) games room calor
gas camping gaz ☎ ⛐
➔ ⌨ ⛐
200⛺ or 200🚐 or 200🚙 awnings

ARDMAIR Highland Map 43 NH19
▶▶**Ardmair Point Campsite** (NH108983)
☎Ullapool 2054
②⓿⚠
Small, well-maintained grass site 3½m N of
Ullapool on A835, with unspoilt views from
Ardmair. 3½acres 45pitches 1static
Etr–Sep must book peak periods last arrival
23.00hrs last departure 12.00hrs 3🚻 individual
pitches 9wc lit all night 1cdp ⌂ washbasins
hc (㋐hc) ☉ (spin, dry) cold storage calor gas
camping gaz ☎ chandlery
➔ stables ⌨ launderette pub ⛐
45⛺£2.40 or 45🚐£2.40 or 45🚙£2.40 (awnings)
SA

AUCHENBOWIE Central Map 34 NS78
▶▶**Auchenbowie Caravan & Camping Site**
(NS795880) ☎Denny 822141
②⓿⚠ signposted
A partly level and sloping grassy site. ½m S of
M80 Snabhead Interchange on A872.
40pitches 20static
Apr–Oct no bookings 6🚻 lit all night 1cdp
washbasins hc ☉ children's playground
calor gas camping gaz paraffin ☎ mobile
shop
➔ cinema ⌨ launderette pub ⛐
40⛺£2.50 or 40🚐£2.50 or 40🚙£2.50 (awnings)
ltr

AUCHENMALG Dumfries & Galloway
Map 30 NX25
▶▶▶**Cock Inn Caravan Park** (NX238518)
☎227
②⓿⚠ signposted
Part level, part sloping, grass site set in
meadowland, close to sea, beach and main
road; A747 Glenluce to Port William road.
Overlooks Luce Bay. 3½acres 70pitches
50static
mid May–Aug rsMar–mid May & Sep–Oct
must book public hols & Jul–Aug last arrival
23.00hrs last departure 11.00hrs 4🚻 individual
pitches wc lit all night 2cdp ⌂ washbasins hc
(6㋐hc) 2☉ (wash) (dry, iron) (cold storage)
calor gas camping gaz toilet fluid ☎ ⛐
➔ ⌨ launderette pub
70⛺£2.75 or 70🚐£2.75 5🚙£2.75 (awnings)

AVIEMORE Highland Map 44 NH81

Cock Inn Caravan Park Auchenmalg

AUCHENMALG, NEWTON STEWART, Wigtownshire. "Get Away from it all", crowds, traffic noise, peaceful, select,
caravan park, situated on Luce Bay, on A747, coastal road between Glenluce and Port William. Adjacent pleasant little beach
and small country Inn. Panoramic views across Luce Bay to the Mull of Galloway and Isle of Man. Sailing, bathing, sea
angling. (Fishing, golf and pony trekking nearby.)
Modern toilet block with showers and laundry room. Shop on site.
Holiday Caravans for hire. TOURERS WELCOME.
SAE for brochure or telephone Auchenmalg 227.

Aviemore contd–Balloch — Camping and caravanning sites

▶▶▶**Aviemore Centre Caravan Park**
(NH894120) ☎810751
①②⚠ signposted
Set amongst pine trees, adjacent to the Aviemore Centre where caravanners can make full use of the facilities. No tents, no motorcycles, no single sex groups 6acres 90pitches
Dec–Oct must book Xmas–Etr & Jul–Aug last arrival 18.00hrs last departure 12.00hrs 8⇔ individual pitches 18wc lit all night 1cdp washbasins hc (fihc) ☉ (wash, spin, dry, iron) 🞋 licensed club/bar children's playground calor gas camping gaz toilet fluid cafe restaurant ☎ 🛒
➔ stables 🄼 cinema ♫ launderette pub
90⇔£2.90 or 90⇌£2.90 (awnings)

▶▶▶**Dalraddy Caravan Park** (NH859083)
☎810330
①②⚠ signposted
A well-secluded site situated off the A9, 4m S of Aviemore, set amidst heather and young birch trees, looking towards the Cairngorm mountains. 25acres 218pitches 52static Dec–Oct must book last arrival 18.00hrs last departure 12.00hrs 22⇔ individual pitches caravans only ⓐ 42wc lit all night 1cdp 🞋 washbasins hc (fihc) ☉ supervised (wash, spin, dry) cold storage children's playground calor gas camping gaz paraffin toilet fluid ☎ hair dryer 🛒
➔ 🄼 ♫ pub
70⇔£2.20 or 70⇌£2.20 150⚐£2 awnings

▶▶▶**Speyside Caravan Park** (NH 895115)
☎810236
①❶⚠ signposted
Level, grass and gravel site with trees and bushes, set in hilly country and woodland, adjacent to River Spey. Immediately S of Aviemore close to junction of A9 and A951. No firearms & no motorcycles 3acres 44pitches 60static
Etr & Jul–Aug rsmid Dec–Mar & Sep–Oct must book Apr & Jul–Aug last arrival 19.00hrs last departure 12.00hrs 8⇔ individual pitches late arrivals enclosure 21wc lit all night 1cdp 🞋 22washbasins hc 8fihc 6☉ (wash, spin, dry, iron) calor gas toilet fluid ☎ 🛒 bicycle hire, fishing, battery charger
➔ cinema ♫ launderette
44⇔£2.20–£3.20 or 44⇌£2.20–3.20 or 44⚐£2.20–£3.20 (awnings) ltr SA

▶▶**Glen More Forest Park** (NH975097)
☎Cairngorm 271
①❶⚠ signposted
Level, grass and gravel site with young trees and bushes set in mountainous moorland and woodland, adjacent to Loch Morlich. From Aviemore follow A951 for 7m. 14acres 221pitches
All year no bookings last departure 12.00hrs 12⇔ individual pitches 32wc lit all night 2cdp washbasins hc fihc ☉ (wash) (dry) private beach calor gas camping gaz toilet fluid cafe ☎ 🛒
➔ 🄼 ♫ launderette
221⇔£2.50–£3.50 or 221⇌£2.50–£3.50 or 221⚐£2.50–£3.50 awnings

AYR Strathclyde Map 34 NS32
▶▶▶**Trax Campsite** (NS348224) Ayr Racecourse, Whitletts Rd
①❶⚠ signposted
A level grassy site near sea. Off A719 Mauchline road. 12acres 250pitches
8–13 Apr, 28 May–11 Sep (except 8–10 Jul, 16–20 Jul & 2–4 Aug) no bookings last arrival 22.30hrs last departure 15.00hrs 10⇔ individual pitches 49wc lit all night 2cdp 33washbasins hc 6central hot water 11fihc 7☉ supervised (wash, spin) TV ☎ free access to racing for campers 28, 29 May & 18 & 19 Jun
➔ stables 🄼 cinema ♫ launderette pub 🛒
250⇔£2.80–£3.50 or 250⇌£2.80–£3.50 or 250⚐£2.80–£3.50 awnings

BALLATER Grampian Map 41 NO39
▶▶**Ballater Caravan & Camping Site**
(NO371955) c/o Leisure & Recreation Officer, Kincardine & Deeside District Council, Viewmount, Stonehaven, Kincardineshire
☎Stonehaven 62001 ext 21
①❶⚠ signposted
A level, grassy site near the river, set in hilly country with nearby woodland and moorland. No awnings 3acres 40pitches 71static
5 Apr–Oct bookings advisable wknds last arrival 20.00hrs last departure 10.00hrs 4⇔ ⓐ 18wc lit all night 1cdp 28washbasins hc (18fihc) 6☉ (wash, spin, dry, iron) games room children's playground ☎ 🛒
➔ stables 🄼 cinema ♫ launderette pub
40⇔£2.50 or 40⇌£2.50 or 40⚐£2.50

BALLOCH Strathclyde Map 39 NS38
▶▶**Tullichewan Caravan Park** (NS381816)
Old Luss Rd ☎Alexandria 59475
①❶⚠ signposted
A quiet and pleasant rural site near Loch Lomond, surrounded by woodland and hills. Close to the A82. No single sex groups 12acres 200pitches 10static
Apr–20 Oct must book mid Jul–mid Aug last arrival 22.30hrs last departure 12.00hrs 7⇔ individual pitches ⓐ late arrivals enclosure 35wc lit all night 3cdp 🞋 washbasins hc fihc

---

AVIEMORE
SPEYSIDE CARAVAN PARK
AND CHALETS

Ideally situated in a sheltered position within half a mile of the Aviemore Centre and main line railway station, and nine miles from the Cairngorm ski slopes. Self-catering chalets and static caravans available for hire throughout the year. Touring caravans and motor caravans welcome.

For full details apply to the resident owners:
**Mr and Mrs H M D McWilliam, Craigellachie House,
AVIEMORE, PH 22 1PX Tel: 0479 810236**

☺ (wash) spin (dry, iron) (games room) CTV (cold storage) children's playground calor gas camping gaz toilet fluid ☎ ⓘ
↩ stables 🅿 ⚠ ♪ launderette pub
170⇔£3.35–£4.30 or 170⇐£3.35–£4.30 30⇗£3.35–£4.30 (awnings) ltr

BALMACARA Highland Map 42 NG82
▶▶**Reraig Caravan Site** (NG815272) ☏285
②●⚠ signposted
Set on level, grassy ground surrounded by trees, the site looks S towards Loch Alsh and Skye. 2½acres 40pitches
May–Sep rsApr bookings advisable Jul & Aug last arrival 22.00hrs last departure 12.00hrs 3⇐ individual pitches 7wc lit all night 1cdp 8washbasins hc (ⓗhc) ☺ supervised cold storage children's playground
↩ ♪ pub ⓘ
40⇔£2 or 40⇐£2 or 40⇗£2 (awnings)

BALMAHA Central Map 39 NS49
▶▶**Cashell Caravan & Camping Site** (NS396939) ☏Drymen 60255
②●⚠ signposted
An attractive and well-wooded site, lying on the eastern shores of Loch Lomond within the Queen Elizabeth Forest Park, offering seclusion to campers and splendid views over the loch. 12acres 200pitches
Apr–Sep last arrival 20.00hrs last departure 12.00hrs 6⇐ individual pitches late arrivals enclosure 24wc lit all night 2cdp 31washbasins hc 10ⓗhc 7☺ supervised (wash, spin) private beach calor gas camping gaz ☎ ⓘ
↩ stables ⚠ ♪ pub
200⇔£2–£2.80 or 200⇐£2–£2.80 or 200⇗£2–£2.80 awnings

BALMINNOCH Dumfries & Galloway Map 30 NX26
▶▶▶**Three Lochs Caravan Park** (NX272655) ☏Kirkcowan 304
③●⚠ signposted
Level, grass and sand site with trees and bushes set in meadowland and woodland with access to river and lake. 5m N of Kirkcowan off A75. 15acres 80pitches 120static
Etr–1st Wk Oct must book peak periods last arrival 21.00hrs last departure 17.00hrs 12⇐ 18wc lit all night 2cdp 🅿 washbasins hc (ⓗhc) ☺ supervised (wash) (dry, iron) games room CTV (cold storage) children's playground calor gas camping gaz ☎ off licence ⓘ
↩
80⇔£3.50 or 80⇐£3.50 or 80⇗£3.50 awnings ltr

BANFF Grampian Map 45 NJ66
▶▶▶**Banff Links Caravan Site** (NJ672646)
Apply to: Banff & Buchan District Council, Director of Leisure & Recreation, 1 Church St, Macduff, Banffshire AB4 1UF ☏Macduff 32861
②●⚠ signposted
Mainly static site set right on sea front, bordered by fine beach and with golf links to one side. Situated off A98. 1m W of Banff. 5acres 37pitches 100static
May–Sep must book last arrival 21.00hrs last departure 9.00hrs 5⇐ 28wc lit all night washbasins hc (central hot water) (ⓗhc) ☺ supervised (wash, spin, dry) licensed club/bar children's playground calor gas camping gaz paraffin toilet fluid cafe restaurant ☎ mobile shop ⓘ
↩ 🅿 ⚠ ♪ launderette pub

27⇔£2.30 or 27⇐£1.80 10⇗£1.20 (awnings)

BARCALDINE Strathclyde Map 39 NM94
▶▶**Barcaldine Garden Caravan Park** (NM955415) ☏Ledaig 348
②●⚠ signposted
Mainly level grass site with young trees and bushes. Set in mountainous woodland country with a lake nearby. 4acres 75pitches
Jun–Oct rsApr & May booking advisable peak periods last arrival 22.00hrs last departure 12.00hrs 4⇐ late arrivals enclosure 17wc lit all night 1cdp ☎ 16washbasins hc (4ⓗhc) ☺ 1dry (1 iron) (cold storage) calor gas toilet fluid ☎ ⓘ private beach, boats for hire & battery charging ⓘ
↩ ⚠ ♪
70⇔ 5⇐ (awnings)

BEAULY Highland Map 43 NH54
▶▶▶**Cruivend Camping & Caravan Site** (NH516446) ☏2367
②●⚠ signposted
Level, grassy site situated off A9 and 1m S of Beauly. 2acres 30pitches 4static
Apr–Sep must book Jul & Aug last arrival 23.00hrs last departure 12.00hrs 2⇐ individual pitches 8wc lit all night 1cdp 7washbasins hc, central hot water) (ⓗhc) ☺ supervised cold storage children's playground calor gas camping gaz paraffin ☎ ⓘ
↩ stables 🅿 ♪ pub
10⇔£2.10 10⇐£2.10 10⇗£2.10 (awnings) ltr
▶▶**Lovat Bridge Caravan & Camp Site** (NH517451) ☏2374
②●⚠ signposted
Mainly level, grass site with trees; direct access to river and main road. 7acres 75pitches 10static
16 Mar–16 Oct booking advisable last arrival 23.00hrs last departure 12.00hrs 6⇐ ⓐ last arrivals enclosure 16wc lit all night 1cdp washbasins hc central hot water (ⓗhc) ☺ supervised (cold storage) children's playground calor gas toilet fluid ☎
↩ stables 🅿 ⚠ ♪ pub ⓘ
75⇔£2.50–£3.10 or 75⇐£2.50–£3.10 or 75⇗£2.50–£3.10 awnings

BENDERLOCH Strathclyde Map 39 NM93
▶▶**Tralee Bay Caravan Park** (NM896393) ☏Ledaig 255
②●⚠ signposted
Attractive site on level ground, sloping gently towards the sea. Outstanding views over Ardmuckmish Bay, towards Oban. A 16th-century castle lies N of the site on the same peninsula. 8acres 70pitches 96static
Apr–Oct no bookings last arrival 19.00hrs last departure 12.00hrs 7⇐ individual pitches ⓐ no cars by tents 4wc lit all night 1cdp washbasins hc (ⓗhc) ☺ supervised wash, spin, dry, iron cold storage private beach calor gas camping gaz toilet fluid restaurant ☎ ⊞ ⓘ stables ⚠ ♪ pub
20⇔£2.60 10⇐£2.20 40⇗£2.60 (awnings) SA

BIRNAM Tayside Map 40 NO04
▶▶▶**Erigmore House Caravan Park** (NO036416) ☏Dunkeld 236
②●⚠ signposted
A predominantly touring site in the tree-studded grounds of 18th-century Erigmore House which offers a wide variety of unusual trees including Japanese maple and cherry. Site well-secluded from the main road and a considerable degree of privacy can be found. Situated on B898 just off

Birnam contd – **Brighouse Bay** — Camping and caravanning sites

A9 through Birnam village. 13acres 164pitches 12static
Apr–early Oct last arrival 21.00hrs last departure 12.00hrs 15↔ individual pitches Ⓐ 36wc lit all night 1cdp washbasins hc central hot water (⇌hc) ladies only (🛁hc) supervised (wash, spin, iron) games room licensed club/bar children's playground calor gas camping gaz toilet fluid restaurant ☎ ⊞ 🛒
↪ stables 🅿 🔺 🅹 launderette pub
164🚐 or 164🚙 20⛺ (awnings)

BLAIR ATHOLL Tayside Map 40 NN86
▶▶▶ **Blair Castle Caravan Site** (NN874656)
☎263
③❶⚠ signposted
This is a predominantly touring site set in tree-studded land within the grounds of Blair Castle and bordered on one side by the River Tilt. Although situated near to the main road there is ample screening by trees to provide seclusion. 32acres 330pitches 82static
Apr–Oct must book Jul & Aug last arrival 22.00hrs last departure 12.00hrs 30↔ individual pitches Ⓐ 99wc lit all night 5cdp 🚰 washbasins hc 🛁hc ⊙ supervised (wash, spin, dry, iron) children's playground calor gas camping gaz toilet fluid ☎ 🛒
↪ stables 🅿 🅹 launderette pub
197🚐£3 34🚙£3 100⛺£3 (awnings)

▶▶▶ **River Tilt Caravan Site** (NN875653)
☎333
①❶⚠ signposted
Level, grass site with trees and bushes set in hilly woodland country with access to River Garry. 7m N of Pitlochry on A9. 4acres 60pitches 40static
All year no bookings last arrival 20.00hrs last departure 12.00hrs 15↔ 20wc lit all night 1cdp 🚰 washbasins hc central hot water 🛁hc ⊙ warden wash spin dry iron games room TV cold storage calor gas camping gaz toilet fluid cafe restaurant ☎ ⊞ licensed club fishing & shooting 🛒
↪ stables 🅿 🔺 launderette pub
50🚐 or 50🚙 10⛺ (awnings)

BLAIRLOGIE Central Map 40 NS89
▶▶ **Witches Craig Farm Caravan & Camping Park** (NS823967) ☎Stirling 4947
②❶⚠
A level grassy site on the main road with tree studded hills to the rear. 5acres 60pitches 8static
Apr–Oct no bookings last arrival 22.00hrs last departure 13.00hrs 2↔ 5wc lit all night 1cdp washbasins hc 🛁hc ⊙ supervised (wash, spin, dry) cold storage children's playground calor gas camping gaz paraffin toilet fluid ☎ 🛒
↪ stables 🅿 🔺 cinema 🅹 launderette pub
30🚐£3 15🚙£2.75 15⛺£3 (awnings)

BLAIRMORE Strathclyde Map 33 NS18
▶▶ **Gairletter Caravan Park** (NS193844)
☎Ardentinny 208
③❶⚠
On the W shore of Loch Long, south of Ardentinny, this site gives outstanding views of mountains and loch. Off A815 from Glasgow. No tents, no motorcycles, no single sex groups 3½acres 6pitches
Apr–Oct must book last arrival mdnt last departure 11.30am 4↔ individual pitches no cars by caravans 8wc 1cdp washbasins hc central hot water (🛁hc) ⊙ supervised (wash,

spin, dry, iron) cold storage calor gas ☎
↪ stables 🅿 🔺 🅹 pub
6🚐£3 or 6🚙£3

BOAT OF GARTEN Highland Map 44 NH91
▶▶▶ **Boat of Garten Camping & Caravanning Park** (NH939191) ☎652
②❶⚠ signposted
Level, grass site with young trees and bushes set in mountainous woodland in the village itself, near the River Spey and Loch Garten. Off A95. 3½acres 60pitches 67static
Closed Nov must book New Year, Whit & Jul–Aug last departure 12.00hrs 7↔ individual pitches ⓐ late arrivals enclosure 24wc lit all night 1cdp 🚰 washbasins hc (🛁hc) ⊙ (wash) (dry, iron) games room CTV (cold storage) children's playground calor gas camping gaz paraffin toilet fluid ☎ ⊞ hair dryers, bicycle hire 🛒
↪ stables 🅿 🔺 cinema 🅹 pub
30🚐£2.80 or 30🚙£2.80 30⛺£2.80 awnings ltr

BOTHWELL Strathclyde Map 34 NS75
▶▶▶ **Strathclyde Park Caravan Site** (NS715585) Bothwellhaugh Rd
☎Motherwell 66195
②❶⚠ signposted
A mainly level grass site with saplings and bushes situated amidst woodland and meadowland. Close to the M74 with direct access through the park to junction 5. 20acres 150pitches
All year no bookings last arrival 22.30hrs last departure 12.00hrs ↔ individual pitches ⓐ late arrivals enclosure 24wc lit all night 4cdp washbasins hc central hot water 🛁hc ⊙ supervised (wash, spin) 🚿 children's playground calor gas camping gaz ☎ 🛒
↪ stables 🅿 🔺 cinema 🅹 launderette pub
100🚐£4 or 100🚙£4 50⛺£3.50 (awnings)

BRIDGE OF ALLAN Central Map 40 NS79
▶ **Allanwater Caravan Site** (NS787981)
Blairforkie Dr ☎832254
②❶⚠
This is a secluded and well-maintained static and touring site set on level grass on the banks of the River Allan. It is surrounded by wooded hills. The site is positioned north of the small town and access is good. 5acres 50pitches 40static
Apr–Sep no bookings last departure 14.00hrs 6↔ 10wc lit all night washbasins hc (🛁hc) ⊙ (wash, dry) iron calor gas ☎ 🛒
↪ stables 🅿 cinema 🅹 launderette pub
50🚐 or 50🚙 no awnings

BRIDGE OF CALLY Tayside Map 40 NO15
▶ **Middleton Farm Caravan & Camping Site** (NO135585) ☎Blacklunans 226
①❶⚠
A level site in hilly and mountainous country near river. 11m N of Blairgowrie on A93. 30static
Etr–Oct 6↔ 6wc lit all night washbasins hc ⊙
↪ stables 🅹
🚐🚙⛺ (awnings)

BRIGHOUSE BAY Dumfries & Galloway Map 30 NX64
▶▶▶ **Brighouse Bay Holiday Park** (NX628458)
☎Borgue 267
③❶⚠ signposted
Part level, part sloping grass site with mature trees and bushes set in downland, wood and meadow country adjacent to sea and wide

sandy beach. 12acres 190pitches 120static Apr–Oct booking advisable peak periods last arrival 21.30hrs last departure 11.30hrs 10⚡ individual pitches ⚠ late arrivals enclosure 24wc lit all night 1cdp ⚡ 32washbasins hc (2⚡hc) 8🚿hc 8⊙ supervised (wash, spin, dry, iron) (cold storage) children's playground calor gas camping gaz paraffin toilet fluid ☎ ⚡ solarium, bicycles & boats for hire, private slipway ⚡
⚡ stables ⚡ ♪ launderette pub 120⚡£3.50 or 120⚡£3.50 70⚡£3.50 (awnings) SA

BRODIE Grampian Map 44 NH95
▶▶▶**Old Mill Inn** (NH980570) ☎244
②❸▲ signposted
Level, grassy site, bordered by trees, with a small river on W side. Well-screened from main road. 3acres 40pitches 60static
Apr–Oct last arrival 22.30hrs last departure 12.00hrs 4⚡ late arrivals enclosure 21wc lit all night 2cdp washbasins hc 🚿hc ⊙ supervised licensed club/bar children's playground calor gas camping gaz toilet fluid cafe restaurant ☎ ⚡
⚡ ♪ pub
40⚡£2–£3.25 or 40⚡£2–£3.25 or 40⚡£2–£3.25 (awnings)

BRORA Highland Map 47 NC90
▶**Riverside Caravan Site** (NC888035)
Stonehouse Doll ☎353
②❸▲ signposted
Part level, part sloping grass site with meadowland adjacent to River Brora. Turn left at red-roofed cottage on right side of road 4m N of Goldspie and 1m S of Brora. 2acres 21pitches May–Oct last arrival 22.30hrs last departure 10.30hrs 2⚡ late arrivals enclosure 4wc lit all night 1cdp washbasins hc central hot water (🚿hc) ⊙ children's playground calor gas
⚡ ⚡ ♪ pub ⚡
6⚡£1.20 6⚡£1.10 9⚡£ awnings ltr

BUCKIE Grampian Map 44 NJ46
▶**Strathlene Caravan Site** (NJ446668)
①❸▲ signposted
Level, stony and grassy site situated 2m from town on A942. 57pitches 40static
9 Apr–Sep 4⚡ individual pitches ⚠ 16wc lit all night 3cdp washbasins hc 🚿hc ⊙ (wash, dry) ⚡ ⚡
⚡ ⚡ ♪ launderette pub
45⚡ or 45⚡ 12⚡ rates on application ltr

CAIRN RYAN Dumfries & Galloway Map 30 NX06
▶▶▶**Cairn Ryan Caravan & Chalet Park** (NX075673) ☎231
①❸▲ signposted
Neatly laid-out site, standing on sloping ground exposed to Loch Ryan. No tents 20pitches 80static
Etr–Oct must book Jul & Aug last arrival 22.00hrs last departure 12.00hrs 5⚡ individual pitches 16wc lit all night 1cdp washbasins hc 🚿hc ⊙ (wash, spin) (iron) ⚡ games room CTV licensed club/bar children's playground calor gas cafe ☎ ⚡
⚡ stables ♪
20⚡£3.50–£5 or 20⚡£3.50–£5 awnings

CALLANDER Central Map 40 NN60
▶▶▶**Callander Holiday Park** (NN615074)
Invertrossachs Rd ☎30265
③❸▲ signposted
This is an attractive, terraced site situated in a tree-studded estate to the NW of Callander with splendid views over the surrounding countryside. The site is well laid out with mature trees and shrubs providing screening and seclusion. No tents 20acres 54pitches 110static
15 Mar–Oct must book 48hrs in advance last arrival 22.00hrs last departure 10.30hrs 8⚡ individual pitches late arrivals enclosure 20wc lit all night 2cdp washbasins hc central hot water (🚿hc) ⊙ supervised (wash) (dry) iron cold storage children's playground calor gas camping gaz ☎ free fishing mobile⚡
⚡ ⚡ ▲ ♪ launderette pub ⚡
54⚡£3.10 or 54⚡£3.10 awnings ltr
▶▶▶**Gart Estate Caravan Park** (NN643070)
The Gart ☎30002
②❸▲
A well-developed, mainly level grass site lying back from main road and screened by shrubs and trees. 1m E of Callander on A84. No tents 5acres 75pitches 70static
Apr–15 Oct must book Etr, Whit, Jul & Aug last departure 12.00hrs 8⚡ individual pitches late arrivals enclosure 15wc lit all night 3cdp washbasins hc 🚿hc ⊙ (wash, spin, dry, iron) cold storage children's playground calor gas toilet fluid ☎ ⚡
⚡ ♪ launderette pub
75⚡fr£2.25 or 75⚡fr£2.25 (awnir.gs) ltr

CAMUSTIANAVAIG Isle of Skye, Highland Map 42 NG53
▶**Braes Campsite** (NG501390)
①❸▲
Part level, part sloping, grass and gravel site with mature trees, set in mountainous, hilly country, with access to sea, beach and loch. 4½m SE of Portree on B883. No tents 1¼acres 10pitches 6static
15 Jun–15 Sep no bookings last arrival mdnt last departure 12.00hrs 3⚡ individual pitches 4wc lit all night washbasins hc (🚿hc) ⊙
⚡ ♪
10⚡£1.50 or 10⚡£1.40 awnings

CARGILL Tayside Map 40 NO13
▶▶**Beech Hedge Restaurant & Caravan Park** (NO165374) ☎Meikleour 249
②❸▲ signposted
Part level, part sloping grass and gravel site, set in hilly woodland area, close to the River Tay and A93 Perth–Blairgowrie road. ½acre 12pitches 8static

Callander Holiday Park
Invertrossachs Road, Callander, Perthshire, Scotland.
Tel. Callander 30265 (STD 0877)
Telephone Bookings accepted 48hrs before your arrival

Cargill contd – Connel — Camping and caravanning sites

Mar–Oct must book peak periods last arrival 22.00hrs last departure 13.00hrs 2⚘ individual pitches 6wc 1cdp ⊞ washbasins hc ⋔hc ☉ supervised (wash, spin, dry, iron) children's playground calor gas camping gaz cafe restaurant ☎ ♨
↔ ♪ pub
12🚐fr£1.50 or 12🚙fr£1.50 or 12⚘fr£1.50 (awnings)

CARRADALE Strathclyde Map 33 NR83
▶▶**Carradale Bay Caravan Site** (NR815385)
The Steading ☎665
②❶△
Rolling grass site near beach. Views over Kilbrannan Sound to Isle of Arran. Approach from north is via Tarbert. Leave Tarbert by A83 Campbeltown road; within 5m turn onto B8001, then B842 Carradale road. This is a 20-mile single track road with passing places. In Carradale take road to the pier, site is ½m distant. 9acres 60pitches
Whit–Sep rsEtr booking advisable last departure 12.00hrs 5⚘ individual pitches ☉ late arrivals enclosure 16wc lit all night 2cdp washbasins hc ⋔hc ☉ supervised spin dry iron children's playground calor gas
↔ stables 🏇 △ ♪ pub 🍴
50🚐£4 or 50🚙£4 10⚘£4 (awnings) ltr

CASTLE DOUGLAS Dumfries & Galloway Map 30 NX76
▶▶**Lochside Park** (NX764619) Apply to: Stewartry District Council, Environmental Health Dept; Dunmuir Rd, Castle Douglas, Kirkcudbrightshire ☎2949
②❶△ signposted
Municipal touring site incorporating park with recreational facilities, situated on southern edge of town in attractive setting adjacent to Carlingwark Loch. The site has two types of standings, asphalted areas with marked pitches and more informal grassed areas. Site is located SW of the town, 150yds off main A75 from Dumfries–Castle Douglas. 5¼acres 161pitches Etr–mid Oct last departure 12.00hrs 7⚘ individual pitches ☉ 26wc lit all night 3cdp 36washbasins hc 16⋔hc 12☉ (wash) (iron) (cold storage) ☎ putting green, boats for hire
↔ stables 🏇 △ cinema ♪ pub 🍴
108🚐£3.50 or 108🚙£3.50 53⚘£3.50 awnings ltr

CASTLE SWEEN Strathclyde Map 33 NR77
▶**Castle Sween Bay Holidays** (NR770858)
②❶△ signposted
Predominantly static site, laid out in terraces on a hillside above Loch Sween. 5acres 40pitches 240static
Mar–Oct no bookings last departure 12.00hrs 4⚘ 12wc lit all night 2cdp (⋔hc) ☉ supervised (wash, spin) iron licensed club/bar children's playground private beach calor gas camping gaz cafe restaurant ☎ bicycle hire, windsurf boards, fishing licences ♨
↔ ♪ launderette pub
20🚐£3 or 20🚙£3 20⚘£1.50 (awnings) ltr

COCKBURNSPATH Borders Map 35 NT77
▶▶**Chesterfield Caravan Site** (NT772701)
Neuk Farm ☎226
②❶△ signposted
Secluded grass site set in Border country, screened by gorse-covered hills. It is about ½m from the village and within 3m of the sea. 40pitches 40static
Apr–Sep rsOct booking advisable Jul & Aug last arrival 21.00hrs last departure 12.00hrs 4⚘ individual pitches ☉ 17wc lit all night 1cdp washbasins hc ⋔hc ☉ supervised cold storage children's playground calor gas
↔ stables ♪ pub ♨
40🚐£2.50 or 40🚙£2.50 or 40⚘£2.50 (awnings) SA

COLDINGHAM Borders Map 36 NT96
▶▶*Scoutscroft Camping Site* (NT908661)
☎338
①❶△ signposted
Part level, part sloping grass site with saplings and bushes. Set in border country adjacent to sea and beach. 3m E of A1 at Reston.
🎪 3acres 50pitches 110static
Jul & Aug rsMar–Jun & Sep–Oct must book Jul & Aug last departure 12.00hrs 5⚘ ☉ late arrivals enclosure 30wc lit all night 1cdp 30washbasins hc central hot water 6⋔hc 2☉ supervised wash, spin, dry, iron games room TV cold storage licensed club/bar calor gas camping gaz toilet fluid cafe restaurant ☎ sauna ♨
↔ 🎬 cinema ♪ launderette pub
50🚐 or 50🚙 or 50⚘ awnings

COLL SANDS Lewis, Western Isles Map 48 NB43
▶*Broad Bay Caravan Site* (NB462383)
☎Stornoway 2053
①❶△ signposted
A sandy site near the beach and sea, situated on the coast road between Tong and Upper Coll.
½acre 20pitches 12static
Apr–Oct must book 2⚘ ☉ wc lit all night 1cdp washbasins hc (⋔hc) ☉ calor gas ☎ ⊞ private beach ♨
↔ ♪
6🚐 6🚙 10⚘ awnings ltr

COMRIE Tayside Map 40 NN72
▶▶▶**Twenty Shilling Wood Caravan Site** (NN763221) ☎411
②❶△ signposted
This secluded site of level pitches on gravel bases is set in tree-studded hill country lying to the west of the picturesque village, off A85. no tents, no motorcycles, no single sex groups 4acres 30pitches 29static
2 Apr–4 Oct last arrival 22.30hrs last departure 15.00hrs 7⚘ 14wc lit all night 1cdp 16washbasins hc (4⋔hc) 3☉ supervised wash, spin (dry, iron) games room cold storage calor gas toilet fluid ☎ ♨
↔ ♪ launderette pub
30🚐£3.40 or 30🚙£3.40 (awnings)
▶▶*West Lodge Caravan Site* (NN785225)
Lawers ☎354
②❶△ signposted
A sloping, grass site set amidst wooded hillside in rolling, Perthshire scenery. The site is adjacent to main road but screened by wall and hedge. 🎪 ½acre 20pitches 40static
Apr–Oct booking advisable peak periods last arrival 21.00hrs last departure 12.00hrs 7⚘ 13wc lit all night 1cdp ⊞ washbasins hc (⋔hc) ☉ supervised (wash, spin) calor gas camping gaz
↔ ♪ ♨
20🚐£3 or 20🚙£2.50 or 20⚘£2.50 (awnings)

CONNEL Strathclyde Map 39 NM93
▶▶*North Ledaig Caravan Site* (NM907863)
②❶△
Spacious touring site, adjacent to main road and

160

Camping and caravanning sites — Corpach–Crocketford

offering fine views out across the bay. 4acres 60pitches
Etr–Sep must book peak periods last arrival 20.00hrs last departure 12.00hrs 5♨ late arrivals enclosure 12wc lit all night 3cdp washbasins hc (central hot water, ♨hc) ☉ supervised dry calor gas camping gaz paraffin toilet fluid cafe ☎ ⊞ private beach ⚓
60➡ (awnings)

CORPACH Highland Map 39 NN07
▶▶▶▶**Linnhe Caravan Park** (NN074771) ☎376
③●△ signposted
Situated 1m W of Corpach on A830, overlooking Loch Eil, with Ben Nevis to the E and mountains of Sunart to the W. Although site is predominantly static, caravans are accommodated on landscaped terracing with uninterrupted views of surrounding countryside.
no tents 5acres 90pitches 100static
Etr–Sep no bookings last departure 14.00hrs 8♨ individual pitches 20wc lit all night 1cdp □ (washbasins hc) (♨hc ☉) supervised (spin, dry, iron) children's playground private beach calor gas ☎ slipway
⊖▶ △ ♪ launderette ⚓
90➡£2.50–£3 or 90➡£2.50–£3 (awnings)

COYLTON Strathclyde Map 34 NS41
▶▶▶▶**Sundrum Castle Holiday Park** (NS405208) ☎Ayr 61464
③●△ signposted
Set in beautiful Burn's country just a 10 minute drive from the centre of the county town of Ayr.
no single sex groups 5acres 75pitches 181static
Etr–Sep rsMar–Etr & Oct booking advisable Public Hols last arrival 21.00hrs last departure 14.00hrs ♨ 15wc lit all night 1cdp washbasins hc (♨hc ☉) supervised (wash) (dry, iron) (▣) games room (licensed club/bar) children's playground calor gas toilet fluid restaurant ☎ ⚓
⊖▶ stables
52➡£2.75–£3.50 or 52➡£2.30–£2.75 25➡£3.20–£4 (awnings) ltr

CRAIL Fife Map 41 NO60
▶▶**Balcomie Links Caravan Park** (NO605084) Balcomie Rd ☎383
①●△
Slightly sloping, grass site with young trees and bushes, set in downland and meadowland adjacent to sea and sandy beach – within the urban area. Junction of A917 and A918. no awnings, no tents ½acre 7pitches 68static
Apr–Sep no bookings last arrival 22.00hrs last departure 12.00hrs 5♨ individual pitches 16wc lit all night washbasins hc (♨hc) ☉ (wash) spin (dry) iron calor gas camping gaz cafe ☎ ⚓
⊖▶ 🛢 △ ♪ launderette pub
7➡ or 7➡

▶▶**Sauchope Caravan Site** (NO623078) Apply to: North East Fife District Council, Dept of Recreation, County Buildings, Cupar, Fife
☎Cupar 53722 or 54941
①●△
This is a sloping grassy site comprising a large stretch of land bordering rocky foreshore on Fife coast. Secluded but somewhat exposed to sea breezes, with panoramic views over the Fife estuary, to the island of May, Bass Rock and Berwick Law. 12acres 15pitches 150static
24 Mar–5 Oct last arrival 20.00hrs last departure 20.00hrs 14♨ individual pitches 30wc lit all night 1cdp 29washbasins hc 16♨hc 4☉ (wash) ☎ ⚓
⊖▶ 🛢 △ ♪ launderette pub
15➡£3 or 15➡£3 or 15➡£1.50–£3 (awnings)

CREETOWN Dumfries & Galloway Map 30 NX45
▶▶▶**Cassencarie Holiday Park** (NX475576) ☎264
②●△ signposted
A mainly level, grassy site with trees and bushes set in meadowland and woodland just off A75, ½m from Creetown. 3½acres 60pitches 9static
Apr–Sep booking advisable Jul & Aug last departure 12.00hrs 4♨ late arrivals enclosure 12wc lit all night 1cdp 16washbasins hc central hot water (4♨hc) 2☉ supervised iron games room TV (cold storage) children's playground calor gas camping gaz toilet fluid slipway for boats, table tennis ⚓
⊖▶ ♪ pub
60➡£2.50 or 60➡£2.50 or 60➡£2.50 (awnings) SA

CRIEFF Tayside Map 40 NN82
▶▶▶**Crieff Holiday Village** (NN857225) Turret Bank ☎3513
③●△ signposted
Level, gravel site with trees and bushes set in woodland within the urban area and with access to river. 1m W of Crieff on A85. 2acres 70pitches 40static
All year booking advisable Jul & Aug last arrival mdnt last departure 12.00hrs 4♨ individual pitches ⊚ late arrivals enclosure 13wc lit all night 1cdp □ washbasins hc ♨hc ☉ supervised (wash, spin, dry, iron) (games room) CTV (cold storage) children's playground calor gas camping gaz ☎ ⚓
⊖▶ stables 🛢 ▣ cinema ♪ launderette pub
60➡£2.87 or 60➡£2.87 10➡£2.87 (awnings)

CROCKETFORD Dumfries & Galloway Map 30 NX87
▶▶▶▶**Brandedleys Cara Farm** (NX830725) ☎250
③●△ signposted
Grass and gravel, part level, part sloping site with trees and bushes, set in hilly meadowland and country adjacent to lake. 4acres 45pitches 20static
Apr–Oct rsMar booking advisable peak periods last arrival 22.00hrs last departure 12.00hrs 3♨ ⊚ late arrivals enclosure 9wc lit all night 1cdp □ 15washbasins hc 4♨hc 2☉ supervised (wash, spin, dry) iron 🛢 ⊤ games room CTV (cold storage) licensed club/bar children's playground calor gas camping gaz toilet fluid cafe restaurant ☎ ⊞ bicycles for hire, putting, badminton ⚓
⊖▶ △ ♪
45➡£3.30–£4.50 or 45➡£3.30–£4.50 15➡£3.30–£4.50 (awnings) SA

▶▶**Galloway Arms Hotel** (NX831728) ☎240
①●△ signposted
Level, grass site with trees and bushes set in downland, woodland and meadowland within the urban area. 9m W of Dumfries at junction A712 and A75. no single sex groups 6acres 60pitches
Apr–Sep must book last arrival 22.30hrs last departure 12.00hrs 3♨ 10wc lit all night 1cdp washbasins hc ♨hc ☉ supervised wash, spin, dry, iron TV cold storage (licensed club/bar) children's playground camping gaz paraffin

161

Crocketford contd–Dornoch

cafe restaurant ☎ ⊞ ♨
 stables 🅐 ♪ pub
30⊕£4 or 30⇔£4 30⚲£4 awnings ltr SA

CROMARTY Highland Map 43 NH76
▶▶**Shore Mill** (NH749658) ☎Poyntzfield 216
② ❹ △
Part level, part sloping grass site set in meadowland with access to sea and beach. 3m SW of Cromarty on B9163. 2½acres 11pitches 4static
Apr–Sep booking advisable mid Jul–mid Aug last arrival 22.00hrs last departure 12.00hrs 3♿ late arrivals enclosure 3wc lit all night 1cdp washbasins hc ⋒hc ☉ supervised calor gas paraffin
⊕ pub ♨
11⊕£2 or 11⇔£2 or 11⚲£2 awnings ltr

CROOK OF DEVON Tayside Map 40 NO00
▶**Drum Caravans & Filling Station**
(NO044006) Fossoway ☎Fossoway 246
① ❹ △
This is a small touring site offering 1½ acres of level grass bordered by trees with pleasant views. 4½m W of Kinross on A977. 12 pitches 3static
All year last arrival dusk 1♿ 4wc washbasins hc ⋒hc ☉ supervised cold storage calor gas camping gaz paraffin toilet fluid ♨
⊕ 🅟 🅐 ♪ pub
12⊕£2.30 or 12⇔£2.30 or 12⚲£2 awnings ltr

CULLEN Grampian Map 45 NJ56
▶▶**Logie Camping & Caravan Site**
(NJ516674) ☎40766
① ❹ △ signposted
Part level and sloping grassy site near sea and beach. ½m E of A98. 72pitches 40static
9 Apr–29 Sep 5♿ individual pitches ⓐ 16wc lit all night cdp washbasins hc central hot water (⋒hc) ☉ (wash, dry) ⊞ ♨
⊕ 🅟 🅐 ♪ launderette pub
60⊕ or 60⇔ 12⚲ ltr

CUMINESTOWN Grampian Map 45 NJ85
▶**A B Caravans** (NJ842516) ☎261
② ❹ △ signposted
Mainly grass site set in agricultural land, 3m NE off B9027 for East Balthangie. 3acres 6pitches 12static
Jun–Oct rsMay must book peak periods last arrival 22.00hrs last departure 12.00hrs 1♿ ⓐ 6wc lit all night 1cdp washbasins hc (central hot water, ⋒hc) ☉ wash, spin, iron games room TV cold storage calor gas camping gaz toilet fluid cafe ☎ ⊞ ♨
⊕ stables 🅟 ♪ launderette pub
6⊕ or 6⇔ or 6⚲ (awnings) ltr

DALMELLINGTON Strathclyde Map 34 NS40
▶▶**Glebe Caravan & Camping Site**
(NS499065) Cumnock Rd ☎550519
① ❹ △ signposted
Level, grassy touring site on the outskirts of the town. 4acres 50pitches
Apr–Sep no bookings 2♿ 12wc lit all night 1cdp 13washbasins hc (6⋒hc) 6☉ (wash, spin) iron children's playground ☎ ♨
⊕ stables ♪
30⊕£2.30 or 30⇔£2.30 20⚲£2.30 (awnings)

DALRYMPLE Strathclyde Map 34 NS31
▶▶**Doon Valley Caravan Park** (NS365145)
☎242
② ❹ △

Camping and caravanning sites

Part level, part sloping grass site with trees and bushes, set in downland and meadowland, with access to main road. 5m SE of Ayr off B742. No tents 2acres 10pitches 90static
mid May–Sep rsOct–mid May must book mid Jul–mid Aug 5♿ individual pitches late arrivals enclosure 9wc lit all night 1cdp 🅚
12washbasins hc central hot water 6⋒hc 1☉ supervised (wash, dry) iron games room CTV cold storage children's playground calor gas camping gaz toilet fluid ☎ ♨
⊕ stables 🅟 ♪ launderette pub
10⊕ or 10⇔ awnings ltr

DAVIOT Highland Map 44 NH73
▶▶**Auchnahillin Caravan & Camping Park**
(NH742386) ☎223
② ❹ △ signposted
Level grassy site surrounded by hills and forest. 7m S of Inverness. 6acres 65pitches 12static
Dec–Oct last arrival 23.00hrs last departure 12.00hrs 8♿ individual pitches ⓐ late arrivals enclosure 12wc lit all night 1cdp 🅚
washbasins hc central hot water (⋒hc) ☉ supervised (wash, spin) dry iron (games room) cold storage children's playground calor gas ☎ ⊞ ♨
⊕ ♪ pub
45⊕£2.25–£3.25 or 45⇔£2.25–£3.25 20⚲£2.25–£3.25 (awnings) ltr

DINGWALL Highland Map 43 NH55
▶▶**Jubilee Park Caravan & Camping Site**
(NH557588) ☎62236
② ❹ △
Close to town centre and well maintained. 2½acres 52pitches
Apr–Sep booking advisable peak periods last arrival 22.00hrs last departure 12.00hrs 3♿ individual pitches late arrivals enclosure 13wc lit all night 1cdp 13washbasins hc 4⋒hc 2☉ supervised games room calor gas camping gaz
⊕ ♨
52⊕ or 52⇔ or 52⚲ awnings SA

DORNOCH Highland Map 43 NH78
▶▶▶**Grannie's Heilan Hame** (NH818924)
☎260
② ❹ △ signposted
This site is in a coastal setting amidst grass and sand dunes. 40acres 234pitches 66static
Jun–Aug rsSep–May last arrival 22.00hrs 20♿ ⓐ late arrivals enclosure 56wc lit all night 1cdp 🅚 washbasins hc (⋒hc) ☉ (wash, spin, dry, iron) games room TV (cold storage) (licensed club/bar) children's playground private beach calor gas camping gaz toilet fluid cafe restaurant ☎ ⊞ take-away meals ♨
⊕ stables 🅟 🅐 ♪ pub
234⊕£1.70–£3 or 234⇔£1.70–£3 or 100⚲£1.70–£3 awnings ltr
▶▶▶**Royal Dornoch Links Caravan & Camping Site** (NH804888) Apply to: District Amenities Officer, Sutherland District Council, Golspie, Sutherland KW10 6RB ☎423 (Golspie 392 Nov–Mar)
② ❹ △ signposted
A level, grass and sand site near the sea and beach, set in hilly woodland and moorland. 2m off A9 on E side of town. 10acres 160pitches 40static
Apr–23 Oct must book Jul & Aug last arrival 22.00hrs last departure 12.00hrs 15♿ 38wc lit all night 3cdp washbasins hc (⋒hc) ☉ (wash, spin, dry, iron) (games room) CTV children's

Camping and caravanning sites
Dinnishadder–Dunvegan

playground ☎ putting green
↪ stables 🅿 🛆
160⊕ or 160⊜ or 160⬥ (awnings) ltr

DRINNISHADDER Harris, Western Isles
Map 48 NG19
▶*Laig House Caravan Site* (NG171951) ☎207
🗓️⓿⚠ signposted
Part level, part sloping, sand-surfaced site with mature trees set in mountainous and hilly country with access to sea and beach. 4½m S of Tarbert. 2acres 24pitches 5static
Apr–Oct must book Jul & Aug last arrival mdnt last departure 16.00hrs 3₷ individual pitches Ⓐ late arrivals enclosure 5wc lit all night 1cdp 🎱 washbasins hc central hot water ☉ supervised iron cold storage children's playground private beach calor gas camping gaz paraffin toilet fluid ☎ fishing mobile🍴
↪ 🅿 🛆 🎵 launderette
8⊕£1.60 4⊜£1.50 12⬥£1.50 (awnings) ltr

DUMFRIES Dumfries & Galloway Map 30 NX97
▶▶*Newbridge Caravan Park* (NX952787)
Glasgow Rd ☎Newbridge 249
🗓️⚠ signposted
Level, grassy site on outskirts of busy town. Long and narrow site with central hard core road. 2m N on A76. ✶ No tents 1½acres 30pitches 90static
3 Mar–Oct no bookings last arrival 22.00hrs last departure 12.00hrs 2₷ individual pitches late arrivals enclosure 5wc lit all night 1cdp washbasins hc Ⓗhc ☉ children's playground calor gas camping gaz toilet fluid 🍴
↪ stables 🅿 🛆 cinema 🎵 launderette
35⊕£2 or 30⊜£2 awnings

DUNBAR Lothian Map 35 NT67
▶▶*Kirk Park Caravan Site* (NT667789)
🗓️⓿⚠
Part level, part sloping site, in meadowland adjacent to A1 off A1087. 22pitches 100static mid Mar–Oct no bookings last departure 10.30hrs 3₷ individual pitches 14wc lit all night 2cdp 16washbasins hc central hot water ⚭hc Ⓗhc ☉ calor gas camping gaz ☎ 🍴
↪ stables 🅿 🎵 launderette pub
22⊕£2.50–£3 or 22⊜£2.50–£3 or 22⬥£2.50–£3
▶▶*Winterfield Caravan Site* (NT673793) West Prom
🗓️⓿⚠ signposted
Level, grassy site with access to the sea and beach. Situated on the corner of the Back Road and Knockenhair Road. 19pitches 72static
Apr–Sep no bookings last departure 10.30hrs 3₷ individual pitches 16wc lit all night 3cdp 12washbasins hc central hot water ⚭hc 2Ⓗhc 6☉ children's playground calor gas camping gaz ☎ 🍴
↪ 🅿 🎵 launderette pub
19⊕£2.50–£3 or 19⊜£2.50–£3 or 19⬥£2.50–£3 (awnings)

DUNDEE Tayside Map 41 NO33
▶▶*Camperdown Caravan Site* (NO361325)
Camperdown Park Apply to: General Manager of Parks, Parks Dept, Dundee District Council, 17 King Street, Dundee DD1 1LD. ☎23141
🗓️⚠ signposted
Modern neatly laid out touring site adjacent to municipal park, just off Dundee by-pass at its western end. Degree of seclusion despite close proximity of industrial estate. 8½acres 90pitches
Apr–Oct must book peak periods last arrival 21.00hrs last departure 12.30hrs 4₷ individual pitches 20wc lit all night 2cdp 10washbasins hc Ⓗhc ☉ (🎫) mobile🍴 🍴
↪ stables 🅿 cinema 🎵 launderette
90⊕£1.75–£2 or 90⊜£1.75–£2 or 90⬥£1.75–£2 awnings

DUNKELD Tayside Map 40 NO04
▶*Inver Mill Caravan Site* (NO015422)
🗓️⓿⚠ signposted
A level and grassy site with mature trees and bushes set in hilly country with nearby moorland, woodland and river. Turn off A9 onto A822 then right to Inver. 2½acres 50pitches 80static
Apr–Oct no bookings last arrival 22.30hrs last departure 12.00hrs 10₷ 15wc lit all night washbasins hc central hot water Ⓗhc ☉ supervised children's playground private beach mobile🍴
↪ stables 🅿 🎵 pub
50⊕ or 50⊜ or 50⬥ (awnings)

DUNNET Highland Map 47 ND27
▶▶*Dunnet Bay Caravan Club Site*
(ND219703) ☎Castletown 319
🗓️⓿⚠ signposted
This is a mainly level grassy site with gravel driveways, set alongside 3 miles of white shell sands. Access is directly onto A836 approx 8m E of Thurso, immediately W of the village of Dunnet. 8acres 45pitches
22 May–22 Sep rs14–21 May must book peak periods last departure 12.00hrs 9₷ individual pitches Ⓐ late arrivals enclosure wc lit all night 1cdp washbasins hc central hot water (Ⓗhc) ☉ supervised (wash, spin, dry) calor gas camping gaz toilet fluid mobile🍴 🍴
↪ stables 🛆 🎵 launderette pub
45⊕ or 45⊜ or 45⬥ (awnings)

DUNOON Strathclyde Map 33 NS17
▶▶*Cowal Caravan Park* (NS183792) Victoria Rd, Hunters Quay ☎4259
🗓️⓿⚠ signposted
Quiet, walled site in former market garden. 2m from Dunoon. ✶ no tents 6pitches 25static All year must book Jun–Aug last arrival 22.30hrs last departure 12.00hrs 3₷ 6wc lit all night 1cdp 4washbasins hc 2central hot water (4Ⓗhc) 1☉ supervised (wash, spin, dry) iron calor gas 🍴
↪ stables 🅿 🛆 cinema 🎵 launderette pub
6⊕ or 6⊜ ltr

DUNVEGAN Isle of Skye, Highland

CAMPERDOWN CARAVAN PARK, DUNDEE

Modern caravan facilities (90 pitches) situated just off the A972. Attractively landscaped creating small, secluded parking sections.
Situated within a large park which offers leisure and recreation facilities for all age groups.
Booking facilities available on site and further details of charges etc, or prior booking can be obtained from the General Manager of Parks, 17 King Street.
Phone Dundee 23141, Ext 413.

The perfect Highland holiday where you can see the trees from the wood.

From a fully inclusive price of just £98* per lodge, per week, or £40* per weekend, you and up to five friends can enjoy the relaxing beauty of the magnificent Scottish countryside from your very own timber lodge at Lochanhully.

Lochanhully, located near Carrbridge faces South to the Cairngorm mountains with a complex of lodges set in the scenic splendour of the Spey Valley.

*Prices correct at time of going to press.

LOCHANHULLY LODGES

Send to: Lochanhully Lodges, Dept. 4, Carrbridge, Inverness-shire, Scotland, PH23 3NA. Please send me a brochure with details.

Mr./Mrs. _____

Address _____

_____

_____

Scotland's for me! AA

© A joint Lochanhully Lodges and Scottish Tourist Board advertisement.

A Lochanhully Lodge holiday offers the widest possible range of relaxing holiday activities.

The site has its own lake, licensed bar and heated covered swimming pool and is ideally positioned for touring, walking, climbing, pony treking, skiing and fishing. You can even visit nearby whisky distilleries.

Each lodge is modern and functional in design and gives a degree of comfort that you and your family and friends will enjoy.

All the lodges are equipped with electricity, hot and cold water, a cooker, TV, fridge, linen and furnishings, all of a high standard and all included in the price together with electricity and V.A.T.

Two of the fifty units have been specially designed to accommodate accompanied wheelchair or physically handicapped visitors, at no extra charge.

Make your next holiday just that little bit different in the natural setting of a Lochanhully Lodge.

For a brochure complete the coupon or phone Carrbridge (047 984) 234.

Map 42 NG24
▶▶**Dunvegan Caravan Park** (NG260477) ☎362
①⚠ signposted
A mainly level site set in hilly moorland. No tents 2acres 33pitches
May–Sep rsApr & May booking advisable Jul & Aug individual pitches 12wc lit all night 1cdp washbasins hc ♿ ☉ (wash, spin)
↔ 🚐 ⚠ ♪
33🚗£2.20 or 33🚐£2.20 awnings ltr

DURNESS Highland Map 46 NC36
▶▶**Sango Sands Caravan Site** (NC406678)
Sangomore (1m E)
②①⚠ signposted
On the outskirts of Durness on A838 this open cliff-top site overlooks Sango Bay, and is mainly grass and sand. 9½acres 75pitches
Apr–Sep no bookings last arrival 22.00hrs last departure 12.00hrs 7🚗 16wc lit all night 2cdp washbasins hc (♿hc) ☉ spin games room cold storage licensed club/bar calor gas camping gaz paraffin toilet fluid cafe restaurant ☎ bicycle hire 🐕
↔ stables ♪ pub
75🚗£1.90 or 75🚐£1.90 or 75⛺£1.90 awnings ltr

EASTRIGGS Dumfries & Galloway
Map 31 NY26
▶**Gemmel Caravan Site** (NY245666) Central Rd ☎304
①①⚠ signposted
Part level, part sloping, grass site set in meadowland and adjacent to sea and river. 4m N of Gretna off A75. 2acres 30pitches
Apr–Oct last arrival mdnt last departure 11.30hrs 1🚗 4wc lit all night ☉ calor gas 🐕
↔ cinema ♪ launderette pub
10🚗£1.50 10🚐£1.50 10⛺£1.50 (awnings)

ECCLEFECHAN Dumfries & Galloway
Map 31 NY17
▶▶▶**Hoddom Castle Caravan Park**
(NY154729) Hoddom ☎251
③①⚠ signposted
Predominantly touring site created within the grounds of Hoddom Castle with the keep and outhouses now housing the site amenities. The site lies 2m SW of Hoddom Bridge which carries the B725 over the River Annan. 24acres 190pitches 29static
Etr–Sep rsOct booking advisable last arrival 22.00hrs last departure 12.00hrs 50🚗 individual pitches ⓐ late arrivals enclosure 54wc lit all night 1cdp washbasins hc ♿hc ☉ supervised (wash, spin, dry, iron) games room TV cold storage (licensed club/bar) children's playground calor gas camping gaz toilet fluid cafe restaurant ☎ Dog kennels, fishing 🐕
↔ stables ♪ pub
90🚗£2.50–£3.50 or 90🚐£2–£2.75 100⛺£2–£3.50 (awnings) ltr SA

EDINBURGH Lothian Map 35 NT27
▶▶▶▶**Morton Hall Caravan Park** (NT265680)
30 Frogston Road East
☎031-664 1533
③①⚠ signposted
Located on the S side of Edinburgh within 20 minutes' car ride of the city centre, this site is part of a 200-acre estate surrounding the 18th-C Morton Hall mansion designed by Robert Adam. 15acres 250pitches
23 Mar–Oct must book Jun–Sep 7🚗 individual pitches ⓐ late arrivals enclosure 48wc lit all night 2cdp 🚿 washbasins hc central hot water ♿hc ☉ supervised (wash, dry) iron games room CTV (cold storage) licensed club/bar children's playground calor gas camping gaz toilet fluid ☎ 🐕
↔ stables 🚼 cinema launderette pub
250🚗 or 250🚐 or 250⛺ (awnings)

ELGIN Grampian Map 44 NJ26
▶▶**Riverside Caravan Park** (NJ197627) West Rd ☎2813 & Lhanbryde 2448 (Winter)
②①⚠
Pleasant grassy site on banks of River Lossie, partly surrounded by trees. Situated ½m W of Elgin on A96. 2acres 72pitches 10static
Apr–Oct no bookings Jul–Aug last arrival mdnt last departure 12.00hrs 5🚗 individual pitches for caravans ⓐ 11wc lit all night 1cdp washbasins hc (♿hc) ☉ supervised wash spin iron games room cold storage children's playground calor gas camping gaz toilet fluid ☎ 🐕
↔ 🚐 ⚠ cinema ♪ launderette pub
52🚗£2.25 or 52🚐£2.25 20⛺£2.25 awnings ltr
▶**Spynie Hall Caravan Site** (NJ182641)
Spynie ☎45344
②①⚠ signposted
A simple site in attractive position on hillside overlooking Moray Firth. 1acre 18pitches
Apr–Sep no bookings last arrival 20.00hrs 1🚗 4wc lit all night 4washbasins hc 4central hot water 1☉ supervised
↔ stables 🚼 ⚠ cinema ♪ launderette pub 🐕
6🚗£1.50 6🚐£1.50 6⛺£1.50 (awnings) ltr

FINDHORN Grampian Map 44 NJ06
▶▶▶▶**Findhorn Bay Caravan Park**
(NJ048637)
①①⚠ signposted
A level, grass and sand site near sea and beach. 4m E of Forres on B9011. 10acres 130pitches 175static
Jul–Sep rsOct–Jun no bookings last arrival 20.00hrs last departure 12.00hrs 4🚗 ⓐ 38wc lit all night 2cdp 45washbasins hc (4central hot water) (13♿hc) 4☉ (2wash, 1dry, iron) calor gas camping gaz toilet fluid ☎ 🎭 theatre/cinema 🐕
↔ stables 🚼 ⚠ cinema ♪ launderette
130🚗 or 130🚐 or 130⛺ (awnings)
▶▶**Findhorn Sands Caravan Park** (NJ040647)
☎2324
②①⚠ signposted
Mainly level site with bushes set in moorland. Facing Moray Firth. 4m N of Forres on B9011. 28acres 50pitches 150static
Apr–Oct last arrival 19.00hrs last departure 19.00hrs 1🚗 8wc lit all night 1cdp washbasins hc (♿hc) ☉ supervised (wash) (dry) calor gas 🐕
↔ stables 🚼 cinema ♪ launderette pub
50🚗£2.50–£3 or 50🚐£2.50–£3 or 50⛺£2.50–£3 awnings ltr

FINDOCHTY Grampian Map 45 NJ46
▶**Findochty Caravan Site** (NJ458679)
②①⚠ signposted
A neat towing site set on sea front overlooking rocky bay, on the edge of a quaint fishing village. 3acres 30pitches 10static
Etr–Sep must book peak periods last arrival 17.00hrs last departure 10.00hrs 2🚗 individual pitches 8wc lit all night 1cdp washbasins hc central hot water (♿hc) ☉ (wash, spin) 🎭 children's playground
↔ 🚐 ⚠ ♪ 🐕
24🚗 or 24🚐 6⛺ (awnings) ltr

165

FOCHABERS Grampian Map 44 NJ35
►►►**Burnside Caravan Site** (NJ350580) Keith Rd ☎820362
☐☐⚠ signposted
This site is on level ground amidst natural landscaping with a burn flowing through ½m E of town off A96. No motorcycles 5acres 120pitches 45static
Apr–Oct last departure 12.00hrs 7⚲ individual pitches ⓐ 24wc lit all night 2cdp 24washbasins hc 4⋒hc 8☉ wash spin (iron, ▨ games room TV children's playground ☎ ⚐
⊕ stables ⛺ ♪ pub
120⇌£2.50 or 120⇌£2.20 40⚑£1.80–£2.50 awnings

FORFAR Tayside Map 41 NO45
►►**Lochside Caravan Park** (NO450505)
☎62528
☐☐⚠ signposted
Pleasant, well laid-out touring site just off the Ring Road. Close to Recreation Centre.
No tents 4acres 48pitches
Apr–mid Oct must book peak periods last arrival 21.00hrs last departure 12.00hrs 4⚲ individual pitches 11wc lit all night 1cdp 6washbasins hc central hot water (4⚑hc) 2☉ wash spin children's playground mobile▨ ⚐
⊕ ⛺ cinema ♪ pub
48⇌£2.20 or 48⇌£2.20 (awnings) ltr SA

FORTROSE Highland Map 44 NH75
►►**Fortrose Site** (NH736563)
☐☐⚠ signposted
A level, grassy site near sea and beach. ½m S of Fortrose on A832. 4½acres 70pitches
May–Sep no bookings 6⚲ individual pitches 12wc lit all night (17washbasins hc) (4⋒hc) 4☉ calor gas ⊞
⊕ ⛺ ♪
70⇌ or 70⇌ or 70⚑

FORT WILLIAM Highland Map 39 NN17
►►►**Glen Nevis Caravan & Camping Park** (NN124722) Glen Nevis ☎2191
☐☐☐⚠ signposted
At the foot of Ben Nevis, bordered by ragged pine-covered forests, the site is 2m from Fort William, in this most impressive glen. The River Nevis runs through tree-lined banks. 19acres 380pitches
5 Apr–4 Oct no bookings last arrival 22.00hrs last departure 12.00hrs 13⚲ 58wc lit all night 1cdp 42washbasins hc (1central hot water) (15⋒hc) 17☉ (wash, spin, dry) iron children's playground calor gas camping gaz toilet fluid restaurant ☎ ⚐
⊕ stables ♪ pub
150⇌£2.20–£2.90 or 150⇌£1.80–£2.60 230⚑£1.80–£2.60 (awnings) SA

FRASERBURGH Grampian Map 45 NJ96
►►**Kessock Road Caravan Site** (NJ999661)
Esplanade, Kessock Rd Apply to: Banff & Buchan District Council, Leisure & Recreation Dept, 1 Church St, Macduff, Banffshire, AB4 1UF ☎Macduff 32761
☐☐⚠ signposted
A level and grassy site near the sea and beach. 100yds off A92 on Kessock Road. 70pitches 50static
Apr–Sep must book last arrival 21.00hrs last departure 09.00hrs 3⚲ 12wc lit all night 1cdp washbasins hc central hot water (⋒hc) ☺ (wash, spin, dry, iron) (▤) children's playground calor gas camping gaz paraffin toilet fluid ☎ mobile▨ ⚐
⊕ stables ⛺ ⚑ ♪ launderette pub
30⇌£2.30 or 30⇌£1.80 40⚑£1.20 (awnings)
►**Esplanade Caravan Site** (NK000662) Harbour Rd Apply to: Banff & Buchan District Council, Leisure & Recreation Dept, 1 Church St, Macduff, Banffshire, AB4 1UF. ☎Macduff 32861
☐☐⚠ signposted
Mainly level, grass and sand site, in urban area, near sea, beach and main road. No tents 1½acres 40pitches 20static
May–Sep must book last arrival 21.00hrs last departure 09.00hrs 2⚲ 12wc lit all night 1cdp washbasins hc (central hot water) (⋒hc) ☺ (wash, spin, dry, iron) (▤) children's playground calor gas camping gaz paraffin toilet fluid cafe restaurant ☎ mobile▨ ⚐
⊕ stables ⛺ ⚑ ♪ launderette pub
40⇌£2.30 or 40⇌£1.80

GAIRLOCH Highland Map 42 NG87
►►**Sands Holiday Centre** (NG758784) ☎2152
☐☐⚠ signposted
Part level site set in moorland, 3m W of Gairloch on B8021. 53acres 360pitches 16static
22 May–Sep rsApr must book peak periods last arrival 22.30hrs last departure 12.00hrs 10⚲ 54wc lit all night 1cdp 57washbasins hc (22⋒hc) 16☉ supervised (wash, spin, dry, iron) private beach calor gas camping gaz toilet fluid ☎ hairdriers ⚐
⊕ ⚑ ♪ launderette
160⇌£3 50⇌£2.70 150⚑£3 (awnings)

GAIRLOCHY Highland Map 39 NN18
►**Gairlochy Caravan Park** (NN187835) ☎229
☐☐⚠ signposted
Site set near river, lake and canal. 2m NW of junct A82/B8004, on B8004. 3acres 20pitches 5static
Apr–Sep last departure 11.00hrs 1⚲ individual pitches ⓐ 4wc lit all night 1cdp washbasins hc ⋒hc ☉ supervised calor gas camping gaz ☎ ⚐
⊕ ⛺ ⚑ ♪ pub ⚐
20⇌ or 20⇌ or 20⚑ (awnings) ltr SA

GARTMORE Central Map 37 NS59
►►**Cobleland Campsite** (NS531989)
☎Aberfoyle 392
☐☐⚠ signposted
Set within the Queen Elizabeth Forest Park, this grass and tree-studded site offers seclusion, views, forest walks, and free fishing on the River Forth which borders the camping area. No

---

FINDHORN SANDS CARAVAN PARK
SITES AVAILABLE FOR SERVICED AND NON-SERVICED STATIC CARAVANS
6/8 berth caravans for hire, off-season rates. New toilet/shower blocks. Laundrette on Site, Shops and hotels nearby. Fishing, Pony-trekking, water ski-ing, safe bathing, yachting, on hand.
Site for touring caravans, caravanettes, tents.
Findhorn Sands Caravan Park, By Forres, Morayshire, IV36 0YE.
Tel. Findhorn 2324.

firearms 5acres 100pitches
Apr–Sep no bookings last arrival before dusk
last departure 10.00hrs 4⚬ 14wc lit all night
1cdp washbasins hc central hot water ⋔hc ☉
supervised
➔ stables 🅿 🛆 ♪
100⚬ or 100⚬ or 100⚬ awnings

GARVE Highland Map 43 NH36
▶**Garve Hotel Caravan Park** (NH393619)
☎205
②❶▲
A large touring site comprising four acres of level grassland bordered on one side by the main road and on the other by the River Blackwater. The site lies on sheltered ground to the S side of the Garve Hotel and is secluded on all sides by mature trees. Site facilities are basic but there is plenty of space on the site which is pleasantly situated amid Highland scenery.
5acres 34pitches
Apr–Oct must book peak periods last arrival 22.00hrs 2⚬ 7wc lit all night 1cdp washbasins hc central hot water ⋔hc ☉ cold storage licensed club/bar children's playground calor gas camping gaz cafe restaurant ☎ Trout fishing ⚓
➔ stables ♪ pub
34⚬£2.50 or 34⚬£2 or 34⚬£1.50 awnings ltr

GATEHOUSE OF FLEET Dumfries & Galloway Map 30 NX65
▶▶▶**Anwoth Caravan & Camping Site** (NX595563) ☎Gatehouse 333
②❶▲ signposted
Compact touring site situated on southern edge of small holiday town. Although the site lies just off the main road behind garage and filling station, trees surrounding most sides still manage to create a degree of seclusion. No motorcycles 3½acres 70pitches 13static
Apr–Oct must book peak periods last arrival 22.00hrs last departure 12.00hrs 5⚬ individual pitches ⓐ 13wc lit all night 1cdp washbasins hc central hot water ⋔hc ☉ supervised (wash, spin, dry, iron) games room (cold storage) calor gas toilet fluid ☎ ⚓
➔ stables 🅿 ♪ launderette pub
47⚬£3.50 or 47⚬£3.50 23⚬£3.50 (awnings)
▶▶**Cardoness Caravan Site** (NX564534)
Cardoness Estate ☎Mossyard 288
②❶▲ signposted
Beautifully situated park created out of the woodland and coastline of the Cardoness Estate, 3m SW of Gatehouse of Fleet. The natural environment has been utilised to every advantage whilst still retaining its unspoilt character. No tents 30acres 24pitches 188static
Apr–Oct must book last arrival 21.00hrs last departure 11.30hrs 5⚬ individual pitches 8wc lit all night 4cdp washbasins hc central hot water (⋔hc) ☉ supervised (wash) (dry) (T) children's playground private beach calor gas toilet fluid ☎ putting green ⚓
➔ stables 🅿 launderette pub
24⚬£3 or 24⚬£3 (awnings) SA

GLENCOE Highland Map 39 NN15
▶▶▶**Glencoe Campsite** (NN111578)
☎Ballachulish 397
②❶▲ signposted
Part level, part sloping, grass, gravel and sand site with young trees and bushes, set in mountainous woodland with direct access to river and main road (A82). 11¼acres 200pitches

No bookings 5⚬ individual pitches 16wc lit all night 1cdp 19washbasins hc (⋔hc) ☉ (wash, spin) calor gas camping gaz ☎
➔ ♪ pub ⚓
200⚬£2–£2.80 or 200⚬£2–£2.80 or 200⚬£2–£2.80 awnings
▶▶**Invercoe Caravan Site** (NN098594)
☎Ballachulish 210
②❶▲ signposted
Level, grass site set in mountains with access to sea, beach and river. On A82 from Fort William, turn left to Kinlochleven. 5acres 100pitches 5static
Etr–mid Oct no bookings last departure 13.00hrs 6⚬ 10wc lit all night 1cdp 8washbasins hc (central hot water) (⋔hc) ☉ supervised (wash) (dry, iron) calor gas camping gaz ⚓
➔ 🅿 ♪ launderette pub
⚬£2.50 ⚬£2.50 ⚬£2.50 awnings

GLENDARUEL Strathclyde Map 33 NR98
▶**Glendaruel Caravan Park** (NS005865) ☎267
②❶▲ signposted
Mainly level grass site in valley adjacent to river and main road. ✝ 3acres 40pitches 30static
Apr–Oct must book peak periods last arrival 22.00hrs last departure 12.00hrs 2⚬ individual pitches ⓐ late arrivals enclosure 10wc lit all night 1cdp 🅆 washbasins hc central hot water supervised (spin, dry, iron) games room cold storage children's playground calor gas camping gaz toilet fluid ☎ off-licence, barbecues ⚓
➔ ♪ pub
40⚬£2.50–£3 or 40⚬£2.50–£3 or 40⚬£2.50–£3 (awnings) ltr

GLENLUCE Dumfries & Galloway Map 30 NX25
▶▶▶**Glenluce Caravan Site** (NX201576)
☎Stranraer 2447 and Glenluce 412
②❶▲ signposted
Partly level site in sylvan surroundings off A75 Stranraer road. Concealed entrance at telephone kiosk in centre of main street. No single sex groups 2acres 40pitches 30static
Etr–Oct must book peak periods last arrivall 21.00hrs last departure 12.00hrs 4⚬ individual pitches ⓐ 13wc lit all night washbasins hc central hot water (⋔hc) ☉ (wash, spin) (iron) children's playground calor gas camping gaz paraffin toilet fluid ⚓
➔ stables 🅿 🛆 ♪ launderette pub
20⚬£2.70 or 20⚬£2.40 20⚬£2.70 (awnings)

GLEN TROOL Dumfries & Galloway Map 30 NX47
▶▶▶**Caldons Caravan and Camping Ground** (NX400790) Apply to: Recreation Forester, Forest Office, Glen Trool, Newton Stewart, Wigtownshire, D68 6SZ ☎Bargrennan 200
③❶▲ signposted
Level, grass site with trees and bushes, set in hilly, wooded moorland country, with access to river and Loch Trool. 7m N of Newton Stewart on A714. 22acres 240pitches
Apr–Sep must book peak periods last departure early afternoon 14⚬ wc lit all night 2cdp 30washbasins hc ⋔hc 6☉ supervised (4drying cabinets) calor gas camping gaz ☎ ⚓
➔ ♪ pub
240⚬£2.20–£3.40 or 240⚬£2.20–£3.40 or 240⚬£2.20–£3.40 awnings
▶▶**Merrick Caravan Park** (NX354775)
☎Bargrennan 280
②❶▲ signposted

167

Glen Trool contd – Hollybush
Camping and caravanning sites

Part level, part sloping, gravel and sand site with trees and bushes, set in mountainous moor and woodland, adjacent to river estuary and lake in the heart of Galloway National Forest Park. Off A714 from Girvan. 1acre 15pitches 25static Mar–Oct must book peak periods last arrival mdnt last departure 12.00hrs 2♣ individual pitches 9wc lit all night 1cdp 12washbasins hc (4fihc) ⊙ supervised cold storage calor gas camping gaz
⊖→ 🐎
15₽£2.50–£3 or 15₠£2.50–£3 awnings

GRANTOWN-ON-SPEY Highland Map 44 NJ02
▶▶▶ **Municipal Caravan Site** (NJ028283)
Seafield Av
②❶▲ signposted
Part level and sloping, grass site with mature trees and bushes near river and site admist hills, mountains, moorland and woodland. ½m from town centre on A939. 20acres 350pitches 70static
Etr–Sep no bookings last departure 12.00hrs 13♣ individual pitches ④ 32wc lit all night 3cdp 39washbasins hc central hot water 5⇨hc 11fihc 25⊙ spin (dry) iron children's playground calor gas toilet fluid ☎ putting green 🛒
⊖→ stables 🐎 ♪
170₽£3 or 170₠£3 180₠£2 awnings

GREENLAW Borders Map 36 NT74
▶▶▶ **Greenlaw Caravan Park** (NT709461)
Bank St ☎341
②❶▲ signposted
Part level, part sloping, grass site amidst various trees and bushes; set in meadowland, adjacent to main A6105 road with direct access to river. 2½acres 35pitches 45static
Etr–Oct must book peak periods last arrival 22.00hrs last departure 12.00hrs 5♣ individual pitches 8wc lit all night 1cdp 8washbasins hc 6fihc 3⊙ (1wash, 1dry) cold storage calor gas camping gaz toilet fluid ⊞ fishing 🛒
⊖→ stables pub
35₽ or 35₠ or 35₠ (awnings) ltr

GRETNA Dumfries & Galloway Map 31 NY36
▶ **Braids Caravan Site** (NY314675) The Braids
☎409
①❶▲ signposted
Small, peaceful touring site bordered by fields on N side of B721, 1m W of the village of Gretna. 1¼acres 30pitches
Apr–Oct must book Jul–Aug last arrival 23.00hrs 2♣ individual pitches ④ late arrivals enclosure 6wc lit all night 1cdp ⊞ washbasins hc (central hot water) (fihc) ⊙ supervised (cold storage) calor gas camping gaz toilet fluid 🛒
⊖→ stables cinema ♪ launderette pub
30₽ or 30₠ or 30₠ (awnings) ltr

GRETNA GREEN (A74 Service Area, northbound) Dumfries & Galloway
Map 31 NY36
▶▶ **Canny Scots Caravan Park** (NY306688)
North Bound Service Area ☎Gretna 598
①❶▲ signposted
Part level, part sloping, mainly grass site with saplings, overlooking the Solway Firth. 1m N of English/Scottish border on A74. 7acres 80pitches
Etr–Oct booking advisable 3♣ wc lit all night 1cdp washbasins hc central hot water ⊙ children's playground cafe restaurant ☎ 🛒

⊖→ stables ♪ pub
80₽£1.50 or 80₠£1.50 or 80₠£1 awnings

GUARDBRIDGE (nr St Andrews) Fife
Map 41 NO41
▶▶▶▶ **Clayton Caravan Park** (NO432182)
☎Balmullo 242
②❶▲
This is a level tree-studded grassy site adjoining farm, in gently rolling hill land. On south side of A91, midway between Cupar and St. Andrews. 6acres 75pitches 150static
Mar–Sep rs early Apr & Oct booking advisable Jul–early Aug last arrival 20.00hrs last departure 12.00hrs 10♣ late arrivals enclosure 15wc lit all night 1cdp ⊞ washbasins hc central hot water (1⇨hc fihc) ⊙ wash, dry games room CTV cold storage licensed clubbar children's playground calor gas camping gaz paraffin toilet fluid ☎ ⊞ putting, gold practice net, fishing 🛒
⊖→ stables 🐎 pub
75₽£2.30–£3.45 or 75₠£2.30–£3.45 or 75₠£2.30–£3.45 awnings SA

HADDINGTON Lothian Map 35 NT57
▶▶ **Monksmuir Caravan Park** (NT548756)
☎East Linton 340
②❶▲
Mainly level site with trees and bushes set in meadowland off A1 Edinburgh–Dunbar road, equidistant to Haddington and East Linton. 5½acres 43pitches 7static
All year rsWinter (cafe closed) no bookings last departure 12.00hrs 7♣ 12wc lit all night 2cdp ⊞ 14washbasins hc 8central hot water 6fihc (2⊙) supervised (wash, spin, dry, iron) (cold storage) calor gas camping gaz cafe ☎ washing-up sinks 🛒
⊖→ stables 🐎 launderette pub
23₽£2.05–£2.50 or 23₠£2.05–£2.50 20₠£2.15–£2.60 (awnings) ltr SA

HARRIS, (ISLE OF) Western Isles Map 48 NG
See **Drinnishadder**

HAWICK Borders Map 35 NT51
▶▶▶ **Riverside Caravan Park** (NT537169)
☎3785
②❶▲ signposted
A level and grassy site near A698 Hawick–Kelso road 2½m E of Hawick. Located on the banks of the River Teviot. 2½acres 48pitches 24static
Apr–Oct last arrival 22.00hrs last departure 12.00hrs individual pitches ④ 16wc lit all night 1cdp washbasins hc (fihc) ⊙ supervised wash, spin (cold storage) children's playground calor gas camping gaz toilet fluid ☎ fishing 🛒
⊖→ stables 🐎 cinema launderette pub
41₽£2.75–£3.50 4₠£2.75–£3.50 3₠£2.75–£3.50 (awnings)

HOLLYBUSH Strathclyde Map 34 NS31
▶▶ **Skeldon Caravans** (NS389144) ☎Dalrymple 202
②❶▲ signposted
A small, secluded touring site on the banks of the River Doon. 2m from Dalrymple on B7034. 3 acres 20pitches 10static
Apr–Sep must book Jul & Aug last arrival 18.00hrs last departure 12.00hrs 4♣ 7wc lit all night 12washbasins hc (fihc) ⊙ supervised children's playground calor gas camping gaz ☎ fishing 🛒

Camping and caravanning sites
Inchture–Inverness

⊖ 🅿 ♪ pub
20⊕fr£2.20 or 20⛺fr£2.20 or 20▲fr£2.20
(awnings) SA

INCHTURE Tayside Map 41 NO22
▶**Inchmartine Nurseries** (NO263277) Carse of Gowrie ☎251
② ❶ ⚠ signposted
A level and grassy site with mature trees and bushes, set amidst hills, mountains, moorland, woodland and downs. Near to A85 Perth–Dundee road. 3acres 45pitches
Apr–3 Oct no bookings last departure 12.00hrs 3⚡ 9wc lit all night 1cdp 9washbasins hc central hot water ♿ ☺ children's playground ☎
45⊕ or 45⛺ (awnings)

INNERLEITHEN Borders Map 35 NT33
▶**Tweedside Caravan Site** (NT338367)
☎Galashiels 830260
① ❶ ⚠ signposted
A spacious site standing on perimeter of village, in a relatively secluded and sheltered position, offering panoramic views of the Tweed Valley and surrounding hills. 6acres 50pitches 60static
Apr–Oct no bookings last arrival 19.30hrs last departure 12.00hrs 3⚡ ⓐ 15wc lit all night 1cdp washbasins hc (central hot water) (♿hc) ☺ (iron) children's playground calor gas
⊖ 🅿 ♪ pub
40⊕£2.50 or 40⛺£2.50 10▲£2.50 awnings ltr

INVERARAY Strathclyde Map 39 NN00
▶▶▶**Battlefield Caravan Park** (NN075055)
☎2285
② ❶ ⚠ signposted
Level site with mainly grass and stoney surface set among wooded hills & overlooking Loch Fyne. 3m S of Inveraray on A83. no single sex groups 11acres 40pitches 248static
Apr–Oct no bookings last arrival mdnt last departure 12.00hrs 4⚡ ⓐ late arrivals enclosure 24wc lit all night 3cdp washbasins hc central hot water ♿hc ☺ supervised iron games room licensed bar children's playground calor gas camping gaz toilet fluid cafe ☎ bar meals 🍴
⊖ stables ⚠ ♪ pub
40⊕£2.20 or 40⛺£1.90 ▲£1.80 (awnings) ltr SA

INVERCHAPEL Strathclyde Map 33 NS18
▶▶▶**Stratheck Caravan Park** (NS144865)
☎Kilmun 472
② ❶ ⚠ signposted
Part level, part sloping, grass site amidst mature trees and bushes, set in mountainous woodland country close to river, loch and main road. 8m N of Dunoon on A815. 8acres 50pitches 50static Etr–Sep must book peak periods last arrival 21.00hrs last departure 12.00hrs 5⚡ ⓐ late arrivals enclosure 18wc lit all night 1cdp 🅿 washbasins hc ♿hc ☺ supervised (wash, spin, dry, iron) games room (cold storage) children's playground private beach calor gas camping gaz toilet fluid ☎ 🕀 off licence, football pitch, putting green, fishing pond, boat launching facilities, bicycle hire 🍴
⊖ stables ⚠ ♪ launderette pub
50⊕£2.87 or 50⛺£2.87 or 50▲£2.87 (awnings) ltr SA

INVERGARRY Highland Map 43 NH30
▶**Faichem Park** (NH285023)
Ardgarry, Faichem

☎226 ② ❸ ⚠ signposted
The site is on a small working farm on Faichem Hill in a park-type setting, ideally situated for fishing & walking. From the A82 at Invergarry take the A87 for one mile, turn right at 'Faichem' signpost, site is on the right. 3acres 30pitches Apr–Oct rsNov–Mar booking advisable Jul & Aug last arrival 21.00hrs last departure 12.00hrs 3⚡ ⓐ 6wc lit all night 6washbasins hc 2♿hc 1☺ supervised cold storage children's playground calor gas children's pony, menagerie
⊖ stables ♪ 🍴
15⊕£3.50 15⛺£3.50 or 15▲£3.50 awnings ltr

INVERMORISTON Highland Map 43 NH41
▶▶**Loch Ness Caravan & Camping Park** (NH424150) Easter Port Clair ☎Glenmoriston 51207
① ❶ ⚠ signposted
Part level, part sloping, grass and gravel site amid mountains and wooded hill country, with access to Loch Ness. 5m N of Fort Augustus. 5acres 85pitches 6static
15 Mar–15 Oct last arrival 23.00hrs last departure 12.00hrs 12⚡ ⓐ late arrivals enclosure 16wc lit all night 3cdp washbasins hc central hot water ♿hc ☺ supervised (wash, spin, dry, iron) (cold storage) children's playground private beach ☎ 🕀 boat hire mobile🍴
⊖ stables ⚠ ♪ launderette pub 🍴
25⊕£3.45 25⛺£3.45 35▲£3.45 (awnings)

INVERNESS Highland Map 43 NH64
▶▶▶**Bught Caravan & Camping Site** (NH658438) ☎36920
② ❶ ⚠ signposted
Level and grassy site with mature trees and bushes near canal and river, set among hills and mountains. 1m W of Inverness on A82. 9½acres 250pitches
Etr–mid Oct no bookings last arrival 22.00hrs last departure 12.00hrs 6⚡ late arrivals enclosure 36wc lit all night 6cdp central hot water ♿hc ☺ supervised (licensed club/bar) (children's playground) calor gas camping gaz cafe restaurant ☎ 🍴
⊖ 🅿 ⚠ ♪ launderette
250⊕£3 or 250⛺£3 or 250▲£3 (awnings)
▶▶▶**Bunchrew Caravan Park** (NH618460) Bunchrew ☎37802
② ❶ ⚠ signposted
A well laid out and carefully maintained site with touring pitches separate from the residential area. 13acres 100pitches 60static
Etr–Sep booking advisable Jul & Aug last arrival 21.00hrs last departure 12.00hrs 12⚡ ⓐ 18wc lit all night 1cdp 🅿 18washbasins hc (8♿hc) ☺ supervised (wash, spin, dry, iron) Children's playground private beach calor gas camping gaz ☎ 🍴
⊖ cinema ♪ launderette
50⊕£2.75 or 50⛺£2.75 50▲£2.75 (awnings) ltr
▶▶**Dochfour Site** (NH616404) Dochgarroch
② ❶ ⚠ signposted
A level, grassy site near the Caledonian Canal and 4m SW of Inverness on A82. 5acres 190pitches 10static
May–Sep no bookings last arrival 20.00hrs last departure 12.00hrs 6⚡ ⓐ 36wc lit all night 1cdp washbasins hc ♿hc ☺ calor gas camping gaz paraffin 🍴
⊖ 🅿 ⚠ ♪ launderette
90⊕£2.50–£2.80 or 90⛺£2.50–£2.80 100▲£2.50–£2.80 awnings

169

Inveruglas – Kilberry

INVERUGLAS Strathclyde Map 39 NN30
▶▶**Loch Lomond Caravan Park** *(NN320092)*
☎224
②❶⚠ signposted
Level site with mature trees and bushes. On A82 between Inverbeg and Ardlui. no tents
Apr–Oct no bookings
last arrival 22.00hrs last departure 22.00hrs
6⛺ 12wc lit all night 1cdp washbasins hc central hot water (fihc) ☉ supervised private beach calor gas toilet fluid
➔ ▲ ♪ pub ⛄
12⛺£3–£4 12🚐£3–£4 (awnings) ltr

ISLE OF WHITHORN Dumfries & Galloway Map 30 NX43
▶▶▶**Burrow Head Holiday Farm** *(NX450346)* ☎Whithorn 252
②❶⚠ signposted
Part level, part sloping grass site with bushes set in hilly moorland country on cliff edge with access to sea for fishing only. 2m W of Isle of Whithorn. 50acres 260pitches 300static
Mar–Oct last departure 14.00hrs 12⛺ wc lit all night 1cdp washbasins hc (fihc ☉ supervised (wash) (dry) iron 🎮 (T) games room CTV licensed club/bar children's playground calor gas camping gaz paraffin toilet fluid cafe ☎ pony trekking ⛄
➔ stables ▲ ♪ launderette pub
260⛺£3 or 260🚐£3 or 260⚓£3 awnings ltr

JEDBURGH Borders Map 35 NT62
▶▶▶**Lilliardsedge Park** *(NT620267)* Ancrum
☎Ancrum 271
②❶⚠ signposted
A part level, part sloping, stony and grassy site with mature trees and bushes set amid woodland, moorland and downs 6m NW on A68. 25acres 190pitches 30static
Whit–Oct rsEtr–Whit & Oct must book Whit & Jul–Aug last arrival 23.00hrs last departure 12.00hrs 18⛺ 49wc lit all night 4cdp 🎮 49washbasins hc (22fihc) 6☉ supervised (wash, spin, dry, iron) TV licensed club/bar children's playground calor gas camping gaz paraffin toilet fluid ☎ ⛄
➔ ▲ ♪
100⛺ 10🚐 80⚓ (awnings)
▶▶▶**Eliot Park** *(NT658218)* Edinburgh Rd
☎3393
①❶⚠ signposted
Smapp touring site on northern edge of town, off A68, and nestling at foot of cliffs close to Jed Water. 3acres 64pitches
Etr–Sep must book in season last arrival 20.00hrs 8⛺ individual pitches 9wc lit all night 1cdp (washbasins hc) fihc ☉ supervised iron ☎ mobile⛄
➔ stables ▲ ♪ pub ⛄
64⛺£3.20–£3.76 or 64🚐£3.20–£3.76 or 64⚓£3.20–£3.76 awnings

JOHN O'GROATS Highland Map 47 ND37
▶**John O'Groats Caravan Site** *(ND382735)*
☎250
①❶⚠ signposted
Situated in open position right above the seashore looking out towards the Orkney Islands. At the end of A9. 2acres 45pitches
May–Sep last departure 12.00hrs 8⛺ 10wc lit all night 1cdp 12washbasins hc (4fihc) 2☉ cold storage calor gas camping gaz
➔ ♪ pub ⛄
45⛺£2.30 or 45🚐£2.30 or 45⚓£2.30 (awnings) ltr SA

STROMA VIEW SITE ▶*(ND373782)* Huna ☎313
①❶⚠ signposted
Slightly sloping, grass site set in downland with cliff scenery and access to sea and beach. 1½m W of John O'Groats on A836. ½acre 15pitches 2static
Apr–Oct booking advisable Jul & Aug last arrival 23.00hrs last departure 11.00hrs 3⛺ 3wc lit all night 1cdp washbasins hc (fihc) ☉ supervised iron cold storage children's playground camping gaz ⛳ mobile⛄ ⛄
➔ ▲ ♪ pub
5⛺£2 5🚐£2 5⚓£1.75 (awnings) ltr SA

KEITH Grampian Map 45 NJ45
▶**Keith Caravan Site** *(NJ435501)*
①❶⚠ signposted
A compact, newly developed site, located on the southern edge of town off the A96. Adjacent to housing estate. 3½acres 33pitches 4static
Etr–Sep must book peak periods last arrival 17.00hrs last departure 10.00hrs 3⛺ individual pitches ⓐ 8wc lit all night 2cdp washbasins hc central hot water (fihc) ☉ (wash, spin) iron ⛳
➔ cinema ♪ launderette ⛄ pub
23⛺ or 23🚐 10⚓ (awnings) ltr

KELSO Borders Map 35 NT73
▶▶▶**Springwood Caravan Park** *(NT720334)*
☎2596
③❶⚠ signposted
The site is located in a secluded position close to the tree-lined River Teviot about 1m W of the town. No tents 4acres 30pitches 175static
Apr–Sep last arrival 22.00hrs last departure 12.00hrs 4⛺ 21wc lit all night 1cdp washbasins hc fihc ☉ (wash, iron) (games room) (cold storage) children's playground calor gas ☎ ⛄
➔ stables ▲ cinema ♪ launderette
30⛺ or 30🚐 (awnings) ltr

KENMORE Tayside Map 40 NN74
▶▶▶**Kenmore Caravan Site** *(NN772458)*
☎226
②❶⚠ signposted
Part level, part sloping, grass site with trees, set in mountains, woods and meadowland, adjacent to River Tay. W of Aberfeldy on A827. 8acres 150pitches 60static
Etr–mid Oct rs late Mar booking advisable Jul & Aug last arrival 21.00hrs last departure 12.00hrs 10⛺ individual pitches caravans only ⓐ late arrivals enclosure wc 2cdp washbasins hc fihc ☉ supervised (spin, dry, iron) (cold storage) children's playground calor gas camping gaz toilet fluid ☎ ⛳ bicycle hire ⛄
➔ stables ▲ ♪ launderette pub
60⛺£3 10🚐£2 90⚓£2 awnings ltr

KILBERRY Strathclyde Map 33 NR76
▶▶**Port Ban Park** *(NR710655)* ☎Ormsary 224
①❶⚠
Secluded site, set on sea-front, with uninterrupted views of Islay and Jura. 1½acres 25pitches 45static
Apr–Oct booking advisable end Jul & Aug last arrival 22.00hrs last departure 13.00hrs 3⛺ 7wc 14washbasins hc 4fihc ☉ supervised (T) games room children's playground private beach calor gas camping gaz toilet fluid ☎ boat hire, putting
➔ ▲ ♪ ⛄

15⊕£2.25–£3.35 or 15⇔£2.25–£3.35 10⚐£2.25–£3.35 (awnings)

KILLIN Central Map 39 NN53
▶▶**High Creagan** (NN594352) Morenish (3m NE A827) ☎449
🅰🅾⚠
Level, grass and gravel site with trees, set in mountainous moorland country adjacent to river and Loch. no tents 1acre 15pitches 15static Apr–Oct must book last arrival 21.00hrs last departure 12.00hrs 4⚓ individual pitches late arrivals enclosure 8wc lit all night 1cdp 9washbasins hc ℏhc ☺ supervised cold storage calor gas toilet fluid ☎
↔ 🅿 🅰 ♩ pub
15⊕£2 or 15⇔£2 awnings

KILMARNOCK Strathclyde Map 34 NS43
▶**Cunningham Head Estate Caravan Park** (NS370418) Cunningham Head ☎Torranyard 238
🅰🅾⚠ signposted
Compact site within the grounds of a farmland estate. 3½m NE of Irvine on B769. 3acres 100pitches 60static
26 May–Sep rsApr–25 May no bookings last arrival 22.00hrs last departure 12.00hrs 7⚓ ⚠ 22wc lit all night washbasins hc ☺ (ℏhc) supervised (wash, spin, dry) games room cold storage licensed bar children's playground camping gaz toilet fluid ☎ ☎
↔ stables 🅿 🅰 cinema ♩ launderette
40⊕£3 20⇔£3 40⚐£3 (awnings)

KILNINVER Strathclyde Map 39 NM82
▶▶**Glen Gallain Caravan Park** (NM843196) ☎200
🅰🅾⚠ signposted
Part level, part sloping, grass and gravel site with young trees, set in mountainous wooded hill country adjacent to River Euchar. 10m S of Oban. 4acres 60pitches
Etr–mid Oct rsMar–Etr & Nov no bookings last arrival 22.00hrs last departure 12.00hrs 2⚓ individual pitches caravans only 6wc lit all night 1cdp washbasins hc (ℏhc) ☺ supervised (28 June–3 Sep) (spin, dry, iron) (cold storage) children's playground calor gas camping gaz paraffin toilet fluid ⊞(28 Jun–3 Sep) ☎
↔ 🅿 ♩
30⊕£3.20 or 30⇔£2.90 30⚐£2.70 (awnings) SA

KINGHORN Fife Map 35 NT28
▶▶▶▶**Pettycur Bay Caravan Park** (NT259865) ☎890241
🅰🅾⚠ signposted
This sloping, hillside, terraced site has splendid views of Edinburgh across the River Forth.
no motorcycles, no single sex groups 4acres 50pitches 360static
end Mar–early Oct booking advisable Jul & Aug last arrival 22.00hrs last departure 12.00hrs 16⚓ ⚠ late arrivals enclosure wc lit all night (⚫hc ℏhc) ☺ supervised (wash) (dry) iron children's playground calor gas toilet fluid cafe ☎ ⊞ ☎
↔ 🅿 cinema ♩ launderette pub
25⊕£3.60 or 25⇔£3.10 25⚐£3 (awnings) ltr SA

KINROSS Tayside Map 40 NO10
▶▶▶**Loch Leven Caravan Site** (NO123019) Sandport ☎63560
🅰🅾⚠ signposted
This level, grassy site is situated behind the town and on the shores of Loch Leven with good views of loch and surrounding countryside. The location is relatively secluded being off the main road. 1½acres 30pitches 44static
Apr–Sep booking advisable Jul & Aug last arrival 23.00hrs last departure 12.00hrs 5⚓ 15wc lit all night 1cdp 🚽 washbasins hc (ℏhc) ☺ supervised (wash) (dry, iron) games room CTV (cold storage) calor gas camping gaz ☎ ☎
↔ 🅿 🅰 cinema ♩ pub
30⊕£2.50 or 30⇔£2.50 or 30⚐£2.50 (awnings) SA
▶**Milk Bar** (NT129985) Hatchbank ☎63506
🅰🅾⚠ signposted
Level, grassy site in hilly country near lake. 2m S of Kinross and ½m N.of Junction 5 of M90. 2acres 30pitches 6static
Apr–Oct rsNov–Mar 1⚓ 10wc lit all night 1cdp washbasins hc ℏhc ☺ wash licensed club/bar children's playground calor gas camping gaz cafe ☎
↔ stables 🅿 cinema ♩ launderette pub
15⊕£2 or 15⇔£2 15⚐£2 (awnings) ltr

KIPPFORD Dumfries & Galloway Map 30 NX85
▶▶**Kippford Caravan Site** (NX844564) ☎636
🅰🅾⚠ signposted
Part level, part sloping grass site with bushes, set in hilly country adjacent to Urr Water estuary, main road and stony beach. 5acres 45pitches 84static
Mar–Oct no bookings last arrival 22.00hrs last departure 22.00hrs 5⚓ individual pitches for caravans ⚠ 12wc lit all night 1cdp 12washbasins hc 4ℏhc 1☺ supervised spin children's playground calor gas ☎
↔ stables 🅰 ♩ pub
45⊕£2.75–£3.45 or 45⇔£2.75–£3.45 or 45⚐£2.75–£3.45 (awnings)

KIRKCALDY Fife Map 41 NT29
▶▶▶**Dunnikier Caravan Site** (NT285942) Dunnikier Rd ☎67563
🅰🅾⚠ signposted
Level, grass site with trees and bushes. Within the urban area on B926. 3acres 95pitches
Apr–Sep booking advisable Jul & Aug last arrival 20.00hrs last departure 12.00hrs 10⚓ individual pitches ⚠ late arrivals enclosure 17wc lit all night 1cdp 🚽 washbasins hc central hot water ℏhc ☺ (wash) (dry, iron) calor gas ☎ ☎
↔ stables 🅿 🅰 cinema ♩ launderette pub
70⊕£2.70 or 70⇔£2.70 25⚐£1.65 (awnings) ltr

KIRKCUDBRIGHT Dumfries & Galloway Map 30 NX65
▶**Silvercraigs Caravan & Camping Site** (NX686508) Silvercraigs Rd
🅰🅾⚠ signposted
Touring site in pleasant elevated location, behind and overlooking the town. Famed for its Artists Colony. 4acres 50pitches
29 Mar–Sep no bookings last departure 12.00hrs 6⚓ individual pitches ⚠ 10wc lit all night 1cdp washbasins hc ℏhc ☺ children's playground ☎ ☎
↔ stables 🅿 🅰 ♩ pub
37⊕£2.50 or 37⇔£2.50 13⚐£2.50 awnings

KIRKFIELDBANK Strathclyde Map 34 NS84
▶▶**Clyde Valley Caravan Park** (NS868441) ☎Lanark 3951
🅰🅾⚠ signposted
Level, grass site with trees and bushes set in mountains and hilly country with access to

171

Kirkfieldbank contd – Lochgilphead | Camping and caravanning sites

river. 4acres 65pitches 60static
Apr–Sep no bookings last arrival mdnt last departure 18.00hrs 5⇨ individual pitches ⓐ 10wc lit all night 1cdp 16washbasins hc central hot water (2ℏhc) ⊙ supervised (wash, spin, dry) iron calor gas camping gaz toilet fluid 🏊
⊕ stables 🅿 🅰 ♪ launderette pub
25⇨ 25⇨ 15⛺ (awnings)

KIRKGUNZEON Dumfries & Galloway
Map 30 NX86
▶▶▶**Mossband Caravan Park** (NX873664)
☎280
①⊕⚠ signposted
Level park on site of old railway station in hilly country with trees and bushes; adjacent to main road, A711 to Dalbeattie. 3½acres 37pitches 3static
Etr–Oct rs1 Mar booking advisable Aug last arrival 22.00hrs last departure 14hrs 6⇨ late arrivals enclosure 10wc lit all night 1cdp 🚿 10washbasins hc 2ℏhc 2⊙ supervised spin 🚽 🅣 cold storage children's playground calor gas camping gaz toilet fluid cafe restaurant 🏊
⊕ 🅿 cinema ♪ pub
37⇨£2.90 or 37⇨£2.90 or 37⛺£2.90 (awnings) ltr

KIRKPATRICK FLEMING Dumfries & Galloway
Map 31 NY17
▶▶**Bruce's Cave & Caravan Site** (NY266705)
☎285
①⊕⚠ signposted
Part level, part sloping, grass, gravel and sand site with trees and bushes, set in wooded country and meadowland, with direct access to the river. Off A74 at Kirkpatrick. 80acres 45pitches 25static
Apr–Sep rsNov–Mar booking advisable Jul & Aug last arrival mdnt last departure 16.00hrs 8⇨ individual pitches late arrivals enclosure 14wc lit all night 1cdp 🚿 washbasins hc central hot water (⇨hc ℏhc) ⊙ supervised iron 🧺 (cold storage) children's playground calor gas toilet fluid cafe restaurant ☎ fishing 🏊
⊕ stables 🅿 🅰 cinema ♪ launderette pub
45⇨£2 or 15⇨£2 15⛺£2 (awnings) SA
▶▶**Greenfield Caravan Park** (NY275706) ☎237
①⊕⚠ signposted
A mainly level, grass and gravel site with young trees and bushes set within the urban area with direct access to main road and river. 2acres 40pitches 20static
All year last arrival 23.00hrs last departure 12.00hrs 3⇨ ⓐ late arrivals enclosure 3wc lit all night 1cdp 🚿 washbasins hc (ℏhc) ⊙ supervised (wash, spin, dry) cold storage licensed club/bar children's playground calor gas ☎ 🏊
⊕ ♪ launderette pub
10⇨£2.50 10⇨£2 20⛺£1 awnings ltr

KIRRIEMUIR Tayside Map 41 NO35
▶▶**Drumshademuir Caravan Park** (NO381509) Roundyhill ☎3284
②⊕⚠
Mainly level, part sloping, grass site with saplings and bushes. Set in a valley in hilly country 2½m S of Kirriemuir on A928. 5½acres 82pitches 28static
Apr–Oct rsNov–Mar must book peak periods 7⇨ individual pitches 15wc lit all night 2cdp 🚿 17washbasins hc ℏhc 4⊙ (1wash, 1spin, 1dry, 1iron) (cold storage) calor gas camping gaz paraffin toilet fluid ☎ 🅣 children's playground 🏊
⊕ 🅿 ♪ pub
82⇨ or 82⇨ or 82⛺ (awnings) ltr
▶**Thrums Caravan Site** (NO394533) Marytown ☎2436
①⊕
Level grassy site just outside town, backed by fruit trees on the B926 to Forfar. No ball games 2acres 30pitches
Apr–Sep no bookings individual pitches 2wc lit all night 🚿 (washbasins hc, central hot water) ⊙ calor gas camping gaz toilet fluid ☎ 🏊
⊕ 🅿 cinema
30⇨ 30⇨ 30⛺ awnings

LAIRG Highland Map 46 NC50
▶**Woodend Caravan & Camping Site** (NC551127) ☎2248
①⊕⚠ signposted
Part level, part sloping, grass site set in hilly moorland and woodland country with access to sea, beach, river and Loch Shin, off A836 to Tongue. 4½acres 45pitches 6static
Apr–Sep booking advisable Jul & Aug last arrival 22.00hrs last departure 12.00hrs 3⇨ 11wc lit all night 1cdp washbasins hc (central hot water) (ℏhc) ⊙ supervised wash cold storage children's playground ☎ 🏊
⊕ stables 🅰 ♪
45⇨£2 or 45⇨£2 or 45⛺£2 awnings

LAUDER Borders Map 35 NT54
▶▶**Thirlestane Castle Caravan Site** (NT536473) Thirlestane Castle ☎542
②⊕⚠ signposted
Mainly level grass site set in the grounds of the impressive Thirlestane Castle. The site is situated off the A697. 60pitches
Apr–15 Oct booking advisable Jul & Aug 4⇨ individual pitches 10wc lit all night 1cdp washbasins hc (central hot water) (ℏhc) ⊙ ☎
⊕ stables 🅿 ♪ pub
60⇨£3 or 60⇨£3 or 60⛺£3 (awnings) SA

LETHAM FEUS Fife Map 41 NO30
▶▶**Letham Feus Caravan Park** (NO369094) ☎Kennoway 350323
②⊕⚠ signposted
This is a grassy site near to a forest. Good southern views obtained over the River Forth and to the Bass Rock. No tents 1acre 11pitches 100static
Apr–Sep must book Jul & Aug last arrival 22.00hrs last departure 12.00hrs 8⇨ late arrivals enclosure 14wc lit all night 1cdp 🚿 18washbasins hc 6ℏhc 4⊙ (wash) (dry, iron) games room TV children's playground calor gas camping gaz toilet fluid 🏊
⊕ cinema ♪ launderette pub
11⇨£2.50 or 11⇨£2 awnings ltr

LOCHGILPHEAD Strathclyde Map 33 NR88
▶▶**Lochgilphead Caravan Site** (NR859881) ☎2003 or 2436
①⊕⚠
Mainly level grassy site set in the most beautiful mountain and loch scenery in Argyll. Fishing and sailing available on the loch. 3acres 30pitches 30static
Apr–Oct must book Jul & Aug last departure 12.00hrs 3⇨ late arrivals enclosure 17wc lit all night 1cdp washbasins hc ℏhc ⊙ supervised calor gas camping gaz toilet fluid 🏊
⊕ stables 🅿 🅰 cinema ♪ pub

172

25⇔ 5⇔ (awnings) ltr

LOCHGOILHEAD Strathclyde Map 39 NN20
▶▶**Lochgoilhead Caravan Site** (NN192013)
☎312
①❶⚠ signposted
A partly level and sloping grass and stony site with mature trees and bushes set in hills, and near river, lake, sea and beach. B828 and B839 to Lochgoilhead then ½m on Carrick Castle road.
No tents ¾acre 10pitches 160static
Apr–Oct last arrival 21.00hrs 1⇔ 7wc lit all night washbasins hc ⋒hc ⊙ supervised (wash) (dry) calor gas camping gaz paraffin ☎ ⚘
10⇔£2 or 10⇔£2

LOCHMABEN Dumfries & Galloway
Map 35 NY08
▶▶**Halleaths Caravan Site** (NY098818) ☎321
①❸⚠ signposted
Level, grassy site with hard standing. Situated within an estate in a sheltered position with a wood on one side and a high hedge on the other. From Lockerbie on A74 take A709 to Lochmaben – ½m on right after crossing River Annan. 3acres 80pitches
Apr–Oct late arrival 22.00hrs 5⇔ individual pitches ⚘ late arrivals enclosure 12wc lit all night 1cdp (washbasins hc) central hot water (⋒hc, ⊙) children's playground
↔ 🏠 cinema 🎵 ⚘
40⇔£3.25 20⇔£2.75 20⚘£2.75 (awnings) SA
▶▶**Kirloch Brae Caravan Site** (NY082825)
②❶⚠ signposted
Mainly level, grass site with mature trees set in meadowland, adjacent to loch and main road.
No tents ¾acre 30pitches
Etr–Oct no bookings 1⇔ 8wc lit all night 1cdp 8washbasins hc ⋒hc ⊙ (spin) ⚘
↔ 🏠 🎵 pub
30⇔ or 30⇔ (awnings) ltr

LOCHNAW Dumfries & Galloway
Map 30 NW96
▶▶**Drumlochart Caravan Park** (NW997634)
☎Leswalt 232
②❶⚠ signposted
Part level, part sloping, grass site with trees and bushes set in hilly woodland – adjacent to Loch Ryan and Luce Bay. 5m SW of Stranraer on A7043. 3acres 24pitches 96static
Mar–Oct last arrival 22.00hrs last departure 14.00hrs 6⇔ ⚘ late arrivals enclosure 14wc lit all night 1cdp washbasins hc ⋒hc ⊙ supervised (wash) (dry, iron) 🎮 games room (cold storage) licensed club/bar calor gas camping gaz ☎ boating & fishing ⚘
↔ stables 🏠 ⚠ 🎵
24⇔£3 or 24⇔£3 or 24⚘£3 (awnings)

LOCKERBIE Dumfries & Galloway
Map 35 NY18
▶▶**Glasgow Road Caravan Site** (NY133823)
①❶⚠ signposted
Level, grass site set in an urban area. Close to A74 on outskirts of town. 55pitches
Etr–Oct no bookings 2⇔ ⚘ 11wc lit all night 1cdp 16washbasins hc (2⋒hc) ⊙
↔ 🏠 cinema 🎵 pub
35⇔ or 35⇔ 20⚘ (awnings) ltr

LOSSIEMOUTH Grampian Map 44 NJ27
▶▶**Silver Sands Leisure Park** (NJ205710)
Covesea, West Beach (2m W B9040) ☎3262
②❶⚠ signposted

8acres 140pitches 160static
Etr & Jun–Aug rsApr–May & Sep–Oct last departure 12.00hrs 14⇔ 38wc lit all night 1cdp washbasins hc ⋒hc ⊙ (wash) (dry) games room licensed club/bar children's playground private beach calor gas camping gaz cafe restaurant ☎ ⚘
↔ 🏠 ⚠ 🎵 launderette pub
140⇔£3.20 or 140⇔£3.20 or 140⚘£3.20 (awnings)

LUIB Central Map 40 NN42
▶**Glen Dochart Caravan & Camping Park** (NN472268) ☎Killin 538
①❶⚠
Mainly level, part sloping, gravel and sand with trees and bushes set in mountainous country adjacent to main road (A85). 7½acres 125pitches 49static
Etr–mid Oct no bookings last arrival 21.00hrs last departure 12.00hrs 5⇔ ⚘ late arrivals enclosure 26wc lit all night 1cdp 25washbasins hc central hot water ⊙ (wash, spin, dry, iron) TV (cold storage) calor gas camping gaz toilet fluid hot drinks vending machine ☎ ⌂ ⚘
↔ ⚠ 🎵 launderette
76⇔ or 76⇔ 50⚘ (awnings)

LUNDIN LINKS Fife Map 41 NO40
▶▶**Woodland Gardens** (NO418031) Blindwell Rd ☎Upper Largo 319
②❶⚠ signposted
A predominantly touring site situated in hilly country at the foot of Largo Law and about ½m from Lundin Links. It has level grass areas and is bordered by well-established trees and shrubs which give seclusion and shelter. ½acre 20pitches 5static
Mar–Oct no bookings last departure 12.00hrs 3⇔ late arrivals enclosure 7wc lit all night 1cdp washbasinshc ⋒hc ⊙ supervised (iron) games room TV (cold storage) children's playground calor gas camping gaz ☎ ⚘
↔ stables 🏠 cinema 🎵 launderette pub
20⇔£2.80 or 20⇔£2.80 or 20⚘£2.80 (awnings)

LUSS Strathclyde Map 39 NS39
▶▶**Camping Club Site** (NS360936) ☎658
②❶⚠ signposted
Grassy site on the west shore of Loch Lomond. No awnings, no caravans or motor caravans
10½acres 90pitches
Apr–Sep must book peak periods last arrival 23.00hrs last departure 12.00hrs 4⇔ late arrivals enclosure 12wc lit all night 1cdp washbasins hc ⋒hc supervised children's playground private beach camping gaz toilet fluid ☎ ⚘
↔ ⚠ 🎵 pub
90⚘£3.20–£3.76

MACDUFF Grampian Map 45 NJ76
▶▶▶**Myrus Caravan Site** (NJ710634)
☎Banff 2845
②❶⚠ signposted
Part level, part sloping, grass site with trees and bushes, set in meadowland. On main A947.
2acres 30pitches 30static
Jul & Aug rsApr–Jun & Sep–Oct must book Jul & Aug last departure 12.00hrs 8 ⚘ 21wc lit all night 1cdp washbasins hc (⋒hc) ⊙ supervised (wash spin dry) iron games room (cold storage) children's playground calor gas camping gaz toilet fluid ☎ bicycles for hire
↔ 🏠 🎵 launderette pub ⚘

173

Macduff contd – Mouswald

⊕£2.30 ⇌£2.30 △£2.30 (awnings)

MAIDENS Strathclyde Map 33 NS20
▶▶**Sandy Beach Caravan Park** *(NS215082)*
☎Turnberry 456
①❶⚠
This is a mainly level, grass site near to the sea and beach. no tents 8pitches 40static Apr–15 Oct rs24 Dec–3 Jan must book peak periods last arrival 19.00hrs last departure 12.00hrs 3⚘ individual pitches late arrivals enclosure 9wc lit all night 1cdp washbasins hc ♨hc ☺ (wash spin) games room cold storage toilet fluid ☎ ☒
⊕ ✉ ⚠ ♪ launderette pub
5⊕£3 3⇌£3 ltr SA

MARYCULTER Grampian Map 41 NO89
▶▶**Lower Deeside Caravan Park** *(NJ855001)*
☎Aberdeen 733860
①❶⚠
A level and grassy site with mature trees, near river. 5m SW of Aberdeen. 3acres 45pitches 60static
Apr–Oct no bookings last arrival 22.00hrs last departure 12.00hrs 4⚘ ⚐ 8wc lit all night washbasins hc central hot water ♨hc ☺ supervised (wash spin dry) iron games room TV children's playground calor gas camping gaz ⚑ ☒
⊕ ♪ launderette pub
15⊕£2.50 or 15⇌£2.50 30△£2.50 (awnings) ltr

MELROSE Borders Map 35 NT53
▶▶**Gibson Park Caravan Site** *(NT545341)*
Apply to: Ettrick & Lauderdale District Council, Council Chambers, Paton St, Galashiels TD1 3AS ☎Galashiels 4751 ext 47
①❶⚠ signposted
A secluded, sloping grass site partially screened by mature trees, with views of Eildon Hills. The site adjoins a recreation park and is situated a short distance from the historic border town shopping centre. no single sex groups 60pitches
Apr–Oct must book last arrival 22.00hrs last departure 12.00hrs 2⚘ individual pitches ⚐ 10wc lit all night 1cdp washbasins hc central hot water ♨hc ☺ (T) games room children's playground ☒
⊕ stables ⚑ pub
60⊕£2.50–£3 or 60⇌£2.50–£3 or 60△£2.50–£3 awnings ltr SA

MEMUS Grampian Map 41 NO45
▶▶**Glens Caravan Site** *(NO426592)*
☎Foreside 258
③❷ signposted
Level, grass site with young trees and bushes set in mountainous meadowland. 5m off A94.
1acre 9pitches 21static
Apr–Oct booking advisable Jul & Aug last arrival 23.00hrs 1⚘ late arrivals enclosure 6wc lit all night washbasins hc (♨hc) ☺ supervised calor gas camping gaz paraffin toilet fluid ☎ ☒

⊕ stables ⚑ ♪
9⊕£2.10 or 9⇌£2.10 2△£2.10 (awnings) SA

MINTLAW Grampian Map 45 NK04
▶▶**Aden Country Park Caravan Park** *(NJ995484)* ☎Macduff 32861
②❶⚠ signposted
Pleasant grassy site set at entrance of country park. Just off A950, this site is partially screened by trees. 4½acres 27pitches 3static
May–Sept must book last arrival 21.00hrs last departure 09.00hrs 4⚘ 6wc lit all night 1ccp washbasins hc ♨hc ☒
⊕ stables ⚑ ♪ pub
23⊕fr£2.10 or 23⇌fr£1.80 4△fr£1 (awnings)

MOFFAT Dumfries & Galloway Map 35 NT00
▶▶**Camping Club Site** *(NT080051)*
Hammerland's Farm ☎20436
②❶⚠ signposted
Well maintained level grass touring site.
5½acres 150pitches
Apr–Sep must book Jul & Aug last arrival 22.00hrs last departure 12.00hrs 4⚘ late arrivals enclosure 1cdp washbasins hc ♨hc ☺ supervised (wash spin dry) iron children's playground calor gas camping gaz ☎ ☒
⊕ stables ⚑ ⚠ launderette pub
150⊕fr£2.44 or 150⇌fr£2.44 or 150△fr£2.44 awnings SA

MONIFIETH Tayside Map 41 NO43
▶▶**Riverview Caravan Park** *(NO502322)*
Apply to: General Manager of Parks, Parks Dept., Dundee District Council, 17 King Street, Dundee DD1 1LD ☎Dundee 23141 ext 413
①❶⚠ signposted
A level and grassy site near sea and beach. 400yds S of A930. Situated approx 7m E from Dundee town centre. 10acres 180pitches
Apr–Oct booking advisable Jul & Aug ⚘ individual pitches 34wc lit all night 4cdp 15washbasins hc (♨hc) ☺ children's playground ☎ ⊞ ☒
⊕ stables ⚑ ⚠ cinema ♪ launderette
180⊕£2.20–£2.50 or 180⇌£2.20–£2.50 or 180△£2.20–£2.50 awnings SA

MONTROSE Tayside Map 41 NO75
▶▶**South Links Site** *(NO725575)* Traill Dr
Apply to: Director of Parks & Cemeteries, Angus District Council, Town House, Montrose, Angus DD10 8QW ☎2044
①❶⚠ signposted
A grassy, sloping site near the sea and beach.
No tents 6acres 116pitches
Etr–23 Oct must book Jun–Aug last arrival 21.00hrs last departure 12.00hrs 6⚘ individual pitches 21wc lit all night 2cdp washbasin hc central hot water ♨hc ☺ (wash spin) children's playground ☒
⊕ stables ⚑ ♪ launderette
116⊕£2.20 or 116⇌£2.20 (awnings) ltr

MOUSWALD Dumfries & Galloway
Map 31 NY07

RIVERVIEW CARAVAN PARK, MONIFIETH

Modern caravan facilities (180 pitches) situated approximately 7/8 miles east from Dundee town centre, on Monifieth foreshore adjacent to a safe sandy beach and Riverview Park which offers leisure and recreation facilities.

Booking facilities available on site and further details of charges etc, or prior booking can be obtained from the General Manager of Parks, 17 King Street.
Phone Dundee 23141 Ext 413.

▶▶Mouswald Caravan Park *(NY060740)*
☎226
②❸⚠ signposted
Level, grass site with mature trees and bushes.
Off A75 Dumfries–Annan road.
35pitches 15static
Etr–Oct no bookings 2⚑ 10wc 1cdp
10washbasins hc (ⁿhc) ☉ supervised (wash spin) (iron) (cold storage) calor gas toilet fluid ☎ mobile 🛒
❂ cinema 🎵 launderette ⛴
25⚐£2.25 5⚑£2.25 5⚑£2.25 (awnings)

NAIRN Highland Map 44 NH85
▶▶▶Delnies Wood Caravan Park
(NH846552) ☎54752
③❸⚠ signposted
An attractive site set amongst pine trees.
7acres 50pitches
Apr–Oct must book high season last departure 10.00hrs 5⚑ individual pitches late arrivals enclosure 10wc lit all night 2cdp
10washbasins hc 2 central hot water 6ⁿhc 3☉ supervised children's playground calor gas camping gaz paraffin toilet fluid ☎ 🛒
❂ stables 🚲 ⛺ cinema 🎵 launderette pub
30⚐£2–£3.25 10⚑£2–£3.25 10⚑£2–£3.25 (awnings)

▶▶▶East Beach Caravan Park *(NH895574)*
East Beach ☎53764
①❸⚠ signposted
A level site bordered by the beach, the River Nairn and golf course. 2¾acres 100pitches 280static
15 Mar–Oct booking advisable peak periods last arrival 21.00hrs last departure 10.00hrs
7⚑ individual pitches ☉ late arrivals enclosure 30wc lit all night 3cdp 30washbasins hc 3 central hot water 6ⁿhc 8☉ supervised (wash spin dry iron) children's playground private beach calor gas camping gaz toilet fluid ☎ ⊞ 🛒
❂ stables 🚲 ⛺ cinema 🎵 launderette pub
50⚐£2–£3.25 20⚑£2–£3.25 30⚑£2–£3.25 (awnings)

NEWTON STEWART Dumfries & Galloway
Map 30 NX46
▶▶▶Creebridge Caravan Park *(NX415656)*
☎2324
①❸⚠ signposted
Level, grass and gravel site with trees set in urban area. ½m E of Newton Stewart on A75.
40pitches 45static
Apr–Oct booking advisable Jul & Aug last arrival 22.00hrs last departure 12.00hrs 9⚑ late arrivals enclosure lit all night washbasins hc ⁿhc ☉ supervised (wash) (dry, iron) children's playground private beach calor gas camping gaz toilet fluid ☎ 🛒
❂ 🅿 cinema 🎵 launderette pub
40⚐£2.50 or 40⚑£2.50 or 40⚑£2.50 (awnings)

NORTH BERWICK Lothian Map 35 NT58
▶▶Rhodes Caravan Site *(NT566850)*
②❸⚠ signposted
Level grass site in meadowland in the urban area with direct access to sea and beach.
Located off A198 Dunbar road. 10acres
350pitches
Apr–Sep no bookings last departure 10.30hrs 17⚑ ☉ late arrivals enclosure 68wc lit all night 8cdp 54washbasins hc 24ⁿhc ☉ (wash, spin) children's playground calor gas camping gaz ☎ 🛒
❂ stables 🚲 cinema 🎵 pub
350⚐£2.50–£3 or 350⚑£2.50–£3 or 350⚑£2.50–£3

PARTON Dumfries & Galloway Map 30 NX67
▶▶▶Loch Ken Holiday Centre *(NX687702)*
☎282
②❸⚠ signposted
A compact touring site on the eastern shores of Loch Ken. 60pitches 17static
Mar–Oct last arrival 15.00hrs last departure 10.00hrs 10⚑ individual pitches ☉ 16wc lit all night 1cdp washbasins hc ⁿhc ☉ (wash) (dry, iron) cold storage children's playground calor gas camping gaz ☎ boats for hire 🛒
❂ stables 🚲 ⛺ cinema 🎵 launderette pub
40⚐£3.50 or 40⚑£3.50 20⚑£3.50 (awnings) SA

PEEBLES Borders Map 35 NT24
▶▶▶▶Rosetta Caravan & Camping Park
(NT245415) ☎20770
②❸⚠ signposted
Part level, part sloping, grass site with mature trees and bushes, set in hilly woodland country. ½m from town centre off A72. 24acres
130pitches
Apr–Oct must book peak periods last arrival 22.30hrs last departure 12.00hrs 5⚑ individual pitches caravans only ☉ 26wc lit all night 2cdp washbasins hc ⁿhc ☉ supervised (wash) spin (dry) iron games room TV cold storage licensed club/bar children's playground calor gas camping gaz toilet fluid ☎ 🛒
❂ stables 🚲 ⛺ 🎵 launderette pub
100⚐ or 100⚑ 30⚑ (awnings)

▶▶▶Crossburn Caravan Park *(NT248417)*
Edinburgh Rd ☎20501
②❸⚠ signposted
A gently sloping, grassy site, in a peaceful and relatively quiet location, despite the proximity of the main road which partly borders the site as does the Eddleston Water. Natural screening by mature and young trees all add to the feeling of seclusion. 2acres 25pitches 95static
Apr–14 Oct booking advisable Jul & Aug last arrival 23.00hrs last departure 12.00hrs 11⚑ individual pitches 17wc lit all night · 2cdp ⛾ 18washbasins hc 9ⁿhc 4☉ supervised (wash, spin) (iron) children's playground calor gas camping gaz toilet fluid 🛒
❂ stables 🚲 ⛺ launderette pub
25⚐£2.75 or 25⚑£2.75 or 25⚑£2.75 (awnings) SA

PERTH Tayside *Perthshire* Map 40 NO12
▶▶Cleeve Caravan Park *(NO095228)* Glasgow

Loch Ken Holiday Centre

Camp site ▶▶▶

Parton, by Castle Douglas,
South West Scotland
Telephone: Parton (064 47) 282

A small caravan and camping park on the shores of loch Ken, in Galloway. Beautifully situated in the Ken/Dee Valley, surrounded by hills and woodland it provides a perfect spot from which to walk, fish and sail. The caravan park is on the A713 Castle Douglas to Ayr Road, and has established a reputation for high standards of cleanliness and service. The park has a grocery shop, play area for children, modern toilet block with H & C water, showers and electric shaving points. Laundry and dish washing facilities. Open from late March to October.   **Proprietors: Mr & Mrs Mungo Bryson.**

Perth contd–Powfoot

Rd ☎25662
②⊘△ signposted
Level grass site with young trees and bushes.
60pitches
Etr–Oct last arrival 18.00hrs last departure
16.00hrs 5⇌ individual pitches wc lit all night
washbasins hc central hot water ⋔hc ☉ ☎ ⊞
children's playground
➔ stables 🅿 △ cinema ♪ launderette pub 🛒
60⇌ or 60⇌ awnings ltr
▶▶Windsor Caravan Park (NO110225)
Windsor Ter ☎23721
②⊘△ signposted
A small, sloping, grass site situated within
residential area of the city but with a pleasant
rural atmosphere owing to effective screening
by bushes and mature trees. An attractive
feature is the waterfall tumbling over a natural
rocky outcrop at one en d of the park. no tents
7pitches 16static
Apr–Sep must book Jul & Aug last departure
11.00hrs 1⇌ individual pitches 6wc lit all
night 1cdp 7washbasins hc central hot water
(2⋔hc) 2☉ calor gas 🛒
➔ stables 🅿 cinema ♪ launderette 🛒
7⇌£2 or 7⇌£2

PITLOCHRY Tayside Map 40 NN95
▶▶▶**Faskally Home Farm** (NN916603) ☎2007
①⊘△ signposted
This site is situated outside the town and on the
banks of the River Gay. Although bordered on
one side by the main road, most of the site is on
gently sloping grassland dotted with trees.
Splendid views. Turn off A9 Pitlochry by-pass ½m
N of town, proceed 1m N on A924. 23acres
400pitches 60static
15 Mar–Oct booking advisable Jul & Aug 24⇌
△ 96wc lit all night 1cdp 🎲 washbasins hc
(⋔hc) ☉ (wash) (dry, iron) (games room) cold
storage children's playground calor gas
camping gaz toilet fluid ☎ 🛒
➔ stables 🅿 △ cinema ♪ launderette pub
255⇌£2.90 or 255⇌£2.80 150⇌£2.40
(awnings) ltr
▶▶▶**Milton of Fonab Caravan Site**
(NN945573) ☎2882
②⊘△ signposted
Level, grass site with mature trees on banks of
River Tummel. ½m S of town. no motorcycles
no single sex groups no tents without car
12acres 154pitches 36static
29 Mar–6 Oct must book Jul & Aug last
arrival 21.00hrs last departure 13.00hrs 20⇌
individual pitches caravans only ☉ 43wc
lit all night 1cdp 50washbasins hc (4⇌hc,
4⋔hc) 16☉ (wash, spin, dry) iron cold
storage calor gas camping gaz toilet fluid

☎ 🛒
➔ stables 🅿 △ cinema ♪ launderette pub
154⇌£2.90 or 154⇌£2.50 or 154⇌£2.90
(awnings)

POOLEWE Highland Map 42 NG88
▶▶▶**Inverewe Stage House** (NG861811)
☎249
②⊘△ signposted
Level, grass and sand site with trees and
bushes, set in mountainous moorland and hills,
with access to sea and beach. 4acres
50pitches
Apr–Sep booking advisable Jun–Aug last
arrival 21.00hrs last departure 12.00hrs 4⇌
individual pitches 10wc lit all night 1cdp
10washbasins hc (4⋔hc, 2☉) (wash, spin, cry)
calor gas camping gaz 🛒
➔ ♪
50⇌£2.50 or 50⇌£2.40 5⇌£2.50 (awnings)

PORTKNOCKIE Grampian Map 45 NJ46
▶**Macleod Park Camping Site** (NJ494684,
☎Cullen 40270
①❶ signposted
A level and grassy site near to the sea and
beach. 30 pitches 5static
9 Apr–Sep ⇌ individual pitches △ 6wc lit all
night washbasins hc (⋔hc) ☉ (wash, dry) ⊞ 🛒
➔ ♪ launderette pub
20⇌ or 20⇌ 10⇌ rates on application ltr

PORTSOY Grampian Map 45 NJ56
▶**Portsoy Links Site** (NJ592662) Apply to:
Director of Leisure and Recreation, Banff &
Buchan District Council, 1 Church St, Macduff,
Banffshire AB4 1UF ☎Macduff 32861
②⊘ signposted
Local authority run site, in pleasant position on
seafront giving unrestricted views over Moray
Firth. 8m NW of Banff. In Portsoy turn north off
A98 into Church Street then in 100 metres turn
right into Institute Street. 2½acres 45pitches
37 static
Apr–Sep must book
last arrival 21.00hrs last departure 09.00hrs
2⇌ 10wc lit all night washbasins hc (central
hot water) (⋔hc) supervised (wash, spin, dry)
children's playground calor gas camping gaz
paraffin toilet fluid mobile🛒 🛒
➔ stables △ ♪ launderette pub 🛒
35⇌£2.10 or 35⇌£1.80 10⇌£1 (awnings)

POWFOOT Dumfries & Galloway Map 31 NY16
▶▶**Queensberry Bay Caravan Park**
(NY140654) ☎Cummertrees 205
②⊘△ signposted
Touring and static site in quiet location beside

MILTON OF FONAB CARAVAN SITE
PITLOCHRY, PERTHSHIRE

Ideally situated on the banks of River Tummel ½ mile south of Pitlochry. All modern amenities — flush sanitation, hot baths and showers, hot and cold in wash basins, electric shaving points, laundry facilities, shop.

This site is renowned for the high standard of cleanliness and the peace and quietness maintained, through strict observance of commonsense rules.

Separate sections for touring caravans, motor caravans, tents with cars. Fully equipped modern caravans for hire. SAE for reply.
Tel: Pitlochry 2882.

Solway Firth adjacent to beach and golf course.
60pitches 50static
Apr–Oct must book peak periods 5⚌ ⓐ
13wc lit all night 1cdp washbasins hc ⓝhc ☺
supervised wash spin dry iron ▣ Ⓣ games
room TV calor gas camping gaz toilet fluid ☎ ⚒
⇨ stables ⬛ cinema ♪ launderette pub
60⚌ ⚍ (awnings)

RAVENSTRUTHER Strathclyde Map 34 NS94
▶▶**Newhouse Farm** *(NS926456)*
☎Carstairs 228
③☺⚠ signposted
Level grass and gravel site, with young trees
and bushes. Situated on A70, Ayr–Edinburgh
road 3m E of Lanark. 2acres 10pitches
Mar–Oct last departure 12.00hrs 1⚌ 4wc lit
all night 1cdp ▣ washbasins hc (ⓝhc) ☺ cold
storage children's playground calor gas
camping gaz
⇨ stables ⬛ ⚠ ♪ launderette pub ⚒
10⚌£1.75 or 10⚌£1.75 or 10⚍£1.75 awnings ltr

REAY Highland Map 47 NC96
▶**Dunvegan Euro Campsite** *(NC960644)*
②☺⚠ signposted
Level and grassy site with slight gradients,
young trees and bushes set in meadowland and
in urban area with access to sea and beach. 12m
W of Thurso. Site is adjacent to A836 in village.
25pitches
Jun–Oct last arrival 21.30hrs last departure
12.00hrs 1⚌ late arrivals enclosure 4wc lit all
night (washbasins hc, central hot water) (ⓝhc)
☺ ☎ ⚒
⇨ stables ⬛ ⚠ ♪
10⚌£1.25 5⚌£1.25 10⚍£1.25 (awnings)

RESIPOL (Loch Sunart) Highland Map 38 NM76
▶▶**Resipole Farm** *(NM725639)* ☎Salen 235
②☺⚠
A spacious and grassy site in isolated roadside
position overlooking Loch Sunart. 8acres
110pitches
15 May–15 Oct rs15 Mar–14 May booking
advisable mid Jul–mid Aug last departure
12.00hrs 5⚌ 15wc lit all night 1cdp
8washbasins hc 4ⓝhc 2☺ cold storage calor
gas camping gaz paraffin toilet fluid ⚒
⇨ stables ⚠ ♪
60⚌£2.40 or 40⚌£2.40 40⚍£2.40 (awnings)

ROSEHEARTY Grampian Map 45 NJ96
▶▶**Rosehearty Caravan Site** *(NJ935675)*
Apply to: Director of Leisure & Recreation, Banff
& Buchan District Council, 1 Church St,
Macduff, Banffshire AB4 1UF☎Macduff 32861
①☺⚠ signposted
A level, grass site near the sea and beach. 4m W
of Fraserburgh on B9031. 1acre 30pitches
10static
May–Sep must book last arrival 21.00hrs last
departure 09.00hrs 2⚌ 9wc lit all night
washbasins hc (central hot water) (ⓝhc) ☺
(wash, spin, dry) children's playground calor
gas camping gaz paraffin toilet fluid mobile⚒
⇨ ⬛ ♪ pub
20⚌fr£2.10 or 20⚌fr£1.80 10⚍fr£1 (awnings)

ROSEMARKIE Highland Map 44 NH75
▶▶**Rosemarkie Site** *(NH739570)*
②☺⚠ signposted
A level and grassy site near sea and beach. ½m E
of Fortrose on A832. 6acres
May–Sep no bookings 6⚌ individual pitches

14wc lit all night (18washbasins hc) (4ⓝhc)
4☺ ⊞
⇨ ⬛ ♪
70⚌ or 70⚌ or 70⚍

ROY BRIDGE Highland Map 39 NN28
▶**Bunroy Caravan Park** *(NN273806)* ☎Spean
Bridge 332
③☺⚠ signposted
Level, grass site sheltered by mature trees and
bordered by River Spean, set in mountainous
country. 300yds off A86. 2acres 30pitches
1static
Apr–Sep no bookings last arrival 22.00hrs last
departure 16.00hrs 3⚌ 8wc lit all night
(washbasins hc, central hot water) (ⓝhc) ☺
supervised
⇨ ⬛ ♪ pub ⚒
30⚌£2.20 or 30⚌£2.20 or 30⚍£2.20 (awnings)
▶**Stronreigh** *(NN258812)* ☎Spean Bridge 275
①☺⚠ signposted
Part level, part sloping, grass and gravel site
with trees and bushes, set in meadowland,
adjacent to River Spean. On A86 11m N of Fort
William. ½acre 10pitches 10static
Apr–Oct must book 4⚌ 4wc lit all night
(washbasins hc) (central hot water) (ⓝhc) ☺
spin cold storage children's playground calor
gas ☎
⇨ stables ⬛ ⚠ ♪ launderette ⚒
10⚌ or 4⚌ 10⚍ awnings ltr

ST ANDREWS Fife Map 41 NO51
▶▶▶▶**Craigtoun Meadows Holiday Park**
(NO483153) Mount Melville ☎75959
③☺⚠ signposted
Set in downland with mixed woodland and
pasture, 2m from sea and sandy beaches. 2m
from St Andrews on the Craigtoun road. 8acres
98pitches 146static
Mar–Oct booking advisable Jul & Aug last
arrival 21.00hrs last departure 12.00hrs 29⚌
individual pitches ⓐ late arrivals enclosure
19wc lit all night 2cdp ▣ washbasins hc ⓝhc
☺ supervised (wash, spin, dry) iron games
room CTV cold storage children's playground
calor gas camping gaz toilet fluid cafe
restaurant ☎ ⊞ bicycle hire ⚒
⇨ stables ⬛ ⚠ cinema ♪ launderette pub
90⚌£2.50–£4.50 or 90⚌£2.50–£4.50 8⚍£2.50–
£4.50 (awnings)
▶▶▶**Kinkell Braes Caravan Site** *(NO522156)*
☎Cupar 53722
①☺⚠
A large predominantly static site in open position
high above the town with fine panoramic views
across St Andrews and Firth of Tay. Lovely
sandy beaches nearby. 29½acres 69pitches
25 Mar–5 Oct must book last arrival 20.00hrs
last departure 20.00hrs 17⚌ individual pitches
late arrivals enclosure 116wc lit all night 1cdp
146washbasins hc 20ⓝhc 31☺ (wash) (dry)
children's playground calor gas camping gaz
☎ ⚒
⇨ stables ⬛ ⚠ cinema ♪ launderette pub
69⚌£3 or 69⚌£3 or 69⚍£1.50–£3 (awnings)

ST FILLANS Tayside Map 40 NN72
▶▶▶**Lochearn Caravan Park** *(NN680239)*
South Shore Rd ☎270
②☺⚠
Part level, part sloping gravel site with young
trees and bushes, set in mountainous country
adjacent to lake. 6m W of Comrie on A85. No
tents 30pitches 204static
Apr–27 Oct no bookings last arrival 20.00hrs

177

St Fillans contd–Stirling   Camping and caravanning sites

last departure 16.00hrs 10⇔ 38wc lit all night washbasins hc (ñhc) ☺ (wash, spin, dry) calor gas camping gaz ☎ ♨
➡ 🅟 ♪ launderette
30☆ or 30⇔ (awnings)

SANDBANK Strathclyde Map 33 NS18
▶**Cot House Garage** (NS154831) Cot House
☎Kilmun 351
①◉△
This level grass and gravel site with trees and bushes is set in mountains in the urban area, adjacent to sea, beach and river. 5m NE Dunoon on A815. 1acre 37pitches 15static
Apr–Oct no bookings 2⇌ ☺ no cars by tents 6wc 1cdp (central hot water) (ñhc) ☺ calor gas camping gaz paraffin cafe restaurant ♨
➡ stables 🅟 ▲ cinema ♪ launderette pub
7☆£1.95 or 7⇔£1.95 30☆£1.95 awnings SA

SANQUHAR Dumfries & Galloway
Map 34 NS70
▶▶**Castle View Caravan Park** (NS786095)
☎291
①◉△ signposted
Small site set behind filling station and general store on edge of village in Upper Nithsdale. 1acre 8pitches 22static
Apr–Sep rsOct–Mar last arrival 22.00hrs last departure 12.00hrs 3⇌ ☺ late arrivals enclosure 3wc lit all night 1cdp 🅘 washbasins hc (ñhc) ☺ supervised wash spin cold storage calor gas camping gaz paraffin ♨
➡ 🅟 ♪ pub ♨
8☆£2.50 or 8⇔£2.50 or 8☆£2.50 (awnings)

SCANIPORT Highland Map 43 NH63
▶**Scaniport Caravan Site** (NH628398)
①◉△ signposted
A level and grassy site with some trees, set in hills, woodland, moorland and near canal. On A862 Inverness–Foyers road about 5m S of Inverness, entrance to site is opposite Scaniport Post Office. 2acres 30pitches
May–Sep no bookings last arrival 20.00hrs last departure 12.00hrs 1⇌ 6wc lit all night (washbasins hc) (ñhc) ☺ calor gas camping gaz ♨
➡ ♪
15☆£1.30–£1.50 or 15⇔£1.30–£1.50 15☆£1.30–£1.50 (awnings)

SCONE Tayside Map 40 NO12
▶▶▶**Scone Palace Camping Club Site**
(NO106173) Scone Racecourse ☎52323
②◉△ signposted
14½acres 150pitches 20static
Apr–Sep must book 1–14 Aug last arrival 23.00hrs last departure 12.00hrs 11⇌ late arrivals enclosure 29wc lit all night 2cdp 28washbasins hc 10ñhc 10☺ supervised (wash, spin, dry, iron) licensed club/bar children's playground calor gas camping gaz ☎ ♨
➡ stables 🅟 ▲ cinema ♪ launderette pub
150☆frf£1.22 or 150⇔frf£1.22 or 150frf£1.22 (awnings)

SCOURIE Highland Map 46 NC14
▶▶**Scourie Caravan & Camping Site**
(NC153446) ☎2217
②◉△ signposted
Mainly level site adjacent to beach and sea. In centre of village off the Kylesku–Laxford road A894. 4acres 80pitches
Apr–Oct no bookings last arrivals 22.00hrs last departure 12.00hrs 2⇌ 10wc lit all night washbasins hc (ñhc) ☺ supervised spin iron cold storage cafe restaurant ♨
➡ ▲ ♪ pub
20☆£2.50 15⇔£2.50 40☆£2.50 (awnings) ltr

SHIEL BRIDGE Highland Map 42 NG91
▶**Shiel Bridge Caravan Site** (NG938185)
Dochgarroch
①◉△ signposted
Level grass and sand site, set in mountainous country with access to sea, beach and river estuary. 15m from Kyle of Lochalsh. 2¼acres 65pitches
May–Sep no bookings last arrival 20.00hrs last departure 12.00hrs 4⇌ ☺ 8wc lit all night 1cdp washbasins hc ñhc ☺ calor gas camping gaz cafe ♨
➡ ♪
40☆£2.50–£2.80 or 40⇔£2.50–£2.80 25☆£2.50–£2.80 awnings

SKYE, ISLE OF Highland Map 42 NG
See Camustianavaig, Dunvegan and Staffin

SOUTHERNESS Dumfries & Galloway
Map 30 NX95
▶▶▶**Southerness Holiday Village**
(NX976545) ☎Kirkbean 256
②◉△ signposted
A large campsite situated in close proximity to sandy beach. 8acres 250pitches 450static
Mar–Oct 24⇌ individual pitches ☺ late arrivals enclosure wc lit all night ⚉ washbasins hc central hot water ñhc ☺ (wash, spin, dry, iron) licensed club/bar children's playground private beach calor gas camping gaz toilet fluid cafe restaurant ☎ mobile ♨ ♨
➡ ♪ launderette pub
150☆£3.25 50⇔£3.25 50☆£3.25 (awnings) ltr

STAFFIN Isle of Skye, Highland Map 42 NG46
▶▶**Staffin Caravan & Camping Site**
(NG496668) ☎213
②◉△ signposted
Level and gently sloping, gravel, grass and sand site with young trees and bushes, set in hilly downland and meadowland, adjacent to sea, beach and river. 16m N of Portree on A855. 2½acres 82pitches 6static
May–Sep rsApr & Oct must book Jul & Aug last arrival 22.00hrs last departure 11.00hrs 5⇌ individual pitches ☺ 8wc 1cdp washbasins hc ñhc ☺ supervised cold storage children's playground private beach toilet fluid
➡ ▲ ♨
20☆£2.50 10⇔£2.50 52☆£2 (awnings) ltr SA

STIRLING Central Map 40 NS79
▶**Cornton Caravan Park** (NS786952) ☎4503
①◉△ signposted
This is a level, grass site situated on the outskirts of the town and near to the main road. Some nearby housing development is apparent but splendid views are obtained of both Stirling and the Wallace monument. 2acres 26pitches 16static
Apr–Oct no bookings 2⇌ 13wc lit all night 1cdp 🅘 washbasins hc ☺ supervised (dry, iron) (cold storage) children's playground calor gas camping gaz toilet fluid fishing ♨
➡ stables 🅟 ▲ cinema ♪ launderette pub
26☆£3 or 26⇔£2.80 ☆£3 (awnings)

Camping and caravanning sites

Stonehaven–Thurso

STONEHAVEN Grampian Map 41 NO88
▶▶▶**Queen Elizabeth Caravan Site**
(NO875866) Apply to: Leisure & Recreation Officer, Kincardine & Deeside District Council, Leisure & Recreation Dept, View Mount, Stonehaven, Kincardineshire.
☎62001 ext 21 or 48
🚽⊕⚠ signposted
A gently sloping grass site offering a good range of recreational facilities, situated between a main road and seafront adjoining a public park.
½acre 40pitches 80static
5 Apr–Oct booking advisable last arrival 20.30hrs last departure 10.30hrs individual pitches 22wc lit all night 2cdp washbasins hc (ñhc) ☉ (wash, spin, dry, iron, ■) children's playground mobile 🛒
⇔ stables 🚲 🏕 🎵 launderette pub
40♣£2.50 or 40🚐£2.50 or 40🔺£2.50 ltr

STRACHAN Grampian Map 41 NO69
▶▶**Feughside Caravan Site** (NO642926)
☎Feughside 669
🚽⊕⚠
Level, grass site with young trees and bushes, set in hilly moorland and woodland country, adjacent to Water of Feugh. 5m W of Banchory and 9m E of Aboyne, just off B976. Situated behind the Feughside Inn, 2m W of Strachan.
No tents ½acre 8pitches 39static
Apr–mid Oct last arrival 22.00hrs 8🚐 individual pitches 9wc lit all night 1cdp washbasins hc (central hot water) ñhc ☉ (wash) (dry) iron games room cold storage children's playground calor gas
⇔ pub 🛒
♣fr£2.75 🚐fr£2 (awnings) ltr

STRACHUR Strathclyde Map 39 NN00
▶▶▶**Strathlachlan Caravan Park** (NN013953)
☎300
🚽⊕⚠ signposted
Mainly level grass site screened by mature trees on edge of river. Views of Loch Fyne. From Strachur follow the A886 for 3m then turn right onto B8000 (Kilfinan) road, site in approx 3m.
No tents 1acre 14pitches 8static
Apr–Oct booking advisable peak periods last arrival 22.00hrs last departure 12.00hrs 5🚐 individual pitches 9wc lit all night washbasins hc ñhc ☉ supervised (wash, spin) calor gas camping gaz 🛒
⇔ 🎵 launderette pub
♣£2.75 🚐£2.75 awnings ltr

STRANRAER Dumfries & Galloway
Map 30 NX06
▶▶▶**Aird Donald Caravan Park** (NX075605)
☎2025
🚽⊕⚠ signposted
Level, grass and sand site with trees and bushes. Set in woodland and meadowland within the urban area. There is a tarmac hard standing for 25 caravans. 12acres 175pitches 25static
All year last arrival 22.00hrs last departure 14.00hrs 8🚐 individual pitches ⓐ late arrivals enclosure 29wc lit all night 2cdp washbasins hc central hot water (ñhc) ☉ supervised (spin, iron) (cold storage) children's playground calor gas camping gaz 🛒 🛒
⇔ stables 🚲 🏕 🎵 launderette
175♣ or 175🚐 or 175🔺 (awnings)
▶▶▶**Wig Bay Holiday Park** (NX034655) Loch Ryan ☎Kirkcolm233
🚽⊕⚠

3m NW of Stranraer off A718. In sheltered position on western shores of Loch Ryan.
3acres 26pitches 100static
Jun–Sep rsMar–May & Oct booking advisable Jul last arrival 22.00hrs last departure 18.00hrs 3🚐 late arrivals enclosure 18wc lit all night 1cdp 18washbasins hc 1central hot water 8ñhc 5☉ supervised (wash) (dry, iron) games room cold storage licensed club/bar children's playground calor gas camping gaz toilet fluid 🛒 paddling pool 🛒
⇔ stables 🚲 🏕 🎵 launderette pub
26♣£3 or 26🚐£3 or 26🔺£3 (awnings) SA

STRATHAVEN Strathclyde Map 34 NS74
▶▶**Gallowhill Caravan Park** (NS708440)
Lesmahagow Rd ☎21267
🚽⊕⚠ signposted
Level grass site with young trees, set in meadowland, adjacent to river. On A726 ½m S of Strathaven. 2acres 30pitches
Apr–Sep no bookings last arrival 23.00hrs 2🚐 individual pitches 6wc lit all night 1cdp washbasins hc (ñhc) ☉ (wash, spin) calor gas camping gaz toilet fluid
⇔ 🚲 🎵 🛒
30♣£2.50 or 30🚐£2.50 or 30🔺£2.50 (awnings)

TARLAND Grampian Map 45 NJ40
▶▶▶**Drummie Hill Caravan Park** (NJ478045)
☎388
🚽⊕⚠ signposted
Landscaped site set on edge of village amidst hill and farmland, five miles north of Deeside.
3acres 30pitches 40static
Apr–mid Oct booking advisable Jul & Aug last arrival 23.00hrs last departure 12.00hrs 6🚐 individual pitches ⓐ late arrivals enclosure 12wc lit all night 1cdp washbasins hc ñhc ☉ supervised (spin) (iron) cold storage children's playground calor gas camping gaz 🛒 🛒
⇔ stables 🚲 🎵 pub
20♣£2.30 or 20🚐£2.30 10🔺£2 (awnings) ltr SA

TAYPORT Fife Map 41 NO42
▶▶**East Common Site** (NO465283) Apply to: North East Fife District Council, Dept of Recreation, County Buildings, Cupar, Fife
☎Cupar 53722
🚽⊕⚠ signposted
Level, grass site set in meadowland, adjacent to River Tay. 4acres 100pitches
24 Mar–5 Oct must book last arrival 20.00hrs last departure 20.00hrs 4🚐 individual pitches 13wc lit all night 1cdp 16washbasins hc (6ñhc) 4☉ (wash, spin) iron games room TV ☎
⇔ 🚲 🎵 launderette pub 🛒
20♣£3 or 20🚐£3 or 20🔺£1.50–£3 (awnings)

THURSO Highland Map 47 ND16
▶▶**Thurso Burgh Caravan Site** (ND111688)
Scrabster Rd
🚽⊕⚠ signposted
A level and grassy site near the sea and beach, ½m from Post Office on A882. 4½acres 130pitches 10static
May–Sep no bookings last arrival 22.00hrs last departure 12.00hrs 8🚐 individual pitches ⓐ late arrivals enclosure 23wc lit all night 1cdp washbasins hc central hot water ñhc ☉ (wash, spin, dry, iron) TV cafe restaurant ☎ 🛒
⇔ stables 🚲 🏕 cinema 🎵 launderette pub
80♣£2.10–£2.50 or 80🚐£2.10–£2.50 50🔺£2.10–£2.50 (awnings) ltr

179

Turriff – Yetholm

TURRIFF Grampian Map 45 NJ75
▶**Kinnaird House** (NJ733506) Banff Rd ☎2550
①❷ signposted
Mainly level grass site with mature trees and bushes, set in woodland adjacent to the A947 road. ½acre 6pitches 2static
Apr–Oct must book last arrival 22.00hrs last departure 10.00hrs 1⚡ individual pitches 2wc lit all night 🚿 washbasins hc central hot water ⓗc ⊙ supervised (wash, spin) iron cold storage children's playground calor gas
⊖➤ stables 🎣 🏌 ♪ pub 🏪
6🚐£1.75 or 6🚚£1.50 🏕£1.50 (awnings) ltr
▶**Turriff Caravan Site** (NJ725494)
☎Macduff 32861
①❶△ signposted
1½acre 25pitches 10static
May–Sep must book last arrival 21.00hrs last departure 09.00hrs 4⚡ 6wc lit all night cdp washbasins hc central hot water (ⓗc) 🏪
⊖➤ 🎣 △ ♪ launderette pub
20🚐£2.10 or 20🚚£1.80 5🏕£1 (awnings)

TUSHIELAW Borders Map 35 NT31
▶**Honey Cottage Caravan Site** (NT295164)
Ettrick Valley ☎Ettrick Valley 246
①❶△ signposted
Pleasantly situated near River Ettrick in quiet Ettrick Valley. 6acres 15pitches 44static
Apr–Oct no bookings 8⚡ ⊙ 16wc washbasins hc ⓗc ⊙ games room TV cold storage children's playground calor gas

camping gaz paraffin toilet wet ☎ 🏪
⊖➤ stables ♪ pub
15🚐 or 5🚚 or 15🏕 (awnings)

WATERBECK Dumfries & Galloway Map 31 NY27
▶▶**Fallford Lodge Caravan Site** (NY268807)
☎275
②❶△ signposted
A quiet, country site picturesquely situated in a fold of the hills besides the Kirtle Water. 1½acres 15pitches
Etr–Oct booking advisable last arrival 22.00hrs last departure 12.00hrs 3⚡ 4wc lit all night 1cdp 4washbasins hc 1ⓗc 1⊙ supervised calor gas (laundering available) ⊖➤ ♪ 🏪
15🚐£3.45 or 15🚚£3.45 or 15🏕£3.45 awnings ltr

YETHOLM Borders Map 36 NT82
▶▶**Kirkfield Caravan & Camping Site**
(NT821281) ☎346
③❶△ signposted
Part level, part sloping, grass site with trees and bushes, set in hilly moorland country adjacent to river. 7m S of Kelso on B6352. 1acre 34pitches 15static
Apr–Oct must book peak periods last arrival 20.00hrs last departure 12.00hrs 3⚡ △ 9wc lit all night washbasins hc ⓗc ⊙ supervised calor gas camping gaz paraffin ☎ 🏪
⊖➤ stables ♪
12🚐£3 22🚚£3 or 22🏕£3 (awnings)

Sites listed in Regions

Places appearing in the gazetteer are here arranged in Regional order. Look for the Region in which you wish to stay to find the names of places where AA recommended sites are situated. These place names appear alphabetically within the Camping and Caravanning section.

BORDERS
Cockburnspath
Coldingham
Greenlaw
Hawick
Innerleithen
Jedburgh
Kelso
Lauder
Melrose
Peebles
Tushielaw
Yetholm

CENTRAL
Auchenbowie
Balmaha
Blairlogie
Bridge of Allan
Callander
Gartmore
Killin
Luib
Stirling

DUMFRIES & GALLOWAY
Amisfield
Annan
Auchenmaig
Balminnoch
Brighouse Bay
Cairn Ryan
Castle Douglas
Creetown
Crocketford

Dumfries
Eastriggs
Ecclefechan
Gatehouse of Fleet
Glenluce
Glen Trool
Gretna
Gretna Green
Isle of Whithorn
Kippford
Kirkcudbright
Kirkgunzeon
Kirkpatrick Fleming
Lochmaben
Lochnaw
Lockerbie
Moffat
Mouswald
Newton Stewart
Parton
Powfoot
Sanquhar
Southerness
Stranraer
Waterbeck

FIFE
Crail
Guardbridge
Kinghorn
Kirkcaldy
Letham Feus
Lundin Links
St Andrews
Tayport

GRAMPIAN
Aberchirder
Aberdeen
Aberlour
Aboyne
Alford
Alves
Ballater
Banff
Brodie
Buckie
Cullen
Cuminestown
Elgin
Findhorn
Findochty
Fochabers
Fraserburgh
Keith
Lossiemouth
Macduff
Maryculter
Memus
Mintlaw
Portknockie
Portsoy
Rosehearty
Stonehaven
Strachan
Tarland
Turriff

HIGHLAND
Applecross
Ardmair

Aviemore
Balmacara
Beauly
Boat of Garten
Brora
Camustianavaig
 (Isle of Skye)
Corpach
Cromarty
Daviot
Dingwall
Dornoch
Dunnet
Dunvegan (Isle of Skye)
Durness
Fortrose
Fort William
Gairloch
Gairlochy
Garve
Glencoe
Grantown-on-Spey
Invergarry
Invermoriston
Inverness
John O'Groats
Lairg
Nairn
Poolewe
Reay
Resipol
Rosemarkie
Roy Bridge
Scaniport
Scourie

Shiel Bridge
Staffin (Isle of Skye)
Thurso

LOTHIAN
Dunbar
Edinburgh
Haddington
North Berwick

STRATHCLYDE
Ardgartan
Ayr
Balloch
Barcaldine
Benderloch
Blairmore
Bothwell
Carradale
Castle Sween
Connel
Coylton
Dalmellington
Dalrymple
Dunoon
Glendaruel
Hollybush
Inveraray
Inverchapel
Inveruglas
Kilberry
Kilmarnock
Kilninver
Kirkfieldbank
Lagganmore

Lochgilphead
Lochgoilhead
Luss
Maidens
Ravenstruther
Sandbank
Strachur
Strathaven

TAYSIDE
Aberfeldy
Birnam
Blair Atholl
Bridge of Cally
Cargill
Comrie
Crieff
Crook of Devon
Dundee
Dunkeld
Forfar
Inchture
Kenmore
Kinross
Kirriemuir
Monifieth
Montrose
Perth
Pitlochry
St Fillans
Scone

WESTERN ISLES
Coll Sands (Lewis)
Drinnishadder
 (Harris)

Scotland by the Sea

In this selection of seaside resorts, some of the larger holiday towns are combined with smaller and lesser-known places. The list reads clockwise, starting in the south-west.

DUMFRIES AND GALLOWAY

Southerness
Old hamlet plus holiday village, with wide, safe sands to the west.

Sandgreen
Low dunes shelter a wide sweep of safe, sandy beach.

Monreith
Quiet little resort has a safe, sandy bay (with outcrops of rock) sheltered by cliffs.

Maryport
Little town on Luce Bay sheltered by the land mass of the Mull of Galloway. Stretches of level sand, with safe swimming.

STRATHCLYDE

Girvan
Girvan combines beautiful surroundings and a sheltered sandy bay. There is access to the gently-shelving beach direct from the mile-long promenade. To the south there are cliffs and sandy coves.

Turnberry
Turnberry's famous golf courses are real 'links', laid out among dunes which back the sandy beaches.

Ayr
Fine sandy beach, lots of entertainment for children and adults, and good sports facilities.

Prestwick
Spacious town with a long sandy beach, seawater 'lake' and views across the Firth of Clyde.

Troon
Sandy beaches stretch to the north and south of the busy harbour. Sports (especially golf) are well catered for.

Saltcoats
Safe bathing and donkey rides at the firm sandy beach here, where fossilised trees are visible at low tide.

Dunoon
Good touring centre on a spur of land flanked by safe shingle beaches.

Carradale
Small resort with harbour on a coast noted for its small rocky bays with unspoilt sandy coves.

Campbeltown
Resort with a natural, sheltered harbour and shingle beach, at head of Campbeltown Loch.

HIGHLAND

Arisaig
Village on wooded peninsula with fine silver sand beaches.

Back of Keppoch
Safe sand beaches backed by dunes.

Gairloch
Fishing harbour with miles of safe, sandy beaches to the west and rocky coves and bays on the wooded southern shore of the loch.

Poolewe
Safe swimming in the warm waters of Loch Ewe from the sand or shingle beaches north of the village.

Gruinard Bay
The eastern, sheltered part has sandy beaches and is safe for swimming.

Balnakeil and Durness
Balnakeil is a village of craftsmen, Durness is a sheep-farming centre, and both have safe, sandy beaches.

Bettyhill
Small holiday and game fishing resort with wide, sandy beaches where semi-precious stones can be found.

Thurso
This resort, the most northerly town on the British mainland, has a sandy beach though most of the bay has a rocky coastline.

Dornoch
Mellow old town with sandy beach sheltered by rocks at the northern end (where bathing is safe) but with quicksands and dangerous currents round Dornoch Point to the south.

Portmahomack
Facing west, though on the east coast of Scotland, this fishing and holiday village has a sheltered sandy bay flanked by rocks.

Rosemarkie
Attractive village sheltered from the north by sandstone cliffs where sea birds nest, and with a shingle-backed beach.

Nairn
Holiday centre with mild, dry climate, safe bathing from beaches where pools form between flat rocks which obtrude from the sands

GRAMPIAN

Burghead
Georgian village with harbour sheltered by rocky headland and with a sandy beach to the west.

Lossiemouth and Branderburgh
Fishing port and holiday town with sandy beach at Branderburgh below rocky headland. There is a long spit of sand and shingle to the east of Lossiemouth but bathing is dangerous near the river mouth.

Cullen
Mostly-Regency holiday resort with old fishing quarter around harbour. To the west is a sandy bay, rocky outcrops and pools.

Banff
Ancient county town with steep streets and a sandy-bottomed harbour now used only by pleasure craft and swimmers, who should keep away from the river mouth.

Cruden Bay
Small but popular family holiday resort with a long sandy beach backed by dunes.

Balmedie
From the well-wooded village a path leads to 10 miles of fine sandy beach backed by grassy sandhills.

Aberdeen
As well as being an important fishing port, this granite city still caters admirably for holidaymakers and has two miles of safe sandy beach backed by grassland.

TAYSIDE

Montrose
Old port is almost surrounded by salt water and has a four-mile dune-backed beach to the north between the rivers South Esk and North Esk. It is safe for bathing except near the river mouths.

Arbroath
Here the beach has many flat rocks in which pools form at low tide. To the east stretch two miles of sandy beach and to the north west are impressive cave-riddled cliffs.

Carnoustie
This town, which has developed during the 20th century around the old fishing village, is a popular resort with a good sandy beach which becomes rocky north of the town. Beautiful coastal walks and a world-famous golf course.

FIFE

St Andrews
Many ancient buildings and historical connections help to make this an interesting place for a holiday even if you are not a golfer. The shore is rocky with patches of sand but there are dangerous quicksands and dangerous currents near the river mouth.

Elie and Earlsferry
Spacious and dignified resort with dark sands broken by black rocks and sandy coves round Elie Ness where garnets may be collected.

Aberdour
The sands which stretch for a mile on either side of this unspoilt and popular boating and holiday centre are split by banks of shingle, and clumps of trees at the edge of the beach.

LOTHIAN

Cramond and Portobello
Contrasting resorts on the outskirts of Edinburgh. From the quaint village of Cramond, which is popular for sailing, it is possible to walk across the sands at low tide to Cramond Island. Portobello is a suburb with a long promenade backing a sandy beach.

Yellowcraig
A coastal park overlooks three bird-sanctuary islands and the sandy beach has outcrops of rock.

North Berwick
Seaside and golfing resort overlooked by a conical hill 613ft high, with beaches of firm sands, broken by rocks where pools form at low tide around a small harbour.

Dunbar
Now-tranquil town with a war-torn history situated on a rocky headland with sandy beaches to east and west and pools to explore among the rocks by the ruined castle.

White Sands
Safe bathing beach with firm sands flanked by flat rocks and backed by dunes.

Places of interest

Ancient Monuments (including opening times)
The National Trust and The National Gardens Scheme

Ancient Monuments **AM** Ancient Monuments in Scotland (with the exception of Holyrood House) are the responsibility of the Scottish Development Department, 17 Atholl Crescent, Edinburgh EH3 8JN.
Due to lack of custodians some establishments may be closed. Certain standard times for Ancient Monuments now include *Sunday opening* from 9.30 between April and September only; these entries have in each case been marked with an † after the word 'open' in the gazetteer. Standard times of opening for all Ancient Monuments in Scotland are as follows:

Apr – Sep:	weekdays 9.30 – 7	Sundays 2 – 7
Oct – Mar:	weekdays 9.30 – 4	Sundays 2 – 4

All monuments in Scotland are closed on 25 and 26 December, also 1 and 2 January.
Some of the smaller monuments may close for the lunch hour and may be closed for one or two days a week. It is advisable to check before visiting. Parties of 11 and over may obtain a 10% discount on admission at most of the monuments.

The National Trust **NTS** National Trust for Scotland, 5 Charlotte Square, Edinburgh EH2 4DU

ABERDEEN Grampian *Aberdeenshire*
Map 45 NJ90
Aberdeen Art Gallery and Museums
Schoolhill. Scottish art from 16th-C to present day, with outstanding collection of 20th-C paintings. Water-colours, print-room, and art library; contemporary sculpture and decorative arts; special exhibitions and events throughout the year. Shop. Open all year (ex 25, 26 Dec & 1, 2 Jan) Mon – Sat 10 – 5 (8 pm Thu) Sun 2 – 5. Free. ⫫ ⚿
(☎ 26333)
Cruickshank Botanic Gardens University of Aberdeen. First developed at the end of the 19th-C, the 7 acres of mature garden include rock and water gardens, a heather garden, collections of spring bulbs, gentians and alpine plants and, under glass, succulent plants. There are also extensive collections of trees and shrubs. Open all year Mon – Fri 9 – 5; also Sat & Sun May – Sep 2 – 5. Free. P. ⚿ (☎ 40241 ext 340 or 348)
James Dun's House 61 Schoolhill. 18th-C house used as a museum with changing exhibitions. Shop. Open all year (ex 25, 26 Dec & 1, 2 Jan) Mon – Sat 10 – 5. Free.
(☎ 26333)
Provost Ross's House Due to open in 1982 as a maritime museum. Contact Aberdeen District Council for details. (NTS) (☎ 25788)
Provost Skene's House Guestrow. A 17th-C house restored as a museum of local history and social life. Furnishings, panelling, and plaster ceilings of 17th- and 18th-C. Open all year (ex 25, 26 Dec & 1, 2 Jan) Mon – Sat 10 – 5. 10p (ch 12 & pen 2p) ⫫ (☎ 50086)

ABERDOUR Fife *Fife* Map 41 NT18
Aberdour Castle A 14th- to 17th-C stronghold, still partly roofed. Fine circular dovecote and gardens. Open Apr – Sep, weekdays 9.30 – 7, Sun 2 – 7; Oct – Mar, weekdays 9.30 – 4, Sun 2 – 4. * 30p (ch 15p). ▲ (AM)
Inchcolm Abbey Remains of an Augustinian Abbey, founded c1123 by Alexander I which are situated on a green island in the Firth of Forth, S of Aberdour. The well-preserved monastic buildings include a fine 13th-C octagonal Chapter House and a fine example of a 13th-C wall painting, depicting a funeral procession of clerics. Open see page 182.
* 30p (ch 15p). Ferry service from S. Queensferry £2 (ch £1.20), includes admission to Abbey.
(☎ Dalgety Bay 823332) (AM)

ABERLADY Lothian *East Lothian*
Map 35 NT47
Myreton Motor Museum A comprehensive collection of cars and motorcycles from 1896, cycles from 1863 and commercial vehicles. Latest addition is a rapidly expanding collection of historic British military vehicles. Picnic area. Open Etr – Oct, daily 10 – 6; Oct – Etr, Sat & Sun 10 – 5. * 50p (ch 16 10p). ▲ ⚿B (☎ 288)

ALFORD Grampian *Aberdeenshire*
Map 45 NJ51
Alford Valley Railway Narrow gauge passenger railway located in Haughton Park. 1½ miles of track through nature trails and historic battlefield. Diesel traction. Alford cavalcade 24 and 25 Jul. Picnic area & Shop. Open Apr, May & Sep weekends only 11 – 5, Jun – Aug daily 11 – 5. 80p return fare (ch 40p). ▲ ⚿ (☎ 2326)

ALLOWAY Strathclyde *Ayrshire*
Map 33 NS31
Burns Cottage Thatched cottage, built in 1757, now museum, birthplace in 1759 of Robert Burns. Open all year, Apr – mid Oct Mon – Sat 9 – 7, Sun, Mar – May & Sep, Oct 2 – 7, Jun – Aug 10 – 7. Closing time 7 or dusk if earlier. Prices under review. ⫫ P. (100yds)
Also **Burns Monument** Built in 1823 to a design by Thomas Hamilton Junior with fine sculptures of characters in Burns' poems by a self-taught artist, James Thorn. Open as cottage. Prices under review. ⚿ P.
(☎ 41215 for cottage or 41321 for monument)
Land O'Burns Centre Robert Burns Interpretation Centre. Audio-visual, multi-screen presentation showing the life of Robert Burns. Burns festival 12 – 20 Jun. Exhibition area. Landscaped gardens. Picnic area. Shop. Open all year daily 10 – 5; 10 – 6 (Jun & Sep); 10 – 9 (Jul & Aug).
* 20p (audio-visual theatre), (ch 14 & pen 10p). ▲ ⚿ (☎ 43700)

ANNAN Dumfries and Galloway *Dumfriesshire* Map 31 NY16
Kinmount Gardens Gardens and signed woodland walks of ½hr, 1hr and 2hr duration. Rhododendrons and azaleas in May and Jun. Picnic area. Open Apr – Sep 9 – 5. * 25p (ch 10, 10p). ▲ (☎ Ecclefechan 244)

ANSTRUTHER Fife *Fife* Map 41 NO50
Scottish Fisheries Museum St Ayles. A 14th- to 18th-C group of buildings around a cobbled courtyard. Contains fishing boats and gear, fisherman's house c1900, a marine aquarium and a Lecture Hall for special displays. Painting Exhibitions 3 – 29 Jul & 7 Aug – 5 Sep. Tourist Info Service in summer. Shop. Open Apr – Oct, Mon – Sat 10 – 12.30 & 2 – 6, Sun 2 – 5; Nov – Mar,

daily (ex Tue) 2 – 5. * 75p (ch & pen 25p). ⌇ P. &B (☎ 310628).

ARBROATH Tayside *Angus* Map 41 NO64
Arbroath Abbey Remains of a Tironensian Monastery founded in 1176 by William the Lion, King of Scotland. Considerable portions of the cruciform abbey remain. Arbroath Abbey Pageant 30 Aug – 5 Sep. * 30p (ch 15 & pen 15p). P. &B
Signal Tower Museum Ladyloan. Collection of local and natural history. Open all year Mon – Sat 9.30 – 1 & 2 – 5. Free. ▲ &B (☎ Montrose 3232)

ARDCLACH Highland *Nairnshire* Map 44 NH94
Ardclach Bell Tower Two-storeyed 14ft-square tower, with upper floor containing fireplace and shot hole. Belfry on side gable built to house the bell formerly used as a warning, or for church services. Built probably in 17th-C. Accessible on application to custodian. Free. (AM)

ARDFERN Strathclyde *Argyll* Map 39 NM80
Argyll Wildlife Centre Arduine, A816. Presented in a natural setting on a small hill with an area of old Caledonian Oak woodland and marshland. Visitors will find birds, mammals, trees, plants etc, formerly or currently native to Scotland. Education and Conservation are primary objects with guided tours provided whenever possible. Picnic area, Shop & garden centre. Open Etr – Oct daily 10 – 6. £1 (ch 50p). Party ⌇ ▲

ARDMINISH Isle of Gigha, Strathclyde *Argyll* Map 32 NR64
Achamore Unique garden of azaleas and rhododendrons, created by the late Sir James Horlick Bt. Shop. Open all year 10 – sunset. 50p (ch & pen 30p). ⌇ ▲ (☎ Gigha 258)

ARDWELL Dumfries and Galloway *Wigtownshire* Map 30 NX14
Ardwell House Gardens Country house gardens and grounds with flowering shrubs and woodland walks. House not open to public. Gardens open Mar – Oct 10 – 6. Voluntary donations. ▲ (☎ 227)

ARMADALE Isle of Skye, Highland *Inverness-shire* Map 42 NG60
Clan Donald Centre Situated ½m N of pier in the restored north wing of Armadale Castle, the Seat of the Macdonalds, a building dating from the early 18th-C. The main building is now a sculptured ruin. Flora Macdonald was married from Armadale in 1750. Picturesque woodland gardens overlook the Sound of Sleat with a tree collection over 200 years old. Museum of the Isles, audio-visual, craft and book shop. Countryside ranger service available for guided woodland walks. Clan Donald Archery Tournament 6 – 10 Jul (tentative). Picnic area. Shop. Open Etr – Oct, Mon – Sat 10 – 5.30; May – Sep, Sun 2 – 5.30. 60p (ch & pen 30p) ⌇ (licensed) ▲ &B (☎ Ardvasar 227)

ARNOL Isle of Lewis, Western Isles *Ross & Cromarty* Map 48 NB34
Black House Museum Good example of traditional Hebridean dwelling. Retains many of its original furnishings. Open Apr – Sep, weekdays 9.30 – 7; Oct – Mar, weekdays 9.30 – 4. * 30p (ch 15p). ▲ & (AM)

ARRAN, ISLE OF Strathclyde *Bute* Map 33
see **Brodick, Brodick Castle**

AUCHINDRAIN Strathclyde *Argyll* Map 39 NN00
Open-Air Museum A folk life museum on ancient Communal-tenancy farm. Original 18th- and 19th-C buildings being restored and furnished. Traditional crops and livestock, also a display centre. Picnic area & craft shop. Open Etr – Sep (other times by appointment), Mon – Sat 10 – 6, Sun 12 – 6. 80p (ch 40p). ▲ & B (☎ Furnace 235)

AUCHINLECK Strathclyde *Ayrshire* Map 34 NS52
Auchinleck Boswell Museum and Mausoleum Church Hill off A76. The Boswell Museum was the family seat of the Boswells whose most famous member was James Boswell 1740 – 1795. The Biographer of Dr Johnson, author of the 'Tour of the Hebrides' etc. The old parish church, of which a portion dates back to c900AD, is where the family worshipped and is now the museum containing books, manuscripts, portraits, china etc. Also represented in the Museum is the famous engineer William Murdoch, 1754 – 1839, who found ways and means of utilising gas for lighting and heating and who made the 1st Steam Road Engine. Attached to the north wall is the Mausoleum where five known generations of Boswells are buried. 12th Annual Boswell dinner 20 Aug. Open Mon & Fri at 6.30pm; otherwise by appointment. Free. ▲ & Curator at 131 Main St. (☎ Cumnock 20757)

AULDEARN Highland *Nairnshire* Map 44 NH95
Boath Doocot A circular 17th-C doocot, or dovecote (exterior only can be seen). The standard of Charles I was raised here, in the battle of Auldearn in 1645. Battle plan on display outside. Donation box: 10p. (NTS)

AYR Strathclyde *Ayrshire* Map 33 NS32
Tam O'Shanter Museum This is considered to be the point where Tam O'Shanter's memorable ride commenced. The house now contains some of Robert Burns belongings. Shop. Open Apr – Sep Mon – Sat 9.30 – 5.30; Oct – Mar Mon – Sat 12 – 4, also Sun, Jun, Jul & Aug 2.30 – 5. * 30p (ch & pen 15p). P. (☎ Ayr 69794).

BALERNO Lothian *Midlothian* Map 35 NT16
Malleny Garden Off Bavelaw Rd. A delightfully personal garden, with shrub roses and shaped yews. Open May – Sep daily 10 – dusk. 40p (ch 20p). ▲ & (NTS)

BALLATER Grampian *Aberdeenshire* Map 44 NO39
McEwan Gallery 1m NW on A939. Built by the Swiss artist Rudolf Christian in 1902. All paintings in the main gallery are for sale. Wildlife exhibition, Aug. Open all year. Mon – Sat 10 – 6, Sun 2.30 – 5. Free. ▲ & B (☎ 429)

BALLOCH Strathclyde *Dunbartonshire* Map 37 NS38
Balloch Castle Park Situated on the shore of the loch, with large area of grassland, suitable for picnics and surrounded by extensive woodlands. Views of the loch from the Castle terrace (c1800). Walled garden. Nature trail. Open all year daily. Park

8 – dusk; garden 10 – 9 (4.30 winter). Free. ⚠ Vistor Centre open May – Sep daily 11 – 7
Cameron Loch Lomond Wildlife Park 1m NW. Drive through acres of parkland where different species of bears, bison, yak and deer roam freely. Other attractions include the children's zoo, waterfowl sanctuary, landscaped gardens, adventure playground, children's assault course, giant slide, paddle boats, canoes, trampolines etc. Picnic area. Shop. Open Etr – Sep daily. Prices under review. ⚐ ⚠ ♿ (☎ Alexandria 57211)
Also **Cameron House,** home of the Smolletts of Bonhill. Contains artifacts and documents collected by the family for over 300 years, including 'Whisky Galore' room, Staffordshire pottery collection, fine porcelain, pictures, furniture, armour, Oriental curios, nursery with children's toys and books. Tobias Smollett Museum. Entrance through Wildlife Park, off unclass road on Lochside. Shop. Open Etr – Sep, daily, 10.30 – 6. Prices under review. Kennels. ⚐ ⚠ ♿B
(☎ Alexandria 57211)

BALMACARA Highland *Ross and Cromarty*
Map 42 NG82
Woodland Garden Situated in magnificent stretch of West Highland mountainous scenery, including Five Sisters of Kintail and Beinn Fhada. Natural History display in coach house. Lockalsh Woodland and Garden. Self-guided and guided walks from Balmacara on the Kyle to Plockton Peninsula. Ranger Naturalist Service. Woodland garden open all year daily. Coach House open Etr – mid Oct, daily 10 – 6. Kiosk Jun – Sep Mon – Sat 10 – 1 & 2 – 6. 30p (ch 15p). (☎ 207) (NTS)

BALMORAL Grampian *Aberdeenshire*
Map 15 NO29
Balmoral Castle Grounds The Highland residence of Her Majesty the Queen. Beautiful Deeside forest setting. Grounds, gardens and exhibition of paintings and works of art in the Castle Ballroom open from May – Jul, daily (ex Sun) 10 – 5. Shop. * 75p (ch 35p). Donations to charities from charges. ⚐ P (400 yds). ♿B
(☎ Crathie 334) (cars for ♿ allowed to enter by separate entrance)

BANCHORY Grampian *Kincardineshire*
Map 45 NO69
Banchory Museum Council Chamber. Exhibition of local history and bygones. Shop. Open Jun – Sep daily (ex Thu) 2 – 5, Sat 10 – 12. ⚠ (☎ Peterhead 77778)

BANFF Grampian *Banffshire* Map 44 NJ66
Banff Museum Exhibition of British birds set out as an aviary. Local history and costumes also on show. Shop. Open Jun – end Sep daily (ex Thu) 2 – 5, Sat 10 – 12, Sun 2 – 5. Free. P. ♿B (☎ Peterhead 77778)
Duff House ½m S, access from bypass south of the town. Designed by William Adam for William Duff (later Earl of Fife). The main block was roofed in 1739, but proposed wings were never built. Although incomplete it ranks among the finest works of Georgian Baroque architecture in Britain. An exhibition illustrating the history of the house can also be seen. Open Apr – Sep. Mon – Sat 9.30 – 7, Sun 2 – 7. * 30p (ch 15p). (AM)

BANNOCKBURN Central *Stirlingshire*
Map 40 NS89

Bannockburn Monument This is the Borestone Site, by tradition King Robert the Bruce's command post before the battle (1314). Bruce is commemorated by a bronze equestrian statue. Rotunda and site always open. Visitor centre and historical exposition in sound and colour, open Apr – Sep, Mon – Sat 10 – 6, Sun 11 – 6 (9 – 6, daily, Jul & Aug). Admission to exhibition 40p (ch 20p). ⚠ (☎ 812664) (NTS)

BARCALDINE Strathclyde *Argyll*
Map 39 NM83
Sea Life Centre Loch Creran. Newest and most modern marine, aquatic life display in Europe. It contains the largest collection of native marine life in Britain. Operated by a fish farming company, it exhibits marine life in unique ways enabling a greater understanding of the underwater world. New seal display, tidepool touch tank and intertidal dump tank. Picnic area. Shop. Open daily, Apr – Oct, 8.30 – 8. £1 (ch 14 50p). ⚐ ⚠ ♿B (☎ Ledaig 386)

BARRA, ISLE OF Western Isles
Inverness-shire Map 48
see **Castlebay**

BATHGATE Lothian *West Lothian*
Map 34 NS96
Cairnpapple Hill Sanctuary and Burial Cairn 2m N. Monumental temple, in the form of a stone circle and ditch, of several dates in the prehistoric period, notably the second millenium BC. It was recently excavated and laid out. Open daily 9.30 – 7 (ex Thu afternoon, Fri), Sun 2 – 7. Closed Winter. * 25p (ch 10p). (☎ 031-229 9321 Scottish Development Dept.) (AM)

BEAULY Highland *Inverness-shire*
Map 43 NH54
Beauly Priory Founded in 1230, one of three houses of the Valliscaulian Order founded in Scotland. Only the church remains, a long narrow building comprising aisleless nave, transepts and chancel. This is the burial place of the Mackenzies of Kintail and contains the fine monument of Sir Kenneth Mackenzie. Open, see page 182 Closed Sat & Sun. * 25p (ch 10p). (AM)

BENMORE Strathclyde *Argyll* Map 33 NS18
Benmore Younger Botanic Garden Woodland and garden on a grand scale, featuring conifers, rhododendrons, azaleas, and many other shrubs. Open from Apr – Oct, daily 10 – 6. 20p (ch & pen 10p). No pets. ⚐ ⚠ 10p. ♿B (☎ Sandbanks (Argyll) 261)

BERRIEDALE Highland *Caithness*
Map 47 ND12
Langwell A residence of the Duchess of Portland, which has fine gardens showing plant growth in exposed areas. The gardens only are shown 2 – 7. Shop. Dates for 1982 not available. 40p (ch 12 & pen 20p). ⚐ ⚠ ♿ (☎ Berriedale 280)

BETTYHILL Highland *Caithness*
Map 47 NC76
Strathnaver Museum Fine stone-built, white harled building, formerly a church, in an area of outstanding beauty. It contains a magnificent pitch pine canopied pulpit dated 1774, a fine collection of home-made furnishings, domestic and farm implements and Gaelic books. The churchyard contains a

carved stone known as the Farr Stone dating back to the 10th-C. Open 1st week in Jun – Sep, Mon – Sat 10 – 12.30, 1.30 – 5. 30p (ch 10p). P. &B

BIGGAR Strathclyde *Lanarkshire*
Map 35 NT03
Gladstone Court Museum Entrance by 113 High St. Interesting museum which portrays an old-world village street, housed in century-old coachwork with modern extension. On display are reconstructed old shops, complete with fascinating signs and adverts, a bank, telephone exchange, photographer's booth, etc. Albion Motors section. Blackwood Murray run mid Aug. Commemorative run for vintage and veteran vehicles held annually in mid Aug. H.Q. Albion Owners Club. Museum shop. Open Etr – Oct, daily 10 – 5 and 2 – 5; Sun 2 – 5. 40p (ch 20p, ch 8 free). P. &B (☎ 20005)
Greenhill Convenanters House Burn Braes. 17th-C farmhouse brought stone by stone 10 miles from Wiston and re-erected at Biggar. Contains relics of the covenanting period, history of Scotland between the Union of the Crowns and the Union of Parliaments. Open Etr – Oct, daily 2 – 5. 40p (ch 20p, ch 8 free) reduced price for joint ticket with Gladstone Court. & &B (☎ 20005)

BLAIR ATHOLL Tayside *Perthshire*
Map 40 NN86
Blair Castle Of 13th-C origin, altered in the 18th-C, and later given a castellated exterior. There are Renaissance-style furnishings, paintings, Jacobite relics, china, and arms displayed in 32 rooms. It is the home of the Duke of Atholl. Open Etr week, each Sun & Mon in Apr, afterwards daily, from first Sun in May to second Sun in Oct, Mon – Sat 10 – 6, Sun 2 – 6; no admission after 5.30pm. Party. ⏚ & &B (☎ 355)

BLAIR DRUMMOND Central *Perthshire*
Map 40 NS79
Scotland's Safari Park Exit 10 off M9, A84 between Doune and Stirling. Features wild animals in natural surroundings, including lions, giraffes, buffalo, zebras, camels, elephants, monkeys and Siberian tiger reserve. Also Pets Corner, Boat Safari, and Astra glide (extra charges). Amusement and picnic areas. Shop. Open Apr – late Oct. * £3.80 per car. ⏚ (licensed). & & (☎ Doune 396 or 456)

BLANTYRE Strathclyde *Lanarkshire*
Map 37 NS65
David Livingstone Centre with 'The Livingstone Memorial'. The birthplace of David Livingstone in 1813 containing personal relics, tableaux and working models. The 'Africa Pavilion' with exhibition describing life in modern Africa and 'Shuttle Row (Social History) Museum'. Picnic area. Gardens. Shop. Open all year Mon – Sat 10 – 6, Sun 2 – 6. * 50p (ch & pen 25p). ⏚ (Apr – Sept). & &B (☎ 823140)

BOAT OF GARTEN Highland *Inverness-shire*
Map 44 NH91
Strathspey Railway The Station. Steam railway covering the five miles from Boat of Garten to Aviemore, a twenty-minute journey Trains can also be boarded at Aviemore. Evening Diner trains Fri & Sat by arrangement. Timetables available from station and Tourist Information Office. Picnic area. Shop. Open mid May – Jun & Sep – mid Oct Sat & Sun. Jul & Aug Sat – Wed. Family fares, party bookings. Basic return fare £1.60. ⏚ (on most trains). & at Boat of Garten; P. 600 yds at Aviemore. & (by arrangement). (☎ 692)

BO'NESS Central *West Lothian*
Map 34 NS98
Kinneil House Situated in a public park, and preserving 16th- and 17th-C wall paintings. Open, see page 182. Closed Tue afternoon, Fri. * 25p (ch 10p). & (AM)
Kinneil Museum Situated in the renovated 17th-C stable block of Kinneil House. The ground floor illustrates the industrial history of Bo'ness, while the main display on the first floor houses the extensive display of local pottery 1850 – 1950. Open all year May – Oct, Mon – Sat 10 – 12 and 1 – 5. Nov – Apr, Mon, Wed & Fri 10 – 12 & 1 – 5. Sat 1 – 5. Free. & &B (☎ Falkirk 24911 ext 2202)

BOTHWELL Strathclyde *Lanarkshire*
Map 37 NS75
Bothwell Castle An impressive, ruined 13th- to 15th-C stonghold. Open, see page 182. Entrance to castle is at Uddington Cross by traffic lights. * 25p (ch 10p). & (AM)

BRAEMAR Grampian *Aberdeenshire*
Map 44 NO19
Braemar Castle Picturesque castle near River Dee. Built in 1628 and burned in 1689 it was purchased by the Farquharson of Invercauld in 1732, and largely rebuilt. Fully furnished family residence with many items of historic interest. Shop. Open May – early Oct, daily 10 – 6. 90p (ch 13 45p). & (☎ 219)

BRODICK Isle of Arran, Strathclyde *Bute*
Map 33 NS03
Rosaburn Heritage Museum Set in part of a former croft farm, the museum illustrates the changing way of life of the island's inhabitants. Features include a working blacksmith's shop, a cottage furnished in early 1920's style, a stable block with six horses and several coaches and an open air display of old farm equipment. Shop. Open Etr – Sep daily (ex Sat & Sun) 45p (ch 20p). & &B (☎ Brodick 2140)
Brodick Castle and Country Park Part dates from the 13th-C, with later extensions, the former stronghold of the Dukes of Hamilton which contains an impressive art collection. Outstanding gardens. Castle open Etr Sun & 10 – 30 Apr, Mon, Wed & Sat 1 – 5; May – Sep daily 1 – 5. Gardens open daily all year 10 – 5. Castle & gardens £1.05 (ch 50p). Gardens only 50p (ch 25p). Party rates, castle & gardens 85p (ch 40p). ⏚ Etr, then May – Sep, Mon – Sat 10 – 5, Sun 12.30 – 5. (☎ Brodick 2202) (NTS)

BRODIE CASTLE Grampian *Morayshire*
Map 44 NH95
6m E of Nairn, off A96. Largely rebuilt after being burned down in 1645 and with additions of the 18th and 19th centuries. Contents include fine furniture, porcelain and paintings. Short woodland walk, bird observations hide. Open Good Fri – 12 Apr & May – Sep, Mon – Sat 11 – 6, Sun 2 – 6 (last

admission 5.15). £1.10 (ch 55p). Parties 85p (ch 40p). Grounds open all year, 9.30 – sunset, admission by donation. (☎ Brodie 371) (NTS)

BROUGHTON Borders *Peeblesshire*
Map 35 NT13
Broughton Place Built on the site of a much older house and designed by Sir Basil Spence in 1938, in the style of a 17th-C Scottish tower house. The drawing room and main hall are open to the public and contain paintings and crafts by living British artists for sale. The gardens, which are open for part of the summer, afford fine views of the Tweeddale hills. Gallery open Etr – Sep daily (ex Wed) 10.30 – 6. Free garden 30p. ▲ ሌB (☎ 234)

BRUAR Tayside *Perthshire* Map 40 NN86
Clan Donnachaidh (Robertson) Museum
Documents, books and pictures associated with the Clan Donnachaidh, one of whose early chiefs fought for King Robert the Bruce. Craft display. Open Etr – 15 Oct, Mon – Sat 10 – 5.30, Sun 2 – 5.30. Closed 1 – 2 for lunch. At other times by arrangement with the curator. Clan gathering 3rd Sat in Jan. Clan items for sale. ⚓ ▲ ሌ (☎ Calvine 264, or Curator's residence Calvine 222)

BUCKIE Grampian *Banffshire* Map 44 NJ46
Buckie Museum and Peter Anson Gallery
Maritime museum with new displays completed in 1981 relating to the fishing industry including exhibits on coopering, navigation, lifeboats and fishing methods. Selections from the Peter Anson watercolour collection of fishing vessels are on display in the gallery. Shop. Open all year Mon – Fri 10 – 8, Sat 10 – 12.30. Free. ▲ ሌ (☎ Forres 73701)

BURGHEAD Grampian *Moray* Map 44 NJ16
Burghead Museum 16 – 18 Grant St. Archaeology of the Laich of Mory from 2500 BC – 1300 AD. Open Tue 2 – 5, Thu 5.30 – 8.30, Sat 9.30 – 12.30. Free. ▲ ሌ (☎ Forres 73701)

BUTE, ISLE OF Strathclyde *Bute* Map 33
see **Rothesay**

CAERLAVEROCK Dumfries and Galloway *Dumfriesshire* Map 30 NY06
Caerlaverock Castle A famous medieval stronghold, mainly 13th- to 15th-C, with a Renaissance wing of 1638. Open, see page 182 *40p (ch 20p). ▲ (AM)
Wildfowl Trust Outstanding hide facilities, observation towers, and observatory, providing impressive views of the flocks of barnacle, and pink-footed geese, whooper and Bewick swans and numerous species of wild ducks that spend most of the winter in the refuge. Open 15 Sep – Apr (ex 24, 25 Dec). Guided tours 11 & 2 daily. 85p (ch 50p, pen 65p). ▲ Party 20 + (☎ Glencaple 200)

CAIRNDOW Strathclyde *Argyll*
Map 39 NN11
Strone House Gardens featuring rhododendrons, azaleas, conifers and daffodils. The tallest tree in Britain, measuring 190ft, is located within the gardens. Picnic area. Open Apr – Sep, 9 – 9. 30p (ch & pen free). ▲ 50p (☎ 284)

CALLANDER Central *Perthshire*

Map 40 NN60
Kilmahog Woollen Mill A once-thriving woollen mill, famous for hand-woven blankets and tweed. Part of the old structure can be seen, also an old water wheel which has been preserved and is still in working order. Woollens can be purchased in the store. Shop. Open all year Mon – Fri 9 – 8, Sat & Sun 9 – 6. ▲ ሌB (☎ 30268)

CALLANISH Isle of Lewis, Western Isles *Ross & Cromarty* Map 48 NB23
Callanish Standing Stones Unique collection of megaliths comprising an avenue 27ft in width, with 19 standing stones, terminating in a 37ft-wide circle containing 13 additional stones. Other stones, burial cairns, and circles in the near vicinity. Accessible at all times. Free. ▲ (AM)

CARDONESS CASTLE Dumfries and Galloway *Kirkcudbrightshire* Map 30 NX55
A 15th-C stronghold, overlooking the Water of Fleet, once home of the McCullochs of Galloway. Notable fireplaces. Open from Apr – Sep, weekdays 9.30 – 7 (Sun 2 – 7); from Oct – Mar 9.30 – 4 (Sun 2 – 4). *30p (ch 15p). ▲ (AM)

CARLOWAY Isle of Lewis, Western Isles *Ross & Cromarty* Map 48 NB24
Dun Carloway Broch Well-preserved broch, or Pictish tower, about 30ft in height, one of the finest in the Western Isles. Accessible at all times. Free. ▲ (AM)

CARNASSERIE CASTLE Strathclyde *Argyll*
Map 39 NM80
Built in the 16th-C by John Carswell, first Protestant Bishop of the Isles, who translated into Gaelic and published Knox's *Liturgy* in 1567. In was taken and partly destroyed in Argyll's rebellion of 1685, and consists of a towerhouse, with a courtyard built on to it. Open, see page 182. Free. ▲ (AM)

CARRADALE Strathclyde *Argyll*
Map 33 NR83
Carradale House Off B879. Overlooks the lovely Kilbrennan Sound. Beautiful gardens, with flowering shrubs, mainly rhododendrons, best vistited Apr – Jun. Plants, vegetables and shrubs for sale. Open Apr – Sep. 20p (ch 12 free). ▲ ሌB (☎ 234)

CARRBRIDGE Highland *Inverness-shire*
Map 44 NH92
Landmark Europe's first 'visitor' centre, with an exhibition on the history of Strathspey, a multi-screen programme in the auditorium showing in sound and vision the story of The Highlands from the last Ice Age to the present day, and evening film shows. Treetop trail opened '81, woodland adventure playground due to open '82. Also craft and bookshop, nature trail, with picnic area, open-air sculpture park. Open summer 9.30 – 10.30, winter 9.30 – 5. Admission to Exhibition & Auditorium 70p (ch 35p). ⚓ ▲ ሌ (☎ 614)

CARSLUITH CASTLE Dumfries and Galloway *Kirkcudbrightshire* Map 30 NX45
A roofless 16th-C tower house on Wigtown Bay. A previous owner was the last abbot of Sweetheart Abbey. Entry free on application to Custodian. Open, see page 182. (AM)

CASTLEBAY Isle of Barra, Western Isles *Inverness-shire* Map 48 NL69

Places of Interest   **Castle Douglas – Corgarff**

Kisimul Castle Facing Castlebay, an early 15th-C island stronghold, the historic home of the Macneils of Barra. Open May – Sep, Sat & Wed. 60p (ch 30p). Accessible by boat from Castlebay. (The Macneil of Barra).

CASTLE DOUGLAS Dumfries and Galloway *Kirkcudbrightshire* Map 30 NX76
Threave Castle Follow A75 SW to Bridge of Dee (3m) then take unclass rd to N. Standing on an islet in the River Dee, this lonely castle, erected by Archibald the Grim in the late 14th-C, is four storeys in height, with round towers guarding the outer wall. It was dismantled by the Covenanters in 1640. Open Apr – Sep, weekdays (ex Thu) 9.30 – 7, Sun 2 – 7. Ferry charge. *30p (ch 15p). Access to castle is by rowing boat. (AM)
Threave Gardens 1m W of Castle Douglas. Fine gardens noted for a splendid Springtime display of over 300 varieties of daffodil. Walled garden and glasshouses. Open all year, daily 9 – sunset, walled garden & glasshouses 9 – 5. (The house is NTS School of Gardening.) Visitor centre open Apr – Oct. 90p (ch 45p). Party 60p each, Schools £5 per coach. ℒ (daily Apr – Sep). & (☎ 2575) (NTS)

CASTLES GIRNIGOE AND SINCLAIR Highland *Caithness* Map 47 ND35
Two adjacent ruined castles of the Sinclairs, in a striking rock setting at Noss Head. Girnigoe is 15th-C and Sinclair dates from the early 16th-C. After c1697 both castles were abandoned. They can be seen at any time. Free.

CASTLE KENNEDY Dumfries and Galloway *Wigtownshire* Map 30 NX15
Castle Kennedy Gardens Situated 3m E of Stranraer on A75. 17th-C and later gardens, with a fine collection of rhododendrons, azaleas, magnolias and other shrubs. Situated on peninsula between two lochs, the gardens offer a choice of walks. Picnic area. Shop. Open Apr – Sep, daily (ex Etr, May Day & August Bank Hol Sats) 10 – 5. £1 (ch 16 & pen 50p). Garden centre adjoining gardens. ℒ ▲ &B (☎ Stranraer 2024)

CAUSEWAYHEAD Central *Stirlingshire* Map 40 NS89
Wallace Monument 220ft-high-tower erected in 1869, in which Sir William Wallace's famous two-handed sword is preserved. No fewer than seven battlefields are visible from the summit of the monument, in addition to a wide panoramic view towards the Highlands. There is a Hall of Heroes. Audio-visual system on life of William Wallace. Picnic area. Shop. Open all year Nov – Jan 10 – 4, Oct & Feb 10 – 5, Sep & Mar 10 – 6, Apr & Aug 10 – 7, May – Jul 10 – 8. *40p. School booked parties ch 15p. ℒ P. at foot of Abbey Craig. (☎ Stirling 2140)

CAWDOR Highland *Nairnshire* Map 44 NH84
Cawdor Castle Home of the Thanes of Cawdor since the early 14th-C and home of the present Earl of Cawdor. It has a drawbridge, an ancient tower built around a tree, and a freshwater well inside the house. Nature trails, pitch and putt & putting green. Picnic area. Open May – Sep daily 10 – 5.30 (last admission 5pm). £1.50 (ch 75p & pen

£1) subject to alteration. Party 20 + £1.25 (ch 60p). ℒ (licensed). ▲ &B (☎ 615)

CERES Fife *Fife* Map 41 NO31
Fife Folk Museum The Weigh House. A regional, rural Folk collection displayed in the historic Weigh House Cottages and terraced garden near Ceres Green. Picnic area. Open Apr – Oct, Mon & Wed – Sat (closed Tue) 2 – 5. Sun 2.30 – 5.30. *40p (ch 20p). P. (200yds). &B (☎ Ladybank 30410)

CLACKMANNAN Central *Clackmannanshire* Map 40 NS99
Clackmannan Tower A fine 14th- and 15th-C tower house, battlemented and turreted, and at one time moated. Now under repair and not open, but can be closely viewed from outside. (AM)

CLAVA CAIRNS Highland *Inverness-shire* Map 44 NH74
Situated on the south bank of the River Nairn, this group of burial cairns has three concentric rings of great stones. They are of late neolithic or early Bronze Age. Open at all times. Free. (AM)

COLBOST Isle of Skye, Highland *Inverness-shire* Map 48 NG24
The Skye Black House Folk Museum On B884. Typical 19th-C house of the area containing implements and furniture of bygone days, with peat fire burning throughout the day. A replica of an illicit whisky still can be seen behind the museum. Open Etr – Oct daily 10 – 7. Prices under review. ▲ (☎ Glendale 291)

COLDSTREAM Borders *Berwickshire* Map 36 NT84
Dundock Wood 1½m W on A697. Magnificent display of rhododendrons and azaleas (mid May to end of Jun depending on season). It is also a large bird sanctuary. The wood and grounds are open at all times. Estate interpretation centre in Hirsel House grounds. Borders Country Fair 22 & 23 May. Nature walks. Picnic area. Admission by collecting box. ▲ &B (☎ 2345 and 2439)

COLPY Grampian *Aberdeenshire* Map 45 NJ63
Williamston House Attractive gardens, with a lochan. Ancient St Michael's Well nearby. Gardens open Jun – Sep, 10 – 7 daily. 30p (ch 15p) by collection box at garden entrance. Garden produce and plants for sale. ▲ & B (☎ Colby 227)

COMRIE Tayside *Perthshire* Map 40 NN72
Museum of Scottish Tartans Occupies an 18th-C building situated in the centre of town on the A85. The collection is the most comprehensive in the world with books, pictures, prints, maps and manuscripts relating to the history and development of Tartans and Highland Dress. Specialised library, and research collection of over 1,300 specimens of Tartans, and a unique system (Sindex) which records details of every known tartan. Quizzes for children. Spinning, weaving, dyeing demonstrations. Museum open all year, summer Mon – Sat 10 – 1, 2 – 5, Sun 2 – 4; winter weekdays 10.30 – 12.30, 2 – 4 (closed Sun). *60p (ch & pen 30p) including brochure. Party. P. & (☎ 779)

CORGARFF Grampian *Aberdeenshire* Map 44 NJ20

Corgarff Castle 16th-C tower, which was besieged in 1571, and is associated with the Jacobite Risings of 1715 and 1745. Later it became a military barracks. Open Apr–Sep, weekdays 9.30–7, Sun 2–7. *30p (ch 15p). ▲ (AM)

CRAIGIEVAR Grampian *Aberdeenshire* Map 45 NJ50
Craigievar Castle Unaltered tower house, built 1610 to 1626, with a notable Renaissance ceiling. Perhaps the most characteristic example of the true Scottish Baronial period. It enjoys a lovely setting between the valleys of the Dee and the Don. Castle open May–Sep, 2–6 daily (ex Fri), last visitors 5.15. Grounds open all year, 9.30–sunset. Castle £1.10 (ch 55p). Parties 90p, school parties 45p; grounds by donation. (☎ Lumphanan 635) (NTS)

CRAIGNURE Isle of Mull, Strathclyde *Argyll* Map 38 NM73
Duart Castle The restored ancestral home of the Macleans which dates from 1250 is in a splendid setting by Duart Point, overlooking the Sound of Mull and Firth of Lorne. Open May–Sep, daily 10–6; in addition Jul & Aug Sat & Sun. £1 (ch & pen 50p). ⚲ (teas). P. 5p. Frequent motor launch service from Oban direct to Castle pier and steamer to Craignure.
Torosay Castle and Gardens 19th-C house containing family portraits, wildlife pictures, a superb collection of Stags' 'Heads' (antlers) and the huge head of a prehistoric Irish elk, dug out of a bog in Co Monaghan. Victorian library and archive rooms with family scrapbooks and photographs covering the last 100 years. 11 acres of Italian gardens and grounds with Venetian statues and a plantation of Australian gum trees and many other Gulf Stream shrubs. Open 10 May–early Oct daily 11–5 (last entry). £1 (ch & pen 50p). Dogs in garden only. ⚲ (teas). ▲ (☎ 421)

CRATHES Grampian *Kincardineshire* Map 45 NO79
Crathes Castle and Gardens 3m E of Banchory on A93. A picturesque 16th-C structure noted for its magnificent painted ceilings and famous gardens. Nature trails. Castle open Good Fri–12 Apr & May–Sep, Mon–Sat 11–6, Sun 2–6; (last admission 5.15). Gardens & grounds open daily all the year from 9.30–sunset. Castle only, 85p (ch 40p); gardens only 45p (ch 20p); grounds, cars 60p, minibuses £1.50, coaches £5. Combined ticket £1.40 (ch 70p). ⚲ Shop & restaurant Apr & 1–26 Oct Wed, Fri, Sat & Sun 12–4; May–Sep Mon–Sat 11–6, Sun 10–6. (☎ 525) (NTS)

CREETOWN Dumfries and Galloway *Kirkcudbrightshire* Map 30 NX45
Creetown Gem Rock Museum and Art Gallery Largest private collection in Great Britain with many of the exhibits collected by the proprietors on their world travels. Lapidary workshops open to view. Craft shop offering gifts and lapidary requirements for sale. Open daily 9.30–10pm. 30p (ch 10p). ⚲ ▲ ♿ (☎ Creetown 357)

CRICHTON Lothian *Midlothian* Map 35 NT36
Crichton Castle A 14th- to 16th-C castle, notable for the Earl of Bothwell's Italianate wing. Open see page 182 (but closed every 2nd Thu) *30p (ch 15p). (AM)

CRIEFF Tayside *Perthshire* Map 40 NN82
Innerpeffray Library 4½m SE of B8062. A late 18th-C building, housing Scotland's second oldest library founded in 1691 (the oldest library founded in 1683 is at Kirkwall, Orkney). Accessible all year weekdays (ex Thu) 10–1 & 2–5 (4, Nov–Feb), Sun all year 2–4. 30p (ch 10p). ▲ (☎ 2819)

CROMARTY Highland *Ross and Cromarty* Map 44 NH76
Hugh Miller's Cottage House c1711 birthplace in 1802 of Hugh Miller, the geologist. Open May–Sep, Mon–Sat 10–12 & 1–5; Jun–Sep also Sun 2–5. 50p (ch 25p). (☎ 245) (NTS)

CULLODEN MOOR Highland *Inverness-shire* Map 44 NH74
Culloden Battlefield The Cairn, built in 1881, recalls the famous battle of 1746, when 'Bonnie' Prince Charles Edward Stuart's army was routed by the Duke of Cumberland's forces. Near the Graves of the Clans is the Well of the Dead, and also the Cumberland Stone. The battle fought around Old Leanach Farmhouse, now a museum. Site always open. There is also a Trust Visitor Centre and exhibition open Good Fri–30 May, Sep–10 Oct daily 9.30–6, 31 May–Aug daily 9.30–8. Admission to Visitor Centre & museum (includes audio-visual exhibition in centre & parking). 90p (ch 45p). Party 20+ 55p (ch 25p). ▲ (☎ 607) (NTS)

CULROSS Fife *Fife* Map 40 NS98
Abbey Cistercian monastery founded by Malcolm, Earl of Fife in 1217. The choir is still used as the parish church and parts of the nave remain. Fine central tower, still complete, bears the arms of abbot Masoun (1498–1513). Open, see page 182. Free. (AM)
Culross Palace Dated 1597 and 1611, and noted for the painted rooms and terraced gardens. Open, see page 182. Prices under review. (AM)
Dunimarle Castle Part of this castle is now a museum, with valuable paintings, silver, books, and rare items of furniture, once belonging to Napoleon. Open Apr–Oct, daily 11–6. 60p (ch 14 30p). ▲ ♿B (☎ Newmills 229)

CULZEAN CASTLE Strathclyde *Ayrshire* Map 33 NS21
18th-C castle, in a fine Firth of Clyde setting of 560 acres. Designed by Robert Adam, it contains fine plaster ceilings, a splendid central staircase, and a circular drawing room. There is a collection of portraits of the Kennedys, Earls of Cassillis, and Marquess' of Ailsa. Guest flat presented to the late General Eisenhower. Open Apr–Sep, daily 10–6. Oct daily 10–4 (last admission ½hr before closing). £1.30 (ch 60p), party 85p per person, schools 60p per person. Jul & Aug £1.20 (ch 60p). No party reduction. (☎ Kirkoswald 269) (NTS)

CULZEAN COUNTRY PARK Strathclyde *Ayrshire* Map 33 NS21
560 acres including 1783 walled garden,

camelia house, orangery, swan pond, aviary. The home farm buildings by Robert Adam have been converted into a Reception and Interpretation Centre. Park open all year. Centre Apr–Sep daily 10–6; Oct daily 10–4. * Pedestrians free, cars £1.20 minibuses & caravans £2.50, coaches £7. (Charges for Apr–Oct only, vehicles ex school coaches, free other times). (☎ Kirkoswald 269) ♿ (NTS)

CUPAR Fife *Fife* Map 41 NO31
Hill of Tarvit Mansion House and Garden 2m S off A916. A mansion house remodelled in 1906 by Sir Robert Lorimer, with a notable collection of furniture, tapestries and paintings. Open 10–12 Apr, then May–Sep daily (ex Fri) 2–6, last admission 5.30. Gardens & grounds open all year 10–dusk. House & gardens 90p (ch 45p); gardens only 35p (ch 15p). Parties 20 + 60p. (☎ 53127) (NTS)

DERVAIG Isle of Mull, Strathclyde *Argyll* Map 38 NM45
Old Byre Visitor Centre Torra Chlachainn, 1m S off B8073. Imaginative museum providing a reconstruction of the crofter's lives at the time of the clearances. Authentic cottage interiors with life-size figures and animals. 1978 winner of special Certificate of Commendation in BTA 'Come to Britain Trophy' competition. 1979 awarded 1st prize in 'Museum of the year award for Scotland' Audio-visual presentations every half-hour. Gift stall. Shop. Open Etr–Oct Mon–Fri 10.30–5, Sun 2–5 (exhibition closes at 5.30 daily). 90p (ch 10 50p). ☕ ⛺ ♿B (☎ 229)

DOLLAR Central *Clackmannanshire* Map 40 NS99
Castle Campbell and Dollar Glen 1m N. 15th-C tower with 16th- and 17th-C additions, in a picturesque Ochil Hills setting above the Dollar Glen, providing splendid views. Open, see page 182. Closed Thu afternoon, Fri. *30p (ch 15p). ⛺ (Castle AM and Glen NTS)

DORNIE Highland *Ross and Cromarty* Map 42 NG82
Eilean Donan Castle Stands at the meeting-point of Lochs Duich, Alsh and Long. Connected to the mainland by a causeway. This Seaforth fortress, erected originally in 1220, was destroyed in 1719, after being held by Jacobite troops, and was restored in 1912. Beautiful mountain setting. Shop. Open Etr–Sep, daily 10–6. Prices under review. ⛺ (☎ 202)

DOUNBY Orkney Map 48 HY22
The Brough of Birsay 6m NW. Ruined Romanesque church consisting of nave chancel and semicircular apse, with claustral buildings on north side. Adjacent to the ruins are remains of Viking dwellings which have been unearthed and are not conserved. Open, see page 182. (Closed on Mon, Tue afternoon in winter.) *30p (ch 15p). Crossing by foot except at high water (no boat). (AM)
Click Mill NW of town, off B9057. Example of one of the rare old Orcadian horizontal watermills, in working condition. Open at all times. Free. (AM)
Skara Brae 4m SW. A notable collection of well-preserved Stone Age dwellings, engulfed in drift sand, including stone furniture and fireplace. The most remarkable survival of its kind in Britain, much of it was first discovered in 1850 after a layer of sand was disturbed by a gale. Open, see page 182. *50p (ch 25p). (AM)

DOUNE Central *Perthshire* Map 40 NN70
Doune Castle Restored 14th-C stronghold, with two fine towers on the banks of the River Teith. Associations with Bonnie Prince Charlie and Scott's Waverley. Shop. Open Apr–Oct, daily 10–6 (ex Thu in Apr & Oct). * 65p (ch 40p) ⛺ (☎ 203)
Doune Motor Museum Situated 9m NW of Stirling on A84. Approximately 40 cars on display. Motor Racing Hill Climbs held in Apr, Jun and Sep. Picnic area, tourist shop. Shop. Open Apr–Oct, daily. *£1 (ch 40p) ☕ ⛺ ♿ (☎ 203)

DRUMCOLTRAN TOWER Dumfries and Galloway *Kirkcudbrightshire* Map 30 NX86
A 16th-C tower house, three-storeys in height and built to an oblong plan, with a projecting tower or wing. Standard hours, apply to key keeper. Free. (AM)

DRUMNADROCHIT Highland *Inverness-shire* Map 43 NH53
Official Loch Ness Monster Exhibition Includes photographs taken between 1933 and 1960; scale model of the loch. Equipment used in the hunt, sonar display and a model of the various underwater investigations. Shop. Open Etr, then May–14 Jun & Sep–Oct daily 9.30–8, 15 Jun–Aug daily, 9am–9.30pm. (Closed Xmas & New Year). Prices under review. ☕ ⛺ ♿ (☎ 573)
Urquhart Castle Historic, mainly 14th-C castle overlooking Loch Ness, destroyed before the 1715 Rising. Open, see page 182. Closed Wed, Thu afternoon. *40p (ch 20p). (AM)

DRYBURGH Borders *Berwickshire* Map 35 NT53
Dryburgh Abbey One of the famous Border group of monasteries founded by David I. The ruins are of great beauty and occupy a lovely situation in a horseshoe bend of the River Tweed. Within the church are the graves of Sir Walter Scott and Earl Haig. Open, see page 182. *40p (ch 20p). ⛺ (AM)

DUFFTOWN Grampian *Banffshire* Map 44 NJ33
Balvenie Castle Mainly 15th- and 16th-C, the ancient stronghold of the Comyns, preserving a remarkable iron 'yett'. Open, see page 182. Closed Wed afternoon, Thu. *30p (ch 15p). ⛺ (AM)
Dufftown Museum The Tower. Small local history museum. Civic regalia, Mortlach Kirk material. Shop. Open Jun–Sep daily 10–5 (7 Jul & Aug). Free. ⛺ ♿ (☎ Forres 73701)
Glenfiddich Distillery N of town, off A941. Situated by the 'Robbie Dubh' or 'Black Robert stream, this distillery was founded in 1886 by Major William Grant in the heart of the Speyside country. A visitor's Reception Centre houses a bar and a Scotch whisky museum. Gift shop. Open 8 Jan–23 Dec. Trained guides give tours Mon–Fri 10–5. (Last tour 4.30). Free. ⛺ ♿B (☎ 20375)

DUFFUS Grampian *Moray* Map 44 NJ16
Duffus Castle Off B9012. Motte and bailey

castle, with 8-acre bailey surrounding rebuilt 15th-C hall and 14th-C tower, now split into two halves. Open all reasonable times. Free. ▲ (AM)

DUMBARTON Strathclyde *Dunbartonshire* Map 37 NS37
Dumbarton Castle Atop 240ft high rock, with ancient gateway preserved. Associations with Mary, Queen of Scots. Open, see page 182. *30p (ch 15p). (AM)

DUMFRIES Dumfries and Galloway *Dumfriesshire* Map 34 NX97
Burns House Robert Burns died in this house in 1796. In the house are displayed memorials and personal relics of the poet. Open all year, Apr–Sep Mon–Sat 10–1, 2–7, Sun 2–7, Oct–Mar Mon–Sat 10–12 & 2–5. *20p (ch, pen & students 10p). P. (☎ 5297)
Burns Mausoleum St Michael's Churchyard. Mausoleum in the form of a Grecian temple containing the tombs of the poet, Jean Armour, Burn's wife, and their five sons. A sculptured group depicts the Muse of Poetry throwing her cloak over Burns at the plough. Opens as Burns House by arrangement with Curator. P. (☎ 5297)
Dumfries Museum and Camera Obscura The Observatory, Church St. Large collection of local history, archaeology, geology, local birds and animals. The Old Bridge House branch museum (on the Old Bridge) contains period rooms portraying the local way of life in the past. Picnic area. Shop. Open all year (Old Bridge House Apr–Sep only) Mon–Sat 10–1, 2–5 (ex Tue), Sun 2–5 Apr–Sep only. Museum & Old Bridge House free. Camera Obscura. *35p (ch 15p) ▲ (disabled only). P. ċB (☎ 3374)
Lincluden College Originally the site of a Benedictine nunnery, founded by Uchtred, Lord of Galloway in 1164. This was suppressed at the end of the 14th-C by Archibald the Grim, 3rd Earl of Douglas, who established in its place a college of eight secular canons under a provost. The present remains are that of the collegiate church, dating from the early 15th-C and the provost's house, dating from the 16th-C. Open, see page 182. Closed Thu afternoon, Fri. *25p (ch 10p). (AM)

DUNBEATH Highland *Caithness* Map 47 ND12
Laidhay Croft Museum Late 18th- to early 19th-C Caithness-type longhouse with dwelling, byre and stable under one roof and detached winnowing barn. All thatched and furnished in typical croft style. Picnic area. Open Etr–Sep dail 9–6. 30p (ch 14 & pen 15p). ċ ▲

DUNDEE Tayside *Angus* Map 41 NO43
Barrack Street Museum Ward Rd. Shipping and industrial exhibits relating especially to local ships built at or associated with Dundee. There are also art and photographic exhibitions. Rebuilding programme may cause changes in displays. Shop. Open from Mon–Sat 10–5.30; closed Sun. P. (☎ 25492 ext 17)
Broughty Castle and Museum Broughty Ferry. 4m E. 15th-C castle rebuilt as an estuary fort in the mid 19th-C. Displays relating to former Burgh of Broughty Ferry, whaling, natural history of the Tay, arms and armour, also Ecology Gallery. Picnic area. Shop. Open all year, Mon–Sat (ex Fri) 10–1 & 2–5.30; Sun (Jun–Sep only) 2–5. Free. ▲ (☎ Dundee 76121)
Central Museum and Art Gallery Albert Sq. Local archaeology, history, natural history, and geology, also a display devoted to the works of Mary Slessor, the missionary. The Art Gallery portrays the principal British and European masters. Rebuilding programme may cause changes in displays. Shop. Open from Sat 10–5.30; closed Sun. Free. ▲ (disabled only). P. ċB
Claypotts Broughty Ferry. 4m E. Claverhouse of Dundee's castle, of unusual appearance, built between 1569 and 1588, showing angle towers with crowstepped gables closed at present. Contact *Scottish Development Dept* on 031-229 9321 for details of opening times & prices. (AM)
Mills Observatory Situated in Balgay Park, the observatory, erected in 1935, is equipped with a 10in Cooke refracting telescope, and two 4in Terrestrial telescopes. Picnic area. Shop. Open Apr–Sep. Mon–Fri 2–7, Sat 2–5; Oct–Mar, Mon–Fri 2–10, Sat 2–5. Closed Sun & public hols. Free. ▲ ċB (☎ Dundee 67138)
Orchar Art Gallery Beach Crescent, Broughty Ferry. 4m E. The gallery displays oil-paintings and water-colours mostly by Scottish artists of the 19th-C. Among the etchings are 36 by Whistler. Open Mon–Sat (ex Fri) 10–1 & 2–5; Sun Jun–Sep only 2–5. Free. ▲ (☎ 77337)
St Mary's Tower Kirk Style, Nethergait. A 15th-C bell tower or steeple containing a magnificent peal of bells also displays relevant to the Tower. Open Etr–Oct, daily (ex Fri) 1–5, Sun 2–5. Free. P. ċB (☎ 25492/3 ext 16)
Spalding Golf Museum Camperdown Park. The museum in Camperdown House portrays the history of golf through three centuries and includes an iron club of c1680. Picnic area. Shop. Open Mon–Thu & Sat 1–5 (closed Fri), also Sun Etr–Oct 2–5. Free. ℒ available at Camperdown House. ▲ ċ B (☎ 645443)

DUNDONNELL Highland *Ross and Cromarty* Map 43 NH18
Dundonnell House 2m SE. An 18th-C house, noted for its fine gardens, featuring Chinese, Japanese, and other rare plants and shrubs. Collection of exotic birds. Teas available on open days. Times, dates and prices published by Scotland's Garden scheme and in the press. ▲ ċB (☎ 206)

DUNDRENNAN Dumfries and Galloway *Kirkcudbrightshire* Map 30 NX74
Dundrennan Abbey The remains of Cistercian house founded by David I and Fergus Lord of Galloway in 1142. Here Mary Queen of Scots spent her last night on native soil before seeking shelter in England. Open, see page 182. *25p (ch 10p). (AM)

DUNFERMLINE Fife *Fife* Map 40 NT08
Andrew Carnegie Birthplace Junction of Moodie St and Priory Lane. The cottage in which the great philanthropist was born in 1835. Personal relics, presentation caskets, Roll of Honour of Carnegie Hero Fund Test displayed in a Memorial Hall. Open

Places of Interest — Dunkeld–East Linton

May–Aug, Mon–Sat 11–1 & 2–6, Sun 2–5; Sep–Apr Mon–Sat 11–1 & 2–5, Sun 2–5. &B (☎ 724302)

Dunfermline Abbey Benedictine house founded by Queen Margaret and the foundations of her church remain beneath the present Norman nave. The site of the choir is now occupied by a modern parish church, at the east end of which are remains of St Margaret's shrine dating from the 13th-C. King Robert Bruce is buried in the choir and his grave is marked by a modern brass. Guest house was a Royal palace where Charles I was born. Situated in Pittencrieff Park. Open, see page 182 but closes at 6pm on Suns, Apr–Sep. Free. (AM)

Dunfermline Museum Viewfield Terrace. Interesting and varied displays of local history, domestic bygones and damask linen. Periodic special exhibitions. Open all year Mon–Sat 11–5. Free. ▲ (☎ 21814)

Pittencrieff House Museum Situated in a rugged glen, with lawns, hothouses, and gardens, overlooked by the ruined 11th-C Malcolm Canmore's tower. Fine 17th-C mansion house, with costume and art galleries. Special Summer exhibitions. Views of Forth estuary and Dunfermline Abbey. Picnic area. Shop. Open May–Sep Mon–Sat (ex Tue) 11–5; Sun 1–5. ▲ &B (☎ 22935)

DUNKELD Tayside *Perthshire* Map 41 NO04
Loch of Lowes Wild Life Reserve Variety of wild life. Great crested grebes and other waterfowl in natural surroundings can be watched through high powered binoculars from observation hide. Exhibition and slide programme in visitor centre. Open Apr–Sep, daily 10–7 Apr, May & Sep; 10–8.30 Jun–Aug. Hide open all times. Free. Special arrangements for parties booked in advance. ▲ (limited). (☎ 337) Apr–Sep, or Ballinluig 267 Oct–Mar)

Trust Visitor Centre 'Little Houses' dating from the rebuilding of village after the Battle of Dunkeld in 1689. Restoration undertaken by NTS and Perth County Council. Visitor Centre open Good Fri–Sep Mon–Sat 10–6, Sun 2–6. Free. (☎ 460) (NTS)

DUNS Borders *Berwickshire* Map 36 NT75
Jim Clark Room Newtown St. Contains motor racing trophies won by the famous driver Jim Clark, who was killed in Germany in 1968. Included are the two world Championship Trophies of 1963 and 1965 and other Grand Prix awards. Clark was the first and only Honorary Burgess of Duns and his parents gifted the trophies to the town. Shop. Open Etr–Sep Mon–Sat 10–1, 2–6, Sun 2–6. 40p (ch 16 20p). Parties during winter by special arrangement. Jim Clark Memorial Rally 3 & 4 Jul 6pm. ▲ & (☎ 2331)

Manderston 1½m E off A6105. A fine Edwardian house with magnificent State Rooms and extensive domestic offices, all completed in 1905, to a high standard of workmanship. Stables, marble dairy, gardens, woodland garden and lakeside walks. Gift shop. Open 17 May–20 Sep, Sun & Thu 2–5.30, also English BHs. Charges not available. Party 20+ by appointment. ☞ ▲ (☎ 3450)

DUNVEGAN Isle of Skye Highland *Inverness-shire* Map 48 NG24
Dunvegan Castle 13th-C and later. Historic and romantic home of the Chief of Macleod since the 13th-C. Pit dungeon and famous 'fairy' flag. Shop. Open Etr–mid Oct Mon–Sat 2–5; late May–Sep 10.30–5. *£1.20 (ch 60p, pen 90p). Gardens only 30p (ch 15p). ☞ ▲ &B (☎ 206)

EASDALE Strathclyde *Argyll* Map 38 NM71
An Cala Garden Featuring cherry trees, azaleas, roses, water and rock gardens. Open mid Apr–mid Sep, Mon & Thu 2–6. 25p (ch 5p). Dogs admitted if on lead. ▲

EAST FORTUNE Lothian *East Lothian* Map 35 NT57
Museum of Flight East Fortune Airfield. (A Royal Scottish Museum Outstation.) The airship base from which the R34 set out in July 1919 to make the first double crossing of the Atlantic, now displays the history of aircraft and rockets. Working exhibits which visitors may operate. Exhibits include Supermarine Spitfire Mk 16, De Havilland Sea Venom, and Hawker Sea Hawk. Open Jul & Aug daily 10–4, also open days yet to be decided. Free. ▲ & (☎ 031-225 7534)

EAST LINTON Lothian *East Lothian* Map 35 NT57
Hailes Castle 1m SW on unclass rd. An old castle or fortified manor house of the Gourlays and Hepburns, with a 16th-C chapel, dismantled by Cromwell in 1650. Open, see page 182. *25p (ch 10p). ▲ (AM)

Preston Mill This is the oldest working water-driven meal mill to survive in Scotland. Conical roof, projecting wind vane and red

The Scottish Experience
West End Princes Street
Tel 031-228 2828

DESTINATION SCOTLAND?
Discover and enjoy THE SCOTTISH EXPERIENCE — a visitor's adventure in the Heart of Edinburgh.

This unique Visitor Centre offers two superb entertainments, Information, Exhibitions, Shop and Refreshments and 33% trade commission. In one hour the visitor can see.

The Making of Edinburgh
A dramatic, multi-vision presentation shown on a giant screen.

Spectacular Scotland
A magnificent panoramic relief model.

There is a friendly Scottish welcome in the Shop. Alison's Kitchen provides home-made Scottish fare in a cosy coffee shop next to the Exhibition and Information area.

Prices: The two shows £1.80 adults; £1.00 children & OAPs. Party Rates and 33% Trade Profit.

For opening hours, Special Shows, Discount Vouchers, Publicity Material, Joint Promotions and further information, please contact: **Mrs. Gay Grossart, The Scottish Experience, West End Princes Street, Edinburgh. Tel: 031-228-2828/9.**

pantiles. Open all year, Mon–Sat 10–12.30 & 2–6.30, closes at 4.30pm Oct–Mar. 60p (ch 30p). Phantassie Doocot, a short walk away, once held 500 birds. (☎ 426) (NTS)

ECCLEFECHAN Dumfries and Galloway
Dumfriesshire Map 31 NY17
Carlyle's Birthplace A characteristic late 18th-C Scottish artisan's house, where Thomas Carlyle was born in 1795. Collection of manuscripts and personal relics. Open Good Fri–Oct, daily (ex Sun) 10–6. 40p (ch 20p). (☎ 666) (NTS)

EDINBURGH Lothian *Midlothian*
Map 35 NT27
Acheson House, Scottish Craft Centre A fine 17th-C mansion in the Royal Mile, opposite Canongate Church. Headquarters of the Scottish Craft Centre. Shop. Open Tue–Sat (ex PH) 10–5. Free. P. &B (☎ 031-5568136/7370)
Canongate Tolbooth Dates from 1591 and shows a curious projecting clock. The J Telfar Dunbar Tartan Collection is on show. Special exhibitions throughout the year. Shop. Dolls Houses exhibition mid Jul–end Festival. Open Jun-Sep, Mon–Sat 10–6, and also Sun 2–5 during Festival; Oct–May 10–5. Free. & (☎ 031-225 1131 ext 6638)
Craigmillar Castle 14th-C stronghold associated with Mary, Queen of Scots, and also the Earl of Mar. Notable 16th- and 17th-C apartments. Open Apr–Sep, weekdays (ex Thu afternoon, Fri) 9.30–7, Sun 2–7; Oct–Mar 9.30–4, Sun 2–4. *30p (ch 15p). & (AM)
Edinburgh Castle An historic stronghold, famous for the Crown Room, Banqueting Hall, Scottish United Services Museum, St Margaret's Chapel (faced by Mons Meg, a 15th-C cannon) and the impressive Scottish National War Memorial. Open Jan–Apr daily 9.30–5.05, Sun 12.30–4.20, May–Oct daily 9.30–6, Sun 11–6, Nov–Dec. *Jan–Apr 50p (ch 16 25p), May–Oct £1 (ch 16 50p), Nov–Dec 50p (ch 16 25p). War memorial free. & (AM)
Edinburgh Zoo The Scottish National Zoological Park. Set in 80 acres of grounds, this zoo is one of the finest in Europe, containing a superb collection of animals, fish, birds and reptiles. Also magnificent panoramic views of Edinburgh and surrounding countryside. Picnic area. Shop. Open all year, summer 9–6 (Sun opens 9.30) (5 or dusk winter). *£1.80 (ch 15 & pen 90p). Party application to Bookings Officer, Zoological Park, Murrayfield, Edinburgh EH12 6TS. ⚲ (also licensed). & (☎ 031-3349171)
George Heriot's School Lauriston Place. Dates from 1628 and was founded by George Heriot, the 'Jingling Geordie' of Sir Walter Scott's Fortunes of Nigel. Open Mon–Fri (ex BH) 9.30–4.30. Free. & &B (☎ 031-2297263)
Georgian House 7 Charlotte Sq. Lower floors open as typical Georgian House, furnished as it might have been by first owners, showing domestic surroundings and reflecting social conditions of that age. Open Apr–Oct, Mon–Sat 10–5, Sun 2–5, Nov–12 Dec Sat 10–4.30, Sun 2–4.30 (last admission ½hr before closing). 90p (ch

45p) (includes audio-visual shows). (☎ 031-225 2160) (NTS)
Gladstone's Land 483 Lawnmarket. Built in 1620, contains fine examples of tempera painting on the walls and ceiling and is furnished as a typical 17th-C home. Ground floor includes shop front and goods of the period. Open Apr–Oct, Mon–Sat 10–5, Sun 2–5; Nov–12 Dec, Sat 10–4.30, Sun 2–4.30 (last admission ½hr before closing). 70p (ch 35p). (☎ 031-2265856) (NTS)
Holyroodhouse At E end of Canongate. Historic Royal Palace of 16th- and 17th-C, built by Sir William Bruce, and associated with Mary, Queen of Scots and Prince Charles Edward. Outstanding picture gallery and state apartments. Ruined 13th-C nave of former Abbey church. Shop. *Open 5 Jan–28 Mar, 25 Oct–31 Dec, Mon–Sat 9.30–4.30. Closed Sun. 29 Mar–24 Oct, Mon–Sat 9.30–6, Sun 11–5.15. Last ticket for admission issued 45 mins before closure. 80p (ch & pen 40p). P. (200yds). &B (☎ 031-5567371)
Huntly House Canongate. Dates from 1570 and houses the City Museum of local history, containing among other things, collections of silver, glass and pottery. Shop. Open Jun–Sep, Mon–Sat 10–6; Oct–May 10–5. During Festival period Sun 2–5. Free. (☎ 031-225 1131 ext 6689)
John Knox's House High St. 15th-C house, preserving old wooden galleries. Built by the goldsmith to Mary, Queen of Scots. Shop. Open weekdays only 10–5. 50p (ch 30p). &B (☎ 031-556 6961)
Lady Stair's House Off Lawnmarket. Restored house, dating from 1622. Museum with literary relics of Robert Burns, Sir Walter Scott and Robert Louis Stevenson. Shop. Open Jul–Sep, Mon–Sat 10–6; Oct–May 10–5 (during Festival period, Sun 2–5). Free. & (☎ 031-225 1131 ext 6593)
Museum of Childhood 38 High St. Children's life in the past. Shop. Open Jun–Sep, Mon–Sat 10–6, Oct–May 10–5, also during Edinburgh's Festival period on Sun 2–6. 40p (ch 15 10p). & (☎ 031-225 1131 ext 6645)
National Gallery of Scotland The Mound. One of the most distinguished of the smaller galleries in Europe, containing collections of Old Masters, Impressionists and Scottish paintings including: Raphael's *Bridgewater Madonna*, Constable's *Dedham Vale*, and masterpieces by Titian, Velasquez, Raeburn, Van Gogh and Gauguin. Drawings, watercolours and original prints by Turner, Goya, Blake, etc (shown on request Mon–Fri 10–12.30 & 2–4.30). Postcards & colour slides on sale at the gallery shop. Museum open daily, Mon–Sat 10–5, Sun 2–5 (Mon–Sat 10–6, Sun 11–6 during Festival). Free. & & (☎ 031-5568921)
National Museum of Antiquities of Scotland 1 Queen St. Extensive collections and national treasures from earliest times to the present day, illustrating everyday life and history. Open Mon–Sat 10–5 (6 during Festival) Sun 2–5 (11–6 during Festival). Free. P. (meters). & (☎ 031-5568921)

Places of Interest

Outlook Tower Exhibition of *camera obscura*, which has operated since 1850. Small working models for use of visitors. Rooftop terrace with telescopes offering unique view of the city. Shop. Open all year 9.30 – 6; winter 9.30 – 4.30. *60p (ch 30p). ▲ (☎ 031-226 3709)

Parliament House East of George IV Bridge. Dates from 1639, but façade was replaced in 1829. Hall has a fine hammer-beam roof. The Scottish Parliament met there before the Union of 1707. Now seat of Supreme Law Courts of Scotland. Open Mon – Fri 10 – 4. ⚃ ▲ &B (☎ 031-225 2595)

Register House East end of Princes St. Designed by Robert Adam, it was founded in 1774. Headquarters of the Scottish Record Office and the repository for National Archives of Scotland. Summer exhibition Jul – Sep. Open all year (ex certain PH) Mon – Fri 9 – 4.45. Free. P. & (☎ 031-556 6585)

Royal Botanic Garden Inverleith Row. Famous garden, noted especially for the rhododendron collection, rock garden, plant houses and exhibition hall. The garden is open all year (ex 1 Jan) Mar – Oct, 9 – 1hr before sunset Mon – Sat, Sun 11 – 1 hr before sunset; Oct – Mar, Mon – Sat 9 – sunset, Sun 11 – sunset; plant houses & exhibition hall open 10 – 5 Mon – Sat, Sun 11 – 5 (during Festival period open on Sun from 10am). Free ⚃ (Etr – Sep). ▲ (Aboretum Road). & Sorry, no animals. (☎ 031-552 7171)

also Scottish National Gallery of Modern Art Inverleith House, Botanic garden. Temporary home since 1960 of the national collection of 20th-C painting, sculpture and graphic art. Among many modern masters represented are Derain, Picasso, Giacometti, Magritte, Henry Moore and Barbara Hepworth. Some sculpture is displayed in the garden immediately surrounding the Gallery. Print room and library also open to the public (closed for lunch). Shop. Open all year, Mon – Sat 10 – 5, Sun 2 – 5 (10 – 6, Sun 11 – 6 during Festival, closes at sunset during winter). Free. ⚃ (Etr – end of Edinburgh International Festival). P. &B (☎ 031-332 3754)

Royal Scottish Museum Chambers St. The most comprehensive display in Britain under one roof comprising the decorative arts, natural history, geology (minerals and fossils), and technology. Colliery locomotive of 1813, many scale-model locomotives, models of ships, Science and Victorian engineering. Lectures, gallery talks and films at advertised times. Special exhibitions. (Mon – Sat 10 – 4) Open weekdays 10 – 5, Sun 2 – 5. Free. ⚃ P. (meters). & (☎ 031-225 7534)

Scottish National Portrait Gallery Queen St. Striking red Victorian building containing portraits of men and women who have contributed to Scottish history. The collection includes such popular figures as Mary Queen of Scots, James VI and I, Burns, Sir Walter Scott and Ramsay MacDonald. Many other artists, statesmen, soldiers and scientists are portrayed in all media, including sculpture. Collections also illustrate the developement of Highland dress. Shop. Open all year, Mon – Sat, 10 – 5, Sun 2 – 5 (10 – 6, Sun 11 – 6 during Festival) Oct – Mar closed 12.30 – 1.30 Mon – Sat. Free. ▲ &B (☎ 031-556 8921)

The Scottish Experience West End Princes St. An ultra modern development inside a 19th-C church. On the ground floor: a spectacular 30 minute multivision show capturing the history, drama and beauty of Edinburgh; on the first floor, a giant three-dimensional walk-round model of the whole of Scotland and the Isles complete with visitor-operated fibre optics, scale models, light shows and complementary exhibition. Very special shop development in the basement. Shop. Open May – Sep, daily 10 – 7; Oct – Apr, Thu – Sat 11 – 4.£1.80 (ch £1). Party by arrangement. ⚃ P. (50yds). &B (☎ 031-228 2828)

West Register House Charlotte Sq. The former St George's church, designed by Robert Reid in the Greco-Roman style in 1811. Auxiliary repository for the Scottish Record Office and houses its museum. Open all year (ex PH) Mon – Fri 9 – 4.45. Free. ▲ (☎ 031-556 6585)

EDZELL Tayside *Angus* Map 41 NO56
Edzell Castle 16th-C, and associated with Mary, Queen of Scots, preserved walled garden from 1604. Open, see page 182 (but closed Tues & Thu am). *30p (ch 15p). (AM)

ELGIN Grampian *Moray* Map 44 NJ26
Elgin Museum The museum conserves and displays the heritage of Elgin and Moray. It contains a world-famed collection of fossils of the Old Red Sandstone. Open Apr – Sep, Mon – Fri 10 – 4, Sat 10 – 12. Under review. P. &B (☎ 3675)

Pluscarden Abbey 6m SW on unclass road. The original monastery was founded by Alexander II in 1230. Restorations and reconstruction took place in the 14th- and 19th-C, and the Abbey has been re-occupied by the Benedictines since 1948. Shop. Open daily 5am – 8.30pm. Free. ▲ & (parking near Abbey). (☎ Dallas 257)

ELLISLAND FARM Dumfries and Galloway *Dumfriesshire* Map 34 NX98
In this farm on the west bank of the Nith, Robert Burns lived from 1788 to 1791 and composed Tam O'Shanter and other poems and songs. Material associated with the poet is on display. No restriction on times of visiting and admission is free. ▲ (limited). &B (☎ Auldgirth 426)

FAIRLIE Strathclyde *Ayrshire* Map 33 NS25
Kelburn Country Centre 1m NE off A78. The historic estate of the Earls of Glasgow, on the Firth of Clyde. Beautiful gardens and spectacular scenery. It offers nature trails, gardens with rare trees and exotic and unusual shrubs from all over the world. Also Kelburn Glen, parts of which have been cultivated and the rest left in its wild state with waterfalls and pools. 18-C farm buildings set round a village square have been turned into shops and a Weaver's workshop, where visitors can watch various articles of clothing being made. Adventure course and pony-trekking available. Picnic area. Open Etr – mid Oct, daily 10 – 6. Winter Sun only 11 – 5. 80p (ch 14 & pen 50p). ⚃ ▲ (☎ Fairlie 685/554)

FALKIRK Central *Stirlingshire* Map 34 NS87
Falkirk Museum District history exhibition with displays relating to clock making, potteries and foundries. Open all year

193

Mon – Sat 9 – 5. Free. ⚐ (☎ 27703)
Rough Castle One of the most remarkable Roman military sites in Britain, situated on the Antonine, or Roman Wall. It covers one acre, with double ditches and defensive pits. Excavations revealing a bathhouse and other buildings made in 1903. Accessible at any reasonable time. Free. ⚐ (AM)

FALKLAND Fife *Fife* Map 41 NO20
Falkland Palace and Gardens Historic former hunting palace of Stewart Kings and Queens, situated below the Lomond Hills. The mid 16th-C buildings include a notable courtyard façade. Chapel Royal and apartments restored. Royal tennis court of 1539, the oldest in Britain. Visitor Centre. Palace & Gardens open Apr – Oct, Mon – Sat 10 – 6; Sun 2 – 6. Last visitors to Palace 5.15. Admission to Palace and gardens £1.10 (ch 55p); gardens only 60p (ch 30p). Parties 80p (school parties 40p). Scots Guards and members of the Scots Guards Association (wearing the Association's badge) Free. (☎ 397) (NTS)

FETTERCAIRN Tayside *Kincardineshire* Map 41 NO67
Fasque Home of the Gladstone family since 1829, the large mansion reflects the life of the original owner, Sir John Gladstone, and of subsequent generations and their families. Four times Prime Minister, William Gladstone, lived at Fasque from 1830 to 1851. Also illustrated is the life and work of the many servants who contributed to the running of the household. Collection of agricultural and other local machinery. Extensive parkland with red deer and Soay sheep. Open May – Sep incl. daily (ex Fri) 1.30 – 5.30 (last entry 5). Prices under review. ⚐ & B (☎ 201)

FINSTOWN Orkney Map 48 HY31
Maeshowe Chambered Cairn Britain's finest megalithic tomb, of Neolithic date (c1800 BC). Masonry in a remarkable state of preservation, showing Viking carvings and runes. Open, see page 14 (closed Sat, Sun). *30p (ch 15p). (AM)
Standing Stones 3m SW on A965. Remains of stone circle, second millenium BC. Nearby is the Ring of Brogar, of c1600 BC, consisting of a splendid circle of upright stones with a surrounding ditch. Open at any reasonable time. Free. (AM)

FINTRY Central *Stirlingshire* Map 37 NS68
Culcreuch Castle Castle dates from 1320 to 1460. Shop. Open every Sun from Etr – Sep. 12.30 Piper's Cold table lunch £2.80 (ch £1), 2.30 – 5.30 Tours of Castle £1 (ch 50p) no reservations necessary. ⚑ (licensed). ⚐ & B (☎ 228)

FORRES Grampian *Moray* Map 44 NJ05
Falconer Museum Tolbooth St. Displays of local history, wildlife, geology, ethnography and archaeological finds from Culbin. Shop. Open May – Sep, daily 10 – 5 (7 Jul & Aug). Free. P. & B (☎ 73701)
Nelson Tower Located on Cluny Hill, within Grant Park, overlooking Forres. The Tower was erected in 1806 by the survivors of the battle of Trafalgar and offers magnificent views of Moray Firth, Black Isle and inland mountains. Key available from Forres Tourist Information Centre at Falconer Museum (£1

deposit). Open mid May – Sep. Daily 10 – 6. ⚐ (☎ Elgin 2666)
Suenos' Stone A notable 20ft high monument, with a sculptured cross on one side and groups of warriors on the reverse. Accessible at all times. Free. (AM)

FORT AUGUSTUS Highland *Inverness-shire* Map 43 NH70
Great Glen Exhibition History and traditions of people of the Great Glen, rare maps and prints. Latest information on the search for Loch Ness Monster. Audio-visual shows. Shop. Open Jun – Sep, Mon – Sat 10 – 6, Sun 2 – 6. *60p (ch 15 30p, pen 40p). P. &

FORT GEORGE Highland *Inverness-shire* Map 44 NH75
Fort George As 18th-C fort, visited by Dr Johnson and Boswell in 1773. Open Apr – Sep, weekdays 9.30 – 7, Sun 2 – 7; Oct – Mar 9.30 – 4, Sun 2 – 4. Prices under review. P. (AM)
Also Queen's Own Highlanders Museum Housed in Fort George which was built 1748 – 1769. Exhibits include regimental uniforms, medals and pictures dating from 1778. Shop. Open Apr – Sep, Mon – Fri 10 – 6.30, Sun 2 – 6.30, Closed Sat. Oct – Mar, Mon – Fri 10 – 4, Closed Sat & Sun. P. (400yds). & B (☎ Inverness 224380)

FORT WILLIAM Highland *Inverness-shire* Map 39 NN17
Inverlochy Castle Well-preserved example of a 13th-C and later stronghold, famous for the battle fought nearby in 1645, when Montrose defeated the Campbells. Now under repair and interior not accessible, but may be viewed from the outside. Free. (AM)
West Highland Museum A museum of local and particularly Jacobite interest, including an exhibition about the '45 rising with the well-known 'secret portrait' of Prince Charles Edward Stuart. Relics from the former fort, archaeology, wildlife, geology, and folk exhibits. Open mid Jun – mid Sep, 9.30 – 9; Oct – May 9.30 – 1, 2.15 – 5. Closed Sun. *20p (ch 10p). P. (600yds). (☎ 2169)

GAIRLOCH Highland *Ross-shire* Map 42 NG87
Gairloch Heritage Museum Achtercairn. A converted farmstead now houses the museum which relates the way of life in the typical West Highland parish of Gairloch from the earliest times to the 20th-C. First prize Scottish 'Museum of the year Award'. Replica croft-house room. External marine display. Shop. Open 19 May – Sep daily (ex Sun) 10 – 1 & 2 – 4. (Jul & Aug 2 – 8). *20p (ch 10 10p). Opening hours & prices under review. Restaurant. ⚐ (☎ Badachro 243)

GALASHIELS Borders *Selkirkshire* Map 35 NT43
Bernat Klein Exhibition Waukrigg Mill. This exhibition is intended to show the stages between the conception of a design idea and the finished product. The exhibition consists of approximately 100 paintings, sketches, photographs, patterns and other objects, specially selected from Bernat Klein's work. It also shows the relationship of his work with the surrounding countryside. Open Apr – Oct daily Nov – Mar Mon – Fri 10 – 4. Free. ⚐ & (☎ 2764)

Places of Interest — Gigha, Isle of – Glasgow

GIGHA, ISLE OF Strathclyde *Argyll* Map 32
See **Ardminish**

GLAMIS Tayside *Angus* Map 41 NO34
Glamis Castle The ancestral seat of the Earl of Strathmore and Kinghorne, family home of Her Majesty Queen Elizabeth, The Queen Mother and birthplace in 1930 of HRH Princess Margaret. Mainly late 17th-C but with an older tower. The drawing room ceiling of 1621 and the painted panels in the chapel are notable. Shop. Open Etr & May – Sep daily 1 – 5 (ex Sat). *£1.30. Grounds only, half-price. Prices under review. ⚓ ♿B (☎242)
Angus Folk Museum Kirkwynd Cottages. Row of restored 19th-C cottages, now housing the Angus Folk Collection of agricultural and domestic equipment and cottage furniture etc. Open May – Sep, daily 12 – 5 (last admission 4.30). 60p (ch 30p). (NTS)

GLASGOW Strathclyde *Lanarkshire* Map 37 NS56
Bellahouston Park Ibrox. 171 acres of parkland only 3 miles from the city centre. Site of the Empire Exhibition of 1938. Sunken garden and rock garden. Multi-purpose Sports Centre situated at west end of park, with all-weather Athletic Centre adjacent and nursery ski slope. Horse show – Pope's visit, Jul. Open daily 7 – dusk. Free ⚓ (in Sports Centre). ⚠ at ski slope and sports centre. ♿ (☎041-427 0558 Park & 041-427 4131 Sports Centre)
Botanic Garden Off Great Western Rd. Established in 1817, it contains an outstanding collection of plants. The Kibble Palace open 10 – 4.45 (4.15 in winter), is a unique glasshouse with, among others, a famous collection of tree ferns. The main glasshouse open Mon – Sat 1 – 4.45 (4.15 in winter), Sun 12 – 4.45 (4.15 in winter), contains numerous tropical and exotic plants. The 40 acres of gardens include systematic and herb gardens, and a chronological border. Open daily 7 – dusk. Free. ⚠ ♿ (Kibble Palace & gardens only). (☎041-334 2422)
Crookston Castle Probably 13th-C, with an earlier defensive ditch. Visited by Mary, Queen of Scots, and Darnley in 1565. Open, see page 182. *25p (ch 10p). (AM)
Glasgow Art Gallery and Museum Kelvingrove Park. Italian, Flemish, Dutch, French and British paintings representing the finest civic art collection in Great Britain. Collections of pottery, porcelain, silver, sculpture, arms and armour. Plus archaeology, ethnography, natural history, selections from the world famous Burrell Collection and the Armour Gallery opened 1980. Shop. Open Mon – Sat 10 – 5, Sun 2 – 5. Closed 25 Dec & 1 Jan. Free. ⚓ ⚠ ♿ (by arrangement). (☎041-334 1134)
Greenbank Garden Clarkston. Off A726 on southern outskirts of the city. Small garden at which has been established a Gardening Advice Centre, particularly suitable for the owners of small gardens. Classes, demonstrations etc. Garden open all year daily 10 – dusk. Garden advice Thu 2 – 5 (at garden or by phone). 50p (ch 25p). ♿ (☎041-639 3281) (NTS)

Haggs Castle 100 St Andrew's Drive. Built in 1585, the castle houses a museum created for children. The theme is exploration of time – particularly the last 400 years since the castle was built. Activities in the adjacent workshop allow young visitors to become practically involved in the past. Picnic area. Open all year (ex 25 Dec & 1 Jan) Mon – Sat 10 – 5.15, Sun 2 – 5. Free. P. (street). (☎041-427 2725)
Hunterian Art Gallery University of Glasgow Collection of works by James McNeill Whistler and Charles Rennie Mackintosh. Also on display are a group of French, Dutch, Flemish, Italian and British 17th- and 18th-century paintings bequeathed by the Gallery's founder Dr William Hunter. A growing collection of contemporary paintings, an outdoor sculpture of old master and modern prints. Open all year Mon – Fri 10 – 5, Sat 9.30 – 1 (please telephone for details of public holiday closures). Free. ⚠ ♿ (☎041-339 8855 ext 7431)
Hunterian Museum The University of Glasgow. The museum is named after the 18th-C surgeon, Dr William Hunter, who bequeathed his own collections to the University. The geological, archaeological, ethnographical, numismatic and historical collections are exhibited in the main building of the University. Shop. Open all year Mon – Fri 9 – 5, Sat 9 – 12. Free. ⚠ ♿ (by prior arrangement). (☎041-339 8855 ext 221)
Linn Park Cathcart. Southern outskirts of Glasgow. Comprises more than 200 acres of pine, deciduous woodland, and riverside walks. Britain's first public park nature trail (1965) features many varieties of flowers, trees, and insects. Children's zoo. Collection of British ponies and Highland cattle. There is also a ruined 14th-C castle, with a Mary Queen of Scots historical plaque. Picnic area. Open daily 7 – dusk. Free. ⚓ (at Mansion House). ⚠ ♿B (☎041-637 3096)
People's Palace Glasgow Green. Contains a fascinating visual record of the history and life of the City. Prehistoric and medieval Glasgow, interesting relics of Mary, Queen of Scots, the Battle of Langside, the Tobacco Lords of the 18th-C, and the history of the music hall. Fine examples of Glasgow craftsmanship, particularly pottery, and special displays illustrating social and domestic life. A wide range of pictures of noteworthy people and places. Shop. Stained glass window exhibition until Apr. Open Mon – Sat 10 – 5, Sun 2 – 5. Free. ⚠ ♿B (☎041-554 0223)
Pollok Park 361 acres, formerly a private estate containing an extensive collection of flowering shrubs and trees in a natural setting. Display rose garden, nature trails, jogging track. Open daily 7 – dusk. Demonstration and display garden open daily 10 – 4. Demonstrations held fortnightly, Sat mornings. Free. ⚠ ♿B (☎041-423 8693)
Also **Pollok House** situated within the grounds, an Adam style building (1752) with Edwardian additions, containing the famous Stirling-Maxwell Collection of Spanish and other paintings, furniture, ceramics, silver, etc. Picnic area. Shop. Open all year Mon – Sat 10 – 5, Sun 2 – 5. Free ⚓ ⚠ ♿B (☎041-632 0271)
Provan Hall Auchinlea Road. Well restored 15th-C house considered most perfect

example of a simple pre-Reformation house remaining in Scotland, set in Auchinlea Park. In the adjacent grounds are formal and informal gardens including garden for the blind. For information on opening hours contact *Glasgow District Council, Parks Dept.* ⚠ ♿ (☎ 041-771 6372) (NTS)

Ross Hall Park Crookson. Beautifully kept gardens with artificial ponds featuring a variety of aquatic plants and stocked with fish. Extensive heather and rock gardens and woodland nature trails. Open Apr – Sep, daily 1 – 8; Oct – Mar, daily 1 – 4. Free. P. ♿ (☎ 041-882 3554)

Rouken Glen Park Thornliebank. Fine park with lovely walks through the glen, waterfall at head of the glen is a noted beauty spot. Large walled garden. Boating on picturesque loch. Picnic area. Open daily 7 – dusk. Free. ♨ ⚠ ♿ (☎ 041-638 1071)

Transport Museum Albert Drive, near Eglinton Toll. A life-size presentation of land transport, showing the development of the bicycle, horse-drawn vehicles, tramcars, Scottish motor cars from vintage to present day and railway locomotives, also the Clyde room with an outstanding collection of ship models and Subway Gallery with a reconstruction of a Glasgow underground railway station. Shop. Open Mon – Sat 10 – 5. Sun 2 – 5. Free. ♨ P. ♿ (☎ 041-423 8000)

Victoria Park Whiteinch. This park has the best known fossilized tree stumps of the prehistoric Coal Age period, discovered in 1887, and housed in the Fossil Grove building. Open Mon – Sat from 8am (Sun from 10am). The park has extensive carpet bedding depicting centennial events. Picnic area. Open daily 7 – dusk. Free. P. ♿ (☎ 041-959 1146)

GLENCOE Highland *Argyll* Map 39 NN15
Glencoe and North Lorn Folk Museum Housed in two heather-thatched cottages, one of cruck construction, in main street of Glencoe. Macdonald relics, local domestic and agricultural exhibits, and Jacobite relics costume and embroidery, ch section. Shop. Open mid May – Sep, Mon – Sat 10 – 5.30. *20p (ch 10p). P.
Glen Coe Visitor Centre Situated at north end of Glen Coe close to site of 1692 massacre. Ranger-Naturalist service available. Open Good Fri – 16 May & 13 Sep – 10 Oct daily 10 – 5; 17 May – 12 Sep, daily 10 – 7. 20p including ⚠. (NTS)

GLENDALE Isle of Skye, Highland *Inverness-shire* Map 48 NG15
Skye Watermill On the shores of Loch Pooltiel, a 200-year-old grain mill and kiln, recently restored to working order. Open Etr – Oct, Mon – Sat 10 – 7. 30p (ch 10p, ch 6 free, pen 15p). ♨ ⚠ (☎ 223)

GLENELG Highland *Inverness-shire* Map 42 NG81
Gleneig Brochs In Glen Beag, reached by way of the steep and winding Marn Rattachen pass, off A87. Remains of two brochs, known as Dun Telve and Dun Troddan. Probably of Iron Age date, some 30ft in height, and showing well-preserved walls, galleries, and courts. Picturesque Highland setting. Accessible at all reasonable times. Free. (AM)

GLENFINNAN Highland *Inverness-shire* Map 39 NM98
Monument Erected in 1815 to commemorate the Highlanders who followed Prince Charles Edward Stuart in 1745. Plaques give a dedication in English, Gaelic, and Latin. The monument stands in a superb setting of mountains at the head of Loch Shiel. Visitor Centre. Open daily Good Fri – Jun 9.30 – 6; Jul – Aug 9.30 – 8; Sep – 10 Oct 9.30 – 6. 40p (ch 20p) including ⚠. (☎ Kinlocheil 250) (NTS)

GLENGOULANDIE DEER PARK Tayside *Perthshire* Map 40 NN75
8m NW of Aberfeldy on B846. A fine herd of red deer, Highland cattle, endangered species and other birds and animals live in the park in surroundings as like their natural environment as possible. Pets must not be allowed out of cars. Picnic area. Shop. Open Apr – Sep daily 9 – two hours before sunset. 35p (ch 25p), cars £1.50. ⚠ (☎ Kenmore 306)

GLENLIVET Grampian *Banffshire* Map 44 NJ12
Glenlivet Distillery Off B9136 12m SW of Dufftown (via B9009 and B9008). The reception centre contains an exhibition of ancient artefacts used in malting, peat cutting and distilling. Distillery tour. Shop. Open Etr – mid Oct, Mon – Fri 10 – 4. Free. ⚠ (☎ Glenlivet 202 ext 10)

GLENLUCE Dumfries and Galloway *Wigtownshire* Map 30 NX15
Glenluce Abbey 2m NW of the village. A Cistercian house founded in 1192 by Roland, Earl of Galloway. The ruins occupy a site of great beauty and are themselves of much architectural interest and distinction. Open, see page 14. Closed Fri & every 2nd Thu. Also closes at 4.30pm on Suns Oct – Mar. *25p (ch 10p). ⚠ (AM)

GOGAR Lothian *Midlothian* Map 35 NT17
Suntrap Gogarbank. 1m S off Gogar Moor – Ransfield road. Small garden containing a Gardening Advice Centre, with lecture hall, glass-houses, demonstrations etc, adapted to help owners of small gardens. Garden open all year, daily 9 – dusk. Centre open all year, Mon – Fri 9.30 – 5 (also Sat & Sun Apr – Sep 2.30 – 5). 50p (ch 25p). Full details from Principal, Oatridge College, Broxburn, West Lothian. ⚠ ♿ (☎ 031-339 7283) (NTS)

GOLSPIE Highland *Sutherland* Map 47 NH89
Dunrobin Castle 1m NE. The ancient seat of the Earls and Dukes of Sutherland. Much of the interior is open to the public and contains a wide variety of furniture, paintings and exhibits. Magnificent garden. Gift shop. Open mid May – mid Sep daily Mon – Sat 10.30 – 5.30, Sun 1 – 5.30. Doors close 5pm. Prices under review. Party. ♨ ⚠ ♿ (☎ 377) (Countess of Sutherland)

GORDON Borders *Berwickshire* Map 35 NT64
Mellerstain House 3m S on unclass road. Adam house with fine plaster ceilings, period furniture and pictures. Terraced gardens and lake. Historic Vehicle display 6 Jun. Shop. Open Etr then May – Sep, Mon – Fri & Sun 1.30 – 5.30 (last admission 5). *£1.10 (ch

14 50p, pen 90p). Prices under review. Dogs must be on a lead. 🍴 ⚠ ♿B (☎ 225)

GREAT CUMBRAE ISLAND Strathclyde
Bute Map 33
See **Millport**

GREENOCK Strathclyde *Renfrewshire*
Map 33 NS27
Mclean Museum and Art Gallery 9 Union St. A museum displaying exhibits relating to local history, ethnography, natural history, geology, and shipping, including river paddle steamers and cargo vessels. There are also relics of James Watt. Inverclyde art exhibition last week in Feb & Mar; Greenock Art Club exhibition in Sep/Oct. Open all year, Mon – Sat 10 – 5 (closed Sat 1 – 2). Free. P. (☎ 23741)

HAMILTON Strathclyde *Lanarks*
Map 37 NS75
Hamilton District Museum Muir St. Collections of local history and crafts, paintings and early photographs, farming, horse and motor transport and period kitchen, all housed in late 17th-C inn with 18th-C Assembly Hall with musicians gallery. Open all year daily (ex Sun) Mon – Fri 10 – 12 & 1 – 5, Sat 10 – 5. Free. ⚠ (☎ 283981)

HARRAY Orkney Map 48 HY31
Corrigall Farm Museum Restored Orkney farmstead dating from mid-19th-C with grain-drying kiln, furnishings and implements of the period. Display room. Shop. Open Apr – Sep Mon – Sat 10.30 – 1 & 2 – 5 Sun 2 – 7. Free. P. ♿ (☎ Kirkwall 3191)

HAWICK Borders *Roxburghshire*
Map 35 NT51
Museum and Art Gallery Wilton Lodge. The museum contains exhibits of natural history, local history, hosiery trade, archaeology, geology, coins and medals. The Art Gallery has exhibitions throughout the year. Open all year, Apr – Oct Mon – Sat 10 – 5 (2 – 5 Sun); Nov – Mar Mon – Sat 10 – 4 (closed Sun). *15p (ch 16 10p). P. ♿B (☎ 3457)

HERMITAGE Borders *Roxburghshire*
Map 35 NY59
Hermitage Castle An old Douglas stronghold, mainly 14th-C, well-restored, with Mary, Queen of Scots associations. Open, see page 182. *25p (ch 10p). ⚠ (AM)

HUNTERSTON Strathclyde *Ayrshire*
Map 33 NS15
Hunterston Power Station Nuclear Power Station of advanced gas-cooled reactor (AGR) type. Guided parties of about 12 are taken on tours of the premises and also see audio-visual presentation on Nuclear Power Generation Open daily, May – Sep Mon – Sat 10 – 11.30 & 2 – 3.30, Sun 2 – 3.30. Free. ⚠ (☎ West Kilbride 823668)

HUNTLY Grampian *Aberdeenshire*
Map 45 NJ53
Agricultural Museum 3½m SE. Contains an interesting collection of about 550 items, including farm implements, horse and cattle equipment, butter- and cheese-making utensils, corn dollies and many hand-tools. Sales dept, selling farm and country antiques. Open Wed, Sat, Sun. Other times by appointment. 40p (ch 20p). ⚠ ♿B (☎ Drumblade 231)

Huntly Castle Formerly Peel of Strathbogie, dates largely from 1602, with elaborate heraldic embellishments. Open, see page 182. *30p (ch 15p). ⚠ (AM)

Huntly Museum The Square. Local history and changing special exhibitions every year. Governed by North East of Scotland Library Committee. Shop. Open all year (ex Mon) Tue – Sat 10 – 12, 2 – 4. Free. ⚠ (☎ Peterhead 77778)

INGLISTON Lothian *Midlothian*
Map 35 NT17
Agricultural Museum Royal Showground. Shows the history of farming and rural life in Scotland. Special exhibition at Royal Highland Show in 3rd week of June. Shop. Open from May Mon – Fri 9.30 – 4. Free. ⚠ (restricted). ♿B (☎ 031-5568921 ext 267 or 031-3332674)

INNERLEITHEN Borders *Peeblesshire*
Map 35 NT33
Traquair House 1m S on B709. Scotland's oldest inhabited, and most romantic house, dating back to the 10th-C. Twenty-seven English and Scottish Kings have stayed here. Rich in association with Mary, Queen of Scots, and the Jacobite Risings. Contains a fine collection of historical treasures, many recently discovered. Unique 18th-C brew-house licensed to sell own beer. Newly planted maze. Woodland walks. Picnic area. 5 craft workshops. Craft Fair 7 & 8 Aug. Gift shop. Antiques and Bric a Brac. Open Etr Sat & mid Apr – mid Oct 1.30 – 5.30. Also Jul & Aug only 10.30 – 5.30 (last admission 5). 🍴 ⚠ ♿B (☎ 830323)

INVERARAY Strathclyde *Argyll*
Map 39 NN00

TRAQUAIR HOUSE
Innerleithen, Peeblesshire

29 miles drive from Edinburgh through beautiful Border country. Scotland's Oldest Lived-in House, inhabited since the 12th century by the Kings of Scotland, the Earls of Traquair and their descendants. A house full of beauty, of mystery and romance and a living mirror of Scotland's past.
Open 1.30 — 5.30 pm. DAILY from Easter Saturday, April 10th until Sunday, October 24th. Also open during July and August only 10.30 am. — 5.30 pm. (Last House admittance 5 pm.)
18th-century working Brewhouse, Craft Workshops, Tea Room, Woodland and River Walks. Newly planted Maze.
Telephone: Innerleithen (0896) 830323.

Inveraray Bell Tower The 126ft tower was planned in 1914, and the ring of ten bells were hung in the great bell chamber in 1931. From the roof of the tower is an excellent view. Exhibition of vestments and campanology and there will be a 'ring-in' daily during Inveraray Week at the end of July. Shop. Open mid May – mid Sep (under review). *30p (ch & pen 15p). P.

Inveraray Castle A fine mansion of the late 18th-C by Robert Mylne and Roger Morris. Ancestral home of the Dukes of Argyll. The great hall, armoury, staterooms, tapestries and furniture are of note. Shop. Open first Sat Apr – Sep daily (ex Fri) 10 – 1, 2 – 6; Jul – Aug weekdays 10 – 6, Sun 2 – 6 (last admission 5.30). £1.50 (ch 16 & pen 80p). Disabled free. ⚲ ▲ ♿B (☎ 2203)

INVERESK Lothian *Midlothian*
Map 37 NT37
Inveresk Lodge Garden New garden featuring numerous varieties of plants for small gardens. Garden only shown all the year, Mon, Wed & Fri 10 – 4.30, on Sun 2 – 5 when house is occupied. 30p (ch accompanied by adults 15p). (NTS)

INVERNESS Highland *Inverness-shire*
Map 43 NH64
Abertarff House Church St. The town house of Lord Lovat, built in 1593, it is now the headquarters of An Comunn Gaidhealach. It has a stone turnpike staircase and contains an exhibition of the origins and history of the Gaels, a sales point for Gaelic books and records and English books on the Highlands. Open all year, Mon – Thu 9 – 5.15 (9 – 4.45 Fri, 10 – 4 Sat). Free. ▲ (☎ 31226)

INVERTROSSACHS Central *Perthshire*
Map 43 NH50
Privately owned nature reserve with trails in extremely fine setting beside Loch Venachar. Picnic area. Open May – Aug by prior appointment only. *50p (ch 20p). ▲ ♿
(☎ Callander 30010)

INVERURIE Grampian *Aberdeenshire*
Map 45 NJ72
Inverurie Museum Town House. Thematic displays changing 4- or 6-monthly. Permanent local history and archaeology exhibition. Reserve collections may be viewed by appointment. Established in 1884, this museum is now governed by the North East Scotland Library Service Committee. Shop. Open all year, Mon – Fri 2 – 5, Sat 10 – 12. Free. P. (☎ Peterhead 77778)

IRVINE Strathclyde *Ayrshire* Map 33 NS34
Eglinton Castle and Gardens Irvine Rd Kilwinning. Late 18th-C castle, built for 13th Earl of Eglinton. Castle ruin set in a 12-acre garden. Site of the famous Eglinton Tournament of 1839. Picnic area. Always open. Free. ▲ ♿B (☎ 74166 ext 373)

ISLE OF ARRAN Strathclyde *Bute* Map 33
see Brodick, Brodick Castle

ISLE OF BARRA Western Isles *Inverness-shire* Map 48
see Castlebay

ISLE OF BUTE Strathclyde *Bute* Map 33
see Rothesay

ISLE OF GIGHA Strathclyde *Argyll* Map 32
see Ardminish

ISLE OF LEWIS Western Isles *Ross & Cromarty* Map 48
see Arnol, Callanish, Carloway

ISLE OF MULL Strathclyde *Argyll* Map 38
see Craignure, Dervaig

ISLE OF SKYE Highland *Inverness-shire*
Map 42
see Armadale, Colbost, Dunvegan, Glendale, Kilmuir

JEDBURGH Borders *Roxburghshire*
Map 35 NT62
Jedburgh Abbey One of the four famous border monasteries founded by David I. The remains of the church are mostly Norman or Transitional. Also small museum, containing many carved fragments of medieval work and some important monuments from the Anglian period. Open, see page 182 (but closed Thu pm & Fri). Prices under review. ▲ (AM)
Castle Jail This is the former county prison, dating from 1820 – 3, on the site of the medieval castle, demolished in 1409. There were three blocks, used for different categories of prisoners. Possibly the last surviving example of its kind. A small museum is also open to visitors. Open Apr – Sep, Mon – Sat 10 – 12, 1 – 5, Suns 1 – 5. *20p (ch 16 15p). P. (100yds).
(☎ Hawick 3457)
Mary Queen of Scots House A historic and picturesque house built in the 16th-C. Now a museum with exhibits relating to the Queen and to the earlier story of Jedburgh and district. Open Mar – Oct daily 10 – 5.30. *30p (ch 16 20p). P. (☎ 3331)
Monteviot House and Gardens (3½m N of Jedburgh off A68/B6400). Home of the 12th Marquis of Lothian, in beautiful grounds by the River Teviot. Included in the family collection are pictures by Holbein and Van Dyck. Shop. Open 6 May – 28 Oct, Wed only 1.30 – 5.30. *£1 (ch 12 50p). ⚲ ▲ ♿
(☎ Ancrum 286 or Crailing 230)

KELLIE CASTLE AND GARDENS Fife *Fife*
Map 41 NO50
Mainly 16th- and 17th-C building, a fine example of the domestic architecture of the Scottish lowlands. Notable plasterwork and panelling painted with 'romantic' landscapes. Audio-visual shows. Castle open 10 Apr – Sep, daily (ex Fri) 2 – 6 (last admission 5.30) gardens and grounds all year daily 10 – dusk. Admission to castle and gardens 90p (ch 45p); gardens only 40p (ch accompanied by an adult 20p). Party 20 + (60p each). ♿B (☎ Arncroach 271) (NTS)

KELSO Borders *Roxburghshire*
Map 36 NT73
Floors Castle Home of Duke and Duchess of Roxbough. Built in 1721 by William Adam with later additions by W H Playfair. Contains superb French and English furniture, tapestries and paintings. Magnificent walled garden and garden centre. Childrens playground. Picnic area. Shop. Open Good Fri – 12 Apr & 2 May – Sep Sun, Tue – Thu 11 – 5.30 (last admission 4.45). Closed Sat & Mon (ex August BH). Open Fri to pre-booked coach parties only. Garden Centre open daily all year 9.30 – 5. £1.10 (ch 55p & pen £1). ⚲ (licensed). ▲ (☎ 23333)
Kelso Abbey Little but the abbey church remains, and that only in imposing fragments.

Places of Interest   Kemnay–Kilsyth

which are almost wholly of Norman and Transitional work. The best preserved portion is the north transept. Open see page 182. Free. (AM)

KEMNAY Grampian *Aberdeenshire*
Map 45 NJ71
Castle Fraser 2½m SW on unclass road. This castle is considered by many to be the most spectacular of the Castles of Mar. The massive Z-plan castle, with splendid architectural embellishments was begun about 1575 by the sixth laird, Michael Fraser, and incorporates an earlier castle. It was completed in 1636. An exhibition tells the story of 'The Castles of Mar'. Open May – Sep daily 2 – 6 (last admission 5.15). Garden and grounds open all year 9.30 – sunset. Castle 90p (ch 45p). Parties 70p, school parties 35p; grounds by donation. ♿ (☎ Sauchen 463) (NTS)

KILBARCHAN Strathclyde *Renfrewshire*
Map 39 NS46
Weaver's Cottage An early 18th-C weaver's house, containing looms, weaving equipment, domestic utensils. Open Apr – May, Sep – Oct, Tue, Thu, Sat & Sun 2 – 5. Jun – Aug, daily 2 – 5. 40p (ch 20p). (NTS)

KILCHRENAN Strathclyde *Argyll*
Map 44 NN02
Ardanaiseig 3m NE at end of unclass road. The gardens have azaleas, rhododendrons, rare shrubs and trees. Magnificent views across Loch Awe. Garden centre. Open Apr – Oct, daily 10 – 8. 50p (ch 16 free). ♿ (☎ 333)

KILDRUMMY Grampian *Aberdeenshire*
Map 45 NJ41
Kildrummy Castle A splendid, ruined, 13th-C fortress, with an imposing gatehouse and notable 15th- to 16th-C additions. Gallantly defended by Sir Nigel Bruce in 1306. Open, see page 182. *25p (ch 10p). ♿ (AM)
Kildrummy Castle Garden Trust Two of the Trustees are the Professors of Forestry and Botany, University of Aberdeen. At foot of the medieval castle lies the Water garden running under a copy of the 14th-C Brig O' Balgownie. Facing south is the shrub bank. The ancient quarry from which the ruins were built, contains a variety of alpines and shrubs from overseas. Plants for sale. Open 1 Apr – 31 Oct, daily 9 – 5. 30p (ch 5p). ♿ 10p (inside Hotel gates). (Coaches 50p by appointment). (☎ 264, 277 & 337)

KILLIECRANKIE Tayside *Perthshire*
Map 40 NN96
Trust Visitor Centre Situated close to site of 1689 battle where Jacobite army, led by 'Bonnie Dundee', routed King William's troops. Battle display. Wooded gorge; walks. Open Good Fri – Jun, & Sep – 24th Oct daily 10 – 6, Jul – Aug daily 9.30 – 6. 20p (ch free). ♿ (☎ 233) (NTS)

KILMARNOCK Strathclyde *Ayrshire*
Map 34 NS43
Burns Museum Outstanding Burns memorial. Panoramic views towards Arran from Tower. Open May – Sep daily 1 – 5, Oct – Apr Sat & Sun 1 – 5. 3p. P. (☎ 26401)
Dean Castle Dean Rd. Fortified tower built 1350 with lower keep, Great Hall and Upper Hall in perfect condition. Exhibitions of European arms and armour, early keyboard and other musical instruments. Palace has Long Gallery, kitchen and tower in equally good condition. Restoration shows Dean Castle as it was in 14th- and 15th-C, 42 acres of gardens and nature trail. Concerts of period music and other historical performances. Picnic area. Shop. Open mid May – mid Sep, Mon – Fri 2 – 5, Sat & Sun 12 – 5 (organised parties throughout the year by arrangement). Free. ♿ P. ♿B (☎ 26401)
Dick Institute Elmbank Av. Exhibits of geology (including fossils), small arms, shells, ethnography, numismatics, and archaeological specimens. Also art gallery (paintings and etchings) and library (Ayrshire and Burns printed books, etc). Open May – Sep, Mon, Tue, Thu & Fri 10 – 8 (Wed & Sat until 5pm); Oct – Apr 10 – 5. Free. ♿ ♿B (☎ 26401)

KILMARTIN Strathclyde *Argyll*
Map 38 NR89
Dunadd Fort 3m S. A816. A prehistoric hillfort incorporating walled enclosures. It was once the capital of the ancient Scots kingdom of Dalriada. Accessible at all reasonable times. Free. (AM)

KILMORY Strathclyde *Argyll* Map 33 NR77
Castle Sween 2½m N. Lonely ruin, situated on the rocky western coast of Knapdale, probably one of the earliest stone castles in Scotland dating from the mid 12th-C. The castle was destroyed by Sir Alexander Macdonald in 1647. Open at all times. Free. (AM)

KILMUIR Isle of Sky, Highland *Inverness-shire* Map 42 NG24
Skye Cottage Museum The museum consists of four thatched cottages portraying the croft house of 100 years ago. It shows a fine selection of implements, tools, etc used by the men and women of the Highlands and a very interesting collection of old letters, papers and pictures are on display. Shop. Open mid May – Sep Mon – Sat 9 – 6. 40p (ch 20p). ♿ ♿ (☎ Duntulm 279)

KILMUN Strathclyde *Argyll* Map 33 NS18
Kilmun Arboretum and Forest Plots A large collection of conifer and broadleaved tree species planted in plots and specimen groups. Established by the Forestry Commission in 1930, and now extending to 100 acres on a hillside overlooking the Holy Loch. Open all year during daylight hours. Free. Entrance and car park at Forestry Commission District Office, Kilmun, from which an illustrated guide book is available. ♿ (☎ 422)

KILSYTH Strathclyde *Stirlingshire*
Map 37 NS77
Colzium House Partly a museum, with attractive walled garden, and associated with Montrose's victory over the Covenanters in 1645. Recreational facilities include pitch and putt and a football field in grounds. House open Mon, Tue, Wed, Fri, Sun 2 – 5 & 7 – dusk (ex when booked for private functions), grounds open at all times. Free. ♿ (Sun, Summer only). ♿ ♿B (☎ 823110)

199

KINCRAIG Highland *Inverness-shire*
Map 44 NH80
Highland Wildlife Park Native animals of Scotland past and present, including wolves, bears, reindeer, wildcat and European Bison. Open daily from 10, 15 Mar – first Sun in Nov. Picnic site, shop, children's park. Prices under review. Kennels for pets at entrance. ⚲ ⚠ ⚙ (☎ 270)

KINGUSSIE Highland *Inverness-shire*
Map 44 NH70
Highland Folk Museum Contains an interesting display of Highland crafts and furnishings; a farming museum; reconstructed Hebridean mill, and primitive 'black house' set in 6 acres of garden. Picnic garden. Open all year Apr – Oct, Mon – Sat 10 – 6, Sun 2 – 6; Nov – Mar Mon – Fri 10 – 3. Subject to review. ⚠ ⚙ (☎ 307)

KINROSS Tayside *Kinross-shire*
Map 40 NO10
Kinross House Gardens Dates from 1685 to 1692, from designs by Sir William Bruce. Gardens only open May – Sep daily 2 – 7. 50p (ch 20p). Prices under review. ⚠ ⚙ (☎ 63467)
Loch Leven Castle Castle Island. From this historic, ruined, 15th-C and earlier island stronghold in Loch Leven, Mary Queen of Scots escaped in 1568, after a year's imprisonment. Scott's novel The Abbot describes the event. It is four storeys in height, with round towers guarding the outer wall. It was dismantled by the Covenanters in 1640. Open Apr – Sep 10 – 6, Sun 2 – 6. Free. *Ferry Charge 50p (ch 25p). (AM)

KINTORE Grampian *Aberdeenshire*
Map 45 NJ71
Balbithan House 2½m N.E. A fine 17th-C house, with an interesting garden, situated near the River Don. Contains small museum with collection of Scottish kitchen antiques. Also gallery of original flower and landscape water-colours, all for sale. Nursery garden with plants for sale. Open May – Sep. *50p (ch 16 20p). ⚠ To view please ☎ 2282

KIRKBEAN Dumfries and Galloway *Dumfriesshire* Map 30 NX95
Arbigland Garden 1m SE adjacent to Paul Jones cottage. The gardens and dower house of this mansion have been evolving through three centuries. Paul Jones the US Admiral worked here under his father, who was the gardener in the 1740s. Woodland, water and formal gardens arranged around a sandy bay. Shop. Open May – Sep, Tue, Thu & Sun 2 – 6. Charges under review. Parties by prior arrangement. ⚲ ⚠ ⚙ (☎ 213)

KIRKCALDY Fife *Fife* Map 41 NT29
Industrial Museum Forth House, 100yds from main museum. Collection of horsedrawn vehicles, blacksmith's forge etc. Open May – Sep, Mon – Sat 2 – 5, other times by arrangement. ⚠ ⚙B (☎ 260732)
John McDouall Stuart Museum Rectory Lane, Dysart. A memorial to the Scottish explorer (1815 – 1866) who in 1861 – 2 was the first man to cross Australia from south to north. Museum of the Year award winner 1978. Open May – Sep daily 2 – 5; other times by arrangement. Opening times under review. Free. ⚠ (☎ 260732)
Museum and Art Gallery War Memorial Grounds. Next to Kirkcaldy station. Local and natural history and archaeology. Collection of local pottery, including the famous Wemyss Ware, other decorative arts and a collection of Scottish Art, which includes works by William McTaggart and Peploe. Temporary exhibitions throughout the year. Shop. Open all year (ex Local Hols) Mon – Sat 11 – 5, Sun 2 – 5. Free. ⚠ (☎ 260732)
Ravenscraig Castle A prominent ruined structure, founded in 1460, and perhaps the first castle designed for defence with firearms. The ashlar masonry is notable. Open, see page 182. Prices under review. (AM)

KIRKCUDBRIGHT Dumfries and Galloway *Kirkcudbrightshire* Map 30 NX65
Broughton House An 18th-C house, noted for the collection of pictures by E A Hornel, a library, and an attractive garden. Open Apr – Oct 11 – 1 & 2 – 5; Nov – Mar, Sat, Sun & Mon 2 – 4 only. 50p (ch 14 to 18 & pen 15 – 20p). P. ⚙ (☎ 30437)
Maclellan's Castle A notable, ruined structure from 1582. Open, see page 182. *25p (ch 10p). ⚠ (AM)
Stewarty Museum A museum displaying objects connected with Galloway, including firearms, domestic and agricultural implements, and a good natural history section. Open Etr – Oct, Mon – Sat 10 – 1, 2 – 5. 40p (ch 14 20p). P. (street). ⚙B (☎ 30797)

KIRKOSWALD Strathclyde *Ayrshire*
Map 33 NS20
Souter Johnnie's Cottage A thatched 18th-C cottage, the former home of the village cobbler, John Davidson, the original Souter Johnnie of Burns' 'Tam O'Shanter'. Life-size figures of the Souter and his friends in the garden. Open Apr – Sep daily (ex Fri) 12 – 5, other times by appointment. 40p (ch accompanied by adults 20p). (☎ 243) (NTS)

KIRKWALL Orkney Map 48 HY41
Bishop's Palace A ruined palace dating originally from the 12th-C. Round tower built by Bishop Reid with addition of c1600 by Patrick Stewart, Earl of Orkney. Open, see page 182. Apply custodian of Earl Patrick's Palace. *30p (ch 15p). (AM)
Earl Patrick's Palace Built c1607 by Patrick Stewart, Earl of Orkney, and considered one of the finest Renaissance buildings in Scotland. Although roofless, much still remains. The oriel windows are notable. Accessible, see page 182, ex Oct – Mar Mon – Sat 9.30 – dusk, Sun 2 – dusk. *30p (ch 15p). (AM)
Tankerness House Broad St. Dating from the 16th-C, this is one of the finest vernacular town houses in Scotland. It is now a museum of Orkney history with archaeological collections. Special exhibitions. Open all year, Mon – Sat 10.30 – 12.30, 1.30 – 5. Free. ⚠ ⚙B (☎ 3191)

KIRRIEMUIR Tayside *Angus* Map 41 NO35
Barrie's Birthplace 9 Brechin Rd. A small house containing personal mementoes of Sir James Barrie, who was born here in 1860. Open May – Sep, Mon – Sat 10 – 12.30 & 2 – 6, Sun 2 – 6; or by arrangement. 50p (ch accompanied by adult 25p). (☎ 2646) (NTS)

KNOCKANDO Grampian *Moray*
Map 45 NJ14
Tamdhu Distillery Visitors are able to see the complete process of whisky being made. Open May – Sep, Mon – Fri 10 – 4. Free. ⚠ &B (☎ Carron 221)

LANGBANK Strathclyde *Renfrewshire*
Map 34 NS37
Finlaystone Estate 1m W. Gardens, garden centre and woodland walks and jogging trail. Open all year Mon – Sat 9 – 5, Sun 2 – 5. Shop. Craft shop and woodlands 40p (ch 30p). House with doll and Victorian collections open to parties by arrangement. 𝒥 (May to Aug, Sat & Sun 2 – 5). &
(☎ 285)

LARGS Strathclyde *Ayrshire* Map 33 NS25
Skelmorlie Aisle A splendid example of a Renaissance monument, erected by Sir Robert Montgomery of Skelmorlie in 1636, stands in an aisle, formerly the north transept of the old church of Largs, and is the only portion now preserved. The monument, which is built in stone, consists of a gallery raised above a partially sunk burial chamber. Open Apr – Sep (see page 182). *25p (ch 10p). (AM)

LAUDER Borders *Berwickshire*
Map 35 NT54
Thirlestane Castle One of Scotlands finest buildings, with magnificent ceilings. Owned by the Maitland family since the 12th-C. Attractive parkland and riverside setting. Home of the Border Country Life Museum, with static and working displays. Picnic area. Shop. Open Whit – mid Sep, Sat, Sun, Wed & Thu 12 – 6 plus Etr, BH & local hols. £1.25 (ch & pen 50p). 𝒥 ⚠ &B (☎ 254)

LAURISTON CASTLE Lothian *Midlothian*
Map 35 NT27
On NW outskirts of Edinburgh, 1m E of Cramond. A late 16th-C mansion, with furniture and antiques, displaying English and French styles. Associated with John Law, the early 18th-C broker. Open Apr – Oct, daily (ex Fri) 11 – 1 and 2 – 5; from Nov – Mar, Sat & Sun only 2 – 4. 70p (ch 15 30p). Grounds 9 – dusk, free. ⚠ & (☎ 031-336 2060)

LAWERS Tayside *Perthshire* Map 40 NN64
Mountain Visitor Centre Ben Lawers, on slopes of Perthshire's highest mountain, 3,984ft, noted for variety of Alpine flowers, and species of birds to be seen. Centre includes exhibition and self-guided and guided trails. Open Good Fri – May & Sep, daily 11 – 4, Jun – Aug daily 10 – 5. 40p (ch 20p). ⚠ (☎ Killin 397) (NTS)

LEWIS, ISLE OF Western Isles *Ross & Cromarty* Map 48
See **Arnol, Callanish, Carloway**

LINLITHGOW Lothian *West Lothian*
Map 34 NS97
Blackness Castle 4½m NE. A 15th-C tower and later stronghold, formerly a Covenanters' prison and at one time used as a powder magazine. Massive 17th-C artillery emplacements. Open, see page 182 (but closed Mon afternoon, Tue). *25p (ch 10p). ⚠ (AM)
House of The Binns 4m E off A904. A 17th-C magnificent house, with plaster ceilings. General Tam Dalyell raised the Royal Scots Greys here in 1681. Panoramic viewpoint in grounds. Open 10/11 Apr, then May – Sep daily (ex Fri) 2 – 5.30. Parkland 10 – 7. 90p (ch 45p). Parties 70p (schools 35p). Members of Royal Scots Dragoon Guards, successors to Royal Scots Greys admitted free when in uniform. (☎ Philipstoun 255) (NTS)
Linlithgow Palace A fine, but ruined 15th-to 17th-C structure, associated with Mary, Queen of Scots (born here in 1542), and also with Prince Charles Edward. Chapel, great hall, and quadrangle fountain are notable. Open, see page 182. *40p (ch 20p). ⚠ (AM)

LOCHAWE Strathclyde *Argyll* Map 39 NN12
Cruachan Power Station 3m W off A85, near Pass of Brander. This important power station of the North of Scotland Hydroelectric Board pumps water from Loch Awe to a spectacular high level reservoir up on Ben Cruachan. Picnic area. The station is open to the public from 9 – 5. 80p (ch 10 – 15 40p; ch 10 accompanied, free) and a minibus service into the underground station is provided for touring motorists during the summer. Prices under review. ⚠
Kilchurn Castle 1½m E on A85. Dates from the middle 15th-C, with addition of the 16th- and 17th-C, in a beautiful mountain setting at the north-east extremity of Loch Awe. Not open to the public but can be viewed from the outside. Free. (AM)

LOCHCARRON Highland *Ross and Cromarty*
Map 42 NG83
Strome Castle 3m SE. A fragmentary ruin of the Macdonalds of Glengarry, blown up by Kenneth Mackenzie of Kintail in 1602. There are wide views across the Inner Sound to Scalpay, Raasay and the Coolins of Skye. Accessible at all reasonable times. (NTS)

LOCHMABEN Dumfries and Galloway *Dumfriesshire* Map 36 NY08
Rammerscales 3m S off B7020. Contains a fine circular staircase, elegant public rooms, and a long library at the top of the house. There are Jacobite relics and links with Flora Macdonald. Also a small collection of works by modern artists. Picnic areas in grounds which have fine views over Annandale. Open 29 Jun – 2 Sep, every Tue, Wed & Thu & alternate Sun from 4 Jul (otherwise by appointment) 2 – 5. 70p (ch 14 30p). ⚠
(☎ 361)

LOCHTY Fife *Fife* Map 41 NO50
Lochty Private Railway Steam trains run on Sun from Lochty to Knightsward, hauled by the restored War Department Tank Locomotive No. 16. Train includes ex LNER Observation Coach, part of pre-war 'Coronation Express'. There are regular services Jun – Sep, Sun from 2 – 5. Return fare 60p (ch 14 40p). ⚠
(☎ Kirkcaldy 4587)

MARYPARK Grampian *Banffshire*
Map 44 NJ13
Glenfarclas Distillery 1m W. One of the finest Highland Malt whiskies is produced here. There is an exhibition, museum, craft shop and visitor centre. Museum and exhibition now in French, German and Swedish. Open all year (ex 25 Dec, 1 & 2 Jan) Mon – Fri 9 – 4.30. Free. ⚠

(☎ Ballindalloch 257)

MAUCHLINE Strathclyde *Ayrshire*
Map 34 NS42
National Burns Memorial and Cottage Homes The memorial tower of 1896 stands north of the town on the Kilmarnock road and has a Burns museum containing many relics of the poet. Open most of the year. 9 – 6. 15p (ch 10p). ⚡ ⚠ (☎ 50213)

MAYBOLE Strathclyde *Ayrshire*
Map 33 NS20
Crossraguel Abbey 2m SW. A cluniac monastery founded by Duncan, Earl of Carrick in 1244. The extensive remains are of high architectural distinction and consist of the church, claustral buildings, outer court with an imposing castellated gatehouse and abbot's house. Open, see page 182 (but closed Wed afternoon & Fri). *25p (ch 10p). ⚠ (AM)

MELROSE Borders *Roxburghshire*
Map 35 NT53
Abbotsford House 2m W off A6091. 19th-C mansion on the River Tweed. Built by Sir Walter Scott, and the place of his death. Contains his library and a collection of historical relics. Open 23 Mar – Oct, Mon – Sat 10 – 5 Sun 2 – 5. 80p (ch 16 60p). Party 70p (ch 35p). (subject to alteration). ⚠ (☎ Galashiels 2043)
Melrose Abbey Probably the most famous ruin in Scotland, owing much of its modern fame to the glamour given to it by Sir Walter Scott. This was a beautiful Cistercian abbey, repeatedly wrecked during the wars of Scottish independence and notably by Richard II in 1385. Most of the ruins belong to the 15th-C reconstruction. The heart of Robert the Bruce is buried somewhere within the church. Open see page 182. *50p (ch 25p). (AM)
Also **Abbey Museum** housed in 15th- to 16th-C former Commendator's House, containing carved stones, etc. and situated in the abbey grounds. Details as above. (AM)
Priorwood Garden Special garden with flowers for drying. Visitor centre and shop, picnic area adjacent to Melrose Abbey. Open Apr & end Oct – 24 Dec, Mon – Fri 10 – 1, 2 – 5.30, Sat 10 – 5.30. May – Oct, Mon – Sat 10 – 6, Sun 2 – 5. Donations. (☎ 2555) (NTS)

MENSTRIE Central *Clackmannanshire*
Map 40 NS89
Menstrie Castle 16th-C fortress now restored partly as modern flats. It was the birthplace in 1657 of Sir William Alexander, the founder of Nova Scotia. The Nova Scotia Commemoration Rooms devised and furnished by the NTS are shown May – Sep, Wed, Sat & Sun 2.30 – 5. Free. (NTS and Clackmannan District Council)

METHLICK Grampian *Aberdeenshire*
Map 45 NJ83
Haddo House 4m N of Pitmedden off B999. Designed by William Adam in 1731 for the Second Earl of Aberdeen. Much of the interior is 'Adam Revival' dating to about 1880. Nava country park run by Grampian Regional Council. House open May – Sep, daily 2 – 6 (last admission 5.15), closed 15/16 May. Garden and park open all year 9.30 – sunset. Visitors centre & shop

May – Sep 11 – 6. House £1.10 (ch 55p), gardens & grounds by donation. Party 85p (schools 40p). ⚠ (☎ Tarves 440) (NTS)

MEY Highland *Caithness* Map 47 ND27
Castle of Mey Gardens Dates from 1606 and is now a home of Her Majesty Queen Elizabeth, the Queen Mother. Fine views across the Pentland Firth towards the Orkneys. Gardens only shown. Opening dates under review. * 40p (ch 12 & pen 20p). ⚡ ⚠ (☎ Barrock 227)

MILLPORT Strathclyde *Bute* Map 33 NS15
Museum of the Cumbraes Garrison House. The museum tells the story of life on and around the Cumbraes and features many old photographs and objects. Also photographs of some of the steamers which achieved fame on the Millport run. Open during summer months Tue – Sat 10 – 4.30 or at other times by appointment. Free. P. (☎ 741)

MILNATHORT Tayside *Kinross-shire*
Map 40 NO10
Burleigh Castle A 16th-C tower house, with a courtyard enclosure and roofed angle tower, dating from 1582. Open, see page 182. On application to key keeper. Free. (AM)

MINARD Strathclyde *Argyll* Map 39 NR99
Crarae Gardens Woodland garden, with rhododendrons, eucalyptus, rare trees, and shrubs, in a Highland glen. Picnic area. Shop. Open Mar – Oct, daily from 9 – 6. *50p (ch 16 free) by collecting box. ⚠ (☎ Furnace 286 or 218)

MOFFAT Dumfries and Galloway *Dumfriesshire* Map 35 NT00
Ladyknowe Mill Small weaving unit, skirtmaking department where garments can be seen in process. Showroom for sale of woollens, tweeds and tartans. Scottish gifts and souvenirs. Shop. Open all year, mid Mar – Oct daily 9 – 5, Nov – mid Mar Mon – Fri 9 – 5. Free. ⚡ (licensed) ⚠ &B (☎ 20134)

MONIAIVE Dumfries and Galloway *Dumfriesshire* Map 11 NX79
Maxwelton House Stronghold of Earls of Glencairn until 1611, and later birthplace of Annie Laurie. Fascinating house, recently restored, covering 500 years of architectural whims. Own chapel, and museum of ancient domestic appliances. Shop. Open May – Sep Wed & Thu afternoon 2 – 5, also 4th Sun in month. £1 (ch 12 20p). No dogs. ⚠ (☎ 385). (Maxwelton House Trust)

MOUSA ISLAND Shetland Map 48 HU42
Mousa Broch Best preserved Pictish drystone tower in Scotland. Rises to a height of 40ft and is exceptionally complete. Reached by boat from Leebotton, on Mousa Sound. Open, see page 182. Apply keeper. Free. (AM)

MUCHALLS Grampian *Kincardineshire*
Map 45 NO89
Muchalls Castle 17th-C castle, with fine fireplaces and plaster ceilings. Shop. Open May – Sep, Tue & Sun 3 – 5. Admission 30p (ch 10p). No dogs. ⚠ (☎ Newtonhill 30217).

Places of Interest

MULL, ISLE OF Strathclyde *Argyll* Map 38
See Craignure, Dervaig

MUSSELBURGH Lothian *Midlothian*
Map 35 NT37
Pinkie House A fine Jacobean building of 1613 and later, incorporating a tower of 1390. Fine painted ceiling in the long gallery. The house now forms part of the well-known Loretto School. Open mid Apr – mid Jul & mid Sep – mid Dec every Tue 2 – 5. Party. ▲ (☎ 031-665 2059)

MUTHILL Tayside *Perthshire* Map 40 NN81
Drummond Castle Gardens 1m N. Beautiful formal gardens. Open (gardens only) Apr – Sep, Wed & Sun 2 – 6. 60p (ch & pen 25p). ▲ ♿ (☎ 257)

NEW ABBEY Dumfries and Galloway *Kirkcudbrightshire* Map 30 NX96
Sweetheart Abbey One of the most beautiful monastic ruins in Scotland, built for the Lady Devorgilla of Galloway, in memory of her husband John Balliol, in 1273. In 1289 the Lady was buried in front of the high altar with the 'sweet heart' of her husband resting on her bosom. Open, see page 182. *25p (ch 10p). ▲ (AM)

NEWTONMORE Highland *Inverness-shire*
Map 44 NN79
Clan Macpherson House and Museum Relics and memorials of the Clan Chiefs and other Macpherson families. Prince Charles Edward Stuart relics, including letters to the Clan Chief (1745) and a letter to the Prince from his father (The Old Pretender). Royal Warrants, Green Banner of the Clan, swords, pictures, decorations and medals. James Macphersons fiddle and many other interesting historical exhibits. Clan Macpherson 36th Annual Rally 6 – 7 Aug. Open May – Sep Mon – Sat 10 – 12 & 2 – 6. Free (donation). ▲ ♿ (☎ 332)

NORTH BERWICK Lothian *East Lothian*
Map 35 NT58
North Berwick Museum Small museum in former Burgh school with sections on local and natural history, archaeology and domestic life. Library in the same building. Open Etr – Sep; Mon – Sat 10 – 1, 2 – 5; Sun 2 – 5. Free. ▲ (☎ 3470)
Tantallon Castle 2m E on A198. A famous 14th-C stronghold of the Douglases facing towards the lonely Bass Rock from the rocky Firth of Forth shore. Nearby earthworks of 16th- and 17th-C. Open, see page 182. Prices under review. (AM)

OBAN Strathclyde *Argyll* Map 39 NM83
Dunstaffnage Castle 3m N on Peninsular. A ruined four-sided 13th-C Campbell stronghold, showing a gatehouse, two round towers, and walls 10ft thick. Once the prison of Flora MacDonald. Open, see page 182 (but closed Thu afternoon & Fri). *30p (ch 15p). ▲ (AM)
Macdonald's Mill ½m S of centre of Oban, on A816. Exhibition of the Story of Spinning and Weaving, and demonstrations of this ancient Scottish industry. Also showroom containing modern products. Open Mar – Oct Mon – Fri 9 – 7.30, Sat 9 – 5; demonstrations Mon – Fri only. Free. ♎ (licensed) ▲ ♿B (☎ 63081)

OLD DAILLY Strathclyde *Ayrshire*
Map 33 NX29
Bargany Gardens 4m NE on B734 from Girvan. Woodland walks; snowdrops, bluebells and daffodils. Fine display of azaleas and rhododendrons round lily pond in May and Jun. Autumn colours. Many ornamental trees. Plants for sale. Picnic area. Gardens open Feb – Oct daily 10 – 7 (4 in winter). Contribution box. ▲ (buses by arrangement). ♿ (☎ 227)

OLD DEER Grampian *Aberdeenshire*
Map 45 NJ94
Deer Abbey The remains of the Cistercian Abbey, founded in 1219, include the southern claustral range, the Abbot's House and the infirmary. The famous Book of Deer, compiled in the former Celtic monastery on a different site, is now in the University Library at Cambridge. The ruins are accessible Apr – Sep, weekdays 9.30 – 7, Sun 2 – 7. *30p (ch 15p). ▲ (AM)

OLDMELDRUM Grampian *Aberdeenshire*
Map 45 NJ82
Glengarioch Distillery Distillery Rd. Distillation of Scotch Whisky and horticultural unit using waste heat from the distillery. Shop. Open all year ex Jul & Aug. Telephone for times. Free. ▲ (☎ 2706)

ORKNEY Map 48
See Dounby, Finstown, Kirkwall, Stromness, Westray

PAISLEY Strathclyde *Renfrewshire*
Map 37 NS46
Paisley Museum and Art Galleries High St. Contains collections illustrating local industrial and natural history of Paisley and district. World-famous collection of Paisley shawls. Art collection with emphasis on 19th-C Scottish artists. Shop. Open all year (ex Sun & PH) Mon – Sat 10 – 5. Free. ▲ (☎ 041-889 3151)

PALNACKIE Dumfries and Galloway *Kirkcudbrightshire* Map 30 NX85
Orchardton Tower A rare example of a circular late 15th-C tower, built originally by John Cairns. Open, see page 182, on application to the Custodian. Free. (AM)

PATHHEAD Lothian *Midlothian*
Map 35 NT36
Prestonhall A late 18th-C mansion designed by Robert Mitchell. Set in parkland with beautiful old trees. Open all year by appointment only. ▲
(☎ Ford [Midlothian] 320309)

PEEBLES Borders *Peeblesshire* Map 35 NT23
Kailzie 2½m SE on B7062. Extensive grounds with fine old trees, Burnside walk with bulbs, rhododendrons and azaleas. Walled garden with herbaceous and shrub rose borders. Pheasantry. Waterfowl pond, Art gallery. Shop. Open Etr – Oct daily 10 – 5.30. 50p (ch 30p). ♎ (licensed) ▲ ♿ (☎ 20007)
Neidpath Castle On the river Tweed. The earliest known owners of the lands of Neidpath were the Frasers. Construction of the Castle apparently began during the 14th-C. It was purchased by the first Duke of Queensberry in 1686 and has passed through several heirs to the present Lord Wemyss' Trust. Shop. Open 8 Apr – 10 Oct, Mon – Sat 10 – 1 and 2 – 6, Sun 1 – 6 (last

visitor 5.30) subject to availability of staff. 35p (ch 5 – 14 15p, pen 20p). Dogs on leads only. ▲ (☎ 20333)

PENCAITLAND Lothian *East Lothian*
Map 35 NT46
Winton House Dates from 1620, with 19th-C additions, a fine example of Scottish Renaissance architecture, with beautiful plaster ceilings, pictures, furnishings, and unique carved stone chimneys. Associations with King Charles I and Sir Walter Scott. Terraced garden. Open to parties by prior written or telephone appointment from Sir David Ogilvy Bt. (☎ 340222). £1. ▲

PERTH Tayside *Perthshire* Map 40 NO12
Branklyn Garden on Dundee Rd, A85. Has been described as the finest garden of its size in all Britain. Little more than two acres, it is noted for its collection of rhododendrons, shrubs and alpine plants. Open Mar – Oct, daily 10 – sunset or by arrangement. 60p (ch 30p). (☎ 25535) (NTS)
The Black Watch Regimental Museum Balhousie Castle, Hay St. Treasures of the 42nd/73rd Highland Regiment from 1725 – 1980 including painting, silver, colours and uniforms. Open May – Oct Mon – Fri 10 – 12 & 2 – 4.30 (Nov – Apr 3.30). Free/donations. ▲ (☎ 26287 ext 3)
Elcho Castle 5m SE on S bank of River Tay. A well-preserved 16th-C stronghold, with wrought-iron window grilles. Open from Apr – Sep, weekends 9.30 – 7, Sun 2 – 7; from Oct – Mar. Weekdays 9.30 – 4, Sun 2 – 4. Prices under review. ▲ (AM)
Fair Maid's House North Port. Situated near the historic North Inch where the battle of the Clans was fought in 1396. In the 14th-C it became the home of Simon Glover, a glovemaker, whose daughter Catherine was the heroine of Sir Walter Scott's *Fair Maid of Perth*. The house was a guildhall for over 150 years. It was renovated in the 19th-C and is now a centre for Scottish Crafts. A recently uncovered wall is said to be the oldest visible wall in Perth. Open all year Mon – Sat 10 – 5. P. ♿ (☎ 25976)
Huntingtower Formerly known as Ruthven Castle. A castellated 15th- and 16th-C structure, with a painted ceiling. Famous as the scene of the so-called 'Raid of Ruthven' in 1582. Open, see page 182. *25p (ch 10p). (AM)
Perth Museum and Art Gallery George St. Purpose-built in 1935 to house collections of fine and applied art, social & local history, natural history, archaeology etc. Special events monthly. Open all year, Mon – Sat 10 – 1 & 2 – 5. Free. ▲ ♿ (☎ 32488)

PETERCULTER Grampian *Aberdeenshire*
Map 45 NJ80
Drum Castle 3m W. The oldest part, the great square tower dates from the late 13th-C. A charming mansion was added in 1619 enclosing a quadrangle. In 1323 King Robert the Bruce gave a charter of the Royal Forest of Drum to William de Irwin. This family connection remained unbroken until the death in 1975 of Mr H Q Forbes Irvine, who bequeathed the castle and over 400 acres of land to the Trust. Open May – Sep daily 2 – 6; (last admission 5.15). 90p (ch 45p). Grounds open all year 9.30 – sunset (by donation). ▲

(☎ Drumoak 204) (NTS)

PETERHEAD Grampian *Aberdeenshire*
Map 45 NK14
Arbuthnot Museum and Art Gallery A Museum specialising in local exhibits, particularly those relating to the fishing industry; includes also Arctic and whaling specimens. British coin collection. Shop. Open Mon – Fri 10 – 12 & 2 – 5, Sat 2 – 5. Free. P. (☎ 77778)

PITCAPLE Grampian *Aberdeenshire*
Map 45 NJ72
Pitcaple Castle Built in the 15th-C, with additions in 1830. Still lived in as a family home. Visitors welcome Apr – Sep. 70p (ch 15 35p). Conducted tour of 19th-C portion 30p (ch 15 15p). ▲ ♿ (☎ 204)

PITLOCHRY Tayside *Perthshire*
Map 40 NN95
Faskally Wayside Centre 2m NW. Incorporates woodland/lochside parking, picnic facilities, children's play area and nature trail. Open May – Sep daily 8 – 7.50. ▲ (☎ Killiecrankie 223)
Pitlochry Power Station Dam and Fish Pass There is a permanent definitive exhibition of hydro-electricity, with audio-visual presentation. The Power Station is not open, but there is a viewing gallery in the exhibition area. Fish Pass observation chamber open during daylight hours. Shop. Exhibition open Etr – Oct daily 10 – 6 (8.30 Jul & Aug, ex Mon). 30p (ch 10p, free if accompanied). ⚲ ▲ (limited) (☎ 031-2251361)

PITMEDDEN Grampian *Aberdeenshire*
Map 45 NJ82
Pitmedden Garden A fine late 17th-C garden, now re-created. Sundials, pavilions, and fountains. Elaborate floral designs. Also Museum of Farming Life. Garden and grounds open all year, daily 9.30 – dusk. Museum and exhibition open May – Sep daily 11 – 6. 60p (30p). ♿ (☎ Udny 445) (NTS)
Tolquhon Castle 2m NE off B999. A late 16th-C quadrangular mansion, now roofless, and enclosing an early 15th-C tower. Fine gatehouse and courtyard. Open, see page 182. *30p (ch 15p). ▲ (AM)

POLMONT Central *Stirlingshire*
Map 34 NS97
Westquarter Dovecot This notable example of a Scottish dovecote is dated 1647 and carries the arms of Sir William Livingstone. May be viewed from the outside. (AM)

POOLEWE Highland *Ross and Cromarty*
Map 42 NG88
Inverewe Garden Remarkable gardens, full of interest and beauty from Mar to Oct (at their best May to early Jun), and containing rare and sub-tropical plants. Magnificent mountain background. Loch Maree lies to south. Open daily (incl Sun), all the year, 9 – 9 (or ½hr before dusk if earlier). Visitor centre. Apr – 9 May, 13 Sep – 15 Oct. Mon – Sat 10 – 5, Sun 12 – 5. May 10 – 12 Sep. Mon – Sat 10 – 6.30, Sun 12 – 6.30. £1.10 (ch 55p), adult parties 70p per person. ⚲ (open Apr - mid Oct). ▲ 10p. ♿ (☎ 229) (NTS)

PORT GLASGOW Strathclyde *Renfrewshire*
Map 33 NS37

Places of Interest

Port Logan – Ruthwell

Newark Castle Dates from the 15th- and 17th-C, preserving a courtyard and hall; the hall carries an inscription of 1597. Fine turrets and remains of painted ceilings: Once a home of the Maxwells. Open, see page 182. *25p (ch 10p). ▲ (AM)

PORT LOGAN Dumfries and Galloway *Wigtownshire* Map 30 NX04
Logan Botanic Garden An annexe of the Royal Botanic Garden in Edinburgh, containing a wide range of plants from the warm temperate regions of the world. Open Apr – Sep, daily 10 – 5. ▲ Car and passengers 30p. No animals. Prices under review. ⚏ ▲ ৬ (☎ Stranraer 86231)

PORT OF MENTEITH Central *Perthshire* Map 40 NN50
Inchmahome Priory The 13th-C ruins of the church and cloisters of an Augustinian house founded by Walter Comyn in 1238. Famous as the retreat of the infant Mary, Queen of Scots, in 1543. The ruins are situated on an island in the Lake of Menteith. Open, see page 182. Ferry subject to cancellation in adverse weather conditions. Advisable to check. *Ferry 50p (ch 25p). Prices under review. (☎ Stirling 62421) ▲ At ferry. (AM)

QUEENSFERRY (South) Lothian *West Lothian* Map 35 NT17
Dalmeny House. Magnificently situated on the shores of the Firth of Forth, 7m W of Edinburgh. Home of the 7th Earl of Rosebery this was the first Tudor Gothic Revival House in Scotland. Collection includes furniture and other items belonging to Napoleon. Also superb 18th-C French furniture, portraits, tapestries and porcelain from Mentmore. Open Etr Sun & Mon, 2 May – Sep, Sun – Thu 2 – 5.30 (last admission 5). *£1.20 (ch 16 & pen 90p). ⚏ ▲ ৬ (☎ 031-331 1888)

Hopetoun House 2m W on unclass road. Residence of the Marquess of Linlithgow MC. Scotland's greatest Adam Mansion. Magnificent reception rooms, pictures, furnishings and spacious grounds: Red and fallow deer and St Kilda sheep. Nature trail. Views of Forth Bridges. Shop. Open Etr & May – Sep, daily 11 – 5.30. £1.50 (ch 70p, students & pen £1.05). ⚏ ▲ ৬B (☎ 031-331 2451)

William Sanderson and Son 27 The Loan. Blending and bottling plant where VAT 69, VAT 69 Reserve, The Antiquary and Glenesk 12 year old Single Malt Highland Scotch Whisky are prepared for United Kingdom and all export markets. Open all year (ex for Edinburgh statutory holidays, first two weeks in Jul & Xmas week), for conducted tours. Mon – Fri at 10 & 2. No tour Fri afternoons. Visits by prior appointment only. Free. ▲ (limited). (☎ 031-331 1500)

QUEEN'S VIEW Tayside *Perthshire* Map 40 NN85
Tummel Forest Centre Exhibits show changes in Tummel Valley since Queen Victoria's visit in 1866. Included are a diorama, a model of a Highland Clachan in the forest, which has recently been excavated and partly restored. Slides and sound show. Information desk. Forest walks. Picnic areas. Regular access. Open Etr – Sep 9 – 6. Free. ▲ ৬ (☎ Killiecrankie 223)

REAY Highland *Caithness* Map 47 NC98
U.K.A.E.A. Dounreay Exhibition 2m NE. Scale models, charts and display panels, relating to fast reactors and nuclear energy; generally housed in a former airfield control tower overlooking the plant, conspicuous for its 135ft sphere and the prototype fast reactor. Tickets from Thurso Tourist Information Centre or the Exhibition. Shop. Open May – Sep, daily 9 – 4. Free. ▲ (☎ Thurso 2121 ext 656)

RHYNIE Grampian *Aberdeenshire* Map 45 NJ42
Leith Hall and Garden 3½m NE on B9002 at Kennethmont. A house built round a courtyard, with Jacobite relics and a fine rock garden. The earliest part dates from 1650. House open May – Sep, Mon – Sat 11 – 6, Sun 2 – 6 (last visitors 5.15). Gardens & grounds open all year 9.30 – sunset. House 80p (ch 40p), parties 65p, school parties 30p per person. Gardens & grounds by donation. (☎ Kennethmont 216) (NTS)

ROTHES Grampian *Moray* Map 44 NJ24
Glen Grant Distillery Established 1840. The whisky produced here is regarded as one of the best, and is used in many first-class blends as well as being sold as a single Glen Grant Malt in bottle. Traditional malt whisky methods of distillation are used together with the most modern equipment. Reception, Shop & Hospitality Bar. Open Etr – mid Oct 10 – 4. Free. ▲ ৬B (☎ 494)

ROTHESAY Isle of Bute, Strathclyde *Bute* Map 33 NS06
Rothesay Castle 13th-C moated castle, with lofty curtain walls, defended by drum towers enclosing a circular courtyard. Open, see page 182, Sun 2 – 4. *30p (ch 15p). (AM)
Bute Museum Contents are all from the county of Bute. Natural history room contains exhibits of birds, mammals and items from the seashore. History room has varied collections of recent bygones including models of Clyde steamers. There is a collection of early Christian crosses. Prehistoric section contains flints and pots from two recently excavated neolithic burial cairns. Recently mounted comprehensive geological survey of the Island of Bute. Details of nature trails on the island are on sale. Open all year, Apr – Sep 10.30 – 12.30, 2.30 – 4.30, Oct – Mar 2.30 – 4.30. Sun Jun – Sep 2.30 – 4.30. 20p (ch & pen 10p). P. (street). ৬ (☎ 2248)

RUTHWELL Dumfries and Galloway *Dumfriesshire* Map 31 NY16
Ruthwell Cross Off B724. One of Europe's most famous carved crosses resting in the Parish Church in an apse built specially for it. The date is probably late 7th-C and the 18ft-high cross is richly carved with Runic characters showing the earliest form of English in Northumbrian dialect. Free. Key of church obtainable from the Key Keeper, Kirkyett Cottage, Ruthwell. (AM)
Henry Duncan Museum First Savings Bank founded here in 1810. Interior set in period furnishings around a peat fire and contains many early savings bank documents, four lock security kist, collection of home savings bank from Great Britain and abroad, International Money Corner etc. Personal

pencil drawings. Open daily. Free. ▲ ㊓
(☎ Clarencefield 640)

ST ANDREWS Fife *Fife* Map 41 NO51
Castle Ruined 13th-C stronghold where Cardinal Beaton was murdered in 1546. Captured by the French fleet in the following year. Open, see page 182. *40p (ch 20p). (AM)

SALTCOATS Strathclyde *Ayrshire* Map 33 NS24
North Ayrshire Museum A museum located in the ancient former Parish Church, with interesting old churchyard gravestones. Exhibits portray local historical items, and early 19th-C exhibits. Picnic area. Open all year Mon–Sat 10–4. School hols 10–4.30. ▲ ㊓B (☎ 64174)

SCALLOWAY Shetland Map 48 HU33
Scalloway Castle Erected by Patrick Stewart, Earl of Orkney, c1600, and designed on the 'two-stepped' plan. Open, see page 182, on application to the Custodian. Free. (AM)

SCONE Tayside *Perthshire* Map 40 NO02
Scone Palace Home of Earl of Mansfield in town famous in Scottish history as the 'Royal City of Scone'. A seat of government in Pictish times, the home of the Stone of Destiny until 1296 when Edward I removed it to Westminster Abbey; Scottish kings were crowned at Scone until 1651. A religious centre for more than 1,000 years. Present palace, largely rebuilt in 1803, incorporates part of the earlier 1580 palace. Fine collection of French furniture, china, 16th-C needlework, including bed hangings worked by Mary, Queen of Scots, ivories and *objets d'art*. The Pinetum has one of the finest collections of rare conifers in the country, and the woodland garden displays rhododendrons and azaleas. Open Etr Sat–11 Oct, Mon–Sat 10–6, Sun 2–6. (Jul & Aug 11–6) (last admission 5.15). No admission after 5.30pm. House & grounds £1.50 (ch £1.20). Grounds £1 (ch 70p). Parties 20 + . ▲ (☎ 52308)

SELKIRK Borders *Selkirkshire* Map 35 NT42
Bowhill 2½m off A708. For many generations the Border home of the Scots of Buccleuch. The house contains an outstanding collection of pictures, porcelain and furniture, Monmouth's saddlery and relics, Sir Walter Scott's proofs and portraits, Queen Victoria relics. Adventure woodland play area and pony trekking. Picnic area. Open Etr weekend & most days May to late Sep. Admission prices not yet decided. ⚲ (afternoon teas). P. ㊓ (☎ 20732)
Selkirk Museum Ettrick Terrace. Occupies first floor of former Town Jail, built in 1803, and includes items of local history. Also mementoes of local celebrities including Sir Walter Scott, Mungo Park and Andrew Lang. Open mid May–mid Sep, Mon, Wed & Fri 2–4.45. Mon evenings 6.30–8.00. Free. P. 30yds. (☎ 20096)

SHETLAND Map 48
See **Mousa Island, Scalloway, Sumburgh**

SKYE, ISLE OF Highland *Inverness-shire* Map 48
See **Armadale, Colbost, Dunvegan, Glendale, Kilmuir**

STIRLING Central *Stirlingshire* Map 40 NS79
Cambuskenneth Abbey Founded in 1147 by David I, this abbey was the scene of Bruce's important parliament of 1326. It is also the burial place of James III and his wife. Open see page 182, Apr–Sep only. *25p (ch 10p). (AM)
Stirling Castle Upper Castle Hill. An historic 13th-C and earlier structure. The Renaissance additions of the 15th-C are notable. Queen Victoria's lookout and the Ladies' Rock are viewpoints. Open Jan–Apr daily 9.30–5.05, Sun 12.30–4.20, May–Oct daily 9.30–7, Sun 11–7, Nov–Dec times under review. *Jan–Apr 25p (ch 10p), May–Oct 50p (ch 25p), Nov–Dec 25p (ch 10p). ▲ (AM)
Landmark Scotland's second Landmark Centre, with exhibition and shop in restored old building overlooking River Forth near castle. Multi-screen presentation of the history of Stirling Castle. Open Mar–Oct 9–6. *Theatre and exhibition 70p (ch 35p). ⚲ ▲ ㊓ (☎ 62517)
Mar's Wark Broad St. A partly ruined Renaissance mansion, with a gatehouse enriched by sculptures. Built by the Regent Mar in 1570. Open at all times. Free. (AM)
The Museum of the Argyll and Sutherland Highlanders Situated in King James V Palace of Stirling Castle. Fine collection of regimental silver and plate, colours, pipe banners, paintings and uniform. Also medals, covering period from Waterloo to present day. Open Etr–Oct, Mon–Sat 10–6, Sun 12–6 (closes at 4 in Oct). Free. P. (☎ Stirling 2356)

STOBO Borders *Peeblesshire* Map 35 NT13
Dawyck Arboretum (Royal Botanic Garden, Edinburgh). On B712, 8m SW of Peebles. Impressive arboretum, noted for collection of trees, shrubs and bulbs. House not shown. No animals. Open Apr–Sep daily 10–5. 50p per car. Prices under review. ▲ (☎ 254)

STONEHAVEN Grampian *Kincardineshire* Map 41 NO88
Dunnottar Castle 1½m S off A92. On a headland facing North Sea, dates from late 14th- to 16th-C. The Scottish regalia kept here for safety in the 17th-C. Open all year (ex Sats in Winter) Mon–Sat 9–6, Sun 2–5. *50p (ch 15 20p). Prices under review. ▲ (☎ 62173)
Stonehaven Tolbooth Once a 16th-C storehouse of the Earls Marischal, later used as a prison. Restored and re-opened in 1963 by the Queen Mother; fishing and local history museum. Shop. Open from Jun–Sep, daily (ex Tue) 2–5 Sat 10–12. Free. ⚲ ▲ (limited) ㊓B (☎ Peterhead 77778)

STROMNESS Orkney Map 48 HY20
Stromness Museum Alfred St. Founded by the Orkney Natural History Society in 1837. Deals mainly with Orkney maritime and natural history, notably in bird and shell collections. There is also a New Stone Age collection. Special exhibition of Orkney interest each summer. Open 11–12.30 & 1.30–5 (from 10.30am in Jul & Aug). Closed Sun, Thu afternoon & local holidays also 3 weeks Feb–Mar. Prices under review. ▲ ㊓B (☎ 850025)
Orkney Arts Centre The Pier Arts Centre

Collection housed in warehouse building on its own stone pier. Also galleries for visiting exhibitions and children's work. Arts library and reading room in adjacent house. Open all year 10.30 – 12.30 & 1.30 – 5, Sun 2 – 5, closed Mon. Free. P. (50yds). &B (☎ 850209)

SUMBURGH Shetland Map 48 HU30
Jarlshof Prehistoric Site Remarkable Bronze Age, Iron Age, Viking, and Medieval settlements. The 17th-C Laird's House is the 'Jarlshof' of Scott's novel *The Pirate*. The remains are accessible, see page 182 (closed Tue & Wed afternoon). *40p (ch 20p). (AM)

TARBOLTON Strathclyde *Ayrshire* Map 34 NS42
Bachelors' Club A 17th-C house, taking its name from the society which Robert Burns and his friends founded there in 1780. Period furnishings. Contains a small museum. Open Apr – Sep daily 10 – 6, other times by appointment. 40p (ch 20p). (☎ 424) (NTS)

TARFSIDE Tayside *Angus* Map 41 NO57
The Retreat 1m E. Former shooting lodge, with museum of local country life and handicrafts. Shop. Open from Etr – 1 Jun, Sun only, 2 – 6; from Jun – Sep, daily 2 – 6. *40p (ch 12 20p). ⚲ (beautiful glen setting). ⚠ &B (☎ 236 & 254)

THORNHILL Dumfries and Galloway *Dumfriesshire* Map 34 NX89
Drumlanrig Castle 4m NW off A76 on west bank of River Nith. 17th-C castle in pink stone. Celebrated collection of paintings, silver and Bonnie Prince Charlie relics.

Woodland walks, picnic areas and adventure playground. Shop. Open Etr then Mon, Thu & Sat, Sun, in May & Jun & BH Mon 12.30 – 5. Daily Jul & Aug (ex Fri) 11 – 5, Sun 2 – 6. Last entry 45mins before closing. Party. *£1.20 (ch 70p) ⚲ ⚠ & (☎ 30248)

TOMINTOUL Grampian *Banffshire* Map 44 NJ11
Tomintoul Museum The Square. Reconstructed farm kitchen. Cobbler's and harness displays, local landscape and wildlife displays. Picnic area. Jun – Sep 10 – 6 (7 Jul & Aug). Free. ⚠ & (☎ Forres 73701)

TONGLAND Dumfries and Galloway *Kirkcudbrightshire* Map 30 NX65
Tongland Tour Tour of SSEB Galloway hydro-electricity scheme. It includes a visit to the dam and power station at Tongland. A fish ladder is an attraction to the tour. Open Jul – Sep. Mon – Sat 9 – 5 by appointment only. Free. & people wishing to make the tour are picked up by bus in Kirkcudbright, and later returned. (☎ Kirkcudbright 30114)

TORPHICHEN Lothian *West Lothian* Map 34 NS97
Torphichen Preceptory This was the principal seat of the knights of St John. The central tower and transcepts of their church still remain. The nave, now the parish church, was rebuilt in the 18th-C. Open, see page 182, ex Wed & alternate Fri when closed all day. *25p (ch 10p). (AM)

TORRIDON Highland *Ross and Cromarty* Map 42 NG85
Trust Visitor Centre Situated at junction of

The Scottish Museum of WOOLLEN TEXTILES
Walkerburn, Scotland
Tel. (089 687) 281/3

**Mill Shop : Coffee Shop
Coach and Car Park**

A wonderful day's outing to the beautiful Borders

A fascinating history of the woollen industry showing how it has evolved from a cottage industry. The old weaver's cottage with a spinning demonstration and the weaver's shed, early wool patterns and cloth patterns, the early tools used are not only wonderfully interesting but educational as well.

Adults 40p; OAP and children under 16, 20p; Family ticket £1; (special rates for parties of school children, students from technical colleges, universities, etc. If arranged in advance by telephone call or letter to the curator.)

Walkerburn is easily reached by car from a wide area as the map shows. For any place on or near the M6 motorway, or routes leading to the A1, A7 and A68 roads will find it an easy journey for a one-day outing. From Easter to October the museum will be open daily and special arrangements can be made for school parties all the year round.

A896 and Diabeg road amid some of Scotland's finest scenery. Audio-visual presentations on wild life and on to Deer Museum 25p (ch 10p), audio-visual display 25p (ch 10p). (☎ 221) (NTS)

TRANENT Lothian *East Lothian*
Map 35 NT47
Prestongrange Historical Site and Mining Museum Site with around 800 years of coal mining history, the centre piece of which is a Cornish beam pumping engine – the only one left in Scotland. Its five-storey building is scheduled as an industrial monument and contains plans and documents. The former power house is now an exhibition hall. Outside are two colliery shunting locomotives, one of which can be seen working on first Sun in month, and a 100-year-old steam navvy. Open Mon – Fri 9 – 4.30, Sat by arrangement, Sun all year round (volunteers at work). ⚐ &B Enquiries to *David Spence, Hon Curator, 24 Woodlands Grove, Edinburgh EH15 3PD* (☎ 031-661 2718) or *Mr G B Duncan, Director, Physical Planning, East Lothian District Council, Haddington.*

TURRIFF Grampian *Aberdeenshire*
Map 45 NJ75
Craigston Castle 4m NE off B9105. Early 17th-C, and little altered since its construction. Viewable by written permission from Bruce Urquhart, Turriff. (☎ King Edward 228)
Delgatie Castle 1m E off main Aberdeen-Banff Rd. The 12th- to 16th-C, with turnpike stair of 97 steps, armour, pictures and furnishings. Oldest archery meeting in Scotland dating back to 1584, held 1st Sat in Jul. Open by previous arrangement at any date or time. *50p. ⚐ 25p.

UDDINGSTON Strathclyde *Lanarkshire*
Map 37 NS66
Calderpark Zoo Birds, mammals, and reptiles housed in spacious new enclosures and buildings. Other attractions include ample picnic sites, souvenir shop, and children's shows. Open all year, daily 9 – 5 (or 7, depending on season). £1.20 (ch, pen & students 60p, ch 3 free). Party. ⚐ ⚐ (☎ 041-771 1185)

WALKERBURN Borders *Peeblesshire*
Map 35 NT33
Scottish Museum of Woollen Textiles
Tweedvale Mill. Museum contains a variety of objects connected with the Scottish woollen industry. Also demonstrations of hand spinning and hand weaving. Shop. Open Mon – Fri 10 – 5, Sun 2 – 6; Etr – Oct. 40p (ch 16 & pen 20p). ⚐ ⚐ & (☎ 281 and 283)

WANLOCKHEAD Dumfries and Galloway *Dumfriesshire* Map 34 NS81
Museum of Scottish Lead Mining On B797 at N end of Mennock Pass. Conserves, displays and interprets the physical and documentary history of lead mining in Scotland. Indoor museum and library. 1½-mile Visitor Walkway links a variety of mining and social structures. Shop. Open Etr – end Sep daily 11 – 4. *30p (ch 15p). Visitor lead mine 40p (ch 20p). ⚐ &B (☎ Leadhills 387)

WEEM Tayside *Perthshire* Map 40 NN85
Castle Menzies Fine example of 16th-century 'Z' plan fortified tower. Castle also houses a small museum. One of the twelve most important castles in the country. Shop. Open Apr – Sep 10.30 – 12.30, 2 – 5. 50p (ch & pen 10p). ⚐ (☎ 031-332 3607)

WHITHORN Dumfries and Galloway *Wigtownshire* Map 30 NX44
Whithorn Priory First Christian church in Scotland, founded by Fergus, Lord of Galloway in the 12th-C. The ruins are scanty, but the Norman doorway of the nave is notable. Group of early Christian monuments, include the Latinus stone dating from the 5th-C. Open, see page 182. *25p (ch 10p). (AM)

WICK Highland *Caithness* Map 47 ND34
Caithness Glass Inveralmond Industrial Estate. All aspects of glassblowing can be seen from the viewing gallery at this purpose built visitor centre. There is also a factory 'seconds' shop. Open all year, Mon – Sat 9 – 5, Sun 1 – 5. Free. ⚐ ⚐ & (☎ Perth 37373)
Castle of Old Wick A four-storeyed, ruined square tower, known also as Castle Oliphant, probably of 12th-C date. Accessible except when adjoining rifle range in use. Free. (AM)
Wick Heritage Centre 19 – 27 Bank Row. A complex of four houses, yards and outbuildings, in the 'Telford' planned area of the town, near the harbour. The museum illustrates history from Neolithic times, with emphasis on the fishing industry in the 19th- and 20th-C. Shop. Open Wed 2 – 5, 7 – 9, Sat 2 – 5. Opening times under review. 50p (ch 16 & pen 25p). ⚐ &B (☎ 4179)

DAY DRIVES

The following fourteen one-day tours have been hand-picked to cover the most beautiful and interesting areas that Scotland has to offer. Places of scenic interest are marked along each route

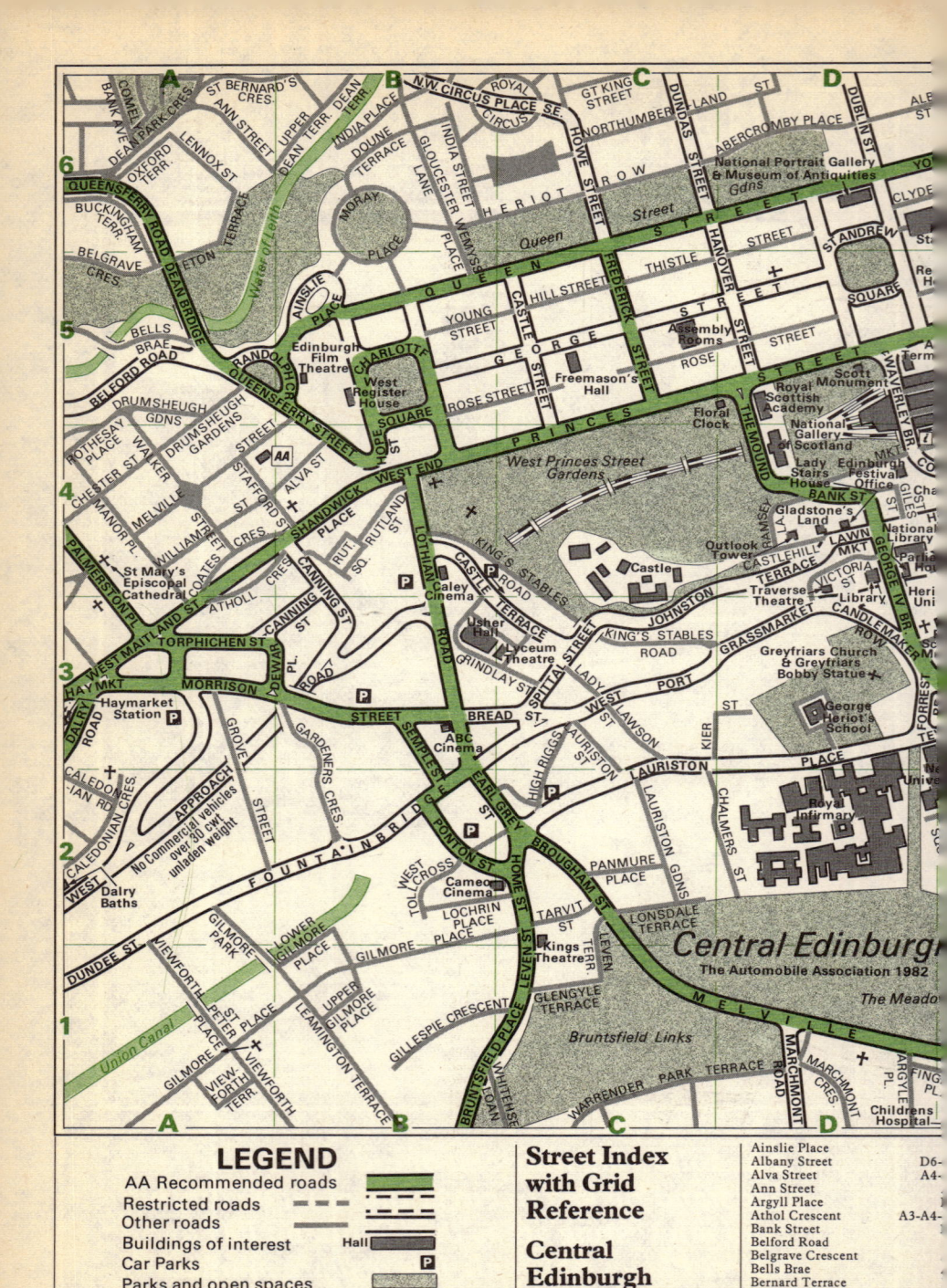

LEGEND
AA Recommended roads
Restricted roads
Other roads
Buildings of interest — Hall
Car Parks — P
Parks and open spaces
AA Service Centre — AA

Street Index with Grid Reference

Central Edinburgh
Street	Grid
Abercromby Place	D6
Adam Street	F3
Ainslie Place	
Albany Street	D6–
Alva Street	A4–
Ann Street	
Argyll Place	
Athol Crescent	A3-A4-
Bank Street	
Belford Road	
Belgrave Crescent	
Bells Brae	
Bernard Terrace	
Blackfriars Street	
Bread Street	B3–

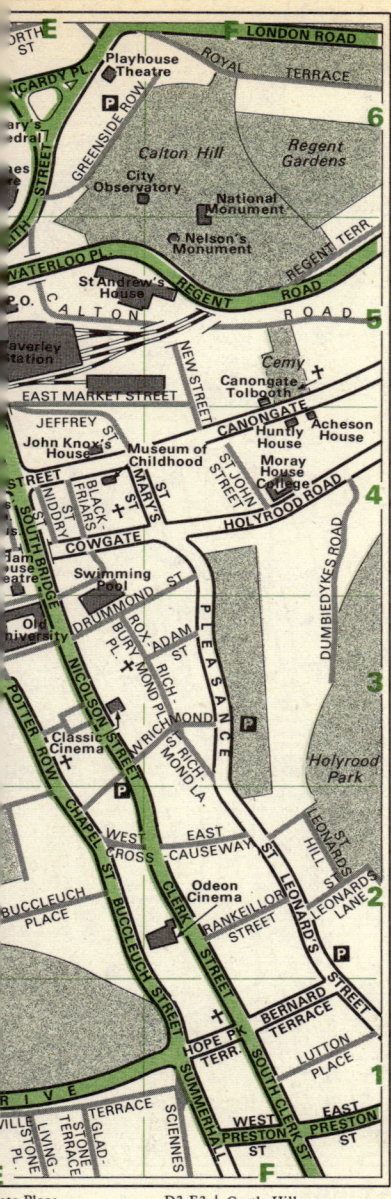

Street	Grid
Cowgate	D4-E4-F4
Dalry Road	A3
Dean Bridge	A5
Dean Park Crescent	A6
Dean Terrace	B6
Dewar Place	A3-B3
Doune Terrace	B6
Dune Terrace	B6
Drummond Street	E3-F3-F4
Drumsheugh Gardens	A4-A5
Dublin Street	D6
Dumbiedykes Road	F3-F4
Dundas Street	C6
Dundee Street	A1-A2
Earl Grey Street	B2-C2
East Cross Causeway	F2
East Market Street	E5-E4-F4-F5
East Preston Street	F1
Eton Terrace	A5-A6
Fingal Place	D1-E1
Forrest Road	D3
Fountain Bridge	A2-B2-B3-C3
Frederick Street	C5
Forth Street	E6
Gardeners Crescent	B2-B3
George IV Bridge	D3-D4
George Square	E2
George Street	B5-C5-D5
Gillespie Crescent	B1-C1
Gilmore Place	A1-B1-B2-C2
Gladstone Terrace	E1
Glengyle Terrace	C1
Gloucester Lane	B6
Grass Market	D3
Great King Street	C6
Greenside Row	E6-F6
Grindlay Street	B3-C3
Grove Street	A2-A3
Hanover Street	C6-D6-D5
Hay Market	A3
Heriot Row	B6-C6
High Riggs	C2-C3
High Street	D4-E4
Hill Street	C5
Holyrood Road	F4
Home Street	C2
Hope Park Terrace	F1
Hope Street	B4
Howe Street	C6
India Place	B6
India Street	B6
Jeffrey Street	E4
Johnstone Terrace	C3-C4-D4
Kier Street	C3-D3
King's Stables Road	B4-C4-C3
Lady Lawson Street	C3
Lauriston Gardens	C2
Lauriston Place	C2-C3-D3
Lauriston Street	C2-C3
Lawn Market	D4
Leamington Terrace	A1-B1
Leith Street	E5-E6
Lennox Street	A6
Leven Street	C1-C2
Leven Terrace	C1-C2
Livingstone Place	E1
Lochrin Place	B1-C1
London Road	F6
Lonsdale Terrace	C2
Lothian Road	B3-B4
Lower Gilmore Place	B1-B2
Lutton Place	F1
Manor Place	A4
Marchmont Crescent	D1
Marchmont Road	D1
Melville Drive	C2-C1-D1-E1-F1
Melville Street	A4-B4-B5
Melville Terrace	E1-F1
Moray Place	B5-B6
Morrison Street	A3-B3
New Street	F4-F5
Nicolson Street	E3-E2-F2
Niddry Street	E4
North Bridge	E4-E5
North West Circus Place	B6
Northumberland Street	C6-D6
Oxford Terrace	A6
Palmerston Place	A3-A4
Panmure Place	C2
Picardy Place	E6
Pleasance	F3-F4
Ponton Street	B2-C2
Potter Row	E2-E3
Princes Street	B4-C4-C5-D5-E5
Queen Street	B5-C5-C6-D6
Queensferry Road	A5-A6
Queensferry Street	A5-B5-B4
Ramsey Lane	D4
Randolph Crescent	A5-B5
Rankeillor Street	F2
Regent Road	E6-E5-F5
Regent Terrace	F5
Richmond Lane	F2-F3
Richmond Place	E3-F3
Rose Street	B5-C5-D5
Rothesay Place	A4-A5
Roxbury Place	E3
Royal Circus	B6-C6
Royal Terrace	E6-F6
Rutland Street	B4
St Andrews Square	D5-D6
St Bernard's Crescent	A6-B6
St Giles Street	D4
St John Street	F4
St Leonard's Hill	F2
St Leonard's Lane	F2
St Leonard's Street	F1-F2
Sciennes	F1
Semples Street	B2-B3
Shandwick Place	B4
South Bridge	E3-E4
South Clerk Street	F1
South East Circus Place	C6
Spittal Street	C3
Stafford Street	A4-B4
Summerhall	F1
Sylvan Place	E1
The Mound	D4-D5
Tarvit Street	C2
Teviot Place	D3-E3
Thistle Street	C5-D5-D6
Torphichen Street	A3
Upper Dean Terrace	B6
Upper Gilmore Place	B1
Victoria Street	D4
Viewforth	A1-B1
Viewforth Terrace	A1
Walker Street	A4-A5
Warrender Park Terrace	C1-D1
Waterloo Place	E5
Wemyss Place	B5-B6
West Approach Road	A2-A3-B3
West Cross-Causeway	E2
West End	B4
West Maitland Street	A3-A4
West Port	C3
West Preston Street	F1
West Richmond Street	E3-F3
West Tollcross	B2
Whitehouse Loan	B1-C1
William Street	A4
York Place	D6-E6
Young Street	B5-C5

The Automobile Association 1982

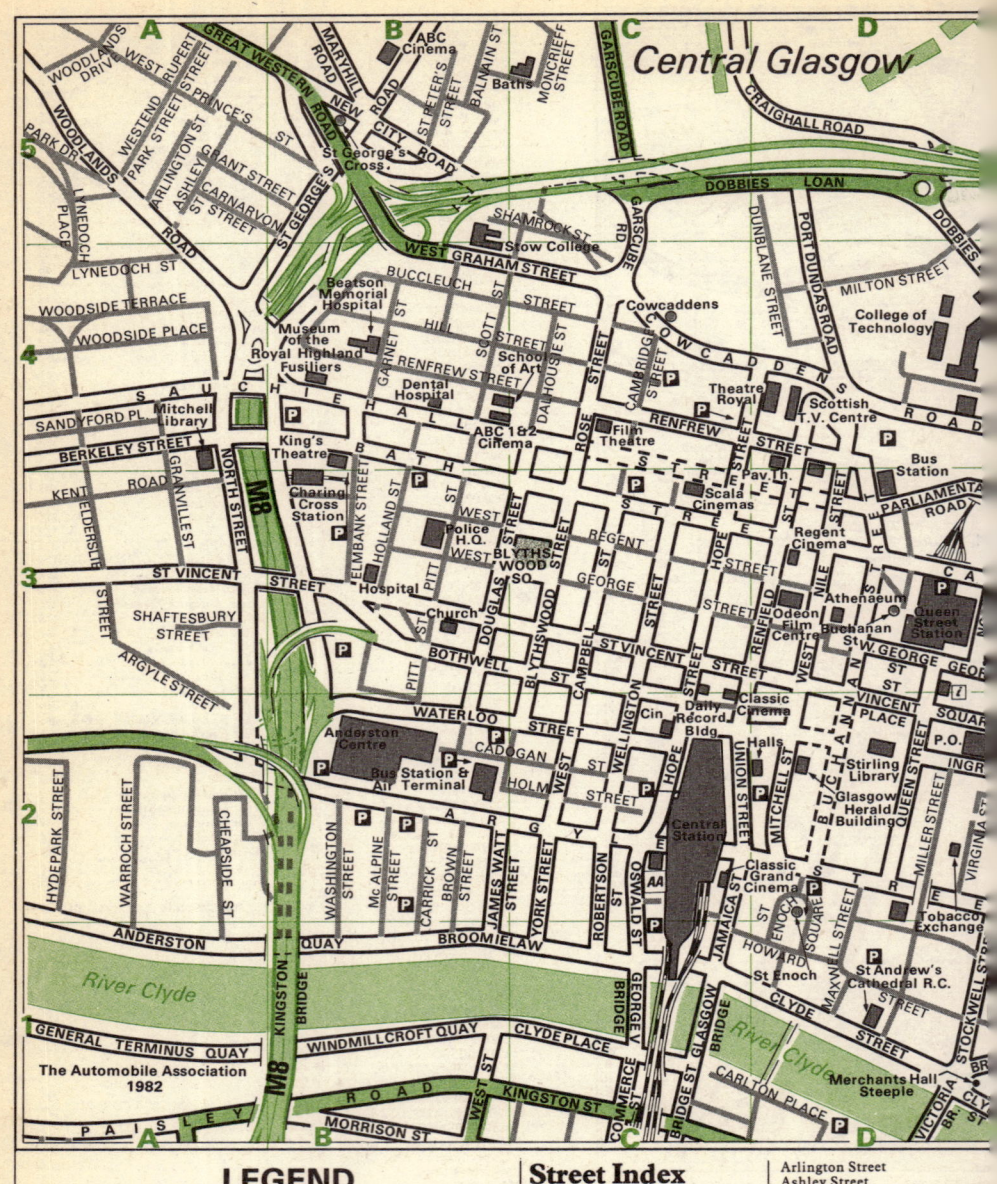

Central Glasgow

LEGEND

- AA Recommended roads
- Other roads
- Restricted roads
- Buildings of intrest
- Parks and open spaces
- Car Parks
- AA Service Centre

Street Index with grid reference

Central Glasgow

Street	Grid reference
Albion Street	E1-E2
Anderston Quay	A2-A1-B1
Argyle Street	A3-A2-B2-C2-D2-E2-E1
Arlington Street	
Ashley Street	
Baird Street	E4-F4-
Balnian Street	
Bath Street	B4-B3-C3-
Bell Street	E2-F2-
Berkeley Street	
Blythswood Square	B3-
Blythswood Street	C2-
Bothwell Street	B3-C3-
Bridgegate	D1-
Bridge Street	
Broomielaw	B1-
Brown Street	B1

The Automobile Association 1982

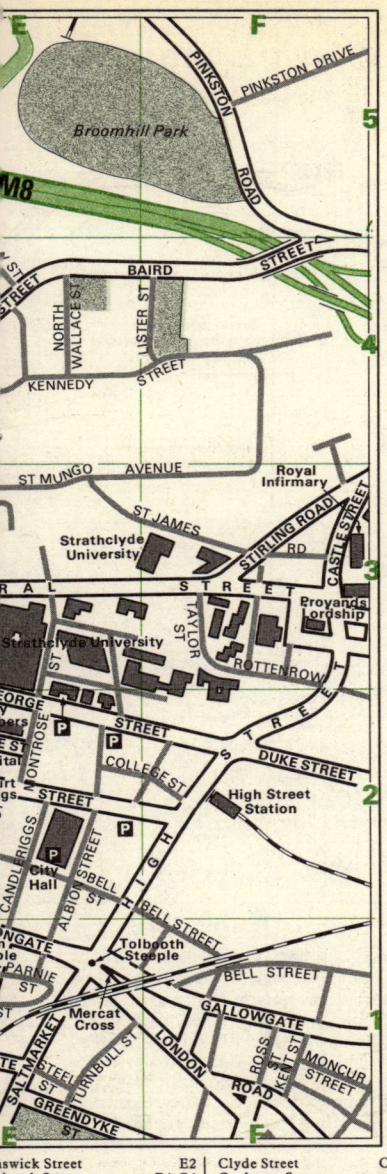

Street	Grid
Garscube Road	C4-C5
General Terminus Quay	A1
Garnet Street	B4
George V Bridge	C1
George Square	D2-D3-E3-E2
George Street	E3-E2-F2
Glasgow Bridge	C1
Glassford Street	D2-E2
Grant Street	A5-B5
Granville Street	A3-A4
Great Western Road	A5-B5
Greendyke Street	E1-F1
High Street	E1-E2-F2-F3
Hill Street	B4-C4
Holland Street	B3-B4
Holm Street	B2-C2
Hope Street	C2-C3-C4-D4
Howard Street	C1-D1
Hutcheson Street	E2
Hyde Park Street	A2
Ingram Street	D2-E2-F2
Irongate	E1-E2
Jamaica Street	C1-C2
James Watt Street	B1-B2-C2
John Street	E3
Kennedy Street	E4-F4
Kent Road	A3
Kent Street	F1
King Street	E1
Kingston Bridge	B1
Kingston Street	B1-C1
Kyle Street	E4
Lister Street	F4
London Road	E1-F1
Lyndoch Place	A4-A5
Lyndoch Street	A4
McAlpine Street	B1-B2
Maryhill Road	B5
Maxwell Street	D1-D2
Miller Street	D1-D2
Milton Street	D4
Mitchell Street	D2
Moncrieff Street	C5
Moncur Street	F1
Montrose Street	E2-E3
Morrison Street	B1
New City Road	B5
North Street	A3-A4
North Frederick Street	E3
North Hannover Street	D3-E3-E4
North Wallace Street	E4
Osborne Street	E1
Oswald Street	C1-C2
Paisley Road	A1-B1
Park Drive	A5
Parliamentary Road	D3-E3
Parnie Street	E1
Pinkston Drive	F5
Pinkston Road	F5
Pitt Street	B2-B3
Port Dundas Road	D4-D5
Queen Street	D2-D3
Renfield Street	D4-D3-C3-C2-D2
Renfrew Street	B4-C4-D4
Robertson Street	C1-C2
Rose Street	C3-C4
Ross Street	F1
Rottenrow	F3
Rupert Street	A5
St Enoch Square	D1-D2
St George's Road	A4-B4-B5
St James Road	E3-F3
St Mungo Avenue	E3-F3
St Peter's Street	B5
St Vincent Place	D2-D3
St Vincent Street	A3-B3-C3-D3-D2
Saltmarket	E1
Sandyford Place	A4
Sauchiehall Street	A4-B4-C4-C3-D3
Scott Street	B4-C4
Shaftesbury Street	A3
Shamrock Street	B5-C5-C4
Steel Street	E1
Stirling Road	F3
Stockwell Street	D1-E1-E2
Taylor Street	F3
Turnbull Street	E1
Union Street	C2-D2
Victoria Bridge	D1
Virginia Street	D2-E2
Warroch Street	A1-A2
Washington Street	B1-B2
Waterloo Street	B2-C2
Wellington Street	C2-C3
West Street	B1
West Campbell Street	C2-C3
West George Street	B3-C3-D3
West Graham Street	B5-B4-C4
West Nile Street	D2-B3-D4
West Prince's Street	A5-B5
West Regent Street	B3-C3-D3
Westend Park Street	A5
Windmill Croft Quay	B1
Woodlands Drive	A5
Woodlands Road	A4-A5
Woodside Place	A4
Woodside Terrace	A4
York Street	C1-C2

The Automobile Association 1982

Street	Grid
nswick Street	E2
cleuch Street	B4-C4
hannan Street	D2-D3-D4
ogan Street	B2-C2
gary Street	E4
dleriggs	E1-E2
bridge Street	C4
ton Place	C1-D1
narvon Street	A5-B5
rick Street	B1-B2
le Street	F3
hedral Street	D3-E3-F3
apside Street	A1-A2
de Place	B1-C1
Clyde Street	C1-D1-E1
Cochrane Street	E2
College Street	E2-F2
Commerce Street	C1
Cowcaddens Road	C4-D4-E4
Craighall Road	C5-D5
Dalhousie Street	C4
Dobbies Loan	C5-D5-D4-E4
Douglas Street	B3-C3
Duke Street	F2
Dunblane Street	D4-D5
Elderslie Street	A3
Elmbank Street	B3-B4
Gallowgate	E1-F1

213

Day Drives

REFERENCE TO DRIVES

Drive route	A40
Alternative route	B69
Motorways	M3 / 6
Other roads	B5913
Places on route	Gralen
Places off route	Helham
Rivers and lakes	R Ure
Woodland	
Heights in feet	▲2323
Crags	
Marshes	
AA viewpoint	
Tower	
Boating centre	
Sandy beach	
Industrial site	
Site of battle	✕
Castle	
Abbey	
Church	†
Houses open to public	
Airport	✈
Other places of interest	■

Scale of Drives (unless otherwise stated)
4 miles to 1 inch
0 1 2 3 4m

Crown Copyright Reserved
©The Automobile Association

INDEX TO DAY DRIVES

Drive	Page	Drive	Page
1 Kelso (76 miles)	214	8 Fort William (104 miles)	228
2 Peebles (70 miles)	216	9 Inverness (91 miles)	230
3 Ayr (101 miles)	218	10 Kyle of Lochalsh (104 miles)	232
4 Stirling (86 miles)	220	11 Lochcarron (91 miles)	234
5 St Andrews (109 miles)	222	12 Gairloch (108 miles)	236
6 Pitlochry (84 miles)	224	13 Oban (102 miles)	237
7 Braemar (115 miles)	226	14 Aviemore (94 miles)	239

Drive 1 Kelso (76 miles)

Scott country and the Cheviots

Kelso, an attractive Border town at the confluence of the Tweed and Teviot, and once the home of Sir Walter Scott, has a courthouse from which a nightly curfew is still sounded. The fine, ruined abbey (AM) dates from 1128. The five-arch Tweed Bridge was built by Rennie in 1803. The 250-mile Pennine Way starts at Kirk Yetholm, 7 miles to the south-east. Leave by the St Boswells-Selkirk road A699, crossing the River Tweed then turning right. Cross the River Teviot and in ½ mile is the site of the former town of Roxburgh, with remains of the castle where James II was killed in 1460. The present hamlet of Roxburgh lies 2½ miles to the south-west. In 9 miles turn right onto the A68, then right again onto the B6404 into St Boswells. Continue forward on the B6404 and in 1 mile cross the River Tweed. In ¼ mile turn left onto the B6356 signed Dryburgh and continue, with views over the river. In 1¼ miles go forward for the ruined 12th-century Dryburgh Abbey (AM), which stands in a riverside setting. Sir Walter Scott and Field Marshall Earl Haig are buried here.

Return along the B6356 and in ½ mile turn left, passing the massive Wallace statue. Half a mile farther on the left is Bemersyde House (not open), the hereditary home of the Haig family. In ¼ mile turn left and in ½ mile pass the famous Scott's View (AA viewpoint), revealing the conical peaks of the Eildon Hills, much loved by Scott. In ½ mile go forward, signed Melrose (unclassified), and descend through woodland to cross the Leader Water. Turn right following signs Jedburgh then turn left to join A68. Cross river bridge and immediately turn right to join B6361. Continue through Newstead to enter the pleasant old town of **Melrose,** famous for the finest of all ruined Border abbeys (AM), founded in 1136 and described by Scott in *The Lay* *of the Last Minstrel.* There is an abbey museum. Follow signs Galashiels A6091 and in 2½ miles at second roundabout take first exit B6360 for Abbotsford House (¼ mile on) the famous 19th-century home of Sir Walter Scott. Return to Melrose and at the roundabout turn right onto the B6359, signed Lilliesleaf and Hawick. Ascend to a summit of 814ft with views ahead of the Cheviots. In 1¾ miles go forward over the cross roads. Three miles farther turn left over the river bridge, continue to Lilliesleaf and turn left signed Denholm. In 3½ miles turn left onto the B6405, passing the twin peaks of the Minto Hills, and 1½ miles farther cross the River Teviot into **Denholm**, birth-place of Scott's friend, the poet John Leyden. Turn right onto the A698, signed Hawick. In 3½ miles turn left onto the A6088, signed Bonchester Bridge and Newcastle. To visit Hawick, keep ahead on A698 (1¼ miles). Gradually ascend a winding road to open moorland, with views of high, rounded hills. To the south are Wyndburgh Hill and Fanna Hill, above the western area of Wauchope Forest. A long descent to Bonchester Bridge, on the Rule Water, is followed by a long climb past the ancient hill-fort on Bonchester Hill to further moorland. A final climb is made before joining the A68 for Carter Bar (1,370ft), the England-Scotland border and a fine viewpoint. There are extensive views to the north-west as far as the Eildon Hills (18 miles). Nearby is the site of the last Border battle, the Redeswire Raid (1575).

Return on the A68, signed Jedburgh, descending to the wooded valley of the Jed Water. **Jedburgh** is one of the most attractive border towns, with many crow-stepped gable houses. There is a ruined 12th-century abbey (AM) and a 16th-century bridge. Queen Mary's House, associated with Mary Queen of Scots, is now a museum. The spired New Gate is unusual. The castle dates from 1823. Continue on the A68 (signed Edinburgh) and in 2 miles turn right onto the A698 for the return along the Teviot Valley to Kelso.

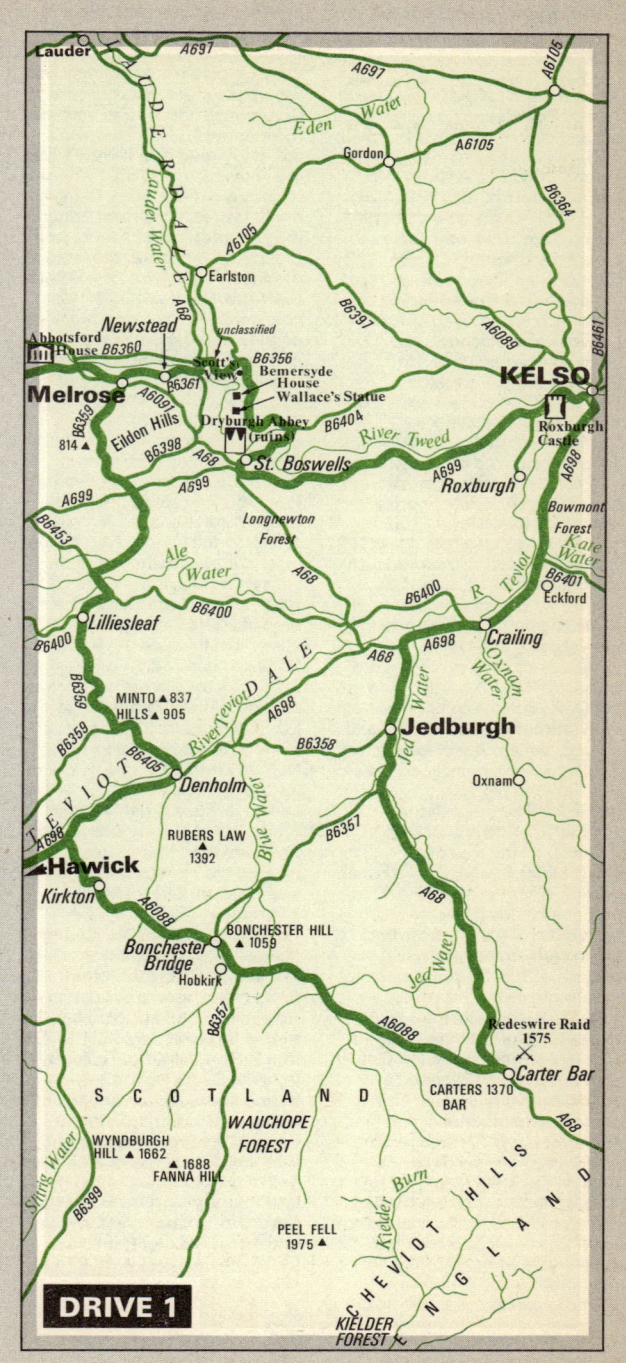

Day Drives

Drive 2 Peebles 70 miles
Through the Tweedsmuir Hills, with St Mary's Loch and the Devil's Beef-tub.

Attractively situated in the Vale of Tweed **Peebles**, an inland resort, angling centre, and royal burgh, is known for its tweed mills. The Tweed Bridge dates from 1467 and remains of Cross Kirk (AM) from 1261. Queensbery Lodging, dating from 1644, now forms part of the Chambers (Dictionaries) Institution and is a museum. The Border Riding ceremony is observed in June. Leave by the Glasgow road A72 along the Tweed Valley. In 1 mile stands the finely situated Neidpath Castle, with walls 11ft thick. *One mile further an unclassified road to the left leads for 8 miles up the Manor Valley, to finish below the slopes of Dollar Law (2,682ft).* Scott described the valley as 'the sweetest vale of all the south'. Two miles beyond this road turn left onto the B712, signed Moffat. At **Stobo** the church, of Norman origin, retains its 'jougs', an iron collar used for punishment. Two miles farther cross the River Tweed, then pass the Dawyck House Gardens, with fine collections of trees and shrubs. Several species new to Scotland were introduced here in the 17th and 18th centuries. Behind the woods rise the Scrape (2,348ft) and Breach Law (1,886ft). In the area of **Drumelzier** Merlin, the Arthurian wizard, is said to be buried. One and a half miles farther turn left onto the A701, signed Moffat. On the left, for several miles, are a series of 1,500ft spurs, leading to a string of summits over 2,000ft. To the right are 1,600ft ridges parallel with the road. At the hamlet of Tweedsmuir the unclassified road (signed Talla) leads to St Mary's Loch. *This route can be taken to avoid Moffat, saving 20 miles. A climb to the edge of Talla Reservoir reveals four peaks over 2,250ft at its eastern end, between which the road climbs, steeply at first. A summit of 1,483ft is reached close to the Megget Stone. To the north stands Broad Law (2,756ft) and to the south, Molls Cleuch Dod (2,572ft), just one of seven summits over 2,500ft in that area. A long descent of the Megget Water leads to Cappercleuch on St Mary's Loch where the main tour is rejoined.* Continue up the Tweed Valley. At the summit (1,334ft) there is a tablet to a mail-coach crew killed in a snowstorm in 1831. Nearby are the sources of the rivers Tweed, Clyde and Annan. In 1¾ miles on the descent is the precipitous hollow at the head of Annandale, known as the Devil's Beef-tub. Hart Fell (2,651ft) is seen to the left across Annandale on the long descent to the market town of **Moffat**. Here, the Colvin fountain, surmounted by a ram, indicates the importance of local sheep-farming.

Bear left onto the A708, signed Selkirk, following the Moffat Water. Beyond the Craigieburn Plantation the valley becomes deeper and U-shaped, with a 2,000ft ridge on the right. Three miles farther, on the left as the valley narrows, is the Grey Mare's Tail, a waterfall with a drop of 200ft. Beyond the 1,108ft summit of the road the Borders Region is entered before descent to Loch of the Lowes, which has a monument to James Hogg, the Ettrick Shepherd. Opposite stands **Tibbie Shiel's Inn.** Named after the landlady, it was visited by Scott and became the centre for literary gatherings; today, it is popular with anglers. The 2½-mile St Mary's Loch beyond the inn was the 'lone St Mary's silent lake' of Scott's *Marmion.*

Continue on the A708, skirting the loch and descending the Yarrow Water to the Gordon Arms Hotel, where Scott and Hogg (who died at Eldinhope, 1 mile to the south-west, in 1835) met for the last time. Turn left onto the B709, signed Innerleithen, and ascend to the summit, at 1,170ft. A long descent leads to Traquair; go forward to reach Traquair House, one of the oldest and most interesting mansions in Scotland. Return to Traquair and turn right onto the B7062 for Peebles, following the Tweed Valley and skirting Cardrona Forest.

DRIVE 2

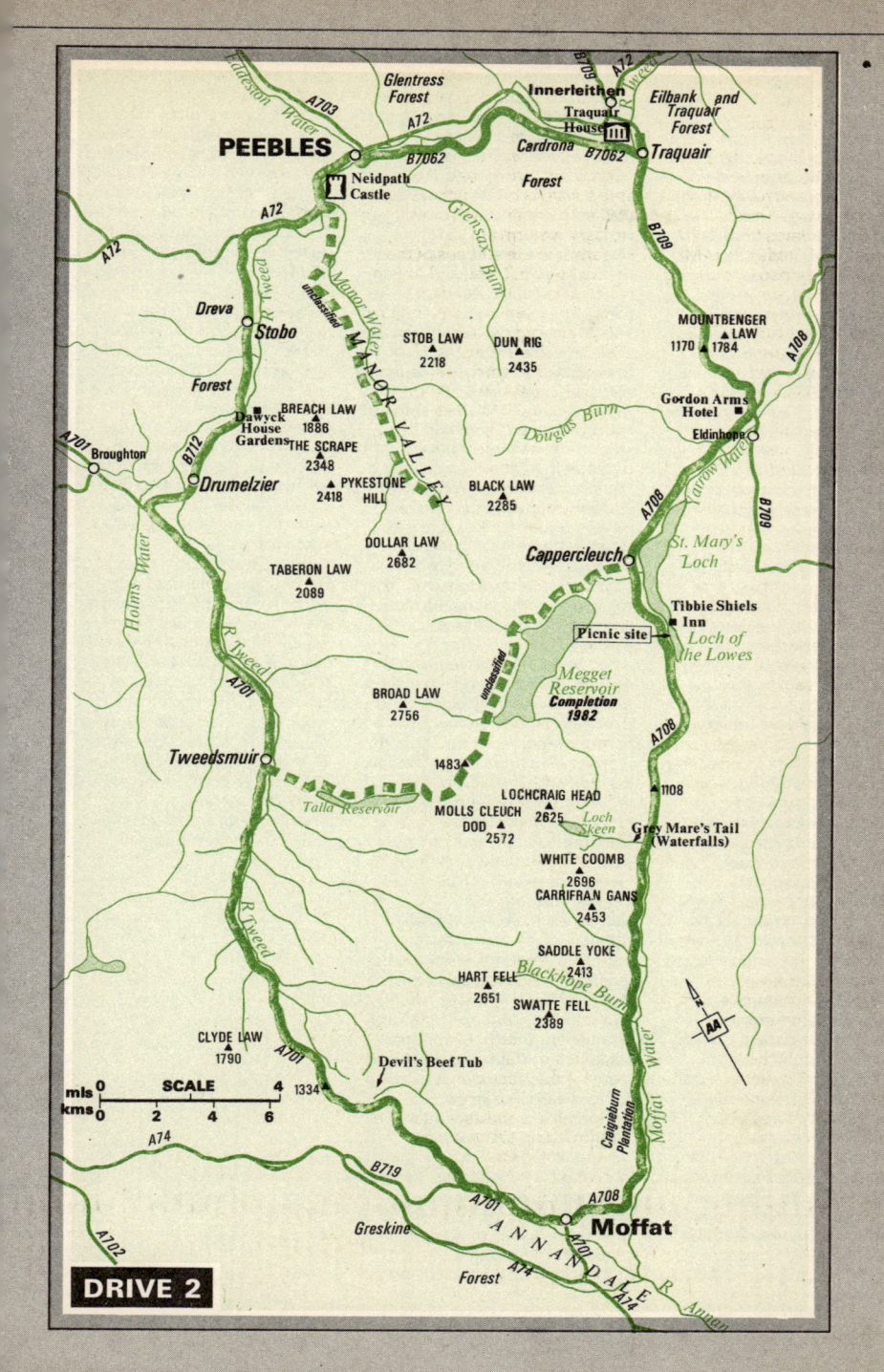

Map labels

- Peebles
- Innerleithen
- Traquair House
- Traquair
- Eilbank and Traquair Forest
- Glentress Forest
- Cardrona Forest
- Neidpath Castle
- Dreva
- Stobo
- Stobo Forest
- Dawyck House Gardens
- Breach Law 1886
- The Scrape 2348
- Stob Law 2218
- Dun Rig 2435
- Mountbenger Law 1170
- 1784
- Gordon Arms Hotel
- Eldinhope
- Broughton
- Drumelzier
- Pykestone Hill 2418
- Black Law 2285
- Dollar Law 2682
- Taberon Law 2089
- Cappercleuch
- St. Mary's Loch
- Tibbie Shiels Inn
- Loch of the Lowes
- Picnic site
- Megget Reservoir Completion 1982
- Broad Law 2756
- Tweedsmuir
- Talla Reservoir
- 1483
- Lochcraig Head 2625
- Molls Cleuch Dod 2572
- Loch Skeen
- 1108
- Grey Mare's Tail (Waterfalls)
- White Coomb 2696
- Carrifran Gans 2453
- Saddle Yoke 2413
- Hart Fell 2651
- Swatte Fell 2389
- Blackhope Burn
- Clyde Law 1790
- Devil's Beef Tub 1334
- Craigieburn Plantation
- Moffat
- Greskine Forest
- ANNANDALE
- R Tweed
- R Annan
- Moffat Water
- Yarrow Water
- Manor Valley
- Glensax Burn
- Douglas Burn
- Eddleston Water
- Holms Water

Roads: A72, A703, A701, A708, A709, B7062, B709, B712, B719, A74, A702

SCALE: mls 0–4, kms 0–6

Day Drives

Drive 3 Ayr 101 miles
Burns country and the west coast

In the heart of Burns Country, the town of **Ayr** is an attractive resort with excellent beaches and a fishing harbour on Ayr Bay. In the vicinity are many places connected with the poet Robert Burns; some are within the town itself, such as the Tam o'Shanter Inn and the 13th-century Auld Brig. One of the most precious relics of the town is the old tower of the Church of St John, the Fort Castle; Robert Bruce's Parliament met here in 1315. Also the restored 16th-century Loudoun Hall is of architectural merit.

There is a racecourse to the east of the town, and a fine esplanade with wide views across the Firth of Clyde to the Isle of Arran. The drive leaves Ayr on the Maidens road A719 and climbs beyond Butlin's Holiday Camp to over 300ft, giving wide seascapes to the Isle of Arran. The small fishing village of Dunure lies to the right below the main road and the remains of a cliff castle can be seen. Two miles farther the drive traverses the 'Electric Brae', where, because of certain factors in the configuration of the land, a car will start to roll backwards although appearing to face a descent. In another 2 miles the drive turns right with the A719 and passes along an attractive wooded valley before reaching the entrance to Culzean Castle. The castle (NTS) was designed in the 18th century by Robert Adam and is set in 500 acres of grounds. In the interior the ceilings and staircase are especially noteworthy. Continue with the A719 and beyond **Maidens,** a small fishing village and resort, the drive reaches **Turnberry,** one of the most famous golfing resorts in the world. The lonely island peak of Ailsa Craig, 1,110ft, lies 12 miles off the coast. In the village turn left on to the Ayr road A77 and proceed to **Kirkoswald,** a village rich in Burns' associations. The graves of 'Tam o'Shanter' and 'Souter Johnnie' are in the churchyard. A thatched cottage (NTS), once the home of Souter Johnnie, now houses Burns relics. Two miles beyond the village the drive passes the ruins of the 12th-century Crossraguel Abbey, with its curious dovecote. At **Maybole,** which now manufactures shoes and agricultural implements, there is a restored 17th-century castle in the High Street. Due to the residence of the road engineer McAdam, the first Macadamized road was traditionally constructed at Whitefaulds Farm, Maybole.

The drives leaves Maybole on the Crosshill road B7023. At **Crosshill** turn right in the village with the Dailly road B7023, and in 1 mile join the B741. The Valley of the Water of Girvan is then followed for 2½ miles before turning left onto an unclassified road, signed Barr. This narrow and sometimes gated road traverses lonely moorland for 5 miles before crossing the river Stinchar and turning right to follow the river to **Barr.** This village is a popular angling resort and nestles beneath the Changue Forest. At the T-junction turn right then turn left onto the B734, signed Barrhill, and after 6 miles left again on to the Newton Stewart road, A714 to **Pinwherry.** Here turn right to cross the Duisk River, passing a ruined castle on the left. The drive continues through the attractive Duisk Valley to **Barrhill,** but then crosses more exposed moorland with fine views of the Carrick Hills to the east. At the hamlet of Bargrennan turn left, signed Straiton, on to an unclassified road, and enter the 165,000 acreage of the Galloway Forest Park. Some of the most picturesque scenery in Scotland is to be found within this Forest Park. *Beyond* **Glentrool Village** *a detour may be made by turning right to visit Glen Trool. The scenery around here is very beautiful, with pine clad hills rising to over 2,300ft from the shores of Loch Trool.*

The main drive continues through the Forest Park for 8 miles before branching right. In this less forested area Merrick 2,764ft, and Shalloch on Minnoch 2,522ft, are among the most prominent hills to be seen to the right, and Craigenreoch, 1,854ft is to the left. A climb is made to the summit (1,407ft) before descending through the Tairlaw Plantation of the Carrick Forest into the Girvan Valley. This road passes some waterfalls before reaching the village of **Straiton,** picturesquely situated beside the Water of Girvan. The church contains a pre-Reformation aisle. The drive turns right in Straiton on to the Dalmellington road B741, and in 6 miles turn left on to the Ayr road, A713. *The iron-working town of Dalmellington lies 1 mile to the right here along the A713.* Several mining settlements for both iron and coal are passed through along the Doon Valley to reach Patna. Three and a half miles farther pass through the hamlet of Hollybush, then in 2½ miles turn left onto an unclassified road, signed Alloway. In 1¾ miles turn right then left crossing the A77 to **Alloway.**

Robert Burns, the Scottish national poet was born here in 1759. His birthplace has been preserved, and there is an adjacent museum with various relics of the poet. The Burns Monument contains bibles belonging to Burns and his 'Highland Mary'. *Spanning the Doon half a mile south off the B7024 is the Old Brig o'Doon, attractively sited and possibly of 13th century origin.*

From Alloway the drive follows the B7024 to return to Ayr.

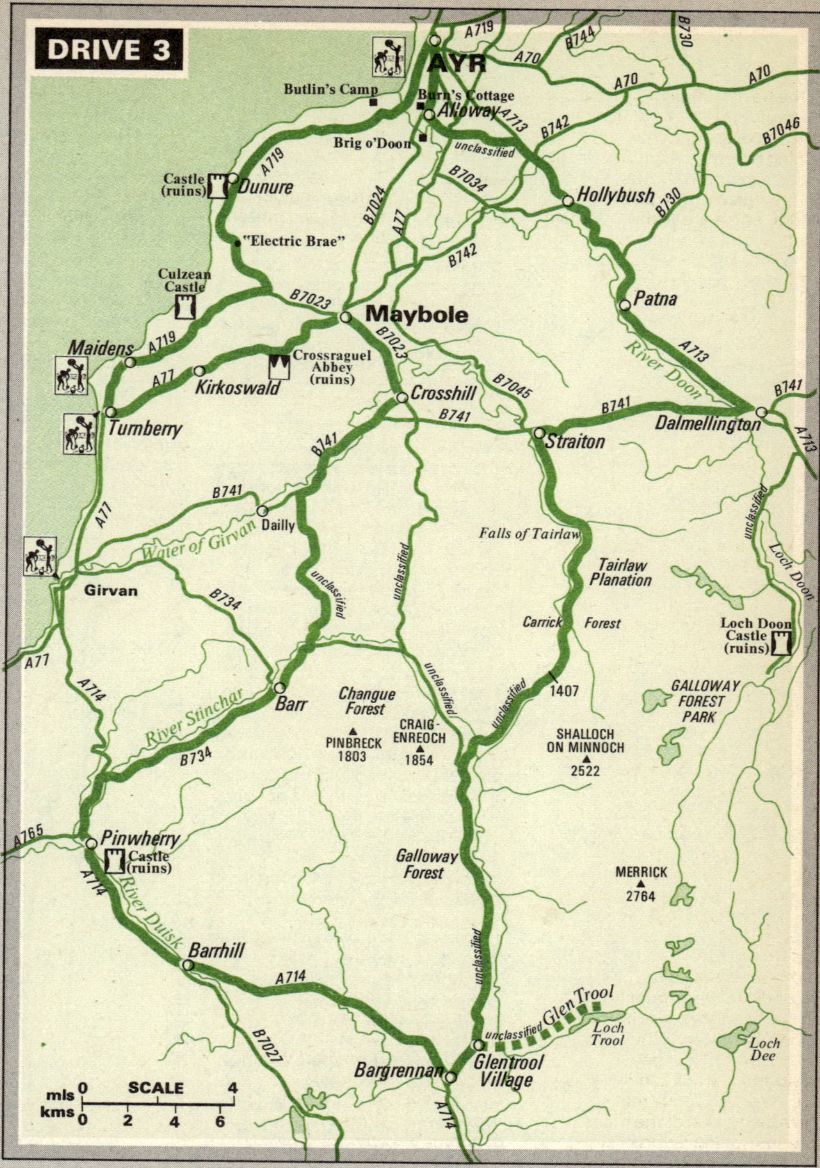

DRIVE 3
AYR
Butlin's Camp
Burn's Cottage
Alloway
Brig o'Doon
Castle (ruins)
Dunure
"Electric Brae"
Culzean Castle
Maidens
Kirkoswald
Crossraguel Abbey (ruins)
Maybole
Turnberry
Crosshill
Hollybush
Patna
River Doon
Straiton
Dalmellington
Dailly
Water of Girvan
Girvan
Falls of Tairlaw
Tairlaw Planation
Carrick Forest
Loch Doon
Loch Doon Castle (ruins)
Barr
River Stinchar
Changue Forest
PINBRECK 1803
CRAIG-ENREOCH 1854
1407
SHALLOCH ON MINNOCH 2522
GALLOWAY FOREST PARK
Pinwherry
Castle (ruins)
River Duisk
Galloway Forest
MERRICK 2764
Barrhill
Glen Trool
Loch Trool
Loch Dee
Glentrool Village
Bargrennan
A719
A70
B744
B730
A713
B742
B7046
unclassified
B7034
B7024
A77
B7023
B7045
B741
A714
B734
A765
B7027
mls 0 SCALE 4
kms 0 2 4 6

Day Drives

Drive 4 Stirling 86 miles
The Trossachs and Campsie Fells

Stirling, on the River Forth, is known as the Gateway to the Highlands. The town is dominated by its imposing castle (AM), standing on a sheer 250ft crag. The present structure dates only from the 15th century, but earlier castles had been built on the site to command the routes across the surrounding region. Scenes from the BBC TV series *Colditz* were filmed at the castle, and it is still used as barracks. Nearby is the Landmark exhibition centre presenting the story of Stirling. The 14th-century Old Stirling Bridge was one of the lowest crossings of the Forth, but is now used only by pedestrians. Notable old houses in the town are Mar's Wark (AM), Argyll's Lodging, and Darnley House. The 15th–16th-century church of Holy Rude has an impressive nave and choir. Crowning Abbey Craig, 1 mile north-east at Causewayhead, is the Wallace monument – a good viewpoint.

Leave Stirling by the A811, signed Erskine Bridge, and travel westwards along the level Forth Valley. In 8¾ miles turn right onto the B822, signed Thornhill, and ½ mile farther cross the River Forth. At Thornhill join the A873, then continue on the B822. The road passes the edge of Torrie Forest before joining the A81 to reach **Callander.** This resort and tourist centre is situated at the confluence of the rivers Teith and Leny. Scenes for the BBC TV series *Dr Finlay's Casebook* were filmed here. Follow the Crianlarich road, the A84, and in 1¼ miles turn left onto the A821, signed Trossachs, and cross the River Leny. The road runs alongside Loch Vennachar with the 2,873ft peak of Ben Ledi to the right. After Brig o'Turk the drive enters the Queen Elizabeth Forest Park beside Loch Auchray. *A quarter of a mile beyond the Trossachs Hotel a diversion can be made by keeping forward to reach the pier on the eastern end of* **Loch Katrine,** *where pleasure steamer trips operate during the summer. The loch, which inspired Sir Walter Scott's poem 'The Lady of the Lake', is set in the heart of the Trossachs area, a delightful combination of mountains, woodland, and water. Ben Venue (2,393ft) is prominent to the south.*

The main drive continues on the Aberfoyle road, which winds through the Queen Elizabeth Forest and, after 2½ miles, affords views of Loch Drunkie to the left. In another 2½ miles the David Marshall Lodge Viewpoint is passed on the descent to the small resort of **Aberfoyle.** *From here a detour may be taken along the B829 for* **Inversnaid,** *picturesquely set on Loch Lomond. This scenic road runs alongside Loch Ard and Loch Chon. The final 4 miles is on an unclassified road passing Loch Arklet. The return is along the same roads and 28 miles should be added if the full detour is made.*

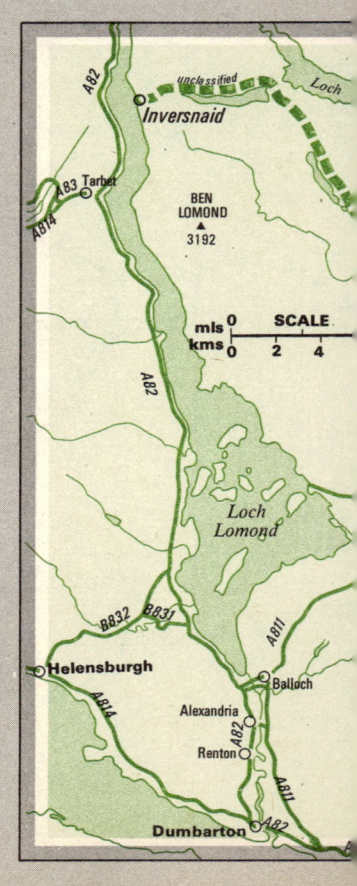

The main drive continues on the Stirling road, A821, and after 1 mile branches left onto the A81, signed Callander. Two and a half miles farther on the right is the Lake of Menteith, where the 13th-century island ruins of Inchmahome Priory are occasionally open to the public. One mile farther turn right onto the B8034, signed Arnprior. *The passenger ferry for Inchmahome Priory is shortly to the right by Menteith Church.* At Arnprior turn right onto the A811, then left onto an unclassified road, signed Fintry. After 2 miles the road crosses the moors below the Fintry Hills and turns right onto the B822 to reach **Fintry**. This village is situated in the valley of the Endrick Water between the Fintry Hills and Campsie Fells, which form the Lennox Hills. Turn right onto the Killearn road, B818, then in 5½ miles join the Glasgow road, A875, and pass through **Killearn**. Two miles farther turn left onto the A81, following Strath Blane to Blanefield and the edge of Strathblane. Here, turn left onto the A891, signed Lennoxtown. At **Lennoxtown** turn left, signed Fintry, onto the B822, which climbs out of the valley and passes the head of Campsie Glen before crossing the moors of Campsie Fells, reaching a height of over 1,000ft. After descending into the valley of the Endrick Water, turn right onto the B818, signed Denny. The road later runs alongside the Carron Valley Reservoir, which is backed by attractive pine forests. One and three-quarters miles beyond the dam, turn left at the Carronbridge Inn onto an unclassified road, signed Stirling. In 1¾ miles the road passes the small Loch Coulter Reservoir (on right). After another 2¼ miles turn left at T-junction. The drive later crosses the M9 Motorway and in ¾ mile turns right and then left to join the A872. Immediately to the left is the Bannockburn Battleground, where an open-air rotunda and equestrian statue of Robert the Bruce commemorate the battle in 1314. The A872 and A9 are taken for the short return into Stirling.

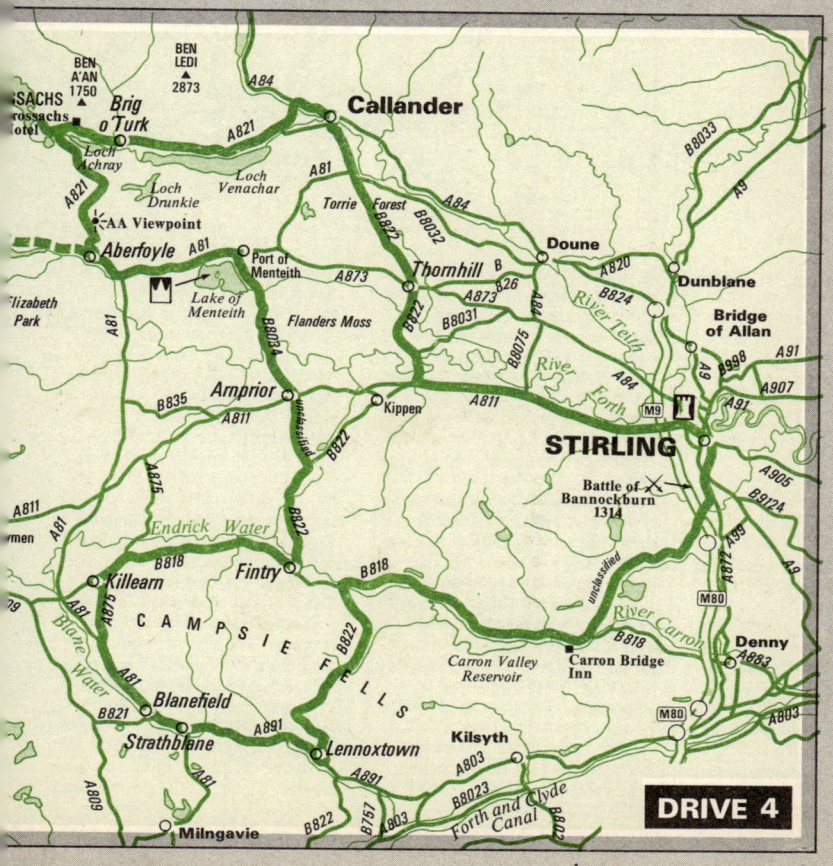

Day Drives

Drive 5 · St Andrews 109 miles
North Fife

St Andrews, a university town and resort, boasts the Royal and Ancient Golf Club, which is acknowledged as the leading authority on golf. The harbour is guarded by steep cliffs, but wide sands lie to the north-west. Completed in the 14th century, the cathedral was in ruins by the 17th century, and the University – the oldest in Scotland – was founded in 1412. Old houses line South Street as far as the West Port of 1589, and the now ruined castle (AM) was built in 1200. The drive follows the Tay Bridge signs to leave by the A91. At **Guardbridge** cross the River Eden and turn right onto the A919 to reach **Leuchars.** The village, known for its RAF base, has one of the finest small Norman churches in Scotland. In 1¼ miles, at St Michael's Hotel, turn right onto the B945 to **Tayport.** There are fine views across the Firth of Tay to Dundee as the B946 proceeds westwards and passes beneath the new Tay Road Bridge into **Newport-on-Tay.** At Wormit there are views of the 2-mile-long Tay railway bridge, completed in 1888. Continue on the B946 inland and, after ¾ mile, branch left onto an unclassified road, signed St Andrews. One mile farther at roundabout take the 2nd exit, then in another 1½ miles turn right onto the A92 and return to St Michael's Hotel. At the crossroads turn right, signed Cupar, and continue through Balmullo. Two miles farther join the A91 to enter **Dairsie.** Here, turn left onto an unclassified road, signed Pitscottie. In 1 mile the drive crosses the River Eden by a 16th-century bridge, and, turning right, offers views of the ruined Dairsie Castle on the north bank. The drive follows the picturesquely wooded Dura Glen – noted for its fossils – to **Pitscottie,** where it turns left and then immediately right onto the B939, signed Kirkcaldy, for the attractive village of Ceres. One and a half miles farther, at Craigrothie, turn right onto the A916 which passes the entrance to Hill Tarvit mansion (NTS). Built in 1696 and enlarged in 1906, this house possesses fine collections of tapestries and furniture. The A916 later descends into the valley of the River Eden and joins the A92 to enter **Cupar,** the main town of the fertile agricultural area known as the Howe of Fife. The town has a fine 15th-century church and an unusual Mercat cross.

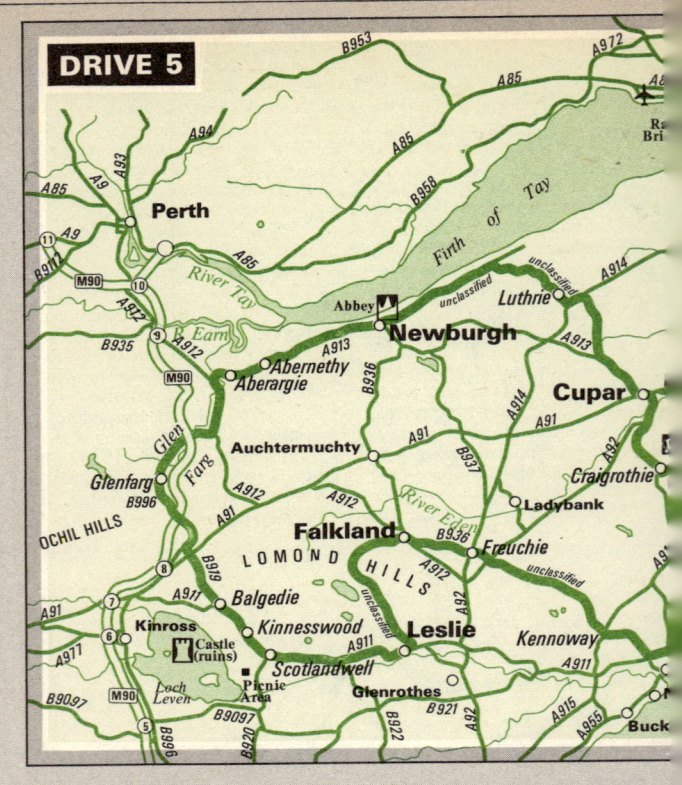

Follow signs Kincardine to leave by the A91 and at end of town turn right onto the A913, signed Perth. One and three-quarter miles farther turn right onto an unclassified road, signed Luthrie, and in another mile pass the ruins of an old castle (on left). At the junction with the A914 turn left and in ½ mile turn right onto another unclassified road for the hamlet of Luthrie. One mile farther the drive bears left and later affords fine views across the Firth of Tay before turning left and following the river to **Newburgh.** On entering the small town the drive passes the remains of Lindores Abbey and turns right onto the Perth road, the A913. Newburgh itself is noted for the manufacture of linoleum and as the site of the Mugdrum Cross, which is more than 1,000 years old.

Continue on the A913 to **Abernethy** where there is an early 12th-century round tower – one of only two on the Scottish mainland. Beyond Aberargie turn left onto the A90 signed Forth Road Bridge and pass through the wooded Glen Farg. Two and a half miles beyond the village of **Glenfarg** turn right at T-junction onto the A91 and then turn left onto the B919. In 1¾ miles, at Balgedie, join the A911 and pass through Kinnesswood, with the Lomond Hills to the left. At **Scotlandwell,** where there is a picnic site, turn left and continue to the small industrial town of **Leslie.** Three hundred yards past the church in the main street, opposite the Clansman PH, turn left (concealed entrance – no sign). This unclassified road crosses the Lomond Hills to reach **Falkland,** a small town of picturesque old houses and cobbled streets. Turn right to enter the town and keep left through the attractive square, passing the interesting 16th-century Palace – former residence of the Stuart kings and queens. Turn right at T-junction onto the A912 and in ¼ mile turn left onto the B936, signed Freuchie. Continue through Newton of Falkland to Freuchie, and at end of village go over the crossroads onto an unclassified road (no sign). At the junction with the A92 turn right, then immediately left onto the Kennoway road to pass through undulating country, and in 4¼ miles turn left to enter **Kennoway.** The drive turns right at the main road in the village and then immediately left, signed Leven. Two miles farther the drive reaches the outskirts of **Leven,** a resort and port on Largo Bay. Turn left onto the St Andrews road, the A915, and continue past Lundin Links to **Upper Largo.** Here take the A917 for **Elie.** Both this resort and Earlsferry are situated on a sheltered crescent-shaped bay and are noted for their fine golf courses.

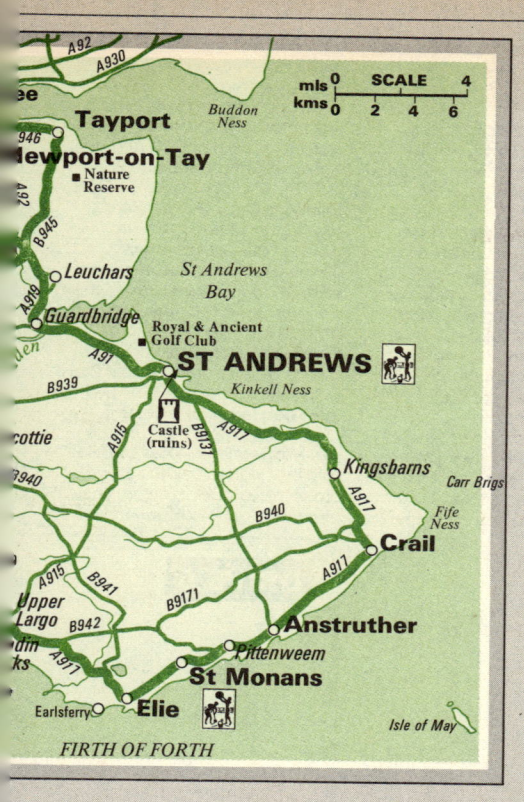

Leave by the Anstruther road, the A917, to follow the next stage of the drive along the East Neuk coastline. The road passes by the fishing villages of St Monans and **Pittenweem** to **Anstruther,** where the Scottish Fisheries Museum is located. Offshore can be seen the Isle of May, a national nature reserve. Continue with the A917 to **Crail,** the easternmost of the East Neuk fishing villages, where an early 16th-century tollbooth is retained. The return to St Andrews is made along the A917 passing through Kingsbarns.

Drive 6 Pitlochry 84 miles
Loch Tummel, Glen Lyon and Loch Tay

Pitlochry is a popular resort beside the River Tummel in an attractive setting of loch, mountains and woods. The modern Festival Theatre presents plays and concerts in the summer. The artificial Loch Faskally was created when the hydro-electric power station was built, and includes an extensive fish ladder with an observation chamber. Both are open to the public during daylight hours. Leave by the Perth road, and in ½ mile turn right onto an unclassified road signed Festival Theatre. Cross the new Aldour Bridge and turn right. In ½ mile turn right onto the A9 and ½ mile farther turn right again onto the unclassified Foss road. The drive continues through magnificent scenery as the road follows the south bank of the River Tummel and Loch Tummel. After 12 miles turn left onto the B846, signed Aberfeldy, and climb out of the valley to a height of over 1,270ft, following the line of a military road constructed by General Wade in the 18th century. A descent is then made into the valley of the Keltney Burn to the Coshieville Hotel. Here, turn right onto an unclassified road for **Fortingall.** Half a mile beyond the village turn right, signed Glen Lyon, and follow the River Lyon into **Glen Lyon,** one of the longest and most picturesque glens in Scotland. After 11 miles turn left, signed Loch Tay, and cross the Bridge of Balgie. This lonely and narrow moorland road

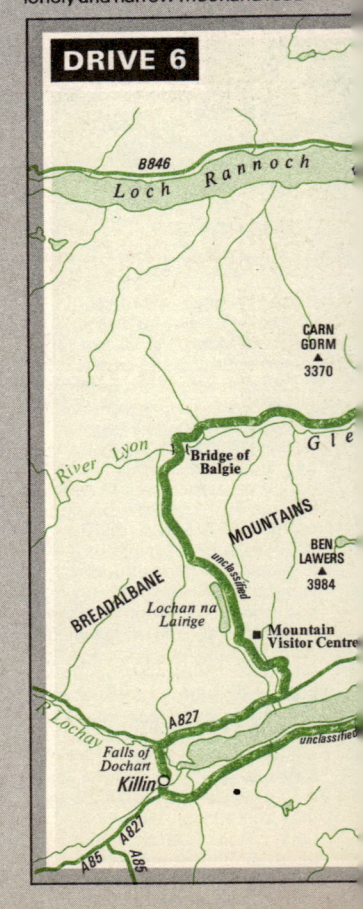

crosses the Breadalbane Mountains at a height of 1,805ft. On the descent there are views of Lochan na Lairige, and, to the left, of Ben Lawers, 3,984ft high and of great botanical interest. Passing the Ben Lawers Mountain Visitor Centre (NTS), in 2 miles turn right to join the A827 along the north side of Loch Tay. At the western extremity of the loch is **Killin,** a pleasant village resort. Cross the River Dochart here and keep right, then take next turning left onto an unclassified road, signed Ardeonaig. This scenic road returns along the south side of Loch Tay, passing through the hamlets of Ardeonaig and Acharn. In 1½ miles turn right onto the A827, signed Aberfeldy.
To the left is the small resort of **Kenmore** *situated at the eastern end of Loch Tay.*
The A827 continues along the valley of the River Tay and to the left is Taymouth Castle (not open). **Aberfeldy** is a market town and holiday centre with a five-arched stone bridge over the River Tay, built in 1733.
Turn left onto the B846, signed Kinloch Rannoch, and cross Wade's bridge for Weem, then turn right onto an unclassified road, signed Strathtay. Follow the north bank of the river to **Strathtay,** and beyond the hamlet join the Ballinluig road, the A827. In 4 miles turn left onto an unclassified road, signed Dunfallandy. This narrow road follows the west bank of the River Tummel before turning right, after another 4 miles, to recross the Aldour Bridge. On the far side turn left for Pitlochry.

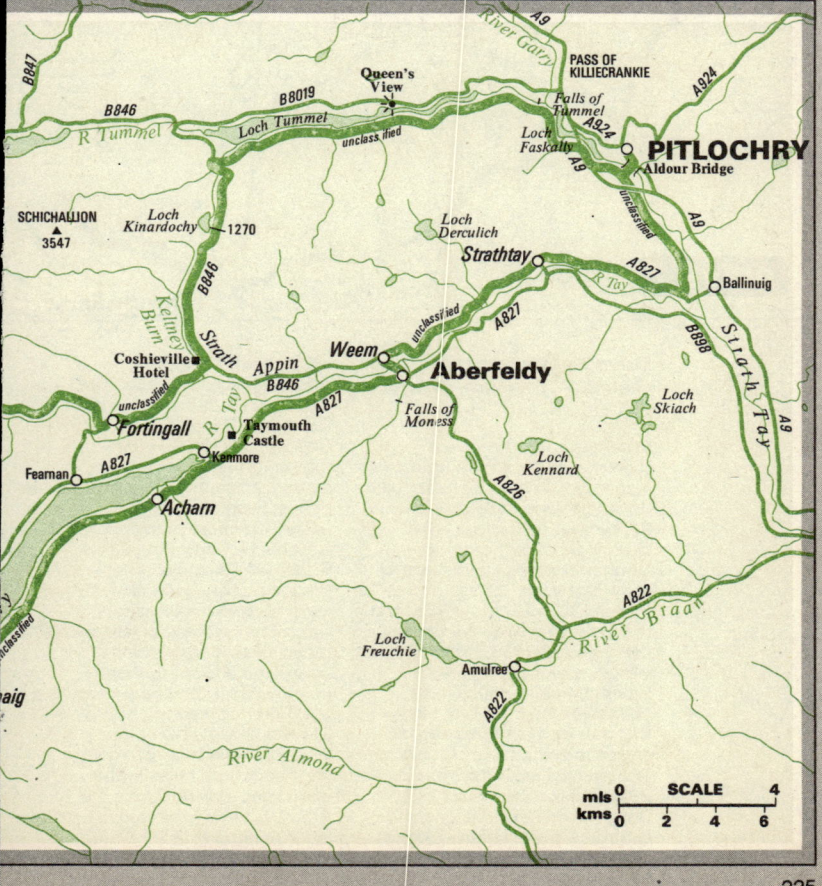

Day Drives

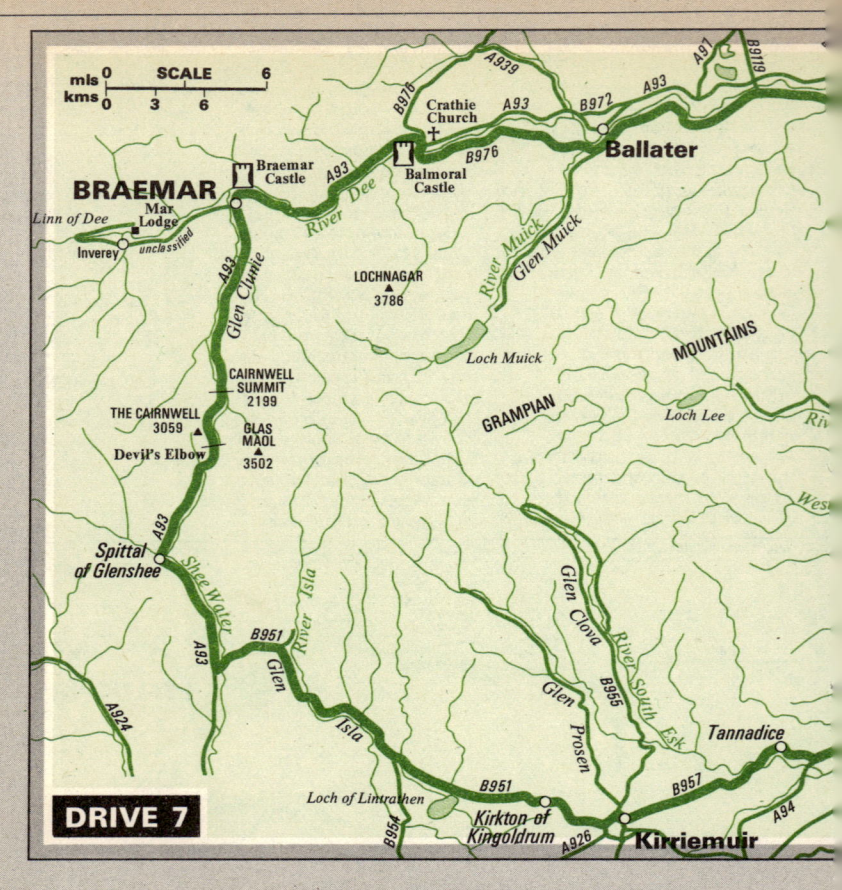

Drive 7 Braemar 115 miles
Glenshee, Glen Isla, Cairn O'Mounth, and Deeside

Braemar is an attractive Highland winter and summer resort, well-known for its annual Royal Highland Gathering, held in September. The village is set high up (at 1,100ft) among heather-clad hills, dominated to the west by the Cairngorm massif of Cairn Toul, 4,241ft, and to the south-east by the Peak of Lochnagar, 3,768ft. North of the village, near the River Dee is Braemar Castle, dating from 1628 and rebuilt in 1748. Leave Braemar by the Perth road, A93, and pass through Glen Clunie. The road gradually rises to 2,199ft at the Cairnwell Pass, Britain's highest main road summit. Here extensive ski-ing developments have taken place, and a chair lift operates throughout the year up to The Cairnwell (3,059ft). To the left is Glas Maol (3,502ft).

Descend the Devil's Elbow by a road once well-known for its severe gradients and hairpin bends, but now realigned with an easier maximum gradient of 1 in 8. Continue down the valley to **Spittal of Glenshee,** another growing resort catering for both summer and winter visitors. Cross Shee water and follow it for 5 miles before passing the new plantation of Strathardle Forest and turning sharp left onto the B951, signed Kirriemuir, Glenisla. Recross the Shee Water and in quarter of a mile keep right. Two miles farther again keep right following the River Isla through attractive Glen Isla. Continue with the Kirriemuir road, then after 6 miles leave the

Continue on the B966, signed Aberdeen, and after 1¾ miles turn right onto the A9 then turn left onto the B966 for **Edzell**, passing through an arch erected in 1887 in memory of the 13th Earl of Dalhousie, before reaching the attractive small town. Continue with the B966 through the Howe of the Mearns, a fertile agricultural area, to **Fettercairn**. This village is also entered through an arch, which commemorates the visit of Queen Victoria in 1861. In the square is the old Kincardine town cross, dated 1670, notched to show the width of 37 inches, a Scottish measurement known as an 'ell'. Follow the Strachan, Banchory road, B974, which recrosses the Grampians over the 1,488ft Cairn o' Mounth, a fine viewpoint. Descend towards Deeside, passing through wooded Glen Dye and later cross the Bridge of Dye which dates from 1680. Two miles farther, turn left onto an unclassified road, signed Aboyne. Cross two fords, and after 2¼ miles turn left onto the B976. Continue 5½ miles, then keep forward with the B976 signed Aboyne, to reach Deeside. *Three and a quarter miles farther, to the right, across the River Dee, lies the small resort of Aboyne.* Keep forward, signed Ballater, and continue along South Deeside, passing through attractive pine forests beside the river. At the edge of Ballater again keep forward, signed Braemar, and in half a mile bear right across the River Muick. Five and a half miles farther, to the right, lies Abergeldie Castle (not open), residence of Edward VII whilst Prince of Wales. After another 2 miles pass the entrance to **Balmoral Castle**, the Queen's Highland residence. The grounds only are open to the public on week-days from May to July. Cross the River Dee to reach the junction with the A93. *A short distance to the right is granite-built Crathie Church, dating from 1895, attended by the Royal Family when in residence at Balmoral.* Turn left to follow the Braemar road along the north side of the Dee, passing through more pine forests with fine views of the eastern-most Cairngorms. Later recross the River Dee and after 2 miles pass the entrance to Braemar Castle, on the right, before the return to Braemar.

valley and 3 miles farther pass the Loch of Lintrathen to enter the fertile Vale of Strathmore. Three miles beyond Kirkton of Kingoldrum turn left onto the A926, then turn right to enter **Kirriemuir**. The small market town is noted for jute manufacture, and as the birthplace (in 1860) of the novelist and playwright Sir James Barrie. The house is open to the public (NTS). Follow the Brechin signs to leave by the B957, and after 5½ miles cross the River South Esk to reach **Tannadice**. One and a half miles beyond the village turn left onto the Aberdeen road, A94. Five miles farther turn right onto the A935 to reach the small city of **Brechin**. The much-restored cathedral has one of the only two round towers on the Scottish mainland, dating from the 10th or 11th century.

Day Drives

Drive 8 Fort William 104 miles

The 'Road to the Isles' and through the districts of Moidart, Ardnamurchan, Sunart, and Ardgour

Fort William is a well-known touring centre standing at the south-western end of the Great Glen (Glen More) and at the head of Loch Linnhe. Ben Nevis, at 4,406ft the highest mountain in Britain, rises behind the town in which is situated the West Highland Museum. To the north-east are aluminium works powered by hydro-electricity produced from water tunnelled through the mountain. South-east of the town, and easily reached by car, lies Glen Nevis, considered one of the most picturesque glens in Scotland. Take the A82 northwards out of the town, passing 15th-century Inverlochy Castle, a ruined stronghold situated between the main road and the River Lochy. Beyond the castle turn left to join the Mallaig road A830, the famous 'Road to the Isles', once notoriously difficult, but now much improved.

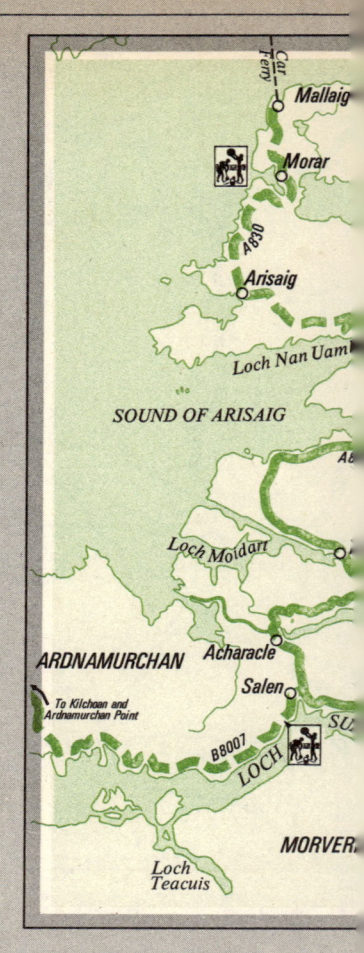

After crossing the River Lochy and the Caledonian Canal, the drive follows the northern shore of Loch Eil and passes a recently-built paper mill at Corpach. At **Glenfinnan,** with its superb view down the 18-mile long Loch Shiel, stands the Prince Charles Edward Monument (NT Scotland), erected in 1815 to commemorate the raising of the Bonnie Prince's standard in 1745. The National Trust of Scotland has an information centre here, and a passenger ferry service runs along Loch Shiel to Acharacle. Continue along Loch Eilt to **Lochailort.**

From here a diversion of 39 miles can be made to Mallaig. Leave Lochailort by the A830, driving alongside Loch Ailort and Loch Nan Uamh. It was here, in July 1745, that Prince Charles Edward landed from France at the start of the second Jacobite rebellion; here also, after the collapse of the rising a year later, he boarded another boat for the beginning of

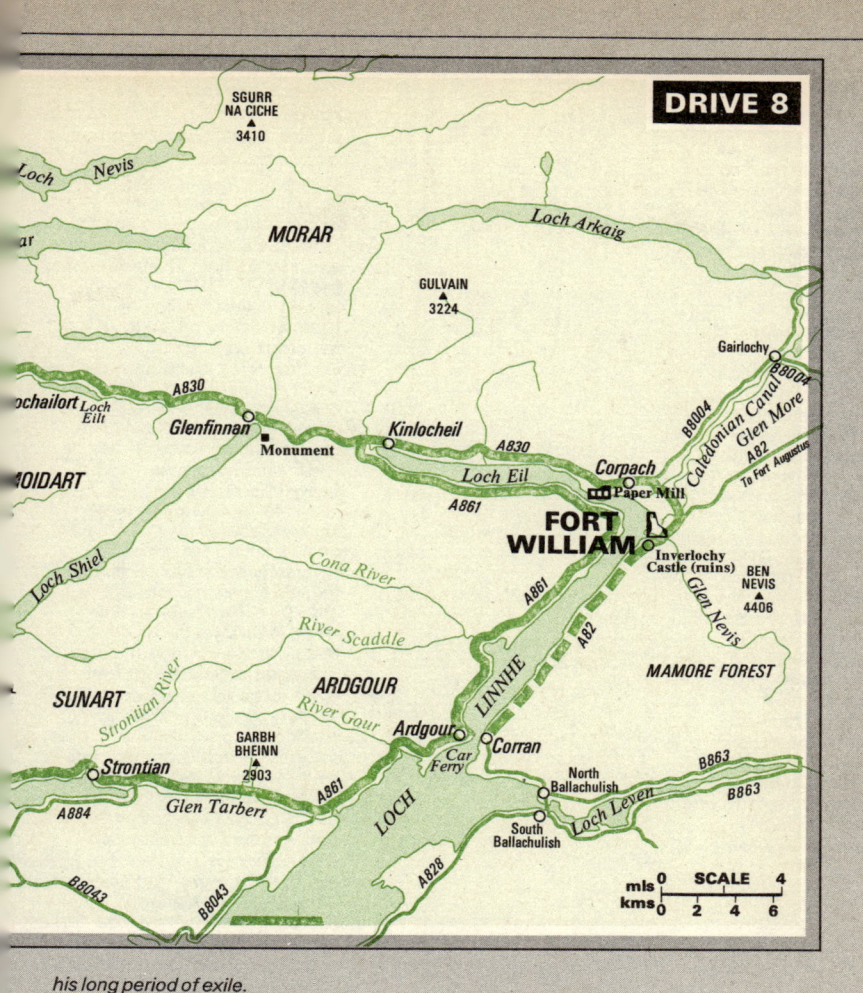

his long period of exile.
Across the Sound of Arisaig the islands of Rhum and Eigg may be seen, and at Arisaig there are lovely views over the sea. Morar, famous for its white sands, stands on the narrow neck of land that separates Loch Morar, 180 fathoms deep, from the sea.
Mallaig, on the Sound of Sleat, is a fishing port and a car-ferry terminal for services to the Isle of Skye.
The main drive takes the A861 out of Lochailort along the eastern shore of the loch and the Sound of Arisaig, before turning south towards Loch Moidart and Acharacle, which stands at the southern end of Loch Shiel and is dominated by Ben Resipol (2,774ft). From **Salen,**

Day Drives

attractively situated on the north shore of Loch Sunart a diversion can be taken to Kilchoan and Ardnamurchan Point. *Take the B8007, a narrow winding road, westwards alongside the loch and then drive inland through the Ardnamurchan Peninsula to Kilchoan.* **Ardnamurchan Point** *and the lighthouse that stands at the most westerly point of the Scottish mainland are 6 miles farther west and offer magnificent marine views. (The detour is 43 miles long.)*
Follow Loch Sunart eastwards from Salen. There are good views across the loch to the Morvern Hills, and Ben Resipol can be seen, rising in the background to the left of the road before the drive reaches **Strontian**. It was near here that the mineral strontianite was first found. After Strontian the drive joins Glen Tarbert and continues to Loch Linnhe. Among the mountains that can be seen on the eastern shore is Ben Nevis. Continue along the west shore of Loch Linnhe, passing the ferry point at Ardgour Hotel before following the shore of Loch Eil round the head of the loch, and turn right onto the A830 for Kinlocheil and Fort William. *Alternatively the ferry may be taken from Ardgour to Corran, and Fort William reached by the A82, cutting the journey by 25¼ miles.*

Drive 9 Inverness 91 miles
Strath Glass, Glen Urquhart and Loch Ness
The ancient 'capital of the Highlands', **Inverness** has become an important road and rail centre in addition to its claim as a historic town. Of interest are the High Church (13th century and later), the clock tower of Cromwell's old fort, and the restored Abertarff House (16th century; NTS). The Mercat Cross and the ancient Clach-an-Cudainn Stone is situated outside the Town House. Also of interest are the Tolbooth steeple and the modern castle.
Leave Inverness by the A9, signed Wick, and follow the southern shoreline of the Beauly Firth. After 11 miles cross the River Beauly and branch left onto the A831, signed Cannich. The drive then follows the thickly-wooded valley of the River Beauly to Struy Bridge. Cross the river and continue along Strath Glass to the village of **Cannich,** the gateway to Glens Cannich and Affric.
Unclassified roads continue into each glen for 10 miles, but they are not through ways for motor traffic. Loch Mullardoch in Glen Cannich and Loch Benevean in Glen Affric have both been dammed for hydro-electricity and there is a power station at Fasnakyle in Glen Affric. The highest mountain peaks north-west of the Great Glen are to be found in this area: they include Sgurr na Lapaich (3,775ft), north of Loch Mullardoch, and Carn Eige (3,880ft) and Mam Sodhail (3,862ft) to the south.
The main drive continues with the Drumnadrochit road which climbs out of the glen onto high ground. Later follow the River Enrick into Glen Urquhart and pass Loch Meiklie. Proceed along the pine-clad slopes of the glen and pass by Milton to reach Drumnadrochit. Here turn right onto the A82, signed Fort William, to enter the Great Glen. After the hamlet of Lewiston join the western shoreline of Loch Ness, passing a lay-by (on the left) which offers views over the ruined Urquhart Castle (AM). Nearly 1½ miles farther, also on

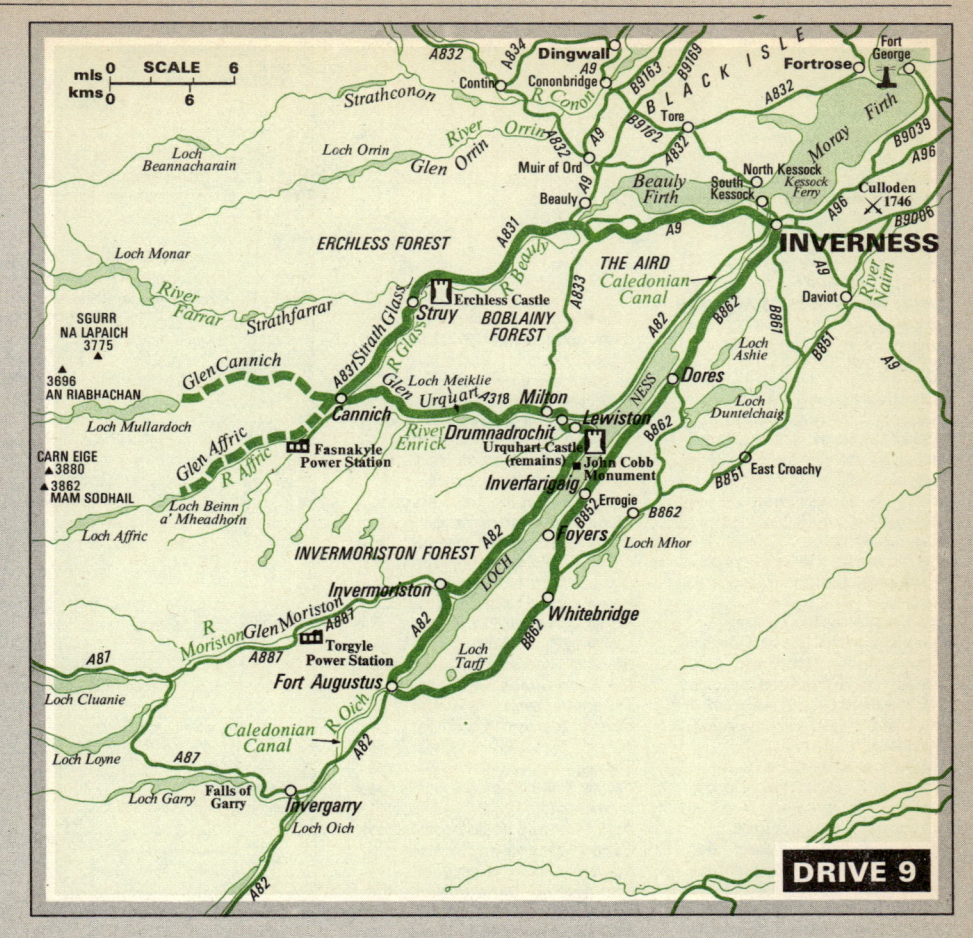

the left, is a memorial to the racing driver John Cobb, who lost his life whilst attempting the world waterspeed record on the loch in 1952.

Continue down the Great Glen to **Invermoriston** and remain on the A82 to reach **Fort Augustus** – situated at the southern end of Loch Ness. The present village takes its name from the fort which was built during the 1700s by General Wade. The fort itself was named after Augustus, Duke of Cumberland, and the remains are now part of a Benedictine abbey. Of interest in the village is the Great Glen Exhibition which displays items of local history, including the latest information on the search for the Loch Ness Monster.

At the far end of the village turn left onto the B862, signed Whitebridge and Dores. After 3 miles the road becomes single-track before passing Loch Tarff. Continue through moorland and woodland scenery to reach **Whitebridge**.

One mile farther turn left onto the B852, signed Foyers, and after another mile pass a picnic site beside the River Foyers. The village of **Foyers** is noted for the first aluminium-smelting works to be built in Britain, erected in 1894. Continue beside Loch Ness through the hamlet of Inverfarigaig, and on to **Dores**. Here rejoin the B862 and follow a two-lane road for the return to Inverness.

231

Day Drives

Drive 10 Kyle of Lochalsh
104 miles

A tour of Skye from Kyle of Lochalsh

Attractively situated at the western extremity of Loch Alsh, **Kyle of Lochalsh** is sometimes known as the 'Gateway to Skye'. A regular car ferry operates across the narrow strait of Kyle Akin and the small town is the railhead of the line from Inverness and the terminal point of one branch of the 'Road to the Isles'.

The drive takes the car ferry to **Kyleakin** on the Isle of Skye and follows the A850 through Breakish to **Broadford,** situated on Broadford Bay. The Broadford group of the Red Hills overlook the village to the west, the highest peak being Beinn na Caillich at 2,403ft. *From here a detour to the left along the A881 can be taken to visit* **Elgol,** *on Loch Scavaig (single-track road throughout). Motor boat trips from Elgol are available to Loch Coruisk, set amid the wild peaks of the Cuillin Hills which provide some of the finest scenery in Britain.*

The main drive continues on the Portree road, with the island of Scalpay to the right. After skirting Loch Ainort there are views – on the left – of the Cuillin Hills, including the peak of Bla Bheinn (3,044ft). Climb onto higher ground, then descend to **Sconser** from where there is a vehicle ferry to the island of Raasay. Continue along the shoreline of Loch Sligachan to the hamlet of **Sligachan,** a noted climbing centre. From here the drive proceeds northwards and later follows the wooded Glen Varragill to the shore of Loch Portree. *The A855, to the right, may be taken to visit* **Portree** *– the 'capital' of Skye.*

This drive remains on the Dunvegan road, A850. In almost 4 miles keep left and shortly pass an inlet of Loch Snizort Beag. Later join a single-track road and continue to **Edinbane** on Loch Greshornish. The road then proceeds westwards and after crossing the Red Burn it becomes double-track again to reach **Dunvegan.** *Pass through the village in order to visit Dunvegan Castle – the ancestral home of the Macleods.*

Leave by the Sligachan road, A863, and after 1¼ miles pass the junction (on the right) with the B884 to Glendale. *This single-track road leads onto the Duirinish Peninsula which is dominated by the twin flat-topped hills known as Macleod's Tables – both over 1,500ft high. Places of interest along this road include the Skye Black House Folk Museum at Colbost and the Skye Watermill on the shores of Loch Pooltiel at Glendale.*

Continue southwards along the A863 and later skirt Loch Bracadale before reaching **Struan.** The drive then rounds Loch Beag before crossing higher ground and later passing the junction with the B8009. *From here a detour can be made alongside Loch Harport to Carbost, noted for its distillery, and on to the small weaving village of Portnalong. An unclassified road off the B8009 near Carbost leads southwards to Glen Brittle – a good climbing centre on the Cuillin Hills.*

Proceed along the A863 to Sligachan, with more fine views of the Cuillins. Here turn right onto the A850, signed Kyleakin. The drive then retraces its route via Broadford and Kyleakin, and crosses the ferry onto the mainland for the return to Kyle of Lochalsh.

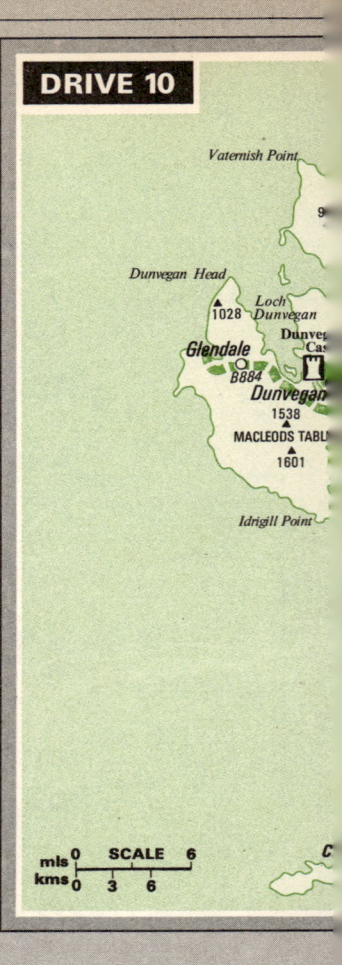

DRIVE 10

Vaternish Point

Dunvegan Head 1028 ▲ Loch Dunvegan
Glendale Dunvegan Cas...
▲ B884
Dunvegan
1538 ▲
MACLEODS TABL...
▲ 1601

Idrigill Point

```
mls  0        SCALE        6
kms  0    3        6
```

Kilmaluag
Port Henderson
B8056
A855
1781
Stenscholl
A832
Uig Bay
Uig
LOCH TORRIDON
RONA
3232
A856
2091
Loch Snizort Beag
THE STORR
2358
SOUND OF RAASAY
A896
Shieldaig
Edinbain
A856
A855
INNER SOUND
2053
A850
APPLECROSS FOREST
A896
A890
Applecross
unclassified
2938
Portree
B885
Glen Varragill
RAASAY
2328
A896
Loch Kishorn
B883
CROWLIN ISLANDS
1442
A850
A863
Glen Drynoch
Sconser
SCALPAY
LOCH CARRON
Stromeferry
A890
Longay
KYLE OF LOCHALSH
1466
Carbost
Loch Ainort
1365
Sligachan
A850
2542
Pabay
A87
1468
3167
A850
Ferry
Loch Alsh
Dornie
GLEN BRITTLE FOREST
Breakish
Kyleakin
A87
2500
A850
CUILLIN HILLS
2424
Bualintur
Broadford
Ferry
3309
3044
unclassified
unclassified
A881
Kylerhea
1984
Glenelg
Loch Brittle
Loch Slapin
SOAY SOUND
Loch Eishort
Elgol
3196
A851
SOAY
SOUND OF SLEAT
LOCH HOURN
980
Teangue
2573
RHUM
Ardvasar
Armadale Bay
1443

Drive 11 Lochcarron 91 miles

Bealach na Ba, Shieldaig, and Glens Torridon and Carron

The drive starts from the attractive village of **Lochcarron**, which lines the shore of Inner Loch Carron. *An unclassified road to the south-west leads past the small fishing harbour at Slumbay to Stromemore, where there are the ruins of Strome Castle.*
Leave by single-track Shieldaig road, A896, and ascend onto high ground. A descent is then made to Kishorn on Loch Kishorn. Across the water can be seen a fabrication yard for the North Sea oil industry. Continue alongside the loch for 1½ miles and turn left onto an unclassified road, signed Applecross. *Alternatively keep forward with the A896 and commence the directions again at Shieldaig. This saves nearly 28 miles.*
The main drive starts to climb the spectacular Bealach na Ba (Pass of the Cattle), following a narrow, winding road with hairpin bends. The maximum gradient is 1 in 5. The summit at 2,053ft makes it one of the highest roads in Britain. An AA Viewpoint has been established here which offers wide views over the Inner Sound to the Isle of Skye. Then follow a long but less difficult descent across rugged terrain to the isolated village of **Applecross**.
Leave by the Shieldaig road and round Applecross Bay. A scenic run is then made along the Inner Sound through remote country with good views towards the islands of Skye, Raasay and Rona. After the settlement of Fearnmore the drive turns south-eastwards beside Loch Torridon. Beyond the turning for Kenmore the road becomes narrower and more winding as it follows Loch Shieldaig to the junction with the A896. Here turn left to reach the edge of **Shieldaig**, a small crofting and fishing village on the loch of the same name.
Continue along the double-tracked Torridon road to round

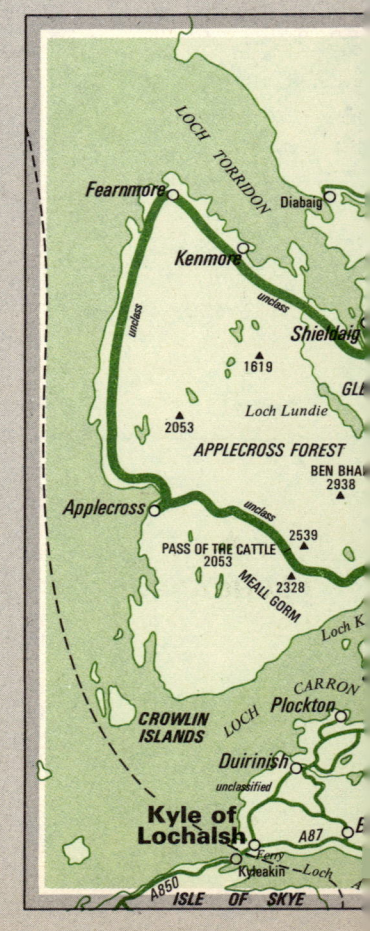

the southern shoreline of Upper Loch Torridon. This road offers magnificent views across the water to the Torridon Mountains – including Beinn Alligin at 3,232ft. Later pass through Annat to reach the turning for **Torridon** village. To the left is the National Trust of Scotland Visitor Centre which includes a deer museum with audio-visual equipment giving information on local wildlife.

The drive then follows the single-track road through Glen Torridon, signed Kinlochewe, with the great red sandstone peak of Liathach (3,456ft) to the left. Later the quartzite peaks of Beinn Eighe come into view – all of which are more than 3,000ft high. The slopes are part of the 10,000 acre Beinn Eighe Nature Reserve.

At **Kinlochewe** turn right onto the A832, signed Achnasheen. Ascend through Glen Docherty and later pass the shore of Loch a' Chroisg to reach the edge of **Achnasheen**. Here turn right onto the A890, signed Kyle of Lochalsh. Cross open moorland, then pass Lochs Gowan and Sgamhain before joining a double-track road through the Achnashellach Forest. The road becomes single-track again as the drive proceeds along Glen Carron. Later join the A896 for the return to Lochcarron.

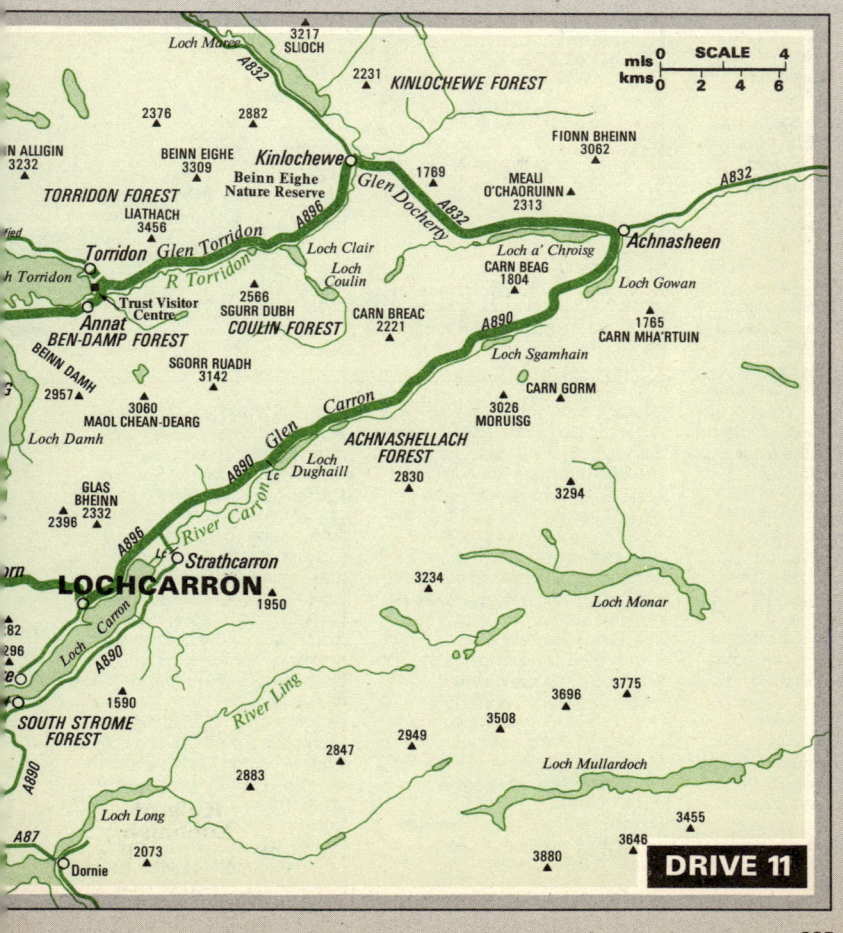

Day Drives

Drive 12 Gairloch 108 miles
Loch Maree, Strath Bran, Corrieshalloch Gorge and Gruinard Bay

The village of **Gairloch** occupies an attractive position on Loch Gairloch and has a fine sandy beach. A converted farmhouse now houses the Gairloch Heritage Museum which displays interesting items relating to the history of the area. Leave by the Kinlochewe road, A832, and proceed inland to follow the River Kerry. The road becomes single-track before passing the Gairloch Dam. Later enter the Slattadale Forest to reach the shore of Loch Maree, with its many small, tree-covered islands. On the far side of the loch are the mountain peaks of Letterewe Forest with Slioch (3,217ft) prominent. The drive joins a double-track road for the run alongside the loch. Approaching Kinlochewe the road skirts the Beinn Eighe Nature Reserve where several nature trails have been provided. At **Kinlochewe** follow the single-track Achnasheen road and ascend through Glen Docherty. Later skirt Loch a'Chroiss to reach the hamlet of **Achnasheen**. Continue forward, signed Inverness, along Strath Bran. The road becomes two-lane again as it rounds Loch Luichart for **Gorstan**. Here turn left onto the A835, signed Ullapool.
The drive now follows the Black Water, and then the Glascarnoch River before passing the Loch Glascarnoch Reservoir. Beyond the loch the bleak Dirrie More is crossed to reach the Braemore Road Junction. Turn left onto the A832 and pass the car park for the Corrieshalloch Gorge (NTS). The Gorge, and the spectacular Falls of Measach, can be viewed from a bridge which spans the deep and narrow chasm.
The A832 climbs onto higher ground before the descent beside the Dundonnell River. Dundonnell House, set beneath the slopes of An Teallach (3,483ft), contains some fine gardens which are occasionally open to the public. At **Dundonnell** the road proceeds along the shoreline of Little Loch Broom. Later cross a headland and rejoin the coast again at **Gruinard Bay** which is noted for its sandy beaches. Gruinard Island in the middle of the bay, was used as a germ warfare testing ground in the Second World War; it is still infected with anthrax and landing is prohibited. At the hamlet of **Laide** the drive turns southwards to reach the outskirts of **Aultbea** – a small crofting village situated on Loch Ewe. Continue along the coast road and after 6 miles pass, on the right, the entrance to **Inverewe Gardens** (NTS). These remarkable gardens, commenced in 1862, contain a fine collection of rare and sub-tropical plants. At **Poolewe** the road turns southwards again and after a mile passes a viewpoint from where the length of Loch Maree can be seen. Higher ground through barren countryside is then traversed before the return to Gairloch.

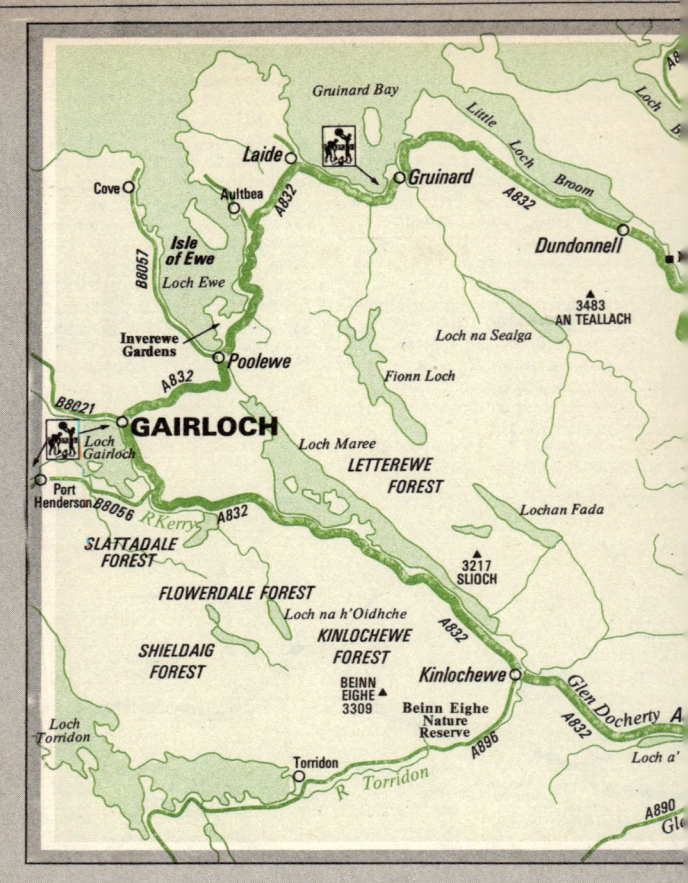

DRIVE 12

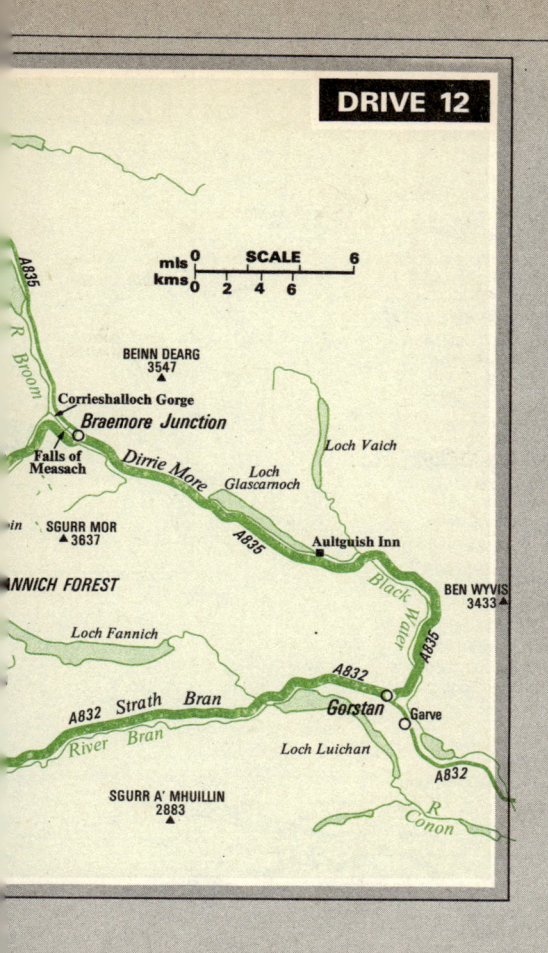

(map showing Braemore Junction, Falls of Measach, Corrieshalloch Gorge, Beinn Dearg 3547, Loch Vaich, Loch Glascarnoch, Aultguish Inn, Ben Wyvis 3433, Fannich Forest, Loch Fannich, Sgurr Mor 3637, Sgurr a' Mhuillin 2883, Strath Bran, River Bran, Gorstan, Garve, Loch Luichart, R Conon, A835, A832)

Drive 13 Oban 102 miles
The Pass of Brander, Glen Coe, and the Appin Coast road

Oban is both a popular resort and the port for goods and car-carrying services to the islands of Mull, Coll, Tireem, Barra and South Uist. The smaller islands of Iona and Staffa can also be reached from Oban.
Take the A85 northwards from Oban, passing in 3 miles, to the left of the road, Dunstaffnage Castle (mainly 15th-century) which guards the entrance to Loch Etive. Later, on the approach to Connel, the Falls of Lora can be seen below Connel Bridge. Follow Loch Etive to **Taynuilt** beyond which twin-peaked Ben Cruachan (3,698ft), one of the highest mountains in Argyll, rises to the left of the road. The drive then enters the wild Pass of Brander with, on the left, the Falls of Cruachan and the Cruachan Reservoir. Cruachan power station is built underground and is open to the public in the summer: a minibus service is provided for visitors. Continue alongside Loch Awe, which is also used in the production of hydro-electricity, to the ruins of Kilchurn Castle, sited on a spit projecting into the loch. *A short cut through Glen Orchy on the B8074 saves 5½ miles between Dalmally and Bridge of Orchy. Numerous waterfalls can be seen alongside the road.* The main drive continues through

237

Day Drives

Glen Lochy to **Tyndrum** with Ben Lui (3,708ft) rising to the right. Leave Tyndrum on the Fort William road A82, with the conical peak of Ben Doran (3,524ft) visible to the right before reaching **Bridge of Orchy**. Beyond the village the road passes Loch Tulla then climbs onto the bleak bog and lochan waste of Rannoch Moor on a stretch of road built in the 1930s to replace the narrow, exposed road over the Black Mount. The Kingshouse Hotel, on the right, faces Buchaille Etive Mor (3,345ft), one of Scotland's most famous rock peaks, in a well-known winter sports district. Descend the wild and impressive Glen Coe, overshadowed by the rugged peaks of Bidean nam Bian, at 3,766ft the highest mountain in Argyll, and its outliers, the Three Sisters. On the right you can see the great ridge of Aonach Eagach (3,000ft).

From Glencoe the drive follows the Fort William road A82. From the Signal Rock in the vicinity of the village, in the winter of 1692, came the signal for the hideous massacre of the Macdonalds of Glencoe by the Campbells of Glen Lyon. More than 40 died in the attack; others fled into the hills to die of hunger and exposure. To the right is Loch Leven, backed by the peaks of the Mamore Forest. Continue through **Ballachulish** and 1½ miles farther at a roundabout turn right onto the Oban road A828. At South Ballachulish is a monument to James of the Glen, wrongly hanged in 1752 after a notorious trial known as the Appin murder case. The identity of the real culprit was never discovered but the story is graphically portrayed by R L Stevenson in *Kidnapped*. Along the Appin shore of Loch Linnhe there are views of the Ardgour Hills across the loch, and Castle Stalker can be seen on an island site at Portnacroish, before the drive meets the edge of Loch Creran. Continue with views of Barcaldine Castle to the right of the road. The fine cantilevered **Connel Bridge** is crossed before the drive turns left along the A85 for Oban.

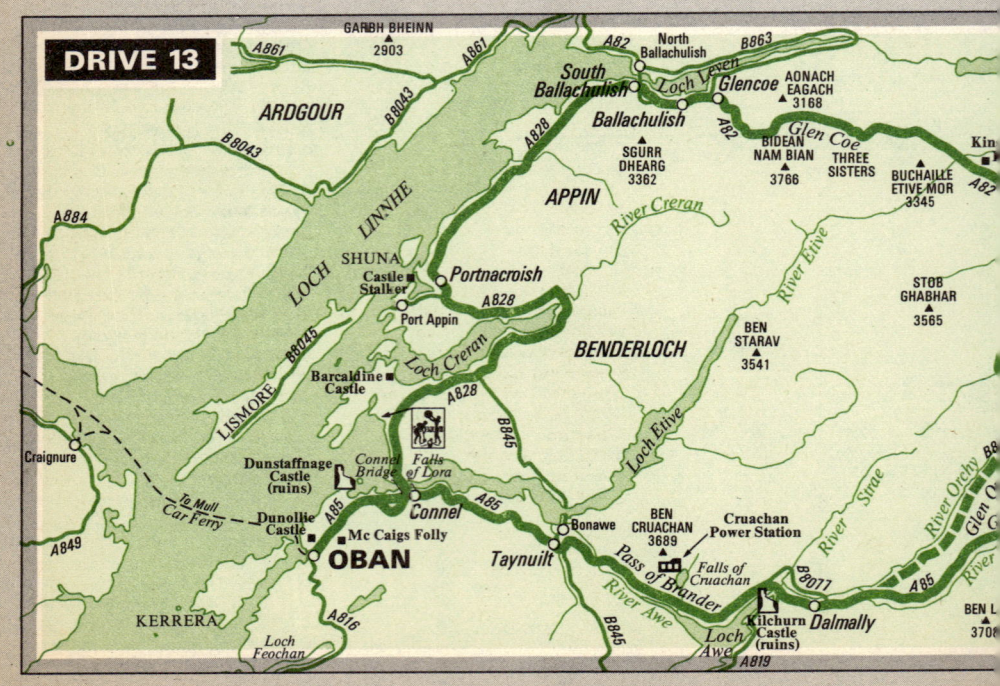

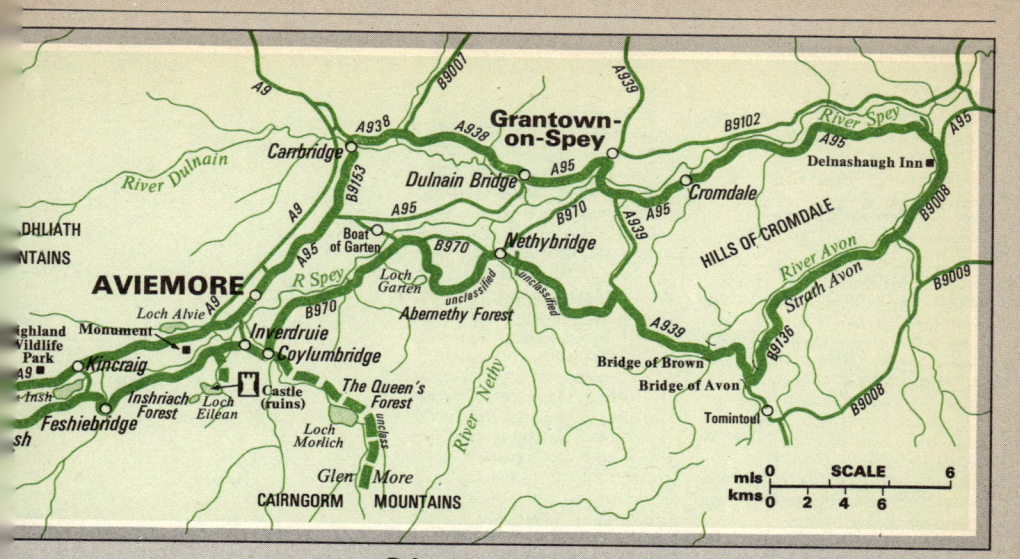

Drive 14 Aviemore 94 miles
Strath Spey, Strath Avon and Carrbridge

Aviemore attractively set beside the River Spey, has recently been affected by the growing popularity of winter sports, which has made the town an all-the-year-round resort. Behind the town rise the Monadlieth Mountains, attaining heights of over 3,000ft, and to the south east the Cairngorm Massif reaches over 4,000ft. Between these two ranges lies the thickly wooded Strath Spey.

Leave Aviemore by the Perth road, B9152 and in 1 mile join the A9. After 2½ miles pass a monument to the Duke of Gordon, set on a hillside to the left. Skirt Loch Alvie. Beyond the village of **Kincraig** is the Highland Wildlife Park where many species of wild animals can be seen. **Kingussie,** the most populated township in upper Strath Spey, has a Highland Folk Museum. Turn left onto the B970, to follow the south side of Strath Spey and pass the remains of Ruthven Barracks, built in 1716 and added to later by General Wade, the famous Highland road maker. One and three quarter miles farther cross the River Tromie and turn left. Continue through the hamlet of **Insh** then in 2½ miles keep forward with the Rothiemurchas road and later cross the River Feshie at Feshiebridge. Beyond this hamlet the drive enters the attractive Inshriach Forest. *After 4½ miles a short detour can be made by turning right onto an unclassified road to visit the shores of Loch an Eilein, where the ruined island castle (not open) was once the stronghold of the notorious Wolf of Badenoch, outlawed son of Robert II, Scotland's first Stuart King.* Continue with the B970 to Inverdruie, then turn right for **Coylumbridge,** a small village situated on the River Druiel. *The unclassified road ahead leads into the Cairngorm Mountains, passing through the Queen's Forest and beside Loch Morlich. This new ski road climbs to nearly 2,250ft. Here ski-tows and chairlifts are open throughout the year, and there are extensive*

Day Drives

views from the car park. This whole area is now part of the Glen More Forest Park, and reindeer have inhabited the mountain slopes since their introduction in 1952. The Cairngorms themselves form a vast National Nature Reserve covering some 60,000 acres. (This diversion would add some 15 miles to the tour.) From Coylumbridge follow sign Nethy Bridge, and continue along Strath Spey. In 6¾ miles turn right onto an unclassified road signed Loch Garten, to enter Abernethy Forest and pass Loch Garten. Half a mile beyond the Loch keep forward onto the Nethy Bridge road and in 2½ miles turn right to rejoin the B970 for **Nethy Bridge,** a small resort on the River Nethy. After crossing the river turn right onto an unclassified road, signed Tomintoul, and in half a mile go over the cross-roads. Continue across bleak moorland and after 4½ miles turn right onto the A939 towards Tomintoul. The Hills of Cromdale rise away to the left whilst the Cairngorms are prominent to the right. The road climbs to a height of over 1,420ft before descending to the Bridge of Brown. A further ascent and descent are made to cross the Bridge of Avon, where the drive turns left onto the B9136, signed Craigellachie, to follow the prettily wooded Strath Avon. In 8½ miles cross the River Livet and turn left to join the B9008 which continues alongside the river. Four miles farther turn left onto the Grantown road, A95, and recross the Avon to enter Strath Spey. Continue along the south side of the Spey, with the Hills of Cromdale to the left, and later pass through the hamlet of Cromdale before reaching **Grantown-on-Spey,** beautifully situated amid woods and mountains. Leave by the Perth road A95 and at Dulnain Bridge keep forward onto the A938, signed **Carrbridge.** This small village is developing fast as a winter sports centre, and is one of Scotland's leading resorts. Attractions at the Landmark Centre include a multi-screen sound and vision presentation of the history of Scotland. Take the Aviemore road B9153, for the return journey to the resort town of Aviemore.